POLITICS IN A CHANGING WORLD

A COMPARATIVE INTRODUCTION TO POLITICAL SCIENCE

FOURTH EDITION

MARCUS E. ETHRIDGE
University of Wisconsin-Milwaukee

HOWARD HANDELMAN
University of Wisconsin-Milwaukee

THOMSON
WADSWORTH

Australia • Brazil • Canada • Mexico • Singapore • Spain • United Kingdom • United States

THOMSON

WADSWORTH

Politics in a Changing World: A Comparative Introduction to Political Science,
Fourth Edition
Marcus E. Ethridge, Howard Handelman

Acquisitions Editor: Carolyn Merrill
Development Editor: Scott Spoolman
Assistant Editor: Rebecca Green
Editorial Assistant: Patrick Rheume
Technology Project Manager: Inna Fedoseyeva
Marketing Manager: Janise Fry
Marketing Assistant: Kassie Tosiello
Marketing Communications Manager: Tami Strang
Project Manager, Editorial Production: Paul Wells
Creative Director: Rob Hugel

Art Director: Maria Epes
Print Buyer: Linda Hsu
Permissions Editor: Joohee Lee
Production Service: Matrix Productions
Photo Researcher: Terri Wright
Copy Editor: Janet Tilden
Cover Designer: Armen Kojoyian
Cover Image: © William Whitehurst/CORBIS
Compositor: International Typesetting and Composition
Printer: Thomson/West

Library of Congress Control Number: 2006930461

ISBN-13: 978-0-495-00741-2
ISBN-10: 0-495-00741-2

Thomson Higher Education
10 Davis Drive
Belmont, CA 94002-3098
USA

For more information about our products, contact us at:
Thomson Learning Academic Resource Center
1-800-423-0563
For permission to use material from this text or product, submit a request online at
http://www.thomsonrights.com.
Any additional questions about permissions can be submitted by e-mail to
thomsonrights@thomson.com.

BRIEF CONTENTS

CONTENTS

III POLITICAL INSTITUTIONS 179

PREFACE

We designed the fourth edition of *Politics in a Changing World* to provide a foundation for understanding political life and the increasingly diverse field of political science.

Although we hope the book will be helpful for those who become political science majors, its primary purpose is to introduce students from a wide range of fields to the discipline. Citizens in every walk of life—not only politicians, government officials, and political analysts—need to understand the consequences of political choices and the processes through which those choices are made.

THE CHANGING WORLD IN THE TWENTY-FIRST CENTURY

Revising a political science textbook through four editions is a wonderfully compelling way to confront the reality of political change. When we wrote the first edition, the United States had never experienced a significant terrorist attack, an elected president had never been impeached, the Institutional Revolutionary Party (PRI) still controlled Mexico, Saddam Hussein seemed to have a firm grip on power in Iraq, ethnic conflicts in southern and eastern Europe were only beginning, no one knew what a "Euro" was, Japan was among the world's healthiest economies while China was not yet a manufacturing power, and the North American Free Trade Agreement was just about to take effect.

Political scientists were only beginning to consider what international affairs would consist of without a cold war to structure them, and no one expected the party controlling the U.S. White House to gain seats in the House of Representatives in a midterm election. (That has now happened twice, in 1998 and 2002!)

It is sobering to consider how inaccurate we would have been if we had attempted to make predictions about particular aspects of political life back in 1994. Nevertheless, the study of politics enables us to understand what factors will be important as government and international relations evolve in the years to come. The increasing importance of international trade will figure in both foreign and domestic policy in nearly all countries, and the protracted state of cultural and ethnic conflict—particularly conflict involving Islamic Fundamentalism—will influence many of the choices governments and citizens will make. The spread of democracy throughout the world has slowed, but the trend toward greater openness in both the political and the economic spheres is firmly entrenched in many areas. Technological advances and the spread of the Internet will shape a great deal of our lives, including commerce, our expectations of privacy, and national security.

We feel that the insights and knowledge produced by the systematic study of political life will be useful in understanding and managing the fundamental changes that are under way. *Politics in a Changing World* focuses on the ways in which accumulated knowledge in political science helps us account for the basic changes taking place in politics, and it explores the ways in which those changes have forced political scientists to revise their concepts, theories, and ideas.

POLITICS IN DIFFERENT NATIONS

Beginning with the first edition of *Politics in a Changing World*, we have worked with the firm conviction that politics cannot be understood fully by considering only a single country. Just as a biologist cannot hope to understand the basic elements of life by studying one species, and just as a physicist cannot hope to understand the nature of combustion by studying only one chemical compound, we cannot understand politics if we restrict ourselves to analysis of a single political system.

Thus, as in the previous editions, a key feature of the fourth edition of *Politics in a Changing World* is its separate chapters on different countries—the United States, Great Britain, Russia (and its predecessor, the Soviet Union), China, and Mexico—along with a chapter on the special problems of developing nations. Although these chapters are not intended even to summarize what is known about those governments, they allow us to give meaningful contexts to our discussions of elections, parties, legislatures, chief executives, courts, and interest groups. They also provide useful historical grounding. For example, the story of Britain's gradual development of democracy is important if we are to understand its current party system, and we need to know something about the Mexican Revolution to appreciate modern political problems and changes in that country.

Most readers of *Politics in a Changing World* are students born in the United States, and most of them have considerable knowledge about the U.S. system of government. But we believe that even a limited understanding of one's own political system is enhanced by coming to understand government and politics in other countries. Government in the United States is unique in many ways, and helping students to appreciate its special nature is one of our objectives in designing this comparative section of the book.

THE PLAN OF THE BOOK

When the discipline of political science reached its adolescence during the 1950s, many leading departments found themselves divided between those who approached their work with advanced statistical tools and quasi-experimental research methods and those who used more traditional approaches. Over the years, that division between "empiricist-quantifiers" and "traditionalists" has all but been replaced by an increasingly diverse array of distinct subfields. Some political scientists study institutions, others study individual behavior, some study ideology, and still others apply economic theories to politics. There is also a great division between those who study government in many nations and those who emphasize a single nation or area.

The divisions in contemporary political science present significant challenges for any introductory text. However, we are convinced that the diversity of perspectives, approaches, and methods in political science is beneficial. Specialists in one subfield often find useful insights generated in other subfields. Indeed, the opportunity to bring together the diverse elements of the discipline has confirmed that impression for us, and we hope our positive feelings about political science as a discipline are communicated effectively to our readers.

We have organized the book into six parts, the first five of which reflect the different objects of mainstream political science: Fundamentals, Political Behavior, Political Institutions, Politics in Selected Nations, and International Relations; the book's Epilogue then explores political prospects and challenges in the first decade of the new century. Each section contains chapters devoted to more specific topics. Part IV comprises the chapters on the United States, Great Britain, Russia, China, Mexico, and the developing world. These chapters can be read as a special unit after the more general chapters are covered, or they may be used as supplementary reading during discussions of political behavior, institutions, or international relations.

Each of the chapters devoted to specific countries contains a map to help readers understand that country's geographical context. Key terms in each chapter are introduced in boldface and are defined in the Glossary. Although the material may be organized in different ways, we have arranged the chapters to correspond to the steps that citizens typically take in approaching politics: Culture and ideology affect us first, then various options for political activity present themselves, and then we consider the institutions we wish to influence. Special issues pertaining to gender transcend the study of ideology, behavior, institutions, and political development, and so appropriate sections devoted to those issues are included in many chapters. Similarly, political economy is relevant to virtually all areas of our discipline, and readers will find that topic addressed throughout the text.

NEW TO THIS EDITION

Several new sections and features enhance the fourth edition of *Politics in a Changing World*. Some of these changes bring the text up to date, and others reflect helpful suggestions from students and instructors.

Extensive Updates Throughout

The effects of the September 11, 2001, attacks on the United States will be felt for many years and in many countries. Increasingly, the U.S. and other political systems must determine the proper balance between national (and individual) security against terrorism and the protection of citizens' civil liberties. Readers will encounter discussions of issues related to those events in several chapters. We examine the implications and importance of continued Republican control of the White House and both Houses of Congress. We discuss the apparent rejection of the EU constitution, the remarkable developments in China and Mexico, and the new challenges for international relations created by the War on Terrorism. And, of course, we include discussion of the war in Iraq.

"Where on the Web?" Boxes

As in previous editions, each chapter contains a boxed display titled "Where on the Web?" listing Web sites relevant to that chapter's subject matter. The World Wide Web contains a staggering array of information ranging from official government documents and survey and election results to partisan propaganda. The resources are impressive, and they are often very current, but Web "surfers" quickly become aware that a great deal of time can be lost searching through addresses that are less useful than their titles suggest. We have sifted through a large number of Web sites to identify resources that are genuinely useful and are likely to be in place for the foreseeable future. Students and instructors are encouraged to consult those addresses for supplementary information, updates, data, and stimulating ideas.

Web-Based Instructional Guide

Wadsworth Press has also created a Web site exclusively devoted to the fourth edition of *Politics in a Changing World*. The site includes suggestions about new Web addresses, new articles and books, and updated information about current political events that will enrich class discussions. Students and instructors are encouraged to use this site, found at http://www.thomsonedu.com/political_science/Ethridge.

ACKNOWLEDGMENTS

One of the most rewarding aspects of writing this new edition was the opportunity for each of us to explore in detail subjects beyond our current specialized interests. Nevertheless, several colleagues have provided valuable assistance in correcting errors and omissions, pointing us to helpful examples, and sharpening our arguments. Shale Horowitz, Uk Heo, Robert Eger, David Garnham, Steve Redd, and Don Pienkos generously gave their time to answer endless questions and to provide sources for us to explore. In addition, the book reflects the suggestions of the following professors and specialists who participated in Wadsworth's rigorous review process: Christopher P. Elmore, Johnson County Community College; Vernon D. Johnson, Western Washington University; F. David Levenbach, Arkansas State University; William Miles, Northeastern University; Kul B. Rai, Southern Connecticut State University; and Paul B. Ethridge, GlaxoSmithKline, Inc.

Marc also wishes to thank Greg and Zach Cigich for their moral support.

Finally, our editor helped to guide this new edition, gently keeping us on schedule and working with us to ensure that it will be stimulating and accessible to students.

About the Authors

Marcus E. Ethridge is professor of political science and chairs the Department of Political Science at the University of Wisconsin, Milwaukee. He is a specialist in the study of American government, focusing on interest group behavior, rational-choice theory, and administrative law. His publications include *The Political Research Experience*, *Legislative Participation in Implementation*, and numerous articles in the *American Journal of Political Science*, *Political Research Quarterly*, the *Journal of Politics*, and other journals. He is completing a new book tentatively entitled *The Case for Gridlock*.

Howard Handelman is emeritus professor of political science at the University of Wisconsin, Milwaukee. He specializes in Latin American politics and the politics of developing nations. His books include *The Challenge of Third World Development* (Fourth Edition), *Democracy and Its Limits: Lessons from Asia, Latin America, and the Middle East* (co-edited), *Üçüncü Dünyanin: Meydan Okuryan Ilerleşi* (Turkish-language edition of *The Challenge of Third World Development*), and *Mexican Politics: The Dynamics of Change*. He has contributed journal articles to the *Latin American Research Review*, *Canadian Journal of Latin American Studies*, and *Studies in Comparative International Development*, among others.

PART I

FUNDAMENTALS

The discipline of political science addresses a wide range of problems, issues, and topics. Nevertheless, there are some concepts that are fundamental for everyone interested in the field, from those doing research on the U.S. Congress to those investigating the developing political systems in Africa. Chapter 1 includes basic information on common definitions of politics and government, an exploration of the functions of government, approaches to classifying governments, and discussions of the stakes of politics and the different ways in which political scientists conduct research.

Chapter 2 is devoted to an overview of the most commonly discussed ideologies that influence the way we think about politics and government. Conservatism, liberalism, Marxism, and other ideologies frame debates about specific political issues, and they also figure in the way we evaluate different countries, the causes of war, and efforts to understand political change. A basic understanding of these ways of thinking about politics and government is essential for all political scientists.

MARINES IN COMBAT U.S. Marines of the 3rd Battalion, 4th Marines, attend to a colleague badly wounded by artillery fire on the Baghdad Highway Bridge, April 7, 2003. This photograph is part of a sequence taken during three days when the 3rd Battalion, 4th Marines of the USMC attacked and captured the Diwanya Bridge, also known as the Baghdad Highway Bridge, prior to driving into Baghdad and pulling down the statue of Saddam Hussein.

© AP/Wide World Photos

1

POLITICS, GOVERNMENT, AND POLITICAL SCIENCE

◆ Politics and Government Defined ◆ Government Functions ◆ Kinds of Governments ◆ The Stakes of Politics ◆ Politics in a Changing World ◆ Approaches to Political Understanding ◆ Conclusion: Why Study Political Science?

The U.S.-led invasion of Iraq in 2003 had major repercussions for international relations and domestic politics. It was a major issue in the 2002, 2004, and 2006 elections in the U.S., it had significant effects on a national election in Spain in March 2004, it strained relations with several key U.S. allies, it changed the role and perceived influence of the United Nations, and it affected the price and availability of oil in international markets. The war has raised new questions about media coverage of military activity, the role of partisanship in U.S. foreign policy, the conflict between due process rights and military activity, and the practicality of building democracy in non-democratic political cultures.

Wars are perhaps the most consequential events in human affairs. Economists, historians, environmental analysts, experts in international law, anthropologists, and many others can help to shed light on the causes and consequences of wars, and their contributions are essential. However, political science research is arguably the discipline most central to understanding the war against Iraq. Every major international or political incident is unique, but the problems and questions that political scientists have studied for generations help to explain what happened and why.

For example, political scientists have studied the idea of a "balance of power" in international conflict for centuries, and insights from research on how this factor influenced decision-making in previous wars may help us understand this one. A great deal of research has been done on the effect of political culture on political development and the prospects for democracy. Electoral systems vary in terms of how well election results reflect citizen preferences, and political scientists have studied this problem in a wide range of settings. Policy makers and analysts will use the knowledge accumulated by political scientists to understand the situations leading up to the war and to make decisions about post-war Iraq for years to come.

While Iraq may be the most urgent issue at present, a great many problems suggest that the beginning of the twenty-first century is a period in which politics and government are particularly pressing subjects for study. Iran's apparent efforts to acquire nuclear weapons (which can be deployed on missiles that the Iranian military already has) continue to raise deep concerns in the international community. It is critical that we come to understand the domestic and international political factors leading Iran to take this step, and it is essential that nations and international organizations rely on accumulated knowledge about government and politics when they respond. The way governments work (or fail to work) has tremendous effects on all of us.

At the same time, we should not lose sight of the fact that politics does not explain *everything*; in fact, many of the best things in life have little or nothing to do with politics. Personal relationships, the satisfaction of learning and working, artistic achievement and enjoyment, the challenges and deep fulfillment of raising a child—we can experience all of those things without doing anything "political." In fact, most aspects of our day-to-day lives do not necessarily involve political institutions, issues, and movements. There is much more to life than politics.

Politics and government have to do with *public* policies and *public* decision making, concerns that most people think about only occasionally. Yet, political decisions do have a huge impact beyond purely "governmental" matters. Political decisions frequently affect parenting, for example. In most countries, the government determines what material children must learn in school and when they will learn it. Often the government mandates what kinds of health-related precautions parents and teachers must take to protect students and what kinds of discipline and religious training children can be given in public schools. Most governments restrict artistic expression to some degree, both to limit exhibitions seen as improper in their cultures and to restrict the dissemination of ideas that may foster dissent and disloyalty.* Virtually everywhere, government regulates membership in selected professions (including not only law and medicine but also plumbing, architecture, and many other fields), limiting and often forcing career choices. Governments are the only organizations that may legally apply the death penalty to their citizens. And, of course, when nations decide to make war on one another, virtually all aspects of their citizens' personal lives may be drastically changed.

Why politics has such pervasive effects is itself a controversial matter. Some contend that government is extensively involved in our lives because much of what people do as individuals affects the economic opportunities of others, the environment, or public safety, and citizens demand that government take action to control those effects. For example, government policies in many countries restrict industrial development because of problems with pollution. Private actions often have public consequences, and many governments regulate those consequences. The nature of modern life thus accounts for a growing governmental role, as societies turn to government to safeguard widely shared interests in an increasingly complex, technological age.

The role of government may also grow for other reasons. Large numbers of citizens in many countries feel that government should be used as a tool to enforce and strengthen certain moral principles. In the United States, contending groups vigorously debate the morality (and legality) of abortion, while in Saudi Arabia the government restricts a woman's right to drive a car. In these and many other instances, people demand government actions that reflect their moral or religious positions, and many governments respond by enacting new restrictions and regulations.

Governments also apply power in pursuit of economic objectives. Sometimes this power is used to stimulate economic growth and opportunity, or to reduce economic inequality, and in other cases government power is employed to increase the wealth of individuals or groups that have gained access to political power. The British National Health Service, established shortly after World War II, is an example of the use of government power to reduce economic inequality; various laws passed under the Somoza regime (1937–1979) in pre-revolutionary Nicaragua employed government power to maintain a privileged status for the ruling family and its allies, making inequality more severe.

In short, government can be beneficial or devastating, but its significance is growing almost everywhere. Given the potential impact of government on so much of our lives, it is important to understand something about how government works, how it changes, how it can be influenced, and why different forms or designs of government operate differently.

Political science is the effort to shed light on these questions through careful, systematic, and informed study.

---

* On February 20, 2006, an Austrian court sentenced David Irving, a British writer, to three years in prison for having written a book in 1989 that denied the existence of gas chambers in the notorious Nazi death camp at Auschwitz. Governmental restrictions on free speech are found in modern democracies, not only in dictatorial regimes in developing countries. And, in March 2006, the government of Afghanistan arrested one of its citizens for converting to Christianity, a crime that could lead to the death penalty for those convicted. The individual was released, following mounting international pressure, and was exiled to Italy.

POLITICS AND GOVERNMENT DEFINED

The study of political science requires that we define *politics, political power, influence,* and *government*—terms about which most students have definite opinions. Consequently, academic definitions of politics and government may strike us as abstract and sterile, often because they are designed to distinguish between popular and scholarly uses of the terms. Definitions in political science are also intended to help us recognize that the scope of our concerns is broad—the terms we employ must apply to systems very different from our own if we are to discover and understand the basic elements of political life. The definitions of two terms are particularly important: *politics* and *government.*

Politics

People commonly use the term **politics** in a negative or pejorative sense, as in "There's only one explanation for her being appointed to be the new ambassador—*politics*"; or, simply, "It's back to '*politics* as usual.'" These statements imply something very basic about politics. A decision was "political" if influence or power was involved in making it. The negative connotation that often surrounds "politics" derives from the idea that a decision about something *should* have been made objectively, on the basis of merit, quality, achievement, or some other legitimate standard. When we find that influence and power had an effect on the decision, most people develop a very cynical attitude, accepting the idea that "politics" is synonymous with cheating or underhanded dealing.

Here are some alternative definitions coined by political scientists:

"Politics is the science of who gets what, when, and how."

Politics is "the authoritative allocation of values."

"Politics [is] . . . the activity by which differing interests within a given unit of rule are conciliated by giving them a share in power in proportion to their importance to . . . the whole community."

Politics is "the processes by which human efforts towards attaining social goals are steered and coordinated."

"Political science is the academic subject centering on the relations between governments and other governments, and between governments and peoples."[1]

The most basic idea contained in these definitions is that politics involves decision making among people in some large group. (An isolated person on a desert island cannot meaningfully be said to act *politically*, although economists could model his or her decisions regarding the investment of time and resources and his or her consumption, and historians could chronicle his or her activities.) More important, the definitions also suggest that political decisions involve influence and power. We can thus contrast political decisions with decisions made through, say, scientific computation or religious revelation. Although some of us may wish that governments would make decisions with the same kind of precision and objectivity that a chemist uses to determine the atomic weight of an element, a key characteristic of political decisions is that they are made in less objective ways. That is what makes the study of politics so interesting, and it is also what sometimes makes politics a "dirty" word. Political decision making involves divergent interests, ideas, and preferences, and it applies power and influence to resolve them. **Politics,** then, is the process of making collective decisions in a community, society, or group through the application of influence and power.

Government

When U.S. citizens think of government, they normally think of the president, the Congress, governors and state legislatures, mayors, and the courts and agencies that implement programs. In primitive societies, a few individuals may constitute the government. Government can be a vast, multifaceted, and complex arrangement, or it can be as simple as one village chieftain or tribal council. However, all governments wield *authority*. Government decisions are normally more coercive than decisions made by other forces in society. (For example, if the Japanese corporation that produces Lexus automobiles decides to make a different model, no one is compelled to buy it or to fund its production. However, if the British Parliament decides to purchase new aircraft for its navy, British citizens are compelled to "buy" the aircraft.)

A **government** is the people or organizations that make, enforce, and implement political decisions for a society.* Accomplishing these tasks involves the performance of certain basic *functions*, which we now explore in more detail.

GOVERNMENT FUNCTIONS

Because actual governments are so different in scale, complexity, and structure, many political scientists have found it useful to itemize the **government functions** performed, in one way or another, in all thriving political systems. Asserting that "all governments have a legislature, an executive branch, courts, and bureaucracies," would imply that a government would have to follow the model of developed Western democracies in order to qualify as a "government." However, identifying universal government *functions* helps us to appreciate that even when a government does not have institutions that seem familiar to us, it is still a government. It simply performs the basic governmental functions in different ways.[2]

Rule Making

Perhaps the most fundamental function of government is **rule making**—that is, making what are normally called *laws* or *orders* or even *constitutions*. These rules define what is legal and illegal, what actions are required, and the rights and responsibilities of citizens. In the United States, Congress (with participation by the president and sometimes the bureaucracy) performs this function; in China, the People's Congress officially makes rules (although most legislative decisions are really made by top Communist Party leaders). Councils of elders often act in this capacity in traditional societies, and the king and his advisers establish rules in the monarchy in Saudi Arabia.

In some way, all governments perform the task of making rules for their citizens. Some rules apply to criminal behavior, others establish economic regulations, and still others create or change public services. A rule is simply an *authoritative act*.

* In the United States, *government* applies broadly to a vast array of national, state, and local institutions. In European parliamentary systems (for example, Great Britain, Italy, Norway), we may speak of "the Government" to apply specifically to the prime minister and cabinet serving at a particular point in time. Thus, when the Italians say that "the Government resigned today," they are using the term in this more restricted sense.

Rule Execution

Rules must be enforced and carried out if they are to have impact; this is what we mean by **rule execution**. A government that proclaims laws and programs will not be very effective if it lacks the ability to put force behind its decision making. Some governments appear to have had the capacity to perform the former function without the latter. For example, many historians noted that the French Fourth Republic (1875–1940) had the ability to make rules (it had an energetic legislature) but that it had a terribly weak executive, a combination that led to protracted periods of instability. Many Latin American governments have passed social legislation in the areas of health care or agrarian reform, but they lack executive establishments capable of enforcing the law. The failure of some systems to thrive can thus be attributed partly to an inability to perform the basic function of rule execution.*

Rule Adjudication

Governments normally apply their laws to specific cases and individuals. If there is a law against murder, for example, there will be situations in which it will be necessary to determine whether a particular killing was murder, manslaughter, self-defense, or even an accident. Laws are frequently ambiguous. As a result, virtually all governments have some way of performing **rule adjudication**. Legal systems, usually with courts and judges, are established to apply and interpret laws that are made in general terms but that must have an impact at the individual level. In most modern societies, institutions for rule adjudication (courts) are at least partly distinct from the bodies that make the rules. In a tribal society or a traditional monarchy, a single governmental group may perform both functions.

Other Functions

Making, executing, and applying rules are the most basic functions of government, but other tasks must be performed for the system to operate effectively. Governments must be able to *communicate* with their citizens. People must be aware of laws if they are to obey them, and they must know about new programs if they are to participate in them. The leaders must also have some way of determining what people want, what they will support, and what they will not tolerate. Governments need some way to *recruit leaders*, perhaps through a party system or through a well-established routine of succession to the throne. It is also necessary that governments have some means of *extracting resources* (such as taxes, military service, or labor in public works projects) from their citizens.

Finally, a healthy political system has some means through which citizens come to support the basic principles and values of their government. Creating this foundation of involvement and awareness is referred to as the process of **political socialization**. Stable political systems also have some established ways for people to present demands for change. Interests must be expressed so that the government is able to take them

---

* Students of early-twentieth-century France point out that the system was held together during periods of political instability in the executive branch during the Fourth Republic (1946–1958) by its strong, stable bureaucracy. See Michael Crozier, *The Bureaucratic Phenomenon* (Chicago: University of Chicago Press, 1964), for the classic discussion along these lines.

into account in its decision making. Political parties, interest groups, and voting systems are some familiar mechanisms through which this function of **interest articulation** is performed.

The concept of government functions helps us to discover what to look for in our efforts to understand and evaluate actual governments. The concept also suggests that basic government functions can be performed in many ways and through many different governmental organizations or processes.

KINDS OF GOVERNMENTS

Governments may be classified in numerous ways. The kind of classification most of us probably encountered as children simply divided governments into free and unfree, or maybe even good and evil. Those concepts can be interesting to discuss, but political scientists have found it valuable to devise somewhat more precise classifications. The Greek philosopher Aristotle (384–322 BCE) constructed one of the first classification schemes, one that focused on who was in charge and in whose interests the ruler ruled. (See Box 1-1.) Many other classification approaches have been devised, some emphasizing economic systems, others reflecting legal arrangements, and still others based on wealth, culture, or even size.

An often useful approach is to classify political systems on the basis of how *developed* they are. The United States, New Zealand, and Sweden have developed political systems, whereas those in Mexico, Nigeria, and Indonesia are termed *developing* (or, alternatively, *underdeveloped* or *less developed*). Unfortunately, the criteria for making these distinctions are often unclear. What determines whether Nigeria or the People's Republic of China is a developed or a developing nation? Are political development and economic development the same thing? If not, does political development require economic development? Was wealthy Kuwait on the eve of the 1990 Iraqi invasion a developed nation? (It was

---

Box 1-1

ARISTOTLE'S APPROACH TO GOVERNMENTS

		Ruler Rules in Interest of:	
		Ruler	**All Citizens**
Type of Ruler	*One*	Tyranny	Monarchy
	Few	Oligarchy	Aristocracy
	Many	Democracy	Polity

Aristotle's classification is remarkable for its combination of an empirically observable factor (is the ruler a single person, a small elite group, or the masses?) with a more value-laden factor (does the ruler rule in his or her own interest or in the interest of all?). Aristotle obviously felt that nations with any of these three governing systems could operate fairly or with great injustice. His categories have suggested questions for political research for centuries.

One notable feature of Aristotle's classification is the assumption that democracy is a bad form of government; this concept was also on the minds of several of the framers of the U.S. Constitution, as we discuss in Chapter 11.

quite wealthy, but it had an ancient form of government.) Does Costa Rica's thriving democracy make it a developed nation (despite its poor economy)?

In their classic book, *Comparative Politics: A Developmental Approach,* Gabriel Almond and Bingham Powell offered one answer. Political systems are developed, they argued, if they can effectively and efficiently carry out the functions of government outlined earlier. To the extent that they cannot, undeveloped governments are often prone to political instability, violence, and military takeovers.[3] We discuss the idea of **political development** in Chapter 15.

What Is Democracy?   Political scientists often compare governments on the basis of how democratic they are. In practice, **democracy**, like political development, is a matter of degree, and so we speak of governments being "more" or "less" democratic. The degree to which a government is democratic depends on several related factors.

First, democratic government requires adherence to the principle of *political equality.* If large segments of the population are denied political rights by virtue of their race, family heritage, economic status, or religious affiliation, then political influence is not in the hands of the people, and the government thus fails to meet a basic principle of democracy. Governments can be undemocratic with respect to this principle in many ways: by giving special political power to the upper echelons of an economic elite or a ruling family, as in El Salvador or Kuwait; by excluding significant parts of society from political life, as South Africa did until the end of *apartheid;* by concentrating power in the hands of the military, as in Nigeria and Burma; or by putting nearly all political power in the hands of a political elite, as in North Korea, Cuba, China, Nazi Germany, and the former Soviet Union.

Even if political equality is generally secure, a government is not really democratic unless there is some process or mechanism through which the people have an opportunity to express their opinions. **Popular consultation** is thus a key component of democracy. It means that the people have a real opportunity to be heard and that this opportunity takes place regularly. (A country would not be very democratic, for example, if its next general election were scheduled for a date 20 years in the future.)

Finally, democracy requires substantial adherence to the principle of **majority rule**. This principle is simple but often controversial. It means that when citizens disagree about a political decision or candidate, as they virtually always do, then the decision made or the candidate selected will be the one preferred by the larger group of people. If a minority (an elite group of landed aristocrats or an exclusive religious leadership, for example) makes political decisions over the objections of the majority of a country's people, the government would not be very democratic.

It is important to recognize, however, that majority rule can lead to the violation of other democratic norms. What if the majority votes to deny electoral rights to a religious or racial minority? Such an action would violate the principle of political equality and would be undemocratic despite the fact that it was adopted through popular consultation and majority rule. Hence, if democracy is to be preserved, the majority must not be allowed to erase fundamental minority rights; democracy implies at least some *limitation* on majority rule. The relationship between majority rule and minority rights is a sticky problem, and it is a central challenge encountered by all democratic governments. As we will see later, although the United States generally appears democratic with respect to the principles of political equality and popular consultation, several features of its Constitution limit majority rule.*

Democratic governments differ in many ways. They have widely varying degrees of government ownership of industry, their citizens engage in different levels and kinds of political participation, and they vary with respect to their economic development and the design of their institutions. Political scientists have devoted great attention, in particular, to the differences between the United States, with its divided powers and "checks and balances," and Great Britain, with its more streamlined, centralized institutions. Other scholars distinguish between *industrial democracies* (those with well-developed economies, such as Germany and France) and less economically developed democratic nations (for example, India and Venezuela), which are less able to provide fundamental services for their populations. We explore the great diversity among democratic governments in later chapters.

Nondemocratic governments also operate in many ways, but most political scientists recognize two well-established types. Both kinds effectively deny political equality, popular consultation, and majority rule, maintaining real political power in the hands of a ruling party, elite group, dictator, or family. The difference between the two types of nondemocratic regimes has to do with the government's long-term goals.

Authoritarian systems require only that citizens obey government edicts and limit their dissent. Africa, Asia, and Latin America have been replete with authoritarian governments in recent decades. Such governments may violently repress opposition groups and torture political prisoners, but ultimately the state simply insists that the people not challenge the orders of the ruling elite. The governments of Haiti and Indonesia are good current examples.

In contrast, **totalitarian systems** energetically seek to change the political thinking and the allegiance of their citizens. The governments of Nazi Germany and Stalinist Russia, for example, sought to indoctrinate their populations into the dominant ideology (fascism or communism), a phenomenon not found in authoritarian regimes. Political recruitment and indoctrination take place in totalitarian regimes largely through a ruling party that dominates public affairs and much of private life as well. Totalitarian systems attempt to politicize virtually all pursuits, including sports and art, that are less constrained in democratic and even in authoritarian societies. For example, under the leadership of Mao Zedong in the 1960s, China's "top ten" pop songs often dealt with such unexpected topics as surpassing Great Britain in steel production or resisting Western imperialism. Without the government's influence and control, one would have expected that popular music would have addressed more typical subjects.

Although citizens have little voice in the affairs of either type of nondemocratic system, authoritarian governments often permit churches, unions, and some interest groups to retain relative independence as long as they do not challenge state authority. Totalitarian governments generally dominate and remove existing organizational features of a society in their attempt to permeate the totality of their citizens' lives.†

---

* See Dahl, Robert A., *How Democratic Is the American Constitution?* 2nd ed. (New Haven, CT: Yale University Press, 2003).

† Totalitarianism is a twentieth-century political concept. Most analysts argue that totalitarianism is possible only in countries with the technology to support mass communications, rapid transportation, and the means to engage in active, comprehensive surveillance of their citizens. Thus, all nondemocratic governments before that century were simply authoritarian. For a classic discussion, see Hannah Arendt, *The Origins of Totalitarianism* (New York: Harcourt, Brace, and World, 1966).

In fact, we might think of democratic, authoritarian, and totalitarian governments as ranging along a continuum; they differ in the degree of independence from government control that they allow individual citizens and groups in society. Democracies are often referred to as *pluralistic* because they permit the greatest diversity of political behavior and viewpoints.

It is important to understand that both democratic and nondemocratic governments can perform the basic functions of government. Both kinds of governments make, enforce, and adjudicate rules; they communicate with their citizens; and they establish some basis for political socialization. Interest articulation occurs in nondemocratic governments as well as in democracies (although smaller segments of citizens articulate a narrower range of demands in nondemocratic governments). Quite simply, whether it operates according to democratic principles or in violation of them, a government is still a government.

Nor are political systems static. Countries may change over time, moving from one form of government to another. During the 1960s and early 1970s, for example, Argentina, Brazil, Chile, and a host of other democratic governments in Latin America collapsed under the strain of internal conflicts. Repressive authoritarian regimes, such as the Pinochet dictatorship in Chile, were established throughout the region. In the 1980s, however, democracy was restored to most of the region. Some Eastern

THE DEADLY TSUNAMI Indonesian men walk past the rubble of buildings destroyed by the Dec. 26 tsunami in Banda Aceh. Indonesia was the worst hit of 11 nations affected by the disaster, though conflicting figures of between 114,978 and 173,981 have been given for its death toll. This photograph was taken one month after the disaster struck.

European countries (Hungary, Poland, Czech Republic) that until rec itarian are now fledgling democracies. On the other hand, Sudan, N each of which was part of the movement toward democracy in the la the twentieth century, have slipped back toward authoritarianism. Other nation Thailand, for example—continue to straddle the line between authoritarianism and limited democracy.

Politics and government constitute the scope of inquiry and analysis for political scientists. The preceding sections describe the kinds of things that political scientists study in their efforts to contribute to our understanding. Through the scientific study of politics we attempt to find out why some forms of government work better than others, how people influence government, how governments change over time, how economic systems influence politics, and many other related matters. Ultimately, however, questions about politics and government are important because of what is at stake when governments act (or fail to act).

THE STAKES OF POLITICS

Most of the important consequences that can be traced to governmental action or inaction fall into one of five categories:

1. The allocation of resources
2. Human rights
3. The physical environment
4. Public services
5. War and peace

These are the "stakes" of politics, the scope of concerns in which politics makes a difference. Although some specific issues may pertain to more than one of these categories, the categories identify distinct aspects of our lives in which government and politics are critical.

The Allocation of Resources

Although politics affects many other things, it is fair to say that the majority of political decisions have to do with the **allocation of resources**.

Government power often has a tremendous impact on how wealth is distributed and on the purposes to which scarce resources are devoted. The word *authoritative* in this definition is crucial. In many countries, a considerable share of national resources is allocated through economic exchange (investing, buying, and selling). This is the normal domain of economic analysis. Some get rich, and others become poor, through the economic choices made by consumers, workers, producers, and investors. In contrast, when governmental acts allocate resources, we refer to the allocation as authoritative.

The distinction is important. When Henry Ford applied assembly-line manufacturing methods to his auto plant, manufacturing costs plummeted, prices fell, and a huge increase took place in the number of people who could afford cars. The labor of thousands of people was diverted from agricultural production and small craft activities to auto assembly. Through an economic process of exchange, a large share of national resources—both materials and labor—was allocated to the manufacture of automobiles.

Yet this allocation was not *authoritative*, because the decisions creating it were made voluntarily—most importantly, by consumers.

In contrast, when the Japanese Diet passes the annual budget, it allocates resources from taxpayers to governmental programs and expenditures. A political decision may be made to increase funding for medical research or to decrease funding for transportation.

New laws may also increase or decrease the proportion of taxes to be paid by the richest and the poorest citizens. These decisions involve allocations, whether they have to do with tax rates or expenditures. And such allocations are authoritative—citizens are required to make the contributions, and the expenditures are made as a matter of law.* Although resource allocation in *all* countries is affected by both economic exchange and authoritative governmental acts, the relative importance of economic and political allocations is very different in different countries. Most of the resource allocation that takes place in Taiwan, for example, is driven by economic exchange. The public sector is relatively small. In Cuba the government directly influences the bulk of resource allocation by making decisions regarding what is produced, at what prices, and with which raw materials. The forces of *both* economic exchange and government authority are important in the United States, Great Britain, Mexico, France, Italy, and most other countries. We use the term *mixed economies* to describe such societies.

Political economy is the study of how political decisions affect economic conditions. Government actions that alter the allocation of resources constitute the basic concerns of political economy. Two basic political problems dominate the field. First, government decisions can fundamentally shift the balance of resources held by the poorest and the richest segments of the population. We discuss the issues of **income distribution** in more detail in Chapter 15. At this point, however, it is important to note that nations differ dramatically with respect to how wealthy they are, and with respect to how that wealth is distributed among rich and poor. See Table 15.1.

Many things contribute to the differences among countries with respect to wealth and the equality with which wealth is distributed. Natural resources, climate, population, access to transportation, and other such factors are obviously important. However, the nature of government and the policies governments enact are profoundly important. In fact, according to Nobel laureate Douglass North, institutions "are the underlying determinant of the long-run performance of economies."[4] Table 1.1 shows the differences among 13 selected countries with respect to governmental corruption, the strength of the rule of law, and the number of days that it takes, on average, to obtain government approval to start a business. As you will see, there are tremendous differences among governments with respect to these factors. In countries in which there is less governmental corruption, a more established rule of law, and more efficient approvals of business start-ups, there are lower infant mortality rates and more wealth. The quality of government makes a tremendous difference in the lives of citizens.

A great deal of the political conflict among people reflects different views regarding the extent to which government effort should be devoted to shifting the allocation of resources from one group of people to another. In developing nations, where gaps

---

* To qualify as authoritative, however, the allocation must be made under *legitimate* public authority. Resources are involuntarily "allocated" from one person to another when a burglar carries off your television and DVD player. It is coercion by *legitimate government power* that makes the allocation authoritative and thus distinctively political.

TABLE 1.1   DIFFERENCES AMONG GOVERNMENTS ARE ASSOCIATED WITH DIFFERENCES IN LIVING CONDITIONS

	Per capita income	Infant mortality	Control of corruption	Rule of law	Number of days to start a business
United States	$39,710	6.5	92.6	92.3	5
Japan	$30,040	3.3	86.2	89.9	31
France	$29,320	4.3	88.7	88.9	8
Russia	$ 9,620	15.4	29.1	29.5	36
Brazil	$ 8,020	48.1	53.2	46.9	152
Thailand	$ 8,020	38.5	49.3	51.7	33
Kazakhstan	$ 6,980	54.9	9.9	17.4	25
Colombia	$ 6,820	24.4	52.2	29.5	43
El Salvador	$ 4,980	70.9	43.8	42.5	115
Philippines	$ 4,890	36.0	36.5	32.4	50
Haiti	$ 1,680	89.4	1.0	2.4	203
Burundi	$ 660	85.8	6.4	6.4	43
Malawi	$ 620	112.5	23.6	45.4	35

NOTE: Per capita income is measured in 2005 U.S. dollars. Infant mortality is the number of deaths to persons under 12 months of age per 1,000 live births. The control of corruption and rule of law measures are indicators of each country's *percentile rankings* on these measures. (For example, Brazil's score of 53.2 on the "control of corruption" variable means that Brazil scored higher than 53.2 percent of the countries, but 46.8 percent of the countries scored higher than Brazil.) For both of these measures, high scores signify better ratings than low scores. The number of days to start a business column indicates how long, in days, it is estimated to take to obtain government licenses and other approvals to start a business.

SOURCES: All data are from the World Bank and the CIA World Factbook. The World Bank material is from its *World Development Report 2006*, Table A3, available at http://siteresources.worldbank.org/INTWDR2005/Resources/complete_report.pdf, its publication, *Governance Matters IV: Governance Indicators for 1996–2004*, available at http://www.worldbank.org/wbi/governance/pubs/govmatters4.html, and its *World Development Report 2005*, Table 1, available at http://siteresources.worldbank.org/INTWDR2005/Resources/complete_report.pdf. Data on the number of days needed to start a business were taken from the World Bank's *Doing Business in 2005: Removing Obstacles to Growth*, available at http://www.doingbusiness.org/documents/DoingBusiness2005.PDF, pp. 89–91. The CIA World Factbook is available at http://www.cia.gov/cia/publications/factbook/.

between rich and poor are often particularly sharp, conflicts between "haves" and "have nots" periodically unleash revolutionary forces (as in Nicaragua, the Philippines, and El Salvador). Extreme inequality in the distribution of income or land increases the likelihood of political instability in developing nations.

In industrial democracies, economic inequality is a less explosive issue but, nevertheless, the major parties in the United States, Great Britain, France, and Germany tend to define themselves primarily by their different positions on resource allocation. More generally, the distinction between "left" and "right" on the political spectrum is largely, although not entirely, a matter of differing positions on what government should do to alter the distribution of resources; those on the left favor more active efforts to redistribute income, whereas those on the right are either less supportive of, or hostile to, such efforts.

Governments are also heavily involved in resource allocations that, though involving large shares of wealth, do not alter the balance between rich and poor. These *intersector allocations* constitute a second set of concerns in the area of political economy. For example, import restrictions alter the allocation of resources. When a government restricts or severely taxes the importation of a particular good, the domestic manufacturers and workers who produce that good find that the demand for what they have to sell is greater (because consumers can no longer buy the imports). Domestic resources that would otherwise be devoted to the production of other goods are then devoted to manufacture of the previously imported good. The trade restriction thus changes the allocation of resources from the production of one good to another, and it increases the income of the manufacturers and workers producing the protected good.

Of course, other groups realize a net decrease in wealth. When the state restricts importation of a good, the total supply of that good is reduced, and the price charged by domestic producers goes up. People who had paid $14,000 for a car before import restrictions were in place may now have to pay $18,000 for the same car. These people have experienced a net wealth reduction of $4,000. The government has "allocated" thousands of dollars from consumers to those involved in the auto industry by enacting the change in trade policy.

Governments also allocate resources in other ways—by adjusting interest rates, changing tax rates and exemptions, nationalizing private industries, and controlling prices and wages. Using these and many other kinds of powers, governments have a

---

Box 1-2

GOVERNMENTS, CAPITALISM, AND DEMOCRACY

With the dramatic decline of communism at the end of the last century, citizens and scholars around the world have become increasingly interested in the possible connection between capitalism and democracy. Ardent advocates of capitalism have long argued that the economic freedoms of capitalism inevitably lead to political freedoms, and that a nation that enjoys genuine political freedom will always construct and maintain a market economy.[5] Although cases can be found to support this argument, the actual record is not so clear.

Historically, the rise of liberal democracy (competitive elections with guaranteed civil liberties) evolved first in Britain and then spread to other parts of Western Europe and the United States at the same time that capitalism was emerging as the new economic system. The tendency of these political and economic systems to develop simultaneously was far from coincidental. As scholars from Karl Marx onward have recognized, it was the rising class of capitalist entrepreneurs and businessmen—often known as the bourgeoisie—who mounted the first major challenges to the political and economic power of the feudal or semi-feudal aristocracy that had previously dominated Europe. The bourgeoisie became the most powerful voice for parliamentary government, wider citizen participation in politics, and notions of guaranteed individual liberties.

In general, capitalism tends to produce democracy because the existence of an independent bourgeoisie in a capitalist society creates centers of economic power independent of the government and makes it easier for political pluralism to flourish. For example, the students who organized China's short-lived democracy movement in 1989 were partly financed by the country's new class of independent businessmen. In a classic study, a leading scholar of political and economic development nicely summed it up by exclaiming "no bourgeoisie, no democracy!"[6]

However, not all capitalist countries are democratic and not all democracies are purely capitalist. From the 1960s through the 1980s, a number of East and Southeast Asian countries became models of capitalist economic development, with very high levels of growth, while at the same time maintaining relatively repressive dictatorships. These countries included South Korea, Taiwan, Singapore, Indonesia, and Malaysia. From 1973 to 1990, Chile's president, General Augusto Pinochet, imposed one of Latin America's more brutal regimes. But, at the same time, led by U.S.-trained economists, the country developed what Nobel Prize–winning economist (and champion of unfettered capitalism) Milton Friedman hailed as one of the world's purest capitalist systems. Moreover, China today seems to be developing an essentially capitalist economy within the confines of an authoritarian, communist political system.

Examples of democracies that are not capitalist are harder to find, and it probably is true that no modern democracy has existed without some elements of capitalism. It should be noted, however, that a number of

tremendous capacity to change economic conditions. Governments can make societies richer or poorer; they can foster a more equal or a less equal distribution of wealth; they can hasten or retard the development of specific industries. Perhaps there is also a connection between government policies that encourage economic freedom and the emergence of democracy. (See Box 1-2.) In short, the widely varying economic conditions among contemporary nations reflect, in large measure, the political choices made by governments.

Human Rights

Although economic issues often seem to dominate politics, many of the political issues that most sharply divide us involve governmental policies in non-economic areas. In the United States, heated debates have focused on prayers in public schools, the achievement of racial balance in public and private organizations, the right to have an abortion, and the rights of homosexuals. In India, Lebanon, Northern Ireland, and

Western European countries have thrived under highly developed democratic political systems and mixed economic systems that combine elements of capitalism and socialism. Norway, Sweden, Denmark, Finland, and Iceland have some of the highest standards of living in the world, socialist welfare systems, and highly democratic politics. It could be argued that in the last years of the Soviet Union (see Chapter 13), President Mikhail Gorbachev's political reforms in the 1980s produced a country that was moderately democratic (competitive elections, multiple parties, a fairly free press, religious tolerance) with an economy that was still primarily state controlled (communist).

But these exceptional cases have proven to be somewhat transitory. Chile, Taiwan, and South Korea have all democratized. Russia's totalitarian political system eventually crumbled, and many analysts think that eventually China's will as well (though this may take a long time and not all experts feel it is certain to happen). Thus, although capitalist societies can be authoritarian, at least for a substantial number of years, and although Scandinavia's mixed economies coexist very smoothly with democracy, there is no question that in the long run capitalist economic systems and democratic political systems seem to reinforce each other.

It should also be noted that the wealth creation that characterizes capitalism may itself undermine democracy. Kevin Phillips, a controversial social critic often seen on public television in the United States, has argued along these lines in a recent book.[7] He states that U.S. capitalism has led to a concentration of

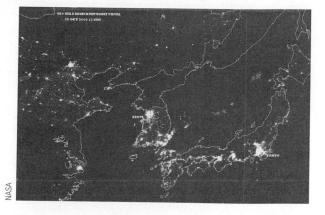

NASA

THE LIGHTS ARE OUT   This nighttime satellite photo provides a striking visual indicator of how different forms of government can create very different living conditions. Although the cities of Seoul, South Korea, Beijing, China, and Tokyo, Japan are very obvious, North Korea is almost completely dark. Its population is 22 million people, about 45% of the population of South Korea.

wealth that is much more pronounced than in earlier periods, and that it threatens the egalitarian conditions that were in place during the Founding period. If the wealthy become too powerful, according to Phillips, the political system will be less democratic.

In short, there is clearly an important connection between capitalism and democracy, but it is far too simple to claim that one always produces or requires the other.

Canada, conflicts over religious or language policies have sometimes erupted in violence. Governments have a tremendous capacity both to protect and to trample on the civil liberties of their citizens.

Nearly everywhere, there is always great disagreement regarding the nature and extent of human rights, and even when people agree that a particular right should be respected, they often differ about when and under what conditions the right may be appropriately abridged. A great deal of political conflict thus involves disputes regarding human rights.

Although issues of human rights can be approached in many ways, two kinds of rights can be distinguished according to how they relate to government. Some rights correspond to limits on government power and are thus called *negative rights*. Examples include the right to free expression, to religious freedom, to a fair trial before punishment, to travel, and so on. They are called negative rights because we enjoy them when government is *prevented* from certain actions. We have freedom of the press, for example, to the extent that the government is *not* free to limit what can be written, printed, or broadcast. In contrast, *positive rights* require governmental action. For example, if we feel that every person has the

---

Box 1-3

FOUR STATEMENTS OF HUMAN RIGHTS

I. THE MAGNA CARTA (THE GREAT CHARTER) [EXCERPTS]

Signed by King John of England in 1215.

—No bailiff for the future shall, upon his own unsupported complaint, put anyone to his "law," without credible witnesses brought for this purpose.

—No freemen shall be taken or imprisoned . . . or exiled or in any way destroyed, nor will we go upon him nor send upon him, except by the lawful judgment of his peers or by the law of the land.

—We will appoint as justices, constables, sheriffs, or bailiffs only such as know the law of the realm and mean to observe it well.

—Wherefore we will and firmly order that the English Church be free, and that the men in our kingdom have and hold all the aforesaid liberties, rights, and concessions, well and peaceably, freely and quietly, fully and wholly, for themselves and their heirs, of us and our heirs, in all respects and in all places forever, as is aforesaid. An oath, moreover, has been taken, as well on our part as on the art of the barons, that all these conditions aforesaid shall be kept in good faith and without evil intent. Given under our hand—the above named and many others being witnesses—in the meadow which is called Runnymede, between Windsor and Staines, on the fifteenth day of June, in the seventeenth year of our reign.

II. THE UNITED STATES BILL OF RIGHTS [EXCERPTS]

Adopted in 1791.

Amendment 1. Congress shall make no law respecting an establishment of religion, or prohibiting the free exercise thereof; or abridging the freedom of speech, or of the press. . . .

Amendment 2. A well-regulated militia being necessary to the security of a free State, the right of the people to keep and bear arms shall not be infringed.

Amendment 4. The right of the people to be secure in their persons, houses, papers, and effects, against unreasonable searches and seizures, shall not be violated. . . .

Amendment 5. No person . . . shall be compelled in any criminal case to be a witness against himself, nor be deprived of life, liberty, or property, without due process of law. . . .

Amendment 8. Excessive bail shall not be required, nor excessive fines imposed, nor cruel and unusual punishment inflicted.

right to a job or to health care, the government must take steps to provide them to people who are unable to obtain private employment or to pay their own .

Both negative and positive rights are contained in th Declaration on Human Rights and in the U.S. Bill of Right controversies about human rights in our discussions of ide ....xt chapter.

A special set of human rights issues involves the treatment of women. In many political systems, the rights of women are severely restricted. The infamous Taliban regime in Afghanistan, which was quickly toppled in 2001 by a coalition of forces led by the United States, placed severe restrictions on the education of women. Taliban policies and laws provided for physical beatings if women failed to observe a wide range of clothing requirements, and these punishments were regularly carried out. Women face restrictions on reproductive choices in China, many Latin American countries, and much of Africa. Although most factors affecting gender equality stem from cultural influences, government policies play a major role in reinforcing or reforming them.

Human rights are important in the stakes of politics because people care deeply about them. In some cases, one person's freedom injures another citizen (as when a

III. THE UNITED NATIONS UNIVERSAL DECLARATION ON HUMAN RIGHTS [EXCERPTS]

Adopted and Proclaimed by the General Assembly Resolution 217 A (III) of December 10, 1948.

Article 1: All human beings are born free and equal in dignity and rights.

Article 2: Everyone is entitled to all the rights and freedoms set forth in this Declaration, without distinction of any kind, such as race, color, sex, language, religion, political or other opinion, national or social origin, property, birth, or other status.

Article 3: Everyone has the right to life, liberty, and the security of person.

Article 4: No one shall be held in slavery. . . .

Article 18: Everyone has the right to freedom of thought, conscience, and religion. . . .

Article 23: Everyone has the right to work, . . . to just and favorable conditions of work and to protection against unemployment.

Article 26: Everyone has the right to education.

Education shall be free. . . .

IV. THE CHARTER OF FUNDAMENTAL RIGHTS OF THE EUROPEAN UNION [EXCERPTS]

Adopted on December 7, 2000

Article 8, Section 1: Everyone has the right to the protection of personal data concerning him or her.

Article 9: The right to marry and the right to found a family shall be guaranteed in accordance with the national laws governing the exercise of these rights.

Article 11, Section 1: Everyone has the right to freedom of expression. This right shall include freedom to hold opinions and to receive and impart information and ideas without interference by public authority . . . .

Article 11, Section 2: The freedom and pluralism of the media shall be respected.

Article 13: The arts and scientific research shall be free of constraint. Academic freedom shall be respected.

Article 17, Section 1: Everyone has the right to own, use, dispose of and bequeath his or her lawfully acquired possessions. No one may be deprived of his or her possessions, except in the public interest and in the cases and under the conditions provided for by law, subject to fair compensation being paid in good time for their loss. The use of property may be regulated by law in so far as is necessary for the general interest.

Article 21: Any discrimination based on any ground such as sex, race, colour, ethnic or social origin, genetic features, language, religion or belief, political or any other opinion, membership of a national minority, property, birth, disability, age or sexual orientation shall be prohibited.

restaurant owner exercises the "freedom" to deny service to African Americans). Citizens are divided in many countries with respect to whether abortion should be legalized. Much of the disagreement has to do with a conflict, in the eyes of many citizens, between the right to privacy and the right of the unborn to live. At times there may be a basic moral conflict between the rights of those accused of crimes and the right of society to be safe from criminals.

In short, people disagree about human rights on many levels, and government action is often demanded either to secure or to modify those rights. Human rights even figure in foreign policy issues. In the United States, the government has been criticized for its present or past affiliation with regimes that have poor records on human rights. One of the justifications that the George W. Bush administration gave for its military action against Iraq was that country's horrendous human rights abuses, including mass murder and the use of chemical weapons against its citizens. In the 1990s, some critics urged the U.S. government to act more forcefully against the Chinese government for its massacre of students at Tiananmen Square in 1989. Especially when a concern for human rights conflicts with other national interests, such as international trade, political decision making becomes very difficult. How human rights should be defined and respected are issues that are very much at stake in political life.

Box 1-4

Rosa Parks and The Struggle for Human Rights

In 2005, one of the most famous and widely respected civil rights pioneers in U.S. history died at the age of 92. Fifty years earlier, Rosa Parks refused to give up her seat on a bus in Montgomery, Alabama to a white person, thereby violating the law in effect at that time, which required African Americans to sit in the rear of buses (she was fined $10 plus court costs of $4). A 13-month boycott of the Montgomery buses ensued, a legal challenge was successful, and Dr. Martin Luther King, Jr. became a national figure as a result of the incident.

The Rosa Parks story demonstrates that a single act of defiance can spark a revolution in a nation's respect for human rights. The law in Montgomery was eventually changed, as were similar laws in several other states. Moreover, national press coverage of the courageous action of this small, dignified woman helped many Americans, most of whom had never observed such blatant and official racist restrictions, see that major changes were needed in order to remove affronts to basic constitutional and moral values. As Rev. Jesse Jackson stated, "She sat down in order that we might stand up."

© AP/Wide World Photos

An Arrest That Moved a Nation　A Montgomery (Ala.) Sheriff's Department booking photo of Rosa Parks taken February 22, 1956, after she was arrested for refusing to give up her seat on a bus for a white passenger on December 1, 1955.

The Physical Environment

Governments play a special role with respect to issues of environmental protection. Most goods and services can be produced entirely through private efforts because investors know that they can be paid for what they produce. But clean air and water, the elimination of toxic wastes, and protection of the natural beauty of the wilderness are "goods" that profit-seeking firms are not necessarily motivated to preserve. If we are to have environmental protection, most people feel that the government must act.

Protection of the environment thus depends almost entirely on governmental action. The continuing controversy over the "greenhouse" effect (the idea that Earth's climate is becoming warmer because of various pollutants entering the atmosphere and because of the destruction of rain forests) is only the most spectacular illustration of the stakes involved—and of the inability of any institution except government to do anything about it.

Although virtually everyone favors protection of the environment, people differ greatly about the priority that environmental protection should be given and about who should pay for it. Should Brazil limit farming in rain forest regions if it means that destitute people in that area will have less food? Should auto makers be forced to produce more electric and hybrid cars, even if it means that consumers will be denied some of the choices they would like to have? In the long run, the quality of human life will be crucially affected by what governments do and fail to do concerning environmental protection.

Public Services

Governments do more than govern. People also look to government for important services—most notably, public education, public transportation, cultural amenities such as museums and libraries, and "infrastructure" support (road repair, street sweeping, and so forth). Although most people accept the need for government to play a role in providing these services, considerable controversy surrounds the scope and nature of this role.

For one thing, public services cost a great deal of money. Paying for them requires taxes, and some taxpayers are reluctant to support the provision of these services. Even the richest of nations can never afford to pay for all desirable services. A 1991 study found that, as estimated in that year, the U.S. Interstate Highway System needed at least $750 billion in repairs, a level of spending made virtually impossible by federal budget problems and highly strained state and local budgets.[8] The problem has not yet been solved. The Federal Highway Administration's 2005 "Report Card" estimated that eliminating problems with bridges alone would cost $9.4 billion annually for 20 years, and that another $10 billion would be needed over the next dozen years to refurbish non-federal dams.[9] Where will that money come from, and what other critical services (education, health care, defense) will be cut? In poor nations, with greater needs and far fewer resources, the choices are yet more difficult.

Provision of public services is also controversial because it can be a way to redistribute income or opportunities. An extensive public education system, such as that in the United States, increases opportunities for poorer children. In South Africa, where secondary education for blacks was limited, or in Colombia, where most secondary schools are private, education reinforces societal inequalities. Similarly, in all countries decisions about where to build roads may be determined by economic development priorities or by political influence. Some win, and others lose.

The government role in provision of public services thus relates to issues that transcend the often mundane concerns of road construction and water utilities. Basic political choices in these areas affect us, since much of the productivity of society depends on the quality of public services.

War and Peace

"War," according to Karl von Clausewitz, is "a real political instrument, a continuation of political commerce . . . by other means."[10] Although a war might be started through accident, and although military leaders can start wars by taking sudden action on their own, most wars begin as a result of deliberate policy choices made by leaders. Those choices may be rational or irrational, well informed or grounded in miscalculation. (Saddam Hussein certainly miscalculated when he believed, in 1990, that he could invade and hold Kuwait. And, the U.S. government acted, in part, on faulty intelligence about Iraq's weapons of mass destruction program when it invaded that country in 2003.) The monumental consequences of war make questions of war and peace a central reason for concluding that politics matters.

We discuss several approaches to understanding the causes of war in Chapter 17. For now, it is important simply to appreciate Clausewitz's notion that war is a "political instrument." Wars can erupt when governments are moved to pursue a moral purpose, when they seek material gain, when they are anxious about their security, or when domestic pressures move them into conflict. In short, the same sets of conflicting passions, interests, and needs that influence political decision making in general are often involved, in one way or another, in the causes of war.

It is important to appreciate the extent to which government action can make a difference in each of the five areas we have outlined. Governments can help provide a basis for economic growth and opportunity, or they can condemn the vast majority of their citizens to poverty and hopelessness. They can plunge their citizens into devastating military conflicts, or they can contribute to peace. Governments can secure or destroy basic rights, protect or savage the environment, and provide or not provide needed public services.

A disinterested extraterrestrial observer, looking at Earth for the first time, would probably be startled by the vast range of conditions in which humans live throughout the planet. Different political choices, made by various kinds of governments, account for much of the diversity in the quality of human life. Perhaps that is why Aristotle referred to politics as the "master science"—political choices have effects, direct and indirect, on virtually everything.

POLITICS IN A CHANGING WORLD

The past quarter-century has been a period of especially momentous changes in political life. Many years from now, historians will write about the fall of communism in the early 1990s, noting that this event marked the end of the Cold War and the beginning of an era in which one country, the United States, became the world's only superpower. For nearly 50 years, virtually every incident, alliance, and issue involving foreign policy had been affected by intense rivalry between the communist and noncommunist blocs, and millions saw Marxist-Leninist ideology as a worthy alternative to democratic government. Beginning in 1989, all of this changed. People around the world were transfixed by pictures of German youth triumphantly climbing and dismantling the Berlin wall, the sounds of Romanian crowds challenging their nation's dreaded secret police (the *securitati*), and the dignity of Lech Walesa and Vaclav Havel as they led the governments of Poland and Czechoslovakia. The end of communism changed the world in profound ways.

It is arguable that the changes in Eastern Europe that began in the late 1980s were but part of a worldwide movement toward democracy. In Latin America, the same period witnessed the restoration of elected civilian governments in such erstwhile rightist military dictatorships as Argentina, Brazil, Chile, Paraguay, and Uruguay. In 1986, a popular uprising toppled the corrupt Marcos dictatorship in the Philippines, while elsewhere in Asia, authoritarian governments in South Korea and Taiwan moved toward limited democracy. Changes during this period in Africa were not limited to Mandela's success; elsewhere in that continent, a number of single-party regimes tentatively began to recognize opposition-party activity.

There are reasons to believe that the democracy movement is continuing. A Harvard-trained banker, Ellen Johnson-Sirleaf, was elected as President of Liberia in January 2006. She is the first woman to serve as head of state of any African country, and the election itself was widely regarded as a legitimate exercise of democracy. During the same month, the voters of Chile elected that country's first female head of state (Michelle Bachelet). If the overthrow of Saddam Hussein leads to a new era of peace and democratization in the Middle East (the outcome is currently far from certain), political scientists and historians will look back on this event as another critical moment in world history. The long-term trend is difficult to deny: As late as the 1970s, there were only 40 countries that could be considered democracies. Today, there are more than 120. Democratic pressures—largely limited to economically developed nations until the 1980s—have spread into all parts of the world, and most of the initial successes have proven enduring.

Nevertheless, serious problems threaten the further spread of democracy. Some contemporary analysts fear that the U.S. actions in Iraq and Afghanistan have only aggravated the tensions in the region, prompting an escalation of violence and instability that will become increasingly severe in years to come. At the time of this writing, the Iranians appear to be well on their way to developing nuclear weapons that can be deployed on missiles capable of reaching Israel, India, and parts of Europe. North Korea remains dangerous and unpredictable. The European Union, Japan, Korea, China, and the United States are still working through the uncertain waters of economic globalization, making it very difficult to predict even near-term developments in politics and economic policy. Given much of Africa's extremely low literacy rates, low GNP per capita, and lack of democratic traditions in national government, the prospects for democratization there seem limited. The futures of Cuba and China are far from clear, although many experts feel that democratic pressures will be hard to resist in the long run. Countries in East Asia, South America, and Eastern Europe (with some still authoritarian and others only marginally democratic) tend to offer better hopes for greater democracy. Even in those more developed countries, deeply rooted class tensions (as in Peru or Colombia) or ethnic hostilities (Bosnia or Malaysia) may undermine democratic forces.

In short, it is not entirely clear that a rosy democratic future stands before us. There is currently much instability among and within many nations. Furthermore, democracy does not solve all societal problems and in some cases may even open a

Pandora's box of new conflicts. In much of Eastern Europe, totalitarian rule held down a host of bitter ethnic rivalries: Serbs against Croatians and Bosnians in the former Yugoslavia; Azerbaijanis against Armenians in the Soviet Union; Bulgarians against the Turkish minority in Bulgaria. Although the governments in these examples are probably semi-democratic at best, it is clear that the tenuous steps that have been taken in that direction have not produced a stable order. The weakening of harsh authoritarian controls has unleashed intense ethnic nationalism, often leading to bloodshed. The march toward stable democracy, if it is under way at all, is neither irreversible nor universal.

The knowledge and understanding accumulated through generations of political science research suggest that the growth of democratic government is rooted in societal forces more fundamental than the actions or vision of particular leaders, or the fallout from single events. Most political scientists conclude that economic growth creates greater social and political diversity as well as heightened political participation and awareness; that all governments need some degree of popular support; and that governments cut off from the pressures of competitive political influences are inherently unstable in the long run. Building on this understanding and related ideas, several leading political scientists and political economists anticipated the breakdown of communist rule as long ago as 1960.[11]

Political science thus presents no clear or universally accepted vision of the future of politics in our changing world. However, there is some basis for predicting that economic growth will create democratic tendencies. Existing research indicates that countries with annual gross national products (GNPs) of under $1,000 per year and literacy rates below 50 percent are very unlikely to achieve democracy. Several years ago, a political scientist found that countries above that economic threshold are far more likely to be democratic, provided that income and wealth are not highly concentrated in a limited number of hands (as in Brazil, Mexico, Saudi Arabia, and Kuwait).[12] Higher levels of economic development, accompanied by a reasonably equitable income distribution, accelerate literacy and the spread of information through newspapers, books, and broadcast media. Together, these conditions produce a more politically informed public, one more capable of holding elected officials accountable. Opinion surveys suggest that more educated populations are more likely to support democratic values.

It is clear that we are living in an era in which political life is both extremely important and highly volatile. As economic growth spreads (unevenly) through the world, and as nations become increasingly interdependent, we will find that the old conflict between communists and anticommunists has been replaced by a more complex pattern of economic, ethnic, and religious relations. The task of political science is to bring sound scientific inquiry to these problems.

Approaches to Political Understanding

The preceding sections present the scope of our concerns and explore why they are worth studying. It is important to understand, however, that political scientists approach their discipline in a variety of ways. More than most fields of study, political science is eclectic: It borrows from other fields to forge its own identity. Although political science enjoys a healthy diversity, it is also one of the most fragmented of academic disciplines.

The first effort to study political life was as a subtopic of *philosophy*. Those studying politics in this manner focus on questions pertaining to the origins of government, the problem of human rights and justice under law, the idea of a "just war," and other basic philosophical concerns. It is important to emphasize, however, that political philosophy includes several very different approaches. Most scholars claim that the field began in ancient Greece with Plato (427–347 BCE) and his student Aristotle. Essential elements of **classical political philosophy** include a distrust of democracy and an emphasis on the problem of designing a political community in accordance with principles of justice. **Modern political philosophy**—beginning with Machiavelli (1469–1527), Hobbes (1588–1679), Locke (1632–1704), and Rousseau (1712–1778)—is distinguished by its emphasis on individualism and its rejection of Plato's search for an ideal state order. Both classical and modern political philosophy include a wide range of more specific perspectives.

The study of *law* was a second major influence on political science. Legal scholars study different approaches to interpreting laws and pri[...]ples pertaining to how courts operate. Legal analysis is also relevant to questions ab[...]t the powers of governmental institutions and their procedures. Much of political sci[...]nce through the [...] quarter of the twentieth century was influenced by legal think[...], and the term **formal-legal analysis** was used to describe pre–World War II political science. During this period, political scientists devoted themselves to issues of constitutional design and formal governmental institutions.

At the beginning of the twentieth century, some political scientists began to criticize philosophical and legal approaches to understanding politics. They argued that we could not fully account for policy choices by considering ethical concerns or legal powers and rights alone. Instead, we should observe actual political *behavior*. The "behavioral revolution" took firm root and, by the 1960s, was firmly established as the mainstream of the discipline. Perhaps the first shot in this revolution was fired in 1908 by Arthur Bentley in *The Process of Government*, an important book that argued persuasively for the observation of behavior in political research.[13] In political science, this approach is known as **behavioralism.**

The behavioral approach to political science necessitated borrowing skills from other disciplines. When we observe behavior—in the form of voting, political demonstrations, voicing opinions, and so on—we usually need to quantify it. How many people voted in the last election, and what caused them to vote as they did? What kinds of people participated in the demonstrations? Analyzing data in a quantified form requires that political scientists have some familiarity with *statistics*. The emphasis on statistical analysis is readily apparent to students exploring political science journals for the first time. Political research often (although not always) involves the use of basic and even highly advanced statistical tools as scholars try to discover and identify patterns in the behavior they observe.

Contemporary political science also owes a great deal to *history* and *sociology*. These disciplines suggested basic questions for political science research. If we are attempting to find out why poor people vote less regularly than rich people, for example, research from sociology is helpful in that it identifies important influences on the behavior of people in different segments of society. Historical knowledge provides an essential context for exploring political changes in both domestic and international relations.

Particularly in the past twenty years or so, political scientists have increasingly drawn from *economics* in their work. (See Box 1-5.) Some have applied the economic concept of the rational, self-interested person in analysis of everything from voting to group membership. The rational choice school is controversial within the discipline

---

Box 1-5

"RATIONAL CHOICE" IN POLITICAL SCIENCE

Political scientists are hotly divided over the role of "rational choice" theory in their discipline. Drawn largely from economic theory, the rational choice approach begins with the assumption that individuals seek to maximize "utility" with their choices and behaviors. This assumption is rarely controversial in economics, where it is used to construct models pertaining to buying and selling oranges, computers, and "widgets," but some political scientists apply it to politics and government. For example, using rational choice logic, one analyst argued that party leaders should be expected to shape their ideological positions in ways that appeal to voters in the center of the ideological spectrum, where the party can "maximize" its votes, just as a retailer shapes a marketing campaign to maximize customers.

Although this example is hardly controversial, other applications are much more contentious. For example, some have used rational choice to construct theories of bureaucratic behavior, predicting that bureaucrats will have a natural urge to expand their agencies in order to increase their personal wealth. One of the most famous rational choice ideas is explored in Chapter 6 (Interest Groups). It holds that people will not willingly participate in collective political efforts because the rational person will realize that one person's contribution is inconsequential and because non-contributors will receive as much benefit from the group's success (if any) as contributors. Political scientists have also used rational choice logic in understanding the emergence of democracy in developing countries.[14]

Advocates of rational choice contend that the approach opens new avenues for understanding political institutions and individual behavior. Others insist that it oversimplifies motivations, that it contains a conservative ideological bias, and that it has not produced any meaningful predictions that could not be derived from other approaches. In a book provocatively entitled *Pathologies of Rational Choice Theory*, two members of the Yale Political Science Department argue essentially that rational choice theory has been a failure.* This volume prompted the publication of *The Rational Choice Controversy*, by another Yale political scientist, which includes essays both criticizing and defending rational choice theory.[†]

The dispute has become even more heated in the last few years. A full-fledged "movement" in political science, termed by its leaders the *"Perestroika"* revolt, emerged when a number of political scientists rebelled against the use of mathematical models and rational choice thinking, arguing that they made the profession's journals irrelevant and unreadable. Political science would be better served, say *Perestroika's* supporters, if researchers would emphasize social and political reality instead of abstract models borrowed from economics and the natural sciences, where they make more sense.**

Specialists in the field continue to argue over these questions. Moreover, some teachers even worry that introducing students to rational choice ideas—with their emphasis on self-interested motives—tends to undermine the development of a civic consciousness among students and teachers. On the other hand, a growing segment of the discipline remains convinced that understanding everything from voting to bureaucracies to elections requires a keen grasp of the choices that rational people make in pursuit of their interests. This debate will figure prominently in the future development of political science.

*Donald P. Green and Ian Shapiro, *Pathologies of Rational Choice Theory* (New Haven: Yale University Press, 1994).

†Jeffrey Friedman, ed., *The Rational Choice Controversy* (New Haven: Yale University Press, 1996).

**See Kristen Renwick Monroe, *Perestroika! The Raucous Rebellion in Political Science* (New Haven: Yale University Press, 2005).

---

because many political scientists believe that it oversimplifies human motivations. But there is general agreement on the relevance of economic concepts and tools in the study of political behavior.

Perhaps in reaction to the dominance of behavioral method and the increasing influence of approaches using economic theory, a significant number of political scientists now argue that there is an important place for less-mathematical research methods.

This way of thinking is sometimes termed "postmodernism" or "postbehavioralist inter-pretivism." Although it is not a very specific approach, its adherents share a conviction that the behavioralists and the rational choice analysts have allowed mathematical rigor to displace the politics in political science. Numbers can tell us some things, but they cannot reveal the whole sense of what is critical about political issues and events, and methods steeped in mathematics may even obscure or distort the essential politi-cal nature of the things they do measure, according to postmodernists.

Political scientists thus attempt to understand politics and government by using a wide range of approaches to study. Sometimes, the differences among political scien-tists with respect to their research methods can become rather heated, and a number of essays have been published attacking and defending various approaches. (See the list of suggested readings at the end of this chapter for some good examples.) We may hope that the decades-long debate over research methods in political science will prove to be useful in moving the discipline to refine and strengthen its ability to pro-duce genuine understanding.

CONCLUSION: WHY STUDY POLITICAL SCIENCE?

Political science encompasses a wide variety of approaches. Sometimes the diversity is enriching and stimulating, but it must be acknowledged that political science is also a highly divided discipline. Some are quite vocal in disparaging the efforts of colleagues who use different tools or methods. Disagreements can be healthy, however, even when they are heated. The diversity and the energy that political scientists bring to their work reflect the deep interest they share in their subject. These are also reasons that political science is fascinating and so involving. The primary answer to the ques-tion "Why study political science?" is simply that it helps us understand the problems and issues that define public affairs. Studying political science is also an excellent foun-dation for careers in law, government, public administration, and other areas, but the most fundamental justification is that it helps us to become more effective participants in the civic life that increasingly affects our future. The passion for political under-standing, shared among professionals and amateurs alike, is nicely captured in the fol-lowing statement by a pioneering political scientist:

> No one can deny that the idea is fascinating—the idea of subduing the phenomena of pol-itics to the laws of causation, of penetrating to the mystery of its transformations, of sym-bolizing the trajectory of its future. . . . If nothing ever comes of it, its very existence will fertilize thought and enrich imagination.[15]

 WHERE ON THE WEB?

http://www.apsanet.org/
The home page of the American Political Science Association provides information about impor-tant publications in political science, career opportunities, internships, and other resources.

http://www.icpsr.umich.edu/
Housed at the University of Michigan, this site is the home page for the Inter-University Consortium for Political and Social Research. It provides a great deal of useful information for anyone interested in advanced political science research and data.

http://www.ucis.pitt.edu/cwes/index.html

The home page of the Center for Western European Studies at the University of Pittsburgh provides useful information about European politics and economics.

http://www.worldbank.org

The home page of the World Bank offers data and links to publications regarding economic development and global poverty issues.

http://www.brook.edu

The Brookings Institution—the nation's oldest think tank—defines itself as "A private, independent, nonprofit research organization seeking to improve the performance of American institutions and government programs and policies." The site lists Brookings studies and personnel.

http://www.cato.org

The Cato Institute, another think tank, states on its home page that it "promotes public policy based on individual liberty, limited government, free markets, and peace."

http://www.psr.keele.ac.uk/thought.htm

This British site focuses on interesting political controversies and provides links to classic, modern, and contemporary political theorists and organizations.

http://www.apsanet.org/~psa/

This is the home page of Pi Sigma Alpha, the national Political Science Honor Society for undergraduate and graduate students majoring or minoring in political science.

◆ ◆ ◆

Key Terms and Concepts_____

allocation of resources	majority rule
authoritarian government	modern political philosophy
behavioralism	political development
classical political philosophy	political economy
democracy	political socialization
formal-legal analysis	politics
government	popular consultation
government functions	rule adjudication
human rights	rule execution
income distribution	rule making
interest articulation	totalitarian systems

Discussion Questions_____

1. What are the most basic functions of government? Explain why a political system cannot be stable and effective unless each of these functions is performed.
2. What is the difference between "positive" and "negative" human rights?
3. If politics means "the application of influence and power in making public decisions," does this mean that politics is underhanded?
4. How are free markets and democracy related to each other?

Notes_____

1. These definitions are adapted from Harold Lasswell, *Politics: Who Gets What, When, and How* (New York: McGraw-Hill, 1936); David Easton, *The Political System*, 2nd ed. (New York: Knopf, 1971); Bernard Crick, *In Defense of Politics*, 2nd ed. (Chicago: University of Chicago Press, 1972); Karl Deutsch, *The Nerves of Government* (New York: Free Press, 1963), and from the Glossary on the "About Economics" Web site, http://economics.about.com/od/economicsglossary/g/political.htm

2. Much of this discussion is drawn from a basic, pioneering work that still influences contemporary political analysis. See Gabriel Almond and G. Bingham Powell, *Comparative Politics: A Developmental Approach* (Boston: Little, Brown, 1966).

3. Ibid.

4. North, Douglas C., *Institutions, Institutional Change and Economic Performance* (Cambridge: Cambridge University Press, 1990, p. 107).

5. One of the most widely read books making this argument is *Free to Choose*, by Milton and Rose Friedman (New York: Harcourt Brace Jovanovich, 1980).

6. Barrington Moore, Jr., *Social Origins of Dictatorship and Democracy: Lords and Peasants in the Making of the Modern World* (Boston: Beacon Press, 1967). For an important refinement of Moore's work, see Dietrich Rueschemeyer, Evelyn Huber Stephens, and John Stephens, *Capitalist Development and Democracy* (Chicago: University of Chicago Press, 1992).

7. Phillips, Kevin, *Wealth and Democracy: How Great Fortunes and Government Created America's Aristocracy* (New York: Broadway Books, 2002).

8. See Kirk Victor, "Paying for the Roads," *National Journal*, February 16, 1991, p. 374.

9. See the "Infrastructure Report Card, 2005," issued by the American Society of Civil Engineers, available at www.asce.org/reportcard/2005/

10. This famous quote is from *On War*, bk. 1, chap. 1, as translated by J. J. Graham (New York: Barnes & Noble, 1956), p. 23.

11. A famous statement of this idea can be found in W. W. Rostow, *The Stages of Economic Growth* (Cambridge: Harvard University Press, 1960).

12. Mitchel Seligson, "Democratizing in Latin America: The Current Cycle," in *Authoritarians and Democrats: The Politics of Regime Transition in Latin America*, ed. James Malloy and Mitchel Seligson (Pittsburgh: Pittsburgh University Press, 1987).

13. Arthur Bentley, *The Process of Government* (Cambridge: Harvard University Press, 1906). Several decades later, David Truman wrote the similarly titled *Governmental Process* (New York: Knopf, 1958), a book that extended and applied Bentley's approach.

14. See Barbara Geddes, "The Uses and Limitations of Rational Choice," in *Latin America in Comparative Perspective*, ed. Peter H. Smith (Boulder, Colo.: Westview, 1995), pp. 81–108.

15. Quoted in David Easton, *The Political System*, 2nd ed. (New York: Knopf, 1971), p. viii.

For Further Reading _____

Arendt, Hannah. *The Origins of Totalitarianism*. New York: Harcourt, Brace, and World, 1966.

Beem, Christopher. *The Necessity of Politics*. Chicago: University of Chicago Press, 2002.

Bentley, Arthur. *The Process of Government*. Cambridge: Harvard University Press, 1906.

Easton, David. *The Political System: An Inquiry into the State of Political Science*. 2nd ed. New York: Knopf, 1971.

Finifter, Ada W. *Political Science: The State of the Discipline III*. Washington, DC: American Political Science Association, 2002.

Friedman, Jeffrey, ed. *The Rational Choice Controversy*. New Haven: Yale University Press, 1996.

Green, Donald P., and Ian Shapiro. *Pathologies of Rational Choice Theory*. New Haven: Yale University Press, 1994.

Held, David. *Models of Democracy*. 3rd ed. Palo Alto, CA.: Stanford University Press, 2006.

Huntington, Samuel P. *The Third Wave: Democratization in the Late Twentieth Century*. Norman, OK: University of Oklahoma Press, 1991.

Landman, Todd. *Protecting Human Rights: A Comparative Study*. Chicago: University of Chicago Press, 2005.

Lowi, Theodore J. *The End of Liberalism*. 2nd ed. New York: Norton, 1979.

Page, Benjamin I., and James R. Simmons. *What Government Can Do*. Chicago: University of Chicago Press, 2000.

Morris, Irwin L., Joe A. Oppenheimer, and Karol Edward Soltan, eds. *Politics from Anarchy to Democracy: Rational Choice in Political Science*. Palo Alto, CA.: Stanford University Press, 2004.

Phillips, Kevin. *Wealth and Democracy: How Great Fortunes and Government Created America's Aristocracy*. New York: Broadway Books, 2002.

Schmidt, Diane E. *Writing in Political Science: A Practical Guide*. 3rd ed. New York: Pearson Longman, 2005.

Warren, Robert Penn. *All the King's Men*. New York: Harcourt, Brace, 1946.

GREENPEACE SAVES A WHALE   Greenpeace is an international organization devoted primarily to raising public awareness about environmental issues. The group often takes direct action to make its points. In this photo, crew members of the Japanese whaling ship *Kyo Maru* use water cannons to disperse Greenpeace activists in the freezing waters of the Southern Ocean off Antarctica in December 2001. The Greenpeace inflatable craft was driven directly in front of the ship to block the capture of a freshly harpooned minke whale.

© Agence France-Presse (AFP)

2

IDEOLOGIES: IMAGES OF POLITICAL LIFE

◆ Liberalism and Conservatism ◆ Capitalism ◆ Marxism ◆ Socialism ◆ Other Ideologies ◆ Conclusion: Ideology Shapes Political Community and Political Conflict

Each of us thinks about politics in a unique way. Our views of political issues, controversies, and values are expressions of our personalities and backgrounds. Some of us want government to make new policies, whereas others feel that it already does enough. Some of us think most about economic problems, others focus on social policies, and still others think about foreign affairs or legal or philosophical principles. Some advocate radical change, and others seek to preserve traditions.

Nevertheless, despite the individualized nature of political orientations, we can identify certain well-established *ideologies* that describe patterns of political thinking among large numbers of people. An **ideology** is a more or less coherent system of political thinking. The most elaborate and complete ideologies, such as Marxism, contain a vision of justice, an identified adversary, a plan for attaining an ideal society, and a conception of good government. Less elaborate ideologies are simply "approaches" to politics, incorporating ideas about good citizenship or assumptions regarding needed policy actions.

Understanding the most important ideologies is useful in two ways. First, the nature of the prevailing ideology that exists in a society affects the way its government works. It will influence the way citizens participate in politics, how the government makes decisions, and what people expect from government. The articulation of interests; the making, adjudication, and execution of rules; the way that people are socialized into political life—all these things are dramatically affected by the ideology that prevails among a nation's citizens. The dominant ideology in North Korea, for example, provides a foundation for widespread deference to state authority in both social and economic affairs, whereas the strong elements of individualism and capitalism in Australia help to produce a very different kind of politics. Second, the degree of ideological consensus in a political system has an important influence on its stability. If a society experiences severe ideological conflict (as Nicaragua did in the 1980s), political life is often violent and unstable, whereas a general ideological consensus contributes to a relatively settled political order, as in Britain or Japan.

In addition to the usefulness of ideology as an aid in understanding the behavior of citizens and governments, studying ideologies helps us to decide for ourselves how we feel about political issues. Many of us have a fairly good idea about the differences between liberalism and conservatism, and we may know something about Marxism, socialism, or other ideologies. But even a brief analysis of the basic principles of these ideologies may help us understand our own political thinking. An individual may find that his or her positions on affirmative action, abortion, and arms control, for example, are manifestations of a political perspective that shapes the development of many other political opinions.

The following sections discuss ideologies that vary considerably with respect to their coherence and comprehensiveness. By some strict definitions, some of them do not fully qualify as "ideologies" at all. In keeping with familiar usage, however, and because of their great practical importance, we discuss each of them here.

LIBERALISM AND CONSERVATISM

Most Americans think of themselves, to some degree, as either liberal or conservative—even people who are generally uninterested in politics. Although being a "liberal" or a "conservative" does not require a consistent adherence to a comprehensive system of thought, there is a meaningful contrast between these ways of thinking about politics.

JOHN LOCKE (1632–1704), one of the foundational philosophers of liberalism.

Liberalism

Liberalism has a long and complex history. Some analysts contend that the first important statement of **liberalism** was contained in the writings of the British political philosopher John Locke (1632–1704), whose ideas influenced the American Declaration of Independence. Perhaps the core idea of Lockean liberalism is simply the recognition that there is a sphere of individual rights that government should respect and leave untouched.

The widespread acceptance of this idea for generations in the U.S. makes it seem obvious to contemporary Americans. However, it is important to realize that other ways of thinking about politics—particularly the classical political philosophy of Plato and Aristotle—attributed no special status to individual rights. An individual's place, and his or her rights, were to be defined with respect to the nature of the social order. Liberalism *begins* with the idea that individual rights come first. Government power is then built around them, so to speak.

Modern liberalism has evolved in ways that have transformed and extended Locke's ideas. Modern liberals oppose the application of state power to enforce conventional moral, religious, or traditional standards of behavior. In this respect, they carry forward a basic component of Lockean liberalism. When some politician or group proposes a law banning abortion or prohibiting flag burning, liberals unite in opposition. In such instances, liberalism advocates the security of individual choices over the state's (or the majority's) demands for the continuation of a single set of values. Liberalism thus emphasizes *tolerance*.

Yet modern liberals advocate the expansion of government authority to counteract corporate economic power and to create social conditions that improve the opportunities for people to engage in a full, satisfying life. This is not necessarily a contradiction, although conservatives often claim that it *is* inconsistent to be simultaneously opposed to state power and also supportive of expanding that power. The consistency is in the liberal's commitment to freeing the individual from forces that interfere with personal advancement and growth. Thus, liberals want to keep the state from enforcing moral conformity, but they support aggressive *government intervention* to provide disadvantaged individuals a way out of the economic and social conditions that condemn them to a bleak, limited future.

Modern liberals see many of society's problems as being rooted in negative social conditions. Again, we can see the common thread running back to the initial concerns of liberal thinking. If, as liberals believe, individuals need to be free both from the restrictions of antiquated traditions *and* from the restrictions created by poverty in order to prosper and develop, it is logical to suppose that many people will fail to thrive when economic distress, racial discrimination, and religious intolerance frustrate their hopes. Poor people turn to crime, teenagers become pregnant and drop out of school, and rates of drug addiction reach epidemic proportions, say liberals, because social conditions deny those people real opportunities.

Although the range of identifiably "liberal" policy positions is quite wide—including everything from advocating gay rights to supporting labor unions to demanding national health plans—modern liberalism is not simply a patchwork quilt of ideas. Its precepts are held together by a faith in the ability of all people to prosper and grow. Liberal policies are thus designed to preserve the rights of individuals and to expand opportunities when social conditions dampen them.

Conservatism

The core features of conservative thinking are notoriously difficult to define. Many capsule definitions begin with the conservative's preference for preserving society's political, social, and economic traditions, thus seeing conservatism as nothing more than support for the status quo. (One of contemporary American conservatism's elder statesmen, William F. Buckley, gave support to this view of conservatism when he famously stated that the role of the conservative is simply to "stand athwart history, yelling Stop!") A second often heard claim is that the essential feature of conservatism is a deep distrust of reason as a solution to social and political problems. Neither of these views gives us a complete view of conservatism.

The most fundamental element of **conservatism** is support for the idea that *traditional values strengthen society*. Although there is considerable variety among conservatives with respect to which values are emphasized and for what purposes, most conservatives feel that humans have natural tendencies toward greed, promiscuity, aggressiveness, and sloth, and that the best way to inhibit those tendencies is through strong traditional values. Churches, schools, and even the state should act to preserve those values, according to conservative thinking, even at the expense of some freedoms.

Sir Edmund Burke (1729–1797) is often considered the father of conservative thinking, particularly in light of his 1790 essay, "Reflections on the Revolution in France."* While liberals applauded the revolution's goals of "Liberty, Equality, and

---

* The text of this classic essay may be found at the Web site of the Constitution Society: http://www.constitution.org/eb/rev_fran.htm

Fraternity," Burke was appalled by the revolution's violent attacks against the aristocracy and the church. He argued that the "customs and traditions" that define the character of a society are essential in preserving stability, culture, and progress. Burke felt
that the French revolutionaries were bent on the destruction of French culture, and
that their success in doing so would create disorder, injustice, and a lower quality of
life for all.

A particularly controversial aspect of Burke's thinking was his acceptance of *class
distinctions*. He argued that society is better off with its aristocratic heritage intact, even
if it perpetuates vast differences between the rich and the poor. Thus, Burke felt that
the trappings of class distinctions, including attendance at different churches for
upper- and lower-class citizens, differences in clothing and accents, deferential forms
of address to one's "betters," among other things, are traditions that make society work.
When people know and accept their places in society, order and stability are possible.
Perhaps reflecting that kind of thinking, all Conservative British prime ministers until
the 1970s had aristocratic roots.

In its modern form, conservatism has two identifiable branches. One focuses on
the moral sphere. According to this aspect of conservative thinking, a good society is
one in which people place greater value on "self-restraint" than self-expression and
pleasure. Conservatives are thus more inclined than liberals to support, for example,
restrictions on obscene artistic expressions, marijuana use, same-sex marriages, and
strict discipline in schools.

Consequently, conservatives often look to *erosions* of traditional moral values as the
primary cause of social ills, while modern liberals are apt to blame poverty or racism.
"Bad conditions do not cause riots, bad men do" is a commonly heard conservative
refrain. Similarly, many conservatives argue that unwanted teenage pregnancies do not
occur as a result of poverty, racism, or inadequate sex education, but as a result of the
erosion of traditional morality. In fact, conservatives often contend that public school
sex education contributes to the perception that sexual behavior has nothing to do
with values. In a wide variety of contexts, conservatism looks to moral standards as a
guide to behavior and claims that liberals, in their emphasis on tolerance, erode the
force of those moral standards, producing disorder, hopelessness, crime, and poverty.

A second identifiable branch of conservatism focuses on economic concerns.
Conservatives who focus exclusively on economics may become indistinguishable
from capitalists in their policy positions (see the following section). Free-market economics is not supported wholly by all conservatives, but it is not a coincidence that
many conservatives blend a traditional perspective on moral issues with support for
the free market. A common thread linking "traditional values" conservatism and "economic" conservatism is support for the work ethic as a traditional value. Conservatives
claim that they defend the work ethic by maintaining an economic system that
rewards initiative, talent, and hard work while penalizing idleness. Conservatives feel
liberals interfere with the market's ability to allocate resources by enacting policies
that restrict initiative and allocate rewards on the basis of need or simply to produce
a more equal distribution of wealth.

American and European conservatives tend to place differing amounts of emphasis on economic freedoms. A strong communitarian perspective is often present
among European conservatives, whereas many American conservatives embrace individualism more firmly. William Bennett, a former Secretary of Education who gained
national fame with his successful volume *The Book of Virtues*, is an exception among

© AP/Wide World Photos

CONTROVERSIAL AND CONSERVATIVE William J. Bennett, former Secretary of Education, is well known for his social conservatism. His *The Book of Virtues* exemplifies the conservative's emphasis on traditional values.

modern American conservatives, emphasizing social values much more than free-market liberties.*

The Policy Relevance of Liberal and Conservative Ideologies

In most industrialized democracies, policies typically reflect a mixture of conservative and liberal thinking. Perhaps the best illustration of this is the changing size and scope of the welfare state. Liberal administrations often expand the welfare state, while conservatives restrain their growth. A comprehensive study of U.S. income distribution policies after World War II confirmed this general impression: "When the Democrats are at average or above-average congressional strength, . . . transfer spending . . . tends to trend upward. . . ."[1] The rate of growth in social programs in this country thus reflects the ever-changing competition between liberal and conservative political influence.

Of course, when policy disputes emphasize moral concerns, it is difficult to make decisions that reflect some measure of both liberal and conservative ideology. Opposing perspectives on abortion severely divide several societies, including the United States. Many proponents of abortion rights tend to view any restriction, even laws requiring parental notification or limits on public funding of abortions, as invasions of a fundamental right. Some of those opposing abortion argue that virtually any abortion, even an abortion to save the woman's life or one to serve the victim of rape or incest, constitutes murder. The U.S. Supreme Court essentially removed this issue from the legislative process with its 1973 *Roe v. Wade* decision, and it is fair to say that many state legislators were glad that they were spared the necessity of taking an official stand.[2] An especially heated fight between liberals and conservatives in the U.S. is now raging over the definition of marriage (see Box 2-1).

* See William J. Bennett, *The Book of Virtues: A Treasury of Great Moral Stories* (New York: Simon & Schuster, 1993), and *Body Count: Moral Poverty and How to Win America's War against Crime and Drugs*, written with John J. Killulia, Jr., and John P. Walters (New York: Simon & Schuster, 1996). Bennett addresses the War on Terrorism in *Why We Fight: Moral Clarity and the War on Terrorism* (New York: Doubleday, 2002).

Box 2-1

LIBERALISM, CONSERVATISM, AND THE PROBLEM OF DEFINING MARRIAGE

There is perhaps no clearer illustration of the contrast between conservative and liberal thinking than the current debate in the United States over the definition of marriage. For several years, gay rights groups have been advocating changes in state and federal law that would give legal recognition to marriages between persons of the same sex. When it became clear that some states could take such steps, the U.S. Congress passed the "Defense of Marriage Act" (110 Stat. 2419) and President Clinton signed it into law on September 10, 1996. According to the Act:

> In determining the meaning of any Act of Congress, or of any ruling, regulation, or interpretation of the various administrative bureaus and agencies of the United States, the word "marriage" means only a legal union between one man and one woman as husband and wife, and the word "spouse" refers only to a person of the opposite sex who is a husband or a wife.

Legal experts have debated the constitutionality of the statute, arguing that it violates the Fourteenth Amendment's requirement that states give "equal protection of the laws" to all their citizens. Following this idea, the City of San Francisco began issuing marriage licenses to several thousand same-sex couples in February 2004, despite the existence of a California law banning such marriages. In August of that year, the California Supreme Court unanimously voided the nearly 4,000 marriage licenses issued in San Francisco, pointing to the existence of both legislation and a voter-approved measure in that state restricting marriage to heterosexual couples.

While the legal controversies raise issues of federalism, equal protection, and civil rights, the debate over the definition of marriage reflects the often stark differences between liberal and conservative approaches to public policy. The following statement from Lambda Legal, a prominent gay rights organization, reflects the liberal's emphasis on tolerance and freedom from restrictions imposed by a dominant majority:

> Marriage is a civil right that belongs to everyone. Loving, committed same-sex couples form families and provide emotional and economic support for each other and for their children just like other couples do. When different-sex couples apply for a marriage license, the state does not ask them

whether their relationship is worthy of its recognition, because the government has no business deciding whom a person should marry. That is a completely private, personal choice that every individual has the right to make for him or herself—a basic principle that should be as true for same-sex couples as for other couples.*

When conservatives express their concerns about same-sex marriages, liberals typically argue that no one should feel threatened by them. In effect, they ask: "How does *my* marrying someone of the same sex endanger *your* marriage?" Such questions reflect the liberal's frustration with those who would needlessly impose on the freedom of others.

Following a very different approach, conservatives emphasize the preservation of traditions that they believe are important to the stability and health of society. "Defend Marriage," a conservative advocacy group, states the conservative position in this way:

> Strong families have always been the essential foundation of every successful society. And for millennia, traditional marriage, defined as the union of a man and a woman, has been essential to the creation and protection of strong families. Legalizing same sex marriage would change forever the role that marriage plays in our society, undermining it and the family.**

A prominent conservative writer went further, arguing that allowing same-sex marriages would eventually mean an end to marriage itself:

> The way to abolish marriage, without seeming to abolish it, is to redefine the institution out of existence. If everything can be marriage, pretty soon nothing will be marriage. Legalize gay marriage, followed by multi-partner marriage, and pretty soon the whole idea of marriage will be meaningless. [This is what many same-sex marriage advocates really want]: an infinitely flexible relationship system that validates any conceivable family

*This statement is taken from Lambda Legal's Web site, www.lambdalegal.org.

**This quotation appears on the home page of "Defend Marriage," www.defendmarriage.org.

(Continued)

Box 2-1

LIBERALISM, CONSERVATISM, AND THE PROBLEM OF DEFINING MARRIAGE (*Continued*)

arrangement, regardless of the number or gender of partners. . .***

Thus, while most liberals approach the same-sex marriage controversy as a matter of individual rights being threatened by intolerance and oppression, most conservatives are concerned about the impact on what they see as necessary traditions. For example, they point

***Stanley Kurtz, *National Review Online*, February 3, 2006, quoted on the home page of the Institute for Marriage and Public Policy, www.marriagedebate.com.

to statistics showing the rising rates of births out of wedlock, and to studies showing that children raised in such households have substantially greater chances of being in poverty and being incarcerated than children raised in "traditional" families. For them, anything that threatens the traditional concept of marriage will only accelerate its demise, leading to more social dysfunction.

The definition of marriage thus goes to the core of the chasm between liberal and conservative ideology. Consequently, this is an issue that is unlikely to be resolved easily or quickly.

Liberals and conservatives often clash on college campuses. In recent years, many colleges and universities have seen passionate debates over the "Academic Bill of Rights," a controversial proposal by a leading conservative advocate. Some conservatives believe that the devotion to **multiculturalism** in nearly all major universities has itself become a source of intolerance. They claim that conservative students and faculty are denied the right to express and hear conservative criticisms of multiculturalism, and that campuses are becoming centers of oppression. The Academic Bill of Rights was designed to "protect students and professors from political bias." Here are a few key passages from the proposal, which has been considered by several state legislatures:

> . . . All faculty shall be hired, fired, promoted and granted tenure on the basis of their competence and appropriate knowledge in the field of their expertise and, in the humanities, the social sciences, and the arts, with a view toward fostering a plurality of methodologies and perspectives.
> . . . Students will be graded solely on the basis of their reasoned answers and appropriate knowledge of the subjects and disciplines they study, not on the basis of their political or religious beliefs.
> . . . Exposing students to the spectrum of significant scholarly viewpoints on the subjects examined in their courses is a major responsibility of faculty. Faculty will not use their courses for the purpose of political, ideological, religious or anti-religious indoctrination.

Is the Academic Bill of Rights a statement of liberal or conservative principles? The passages excerpted above are certainly consistent with the ideas of tolerance for diversity and dissent that are core aspects of liberalism. However, many academics have argued that, if implemented in law, it would be used to stifle the discussion of leftist views in social science and humanities classes. Some professors would be concerned that they might not be able to cover the other side adequately, thereby making them vulnerable to disciplinary action. The safest course would be to avoid controversy altogether. If the Academic Bill of Rights were fully implemented, it is difficult to say whether it would restore diversity and tolerance, as David Horowitz and his supporters claim, or whether it would usher in a new era of inhibited political discussion on college campuses.

The full text of the Academic Bill of Rights is available at http://www.studentsfor academicfreedom.org/. An essay highly critical of Horowitz and his proposal is available at http://chronicle.com/free/v50/i23/23b01301.htm.

CAPITALISM

Capitalism refers both to an economic system and to an ideology. As an economic system, capitalism may be defined by its reliance on *economic exchange* and *private owner-ship* to allocate society's resources. A capitalist system is one in which profit-seeking behavior, not governmental decision making, determines what happens in the econ-omy. Capitalist ideology provides philosophical and analytical support for such a system.*

Capitalism, like liberalism and conservatism, is not a complete ideology. It does not contain an explicit view of human history, it does not identify a specific adversary, and it does not present a picture of some future state of perfect human development. Some capitalist thinkers certainly have views on such matters, but their positions are not intrin-sic to capitalist thinking. Nevertheless, capitalism is a powerful ideology, one that con-tinues to exert considerable influence on political movements and on policy making.

The Elements of Capitalist Ideology

There are two complementary, but separately identifiable, elements in capitalist ideol-ogy. First, capitalism places a heavy emphasis on **individualism.** Whereas socialists focus on communal values and needs, those drawn to capitalism tend to emphasize individual accomplishments and talents and the private sphere of life. Advocates of capitalist ideology typically believe that the general good is best served when each individual seeks his or her economic self-interest. Adam Smith stated this idea in 1776 in his landmark treatise *An Inquiry into the Nature and Causes of The Wealth of Nations:* "[An individual who] intends only his own gain [is] led by an invisible hand to promote an end which was no part of his intention. . . . By pursuing his own interest he frequently promotes that of the society more effectually than when he really intends to promote it."[3] Factories are built, jobs are provided, and wealth is generated—all as the result of free individuals seeking profits in a free marketplace.

Second, capitalist thinking is often associated with *distrust of government control* of social resources. The capitalist sees central bureaucracies as inherently wasteful and inefficient, whereas the market, with its multitude of individual decisions driven by self-interest, is rational and productive. Government decisions are driven by the vague, ill-informed, and misguided motivations of leaders, not by the precise incentives of profit seeking. Thus, those favoring a capitalist economy point with great satisfaction to the vast differences between what used to be East Germany and West Germany. Two states with essentially similar people, a similar culture, and the same climate had very differ-ent economic growth rates and conditions between 1947 and 1990. In 1988, before German Unification, the gross domestic product (GDP) per capita was $18,480 in West Germany and only $11,860 in East Germany. An even starker contrast exists today

* The French phrase *laissez faire,* meaning "leave alone," is commonly employed to designate the essence of what we here term *capitalist* ideology.

between North and South Korea. The GDP per capita is over $20,000 in South Korea but only $1,800 in North Korea. Differences of this magnitude reflect the tremendous impact of ideology on the lives of people.[4]

Policy Implications of Capitalist Ideology

Believing in individualism and free-market economics does not require one to favor the elimination of government's role in society. If it did, capitalist ideology would have little practical relevance to real-world politics. Capitalist ideas can find their way into policy making in less radical ways.

For example, political leaders who support capitalist ideology often advocate tax policies that de-emphasize the goal of economic equality. Proportional tax rates take the same percentage of income from each citizen, regardless of income, whereas progressive systems take an increasing percentage from wealthier citizens. The rich pay more taxes than the poor under both approaches, but progressive taxes are slanted more toward the advantage of the poor. Capitalists claim that steeply progressive taxes stifle the initiative of talented people (since economic success is "penalized" by placing high earners in a higher tax bracket).

Capitalist thinking similarly supports policy choices that emphasize or strengthen private production of goods and services and that give consumers a wider range of choices. (See Box 2-2.) During the Reagan administration (1981–1989), some significant changes along those lines were made in the United States, resulting in a considerable increase in what is called *contracting out* for public services. The current trend in many Latin American societies is also toward greater privatization of state enterprises. In this arrangement, private contractors submitting the lowest qualified bid provide services previously provided by public employees. Capitalist ideology welcomes this approach as a way to harness the power of competition.

Capitalists similarly support **deregulation**. The distrust of purely profit-driven decisions has, in most industrialized nations, led to an extensive framework of regulations that restrict pricing decisions and require safety measures for workers, consumers, and the environment. Capitalist ideology supports the removal of many such regulations, both because the capitalist wants to rely on individual choice as a way to keep prices low and product quality high and because they distrust government power. Critics of capitalist thinking doubt that free-market forces would induce private enterprise to control pollution emissions, properly dispose of hazardous waste, or install sufficient safety protection in automobiles or in the workplace.

MARXISM

Strictly speaking, Marxism is the set of ideas derived from the German philosopher Karl Marx (1818–1883). In contrast to liberalism and conservatism, Marxism is an elaborate, detailed system of thought. It is therefore arguably the most complete example of an ideology. Marxism incorporates an interpretation of history, the identification of an adversary, a plan for the future, and a conception of the just society. Marx was convinced that everything important in society, even the beliefs of people, could be accounted for through the impact of class struggles: "It is not the consciousness of men that determines their existence, but, on the contrary, their social existence determines

Box 2-2

IDEOLOGY AND THE CONTROVERSY OVER "SCHOOL CHOICE"

Many analysts and citizens agree that American public schools have deteriorated during the last 30 years. Since the early 1960s, test scores have dropped, and college professors regularly complain that basic writing and math skills are lacking among high school graduates. One controversial solution, often simply termed "school choice," is remarkable for how closely it reflects capitalist thinking.

Parents and students have always had a choice about whether to attend a public school or a private or parochial school. The controversial aspect of school choice is that the state or school district would be required to give some of the tax funds that the public school would expend in educating the student to a private or a parochial school if the student chooses not to attend a public school. (The details of these proposals vary widely; some provide a voucher to parents that can be used to help pay tuition, and other plans send funding directly to the school chosen by the student and parents.)

Capitalist ideology strongly supports school choice. Proponents of the policy often point out that vigorous competition among universities has made American higher education the envy of the world, whereas the traditional system of public elementary and high schools is the closest thing in America to a purely socialist arrangement, producing inefficiencies and low-quality service. According to this point of view, when a school's administrators know that students and parents dissatisfied with their school can choose a competing school, they will make their schools better, just as Dell Computer's fear of losing business to Gateway makes them work hard to produce innovations and high-quality goods.

Opponents of school choice argue that the capitalist assumptions break down in this policy area. Even with taxpayer funds in the form of vouchers, the poorest parents often will not be able to afford the additional amount needed to pay tuition at the best private

schools; therefore, public schools will overwhelmingly become populated by students from poor families, who are more likely to have academic difficulties. Opponents also feel that public education provides a setting in which widely shared values can be instilled in students and that society will become more fragmented without the common denominator of public school experience.

In June 2002, the U.S. Supreme Court handed down a landmark decision upholding the constitutionality of a voucher program in Ohio that used taxpayer funds to pay for education in private and parochial schools. Since most private schools in the United States have a religious affiliation, one of the most controversial aspects of school choice programs is the fact that most of them permit parents to direct taxpayer funds for tuition at religious schools. Some argue that this violates the First Amendment's prohibition of the establishment of a state religion. However, in *Zelman v. Simmons-Harris* et al., the Supreme Court concluded that the Ohio program was constitutional, primarily because it allowed the parents (and not a state official) to decide which schools would receive the state money. The decision was a very close one, and this issue will continue to divide liberals and conservatives for many years.

See John E. Chubb and Terry M. Moe, *Politics, Markets, and America's Schools* (Washington, DC: Brookings Institution, 1990), for the argument favoring school choice; and see Kenneth J. Meier and Kevin B. Smith, *The Case against School Choice* (Armonk, NY: Sharpe, 1995), for the opposing view. Joseph Viteritti has written a newer book supporting the Chubb/Moe position, titled *Choosing Equality: School Choice, the Constitution, and Civil Society* (Washington, DC: Brookings, 1999). Also see Michael Mintrom, *Policy Entrepreneurs and School Choice* (Washington, DC: Georgetown University Press, 2000); and William G. Howell and Paul E. Peterson, *The Education Gap: Vouchers and Urban Schools*, rev. ed. (Washington, DC: Brookings Institution Press, 2006).

their consciousness."[5] Despite the recent decline of communism, Marxism still exerts a strong political influence in today's changing world.

Marxism can be defined as *the belief that economic conflict between a ruling class and an exploited lower class is the driving force in social and political life.* The elements of this definition require some elaboration.

Economic Exploitation and Economic Determinism

Marxism begins with the idea that people are divided into social classes, one of which suffers severe exploitation by the other. Although many other thinkers focused on this problem before and after him, Marx's analysis of the problem was fundamentally different. Conventional social critics argue that selfishness and shortsightedness among those in power are the ultimate causes of class struggles. Marx rejected this line of reasoning because it implied that the problems of society could be corrected by getting the "right" people into positions of power, perhaps by electing members of a progressive party.

Marxists believe that such strategies always fail. They argue that **economic determinism,** the belief that economic forces largely determine ideas and political movements, is the real source of everything in political life. In Marx's view, poor people are exploited not because some people are greedy or because not enough people fully understand the social costs of poverty, but because *the economic structure of society makes exploitation of the poor inevitable.* Thus, human history is the process of economic forces pushing society from one stage of development to another, until the inevitable end point is reached.

The Stages of Prehistory

The distinguishing feature of the first human societies, according to Marx, was the sharing of the basic resources of life. Primitive communism, or **communalism,** was the economic system that existed before the evolution of private property, slavery, or classes. Small bands of humans lived together in joint control over the land, wildlife, and food supplies. Marx claimed that the egalitarian, communal nature of primitive society was created by an economic fact. It was not simply that no person had yet discovered self-interest; *communal society existed because the primitive level of agricultural productivity made land ownership and slavery economically impossible.*

Why would this be true? Since each person could produce only enough to stay alive, a slave would have had to consume all that he or she produced, leaving nothing for a master to save or consume. Because nearly all one's time was spent gathering food, it was also impractical to devote resources to defending a territory. Thus, human society began as "communism by default," entirely because the primitive state of productivity made any other arrangement impractical.

Feudalism arose when agricultural productivity advanced. As some people found that they could produce more than they and their families consumed, some of them hired soldiers (fed with food not needed by the owners) to defend estates. Land ownership produced power, since large acreages could support armed strength. Feudalism thus created the first *class divisions:* in one group were those who owned the land, and in the other were those who worked on it.

Capitalism emerged as a consequence of further economic development. Greater farm productivity made resources available for enterprises other than agriculture, and people acquired power through their ownership of *capital.* They invested that capital in factories, hiring workers to trade their labor for wages. The "surplus value" created by the workers was then taken by the capitalists, who used it to add to their wealth and power.

A core idea of Marxism holds that capitalism contains flaws (Marxists call them "contradictions") that make its demise inevitable. Capitalists would eventually have to compete aggressively with one another, forcing them to exploit workers ever more severely. Wages would drop, work hours would increase, and work conditions would deteriorate. And, unlike the exploited serfs under feudalism, the increasingly exploited workers under capitalism (the "proletariat") lived and worked together in large numbers in factory settings.

This was a fatal "contradiction" of capitalism, entirely created by the *economic facts* regarding industrial production: Masses of workers were exploited with increasing cruelty at the same time that they were brought into close contact with one another, thus becoming a potentially powerful political force. The downtrodden workers would achieve a sense of class consciousness, realizing their common bond and their common capitalist class enemies. Capitalism would have to fall.

The resulting system would be the next stage: *socialism*. Under the new system, workers would be paid fairly, industrial production would be driven by the real needs of the vast majority of people, and, most important, there would no longer be a ruling class. Eventually, productivity would increase to the point at which all the real needs of society could be satisfied without government help. *Communism* would eventually emerge, the state would "wither away" with no class conflict to resolve, ownership of the means of production would pass from the state to the workers, and "true" history would finally begin.

The Political Relevance of Marxist Ideology

In discussing how Marxism has affected government and politics, it is essential to remember that Marx himself was primarily an economic philosopher and his main contribution was the development of a theory. The real "founding father" of **communism**—and of the first communist system, the Soviet Union—was Vladimir Ilyich Ulyanov, better known as Lenin (1870–1924). Hence, we usually speak of the guiding ideology of communist systems as "Marxism-Leninism."*

Lenin developed the idea of the Communist Party as the "vanguard of the proletariat," a firmly organized unit that could understand the needs of the working class even when workers themselves were confused or misled. Lenin emphasized measures to ensure the expansion of the party's exclusive position of power. In fact, much of what is distinctive about actual communist political systems derives from Lenin's ideas regarding party organization and control. There are at least two characteristic aspects of communist systems.

First, the premise that political conflict is essentially a conflict between workers and those who exploit them leads to a restricted view of politics. Competitive political party systems are illegitimate in Marxist-Leninist thinking because only the Communist Party is believed to have the true interests of the people (that is, the working class) at heart. Until very recently, countries dominated by Marxist-Leninist thinking have all been one-party states. Only after the influence of Marxism receded have competitive electoral processes been established in formerly communist countries.

---

* Similarly, Chinese communism is sometimes termed "Marxism-Leninism-Maoism" because of the importance of Mao Zedong's influence on that version of the ideology. In addition to Lenin and Mao, Fidel Castro, Ché Guevara, and others adapted and altered Marxist concepts in the course of revolutionary movements. We outline the most crucial of the extensions of Marxism in discussing Russia and China (Chapters 13 and 14).

Second, communist governments have frequently used the idea of class conflict as the intellectual justification for repressing political, religious, and artistic expression.* Drawing on Marx's contention that "religion is the opium of the people," Marxist governments in Europe and elsewhere have restricted religious freedom, viewing the Orthodox and Catholic churches as distracting the working class from its true political interests.

Although precise data are often lacking, there is some evidence that Marxist revolutions in underdeveloped nations have produced greater economic equality and more social welfare programs for the poor. For example, whereas most of Latin America is characterized by great income disparities between rich and poor, the Cuban Revolution created far greater economic equality as well as the region's most extensive educational and health-care programs. Proponents of Marxism like to note that Cuba has the highest literacy rate, lowest infant mortality, and longest life expectancy of any nation in Latin America. Comparisons favorable to Marxism are more difficult to find in the developed world; pre-1990 Germany was divided into a communist side with a low standard of living (with a somewhat more equal distribution of income), terrible pollution problems, and other difficulties, and a capitalist side with such superior economic and social conditions that a wall had to be built to prevent migration from East to West.

SOCIALISM

Socialism is a much more generalized ideology that actually predates Marxism. Although many socialists, particularly in years past, have shared many Marxist beliefs, others have not. Socialism shares with Marxism a deep concern about the divisive effects of private property, and it too is driven by a hope that greater social and economic equality can be achieved. Some socialists would even agree that the best way to make progress is to work toward a revolution, although socialist ideology does not require such a position. Once we get beyond the basic problem of social inequality, it becomes clear that *socialism* is a term applied to a rather diverse range of approaches to politics.

Socialism: A Confusing Political Term

The term **socialism** is used in many different ways, creating enormous confusion. Marx used the term specifically, to mean the stage of "prehistory" subsequent to the fall of capitalism and before the "withering away of the state" under communism. Marxist regimes in the former Soviet Union, China, Cuba, and Eastern Europe have referred to themselves as socialist in that sense, because the state has not withered away, nor has it given direct control over the means of production to the workers.

In twentieth-century Western Europe, however, socialism took on a far different meaning. Competing socialist and communist political parties, often sharply antagonistic toward each other, developed in nations such as France and Italy. The communist parties (with the notable exception of the Italian communists) generally accepted the political supremacy of the Soviet Union and its authoritarian political system. In contrast,

---

* Many contemporary Marxist political thinkers and intellectuals, particularly in Europe, strongly support democratic principles, arguing that there is no necessary contradiction between Marxist theory and democracy. However, the record of Marxist regimes in practice has not been tolerant of opposing points of view.

most socialist parties throughout Western Europe were highly critical of the Soviet Union and strongly committed to democratic principles.

At one time or another during the past two decades, socialist political parties have governed Great Britain, France, West Germany, Greece, Spain, Portugal, Sweden, Norway, and other Western European democracies. Even in the United States, a few cities have had socialist mayors, and Vermont now has a socialist congressman (though he is officially listed as an independent). These leaders—as well as former French President François Mitterrand, former West German Prime Minister Willy Brandt, and other Western European socialist politicians—have a different view of socialism from that associated with the leaders of China and North Korea. Indeed, Brandt and many Western European socialist leaders were noted for their strong attacks on Soviet foreign policy and for their support of democratic political rights. In this discussion, then, we are considering socialism as an identifiable ideology that can be distinguished from Marxism. In its most moderate forms, European-style socialism is referred to as *social democracy*.

Fundamental Elements of Socialism

The core idea of socialism is the assumption that a just society requires purposeful social action, or, to put it negatively, that actions based on *private interests* prevent the achievement of a fair society. Socialists focus on the potential for *community* and *public interest*, opposing what they see as an excessive emphasis on profit seeking and self-interest in other approaches to political life. Clearly, the most important fault socialists find in capitalist systems is social and economic inequality, but the creation of greater equality is not their only goal. Socialists also want to establish a greater public role to counter the forces dividing society and the selfishness unleashed by private interests.

Nowhere is this sentiment more wonderfully captured than in the following statement by French philosopher Jean-Jacques Rousseau (1712–1778):

> The first man, who after enclosing a piece of ground, took it into his head to say, *this is mine*, and found people simple enough to believe him, was the real founder of civil society. How many crimes, how many wars, how many murders, how many misfortunes and horrors, would that man have saved the human species, who . . . should have cried to his fellows: Beware of listening to this impostor; you are lost, if you forget that the fruits of the earth belong equally to us all, and the earth itself to nobody![6]

Beyond their agreement with that idea, socialists are a diverse lot. The person generally regarded as the first to use the term *socialism* was a British industrialist named Robert Owen (1771–1858). He supported the free-market system in most respects, although he advocated the establishment of state schools and supported the idea, radical for its time, that children under 12 years of age should not be permitted to work a full (thirteen-hour) day. Although one does not have to be a socialist to agree wholeheartedly with those reforms, they do embody the essence of socialism: The force of the public interest must be brought to bear as a restraint on the forces of private interest.[7]

For most socialists, profit-motivated behavior is less fair and even less efficient than public decision making, and thus socialists favor public ownership of much industrial production. Democratic socialist governments in Western Europe have taken control only of certain key industries, such as steel, electric power, or railroads. Public ownership means, for a socialist, that prices and wages will be set equitably, the environment will be protected, work conditions will be safe, and consumers will obtain reliable products and services. It should be noted, however, that, in practice, European socialist parties in countries such as France and Spain have recently become far more skeptical about the value of state ownership in the economy. Still, they continue to believe that the state should be able to allocate scarce resources to where they are most needed, not simply to where the market demands them.

Democratic Socialism and Marxism

It is often argued that democratic socialism and Marxism share a common view of social injustice but that they diverge with respect to what should be done about it. Marxists (especially those who accept Lenin's ideas) typically advocate revolution, whereas democratic socialists believe in working for change through democratic political channels. Although some people who consider themselves Marxists would not agree, most Marxists assume that political decision making in a prerevolutionary society is inevitably driven by the interests of a ruling capitalist class or landed gentry.

Most Marxists reject the idea that capitalists can be "voted out" of power, and they therefore distrust elections.* (An important exception to this generalization was the Marxist-Leninist Sandinista Party in Nicaragua, which allowed elections in which opposition parties voted it out of power in 1984.) In contrast, democratic socialists work for progressive policies and programs in hopes of creating greater equality of economic conditions and opportunities and bringing communal interests to bear on social choices.

Perhaps the most important aspect of this divergence has to do with the problem of democracy itself. Democratic socialists accept the idea of democracy as a *process*. When people are able to express their views and choose among competitive parties, socialists expect to be able to achieve their objectives. Many Marxists define democracy as an *outcome*—namely, a just distribution of wealth. Democracy, for a Marxist, thus requires the elimination of class divisions; as long as class differences exist, the democratic process is empty, misleading, and doomed to fail.

The Political Relevance of Socialist Ideology

Despite the diversity among those who support socialism, there is an identifiable pattern of policy choices associated with this ideology. First, as noted earlier, socialist systems usually have adopted some degree of *public ownership* of banking, communications, transportation, and steel production, among other industries, to ensure that allocations are in the public interest.

Second, socialist governments usually *regulate private industries* extensively. A distrust of profit-driven decision making leads to government requirements regarding worker safety, equity in compensation of employees, consumer safety, and environmental protection. Although all modern governments have adopted at least some regulatory initiatives, socialist ideology is associated with more extensive and more comprehensive regulation of private industry.

---

* Marx hedged somewhat on this question late in his career when he conceded that workers might be able to seize power democratically in Great Britain.

Third, socialist countries have *large, expensive welfare systems*. The government sector of the economy employs a large proportion of the workforce in implementing programs for social security, education, income maintenance, and health care. Many socialists contend that a basic income and adequate medical care are fundamental human *rights*, not simply advantages that those with good fortune can enjoy. Along with a large **welfare state** (an extensive array of government programs in housing, health care, and education), socialist ideology generally leads to higher public spending relative to the size of the economy. For example, socialist thinking has long influenced politics in Sweden, and government spending there is quite high, but it is much lower in less-socialist Paraguay.

The high taxes and extensive welfare state associated with socialist ideology are also linked to a fourth policy implication of socialism: *redistribution of income*. Socialists, as discussed earlier, are often drawn to their ideology by a concern for the plight of the poor and by a corresponding discomfort at the opulence of the rich. Socialists contend that taking from the rich does not rob them of anything they genuinely need (since they have enough left to provide for themselves), but that it does make the difference between stark poverty and a minimally acceptable standard of living for the poor. Hence, not only do socialist systems have high taxes, but their tax systems also take a larger proportion of taxes from those with high incomes. (See Box 2-3.)

Despite the socialist emphasis on income equality, it is not always true that socialist systems as a whole are strikingly more egalitarian than other systems. Some comparisons suggest that socialism leads to greater equality—for example, largely socialist Sweden has greater income equality than France. Yet capitalist South Korea and Taiwan both have very high income equality, approaching a distribution of wealth similar to that in communist China.

In a controversial empirical study, two prominent political scientists attempted to determine the effect of socialism on economic equality. Although individual comparisons can be found to support the idea that socialist ideology promotes greater equality, the results of this study supported the idea that *higher levels of economic development are, in general, associated with greater equality* and that the degree to which the country adopts socialist policies makes little difference.[8] For example, on the "Gini Index" measure of income inequality (in which higher scores indicate greater inequality), China's score of 44.7 is considerably higher than the U.S. score of 40.8, and South Korea's 31.6 score indicates greater equality than in Mexico, which received a score of 54.6.[9] Obviously, there is no simple explanation for differences among nations with respect to income inequality.

Fifth, socialist ideology usually favors *public service delivery* over private services. Support for public education is actually widespread in most industrialized countries, but public education is especially central to socialist thinking. Reliance on private institutions to provide educational services would be contrary to socialist principles both because, according to socialists, it would foster elitism and because a public educational institution is the most effective way to instill communal, shared ideals in the citizenry. Socialists favor public over private service delivery in other areas, of course, including most municipal services (public safety, road building and repair, garbage collection, prison administration, and many others). The public role in these areas allows the government to make policy choices in accordance with community purposes, and, as an additional socialist benefit, it enables government to provide employment opportunities to those who may not be able to obtain private jobs.

Box 2-3

THE "THIRD WAY"

The 1980s saw a substantial decline in the fortunes of left-leaning parties with socialist sympathies in several Western nations. Ronald Reagan and Margaret Thatcher became two of the world's most powerful leaders, and their support of most principles of capitalist ideology was a central part of their approaches to government. Supporters of movements toward greater socialism concluded that their parties needed to change their message in order to return to power.

British Prime Minister Tony Blair successfully advocated a "Third Way," blending substantial state activism in education, welfare, public transportation, and other areas with a strong dose of economic prudence and traditional management principles. His good friend Bill Clinton also won two elections quite handily by using this approach in his campaigns. For both Blair and Clinton, the "Third Way" was presented as tough on crime and generally friendly toward business, while supporting most feminist and minority concerns and maintaining a strong role for the state in providing social services.

The precise meaning of the "Third Way" is open to dispute. Some observers claim that it has no new substance, and that it is simply an attempt by traditional left-leaning politicians to disguise their more liberal policy positions to get votes from moderate citizens. However, at least with respect to Blair and Clinton, it is arguable that they forged a combination of policy positions that was genuinely distinctive. For example, Bill Clinton publicly supported the death penalty, he signed the "Defense of Marriage Act," and his most important achievements as president were his success in obtaining U.S. ratification of the North American Free Trade Agreement (NAFTA) and his decision to sign a Republican-sponsored welfare reform plan. A very high percentage of Democrats opposed those policy positions. Although the death penalty is not a significant issue in Britain, Tony Blair has frequently supported internationalist policies. At the same time, both Clinton and Blair supported trade unions, affirmative action programs, and expansions of national health insurance, policy positions strongly supported by those on the left. Another elected leader who embraced the "Third Way" was former Prime Minister Adolfo Suarez of Spain.

George W. Bush has arguably moved toward some of the same middle ground. While much of his party's base remains solidly conservative and opposed to any kind of activist government policies, he has successfully expanded the U.S. welfare state more than any president since Lyndon Johnson in the 1960s. With an increased public role in education and in providing prescription drug benefits to older Americans, Bush's policies may be seen as attempting to graft some conservative principles onto "big government" programs. According to political scientist Jonathan Rauch, Bush's ideas accept a much stronger government role than conservative Republicans have traditionally accepted: "government curtails freedom not by being large or active but by making choices that should be left to the people. . . . If he needs to expand government to deliver more choices—well, he can live with that."*

The leading books on this subject are by Anthony Giddens, the sociologist who coined the term: *The Third Way* (London: Polity Press, 1998), *Beyond Left and Right* (Polity Press, 1994), and *The Third Way and Its Critics* (Polity Press, 2000).

*Jonathan Rauch, "The Accidental Radical," *National Journal*, July 25, 2003, http://www.nationaljournal.com/about/njweekly/stories/2003/0725nj1.htm

---

OTHER IDEOLOGIES

Most contemporary political systems make policies that, in varying degrees and mixtures, reflect the ideologies already discussed. Still other ideological strains can be identified, however, and although they have not been as pervasive, these other ideologies have exerted considerable influence on policy decisions, important political movements, or both.

Feminism

Feminism actually applies to two rather different sets of ideas. On one hand, feminism is the demand that females should enjoy the same rights and responsibilities enjoyed by males and that laws and practices placing females in a lower status are unfair, foolish, and wasteful. This type of feminism is largely a statement of basic liberal principles specifically applied to the rights of women. On the other hand, feminism also refers to an approach that attempts to identify special feminine (and masculine) qualities, usually arguing that feminine qualities have not been fully appreciated and that masculine qualities have dominated and distorted social and cultural development.

The first variety of feminism is a widespread, sustained movement that focuses on opening opportunities for women with respect to voting and other civil rights and the removal of gender restrictions in various occupations and in the armed services. For example, a woman may not legally drive a car in contemporary Saudi Arabia, and the former Taliban government of Afghanistan prevented women from obtaining education and mandated severe beatings for women who appeared in public without the *burkas* that covered them literally from head to toe.

Although the Taliban regime was perhaps the most extreme form of widespread restrictions on women's rights, it is important to note that women were denied the vote in virtually all democracies until the early 1900s. In its simplest forms, feminism is a demand that these kinds of inequities be removed. Often, feminists argue that removing legal or even constitutional restrictions is not enough; there must be representation of women where traditions and "old boy" networks effectively exclude them, even when laws officially open the doors to all applicants. Hence, feminists have fought for the appointment of more women to leadership positions in government, universities, and professions historically considered beyond their reach (firefighting, science teaching, space programs).

Feminism also embraces noneconomic policies. The abortion issue occupies a central place among feminist policy demands in the United States, and it is related to the status of women in several ways. Most feminists argue that laws restricting abortion lead women to obtain dangerous illegal abortions, and they note that men are not subject to any parallel restriction. More fundamentally, they see abortion restrictions as a violation of privacy. In Africa, many feminists battle against forced female circumcision, a painful procedure designed to minimize women's enjoyment of sex.

Relatedly, feminists argue that the burdens of childrearing fall disproportionately on women and that the government should act to eliminate this disparity. In many industrialized democracies, taxpayers provide day-care services to any woman needing them, and many feminists argue that this policy should be widely adopted. Without such a policy in place, most men are able to advance their careers while many women are forced to compromise theirs, inevitably falling behind. State-sponsored child care is one way to spread the burden of this essential social function equally between the sexes. (In Cuba, the nation's Family Code requires both spouses to share equally in housework, although it is not clear that the provision is well enforced.)

The second variant of feminism (sometimes termed "radical" or "gender" feminism) generally supports those and other efforts to achieve social and economic equality, but it focuses more on the *differences* between the sexes. Some of these feminists contend that females have greater humanism, are more pacifist, and have a broader ability to nurture than males do, and that these characteristics stem from fundamental biological differences.[10] The fact that men continue to hold dominant positions in corporations, government, and education suggests that the nature of private and public life is driven by the "male" traits of competition and individualism. Identifying essential feminine characteristics helps us to see, according to these feminists, that society would become more peaceful, more humane, and more community-oriented if females achieve equal status.

Both strands of feminist thinking will likely grow in importance in the years ahead. At least in the industrial democracies, women have become influential players in national leadership positions, and feminists have acquired a strong voice in academic and policy-making circles. Although it is important to note that feminism embodies a very diverse set of ideas, this ideology will have considerable impact on virtually all areas of public policy in future decades.

Libertarianism

The basic feature of libertarian ideology is its insistence on *liberty* from government control. The movement thus shares some of the views of both liberalism and capitalism. Libertarians oppose laws restricting abortion or the freedoms of religion and expression. They also oppose the military draft, restrictions on drug use, occupational-safety legislation, and most pollution-control laws. They support an isolationist foreign policy, primarily because an active foreign policy usually requires extensive preparations for war, which interfere with personal freedom on many levels.

Libertarians differ sharply, however, with the modern liberals' support of government as a force to create or maintain better conditions for the poor and disadvantaged. For example, most libertarians oppose the minimum wage law. If a person wants to sell his or her labor for $4 per hour, and if an employer wants to buy it at that price, libertarians believe that government has no right to interfere. Moreover, they contend the government has no right to force people to use seat belts in a car or to wear helmets while riding motorcycles. Libertarians disagree with conservatives regarding laws that would ban illegal drug use, prostitution, or obscenity.

Thus, both left and right are attracted and repelled by **libertarianism.** Both liberals and conservatives support the ideal of privacy in different ways, but each also advocates principles regarding the public interest, and each contains some idea of "civic virtue." Liberals suggest that the public interest requires certain activist social policies, and conservatives argue that the public interest demands the support of traditional values that nurture and preserve culture. In very different ways, then, both liberalism and conservatism advocate an activist government. In contrast, libertarianism will probably always be a limited movement because its ideas cannot incorporate any positive idea of the public interest.

Environmentalism

A great number of people, primarily in developed societies, are deeply concerned about the physical environment, and some of them approach politics and government largely through those concerns. There are many interest groups and at least one well-known political party, the Green Party, for which environmental issues are central. At the beginning of the twenty-first century, **environmentalism** has become large and influential enough to be considered an ideology.

For most people, environmental issues are simply one kind of important issue, to be considered and debated alongside other issues, such as poverty, national defense, economic security, and education. But quite a few citizens in the United States, Western Europe, Japan, and elsewhere are convinced that current threats to the environment are so critical that virtually every policy decision should be made on the basis of its potential impact on the environment. Thus, these people are interested not only in specific pollution control plans but also in the globalization of the economy, public transportation, public management of housing patterns, and foreign aid programs, among many other kinds of policies. As was evident in Seattle, Washington in 2000, and in Hong Kong in 2005, protesters concerned about the environment can become violent in opposing globalization of commerce.

The environmental movement focused on fairly specific policy objectives a few decades ago. The publication of Rachel Carson's *Silent Spring* was a landmark event, depicting how pesticides such as DDT had devastated several endangered bird species.[11] Serialized in 1962 in *The New Yorker*, Carson's book eventually led to severe restrictions on pesticide use. Environmentalists were also key players in the development of regulations on automobile emissions. However, the more recent issue of "global warming" has produced an even more contentious debate, largely because the actions proposed to address the issue would arguably shake the foundations of industrial society.

There is considerable uncertainty regarding the impact of human activity on global temperatures. Lonnie Thompson, professor of geological sciences at Ohio State, claims that massive glaciers and ice caps around the world will melt in the next 15 years as a result of an increase in global temperatures caused by human activity.[12] The environmental movement has seized on this kind of report, arguing that dramatic reductions in automobile and industrial emissions must be made immediately. Storms will become more severe, drought will kill millions, and coastal cities will be flooded, all because of the influence of industrialization on the atmosphere, according to this position. A special-effects laden Hollywood blockbuster, "The Day After Tomorrow" (2004), built on the idea of global warming and the need to take severe steps to stop it.

The Kyoto Treaty (official name: Kyoto Protocol to the United Nations Framework Convention on Climate Change) was negotiated in 1997 and became effective after Russia's decision to sign it in 2005. It was designed to scale back the production of hydrocarbon emissions, primarily in the industrialized nations, and the refusal of the United States to ratify it remains controversial. Critics of the treaty point out that it would not affect the growth of emissions in India or China, two massive areas in which emissions are currently growing at dramatic rates. They also point out that many scientists are skeptical about how significantly the treaty's provisions would affect the environment. Supporters see it as a vital step to protect the globe from catastrophic events.

One critic of Kyoto, Richard Lindzen, a professor of meteorology at the Massachusetts Institute of Technology, complained that the U.S. National Academy of Sciences Report on Climate Change, of which he was a coauthor, has been seriously misinterpreted by the press. He concluded that "the Kyoto Protocol would not result in a substantial reduction in global warming" and that "we are not in a position to confidently attribute past climate change to carbon dioxide or to forecast what the climate will be in the future."[13] The controversy will not end as long as developed and developing nations continue to use millions of tons of fossil fuels, raising important questions about the effects of industrialization on the environment.[14]

With the demise of communism, a great deal of political energy that was previously expended on class-based revolutionary struggle and other such issues is now being devoted to environmental problems. Left-leaning parties in industrialized countries have incorporated environmental concerns into their platforms, but it is fair to say that environmentalism transcends traditional party lines. In the United States, for example, a substantial number of upper-class voters, most of whom support the Republican Party, have become ardent advocates for environmental preservation, especially wilderness protection. The environmental debate will doubtlessly grow in importance in the years to come.

Fascism

As an ideology, **fascism** is short on intellectual content and long on emotion. All ideologies have an element of emotional appeal, of course; people have been known to wax sentimental over socialism, Marxism, and even capitalism. But fascist thinking seems to thrive on emotion. Fascism is aimed more at the heart than at the mind.

The components of fascism vary with culture and the particular historical context in which it takes root. However, all fascist thinking includes an extreme belief in *political obedience,* a pathological *distrust of foreigners,* and the conviction that *progress is possible only through conquest and war.* The following "Commandments of the Fascist Fighter" capture the essence of fascist ideology: "Whoever is not ready to give himself body and soul for his country and to serve . . . without discussion, is not worthy. . . . Discipline is not only a virtue of the soldiers in the ranks, it must also be the practice of every day. And thank God every day for having made you Fascist and Italian!"[15] Although those statements were written to inspire Benito Mussolini's Fascist movement in Italy in the 1930s, they reflect the general character of fascism: slavish obedience, an appetite for war, and extreme nationalism.

The policy content of fascist ideology is vague, except that it always supports a large military establishment and a sense of "supernationalism." In addition, fascist distrust of foreigners typically promotes racist or ethnic divisions, as when Hitler targeted the Jews as enemies of German culture, when ultrarightists in South Africa attacked blacks, or when Iraq's Saddam Hussein effectively designated the Kurds as a group to be eliminated. In Europe, where the ideology originated, fascism was historically associated with anti-Semitism and has retained that feature in almost all settings. Fascism clearly rejects the liberal's notion that all people have equal rights that should be protected and enhanced. But fascism does not speak directly to questions regarding economic systems or many specific problems of social policy.

Some have argued that fascism is simply an extreme form of conservatism, since it is primarily driven by a fanatical attraction to the traditions of the dominant culture. Historically, extreme conservatives in Europe and Latin America have on occasion joined forces with fascist movements. Fascism, however, usually destroys the institutions from which the customs and traditions of a society derive. Whereas conservatives often support traditional religious values, fascists usually permit only a state-approved version of religion (or no religion at all) to exist as a source of influence. Fascists also dominate business and economic enterprise, subordinating those private affairs to the needs of the state. Even extreme conservatism thus breaks with fascism; the elimination of all pillars of traditional society is necessary for fascists but abhorrent to conservatives.

Given their emphasis on supernationalism and military might, it is not surprising that fascist governments have often brought their countries to war. Although people may quibble over which countries may fairly be considered fascist, Hitler's Germany, Mussolini's Italy, and Saddam Hussein's Iraq were arguably fascist states, and all were thoroughly defeated in war.

Islamic Fundamentalism

We normally don't think of religions as political ideologies, and Western religions generally have restricted themselves to the spiritual realm, at least in modern times. But, it should be noted that the Catholic Church has been closely linked to important Christian Democratic political parties in Europe and Latin America and those parties have, in turn, based their ideologies substantially on church teaching. And, the so-called "Christian Right" of American Protestantism has been closely linked to the conservative wing of the Republican Party and other conservative movements. Similarly, leftist politicians such as Jesse Jackson and Al Sharpton have used their religious backgrounds as a base of political support in the Democratic Party.

In the Islamic world there has always been a far closer link between politics and religion. For example, in the Turkish empire that dominated the Middle East for several centuries, the Caliph was both the temporal ruler of the empire and the top official of the Muslim religion. Today in the Muslim world (stretching from Indonesia to Turkey), there are some countries in which there is a very close linkage between the political and the religious systems (Saudi Arabia and Iran, for example) and others in which there is more of a separation of church and state (Egypt and, especially, Turkey). Adherents of Islam themselves vary from very secular Muslims to fundamentalists who believe that the Koran, the Muslim holy book, must be interpreted literally and that government laws and policies should reflect traditional Islamic values in all aspects of human life.

Just as fundamentalists are a minority of Christian believers in the Western world, Islamic fundamentalists are a minority in the Middle East and other parts of the Muslim world. Moreover, even within the fundamentalist minority, most reject violence and some (including the Saudi royal family) are strongly pro-Western.

Despite their minority status, adherents of fundamentalist beliefs and militant (violent) fundamentalist Islam have multiplied recently in the Middle East and other parts of the Islamic world (most notably in Afghanistan and Pakistan). Militant **Islamic Fundamentalism** has the qualities both of a political ideology and of a religious theology. It envisions an ideal political system in which political leaders are inspired by the Koran, in which Western and other non-Islamic values are largely purged from society, and in which citizens are required to live according to traditional Islamic codes. In February 2006, Abdul Rahman, a citizen of Afghanistan who had converted to Christianity, was on trial for his life for his religious beliefs. U.S. Secretary of State Condoleezza Rice and others put considerable pressure on the government of Afghanistan, and Rahman was finally released. He is now living in exile in Italy. This incident illustrates the conflict between Islamic Fundamentalism and the most basic freedoms associated with democracy.

In some cases, the spread of fundamentalist Islamic beliefs has been driven by bitterness against those countries' corrupt and repressive governments (Egypt, Pakistan, Iran, and others), which has generally been transferred to hatred of the United States and other Western countries. For example, the first Islamic revolution took place in Iran, whose Shah (emperor) had been closely linked to the West. Following the revolution,

© AP/Wide World Photos

IDEOLOGY AND LEADERSHIP   Iranian President Mahmoud Ahmadinejad speaks during a conference on Wednesday October 26, 2005 in Tehran entitled "The World without Zionism." He has said that Israel should be "wiped off the map."

the fundamentalist clergymen who ruled Iran referred to the United States as "the great Satan." Moreover, because Islamic fundamentalist movements were often among the first to risk protesting against those unpopular governments and were willing to go to jail or to die for their political principles, many Muslims came to identify the Islamic fundamentalist movement with democracy; because Western-style economic modernization in countries such as Iran, Jordan, and Egypt has failed to improve the lives of many citizens, many of the poor and middle classes have bitterly turned away from Western development models and toward fundamentalism. Finally, fundamentalist movements have successfully linked Israel with Western modernization and have used Arab enmity toward Israel to appeal to their countrymen.

The influence of Islamic Fundamentalism is apparent in both the domestic and the foreign policies of several nations, and it motivates important political movements that challenge the governments of countries not officially run by fundamentalists. Some contend that this way of thinking is on the wrong side of history, with its anti-modern, anti-democratic features, but others see it as a force that will grow for decades to come. At least for the present, Islamic Fundamentalism is an ideology that demands our attention.[16]

Anarchism

The idea of a society without government, or **anarchism**, appears in many different contexts. Some religious traditions contain elements of anarchism in their belief that secular influences (such as government) should be limited or are unnecessary. Some early socialists believed that once private property was eliminated, a common bond would develop among all people, making government obsolete. Serious anarchists consistently paint an idealized picture of human society, one in which community and sharing replace individual interests and competition. In such a world, government becomes a useless relic and is soon discarded.*

More radical anarchists work to destroy government by force and violence. Although usually motivated by some particular concern, violent anarchists put their energy more into destruction than into creating a new order or demanding innovative policies. As an ideology, anarchism is thus profoundly limited, both in practical and in philosophical terms.

CONCLUSION: IDEOLOGY SHAPES POLITICAL COMMUNITY AND POLITICAL CONFLICT

Any overview of ideology will necessarily omit some perspectives or movements that some people consider important. The New Left, certain racially based movements, extreme religious sects, and other approaches to politics also could have been discussed as examples of ideologies. The ideologies considered here are those with the greatest political significance.

Most people are not, strictly speaking, ideologues. The typical citizen rarely thinks about politics in the systematic, philosophical manner characteristic of ideology. Moreover, when most people consider fundamental political principles, they often combine aspects of different ideologies in their thinking. Some people with strong socialist impulses, for example, are also favorable toward certain aspects of capitalism.

Nevertheless, although only a small percentage of citizens are ideologically inclined, appreciating the elements of existing ideologies is a necessary part of learning the language of political life.

* Some of the counterculture leaders of the 1960s in the United States and Western Europe articulated heartfelt notions along these lines. In a highly euphoric state, many interpreted the famous Woodstock festival, in which 300,000 people lived together for three days of "peace, love, and music," as confirmation that people could live together without government if they only had the right frame of mind.

 WHERE ON THE WEB?

http://www.sosig.ac.uk/roads/subject-listing/World-cat/polideol.html
Includes links to dozens of other sites relevant to the main ideologies discussed here.

http://www.swif.uniba.it/lei/filpol/filpole/homefpe.htm
An Italian site (in English) that provides a great amount of material related to political philosophy.

http://www.conservative.org
The Web page of the American Conservative Union; includes ratings of members of Congress as measured by the extent to which they vote in accordance with conservative principles.

http://www.adaction.org/main.html
The Web page for the Americans for Democratic Action, "the nation's oldest liberal political organization." The ADA is perhaps best known for its rating of members of Congress as measured by the extent to which they vote in accordance with liberal principles.

http://www.thefire.org/

As stated on its Web page, the Foundation for Individual Rights in Education is a "nonprofit educational foundation devoted to free speech, individual liberty, religious freedom, the rights of conscience, legal equality, due process, and academic freedom on our nation's campuses."

http://cc.org

The Web page of the Christian Coalition, a conservative religious organization with significant political activities in the United States.

http://www.now.org

The Web page of the National Organization for Women, a liberal/feminist political organization based in the United States.

http://www.cwfa.org/

The Web page of the Concerned Women for America, a conservative women's group based in the United States.

◆ ◆ ◆

Key Terms and Concepts_____

anarchism	feudalism
capitalism	ideology
communalism	individualism
communism	Islamic Fundamentalism
conservatism	liberalism
deregulation	libertarianism
economic determinism	Marxism
environmentalism	multiculturalism
fascism	socialism
feminism	welfare state

Discussion Questions_____

1. Give two examples of policy choices or positions associated with liberal and conservative ideology.
2. What is the role of economic analysis in Marxist ideology?
3. Is feminism one ideology or two?
4. What do you think makes some people more rigid than others in their adherence to an ideology?

Notes_____

1. See Douglas A. Hibbs, Jr., and Christopher Dennis, "Income Distribution in the United States," *American Political Science Review* 82 (June 1988): 482, 485. A more recent study confirms the pattern, particularly with respect to taxation policy. See Carla Inclan, Dennis P. Quinn, and Robert Y. Shapiro, "Origins and Consequences of Changes in U.S. Corporate Taxation: 1981–1998," *American Journal of Political Science* 45 (January 2001): 179–201.
2. More recent decisions have given state legislatures more latitude in which to enact limits on abortion practices. See *Webster v. Reproductive Health Services*, 109 S.Ct. 3040 (1989), and *Planned Parenthood v. Casey*, 112 S.Ct. 2791 (1992). Neither of these cases held that the right

to seek an abortion is not protected by the Constitution (a right established in 1973 in *Roe v. Wade*, 410 U.S. 113), but they upheld state laws requiring, among other things, a waiting period before an abortion can be performed. On the other hand, in *Stenberg v. Carhart*, 530 U.S. 914 (2000), the Supreme Court struck down a Nebraska law that prohibited what some abortion-rights opponents term "partial birth abortion," because the law arguably created unclear limits on the right to an abortion.

3. Adam Smith, quoted in Milton Friedman and Rose Friedman, *Free to Choose* (New York: Harcourt Brace Jovanovich, 1980), p. 2.

4. Figures for Germany are taken from Michael J. Sullivan, ed., *Measuring Global Values* (New York: Praeger, 1991), p. 102; and figures for North and South Korea from the *CIA World Factbook*, http://www.cia.gov/cia/publications/factbook/rankorder/2004rank.html.

5. Karl Marx, "A Contribution to the Critique of Political Economy, Preface," in *Marx and Engels: Collected Works*, vol. 29, *Marx: 1858–1861* (New York: International Publishers, 1987), p. 263.

6. Jean-Jacques Rousseau, *The Social Contract and Discourse on the Origins of Inequality*, bk. 1 [1762] (Harmondsworth, England: Penguin, 1968).

7. See Robert Owen's collection of essays titled *A New View of Society* (London: Cadell and Davies, 1813).

8. Thomas R. Dye and Harmon Zeigler, "Socialism and Equality in Cross-National Perspective," *PS: Political Science and Politics* 21 (Winter 1988): 45–56.

9. Data from the *Human Development Report–2005*, a publication of the United Nations' Development Programme, available at http://hdr.undp.org/statistics/.

10. See, for example, Lynne Segal, *Is the Future Female?* (New York: Peter Bedrick, 1988); Adrienne Rich, *Of Woman Born* (London: Virago, 1977); Susan Griffin, *Rape, the Power of Consciousness* (San Francisco: Harper and Row, 1986); Andrea Dworkin, *Pornography: Men Possessing Women* (New York: Putnam, 1981); Nancy J. Hirschmann, "Freedom, Recognition, and Obligation: A Feminist Approach to Political Theory," *American Political Science Review* 83 (1989): 1227–1244; and Mary L. Shanley and Carole Pateman, *Feminist Interpretations and Political Theory* (College Park: Penn State Press, 1991). For a controversial and very different view, see Christina Hoff Sommers, *Who Stole Feminism? How Women Have Betrayed Women* (New York: Simon & Schuster, 1994).

11. Rachel Carson, *Silent Spring* (New York: Mariner Press, 1994; originally published 1962).

12. The current U.S. Environmental Protection Agency studies on global warming can be found at http://yosemite.epa.gov/oar/globalwarming.nsf/content/ResourceCenterPublications.html.

13. Lindzen wrote a widely disseminated editorial on June 16, 2001. It is available at http://eaps.mit.edu/faculty/lindzen/OpEds/LindzenWSJ.pdf.

14. More recently, Patrick J. Michaels edited a book, *Shattered Consensus: The True State of Global Warming* (Lanham, MD: Rowman and Littlefield, 2005) that reflects the controversial nature of this ongoing issue.

15. Cited in Roy C. Macridis, *Contemporary Political Ideologies*, 2nd ed. (Boston: Little, Brown, 1983), p. 204.

16. A new book on Islamic Fundamentalism provides excellent historical background and informed analysis. See Mansoor Moaddel, *Islamic Modernism, Nationalism, and Fundamentalism*. Chicago: University of Chicago Press, 2005.

For Further Reading _____

Anderson, Charles W. *Pragmatic Liberalism*. Chicago: University of Chicago Press, 1990.

Burke, Edmund. *Reflections on the Revolution in France*. Chicago: Henry Regnery, 1955.

Carson, Rachel. *Silent Spring*. New York: Mariner Press, 1994. Originally published 1962.

Crick, Bernard. *In Defense of Politics*. 2nd ed. Chicago: University of Chicago Press, 1972.

Dworkin, Andrea. *Pornography: Men Possessing Women.* New York: Putnam, 1981.

Euben, Roxanne L. *Enemy in the Mirror: Islamic Fundamentalism and the Limits of Modern Rationalism,* Princeton, NJ: Princeton University Press, 1999.

Hashmi, Sohail H. *Islamic Political Ethics: Civil Society, Pluralism, and Conflict.* Princeton, NJ: Princeton University Press, 2002.

Hirsch, H. N. *A Theory of Liberty.* New York: Routledge, 1992.

Hitler, Adolf. *Mein Kampf.* Translated by Ralph Manheim. Boston: Houghton Mifflin, 1943.

Kirk, Russell. *The Portable Conservative Reader.* London: Penguin, 1982.

Lenin, V. I. *State and Revolution.* New York: International Publishers, 1932.

———. *Imperialism: The Highest Stage of Capitalism.* New York: International Publishers, 1939.

Meyer, Alfred G. *Leninism.* New York: Praeger, 1957.

———. *Communism.* 4th ed. New York: Random House, 1984.

Mill, John Stuart. *On Liberty and Considerations on Representative Government.* Fair Haven, NJ: Oxford University Press, 1933.

Moaddel, Mansoor. *Islamic Modernism, Nationalism, and Fundamentalism.* Chicago: University of Chicago Press, 2005.

Pettit, Philip. *Contemporary Political Theory.* New York: Macmillan, 1991.

Roy, Oliver. *The Failure of Political Islam.* Cambridge: Harvard University Press, 1998.

Shapiro, Ian. *The State of Democratic Theory.* Princeton, NJ: Princeton University Press, 2003.

Susser, Bernard. *Approaches to the Study of Politics.* New York: Macmillan, 1992.

Thiele, Leslie Paul. *Thinking Politics,* 2nd ed. New York: Cheltham House, 2003.

Wolin, Sheldon S. *Politics and Vision,* expanded edition. Princeton, NJ: Princeton University Press, 2006.

PART II

POLITICAL BEHAVIOR

We cannot understand political systems by merely looking at written constitutions and other documents describing them. The beliefs and actions of citizens shape the way political systems work, how stable and democratic they are, and their prospects for the future. Nearly all political systems have an identifiable political culture—sometimes several *conflicting* political cultures, as explored in Chapter 3. Political culture influences what people expect from politics, what kind of role they feel they should have in government decisions, and the rights they demand. Chapter 4 focuses on elections and public opinion. Elections are increasingly common in political life everywhere, but the behavior of voters in different countries varies dramatically. Some people choose not to vote, and those who do are influenced by a number of important factors that help us predict voter choices. Finally, Chapters 5 and 6 address political parties and interest groups. Parties and interest groups provide citizens with additional opportunities for political participation, and understanding their impact on political systems is a central problem in political science.

SPREADING FUNDAMENTALIST CULTURE   A boy awaits classes in front of a *madrasa*, or Islamic school, outside of Peshawar, Pakistan, a city largely populated by Afghan refugees at that time (2001). Many of the fundamentalist *madrasas* for refugees were funded by the Saudi government. Subsequently, many of their graduates became Taliban activists.

© AP/Wide World Photos

3

POLITICAL CULTURE AND SOCIALIZATION

◆ Political Culture: Origins of the Concept ◆ Agents of Political Socialization ◆ Classifying Political Cultures ◆ The Evolution of Political Cultures ◆ The Utility of Political Culture

For many people, one of the most exciting and interesting aspects of foreign travel is the opportunity to observe and interact with cultures that are very different from their own. When one of this book's authors traveled to Bangkok, he was impressed by a large group of Thai high school students who were sitting on a museum staircase, but leaped up to clear a passage as soon as he appeared at the top of the stairs. This reaction was indicative of both the Thai culture's stress on courtesy and its valuation of personal space, which enables throngs of pedestrians to walk the streets of Bangkok seemingly without ever colliding with each other. A visitor to Saudi Arabia or Pakistan would soon observe that these cultures have a view of women's "proper" behavior, employment, and dress that is far more restrictive than in the United States or Western Europe. Other cultural values are less immediately obvious. Indians or Colombians are more prone than are Canadians or Norwegians to judge people on the basis of their caste or class origins. Survey research reveals that the percentage of the population that believes that "most people can be trusted" is substantially lower in the U.S. and Britain than in Sweden or Finland, but much higher than in Chile and Romania.[1] Since the 1960s the level of trust has also dropped in the United States and other countries.

People in another culture may hold different views about voting, the morality of engaging in political violence, the value of political participation, the rights of other ethnic or social groups in their society, and a host of other politically relevant issues. Nations or regions also vary in the extent to which their populations follow politics or understand how their political system works.

Political culture is defined as "a people's predominant beliefs, attitudes, values, ideals, sentiments and evaluations about the political system of its country, and the role of the self in that system."[2] It most clearly includes knowledge about political institutions and processes, evaluations of how well those work, and assessments of the political system as a whole. But it also encompasses attitudes toward family, neighbors, religion, and other factors that shape and influence people's political outlook.

Scholarly observation and survey research clearly demonstrate that political cultures vary around the world and within individual nations. Russians are more skeptical than Australians about the advantages of democracy. The French are more inclined than Indonesians to pay attention to politics. But political scientists remain divided over how well we can measure political cultures, what the relationship is between political culture and political behavior, and what limits, if any, a nation's or region's political culture imposes on its political system. In short, for many years they have continued to debate the question, "Does political culture matter? Or, perhaps more precisely, "How much does political culture matter?"[3]

Those who believe strongly in the influence of political culture on politics argue that cultural values affect the likelihood that a specific country or a region will establish or maintain democracy. Thus, for example, many contemporary political scientists have argued that the reason so few Islamic nations are democratic is that many of that religion's cultural values violate democratic norms. Specifically, they see Islam's merger of Church and State and its confinement of women as obstacles to democratization.

Few would contend that political culture *determines* whether or not a country's political system is, say, stable or democratic. But culturalists argue that a country's political values and beliefs may either facilitate achieving these goals or hamper it. Conversely, few would claim that political culture is irrelevant, but critics insist that it is more malleable than culturalists admit and that new political institutions (such as competitive elections) can change popular attitudes and values relatively quickly. Thus, as Gabriel Almond notes, "political culture affects governmental structure and performance—constrains it, but surely does not determine it."[4]

In discussing a political culture or subculture, the unit we are analyzing may be a country, a portion of a country, a continent, or a religion. Thus, we may speak about European political culture (assuming that the region has important common values that are distinguishable from those of other continents or regions), Irish political culture (presumably different from, say, Finland's), and Irish Catholic political culture (as opposed to Irish Protestant cultural values). Similarly, there may be values in American political culture—belief in equality of opportunity, a pragmatic (rather than ideologically determined) approach to solving political problems—that distinguish it from Colombian or Indian cultures. At the same time that Americans may share many common values, however, there may also be somewhat distinct Southern, Midwestern, Evangelical, or Chicano subcultures within the U.S., each with its own distinguishing characteristics.

We study political culture because it helps us understand political life. For example, why do different ethnic groups cooperate reasonably well in Switzerland but not in Bosnia or India? Why are Russians more inclined than Canadians to support an all-powerful leader (such as President Putin)? Why has political corruption been a serious and long-standing problem in Mexico but not in Chile? Political culture may provide at least partial answers.

Although ideology (Chapter 2), political culture, and public opinion (Chapter 4) all explain how people feel about politics, they are distinct concepts. Ideologies reflect *intellectual efforts*—often identified with individuals, such as Locke or Marx—to project political ideals. In contrast, political culture encompasses the actual *values, attitudes, and beliefs* that most people hold in a society. Thus, although many individuals lack a well-defined ideology, they still have feelings about politics and thereby share in their society's political culture.

Although political culture and public opinion both measure people's feelings, they also are distinct concepts. Public opinion reflects short-term outlooks, such as how French citizens rate their president, whether or not the U.S. public supports the war in Iraq, and how people feel about a local school bond issue. Such attitudes may vary considerably within a country and may change from week to week. Political culture, on the other hand, measures a society's more deep-seated values, such as what role people feel organized religion should play in politics or how tolerant citizens are of those holding very different political views—attitudes that are more pervasive and change far more slowly than public opinion. But, as we will see, political cultures are not totally static. They do change over time, and sometimes that change can be hastened.

Political Culture: Origins of the Concept

As far back as the 1960s, as political scientists expanded their understanding of political systems throughout the world, they realized that institutions such as political parties or national legislatures operate differently from one society to the next, even when they are structured in similar ways. Moreover, they observed that distinct forms of political behavior, such as voting, have different meanings for, say, Mexicans or Russians than for Icelanders or Costa Ricans. So merely studying political parties, the bureaucracy, or interest-group membership does not afford a full understanding of a nation's political processes. We also need to consider the cultural foundations within which political systems operate.

Just as anthropologists and psychologists once analyzed the "national character" of countries such as Germany or Japan, political scientists today study political cultures. Do Russians believe that democracy is worth making sacrifices for? Do South Africans trust their fellow citizens? Do Indonesians feel that they can influence their own political system? Answers to such questions offer important insights into the nature of particular political systems and help us predict change.

It is also important to recognize, however, that *within a single nation there is often a degree of cultural diversity.* When we describe the Nigerian and Indian political cultures in a certain way, we are not claiming that *all* Nigerians and *all* Indians have the same beliefs. We are merely identifying a distinctive national pattern while acknowledging substantial variation among individual citizens.

Moreover, not only do *individuals* in any society vary in their political values, but *groups* within a society also often have distinctive political orientations. In other words, any given political culture may have a number of **political subcultures**. In the United States, for example, there is a national political culture encompassing our society's general political value system. There are, however, also distinctive political subcultures in different regions of the country, or among African-Americans, Hispanics, and Whites, or within various religious groups. These differences can be accommodated in a healthy political system that both respects diversity and imposes certain guidelines on all sub-cultures. If, however, regional, religious, ethnic, or other subcultural characteristics become so distinctive and separate that no discernible "national" culture seems to exist—as was true in Bosnia among its Serb, Croatian, and Muslim populations—political stability is likely to be threatened.

Another complicating factor in the study of political culture is the possibility that political behavior that appears to be based in a distinct cultural value may be instead just a reflection of objective conditions. For example, survey research indicates that Mexican workers have less confidence in their country's legal system than do their middle- or upper-class counterparts and are also less likely to sign political petitions.[5] Is that a reflection of working-class political culture? Do Mexican workers have a weaker sense of political *efficacy* (that is, less confidence in their personal ability to influence government) and distrust the courts because they are less educated or because they had less opportunity to voice their opinion at home when they were growing up? Or might cultural explanations not be the answer here? More likely, working-class opinions merely mirror the harsh reality that Mexican government officials (including judges) are less likely to give the poor a fair shake.

Of course, change in objective conditions can produce changes in political culture, which in turn lead to changes in the way the government works. As the educational levels of South Koreans and Mexicans rose in the last decades of the twentieth century, and as more people achieved middle-class lifestyles, political values changed. As citizens of these countries became more educated, affluent, and urban, they began to demand a more open political system, forcing their authoritarian governments to democratize.

Historical factors—particularly dramatic events such as wars, revolutions, and economic depressions—can also alter a nation's political culture. For example, the Great Depression of the 1920s and 1930s made many Americans and Europeans more sympathetic to government intervention in the economy (guaranteeing bank savings, for example, and providing Social Security). These major historical events have enduring political effects long after they are over. From World War II through the 1970s, the role of government (as expressed by its percentage of the GNP) grew substantially in Europe and the U.S. as citizens sought the protective blanket of government social welfare programs. Since the 1970s, however, new generations of voters have come on board who were raised in the growing prosperity of the postwar years and see less need for government protection.

Even more profoundly, the Nazi era had an enduring impact on German political culture. In their landmark study of political culture, Gabriel Almond and Sidney Verba discovered that in the decades after World War II, even though West Germans were more likely than Mexicans to expect fair treatment from local government officials, they were less proud of their political institutions. Moreover, despite their higher educational level, Germans felt less obligated than did Mexicans to participate in local politics. The Germans' more negative view of government probably reflected a wariness stemming from their country's Nazi past. Mexicans, in contrast, although critical of specific government behavior, expressed general pride in their political system, reflecting the sense of unity and stability that eventually emerged from their 1910 revolution.[6] Since that study was completed, further historical changes have made the German population far more confident of its democracy. But even today, Germany's political culture remains influenced by events that occurred more than 60 years earlier. Germans oppose virtually any foreign military involvement (they most recently rejected the use of force against Iraq) because they had been influenced by their country's suffering in World War II and the international notoriety that military aggression had brought them.

Political culture is a simple concept, but it can easily be misunderstood. The fact that we may characterize a given nation's culture in some way should not lead us to underestimate the importance of cultural diversity within that nation. Similarly, the fact that political culture may serve as an explanatory factor should not lead us to overlook the possibility that objective conditions within a country may be responsible for attitudes and behaviors often attributed to culture.

AGENTS OF POLITICAL SOCIALIZATION

How do individual citizens in any country acquire the values and feelings that constitute their political culture? **Political socialization** is the process of shaping and transmitting a political culture. It involves the transfer of political values from one generation to another and usually entails changes over time that lead to a gradual transformation of the culture.[7]

Agents of political socialization are individuals, groups, or institutions that transmit political values to each generation. Obviously, the importance of specific socialization agents differs from culture to culture and from individual to individual. Nevertheless, the following agents are important in virtually every society.

The Family

As in so many other aspects of life, the family is the first, and frequently the most important, source of political values. For example, in the United States and Japan, people tend to vote for the political party their parents supported.[8] But the political influence of family goes far beyond the development of partisan identification. In Argentina or Russia, many young people at the dinner table repeatedly hear their parents complain about corrupt politicians and, as a consequence, often become cynical about political participation. Meanwhile, in the Netherlands, parents may depict political involvement as a more noble calling.

Because the family exerts its influence from such an early age, when people are most impressionable, some political scientists view the family as the most critical agent for transmitting broad moral and political values during a person's formative years. "Other individuals may have profound influence on a person's political outlook, but none of them is typically credited with as much influence as the child's parents."[9] As people advance toward middle age, however, they are more prone to develop some values and orientations that are distinct from those of their parents.[10]

Family impact seems to be greatest in cultures, such as our own, where people often discuss politics at home. In nations such as France (where there are fewer political conversations at home) or China (where the state plays a dominant role in the socialization process), the family may have less political importance.

Education

From their kindergarten days of making Thanksgiving decorations through high school civics and college political science courses, most American students acquire important political values from the educational system: patriotism, the importance of voting, or the value of constitutional rights, for example. In communist nations such as Cuba, schools have been an important agent socializing youth into the values of Marxism-Leninism. Similarly, during the long struggle to free Afghanistan from Soviet occupation, the Saudi government established schools in Afghanistan and in the many Afghan refugee camps across the border in Pakistan. Those schools taught a fundamentalist version of Islam, called Wahhabi, which helped give birth to the Taliban, the army of religious extremists that eventually seized control of Afghanistan after the Soviets were ousted from that country, and subsequently hosted Osama bin Ladin and al-Qaeda.

Peer Groups

Although family and school are the most influential early influences on political values, the socialization process continues into our adult years. As people grow older, their political values are influenced by their friends and co-workers. During adolescence, peers compete with parents and teachers as the most important source of values.[11] The impact of friends and co-workers seems to be especially strong in economically developed societies, where the influence of family elders, kinship groups, or religion is weaker than in Third World nations. As we will see (Box 3-1), even membership in social clubs and bowling leagues may influence the political culture.

The Media

In advanced industrialized societies, people receive much of their political information and many of their political values from the mass media. Newspapers, news magazines, and especially radio and television play an increasingly important role in transmitting

---

Box 3-1

SOCIAL CAPITAL, TRUST, AND BOWLING ALONE

From his extensive study of Italian politics over a 20-year period, Robert Putnam and his associates concluded that there were marked differences in the quality of performance by the country's regional governments and that those disparities could be linked to cultural and historical factors. Regional governments were more effective and better able to stimulate economic growth in northern Italy than in the south. In turn, differences in political and economic performance, they found, were linked to the degree of civic engagement by the region's citizens, including their interest in furthering the good of the community rather than just the benefit of their family and friends.

People in the northern, more civic-minded regions were more likely to belong to local associations, ranging from sports clubs to associations of bird watchers, causing them to interact with others in their community and to work cooperatively with them. A region's "**social capital**" was a measure of the density of associational involvement in a town, region, or country and the norms and social trust that these group activities produced.[12]

Regions or communities with high levels of social capital, according to Putnam's research, produced citizens who were more law abiding and more trustful of their neighbors, including those whom they did not know very well. These attitudes, in turn were conducive to effective democratic government. But not all involvement in clubs, associations, or groups produces social capital, argued Putnam. Relationships between members must be "horizontal"—between relative equals. If, however, relationships are "vertical"—with a top-down, hierarchical structure like the Mafia in Sicily—such group membership does not build social capital. Since Russia, Romania, and other post-communist nations had no network of *independent* clubs and groups (all were under government control), social capital and, hence, trust, is very low in those nations.

In his best-selling book, *Bowling Alone*, Putnam notes that the United States has always been known for its dense network of groups, clubs, and associations, while it still ranks strongly compared to many other nations, "the vibrancy of American civil society has notably declined over the past few decades."[13] Symbolic of this decline in social engagement, he suggests, has been the fact that in recent decades Americans have increasingly chosen to "bowl alone" or with a small number of friends or family members and have been less inclined

to bowl in leagues, where they would network with people whom they know less well. Thus, between 1980 and 1993, the number of bowlers in the U.S. increased by 10 percent, but the number of people in bowling leagues *decreased* by 40 percent (and that decline had continued into the twenty-first century). There have been similarly sharp declines in the past 30 to 50 years in the number of Americans belonging to parent-teacher associations (PTA), the League of Women Voters, the Red Cross, the Shriners, and the Masons, as well as fewer adult volunteers for the Boy Scouts. It is true that some organizations have increased their membership greatly during this period, including the American Association of Retired Persons (AARP) and the National Organization for Women (NOW). But, unlike the associations just mentioned with sharply declining memberships, these expanding organizations involve little or no face-to-face contacts between members. And despite gains by some groups, total membership in associations declined by almost 30 percent from 1967 to 1993, a trend that continued through the 1990s.

The reasons for the decline in groups such as the PTA and bowling leagues are complex and varied: many people are busier with their careers; watching television and DVDs, playing video games, surfing the Web, and other relatively solitary activities have become more prevalent; and traditional families, which are often the hubs of associational activity (Boy Scouts, PTA) have been weakened by rising divorce rates and the increased numbers of people who elect to postpone or avoid marriage.

Whatever the reasons (and there are others), Putnam argues that America's stock of social capital has eroded, a decline that has significant social and political consequences. During the past 40 years or so, as fewer people have joined associations that bring them into contact with new people, as people less frequently invite neighbors to their homes for dinner, as the percentage of Americans attending church has declined modestly since the 1950s, the percentage of people who give to charity and the share of total national income given to charity has also declined. Equally disconcerting, during the last decades of the twentieth century, the percentage of people who had worked for a political party fell 42 percent, the proportion of those who had attended a political rally or speech declined

(Continued)

Box 3-1

SOCIAL CAPITAL, TRUST, AND BOWLING ALONE
(Continued)

by 34 percent, and the percentage who had written to their congressman or senator fell by 23 percent. At the same time Americans have become less trustful of each other. Moreover, states with the highest social capital (such as South Dakota, Minnesota, and Vermont) tend to have significantly higher rates of compliance with tax laws (i.e., lower rates of criminal charges brought by the IRS), higher levels of tolerance for racial and gender equality, and lower mortality rates (people who belong to clubs have higher life expectancy than those who don't) than do states with the lowest levels of social capital (Nevada, Mississippi, and Georgia). They also have school systems that are more effective. These findings suggest to Putnam and others that the growing tendency of Americans to "bowl alone" and reduce social contacts with co-workers or neighbors is troublesome for American democracy and civil society.

A recent book by Russell J. Dalton discusses a somewhat related phenomenon in 18 advanced, industrial democracies. Data from the World Values Survey and the Eurobarometer shows that in 16 of those 18 nations there has been a clear decline in citizen support for and trust in their country's political institutions (such as parliament or congress). Such declines were frequently not related to government performance or contemporary events. For example, in the United States:

> In . . . 1966, with the war in Vietnam raging and race riots in Cleveland, Chicago, and Atlanta, 66 per cent of Americans *rejected* the view that 'the people running the country don't really care what happens to you.' In . . . 1997, after America's cold war victory and in the midst of the longest period of peace and prosperity in more than two generations, 57 per cent of Americans *endorsed* the same view.[14]

Similar declines in support for government, the courts, and other government institutions took place in almost all advanced democracies during those three decades (and continued into the twenty-first century). For example, the percentage of Swedes who expressed confidence in their parliament declined from 51 percent in 1986 to 19 percent in 1996. Despite growing public distrust of government, the level of support for

democracy as the best form of government has remained high (or even risen) in all 18 nations, ranging from a high of 99 percent support in Denmark and 97 percent support in Iceland, Austria, and West Germany to a low (within this group) of 78 percent in Britain and 86 to 87 percent in the Netherlands and the U.S.[15] Still, Dalton and others argue that if distrust of government and negative evaluations of government institutions continues to grow, this trend could well undermine democracy.

Thus, for example, since growing cynicism about government is associated with reduced participation in politics, a vicious cycle can develop whereby politicians, who are less closely scrutinized by a "turned-off" citizenry, become less responsible to the voters and generate further political apathy. Furthermore, survey research across these nations indicates that citizens who express lower trust in and support for the political system reveal a somewhat greater willingness to cheat on their tax payments and to break the law more generally. They are also less willing to fulfill civic duties such as sitting on juries.[16] All of these data suggest that growing alienation from the political system should be a cause for concern.

Survey data also indicate that dramatic events such as corruption scandals in Italy and Japan, Watergate or the Vietnam war in the U.S., or even poorer economic performance do not account for citizens' increased political distrust. Although there are multiple causes of increased political dissatisfaction, ironically the data suggest that two important reasons seem to be increased educational levels and growing concern for such "post-material" issues as protecting the environment, protecting free speech, and increased community linkages (see Box 3-3 on post-materialism). The evidence suggests that post-materialists (those more concerned with the issues just named than in their own material interests) and more educated citizens are more likely to have higher expectations of government and, consequently, greater disappointment with the political system. At the same time, post-materialists (generally more educated) express the highest level of support for civil liberties such as free speech.

political culture. In some countries, young children and adolescents typically spend several hours daily in front of the television set. One study of nearly two thousand American high school seniors concluded that the mass media equaled parents in importance as an agent of political socialization.[17] In recent years, U.S. radio talk shows have become a potent influence on adults' political values. The Internet is also becoming a major source of political ideas and values, particularly among young people. Even in developing nations, radios are fairly universal, and in many countries televisions are increasingly widespread. Well aware of television's potential for shaping political values, the Cuban government has supplied a free television set to most recipients of public housing. The spread of television in many societies has tended to homogenize political culture—that is, to reduce regional or urban-rural differences. Laurence Wylie's classic study of small-town France several decades ago indicated that villagers were quite suspicious of outsiders and distrusted national politicians.[18] Subsequent research indicated that, more generally, the French tended to close themselves off from influences outside their extended family and were less likely than other Western Europeans or Americans to join political organizations.[19] In recent decades, however, the spread of television has helped break down regional and urban-rural cultural differences.[20] Survey research indicates that the French are far less distrustful today than they were two or three decades ago of people outside their circle of friends and family.[21]

Business and Professional Associations, the Military, Labor Unions, and Religious Groups

Unlike schools, these organizations are all examples of "secondary groups"—organizations that people join for a common goal. Like the family, schools, and the media, their primary role is not to influence political values, yet each of these groups may exert important political influence over its members. That influence may be direct, as when business groups distribute material to their members criticizing government intervention in the economy. Or it may be indirect, as when the leaders of a religious group promote patriarchal (male-dominant) family values. Traditionally, the Catholic Church in Latin America and parts of Europe, Judaism in Israel, as well as Islamic religious institutions in the Middle East, North Africa, and parts of South Asia have exercised an especially strong influence on those regions' political cultures. In Israel, which has virtually universal military service for young men and women, the armed forces have effectively integrated generations of young immigrants into the nation's political culture. The military often plays a similar role in the Third World, socializing recruits into national values.

Voting patterns in countries such as Chile and Italy illustrate the influence of secondary groups. In both countries, men have generally been more prone to support leftist political parties than have women who were more likely to support the Christian Democratic Party or other centrist to right-wing parties. A major cause of that gender gap has been the influence of two agents of socialization, labor unions and the church. Since men are more likely than women to work in factories or other sites where labor is well organized, they are more likely to belong to unions. In both Chile and Italy, most unions have supported the political left. In contrast, women in Chile and Italy tend to be more devout Catholics. Consequently they were more influenced by the Christian Democratic orientations of most parish priests.

CLASSIFYING POLITICAL CULTURES

Survey research on culture has produced a gold mine of information that can be invaluable at cocktail parties or in trivia games. We know, for example, that among western and southern Europeans, the Irish are most prone to feel that divorce can *never* be justified, whereas the Danes and the French are most likely to accept it. The Netherlands and Denmark have the highest proportion of respondents who answered that they were "very happy," and Portugal and Greece have the fewest.[22] Although such facts are interesting, what do they tell us about the political process? How do different cultures make government work differently?

When Almond and Verba wrote their landmark study of political culture, *The Civic Culture*, they did more than merely describe the political knowledge, values, and beliefs of the five countries that they had examined (the United States, Great Britain, West Germany, Italy, and Mexico). Beyond that, they asked which political values are most compatible with democracy. As many Third World nations have found, simply copying political institutions from the West is not enough to produce stable democracy. "A democratic form of participatory political system requires as well a political culture consistent with it."[23]

Much of the subsequent research into political culture has examined the compatibility of a specific society's values with desired political goals. For example, this text's discussions of politics in selected nations (Chapters 11 through 17) note that political values in the United States and Great Britain are more supportive of democratic practices and institutions than are the cultural orientations of Russia or China (with Mexico falling in between). Indeed, both Russia and China seem to have had authoritarian beliefs and attitudes that long preceded the rise of communism.

Another issue often examined by political scientists is the relationship between political culture and stability. If people in a society distrust one another or are sharply divided along racial, religious, ethnic, class, or linguistic lines, prospects for political stability are obviously reduced. Northern Ireland, Rwanda, Bosnia, and Iraq come to mind. A certain degree of stability is, in turn, clearly a prerequisite for democracy. At the same time, however, the political cultures of nations such as Mexico (until recently) or China may have placed so high a value on stability that many people have rejected democratic challenges to the government that might create disorder.

As we have noted, the core values of a political culture change more slowly than do voter preferences or public opinion. American support for the war in Iraq (a measure of public opinion) may change drastically within months. Candidates for office may start off with wide voter backing in September, only to see that support evaporate by election day, two months later. Basic cultural values, however, normally take years or even generations to change. More than half a century ago, European sociologist Gunnar Myrdal noted "an American dilemma," a disconnect in our political culture between our belief in the fundamental equality of all citizens and our persistent racial prejudices.[24] Even though American racial attitudes have changed significantly since that time and institutionalized racism has been greatly reduced, racial prejudice continues to linger in our culture. For decades, Western European voters have been more likely than Americans to support extensive social welfare programs and to accept the tax burden that those programs entail. Western European nations also enforce tighter gun controls than does the United States. Political culture helps explain some of those attitudinal differences. American political culture has historically placed a greater value than European culture does on individuality and the right of individual citizens to be protected from government intervention. Conversely, the French, Germans, and Swedes place greater emphasis than Americans do on government's obligation to provide help to society's disadvantaged citizens. Those cultural differences have remained fairly constant for at least 60 years.

Still, over time *political cultures do change!* Sometimes those changes are the result of conscious government or societal planning as, for example, the concerted efforts after World War II by the schools, mass media, labor unions, and other agents of political socialization in both Germany and Japan to erase fascist and supernationalistic sentiments and to create a more democratic political culture. (See the discussion of political resocialization, later in this chapter.) At other times, cultural change is more unconscious. In Mexico, decades of rising educational levels, greater exposure to the mass media, and increased urbanization all helped create a more informed and participatory political culture.

Over time, political scientists have categorized various kinds of political cultures. We define some of them next and briefly refer to others. These are not necessarily mutually exclusive categories, as a society can have, for example, both a democratic and participatory political culture.

Democratic Political Culture

Although the cultural prerequisites for democracy are quite varied and not always fully clear, certain attitudes clearly are helpful. Democracy is most likely to take hold or persist in societies with widespread tolerance for diverse outlooks, including unpopular or dissenting viewpoints. When the U.S. Supreme Court ruled that individuals have the right to burn the American flag as an expression of free speech, it took this principle beyond the point that many Americans thought reasonable. Despite some initial outrage, however, Congress chose not to introduce a constitutional amendment to ban flag burning. In Western European democracies, there is also a general agreement that people have the right to express ideas that most citizens view as foolish or wrong, even when those ideas are hostile to democracy.

As democratic values become more firmly entrenched in a country's political culture, the nation can more easily tolerate antidemocratic political actors. Nations struggling to create or stabilize democracy in a formerly authoritarian setting, however, may initially find it necessary to exclude political parties or groups that do not accept democratic principles. Thus, in postwar West Germany, the Nazi Party was barred from political participation in elections. In 1992, following a series of neo-Nazi attacks on immigrants, the German parliament, mindful of the country's history, restricted the speech rights of hate groups.

Other important components of a democratic political culture include "moderation, accommodation, restrained partisanship, system loyalty and trust."[25] Survey research indicates that levels of trust (in one's fellow citizens and in government) are very low in Russia and many other former communist nations in Eastern and Central Europe. Those who lack trust are less likely to accept the results of elections as definitive, more likely to accept repression of those with unpopular points of view, more likely to evade taxes, and less likely to extend business credit, thereby inhibiting both democracy and economic growth.

Authoritarian Political Culture

Despite the growing strength of democratic values worldwide, most political cultures have some authoritarian strains. In the developing world, only a few nations—such as Costa Rica and India—have long-established democratic traditions. And even in India, where competitive elections and parliamentary-style government have been the norm, most of the population lives in villages, where the caste system, domination by powerful landlords, and local political machines create undemocratic conditions.

What do we mean when we describe Indonesia, Russia, or Iran as having authoritarian political cultures or subcultures? The phrase suggests that both the leaders of the country and much of the population have values that run contrary to democratic beliefs in majority rule and minority rights. In particular, authoritarian political cultures are less tolerant of dissenters and of ethnic or religious minorities. In Iran, for example, Islamic Fundamentalism denies the legitimacy of other religions or political viewpoints. In both communist North Korea and capitalist South Korea, many citizens believe that journalists have no right to publish material that would contradict the country's prevailing political ideology or potentially destabilize society. And the political culture of politically active Guatemalans features *caudillaje*, a set of values that makes the pursuit of power the "referent for life's activities." Such beliefs produce political leaders with "manipulative, exploitative, and opportunistic" personalities.[26]

Authoritarian political cultures greatly value stability and order. The rough-and-tumble of democratic competition may seem threatening to that order. In Russia, many citizens feel threatened by the crime and economic disarray that followed the collapse of communism, leading voters to overwhelmingly reelect President Putin in spite of his repeated assault on democratic institutions. When asked if they approved or disapproved of strong authoritarian leaders, respondents in countries such as Denmark, the Netherlands, Spain, and Iceland overwhelmingly disapproved, while Tanzanians, Jordanians, Nigerians, and Romanians were more likely to approve.[27] Many authoritarian cultures believe in traditional authority structures and hierarchy. For example, women are told to unquestioningly obey their husbands. Similarly, authoritarian political cultures maintain that the nation's leaders know what is best for society and should not be doubted. Some Mexican anthropologists argue that the country's children are raised to accept unquestionably their father's authority, and so when they grow up, many transfer that obedience to the nation's president and to other authority figures.[28] That paternalistic perspective applies to Marxist-Leninist (communist) "vanguard parties" that claim to know with scientific certainty what is good for the people (discussed in Chapters 13 and 14). It also prevails in the authoritarian cultures of Confucian (and capitalist) Singapore and Islamic Saudi Arabia.

In recent years, a debate has raged among scholars (and some political leaders) as to whether democratic values can easily flourish in Islamic cultures or in Asian ones. Some have argued, for example, that there are aspects of Islamic and Confucian values that are incompatible with democratic norms (see Box 3-2). In some cases, political leaders, such as the former prime minister of Singapore, have used such arguments to justify nondemocratic practices in their own countries. Others, however, find such arguments ethnocentric if not racist. They object strenuously to the idea that Muslims in, say, Malaysia, or Confucians in Singapore, are somehow culturally predisposed against democracy.[29]

In fact, it can be demonstrated that countries with certain dominant religions are more likely than others to be democratic *even when we statistically control for the educational*

Box 3-2

ISLAM AND DEMOCRACY

The relationship between a society's dominant religious beliefs and its political beliefs and behavior has been the subject of sharp debate. As we have noted, historically Protestant countries have been most likely to be democracies, Islamic countries least likely. In the late 1980s, noted political scientist Samuel Huntington wrote *The Clash of Civilizations and the Remaking of World Order*, a book that reached a wide readership and inspired substantial controversy. In it he argued that there were nine primary civilizations in the world today, which could be distinguished primarily (but not exclusively) by their religion.[30] These included Western Christianity, Christian Orthodox (Russian and Greek), Muslim, Hindu, and Sino-Confucian. Furthermore, he predicted, major international strife would occur in the future not as in the cold war between ideological blocs, but rather between clashing civilizations. He saw conflict as most likely to develop between Western versus Islamic and Confucian cultures in part because of the latter civilizations' alleged rejection of democracy.

In one of Huntington's most controversial statements, he warned that "the problem for the West is not [just] Islamic fundamentalism; it is Islam." Islamic civilization, he argued, is culturally opposed to Western democracy. Not surprisingly, other scholars have strongly challenged that assertion, noting, for example, that Muslims have a wide range of political attitudes and that it made little sense to lump them all together as undemocratic.[31] But, several years later, when al-Qaeda's September 11 attack took place, Huntington's critical view of Islam gained new support. Prompted by Huntington's work and growing Western suspicion of Islam, a number of scholars have examined systematically the proposition that Islamic culture presents barriers to democracy.

Alfred Stepan and Graeme Robertson recently compared the extent of free and fair elections (electoral democracy) in 47 nations with Muslim-majority populations, separating them into two groups: 16 Arab countries and 31 non-Arab states.[32] Specifically, they wanted to see what percentage of the countries in each group had been able to sustain electoral democracy for at least five consecutive years during the period from 1972 to 2000. They found that while not a single Arab state had met that standard, 8 of the 31 non-Arab Muslim countries had. This suggests that it is Arab history or culture rather than Islamic culture that creates obstacles to democracy.

But even *non-Arab* Islamic countries still have a lower rate of electoral democracy than non-Islamic countries do. Like other critics of the *Clash of Civilizations*, Stepan and Robertson suggested that this "democracy gap" might be attributable to factors other than religion. Might the poorer democratic performance of Muslim countries be caused by their poverty rather than their culture? We know that very poor countries (with per capita incomes below $1,500) are less likely to sustain democracy, while countries with average incomes exceeding $5,500 annually are far more likely to sustain it. Hence, any very poor country that had a sustained period of electoral democracy could be called an "overachiever," while more affluent states that were unable to sustain free and fair elections were labeled "underachievers."

By those standards, the authors found that half of the Arab countries (including Libya, Kuwait, and Saudi Arabia) had been "underachievers" over the previous 30 years while none had been "overachievers." But, among the 29 non-Arab, Muslim countries, one-fourth of them (including Albania, Bangladesh, and Nigeria) were overachievers and none were underachievers. Looking at it from a different angle, the authors studied the 38 poorest countries in the world (including 1 Arab country, 15 non-Arab predominantly Muslim states, 10 predominantly Christian countries, and 12 with other religions). As expected, most of these countries lacked a record of sustained electoral democracy, but almost one-third of them had exceeded expectations. How did the record of the poor, non-Arab, Muslim nations compare to that of poor non-Muslim countries? While 30 percent of the predominantly Christian nations had overachieved, 33 percent of the non-Arab Muslim countries and 33 percent of the countries with other religions did so as well.

Rather than comparing the past political *performance* of Muslim and non-Muslim countries, Pippa Norris and Ronald Inglehart compared the attitudes towards democracy of citizens in Muslim and non-Muslim countries.[33] Drawing on survey research findings for 43 countries of all types, they examined citizens' attitudes. To make sure that any differences they found between religious groups were not caused by other factors, they statistically controlled for the level of economic and political development in each country

(Continued)

Box 3-2

ISLAM AND DEMOCRACY (*Continued*)

and for the individual respondents' age, gender, education, income, and strength of religious belief.

Once all those factors were controlled, the surveys showed that citizens of Islamic countries are as supportive of democracy as Westerners are. By contrast, the populations of Eastern and Central Europe (the former communist bloc) and of Latin America were less supportive. There *is* a cultural gap between Muslim nations and the West, they found—not in their attitudes toward democracy, but rather in the Muslim population's more conservative *social* values toward gender, equality, and sexual liberalization.

or income differences that are known to affect the likelihood of democracy in a given country. In other words, when we compare countries of comparable educational and income levels with one another, Protestant nations are most likely to be democratic and Islamic nations are least likely. Some scholars have argued that Protestantism emphasizes individuality, which contributes to democratic government, whereas Islam believes in a merger of church and state that retards democratic development.

Although there is likely some truth to these assertions, and although the statistical correlations cannot be denied, it is important to keep in mind our previous assertion that *though cultures are generally slow to change, they can and do change!* Historically, Catholic countries in the West have been less hospitable to democracy than Protestant nations. Not long ago, Spain, Portugal, Brazil, Mexico, and a large percentage of other Catholic nations had authoritarian regimes. Some analysts attributed this to the hierarchical nature of the Catholic Church and its belief in papal infallibility in matters of faith. But, in the Third Wave of democratization, starting in the early 1970s, Catholic countries in Europe and Latin America have been among the most important players. Indeed, the Third Wave started in the Catholic nations of Portugal and Spain. Similarly, cultural arguments were once used to explain why South Korea and Taiwan, both Confucian, remained authoritarian despite their relatively high levels of income and education. Today, however, both have become democracies and they are also cited as evidence that religious and other cultural traditions may inhibit democratization for a period of time, but they don't make democratic change *impossible*.

Thus, when some political scientists say that a country such as Russia or Pakistan lacks important elements of a democratic political culture, they are pointing to important cultural hurdles impeding those countries' transitions to democracy. However, that does not mean that those hurdles are permanent or that authoritarian cultural values cannot be replaced. Surveys in twenty-first-century Russia, for example, clearly indicated that younger citizens—partly or wholly socialized since glasnost (the Soviet Union's political opening in the late 1980s) and the postcommunist era—are more inclined to hold democratic values than are older Russians. On the other hand, it is certainly possible that countries that have endured long periods of ineffective or corrupt rule by a democratic government may experience a decline in pro-democratic values.

Consensual and Conflictual Cultures

We may also classify political cultures according to their degree of consensus or conflict over crucial political issues. In **consensual political cultures**—such as Great Britain, Japan, and Costa Rica—citizens tend to agree on basic political procedures (for example, the legitimacy of free elections) and on the general goals of the political system. **Conflictual political cultures**—in nations such as Rwanda, Bosnia, and Guatemala—are highly polarized by fundamental differences over those issues. In Central America during the 1980s, deep ideological divisions between left-wing and right-wing political subcultures brought El Salvador, Guatemala, and Nicaragua to civil war.

Countries may also be polarized by ethnic, religious, or racial divisions. The people of Bosnia have been violently divided by ethnic nationalism pitting Muslims, Serbs, and Croats against one another. Similarly, in Lebanon, militias representing various Christian and Islamic denominations decimated one another for years. In 1994, Hutus in Rwanda massacred perhaps 800,000 of their Tutsi countrymen. Obviously, relatively homogeneous cultures (which share a common language, religion, and ethnicity) are more likely to achieve a consensual political culture than are nations that are multiracial or multicultural. Thus, it is much easier to achieve political stability and consensus in Denmark or Japan than in India (a nation split into three major religions and dozens of languages) or Rwanda. Nevertheless, Canada, Switzerland, and the United States demonstrate that some heterogeneous societies have developed consensual cultures despite the obstacles. Figure 3.1 suggests the difference between consensual and conflictual political cultures.

Other Cultural Classifications

Along with the classifications we have already mentioned, political scientists have used a host of other classifications of political cultures. Observers of Cuban, North Korean, and Chinese politics have often spoken of those countries' revolutionary or Marxist political cultures. Some authors write of countries with a capitalist political culture, indicating that the values are congruent with a free-market ideology. And as we have seen, still other scholars have focused on religion as the central component of political values in a specific region or nation. They speak of a Confucian political culture in Taiwan, Korea, and Singapore; a Hindu culture in the Indian subcontinent; and an Islamic political culture in Iran and Algeria. Finally, a number of political scientists have felt that particular geographic regions have distinct values and orientations that define a Latin American, African, or Mediterranean political culture.

All these classifications are reasonable if they capture a distinctive set of political values and attitudes that characterize a society or region and distinguish it from other political cultures. Thus, the label "Islamic political culture" is scientifically meaningful only if it describes important political values that are common to most Muslims and are distinct from the values of other cultures. If the classification does not do that, then it is not useful.

THE EVOLUTION OF POLITICAL CULTURES

Political cultures may reflect a balance of *stable* values that may have endured for centuries, *gradual changes* in beliefs that transpire over many years, more rapid value changes resulting from social development (increased educational levels, industrialization, and the like), and even more dramatic events, such as war or revolution. Thus, although all cultures change (some more rapidly than others), the cultural foundations

FIGURE 3.1   HOMOGENEOUS AND HETEROGENEOUS POLITICAL CULTURES

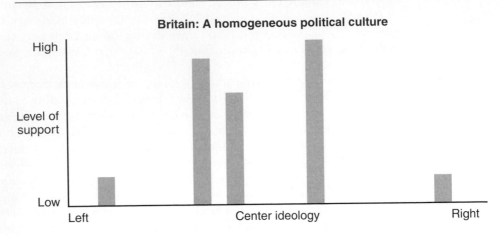

Britain: A homogeneous political culture

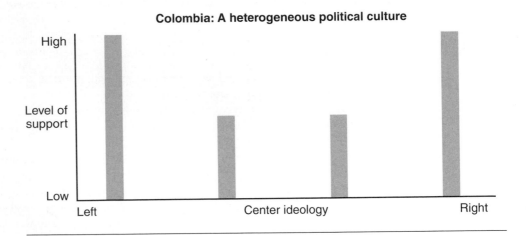

Colombia: A heterogeneous political culture

of political systems are not transformed overnight. Like all value systems, traditional beliefs may serve as anchors of stability in an otherwise confusing world or may be impediments to progress. Hindu religious beliefs support the caste system, which limits the opportunities available to many Indian citizens and contributes to hierarchical political values. On the other hand, many experts argue that Hinduism's separation of church and state and its lack of church hierarchy helps explain why India, despite its abysmal poverty and low literacy rate, has been such a stable democracy.

Because all political cultures change, our understanding of individual societies needs to be constantly reexamined. Clearly, neither Nigerians nor Spaniards nor Americans believe the same things today that they did twenty or thirty years ago. Sometimes, substantial cultural changes are the unintended consequence of rapid urbanization, economic modernization, or increased education. At other times, however, cultural change occurs through **political resocialization**, a conscious effort by

TABLE 3.1   RESPONSES TO QUESTION: HOW MUCH DO YOU TRUST THE [NATIONAL] GOVERNMENT TO DO WHAT IS RIGHT? (PERCENTS, LATE 1970s)

	Britain	Germany
Just about always	7	9
Most of the time	32	39
Only some of the time	47	39
Almost never	10	7
Don't know	4	6

SOURCE: David Conradt, "Changing German Political Culture," in *The Civic Culture Revisited,* ed. Gabriel Almond and Sidney Verba (Boston: Little, Brown, 1980), p. 235.

government leaders to transform their society's political culture. And sometimes, cultural change is a byproduct of both conscious and unconscious factors.

Nearly two decades after *The Civic Culture* was published, research indicated that Germany's political culture had been "remade."[34] West Germans in the late 1970s were far prouder of their political system and more committed to democracy than they had been twenty years earlier. Indeed, one survey revealed that Germans were slightly more confident than Britons (living in an allegedly "model" democracy) that their national government would "do what is right." (See Table 3.1.) Today survey research indicates that Germans (at least those who lived in the former West Germany) have one of the most democratic political cultures in Europe.

Of course, in recent decades some aspects of American political culture also have undergone change. In 1959, Almond and Verba found that Americans had more confidence in their political institutions than did citizens in any of the other four countries studied. That confidence eroded during the late 1960s and the 1970s as a result of the assassinations of President Kennedy and Martin Luther King, an unpopular war in Vietnam, and the Watergate scandal, which almost led to the impeachment of President Richard Nixon. Although the Reagan presidency, the Gulf War, and even the September 11 terrorist attacks all rekindled national pride, Americans today still express less faith than they once did in their political institutions, such as Congress (as evidenced by opinion polls).

Deliberate government efforts to "transform" culture are always difficult and sometimes disastrous. Just as it is hard to "teach an old dog new tricks," it is not easy to change long-standing cultural traditions rapidly. Such efforts are most likely to take place when a war or a revolution has radically altered the political system or the government's political ideology. In our analysis of Chinese politics in Chapter 14, we discuss how Mao Zedong's government conducted political campaigns to create mass commitment to volunteer labor, social equality, and other revolutionary values.

Following the Cuban Revolution, the government introduced a mass adult literacy campaign and created local political units, called Committees for the Defense of the Revolution (CDRs), throughout the nation. The literacy campaign used reading primers with overtly political messages about the benefits that Fidel Castro had brought to the island. CDRs stressed the value of hard work; individual sacrifice for the good of society; and racial, class, and sexual equality. Richard Fagen's study of Cuban revolutionary culture suggested a number of impressive results. Surveys of high

© UNESCO/Asbel Lopez

READING AND POLITICS   Cuba's adult literacy program was designed both to achieve universal adult literacy and to inculcate students with revolutionary values. A volunteer in the program is shown here.

school students indicated that boys were developing less sexist attitudes toward females. Violent crime rates diminished. Volunteer labor for government development projects rose throughout the first decade of the revolution. Over that same period, an increasing percentage of the young people surveyed expressed confidence in their ability to get ahead in life through continued education.[35] In short, the Cuban government had seemingly used education and mass mobilization to reduce prejudice, fatalism, and other prerevolutionary values.

Yet, the radical transformation of any political culture has its costs. Although Cuban crime rates went down, visits to psychiatrists rose, because many Cubans were constantly told that the values they had long held were unrevolutionary and wrong. The introduction of feminist concerns into a *macho* political culture improved sexual equality (husbands, for example, were required to do housework, and women were encouraged to enter the labor force) but likely also contributed to a steep rise in the country's divorce rate.

Other studies have suggested that rapid, government-directed cultural transformations sometimes have been more apparent than real. Although revolutionary activists in Cuba readily mouthed the "correct" political slogans, a number of them privately felt or acted differently. To be sure, many activists in the CDRs were undoubtedly enthusiastic revolutionaries. But one study of a Havana slum found that local CDR leaders in that neighborhood were using the organization as a front for gambling and prostitution operations, decidedly not part of the revolutionary political culture.[36] Other evidence from both Cuba and Nicaragua suggests that although many people accept at least some revolutionary values, others just go through the motions or feign a cultural transformation for the sake of personal advancement. The Cuban economy's sharp decline following the collapse of the Soviet Union and periodic evidence of government corruption have undermined revolutionary values and likely diminished support for the regime.

Following the fall of Central European communism, the governments of the Czech Republic, Hungary, and Poland, among others, have confronted the problem of transforming their political culture. Having grown up under communism, many citizens still feel that government should guarantee them a job, that workers should never be fired, that prices should remain stable (controlled by the government), and that substantial business profits are immoral. In varying ways, these old values are obstacles to the creation of a capitalist economy. In some countries, the demise of communist authority has allowed old prejudices and ethnic animosities to resurface. In Romania, for example, there has been a rise in anti-Semitism and hostility toward Gypsies. Countries that had a democratic tradition before they were communist—most notably the Czech Republic—seem to have had an easier time moving toward a democratic political culture than have countries such as Russia that lack such a tradition.

Postmaterialism and Cultural Change

The phenomenon of **postmaterialism** is one of the most dramatic examples of cultural transformation created by far-reaching social changes. During the quarter century that followed World War II, the industrial democracies of North America and Western Europe enjoyed one of the most rapid improvements in living standards that the world has ever known. Drawing on survey data collected over the past few decades in Western Europe and other economically advanced countries, Ronald Inglehart argued that this economic change substantially altered the political culture of industrial democracies.[37]

He noted that individuals who grew up during the growing prosperity of the postwar period (1945 through the late 1970s) generally felt more economically secure than did their parents and grandparents, many of whom had suffered through the Great Depression or the ravages of war. Having enjoyed relative economic security during their formative years, postwar generations tended to be less preoccupied than their elders with economic stability and growth and to be more concerned with issues such as environmental protection and military disarmament.

Based on their responses to survey questionnaires, individuals in economically developed nations may be classified as materialists, postmaterialists, or a combination of the two subcultures. Materialists, still the largest portion of the population, tend to make political decisions based on economic self-interest. Thus, a middle-class materialist would oppose higher taxes, whereas a poorer materialist would favor expansion of social welfare programs. In addition, materialists are especially concerned about domestic order, a strong national defense, maintaining a stable economy, and controlling inflation.

Postmaterialists, whose numbers have risen sharply in recent decades, may now account for almost half of Western Europe's population, according to Inglehart. Although they are sympathetic to many of the materialists' aspirations (hardly anybody,

© AP/Wide World Photos

ENVIRONMENTAL PROTEST IN DETROIT   Environmental activists hang a banner in the home of the U.S. auto industry criticizing Ford Motor's failure to produce more fuel-efficient vehicles.

after all, likes street crime, inflation, or economic instability), postmaterialists put those goals somewhat lower on their political agenda. At the same time, they are more concerned than materialists are about "moving toward a society where ideas count more than money," "moving toward a friendlier, less impersonal society," protecting the environment, increasing grassroots participation in politics and at the workplace, and defending free speech and other civil liberties.[38] Postmaterialists tend to be more liberal concerning social issues such as divorce, abortion, and homosexuality. They are also more sympathetic to feminist concerns, more committed to disarmament, and less religiously conservative.[39]

Postwar Germany provides an excellent example of what Inglehart calls "culture shift" and the expansion of postmaterialist culture. Over the years, various national surveys asked Germans which of the following four freedoms they felt was most important to them: freedom of speech, freedom of worship, freedom from fear, or freedom from want. In the years after World War II, when the German economy was still in shambles, freedom from want was selected well ahead of any of the others. By 1959, however, as people felt more economically secure, freedom of speech was chosen more often than the other three choices combined.[40]

As the number of postmaterialist voters in Western Europe and the United States grew, Inglehart argues, pocketbook issues played a lesser role in elections, and social class diminished as a determinant of voting.[41] As we will see in Chapters 4 and 5, traditionally, working-class voters have been more likely to support left-of-center parties in Europe and the United States, whereas the middle and upper classes have tended to vote for more conservative candidates. In recent decades, however, that relationship has diminished. Today, many middle-class postmaterialists vote for left-of-center candidates (attracted by factors such as their environmental commitment or their defense of civil liberties) and increasing numbers of workers vote for conservative candidates (sometimes based on the voters' conservative religious values).

Using extensive European survey data over the past decades, Inglehart noted that the number of people in the postmaterialist political culture has grown steadily as young people raised in postwar affluence have entered the political system and as older materialists have died or retired from politics. That trend helps explain the growth of ecologically oriented Green parties in recent years and suggests that issues such as the environment will become increasingly important. If postmaterialist culture continues to grow, liberal parties that stress disarmament, feminist issues, and the environment are likely to benefit, whereas conservative and religiously affiliated parties (such as the German Christian Democrats) could lose ground. There are some signs of this happening already in Western Europe, but certainly not in the U.S. up to this point.

At the same time, however, as Western Europeans became more economically secure and postmaterialist culture expanded, class divisions diminished and voters became less attracted to the welfare-state programs once so favored by the Continent's leftist political parties. As a result, a traditional Marxist party, the French Communist Party—unable to adapt to changing public attitudes—saw its proportion of the vote decline from more than 25 percent in the late 1940s to less than 10 percent today. The French and German socialist parties, perhaps as a response to spreading postmaterialism, have largely abandoned Marxist economics and have increasingly stressed social issues in their campaigns. By expanding beyond its traditional electoral base of workers and teachers, and by attracting the support of middle-class postmaterialists, the French Socialist Party became the nation's largest party in the 1980s and 1990s.

Inglehart's theories have greatly influenced the study of political culture in advanced industrial democracies. However, given the economic insecurity facing many young Americans and Europeans entering the job market since the late 1980s, it remains to be seen whether postmaterialist culture will continue to grow at the same rate. In Europe, especially, high unemployment rates over an extended period have contributed to rising support for France's neofascist National Front Party and for neo-Nazi, skinhead activity in Austria and Germany. These groups express views that are quite the opposite of postmaterialist beliefs. (See Box 3-3.)

THE UTILITY OF POLITICAL CULTURE

Some years ago, Harry Eckstein, a leading political scientist, argued that political culture theory has been one of the two most important developments in political theory during the past 40 years. (We discuss the other development, rational choice theory, in Chapter 6).[42] Culturalist theories have enabled us to progress beyond the study of government institutions in order to understand more fully how politics differs in nations throughout the world. After a period of some disuse, cultural approaches to understanding politics have experienced a revival in recent years, examining such subjects as the prospects for democracy in Eastern Europe and the Middle East, and the relationship of religious values to political beliefs.[43]

Like any important theory, however, cultural explanations of politics have not been without their critics. One significant criticism is that survey research on political

Box 3-3

POSTMATERIALISM IN WESTERN EUROPE AND THE UNITED STATES

Virtually all developed Western nations have experienced the growth of postmaterialist values. Yet, not surprisingly, concerns over materialist issues such as the state of the economy remain strong. Survey data from the start of the 1990s showed that postmaterialist concerns are less prevalent in the United States than in Western Europe and materialist issues are correspondingly more important. The following table lists the values that were most cherished by Americans, Britons, (West) Germans, and French, based on data drawn from the World Values Survey.

Materialist Values	United States	Britain	W. Germany	France
High economic growth	76%	67	65	72
A stable economy	71	62	66	47
Fighting crime	65	64	49	55
Postmaterialist Values				
More say in work/community	55	69	59	68
Protection of free speech	48	45	61	63
More humane society	33	43	55	57

SOURCE: Russell J. Dalton, *Citizen Politics*, 2nd ed. (Chatham, NJ: Chatham House, 1996), p. 95.

Americans were most committed to such traditional materialist values as a stable economy, a growing economy, and fighting crime. Not only were these the most preferred values of the American respondents, but also, in all three cases, Americans chose them more frequently than did British, German, or French respondents. Similarly, Americans had a lower preference for the postmaterialist values listed in this table and almost always selected them less frequently than their European counterparts did. Only one popular postmaterialist value (not shown in the table) was more commonly preferred by Americans than the Europeans—having more say in government.

values and beliefs sometimes uses questions that are not meaningful in other cultures or are translated into terms that have different meanings in different languages. To some extent, that problem can be addressed by more careful translation and greater concern for cultural differences.

A more subtle criticism raised against much of the political culture research is that it has implicit cultural or ideological biases. Carole Pateman has argued that *The Civic Culture* was based on the erroneous assumption that British-American-style democracy is the ideal form of government and consequently that political cultures throughout the world should be judged by the degree to which they support that form of democracy.[44] Richard Wilson goes a step further by arguing that all political cultures consist of widely held (or inculcated) values that justify the political system.[45] Thus, both British and Chinese schoolchildren are politically socialized to support their own system.

Perhaps the most telling criticisms of political culture theory are that too often it is vague and imprecise and that it frequently fails to explain or predict important political changes.[46] For example, we noted earlier the frequent assertion that Latin America has an authoritarian political culture. Yet that assertion fails to explain why Costa Rica has been able to establish a stable democratic order or how Venezuela—historically one of the least democratic nations in South America—was able to transform itself in the late 1950s into one of the region's most stable democracies and then regressed to a limited form of democracy in the 1990s. Similarly, there do not appear to be any identifiable cultural traits that explain why India has been democratic most of the time since its independence, yet virtually none of its neighbors in South Asia has a similar record.

Too often, analysts use culture as a "second-order" or residual explanation.[47] In other words, if political scientists cannot explain why Indian and Pakistani politics are different or why Canadians have less political violence than Americans, they simply chalk it up to culture. Thus, political culture frequently becomes a catchall explanation for anything that cannot be explained by other means. In other words, when scholars are unable to explain differences between two political systems, they often assume that the explanation lies in their political cultures.

These criticisms indicate that some culturalist research and some culturalist explanations are weak. Clearly, political scientists must be careful not to overstretch these theories or to use their own political values as measuring sticks for evaluating other cultures. These criticisms notwithstanding, most political scientists recognize the substantial value of political culture theory when it is carefully and prudently applied.

 ## WHERE ON THE WEB?

http://www.fmv.vse.cz/depts/kpol/pecka.htm

Traces the development of political culture and the transition to democracy in the Czech Republic.

http://www.europa.eu/int/comm/dg10/epo/

Provides information on the Eurobarometer, the most comprehensive survey of European public opinion.

http://www.socialstudieshelp.com/APGOV_Political%20Culture.htm

Offers a discussion of U.S. political culture.

http://religionanddemocracy.lib.virginia.edu/programs/survey/section3.html

Analyzes religion and political culture in the United States.

http://www.library.appstate.edu/reference/polsoc.html

Serves as a guide to sources on political socialization and political culture.

http://www.upenn.edu/museum/Mongolia/section4.html

Discusses modern Mongolian political culture, offering an interesting look at a culture that is way off the beaten track.

http://www.jcpa.org/dje/articles3/elect99.htm

Provides an in-depth examination of Israel's national elections and the implications for Israel's political culture.

◆ ◆ ◆

Key Terms and Concepts_____

agents of political socialization
conflictual political cultures
consensual political cultures
political culture
political resocialization

political socialization
political subcultures
postmaterialism
social capital

Discussion Questions_____

1. Discuss the ways in which a society transmits its political values to its members, particularly to new generations. What are the principal agents of political socialization in the United States, and how might their role in the United States differ from their role in socioeconomically underdeveloped nations?

2. Compare the primary characteristics of a democratic political culture with those of an authoritarian political culture. When analysts characterize countries such as Russia or Egypt as having an authoritarian or semiauthoritarian political culture, what does that say about those countries' chances of ever becoming democratic?

3. If you were the president of a newly independent nation, what government measures might you propose to help develop a democratic political culture in your country?

4. Even in societies that favor a separation of church and state, organized religions play important roles as agents of political socialization. Discuss ways in which political socialization through institutionalized religion can play a positive role in establishing political stability and democracy. Then discuss the ways in which such socialization can play a negative role.

5. Discuss Inglehart's notion of postmaterialism. Specifically, in which countries (or kinds of countries) did postmaterialist values develop? Which types of people are most likely to be postmaterialists? What values distinguish postmaterialists from other people? What are the political consequences of postmaterialist values?

6. What evidence is there to support the claim that Islamic political cultures are less receptive to democracy? What evidence suggests that the preceding argument is untrue?

7. What is the basic argument that Robert Putnam presents in *Bowling Alone*? What are the dangers of a loss of social capital?

Notes_____

1. World Values Survey data in Ronald Inglehart, *Modernization and Postmodernization: Cultural, Economic, and Political Change in 43 Societies* (Princeton, NJ: Princeton University Press, 1997), p. 174.

2. Larry Diamond, "Introduction: Political Culture and Democracy," in *Political Culture and Democracy in Developing Countries*, ed. Larry Diamond (Boulder, CO: Lynne Rienner, 1993), pp. 7–8.

3. Richard J. Ellis and Michael Thompson, eds. *Culture Matters: Essays in Honor of Aaron Wildavsky*. (Boulder, CO: Westview, 1997).

4. Gabriel Almond, "The Study of Political Culture," in *A Divided Discipline: Schools and Sects in Political Science*, ed. Gabriel Almond (Newbury Park, CA: Sage, 1990), p. 144.

5. Data from the World Values Survey cited in Frederick C. Turner, "Reassessing Political Culture," in *Latin America in Comparative Perspective*, ed. Peter H. Smith (Boulder, CO: Westview, 1995), p. 202.

6. Gabriel Almond and Sidney Verba, *The Civic Culture* (Boston: Little, Brown, 1965).

7. Richard Dawson and Kenneth Prewitt, *Political Socialization* (Boston: Little, Brown, 1969), p. 27.

8. Akira Kubota and Robert Ward, "Family Influence and Political Socialization in Japan," in *Comparative Political Socialization*, ed. Jack Dennis and M. Kent Jennings (Beverly Hills, CA: Sage, 1970), pp. 11–46.

9. Paul Allen Beck and M. Kent Jennings, "Family Traditions, Political Periods, and the Development of Partisan Orientations," *Journal of Politics* 53, no. 3 (August 1991): 743.

10. Ibid., 742–763.

11. James Coleman, *The Adolescent Society* (New York: Free Press, 1961).

12. Robert Putnam with Robert Leonardi and Raffaella Nanetti, *Making Democracy Work: Civic Traditions in Modern Italy* (Princeton, NJ: Princeton University Press, 1993).

13. Robert Putnam, "Bowling Alone: America's Declining Social Capital," *Journal of Democracy* 6, no. 1 (1995): 65; Robert Putnam, *Bowling Alone* (New York: Simon and Schuster, 2000).

14. Russell J. Dalton, *Democratic Challenges, Democratic Choices* (New York: Oxford University Press, 2004), p. 191.

15. Ibid, p. 42.

16. Ibid, pp. 165–171.

17. M. Kent Jennings and Richard Niemi, "The Transmission of Political Values from Parent to Child," *American Political Science Review* 62 (March 1968): 169–184.

18. Laurence Wylie, *Village in the Vaucluse* (Cambridge: Harvard University Press, 1974).

19. Michael Crozier, *The Stalled Society* (New York: Viking, 1973).

20. John Ardagh, *France in the 1980s* (New York: Penguin, 1982).

21. William Safran, *The French Polity* (New York: Longman, 1991), pp. 47–48.

22. Ronald Inglehart, *Culture Shift in Advanced Industrial Society* (Princeton, NJ: Princeton University Press, 1990), pp. 197, 449.

23. Almond and Verba, *Civic Culture*, p. 3.

24. Gunnar Myrdal, *An American Dilemma* (New York: McGraw-Hill, 1962; Twentieth Anniversary Edition).

25. Diamond, "Introduction: Political Culture and Democracy," in *Political Culture and Democracy*, p.5.

26. Glen C. Dealy, *The Public Man: An Interpretation of Latin America and Other Catholic Countries* (Amherst: University of Massachusetts Press, 1977), pp. 34–35; and Roland Ebel, "Guatemala: The Politics of Unstable Stability," in *Latin American Politics and Development*, ed. Howard J. Wiarda and Harvey F. Kline (Boulder, CO: Westview, 1990), pp. 508–509.

27. World Values and European Values surveys 1995–2001 as cited in Pippa Norris and Ronald Inglehart, *Sacred and Secular: Religion and Politics Worldwide* (New York: Cambridge University Press, 2004), p. 147.

28. Turner, "Reassessing Political Culture," p. 209.

29. See, for example, Samuel P. Huntington, "The Clash of Civilizations," *Foreign Affairs* 72, no. 3 (Summer 1993): 22–49; Donald Emerson, "Singapore and the Asian Values Debate," *Journal of Democracy* (October 1995): 95–105; Mohamed Elhachmi Hamdi, "The Limits of the Western Model," *Journal of Democracy* (April 1996): 81–85; Adrian Karatnycky, "Muslim Countries and the Democracy Gap," *Journal of Democracy* (January 2002): 99–112.

30. Samuel Huntington, *The Clash of Civilizations and the Remaking of World Order* (New York: Simon and Schuster, 1996).

31. For one of the many challenges to Huntington, see Mark Tessler, "Do Islamic Orientations Influence Attitudes toward Democracy in the Arab World?" *International Journal of Comparative Sociology* 43 (2003), no. 3–4: 229–249; Shireen T. Hunter, *The Future of Islam and the West: Clash of Civilizations or Peaceful Coexistence?* (Westport, CT: Praeger, 1998).

32. Alfred Stepan and Graeme B. Robertson, "An 'Arab' Rather than a 'Muslim' Electoral Gap," *Journal of Democracy* 14, no. 3 (July 2003): 30–44.

33. Norris and Inglehart, *Sacred and Secular*, pp. 133–155.

34. David Conradt, "Changing German Political Culture," in *The Civic Culture Revisited*, ed. Gabriel Almond and Sidney Verba (Boston: Little, Brown, 1980).

35. Richard Fagen, *The Transformation of Cuban Political Culture* (Stanford, CA: Stanford University Press, 1969).

36. Douglas Butterworth, "Grass Roots Political Organization in Cuba: The Case of the Committees for the Defense of the Revolution," in *Latin American Urban Research*, vol. 4, ed. Wayne Cornelius and Felicity Trueblood (Beverly Hills, CA: Sage, 1974).

37. See, especially, Ronald Inglehart, *Culture Shift in Advanced Industrial Society;* Ronald Inglehart, *The Silent Revolution: Changing Values and Political Styles among Western Publics* (Princeton, NJ: Princeton University Press, 1977); and Inglehart, *Modernization and Postmodernization.*

38. Inglehart, *Culture Shift*, pp. 74–75.

39. Inglehart, *Modernization and Postmodernization*, pp. 276–292.

40. Inglehart, *Culture Shift*, p. 71.

41. Inglehart, *Modernization and Postmodernization*, pp. 240–243.

42. Harry Eckstein, "A Culturalist Theory of Political Change," *American Political Science Review* 82, no. 3 (September 1988): 789–804.

43. Some of the many interesting works include Nicolai N. Petro, *The Rebirth of Russian Democracy: An Interpretation of Political Culture* (Cambridge: Harvard University Press, 1995); Daniel Price, *Islamic Political Culture, Democracy, and Human Rights: A Comparative Study* (Westport, CT: Praeger, 1999); Norris and Inglehart, *Sacred and Secular.*

44. Carole Pateman, "The Civic Culture: A Philosophical Critique," in Almond and Verba, *Civic Culture Revisited.*

45. Richard W. Wilson, *Compliance Ideologies: Rethinking Political Culture* (New York: Cambridge University Press, 1992).

46. Paul Warwick, *Culture, Structure or Choice* (New York: Agathon, 1990), pp. 3–24.

47. David Elkins and Richard Simeon, "A Cause in Search of Its Effect, or What Does Political Culture Explain?" *Comparative Politics* (January 1979): 127–145.

For Further Reading _____

Abraham, Paul R., and Ronald Inglehart. *Value Change in Global Perspective.* Ann Arbor: University of Michigan Press, 1995.

Almond, Gabriel, and Sidney Verba. *The Civic Culture.* Boston: Little, Brown, 1965.

Beck, Paul Allen, and M. Kent Jennings. "Family Traditions, Political Periods, and the Development of Partisan Orientations." *Journal of Politics* 53 (August 1991): 742–763.

Dalton, Russell J. *Citizen Politics.* 3rd ed. Chatham, NJ: Chatham House, 2002.

————. *Democratic Challenges, Democratic Choices.* New York: Oxford University Press, 2004.

Fife, Brian L., and Geralyn M. Miller. *Political Culture and Voting Systems in the United States: An Examination of the 2000 Presidential Election.* Westport, CT: Praeger, 2003.

Inglehart, Ronald. *Culture Shift in Advanced Industrial Society.* Princeton, NJ: Princeton University Press, 1990.

————. *Modernization and Postmodernization: Cultural, Economic, and Political Change in 43 Societies.* Princeton, NJ: Princeton University Press, 1997.

Norris, Pippa, ed. *Critical Citizens: Global Support for Democratic Government.* Oxford and New York: Oxford University Press, 1999.

————, and Ronald Inglehart. *Sacred and Secular: Religion and Politics Worldwide.* Cambridge, England: Cambridge University Press, 2004.

Petro, Nicolai N. *The Rebirth of Russian Democracy: An Interpretation of Political Culture.* Cambridge: Harvard University Press, 1995

Putnam, Robert D. *Bowling Alone: The Collapse and Revival of American Community.* New York: Simon & Schuster, 2000.

————., ed. *Democracies in Flux: The Evolution of Social Capital in Contemporary Society.* New York: Oxford University Press, 2002.

Wilson, Richard W. *East Asian Political Culture.* Piscataway, NJ: Transaction Periodicals Consortium, 2002.

A NEW VOICE IN AFRICA Liberia's President Ellen Johnson-Sirleaf sits in the presidential chair during her inauguration at the Capitol Building in Monrovia, Liberia, Monday January 16, 2006. In a ceremony attended by U.S. first lady Laura Bush and other dignitaries, Johnson Sirleaf became Africa's first woman elected head of state.

4

PUBLIC OPINION AND ELECTIONS

◆ Influences on Public Opinion and Voting Choice ◆ Voter Turnout ◆ Belief Systems ◆ The Electoral Process and Campaign Money ◆ Electoral Systems ◆ Public Opinion Polling ◆ Conclusion: Elections and Public Opinion—The People's Voice?

People participate in politics in many ways. They write to government officials, join political parties and interest groups, take part in demonstrations (violent and nonviolent), and discuss politics with relatives and friends. When governments attempt to suppress political involvement, creative people participate in politics in more subtle ways, perhaps by creating literature or music or films containing political messages. In some countries, most notably in the Middle East, Latin America, and parts of Eastern Europe, church-related activities constitute an important setting for political involvement.

Nevertheless, the act of *voting* occupies a central place in political behavior. Elections are a direct and generally accepted approach to popular consultation and are a basic component of democratic government. By selecting one candidate or party over another, citizens express preferences regarding who should govern them and which government policies should be adopted or changed. Apart from voting choices, *public opinion* itself is an important aspect of political behavior. By studying voting and public opinion, we are able to understand a great deal about politics, at least in democracies.

Of course, non-democratic political systems hold elections as well, with the voters often given a "choice" of a single slate of candidates. Such single-party elections are held in China, Vietnam, North Korea, and many African nations. They were the norm, until recently, in the former Soviet Union and Eastern Europe.* Other nations have held elections in which weak opposition parties have been permitted to nominate candidates but have not been given an opportunity to win. In Nicaragua, for example, before the *Sandinista* revolution (1979), the Somoza dictatorship regularly staged such elections. In Mexico, the Institutional Revolutionary Party (PRI) controlled the lower house of Congress for 70 years, until July 1997, and it held the presidency until July 2000, when Vicente Fox, the National Action Party (PAN) candidate was elected (see Chapter 16). Because of the obvious predictability of rigged elections, they tell us little about public opinion or electoral behavior. Hence, this chapter focuses on elections in democratic systems.

The bulk of the study of public opinion and voting focuses on factors that influence how citizens vote and why people hold different views on policies and candidates. Researchers are also interested in the strength and distribution of opinions. Analysts want to know what kinds of people support each political party, how the rich and poor or people of different religions differ with respect to opinions and voting choices, how economic conditions and foreign policy crises affect elections, and how a candidate's personality or character amplifies or restricts his or her support. Our understanding of many kinds of political activity is built mainly on information regarding these matters. And, as a practical matter, the study of voting and public opinion is crucial to strategists who manage campaigns and allocate scarce campaign funds.

In this chapter, we discuss six important problems: factors influencing the direction of public opinion and voting choices, factors affecting voter turnout, the development of belief systems, campaign financing, electoral laws and procedure, and public opinion polling.

---

* Single-party governments still rule most of Africa. Since the collapse of communism in Eastern Europe and the rise of opposition candidates in the states of the former Soviet Union, however, many African governments have come under pressure to allow competitive elections. Some, such as Zambia, Benin, and Togo, have turned power over to electoral opponents.

INFLUENCES ON PUBLIC OPINION AND VOTING CHOICE

In our discussion of political culture (Chapter 3), we noted major agents of political socialization—family, education, friends, religious and social groups, and the media—and analyzed their impact on political culture. In this section, we shift our focus to consider the determinants of *specific* political opinions and voting choices: What led some Canadians to support the Conservative Party of Stephen Harper and others to prefer the Liberal Party's Paul Martin in 2006? How can we explain the choices of some Israeli citizens to support U.S. action against Iraq much more avidly than others?

Orientations to Politics: How Citizens "Filter" Political Information

In a modern industrial democracy, citizens are flooded with complex and detailed information about political issues, national events, and candidates. People need to interpret that information before it will affect their opinions or votes. Political scientists have identified two important ways in which people "filter" political information, helping them to develop their preferences and their votes: party identification and ideology.

Party Identification   Imagine that your instructor asks you to come to the front of the room, and then asks you to guess which way a randomly selected fellow student (with whom you are not acquainted) voted in the last presidential election. If you guess correctly, you will win an all-expenses-paid spring break in Cancun. Before guessing, the instructor tells you that you can ask the student *one* question to help you guess. What question should you ask?

Political scientists would not hesitate—if they had to guess which way a given citizen voted in a democratic country's national election, and if they could only have one piece of information to help them, the one thing they would want to know to help them guess is the person's **party identification**. The more strongly an individual identifies with a particular political party (Democratic, Republican, Conservative, Labour, and so on) and the longer that identification has been held, the more likely it is that the person's political opinions and voting choices will be influenced by that party. Even when it is relatively weak, party identification affects people's political opinions.

Both the 2000 and the 2004 presidential elections in the U.S. were very close. Thus, an unaided guess about the vote of a randomly chosen individual would be correct in only about half of all tries. You would have a very good chance of making an accurate guess, however, with information on the individual's party identification. In 2000, fully 86 percent of voters considering themselves to be Democrats voted for Al Gore, and 91 percent of those considering themselves Republicans voted for George W. Bush. In 2004, 89 percent of voters considering themselves Democrats voted for John Kerry, while 93 percent of those considering themselves Republicans voted for George W. Bush.[1]

A renowned American political scientist, V. O. Key, Jr., observed in 1952 that "the time of casting a ballot is not a time of decision for many voters; it is merely an occasion for the reaffirmation of a partisan faith of long standing."[2] The voter begins with the belief that one party supports his or her interests and simply chooses the candidate nominated by that party. Thus, according to Key, the typical voter rarely evaluates candidates objectively. A person may not immediately know anything about, say, Lamar Alexander (Republican senator from Tennessee) or Herb Kohl (Democratic senator from Wisconsin), but upon discovering each politician's party affiliation, most people will quickly develop an evaluation. If a voter identifies with the candidate's party, he or she almost always concludes that the candidate favors the right proposals.

Party identification even influences the way people evaluate a politician's character. The Watergate scandal (1972–1974) produced a wide range of opinion about the nature and significance of actions taken by Richard Nixon and his advisers, and many people formed their opinions under the influence of partisan identification. Those considering themselves Republicans were far more likely than Democrats to conclude that Richard Nixon's illegal activities were excusable or unimportant.

Bill Clinton's second term (1997–2001) was overwhelmed by the scandal surrounding his testimony about his relationship with intern Monica Lewinsky in a sexual-harassment lawsuit. Although polls regularly indicated that nearly all Americans disapproved of his behavior, those identifying with the Democratic Party tended to conclude that Clinton's actions were a personal issue only, whereas Republicans focused on the perjury and obstruction of justice charges. The power of party identification has rarely been seen more clearly.

The stronger an individual's identification with a particular party, the greater the likelihood that party identification will influence that person's policy views and voting choices. A recent U.S. study of the impact of character on voter judgments confirmed that "partisan bias promotes reliance on impressions of character weakness." In other words, "the more strongly people identify with the party" opposing the candidate, the more their negative impression of the candidate's character influences their impressions of his or her overall performance.[3]

Why does party identification play such a role? For one thing, people get much of their political information from parties or from advertisements paid for by parties, and information is always presented in ways that show the party's position to full advantage. Few of us have the time or the inclination to unearth detailed information independently; parties collect and digest the raw data regarding government and politics, presenting it to their supporters (and potential supporters) in an intelligible way.

Considerable, though not uncontested, evidence suggests that the influence of party identification has diminished in contemporary industrial democracies, particularly in Western Europe and the United States. A study of 21 Western nations concluded that party identification has steadily declined in 19 of them, including the United States, Britain, France, Germany, Sweden, Austria, and Italy.[4] Moreover, a recent study of Venezuela found that party identification there has become less stable in recent elections, making it difficult for a winning party to be assured of holding onto its electoral majority.[5] Where identification is weaker, it has less impact on political behavior, and its impact may be less secure.

Perhaps the most dramatic evidence of this change is the ticket splitting that has become so apparent in the United States. In national elections in the early part of the twentieth century, majorities of voters in over 90 percent of the voting districts chose candidates from the same party for both presidential and congressional races. During the 1980s, majorities of voters in more than one-third of the districts selected a presidential candidate from one party and a congressional candidate from another.[6] This trend has continued. For example, in 2000, 40 of the House districts

won by George W. Bush elected Democrats to Congress. Clearly, although party identification remains an important influence on voting choices and opinions, other factors are also important, leading many citizens to oppose their chosen parties with
some of their votes.

Ideology   The most significant influence on political opinions after party identification
is *ideological orientation*. As discussed in Chapter 2, we often speak of a person's being
liberal or conservative, suggesting a predisposition to interpret political issues from a
particular viewpoint. As with party identification, ideological orientations shape voters'
opinions. Conservatives tend to discount allegations of impropriety on the part of conservative politicians, and liberals tend to do the same with liberal politicians. Moreover, someone may hear of a specific issue or policy question on which he or she is
initially undecided. If this person considers himself or herself a "liberal," and then
finds out which side is the "liberal" side, he or she will tend to support that position
(unless other influences operate in the opposite direction). Of course, conservatives act
this way as well.

Thus, liberals vote for liberal candidates and conservatives vote for conservative
candidates. In 2004, conservatives rated George W. Bush nearly twice as highly as liberals did. Liberal and conservative votes showed the same pattern.

In short, if we want to understand how to account for the public's opinions on candidates or issues, it is useful to begin with party identification and ideological orientation.
These general frameworks often determine how citizens make their specific political
choices. Although most voters occasionally disagree with their party or with ideologically
similar friends about some issue or candidate, predictions about a person's vote are likely
to be much more accurate if we have firm data about that person's partisan and ideological orientations.

Sources of Party Identification and Ideological Orientation

Where do these important influences on vote choice and public opinion come from?
People develop their party identification and ideological orientation through the
influence of family, education, work groups, religious affiliation, the media, unions and
professional associations, and other important relationships. Despite the individualized nature of this process, however, some general patterns can be identified.

Socioeconomic Status (SES)   For some time, social scientists have discussed the
importance of **socioeconomic status,** or **SES.** A person's SES is determined by income,
education, and job status. (Successful neurosurgeons and certified public accountants with
leading firms have "high" SES; the typical migrant farm laborer has "low" SES.) Political
scientists, sociologists, and campaign strategists have noted a strong relationship between
SES and partisan and ideological orientations, at least among people in industrialized
democracies.

Simply put, people with high SES tend to support conservative parties and right-
wing ideology, and low-SES people tend to support leftist parties and ideology. This
relationship has been observed in many countries and over a long period of time. A classic study of U.S. public opinion found that in 1964 nearly 50 percent of self-identified
"working-class" respondents identified themselves as "completely liberal," compared with

only 20 percent of respondents from higher classes.[7] The same pattern was evident in recent presidential elections. In both 1992 and 1996, Democrat Bill Clinton received 59 percent of the votes cast by citizens with annual incomes under $15,000. Wealthier voters found him and his party far less appealing. Clinton received only 35 percent of the votes cast by people with household incomes over $75,000 in 1992, and only about 40 percent of the votes from this group in 1996.[8] In 2004, Democrat Kerry beat Republican Bush 63 percent to 36 percent among the lowest income group, while Bush won handily among those making $200,000 or more, 63 percent to 35 percent.[9] The tendency for SES to influence partisan and ideological orientation is also regularly found in Great Britain, France, Germany, Sweden, and many other democratic political systems.

Two important facts must be noted about this relationship. First, the relationship between SES, on the one hand, and ideology or party identification, on the other, is valid only in the *aggregate*. A thousand randomly selected wealthy Britons will include more Conservatives than will a thousand randomly selected blue-collar workers. One will also find more Democratic Party supporters among a thousand randomly selected American blue-collar workers than among a thousand wealthy Americans. It should be obvious, however, that there will be many exceptions.

Second, the impact of SES has been declining in the United States and Europe over the past five decades. In the United States and Great Britain, as working-class voters have become more economically comfortable (particularly as they have become homeowners), many have become less attached to the economic policies of the Democratic and Labour parties. Substantial numbers of them voted for Ronald Reagan and George Bush in the United States and for the Conservative Party in Great Britain. At the same time, increasing numbers of high-SES citizens are drawn to leftist parties and candidates who advocate more vigorous environmental regulation. Both trends run counter to the traditional relationship between SES and opinion/voting choice.

In the previous chapter, we discussed Ronald Inglehart's evidence of a "culture shift" associated with the rise of what he terms post-materialist values in the industrial democracies of Europe and North America.[10] As societies move beyond struggles over industrial and economic policy, political issues become immersed in other matters, and the impact of SES on party and ideology is less straightforward.

Figure 4.1 shows how the political effect of SES changed in four democracies during the second half of the twentieth century. The vertical axis is the "Alford Class Voting Index," which is simply the "difference between the percentage of the working class voting for the left and the percentage of the middle class voting left."[11] Thus, where the curves are in the upper part of the graph, it indicates that the influence of SES on vote choice was very strong—that the percentage of *working-class voters* who voted for leftist parties was much higher than the percentage of *middle-class voters* who chose such parties. Where the curves are in the lower part of the graph, there was little difference between lower and middle classes with respect to their support for leftist parties. In 1948, 75 percent of Swedish working-class voters favored the Socialist Party, whereas only 25 percent of middle-class Swedes did the same (producing a difference score of 50 points). The 1948 presidential election in the United States between Harry Truman and Thomas Dewey produced almost as big a gap, with working-class voters 45 points more favorable to Truman than middle-class voters were.

Figure 4.1 shows a fairly sharp drop in the relationship between class and vote during the second half of the twentieth century in the United States and in three countries in Western Europe. In the 1972 U.S. presidential race (Democrat George McGovern

FIGURE 4.1   THE DECLINE OF "CLASS-BASED" VOTING

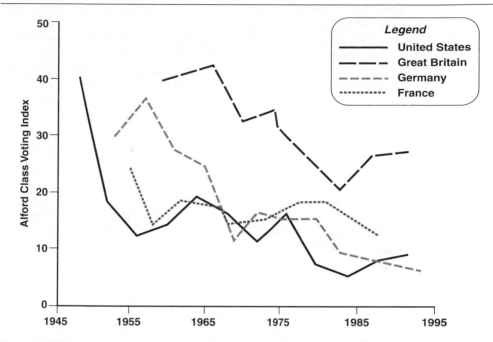

SOURCES: *United States,* 1948–92, American National Election Studies. *Great Britain,* 1959, Civic Culture Study; 1964–92, British Election Studies. *Germany,* 1953–94, German Election Studies. *France,* 1955, MacRae (1967, 257); 1958, Converse and Dupeux study; 1962, IFOP survey; 1967, Converse and Pierce study; 1968, Inglehart study; 1973–88, Eurobarometer studies. Reprinted from Russell J. Dalton, *Citizen Politics* (Chatham, NJ: Chatham House, 1996) p. 172. Reprinted by permission.

versus Republican Richard Nixon), for example, there was virtually no difference in the percentages of working-class and middle-class voters favoring the liberal candidate. Among the countries in Figure 4.1, Britain retains the strongest relationship between class and voting preference, whereas in the United States and Germany that linkage is quite low. During the 2000 U.S. presidential election, there was only a 20-percentage-point difference in the lower-class votes received by the leftist candidate. A recent study of public opinion in Russia presents further evidence suggesting that the traditional relationship between SES and political attitudes is not as simple or as strong as it once was. According to Ada Finifter, the belief that the individual—not the state—is primarily responsible for a person's well-being (a basic axiom of conservatism) is not strongly related to the respondent's level of education.* Contemporary Russian public opinion thus does not confirm the traditional pattern of high-SES conservatism.

As discussed in Chapter 3, the reasons for the declining importance of SES are complex, but they have to do with the increasing economic security and accumulated property on the part of lower-income voters and the increasing concern for non-economic values (for example, environmental protection) among the more affluent. Thus, more

* See Ada W. Finifter, "Attitudes toward Individual Responsibility and Political Reform in the Former Soviet Union," *American Political Science Review* 90 (1996): 138–152. The study also reported results from 39 other countries, suggesting that educational level is only weakly related to conservative views on this issue.

low-SES voters are drawn to conservative parties than in earlier decades, and more high-SES voters support liberal parties. The traditional pattern—high-SES conservatives and low-SES liberals—becomes weaker.

Despite the contemporary erosion of the relationship between SES and party/ideological orientations, this basic feature of modern politics is far from obsolete. Liberal candidates generally do not spend a major share of their time or money campaigning in the wealthier suburbs of British or Australian cities, for example, and conservative Republicans rarely hold rallies in low-income urban neighborhoods. These strategies (and many others) are based on the widely recognized relationship between SES and partisan and ideological orientations. SES remains the best predictor of party and ideological orientations, even though such predictions are less secure than they used to be.

Gender   During the 1980s, political scientists and journalists noted that the distribution of opinion among women and men was conspicuously different in many industrialized democracies. The phenomenon has become a hotly debated issue. Polls show that women are likely to be somewhat more liberal than men on foreign policy, domestic spending priorities, and several other policy issues. Hence, analysts now often speak of a **gender gap,** suggesting that gender is an increasingly important influence on opinion formation and voting choices.

Figure 4.2 shows the influence of gender on political attitudes in a large array of countries, including both industrial and developing nations. The data are from a survey in which respondents were asked if they think that the government or private industry should be given increased influence in society. Those favoring private industry were judged to be "right-wing," and those favoring a stronger government role were judged to be "left-wing." When the bar on the figure corresponding to a given country is on the left side, it indicates the degree to which women in that country are more liberal than men.[12] When it is on the right side, it indicates the degree to which women are more conservative than men. The data show that the tendency for women to be more liberal than men is almost universal, at least since the 1990s.

The idea that men and women approach politics differently is not new. In the early years of the twentieth century, in both the United States and Great Britain, supporters of voting rights for women argued that the political impact of such a reform would be dramatic. Wars would be avoided, there would be less corruption, and family values would be strengthened if women were allowed to vote. Early empirical work suggested that those predictions were wrong. In the 1960s, Almond and Verba's *The Civic Culture* concluded that "women differ from men . . . only in being somewhat more . . . apathetic, parochial, conservative, and sensitive to the personality, emotional, and aesthetic aspects of political life and electoral campaigns."[13]

Contemporary studies indicate that things have changed. In the United States, women are clearly more supportive of the Democratic Party than are men, and they adopt somewhat more liberal positions on policy. Women are less sympathetic to large defense expenditures than men are, and, in general, women are less "hawkish." Opinion surveys show that women were more opposed than men to the war in Vietnam, more critical of U.S. support for the Nicaraguan *contras,* and, at least initially, more hesitant about entering the 1991 Gulf War against Iraq and the 2003 invasion of Iraq. Women are also more likely than men to see a need for state intervention in the economy. Why this gender gap has occurred is a matter of considerable complexity.

FIGURE 4.2 THE POLITICAL GENDER GAP AROUND THE WORLD

The lengths of the bars indicate the gender gap for each country. When the bar is to the left of the zero line, it indicates that women are more supportive of left-wing ideologies than men are; for the few countries in which the bar is to the right, it indicates that women are more supportive of right-wing ideologies than men are.

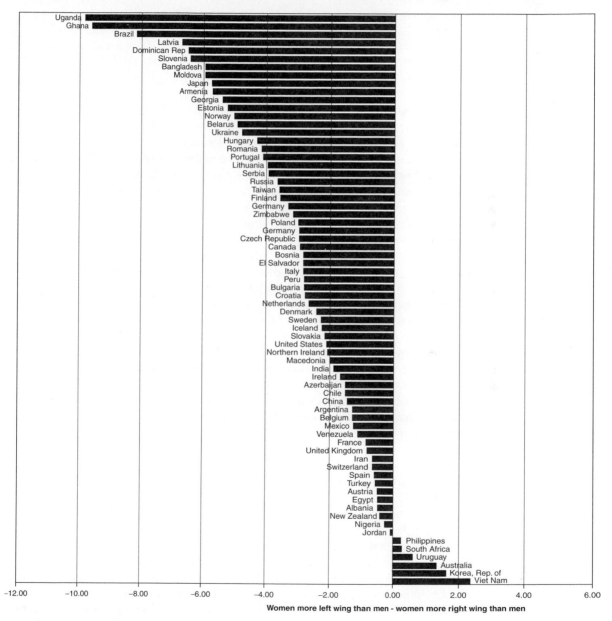

SOURCE: Ronald Inglehart and Pippa Norris, *The Rising Tide: Gender Equality and Cultural Change Around the World* (Cambridge, UK: Cambridge University Press, 2003), p. 82

TABLE 4.1   ELECTORAL RESULTS FROM RECENT U.S. PRESIDENTIAL ELECTIONS, BY GENDER (PERCENT)

| | 1980 | | 1984 | | 1988 | | 1992 | | | 1996 | | 2000 | | 2004 | |
	Reagan	Carter	Reagan	Mondale	Bush	Dukakis	Clinton	Bush	Perot	Clinton	Dole	Bush	Gore	Bush	Kerry
Men	55	36	62	37	57	41	41	38	10	43	44	53	42	55	44
Women	47	45	56	44	50	49	48	37	7	54	38	43	52	48	51

SOURCE: Exit poll data. *New York Times* on the Web at www.nyt.com. Results for the 2000 election from CNN exit poll at http://www.cnn.com/ELECTION/2000/epolls/US/Pooo.html/. and for the 2004 election at http://www.cnn.com/ELECTION/2004/pages/results/states/US/P/00/epolls.0.html.

Many observers (and nearly all journalists) attribute the gender gap in the U.S. to the feminist movement. By "raising women's consciousness," feminist organizations have made women see that their interests demand leftist policies, according to this view. Moreover, as women have entered the workforce in greater proportions, their traditional roles have all but vanished. Many women thus have acquired a pronounced feminist perspective regarding such issues as child care, nuclear disarmament, and abortion. Perhaps the modern gender gap has been created by the fact that the remaining vestiges of traditional gender roles seem increasingly antiquated and unfair in modern life.

However, an important study in the *American Journal of Political Science* evaluated data on U.S. elections beginning in the 1950s and concluded that the "gender gap is the product of the changing partisanship of *men*."[14] In other words, the observed differences between male and female voters has grown not because women have deserted the Republican Party *but because men have deserted the Democratic Party*. (See Table 4.1)

Nevertheless, the extent to which the sexes hold different opinions is often exaggerated. For example, although female voters in the United States have been more sympathetic than males to Democratic presidential candidates in recent years, women as a group still favored Ronald Reagan over Jimmy Carter in 1980 and Reagan over Walter Mondale in 1984, and they were evenly split between George Bush and Michael Dukakis in 1988. Table 4.1 also shows that both men and women preferred Clinton to Bush in 1992, although the margin among women was considerably larger. The 1996, 2000, and 2004 results were remarkable in that in all three elections, U.S. men and women actually preferred different candidates. In 1996, men slightly favored Dole (44 to 43 percent), whereas women clearly favored Clinton (54 to 38 percent); in 2000, men favored Bush (53 to 42 percent), whereas women favored Gore (54 to 43 percent); and in 2004, men favored Bush (55 to 44 percent), whereas women favored Kerry (51 to 48 percent). And although large numbers of American women have demonstrated in favor of abortion rights, many other women have been active in the anti-abortion movement. Given polls that show that a higher percentage of American men than women support the right to an abortion, and that more men than women favor the Equal Rights Amendment (a proposed constitutional provision, defeated in the 1980s, making sex discrimination unconstitutional), it is important not to overstate the gender gap phenomenon.*

The gender gap is the subject of a great deal of contemporary research in psychology and sociology. Some analysts emphasize that more women than men are primary

* See Kay Lehman Schlozman, Nancy Burns, Sidney Verba, and Jesse Donahue, "Gender and Citizen Participation: Is There a Different Voice?" *American Journal of Political Science* 39 (May 1995): 267–293. According to the authors, in the early 1990s, "[U.S.] men are somewhat more pro-choice than women."

caregivers to both children and the elderly and that these experiences generate concern for social programs advocated by liberal parties. Others contend that the root of the gender gap is deeper, having to do with the differences between the way male and female infants relate to their mothers. According to this controversial argument, the male child has a greater need to emphasize his separateness, leading men to be more aggressive and competitive, eventually becoming more supportive of defense spending and less drawn to social welfare efforts.[15]

Religious differences between men and women is another factor explaining gender differences with respect to politics. As we noted in Chapter 3, opinion surveys and voting results from Italy, Chile, and Ireland suggest that in Catholic countries, religious women have traditionally been more likely than men to support conservative political parties, although this tendency has diminished substantially in recent decades. This pattern reflected the church's opposition to leftist or liberal parties in those countries and a higher level of religiosity among women than among men. Yet, a recent study of political attitudes among Egyptians, Kuwaitis, and Palestinians in Kuwait (before the 1991 Gulf War) indicated that in those less traditional Islamic societies, women are more liberal than men about a number of important issues.[16] All of this suggests that while gender will have a unique political impact in each country and culture, there is a clear overall pattern relating gender and ideology throughout much of the world.

Other Influences on Party Identification and Ideological Orientation   Several other factors influence partisan and ideological orientation. In many countries, *race* continues to be critical, often overriding the effects of party or ideology. Most observers of U.S. politics are aware, for example, that fewer than 12 percent of African Americans have voted for Republican presidential candidates in recent elections. Race and ethnicity are also profoundly important factors in elections in Israel, where Sephardic Jews (those descended from Jews in Spain, Portugal, the Middle East, and North Africa) are traditionally more supportive of the conservative Likud Party, while Ashkenazi Jews (Jews of European origin) are more likely to vote for leftist parties.

Religion remains a major political influence in some countries. French and Italian citizens who regularly attend church have more conservative beliefs than those who do not.[17] Voters in different *regions* of some countries approach politics in distinctive ways, revealing modern echoes of ancient conflicts.

Psychological factors constitute a rather different (and often questioned) influence on partisan and ideological orientations. A famous U.S. study in the 1950s concluded that people who held conservative beliefs tended to have psychological traits that were different from liberals. People suffering from significant anxiety, for example, supposedly developed an aversion to change and thus chose to support conservative leaders and parties.[18] Although the methods and data used in that study have been widely criticized, many analysts feel that psychology and political attitudes are related.

Candidate Evaluation: A Confounding Element in Public Opinion

Citizens do not always form opinions or make their voting choices on the basis of party identification and ideological orientation. It is well established that people often react strongly to the personality, style, or "charisma" of a particular candidate. Such reactions, positive or negative, can influence not only a person's vote but also his or her opinions regarding policies and political controversies.

This simple, obvious fact often makes public opinion and voting behavior unpredictable. The influence of **candidate evaluation** was extensively discussed in the United States in the 1980s when Ronald Reagan persuaded large numbers of Democratic Party identifiers to vote for him. Democratic party leaders claimed that most of those voters really supported their policies but were deluded into voting for Reagan by his winning personality and his professional actor's gifts for communication. Similarly, many political analysts argued that Robert Dole lost in 1996 in part because his dour personality (at least on television) made him less appealing than Bill Clinton. Boris Yeltsin made several efforts to enhance his personal appeal during the 1996 Russian elections by, among other things, dancing to a rock band in a staged photo opportunity. In Britain, Labour Party leader Tony Blair used his John Kennedyesque appeal to pull his party into the lead. On the other hand, Stephen Harper, whose Conservative Party won a 2006 election in Canada, is generally considered rather introverted and has a reputation for stiffness in public appearances. While candidate personality and appeal may matter, other things obviously can overwhelm their effects.

Generally speaking, candidate evaluation can be especially important in elections in which the mass media figure prominently and when highly paid consultants manipulate a candidate's "image." Candidate evaluation presents a problem for political analysis, however, because it is so unpredictable. Since citizens can be influenced by factors as changeable as the prevailing image of a candidate's personality, predictions of electoral results on the basis of partisan identification and ideological orientation will often be wrong.

The Impact of Mass Media

In most countries, the mass media, especially newspapers and television, influence voters significantly. The media can amplify or undercut support for a specific candidate; over time, they may even influence deep-seated ideological and partisan attachments. Questions pertaining to the actual workings and effects of the media in these matters are thus critical to the study of public opinion and electoral behavior.

At the outset, it is vital to recognize that not all countries have the same mass media influences. Americans (as well as French and British citizens) rely heavily on television for their political information. Japanese voters read newspapers, which, unlike American papers, "play the role of the constructive critic of the government."[19] In rural areas of the developing world, radio has a great influence. In virtually all societies, however, mass media of some form exert an influence on public opinion.

Gauging the impact of the media on opinions and voting choices is difficult because it is so hard to separate the influence of the media from the influence of party affiliation, family and peer groups, and other organizational relationships. The most difficult questions have to do with the bias allegedly created by broadcasters and newspapers in democratic societies. There is an intriguing symmetry to the charges of bias; nearly always, activists and politicians on *both* the right and the left present charges that the media slant the news. Richard Nixon was strident in his repeated attacks against media bias. He often claimed that the media "kicked him around," and revelations during the Watergate period indicated how much he resented the media. (Nixon was found to have had an "enemies" list that included correspondent Daniel Schorr and other journalists.)

Although not as aroused as Nixon was by the media, virtually every president has argued that journalists are unfair. A 1986 study suggested that some truth may lie behind such claims but that the problem does not arise from partisan or ideological bias. Using a complex approach to measuring the "tone" (positive or negative) of television news statements about the U.S. president, researchers could detect a consistent pattern of increasingly negative coverage for *all* presidents, regardless of party. Every president from Nixon to Reagan began his term(s) with positive television coverage, which then deteriorated. The pattern is too consistent to conclude that it mirrors actual presidential performance over time. Instead, the findings suggest that television focuses on negative aspects of presidents because that is what makes good entertainment. Coverage becomes systematically more negative over time—*regardless of what the president does and regardless of the president's party*—because the television reporters get better at finding negative items to put on the air.[20]

Beyond bias, the most troubling political problem associated with the media has to do with the tendency to oversimplify and distort serious political issues, thereby degrading political discourse. Television seems particularly susceptible to damaging manipulation, but sophisticated campaign managers are often creative in achieving the same effects in other contexts. One famous example of an oversimplifying, emotional political advertisement occurred during the 1964 U.S. presidential campaign, when Democrat Lyndon Johnson's campaign ran a television spot—designed to discredit Republican candidate Barry Goldwater—showing a little girl playing with a flower. A narrator spoke in ominous tones about Goldwater's allegedly "warmongering" policy proposals, and then the girl looked up as a mushroom cloud rose from an atomic bomb. Although the commercial aired only once, it demonstrated the power of television to use emotion in influencing voters. During the 2000 U.S. presidential election, groups opposed to George W. Bush ran a television spot implying that the then Texas governor's reluctance to support additional hate-crime legislation led to the brutal death of an African American who had been chained to a pickup truck. And, in 2004, perhaps the most controversial ads on television were those run by the Swiftboat Veterans for Truth, a group claiming that Democrat John Kerry had misrepresented his combat record in Vietnam. In all these cases, television treated important and complex issues in emotional, manipulative ways and made little contribution to rational analysis.

Nevertheless, a recent study found that "political advertising [in the United States] contributes to a well-informed electorate."* Researchers found that U.S. respondents who paid attention to paid political advertisements had more information about the candidates' issue positions than those who only read newspapers and watched television news. Apparently, campaign commercials transmit at least some real information along with the "sound bites."

Contemporary democracies vary with respect to regulation of political advertising. Paid political advertisements are permitted in Australia, Canada, and Japan but have been prohibited in Great Britain, Sweden, Italy, India, France, and Germany, among other countries. The new Bipartisan Campaign Reform Act of 2002, signed into law by President Bush on March 27, 2002, regulates contributions and some issue ads in the United States, and we will discuss this legislation in detail in Chapter 11. Most of

---

* See Craig Leonard Brians and Martin P. Wattenberg, "Campaign Issue Knowledge and Salience: Comparing Reception from TV Commercials, TV News, and Newspapers," *American Journal of Political Science* 40 (1996): 172–193.

Box 4-1

AL-JAZEERA AND THE PROBLEM OF MEDIA BIAS

Al-Jazeera (from the Arabic word for "island" or "peninsula") is currently one of the world's most successful and most controversial media outlets. It came to international attention when the network broadcast video statements from Osama bin Laden shortly after al-Qaeda's attacks on September 11, 2001. Millions of people throughout the Middle East get the majority of their news from Al-Jazeera's daily news programs, broadcast by satellite to dozens of countries, with a viewership that exceeds 50 million. Al-Jazeera has for some years worked closely with the British Broadcasting Corporation, and it has expanded into a full array of channels devoted to sports, children's programming, and other specialized content, leading some to term it the "CNN of the Middle East." In 2006, Al-Jazeera launched "Al-Jazeera International," a 24-hour English language news and current affairs channel.

Because Al-Jazeera has little competition in the Middle East, the question of its political influence in these unsettled countries is profoundly important. U.S. government officials have argued that Al-Jazeera's news coverage is anti-American, anti-Israeli, and that it gives implicit support to al-Qaeda and other terrorist organizations. In 2003, Paul Wolfowitz, the Deputy

Secretary of Defense, claimed that Al-Jazeera was "slanting news incredibly" regarding the war in Iraq, and that its broadcasts incited violence and endangered the lives of American troops. In an interview with Fox News, Wolfowitz claimed that "Al-Jazeera ran a totally false report that American troops had gone and detained one of the key imams in this holy city of Najaf . . . . It was a false report, but they were out broadcasting it instantly."*

Also in 2003, Dr. Walid Phares, a professor of Middle East Studies and comparative politics at Florida Atlantic University, stated that Al-Jazeera misrepresented a pro-democracy demonstration in central Baghdad. In December of that year, some 20,000 men and women marched through the streets shouting *"La' la' lil irhab. Na'am, na'am lil dimurcratiya."* ("No, no to terrorism. Yes, yes to Democracy!") Instead of reporting that a significant demonstration had taken place that supported the U.S. and coalition activities, the Al-Jazeera coverage stated that about half that many people marched, and that they "were 'expressing views against what they call terrorism.'" Phares claims that ever since September 11, the network "has systematically

*Transcript available at Foxnews.com.

---

the countries that prohibit paid ads reserve free broadcast time for parties, typically allocated to each in proportion to its voting strength. The objective is to ensure that broadcast media will bring information to voters while minimizing the chances that money and clever tactics will manipulate the voters. However, in many Third World countries, one party often has much more money for media advertising than others, giving it a distinct advantage.

Perhaps the most critical factor is the *diversity* of mass media; if no single voice controls newspapers and broadcasting, it is much more difficult to produce significant shifts in support and opposition through the media. (See Box 4-1.) A state-controlled or censored press—such as has existed in Chile, Vietnam, China, and elsewhere—is clearly an influential tool. Television, radio, and newspapers in these countries are used to generate support, direct citizens, and retain power. Yet, the demise of repressive regimes in Eastern Europe, Chile, and elsewhere suggests that the power of state-owned media to control public opinion has its limits. Where the press is free and open, some alternative spokesperson will find an outlet to criticize the government or the ruling party, and some people will listen. The impact of the media is substantially blunted when real media diversity exists, and it is greatly multiplied when all media are in the hands of one ruling party or group.

THE FACE OF TERROR   Osama bin Laden is seen at an undisclosed location in this image taken from video broadcast by Qatar's Al-Jazeera television on Saturday November 3, 2001.

added '*what they call terrorism*' to each sentence reporting terror attacks by al-Qaeda."** Remarks along these lines have led other observers to criticize Al-Jazeera as well. James Morris, of the Institute of Arab and Islamic

**The Phares essay is available at http://www.frontpagemag.com/Articles/ReadArticle.asp?ID=11259.

Studies at the University of Exeter in Britain, concluded that the network is simply "Osama bin Laden's loudspeaker."

Al-Jazeera's spokespersons vigorously deny the allegations of bias. According to one observer, Al-Jazeera has "earned a reputation as an oasis of free speech in a region dominated by government censors," and is often criticized by radical Islamic fundamentalists as serving as a mouthpiece for the West.*** The network, according to its defenders, simply presents both sides of all issues. They also point out that errors in translating their stories into English have been responsible for some of the apparent bias in the stories Al-Jazeera broadcasts.

If democracy succeeds in Iraq, Al-Jazeera will be an increasingly important influence on voters. Voters in the U.S., Canada, Europe, and elsewhere have a broad array of media outlets, making the influence of a single network—however fair or biased—less critical. However, because of its commanding leadership in broadcasting in the Middle East, Al-Jazeera is positioned to have an unusually significant effect on elections in a number of countries.

***Warren Richey, "Arab TV Network Plays Key, Disputed Role in Afghan War," *Christian Science Monitor*, http://www.csmonitor.com/2001/1015/p1s3-wosc.html .

Perceptions of the Government's Economic Performance

Significant evidence shows that the state of the economy often overrides the effects of other influences on voting choices, even the effects of party and ideology. Many citizens vote for or against the incumbent party on the basis of their perceptions regarding the government's economic performance. If economic growth and employment are high and inflation is low, the incumbent party will generally do well with voters, regardless of party and ideology.

A study from the 1980s concluded that, in British elections, "economic variables [exceeded] the impact of partisan identification," and those variables were generally as important as party identification in Germany.[21] Using data from presidential elections between 1956 and 1988, a prominent U.S. political scientist concluded that "each 1 percent increase in real disposable per capita income is estimated to result in a 2 percent direct increase in the incumbent's vote share, other factors held constant."[22] A 2002 study of eight European countries confirms that voter perception of economic performance has a significant impact on elections in those systems, particularly when voters assign clear responsibility for economic conditions. [23]

An exhaustive analysis of data from several countries, both developed and developing, concluded that this factor is often critical:

> The powerful relationship between the economy and the electorate in democracies the world over comes from the economic responsiveness of the electors, the individual voters. Among the issues on the typical voter's agenda, none is more consistently present, nor generally has a stronger impact, than the economy. Citizen dissatisfaction with economic performance substantially increases the probability of a vote against the incumbent. In a sense, the volatility of short term economic performance makes this factor a particularly interesting influence on voter choices—it has its greatest effect on those with low levels of partisan attachment, and can therefore change the outcomes of elections where the parties are of relatively equal strength. Thus, in these situations, the fall of a government is more likely to come from a shift in economic evaluations than from a shift in party attachments.[24]

Given that voters in many countries appear increasingly willing to stray from their party loyalties, contemporary economic conditions will probably become even more important in future elections.

However, it is important not to overstate the importance of this factor. The relatively poor state of the U.S. economy during the months preceding the 1992 election clearly hurt George H.W. Bush, just as a strong economy obviously helped Bill Clinton in 1996. Nevertheless, in 2000, the U.S. economy had started to stall during the two quarters before the November election, and the stock market had fallen considerably over the summer. Because the economy had been strong for several years, traditional indicators suggested that the incumbent party would do extremely well. Although Democrat Al Gore received slightly more of the popular vote than Republican George W. Bush, he received far less than models based on economic performance variables predicted. The predictive models were far more accurate in 2004, suggesting a slight advantage for the incumbent Republican.[25]

A Model of Voting Choices and Opinion Formation

As the preceding sections show, the influences that shape voting choices and public opinions are diverse, complex, and changing. Figure 4.3 is a model illustrating the ways in which several influences act on voters. The idea of the model is to indicate the most important factors in general terms; in a given election in a particular country, some of those influences will be more important than in other settings. The most critical point is that research has demonstrated that voting and opinion are not random behaviors but can often be predicted and understood as the results of a complex set of known influences.

The model implies that SES normally works on opinion formation and voting choice indirectly, by determining party identification and ideological orientation. Gender, race, religion, regional identifications, and psychology, in contrast, often determine both partisan/ideological attachments and specific opinions and voting choices.

Candidate evaluation appears in the model as a factor acting independently on votes and opinions. A particularly strong candidate evaluation can also change party and ideological attachments—some citizens may change their party or even their ideology as a result of their attraction to a particular individual. (The personal popularity of Franklin Roosevelt led many Americans not only to vote for him but also to become liberal Democrats in the 1930s.) Finally, it should be noted that the media's primary potential effect is on opinions and voting choices. On the other hand, newspapers,

FIGURE 4.3 A MODEL OF VOTING CHOICE AND OPINION FORMATION

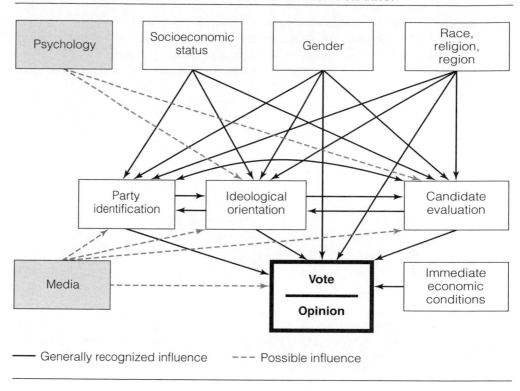

radio, and television may have a longer-term impact, even one that changes partisan and ideological orientations, when the media are under the control of the state or a single dominant interest.

The model helps us understand why research on voting and public opinion is so important a part of political science. Simple explanations (e.g., "John Kerry lost because voters perceived him as weak on national defense," or "Stephen Harper became Canada's new Prime Minister because Canadian voters were more supportive of the United States than the previous Canadian government was," etc.) are almost always incomplete. Accumulated knowledge drawn from political science research makes it clear that voting outcomes and the changing distribution of public opinion are very difficult phenomena to explain and predict, but we have made great progress in terms of identifying which influences are important.

VOTER TURNOUT

Although research on public opinion and voting often focuses on the nature of the respondents' opinions or their vote preferences, it also deals with the question of **voter turnout**. The percentage of citizens who actually vote varies considerably across countries. (See Table 4.2.) The reasons for variations in turnout are many, including

TABLE 4.2   TURNOUT RATES FOR SELECTED DEMOCRACIES

Percent of registered voters voting in all national elections from 1945 through 2005 (number of elections held during the period is shown in parentheses)

Australia (22)	94.5
New Zealand (19)	90.8
Italy (15)	89.8
Sweden (17)	87.1
Denmark (22)	85.9
Germany (14)	85.4
Chile (11)	78.9
Nicaragua (6)	75.9
Panama (4)	75.5
France (15)	73.8
Ireland (16)	73.3
United States (17)	66.5
Algeria (2)	62.3
India (13)	59.4
Poland (5)	50.3
Colombia (18)	47.6
Mali (2)	21.3

NOTE: Turnout percentages are for national elections to the lower house of the national legislature, except for Chile, France, Mali, Panama, Poland, and the United States, where turnout percentages are for presidential elections.

SOURCE: Institute for Democracy and Electoral Assistance (Stockholm, Sweden) at http://www.idea.int.

factors related to voters themselves (such as economic position, psychological orientation to politics, education, and access to transportation) and factors involving the political system (legal requirements pertaining to voting, the activities of parties and other organizations to encourage turnout, and the expected closeness of elections).[26]

Cultural norms are often important in determining voter turnout—in some countries, citizens consider voting a moral duty, and people vote for that reason even when they are unconcerned about the outcome of the election. Public opinion surveys in Venezuela and Mexico, for example, show that most voters feel that elections make little difference in determining government policy. Yet respondents in both countries stated that it was very important to vote.

A decline in partisan loyalty can also reduce turnout. People vote less often when they lose a sense of partisan loyalty, voting only when the few special issues they care about are at stake. In contrast, strong partisans would vote regularly because of their commitment to the party itself.

Legal considerations significantly affect voting turnout. Voter registration is still relatively cumbersome in many states in the United States, often requiring a special visit to city hall; easier voter registration in some other industrial democracies thus helps to explain why U.S. turnout is lower. Other legal factors can increase or decrease turnout. In a number of Latin American countries, parents cannot register their children in school unless they have a stamped identification card proving they voted in the last election (although such requirements can be overcome by paying fines or bribes). Large numbers

© AP/Wide World Photos

VOTING IN IRAQ, 2005 Iraqi Industry Minister Hajim al-Hassani, a Sunni Arab, casts his vote at the National Assembly session in Baghdad, Iraq, Sunday April 3, 2005. Iraqi lawmakers elected al-Hassani as parliament speaker Sunday, ending days of deadlock and moving forward on forming a new government two months after the country's historic elections.

of Italian citizens working in other parts of Europe return home to vote. Although some of these Italians may be simply acting on a sense of civic duty, their behavior is also influenced by the fact that the government pays their passage home on such occasions. Moreover, many nations schedule national elections on Sunday, when people are not at their weekday jobs. Voting is compulsory in some nations, most notably Australia, which regularly ranks as the nation with the highest turnout percentage. Part of the drop in the U.S. turnout rate since the 1960s is related to the lowering of the voting age from 21 to 18, since turnout among younger voters is usually low.

Considering the reasons for different levels of voting turnout may help us understand how well, or how poorly, democracy works in practice. For example, turnout may be very low in less developed regions because of poor transportation, literacy requirements, or even intimidation. According to International IDEA (The International Institute for Democracy and Electoral Assistance, based in Sweden), literacy has a substantial influence on turnout: the 57 countries with 95 percent or better literacy rates have an average turnout of 73 percent, while less literate countries have an average turnout rate of only 66 percent. In Guatemala, where large portions of the nation's population are Indians who speak no Spanish, literacy requirements particularly suppress the vote. Violence and the threat of violence also keep citizens away from the polls.

A new study of voting turnout by IDEA found that the gap in voting turnout between "established democracies" and newer democracies has diminished since the 1990s. (For this study, "established democracies" are democracies with a population of at least 250,000 that have been democratic for at least the last 20 years.) Figure 4.4 shows that turnout rates in both old and new democracies have declined a bit in recent years, a disturbing trend.

FIGURE 4.4   VOTER TURNOUT IN ESTABLISHED AND OTHER DEMOCRACIES SINCE 1945

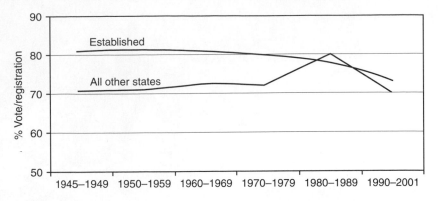

SOURCE: International IDEA.

National voter turnout figures typically obscure great disparities in voting among different segments of society. Perhaps the most consistent research finding regarding turnout is that people of different economic conditions have different turnout rates. Before careful statistical analysis was applied to the question, many observers speculated that poorer people would probably vote more regularly than the rich because the poor were more dependent on government. This "mobilization" hypothesis suggested that the effect of economic distress on turnout would be to mobilize the poor to participate in politics more that the rich. Others argued for the opposite view (termed the "withdrawal" hypothesis), which is the idea that economic distress destroys a voter's sense of self-worth and hope for the future, diminishing interest in elections and leading to lower turnout among the poor.

It is well established that the mobilization hypothesis is completely wrong. Although some poor people doubtlessly respond to their economic distress by voting, a disproportionate number of them withdraw from such activities. In an often cited study from the early 1980s, Steven Rosenstone explored the extent to which this factor affects turnout in the U.S.[27] He found that people who had low incomes or who were unemployed were less likely to vote than those with high incomes and with jobs, and the negative effect on turnout increased with the severity of economic distress. More recent data confirm that not only do the poor vote less regularly than the rich but also, at least in the United States, the disparity is growing.

Census Bureau statistics reported in the August 11, 1996, *New York Times* reveal a trend that points to severely diminished political influence on the part of the poor. As recently as 1984, only 38 percent of the poorest citizens voted, whereas 76 percent of the rich showed up at the polls. In 2000, middle-class voters (those with family incomes between $50,000 and $75,000) made up only 21.6 percent of the population, but they accounted for 25 percent of the votes cast. In contrast, those with incomes lower than $15,000 made up 9.6 percent of the population, but accounted for only 7 percent of the votes cast. Finally, the Census Bureau reported that over 82 percent of citizens with incomes above $100,000 voted, compared to fewer than 49 percent of those with low incomes.[28]

A 2005 study of political inequality in 18 democracies reported that a strong association between socioeconomic status and voter turnout is not exclusively a

TABLE 4.3   VOTER TURNOUT IS HIGHER FOR THE WEALTHY AND BETTER EDUCATED

Country	Income Bias	Education Bias	Year of Election
Australia	5.1	4.4	2004
Britain	6.8	2.2	1997
France	10.8	7.9	2002
Germany	3.8	6.3	2002
Israel	5.9	4.4	2003
Sweden	12.3	6.8	2002
U.S.	30.0	32.9	2004

SOURCE: Data from the Comparative Study of Electoral Systems (www.cses.org), as compiled in Miki Caul Kittilson, "Rising Political Inequality in Established Democracies: Mobilization, Socio-Economic Status, and Voter Turnout, 1960s to 2000," paper presented at the 2005 Annual Meeting of the American Political Science Association.

U.S. phenomenon.[29] Table 4.3 reports the "bias" in turnout created by income and education differences for eight democracies. The table entries indicate the degree to which the turnout rate is higher among citizens in the highest income or education category, compared to the turnout rate among citizens in the lowest income or education category. (For example, the 10.8 percent "income bias" for France means that voter turnout by wealthy French citizens is 10.8 percent higher than it is for poorer French citizens.)

In all these democracies, citizens with wealth and education vote at considerably higher rates than other citizens. To the extent that these citizens have different political interests or preferences than poorer, less educated citizens, the fact that they vote in greater numbers means that electoral outcomes will disproportionately favor their interests. This creates a significant challenge for virtually all modern democracies—the ballot box is not, in practice, the "voice of all the people."

Why do the poor vote less often? Wealthier citizens are more likely than the poor to be literate, to read newspapers and books, and to be members of civic associations. These activities and associations help them develop a strong interest in politics. The rich vote more because they are more involved and more informed, and because they are more likely than the poor to have developed a sense of political efficacy. Yet another problem depresses voter turnout among the poor: complicated voter registration requirements constitute obstacles to voting that are particularly difficult for the poor and uneducated. Sometimes these obstacles are intentionally designed to have this effect.

Before the Civil Rights Act of 1964, it was extremely difficult for many African Americans, particularly if they were poor, to register to vote in rural areas of the South. In many Third World countries, candidates may be so closely identified with economic elites that the poor see no purpose in voting. In Colombia and Mexico, for example, long-term declines in voting are often attributed to the perception among poor voters that the political system offers them little.

Changes in Turnout over Time

It is difficult to interpret the meaning of changes over time in voting turnout. In the United States, turnout has fallen in recent years: 62.8 percent of the voting-age population voted in the presidential election in 1960, only 52.8 percent in 1980, 53.3 percent in 1984, and only 50.3 percent in 1988. Then, after rising to 55.2 percent in 1992, turnout fell in 1996 and was only 50.3 percent in 2000. In 2004, it rose to 55.5 percent, but remained considerably lower than turnout in the 1960s and before.[30]

Some are quick to suggest that declining turnout is a sign of increased alienation. Large segments of the population, say such analysts, are disgusted by scandal or hopeless about the future. Others argue that the decline in American voter turnout reflects the fact that, compared with the period before the 1960s, Americans discuss politics less often with others. Since that time, there has been a "decline in peer interaction itself, caused by a decline of the traditional family, suburbanization, and increased television watching." On the other hand, the Internet appears to have a positive impact on voting participation.[31]

Research on the causes of variations in voter turnout is an important area of political inquiry. Because of the central place of voting in democratic government, understanding variations in voting across classes or across different time periods helps us to see who the "people" are in "government by the people"—an essential question as we gauge the health of a political system.

BELIEF SYSTEMS

Do citizens typically have well-developed, coherent approaches to making voting decisions, or are their choices haphazard reactions to chance events and personalities? In a now classic study, Philip Converse explored the idea of a **belief system**, which he defined as "a configuration of ideas and attitudes in which the elements are bound together by some form of constraint."[32] A strong belief system "constrains" the voter to be consistent in selecting candidates and issue positions, and is therefore not easily swayed by superficial or extraneous information. In terms of our discussion in Chapter 2, such a person is highly *ideological*; his or her political choices are coherent and are firmly connected by some fundamental concern or orientation.

Determining the extent to which people in society can be said to have developed belief systems helps us to interpret how much real substance there is in their opinions. For example, if a large proportion of the population can be said to have recognizable belief systems, then the attractiveness of an individual candidate's personality would have less impact. Parties would offer meaningfully contrasting platforms reflecting the belief systems that shape the political views of large segments of the population. In the absence of such systems—that is, when voters' opinions are more individualized and random—parties may attempt to attract votes by emphasizing a candidate's personality, by sensation and scandal, or by other ploys.

Those who advocate democratic government thus typically hope to find some evidence of belief systems in public opinion. When citizens have coherent, systematic views of politics, a victory by one party reflects a genuine policy preference, making us confident that elections really convey demands about what people want. In contrast, if people vote mainly on the basis of personality and scandal mongering, those elected are free to make any policies they wish, knowing that reelection will have little to do with policy.

Consequently, many observers were disappointed when Converse concluded that "large portions of the electorate . . . simply do not have meaningful beliefs, even on issues that have formed the basis for intense political controversy."[33] His study built on the findings reported in *The American Voter*, one of the most famous political science books ever written. Analyzing public opinion surveys from the 1950s, the authors concluded that the typical American has a rather low "level of conceptualization" regarding political issues.[34] Even by the most generous estimate, the authors found that no more than 10 percent of the population approached political issues from a well-developed ideological perspective. At best, the typical voter had only a vague idea that one of the two parties was more likely to represent his or her interests.

Other research suggests that this conclusion remains accurate, both in the U.S. and in Europe.[35] Even the rapid spread of Internet technology has failed to have an impact: "Our more well-educated, media-soaked public simply has not exhibited any significant increase in knowledge about public affairs . . . nor any increase in political sophistication."[36]

However, there is evidence to support the claim that voters in contemporary democracies *are* becoming somewhat more systematic in their political thinking. As the main parties in the U.S. have adopted more distinct and antagonistic issue positions, an increasing number of citizens have become more meaningfully ideological. In the 1950s, the Democrats and Republicans had far more similar positions on civil rights and foreign policy than they do today. In fact, a recent cross-national study lends support to the idea that the degree to which voters develop belief systems is affected by the main parties, the electoral system, and other institutions.[37] Where policy controversies and partisan conflict mobilizes citizens and generates heated political conflict, a larger number of citizens acquire "belief systems."

Research on belief systems will continue to be a major focus of study for political scientists. Although it is well established that there will always be a large segment of the population that is not politically sophisticated, the size of this segment may increase or decrease in response to the influence of parties, leaders, and events. As research continues on the content and coherence of the public's opinions, we will learn more about the ways in which the real needs and policy preferences of citizens are related to their votes.

THE ELECTORAL PROCESS AND CAMPAIGN MONEY

One of the most controversial aspects of modern elections is the impact of campaign contributions. In some countries, publicly owned broadcasting systems provide free television and radio time for candidates to present their views to voters, but candidates and their parties usually must pay for printing and dissemination of literature, for staff support, and for travel expenses. Candidates in major U.S. elections pay for most of their media time, making campaign dollars an extremely important resource.

Campaign expenditures vary widely across nations. According to a study completed in the 1980s, candidates in Great Britain spent (in total) about $0.50 per voter in national elections, compared with $3.25 per voter in the United States, $1.43 in Canada, $4.34 in Israel, and an astonishing $26.35 in Venezuela.[38] Where most of these expenditures are covered by public funding, candidates and parties do not have to raise the funding themselves, but fund-raising becomes a vitally important task where there is less public funding. For example, the typical Senate campaign in the United States costs the candidate over $2 million, requiring that an incumbent raise an average of nearly $7,000 *per week* during the six years he or she is in office in order to run for reelection. Since the Supreme Court, in the 1976 *Buckley v. Valeo* ruling, has said that a person can spend unlimited shares of his or her own funds in an election campaign, wealthy individuals are often able to gain a decisive advantage over their rivals who must

TABLE 4.4   POLITICAL FINANCE LAWS IN SELECTED NATIONS

Country	Must Contributions to Parties be Disclosed?	Is There a Maximum on Contributions to Parties?	Is There a Ban on Foreign Contributions to Parties?	Are Contributions from Corporations or Unions Banned? Corps.	Unions	Do Parties Receive Public Funding?	When?
Australia	yes	no	no	no	no	yes	1
Austria	no	no	no	no	no	yes	1
Denmark	yes	no	no	no	no	yes	3
El Salvador	no	no	no	no	no	yes	2
France	yes	yes	yes	yes	yes	yes	1
Germany	yes	no	no	no	no	yes	1
India	yes	no	no	no	no	no	
Mexico	yes	yes	yes	yes	no	yes	1
Nicaragua	yes	no	no	no	no	yes	2
Norway	yes	no	no	no	no	yes	1
Peru	yes	no	no	no	no	no	
Poland	yes	yes	yes	yes	yes	yes	1
Russia	yes	yes	yes	no	no	yes	2
Switzerland	no	no	no	no	no	yes	3
Ukraine	yes	yes	yes	no	no	no	
United Kingdom	yes	no	yes	no	no	yes	1
United States	yes	yes	yes	yes	yes	no	

NOTE: For the last column, 1 = "election period *and* between elections," 2 = "election period only," and 3 = "between elections only."
SOURCE: Reginald Austin and Maja Tjernstrom, eds., *Funding of Political Parties and Elections Campaigns*, International IDEA Handbook Series, Stockholm, Sweden: International Institute for Democracy and Electoral Assistance, 2003, pp. 181–238.

observe strict individual contribution limits in gathering funds. For example, Senators Herbert Kohl (D.-Wisc.) and John D. Rockefeller (D.-W. Va.)—among the richest men in the Senate—spent millions of their own fortunes to win their elections.

Table 4.4 provides information on the differences among modern nations with respect to the laws governing campaign finance. There is considerable variation among the countries in this table, reflecting different cultural and political attitudes about elections and campaigns. Consider this summary statement comparing Canada and the U.S.:

> Canada pursues a more egalitarian approach, providing public financing of about two-thirds of candidate and party costs, while seeking to achieve a "level playing field" by imposing expenditure ceilings on candidate, party, and even "third party" or interest group spending. On the other hand, the United States follows more of a libertarian or free-speech approach, with more dependence upon private financing through more generous contribution limits from individual, political action committee and political party sources.[39]

It is difficult to determine precisely the degree to which campaign spending affects electoral outcomes. In Great Britain, analysts have typically assumed that the national campaign—largely driven by publicly funded broadcasts—is the primary factor in determining the results of parliamentary elections, although a study from the

1990s suggested that local spending may have an impact in constituencies where neither party is dominant.[40]

Recent U.S. elections suggest that campaign spending can be a major factor, not only in Senate races, but also in presidential contests. Most observers believe that the very close victory of Republican Richard Nixon over Democrat Hubert Humphrey in 1968 would have been reversed if the Democratic Party had not exhausted its funds during the last weeks of the campaign. More recently, President Clinton's 1996 reelection bid was certainly made easier by the fact that his opponent, Senator Robert Dole, had to spend millions during a difficult primary contest, exhausting the spending limits that applied until after the August conventions. During the long months between April and August, the Dole campaign was relatively silent, while Clinton maintained a consistent presence on the airwaves. In 2000 and 2004, both parties had large war chests, and both elections were close.

Because candidates and parties may be expected to make promises and commitments to groups and individuals in exchange for contributions, most countries have strict limits on such contributions, and many limit the amount that can be spent, regardless of the source of the funds. There have been troubling reports of campaign finance problems in the U.S. for decades, and the problems have involved both major parties. In 1996, the Democratic Party allegedly accepted donations funneled through a Buddhist monastery and an Indian tribe, and there were indications that the government of China had directed campaign funds to both parties in an effort to influence U.S. policy in the Far East. Similar concerns arose regarding both parties again in 2000, and a great deal of controversy surrounded campaign contributions from the failed Enron Corporation. Contributions from oil and tobacco interests to Republican candidates have been examined for many years. Concerns about these contribution patterns, coupled with the persistent efforts of Senators McCain and Feingold and others, led to the passage of the Bipartisan Campaign Reform Act of 2002, as noted above.

ELECTORAL SYSTEMS

The "people" can be said to have a real voice in any electoral system in which the right to vote is secure, the votes are counted honestly, the choices are meaningful, and the elections are regularly scheduled. Even when those conditions are met, however, the nature of the electoral system can have an important impact on electoral outcomes. In the following sections, we consider the most important kind of variation among election systems as well as the issues of malapportionment and redistricting.

Single-Member Districts versus Proportional Representation

Electoral systems based on **single-member districts** divide the nation into a relatively large number of legislative districts with one legislative seat for each. For example, elections for the House of Commons in Britain divide the country into 659 districts of roughly equal population, and each elects one Member of Parliament. Elections for the U.S. House of Representatives also follow this model. The system is sometimes called "winner take all," because the candidate who receives the most votes in a given district wins "all" the legislative power from that district. No seats are awarded to the losers, even if the election is very close. Approximately half of the democracies around the world use some form of the single-member-district system.

Proportional representation (PR) divides the nation into a smaller number of larger electoral districts and assigns several seats to each district. (In Israel, the whole country is a single district.) Rather than vote for an individual candidate, voters normally choose among "party slates" of candidates.* When the votes are tallied, each party receives seats in the legislature in proportion to the share of the popular vote its slate received. Thus, if Party A receives 40 percent of the vote, and there are five seats in that district, two seats will go to candidates on Party A's slate. The other seats will be awarded to the other parties, in proportion to the votes they receive.† About one third of the countries around the world use a PR system. The remaining countries—New Zealand and Germany, for example—use some combination of the two systems.(See Box 4-2 and Table 4.5.)

It may appear that the choice between these two electoral arrangements makes no difference—as long as the principles of majority rule and universal suffrage are followed, both systems are democratic. However, the choice of electoral system can have tremendous political effects, influencing the decisions of both parties and citizens.

In a single-member-district system, party leaders realize that they will get zero representation for their party in any given district if any opposing candidate receives one more vote than their candidate receives. Candidates and party leaders in such systems tend to take moderate positions likely to attract a winning majority or plurality of voters in many districts. Thus, all other factors being equal, systems using single-member-district electoral arrangements tend to have a small number of centrist parties. (See Table 4.5.)

The big losers in a single-member district are smaller parties trying to establish a base of support. It can be done, as the U.S. Republican Party proved in the nineteenth century and the British Labour Party showed in the twentieth century. But doing so is quite difficult. If an up-and-coming third party succeeds in attracting 20 or 30 percent of the national vote, it will still receive virtually no seats because it will fail to come in first in many districts.

For example, as we discuss in Chapter 12, that was precisely the experience of the British Alliance and its successor, the Liberal Democrats. The Alliance (1983 and 1987) and the Liberal Democrats (1992 to the present) received 17 to 25 percent of the popular votes in the last four national elections, but they never received more than 8 percent of the seats in the House of Commons. Proportional representation would have resulted in a stronger British Alliance or Liberal Democratic presence in the House.

Party leaders are well aware of the effects of electoral systems, and sometimes parties with a majority in the legislature enact new electoral laws to benefit their own electoral chances. In a 1959 national referendum, for example, the conservative majority in France introduced a new constitution that moved the country from proportional representation to single-member districts. A major objective was to weaken the Communist Party in the parliament. Of course, sometimes the strategy fails. In 1986, the socialist parliamentary majority reinstituted PR in an effort to dilute the conservative opposition (they hoped PR would produce several new parties, taking voters from the conservatives). The conservatives won anyway and reinstituted single-member districts.

A comprehensive study of comparative electoral systems by Pippa Norris makes a strong case for the importance of electoral systems.[41] She argues that the basic

---

* In some countries, voters choose a party slate and indicate their top choices of individuals on the slate.

† Actual PR systems have detailed rules regarding, among other things, a "threshold" of votes that a party must receive to win any seats.

Box 4-2

NEW ZEALAND'S NEW HYBRID ELECTORAL SYSTEM

New Zealand adopted a new system for electing its parliament in a 1993 referendum. The new system, called *mixed-member proportional,* or *MMP,* includes elements of both a single-member-district and a PR system.

Under an MMP system, each citizen has *two votes:* an "electorate vote" and a "party vote." Half the 120 Members of Parliament (MPs) will be chosen by voters under the single-member-district system, using their "electorate votes" to select named candidates running for election in each electorate (or district). The other 60 winners will be "list MPs," selected from lists of candidates nominated by the political parties. Among these 60 MPs, the total number of MPs from each party will correspond to each party's share of the party votes. New Zealand's new MMP system stipulates, however, that a party must win at least 5 percent of the party votes *or* win at least one electorate seat to receive a proportional allocation of the seats for list MPs.

The sample ballot shown here is based on the one distributed to voters by the government of New Zealand for educational purposes.

The MMP system in New Zealand is an effort to secure some of the advantages of both PR and single-member-district systems. Any party that can command even 5 percent of the nation's party vote will have at least one of its members in Parliament. Such parties would never win a seat in single-member-district systems.

However the electorate votes, the system should ensure that large, established parties will continue to be dominant, since half the seats in Parliament will be awarded to candidates who have received the highest vote totals in their respective electorates. Thus, candidates receiving small percentages of the votes in each electorate will always lose. The hybrid system will produce a more diverse range of partisan voices than would a pure single-member-district system, but it will have more built-in stability than a pure PR system (since the single-member-district system for the electorate votes will ensure that large, established parties continue to dominate).

SAMPLE BALLOT—NEW ZEALAND
NATIONAL PARLIAMENTARY ELECTION

You Have Two Votes

Party Vote	**Electorate Vote**
(This vote decides the share of seats that each of the parties listed below will have in Parliament.)	(This vote decides the candidate who will be elected Member of Parliament of the ———— electorate.)

Vote for One Party		*Vote for One Candidate*	
Carrot Party	————	Allenby, Fred	————
Peach Party	————	Barnardo, Mary	————
Squash Party	————	Dummlop, Alice	————
Banana Party	————	Edlinton, Tony	————
Broccoli Party	————	Nectar, Lizzy	————
Pear Party	————	Omega, Richard	————

character of the political system is substantially determined by its electoral laws. Single-member-district systems produce **adversarial democracy,** where the losing side is excluded from power until the next election, whereas proportional representation systems produce **consensual democracy,** because these systems require a wide range of parties (including those with relatively small shares of the nation's

TABLE 4.5   ELECTORAL SYSTEMS FOR SELECTED NATIONS (LOWER HOUSE OF PARLIAMENT OR GENERAL ASSEMBLY OF REPRESENTATIVES)

	Threshold % of vote needed for seat	Effective number of parliamentary parties*
Majoritarian (Single-Member District)		
Australia	n/a	2.61
Canada	n/a	2.98
United Kingdom	n/a	2.11
United States	n/a	1.99
Combined Systems		
Germany	5	3.30
Mexico	2	2.86
Rep. of Korea	5	2.36
Russia	5	5.40
Taiwan	5	2.46
Ukraine	4	5.98
Proportional Representation		
Czech Rep.	5	4.15
Denmark	2	4.92
Israel	1.5	5.63
Netherlands	0.67	4.81
Norway	4	4.36
Peru	0	3.81
Poland	7	2.95
Romania	3	3.37
Slovenia	3	5.52
Spain	3	2.73
Sweden	4	4.29
Switzerland	0	5.08

*The *Effective number of parliamentary parties* is a measure that estimates the number of political parties that have enough strength to constitute a meaningful influence in parliamentary activity.

SOURCE: Pippa Norris, *Institutions Matter* (Cambridge, UK: Cambridge University Press, 2003).

votes) to cooperate in forming governments. There are arguments to be made for both arrangements:

> For advocates of adversarial democracy, the most important considerations for electoral systems are that the votes cast in elections should decisively determine the party or parties in government. . . . At periodic intervals the electorate should be allowed to judge the government's record. . . . Minor parties in third or fourth place are discriminated against by majority elections for the sake of governability . . . [and] proportional systems are [seen as] ineffective since they can produce indecisive outcomes, unstable regimes, . . . and a lack of clear-cut accountability. . . .
>
> By contrast, proponents of consensual democracy argue that majoritarian systems place too much faith in the winning party. . . . For the vision of consensual democracy, the electoral system should promote a process of conciliation, consultation, and coalition-building within parliaments. [According to this view], majoritarian systems over-reward the winner,

producing 'an elected dictatorship' where a government based on a plurality can steam-roller its policies, and implement its programs, without the need for consultation and com-promise with other parties in parliament or other groups in society.[42]

The electoral system makes an important political difference in two ways. First, it changes the relative fortunes of small and large parties. Proportional representation increases the electoral opportunities of new or narrow-based parties. A party able to obtain only a small share of the popular vote would still win a proportional number of seats in the legislature. Supporters of small parties would not feel that they are wast-ing their votes by voting for them, and potential donors would not feel that they are wasting their money by contributing. Not surprisingly, countries such as Israel and the Netherlands, which use PR electoral systems, are more likely to have multiparty sys-tems with a number of small parties represented in the parliament.

As noted earlier, single-member-district systems usually hurt extreme leftist and rightist parties. The French experience shows how both the far-left Communist Party and the far-right National Front gained more electoral seats when the country used PR. But the single-member-district system tends to hurt *moderate* third parties as well (par-ties that are not in the top two). In Great Britain, the party that would gain most in a switch to PR—the Liberal Democrats (successors to the Alliance)—is more moderate than either the Labour Party or the Conservative Party. Similarly, in Germany, if PR were eliminated, the biggest loser would be the centrist Free Democrats. It is therefore more accurate to say that the single-member-district system creates an obstacle for *less established* parties, regardless of whether they are extreme or centrist.

Second, the electoral system affects the political system in other ways, particularly with respect to stability, voter turnout, and the quality of representation. As we discuss in Chapter 5, the nature of the existing political divisions in society is a key factor in determining whether a country has two or three large moderate parties instead of a large number of smaller, more ideologically distinct parties, but it should be noted that most of the countries of Western Europe use some variant of PR and that most of them have maintained very moderate and stable political systems. If a country has a con-sensual political culture, a generally centrist electorate, and an established two-party system, as in the United States, switching to PR may have little impact. However, if a society is more conflictual and ideologically diverse, such as Israel or Italy, PR tends to produce larger numbers of parties with more polarized ideologies. Although this encourages active input from a wide range of diverse political interests, PR systems can lead to political instability, since elections will often produce a result in which no single party has enough support to govern. To minimize the problem, most PR systems have a "threshold" provision, requiring that parties receive at least a certain percentage of the vote to be represented in the parliament. (See Table 4.5.)

Instability is often a serious problem for PR systems: during the past 50 years, Italian elections have never produced governments (that is, prime ministers and cabinets) backed by stable parliamentary majorities. Italian governments have been forced to resign, on average, every 15 months.* Italy's 1993 reform created a system in which three-fourths of the legislators are elected in single-member districts. This change may increase cabinet stability in the long run. On the other hand, PR systems generally

---

* As we see in our discussion of British politics (Chapter 12), under a parliamentary system, the government (the prime minister and cabinet) needs to be supported by a majority of Parliament. If the prime minister and cabinet lose that support, they must resign.

have higher voter turnout, most likely as a consequence of the wider range of choices that citizens have. According to recent data compiled by International IDEA, countries with PR systems had an average turnout rate of nearly 70 percent, while countries with single-member-district systems had an average turnout rate of only 58 percent.

Malapportionment and District Boundaries

Whatever electoral system is chosen, **malapportionment** (having electoral districts with vastly different numbers of citizens) can also affect electoral results. In severely malapportioned systems, a rural district may be so sparsely populated that its one representative represents only 15,000 citizens. An adjacent urban district may also have only one representative for its 600,000 citizens. The political result can be easily anticipated: A legislature made up of representatives elected through such a malapportioned system would give much greater weight to rural political concerns than would be warranted on the basis of population. Put another way, each citizen in the rural district has 40 times more political power than a citizen in the urban district.

Malapportionment was held unconstitutional in the United States in the landmark *Baker v. Carr* decision in 1962.[43] The Court argued that severe malapportionment effectively violated the Constitution's grant of equal voting power to all citizens. Because of continuing population shifts, this decision requires that the allocation of representatives to each state be reviewed every decade and that states use **redistricting** to correct imbalances among districts. Even when the *number* of citizens in each district is roughly the same, districts can be drawn in ways that affect the ability of the electoral system to represent all voters.

As mentioned previously, when there is widespread knowledge of which parts of a metropolitan area or region support which parties, a party with a majority in the state legislature (which redraws the congressional district lines) and control of the governor's office (who must sign the redistricting) is often able to take this knowledge into account in drawing district boundaries. The requirement that electoral districts be roughly equal in population does not prevent some creative redistricting in ways that diminish the chances of one's opponents.* The areas in which the opposing party is strong are simply divided, and the portions are then included in districts where the favored party has a clear majority.† Strategic redistricting thus creates another way to distort the vote.**

The most controversial issue surrounding the drawing of district boundaries in the United States has to do with the issue of race. The Voting Rights Act of 1965 made it

---

* In 1812, Governor Elbridge Gerry of Massachusetts helped engineer a particularly creative example of this practice. When it was remarked that the district drawn to his party's advantage looked like a salamander on the map, someone pointed out that it wasn't a salamander; it was a *Gerrymander*. The term has stuck as a description of partisan redistricting.

† William E. Brock, chairman of the Republican National Committee from 1977 to 1981, claimed that the Democrats used their control of state legislatures to draw district boundaries so that the Republicans routinely won far fewer congressional seats in the 1970s than their vote totals would have predicted. See John Aldrich et al., *American Government* (Boston: Houghton Mifflin, 1986), p. 238.

** A controversial example of strategic redistricting in the U.S. was applied in Texas in 2003. The new district lines in that state were drawn so that Republicans would gain several seats in Congress, and the strategy bore fruit in the 2004 election. The plan is under scrutiny in a case before the U.S. Supreme Court (*Jackson v. Perry*). The plaintiffs claim that it is a violation of the Constitution's guarantee of equal protection for a state to re-draw congressional districts in the middle of a decade purely for partisan gain, and that the Texas plan violated the Voting Rights Act. As of this writing, the result is not known.

illegal to draw district lines in ways that reduce the ability of racial minorities to elect a candidate to represent them. In 1986, the Supreme Court held that districts could be found illegal if minority voting power is diluted, even if there is no specific intent on anyone's part to create such a dilution.[44] The Voting Rights Act required that Southern states obtain Justice Department approval of their congressional districts, and, in many cases, boundaries were drawn that created "majority-minority" districts (in which racial minorities made up the majority of citizens). In several cases—*Shaw v.Reno* (509 U.S. 630, 1993); *Miller v. Johnson* (132 L.Ed.2d 762, 1995); and *Bush v. Vera* (135 L.Ed.2d 248, 1996)—the Supreme Court has held that districts which are drawn *primarily* on the basis of race are unconstitutional. The controversy rages on, with one side arguing that the government should not assume that members of minority groups are unrepresented unless a person of the same race is elected from their district, and the other side arguing that district boundaries drawn without regard to race will effectively preclude the election of minority representatives.

PUBLIC OPINION POLLING

Much of what we know about public opinion depends on the familiar **public opinion polls** we hear about so frequently during presidential campaigns. Candidates have their own polls, but in most industrialized democracies private organizations have been established to provide independent polling services. (In the United States, the Gallup, Harris, NBC/*Wall Street Journal*, CBS/*New York Times*, and ABC/*Washington Post* polls are the best known.) Opinion polls are essential to those running campaigns, since they help strategists identify where scarce funds should be spent and how the candidate's messages should be crafted. Polls are important in other respects, too, raising questions of real significance for the health of modern democracy.

First, the accuracy of polls is often questioned. Since it is obviously impossible to determine every citizen's views, modern opinion polling works through *sampling*. In the United States, national polls usually are based on responses from no more than two thousand people. If the sample is chosen carefully, the poll will be accurate enough to be useful.* For example, the Gallup, Harris, and CBS/*New York Times* polls were off by no more than 4 percentage points during recent elections and generally predicted the result within 1 or 2 points.[45]

The second issue raised by opinion polls has to do with their possible effects on elections. The argument is often made that undecided voters may make their final choice on the basis of which candidate is ahead in the polls. This possibility is particularly disturbing when we realize that so many news items, in both broadcast and print media, are devoted to poll results. It is not well established that polls have a predictable or significant effect along those lines, but the potential for such influences was enough to prompt the French government to adopt restrictions on poll coverage during the weeks preceding elections.

---

* Perhaps you have heard a national commentator report of poll results with a statement like this: "The results have a margin of error of plus or minus 3 points." This is not precisely correct. The logic of sampling means that if 44 percent of those polls support a given candidate, for example, and if we have a margin of error of plus or minus 3 points, we can be very sure (usually 95 percent sure) that the candidate's support in the whole population is between 41 and 47 percent. This level of certainty requires that the citizens polled constituted a random sample, meaning that every person in the whole population had an equal chance of being included in the sample.

CONCLUSION: ELECTIONS AND PUBLIC OPINION—THE PEOPLE'S VOICE?

The study of public opinion and voting increasingly reveals the complexity of individual political choices. Because of ample data and sophisticated analytical tools, political scientists have developed a large body of knowledge regarding public opinion and voting behavior, making predictions in these areas more useful than in any other set of subjects in the discipline. Nevertheless, our knowledge tells us that useful predictions cannot be based on simple models and that results are often surprising. The most practical bit of knowledge derived from voting and opinion studies is the critical realization that opinions and votes are often influenced by organized entities, particularly political parties, the subject of our next chapter.

 WHERE ON THE WEB?

http://www.electionstudies.org/

Home page for the American National Elections Studies, an ongoing project of the Center for Political Studies at the University of Michigan. From this page, it is possible to access the National Election Studies, which provide data on responses to a wide range of survey questions gathered during national elections.

http://www.gallup.com

Home page for the Gallup Poll, one of the most widely recognized polling organizations in the world.

http://www.fec.gov/pages/bcra/bcra_update.shtml

The U.S. Federal Election Commission's Web site for materials related to the Bipartisan Campaign Reform Act of 2002.

http://www.cfinst.org/studies/vital/index.html

Home page of the Campaign Finance Institute, containing a wide range of recent data.

http://www.ropercenter.uconn.edu/

Home page of the Roper Center for Public Opinion Research.

http://ssdc.ucsd.edu/ssdc/pubopin.html

A guide to "Published Public Opinion Poll Statistics," from the Social Sciences Data Collection at the University of California at San Diego.

http://www.gallup-europe.be/epm/default.htm

Home page of Gallup Europe, containing data on public opinion and elections in several European countries.

http://europa.eu.int/comm/public_opinion/index_en.htm

Web site for the Public Opinion Analysis Sector of the European Commission.

http://www.ropercenter.uconn.edu/jpoll/JPOLL.html

Provides access to JPOLL, "the only comprehensive database of Japanese public opinion."

http://www.cses.org/

Home page of the Comparative Study of Electoral Systems, a "collaborative program of cross-national research among election studies conducted in over fifty countries."

◆ ◆ ◆

Key Terms and Concepts_____

adversarial democracy

belief system

candidate evaluation

consensual democracy

gender gap

malapportionment

party identification

proportional representation
  (PR)

public opinion polls

redistricting

single-member districts

socioeconomic status (SES)

voter turnout

Discussion Questions_____

1. Compare the "mobilization" and "withdrawal" hypotheses as explanations for differences between economic classes with respect to voter turnout.
2. Why is proportional representation (PR) thought to create "consensual" democracy?
3. Why do "single-member-district" systems create "adversarial" democracy?
4. How does the rise of "postmaterialism" affect the impact of socioeconomic status (SES) on the voting preferences of upper- and lower-class voters?

Notes_____

1. Data from CNN Exit Poll data, available at http://www.cnn.com/ELECTION/2004/pages/results/states/US/P/00/epolls.0.html.
2. V. O. Key, Jr., *Politics, Parties, and Pressure Groups* (New York: Crowell, 1952), chap. 20.
3. See Paul Goren, "Character Weakness, Partisan Bias, and Presidential Evaluation," *American Journal of Political Science* 46 (July 2002): 627–641.
4. Russell J. Dalton and Martin Wattenberg, eds., *Parties Without Partisans: Political Change in Advanced Industrial Democracies* (Oxford: Oxford University Press, 2000), chap. 2.
5. Jose E. Molina, V., "The Presidential and Parliamentary Elections of the Bolivarian Revolution in Venezuela: Change and Continuity, 1998–2000," *Bulletin of Latin American Research* 21, no. 2 (2002): 219–247.
6. Morris Fiorina, "The Electorate in the Voting Booth," in *The Parties Respond*, ed. L. Sandy Maisel (Boulder, CO: Westview, 1990), p. 119. See also Fiorina's discussion in *Divided Government* (New York: Macmillan, 1992), in which he notes that party identification for many Americans has been weakened by the perception that the two major parties have become increasingly more ideological and extreme.
7. Lloyd A. Free and Hadley Cantril, *The Political Beliefs of Americans: A Study of Public Opinion* (New York: Simon & Schuster, 1968), p. 216.
8. *New York Times* exit polls, November 5, 1992, and November 11, 1996.
9. Data from CNN Exit Poll data, available at http://www.cnn.com/ELECTION/2000/ epolls/US/P000.html, and http://www.cnn.com/ELECTION/2004/pages/results/states/US/P/00/epolls.0.html.
10. Ronald Inglehart, *Culture Shift in Advanced Industrial Society* (Princeton, NJ: Princeton University Press, 1990).
11. See Russell J. Dalton, *Citizen Politics: Public Opinion and Political Parties in Advanced Western Democracies*, 2nd ed. (Chatham, NJ: Chatham House, 1996), pp. 167–176.
12. Ronald Inglehart and Pippa Norris, *The Rising Tide: Gender Equality and Cultural Change Around the World* (Cambridge, UK: Cambridge University Press, 2003).
13. Gabriel Almond and Sidney Verba, *The Civic Culture* (Boston: Little, Brown, 1965), p. 325.
14. Karen M. Kaufmann and John R. Petrocik, "The Changing Politics of American Men: Understanding the Sources of the Gender Gap," *American Journal of Political Science* 43 (1999): 864, 887.

15. Nancy J. Hirschmann explored this controversial idea in "Freedom, Recognition, and Obligation: A Feminist Approach to Political Theory," *American Political Science Review* 83 (1989): 1227–1244.

16. Jamal Sanad, "Religion and Politics: Islam and Sociopolitical Change" (doctoral diss., University of Wisconsin, Milwaukee, 1990).

17. See Ivor Crewe and David Denver, *Electoral Change in Western Democracies* (London: Croom Helm, 1985), pp. 218–219.

18. See Herbert McClosky, "Conservatism and Personality," *American Political Science Review* 52 (1958): 27–45.

19. William Horsley, "The Press as Loyal Opposition in Japan," in *Newspapers and Democracy: International Essays on a Changing Medium,* ed. Anthony Smith (Cambridge: MIT Press, 1980), p. 212.

20. Fredric T. Smoller, *The Six O'Clock Presidency: A Theory of Presidential Press Relations in the Age of Television* (New York: Praeger, 1990).

21. Michael S. Lewis-Beck, "Comparative Economic Voting: Britain, France, Germany, Italy," *American Journal of Political Science* 30 (1986): 315–346.

22. Gregory B. Markus, "The Impact of Personal and National Economic Conditions on Presidential Voting, 1956–1988," *American Journal of Political Science* 36 (August 1992): 830.

23. Richard Nadeau, Richard Niemi, and Antoine Yoshinaka, "A Cross-National Analysis of Economic Voting: Taking Account of the Political Context Across Time and Nations," *Electoral Studies* 21 (2002): 403–423.

24. Michael S. Lewis-Beck and Mary Stegmaier, "Economic Determinants of Electoral Outcomes," in *Annual Review of Political Science* 3 (2000): 211.

25. See Robert S. Erikson, Joseph Batumi, and Brett Wilson, "Was the 2000 Presidential Election Predictable?" *PS: Political Science and Politics* 34 (2001): 815–819; and Alfred G. Cuzan and Charles M. Bundrick, "Deconstructing the 2004 Presidential Election Forecasts: The Fiscal Model and the Campbell Collection Compared," *PS: Political Science and Politics* 38 (April 2005): 255–262.

26. Ivor Crewe, "Electoral Participation," in Butler et al., *Democracy at the Polls,* p. 239.

27. Steven Rosenstone, "Economic Adversity and Voter Turnout," *American Journal of Political Science* 26 (1982): 25–46.

28. U.S. Census Bureau, Current Population Survey, November 2004.

29. Miki Caul Kittilson, "Rising Political Inequality in Established Democracies: Mobilization, Socio-Economic Status, and Voter Turnout, 1960s to 2000," paper presented at the 2005 Annual Meeting of the American Political Science Association.

30. Data from the U.S. Census Bureau, Statistical Abstract of the United States, 2006, table 407, "Participation in Elections for President and U.S. Representatives: 1932 to 2004."

31. Carol A. Cassell and David B. Hill, "Explanations of Turnout Decline," *American Politics Quarterly* 9 (1981): 193. See also Caroline J. Tolbert and Ramona S. McNeal, "Unraveling the Effects of the Internet on Political Participation," *Political Research Quarterly* 56 (June 2003): 175–185.

32. Philip E. Converse, "The Nature of Belief Systems in Mass Publics," in *Ideology and Discontent,* ed. David E. Apter (New York: Free Press, 1964), p. 207.

33. Converse, p. 245.

34. Angus Campbell, Philip Converse, Warren Miller, and Donald Stokes, *The American Voter.* New York: Wiley, 1960.

35. See Erik R.A.N. Smith, *The Unchanging American Voter* (Berkeley, CA: University of California Press, 1989); Robert Luskin, "Explaining Political Sophistication," in *Controversies in Voting Behavior,* 3rd ed., Richard G. Niemi and Herbert Weisberg, eds. (Washington, DC: Congressional Quarterly, 1993): 114–136; and Richard S. Flickinger and Donley T. Studlar, "The Disappearing Voters? Exploring Declining Turnout in Western European Elections," *West European Politics* 15 (April 1992): 1–16.

36. See Bruce Bimber, "The Internet and Political Transformation: Populism, Community, and Accelerated Pluralism," *Polity* 31 (Fall 1998): 133–160.

37. See Geoffrey C. Layman and Thomas M. Carsey, "Party Polarization and 'Conflict Extension' in the American Electorate," *American Journal of Political Science* 46 (October 2002): 786–802; Paul Goren, "Political Sophistication and Policy Reasoning: A Reconsideration," *American Journal of Political Science* 48 (July 2004): 462–478; and Stacy B. Gordon and Gary M. Segura, "Cross-National Variation in the Political Sophistication of Individuals: Capability or Choice?" *Journal of Politics* 59 (February 1997): 126–147.

38. See Howard Penniman, "U.S. Elections: Really a Bargain?" *Public Opinion* (June–July 1984): p. 51.

39. Herbert E. Alexander, "Comparative Analysis of Political Party and Campaign Financing in the United States and Canada," in *The Delicate Balance Between Political Equality and Freedom of Expression: Political Party and Campaign Financing in Canada and the United States*, Steven Griner and Daniel Zovatto, eds. Washington, DC: Organization of American States, 2005.

40. Charles J. Pattie, Ronald J. Johnston, and Edward A. Fieldhouse, "Winning the Local Vote: The Effectiveness of Constituency Campaign Spending in Great Britain, 1983–1992," *American Political Science Review* 89 (1995): 969–983.

41. Pippa Norris, *Institutions Matter* (Cambridge, England: Cambridge University Press, 2003).

42. Norris *Institutions Matter*, Ch. 2.

43. 369 U.S. 186 (1962).

44. See *Thornburg v. Gingles*, 106 S.Ct. 2752 (1986).

45. See the compilation of figures in James MacGregor Burns and Jack Peltason, *Government by the People: The Dynamics of American National, State, and Local Government*, 11th ed. (Englewood Cliffs, NJ: Prentice Hall, 1989), p. 217. Also see Philip E. Converse, "The Advent of Polling and Political Representation," *PS: Political Science and Politics* 29 (December 1996): 649–657.

For Further Reading _____

Adams, James. *Party Competition and Responsible Party Government*. Ann Arbor, MI: University of Michigan Press, 2001.

Brockington, David. "The Paradox of Proportional Representation: The Effect of Party Systems and Coalitions on Individuals' Electoral Participation. *Political Studies* 52 (2004): 469–490.

Campbell, Angus, Phillip E. Converse, Warren E. Miller, and Donald E. Stokes. *The American Voter.* New York: Wiley, 1960.

Conover, Pamela Johnston. "Feminists and the Gender Gap." *Journal of Politics* 50 (1988): 985–1010.

Dalton, Russell. *Democratic Challenges, Democratic Choices: The Erosion in Political Support in Advanced Industrial Democracies*, Oxford: Oxford University Press, 2004.

Downs, Anthony. "An Economic Theory of Political Action in a Democracy," *Journal of Political Economy* 65 (1957): 135–150.

Elazar, Daniel J., and Shmuel Sandler. *Israel at the Polls, 1992.* Lanham, Md.: Rowman and Littlefield, 1995.

Finifter, Ada W. "Attitudes toward Individual Responsibility and Political Reform in the Former Soviet Union." *American Political Science Review* 90 (1996): 138–152.

Gschwend, Thomas and Leuffen, Dirk. "Divided We Stand—Unified We Govern? Cohabitation and Regime Voting in the 2002 French Elections," *British Journal of Political Science*, 35 (2005): 691–712.

Holbrook, Thomas M. *Do Campaigns Matter?* Thousand Oaks, CA: Sage, 1996.

Holbrook, Thomas M. "A Post-Mortem Update of the Economic News and Personal Finances Forecasting Model," *P.S. Political Science and Politics* 38 (2005): 35–36.

Huber, John, Kernell, Georgia, and Leoni, Eduardo L. "Institutional Context, Cognitive Resources and Party Attachments Across Democracies," *Political Analysis* 13 (2005): 365–386.

Karp, Jeffrey A., and Brockington, David. "Social Desirability and Response Validity: A Comparative Analysis of Over-Reporting Turnout in Five Countries," *Journal of Politics*, 67 (2005): 825–840.

Kedar, Orit. "How Diffusion of Power in Parliaments Affects Voter Choice." *Political Analysis*, 13 (2005): 410–429.

Nicol, Mike. *The Waiting Country: A South African Witness*. London: Gollancz, 1995.

Nie, Norman, Sidney Verba, and John Petrocik. *The Changing American Voter*. Cambridge: Harvard University Press, 1976.

Norris, Pippa. *Electoral Engineering: Voting Rules and Political Behavior*. New York: Cambridge University Press, 2005.

Norris, Pippa. *Institutions Matter*. Cambridge, UK: Cambridge University Press, 2003.

Norris, Pippa, Montague Kern, and Marion Just, eds. *Framing Terrorism: The News Media, the Government, and the Public* New York: Routledge, 2003.

Norris, Pippa, and Ronald Inglehart, *Sacred and Secular: Religion and Politics Worldwide*. Cambridge, UK: Cambridge University Press, 2004.

Pattie, Charles J., Ronald J. Johnston, and Edward A. Fieldhouse. "Winning the Local Vote: The Effectiveness of Constituency Campaign Spending in Great Britain, 1983–1992." *American Political Science Review* 89 (1995): 969–983.

Powell, G. Bingham. "American Voter Turnout in Comparative Perspective." *American Political Science Review* 80 (March 1986): 17–44.

Seligson, Mitchell A., and John A. Booth. *Elections and Democracy in Central America, Revisited*. New and enlarged ed. Chapel Hill: University of North Carolina Press, 1995.

Wattenberg, Martin P. *Where Have All the Voters Gone?* Cambridge: Harvard University Press, 2002.

White, Stephen, Richard Rose, and Ian McAllister. *How Russia Votes*. Chatham, NJ: Chatham House, 1997.

White, Stephen, D. Stansfield, and P. Webb, eds. *Political Parties in Transitional Democracies*. Oxford: Oxford University Press, 2005.

© AP/Wide World Photos

5

POLITICAL PARTIES

◆ What Are Political Parties? ◆ The Functions of Political Parties ◆ The Origins of Political Parties ◆ Party Systems ◆ Types of Political Parties ◆ Parties in a Changing World

However [political parties] may now and then answer popular ends, they are likely, in the course of time and things, to become potent engines, by which cunning, ambitious, and unprincipled men will be enabled to subvert the power of the people, and to usurp for themselves the reins of government.

—*Washington's Farewell Address*

Since the time of the founders, many Americans have shared George Washington's suspicion of political parties. They have regarded parties as divisive and self-serving, more interested in winning elections or representing narrow constituencies than in furthering the national good. Washington believed that government leaders should selflessly work to advance the common interest and that parties would undermine public-spirited cooperation. In recent decades, growing numbers of Americans and Europeans have viewed political parties and partisanship negatively. Indeed, Americans increasingly identify themselves as "independents," loyal to neither major party. Similarly, news analysts often accuse some congressional representatives or senators of engaging in partisan politics, just as they also praise others for "rising above party politics."

Political scientists, on the other hand, have a much more positive view of political parties as institutions, even if they are often critical of how parties currently perform in the U.S. or elsewhere. Rather than viewing parties as inherently divisive or unscrupulous (although some parties may be), they consider them indispensable vehicles for organizing widespread citizen participation, essential to the maintenance of democracy and political stability. To appreciate readily the positive impact of parties, we need only consider examples of contemporary governments that have none. For example, Saudi Arabia has no parties; critical political decisions are made by the royal family and its advisers. In Afghanistan, where tribal chieftains have dominated the political system, parties have only recently gained some significance. One of the gains of the U.S.-sponsored Afghan national elections has been the development of parties for the first time. Until 2005, Uganda had no legal parties under the absolute rule of Yoweri Museveni. Elsewhere, recent authoritarian military governments in Latin America and Africa have often banned political party activity after they seized power.

So it is obviously *possible* for governments to function without parties—but only in societies with very limited socioeconomic development (and, hence, low levels of citizen politicization) or in countries, typically run by the military, where citizen participation is repressed. By definition, then, nonparty systems are politically underdeveloped and undemocratic. But, even though democracy at the national level *requires* active political parties, the existence of parties does not *guarantee* that a country will be democratic.

Indeed, all **totalitarian** regimes and many **authoritarian** governments establish a ruling political party in an attempt to mobilize the population behind them. In totalitarian regimes, the ruling party (which is the only party permitted) seeks a large membership and penetrates virtually all aspects of public life. In communist countries, party membership affords party members certain privileges, but the party is not limited to a tiny ruling clique. It includes workers, doctors, teachers, farmers, and the like, most of whom have no real say in government decision making. For example, more than 66 million people currently belong to the Chinese Communist Party, and the Soviet Communist Party had 19 million members at its peak. Similarly, millions joined the

Italian Fascist Party and Germany's Nazi Party in the 1930s, motivated either by conviction or by opportunism.

In those countries, the government encouraged widespread political participation but only under the tight control of the ruling party. Similarly, the ruling political party in an authoritarian nation such as Zimbabwe may simultaneously promote mass political participation and government control over political life.

To appreciate how parties affect government and society, we must first define what distinguishes them from related political organizations and then identify their basic functions.

WHAT ARE POLITICAL PARTIES?

The enormous differences among political parties make it difficult to devise a definition that fits all of them, but all share a few characteristics. A **political party** is a political organization that unites people in an effort to place its representatives in government offices in order to influence government activities and policies. Many parties, perhaps most, explicitly or implicitly espouse an ideology or at least a set of principles and beliefs, although these vary tremendously in coherence and consistency. The British Conservative and French Socialist parties proclaim their respective ideologies in their party names. America's major political parties do not, but those who follow U.S. politics know that the Republican Party is the more conservative of the two and the Democratic Party the more liberal. In democratic political systems, parties compete to elect their leaders to public office, and voters use party labels to identify and classify candidates. Although many authoritarian and totalitarian regimes hold elections as well, their real purpose is to *legitimize* the leaders in power rather than to allow meaningful opposition.

Political parties differ from interest groups—the subject of our next chapter—in that they usually seek to control the reins of government (alone or as part of a governing coalition), whereas interest groups merely seek to influence government decisions in their area of special concern. Thus interest groups in the United States seek to influence government policy in such areas as labor legislation and minimum-wage law (unions), environmental preservation (The Wilderness Society), manufacturing regulations (the National Chamber of Commerce), and firearms regulation (the National Rifle Association).

THE FUNCTIONS OF POLITICAL PARTIES

The fact that parties have become such a pervasive and central component of modern political systems suggests that they perform vital functions. An examination of those functions allows us to appreciate how parties contribute to the political process.

Recruitment of Political Leadership

Every political system must have some means of recruiting its leaders. In premodern political systems, leaders inherited their positions as kings, feudal lords, or tribal chieftains. As the extent of mass political participation grew—first in Western Europe and the United States and then in other parts of the world—an *institutionalized* process of **leadership recruitment** through political parties became a key feature of their political systems. Conversely, governments operating without an established arrangement for selecting new leaders almost always face a crisis when the existing leaders die, resign, or are removed from office.

By spelling out their ideologies or programs over time, political parties give the population signals about what the new leaders from their ranks will do if elected. Neither George Bush (United States) nor Vicente Fox (Mexico) has carried out all of his campaign pledges, but the supporters of each of those leaders had a general idea about where he was heading when they elected him. That is less true in many developing countries, where prominent political figures sometimes create ad hoc, "personalistic" parties solely for the purpose of getting themselves elected president. Since such a party has no track record and expresses few objectives other than to elect its leader, voters have little idea of what to expect if the party's candidate is elected. Such was the case, for example, in Peru when Alberto Fujimori came out of obscurity to form his own **personalistic party** and win the 1990 presidential election. While running on a very vaguely defined platform, Fujimori rejected the economic stabilization program proposed by his leading opponent. Once he took office, however, the new president quickly implemented the very economic program he had just run against.

On the other hand, in countries where political parties are more established and more entrenched, potential leaders usually must have previously completed a de facto apprenticeship (running for lesser offices), working with local party groups and identifying with at least some of that party's ideology. The most successful of these individuals rise up the electoral ladder and eventually become contenders for national leadership. Any person hoping to become a president or a prime minister in a country with a modern political system must usually first become active in a major political party and attain its nomination. During the 1990s, Ross Perot, a Texas multimillionaire, twice tried to break that pattern by running for the U.S. presidency as an independent, backed by his personalistic Reform Party. Despite initially looking strong in public opinion polls, Perot ultimately failed to win a single state in either election.

Vendors at major-league baseball parks yell to entering fans that "you can't tell the players without a scorecard." So, too, parties provide voters with "scorecards" for evaluating what might otherwise be a bewildering array of individuals seeking office. By knowing the candidates' party labels, voters have important clues about their positions on major issues—whether the candidate is liberal, conservative, or social-democratic, for example. Using that party label as a clue, a substantial—although falling—number of Americans vote repeatedly, even reflexively, for the candidates of one party. Even voters who call themselves independents often vote fairly regularly for one party. Because European parties are generally more tightly organized and, at least until recently, more ideologically unified than American parties and because their Parliamentary representatives are more likely to vote as a bloc in Parliament, European voters are generally less interested than are Americans in the candidate's personal characteristics and comparatively more interested in his or her party label. Knowing a candidate's party affiliation is all the information that many voters need to determine their votes. Indeed, most European countries elect their parliaments through proportional representation (Chapter 4), an electoral system that requires voters to vote for a party list of candidates rather than for individual candidates.

Even in nondemocratic political systems, parties are often very important for recruiting political leaders. In China, for example, aspiring political activists must first rise through the ranks of the Communist Party. As individuals work their way up, those with more powerful political patrons, greater commitment, or greater talent are presumably selected for party and government leadership positions. A similar process takes place within Syria's Baath party.

As we have noted, a number of military regimes and some monarchies in the developing world have governed without parties. Most have not held power for extended periods of time, however, falling victim to their lack of popular support, internal struggles for power, or both. In the past two to three decades, the number of military or other **no-party regimes** has declined rapidly, as democratic or semidemocratic governments have replaced them in many developing nations (see Chapter 15). Even military leaders have retained power longer when—as in South Korea, Brazil, and El Salvador—they have organized a political party to rally popular support behind them. The major exceptions of long-lived, no-party rule are the several remaining absolute monarchies, including Saudi Arabia and Brunei. While the number of military governments has declined sharply, a few no-party military regimes remain in countries such as Myanmar.

Formulating Government Policies and Programs

Parties do more than merely select candidates or name government leaders. They also help formulate government programs. All societies, particularly democratic ones, have a multitude of interest groups seeking to influence government policy. A major function of parties is **political aggregation**—that is, reducing the multitude of conflicting political demands to a manageable number of alternatives.[1]

Every four years, the Democratic and Republican national conventions devote considerable energy to the construction of a **party platform,** a long document outlining in

PROJECTING A CAMPAIGN MESSAGE   As President George Bush, with first lady Laura Bush, get ready for the 2004 Republican Convention, the banner above them promotes his image as a strong leader fighting world terrorism to secure peace.

detail the party's position on issues. Hardly any voters actually read the platforms; indeed, shortly after the 1996 Republican convention, even the party's nominee, Bob Dole, indicated that he had not done so. Nevertheless, a platform reflects a party's efforts to turn the raw demands of citizens and pressure groups into policy proposals; parts of the platform may become the subject of heated debate.

At the 1948 Democratic convention, a number of segregationist, southern delegates ("Dixiecrats")—led by South Carolina Senator Strom Thurmond—left the party after it inserted a pro-integration plank into the platform. In the 55 years since that split, the Democrats have been identified with civil rights for minorities, and the South, once solidly Democratic, has turned largely Republican. More recently, the lead-up to the 1996 Republican convention featured a bitter internal conflict over the party's stance on abortion. For party nominee Bob Dole, that created a difficult dilemma. If the platform moderated the party's "pro-life" position, it would alienate some of its most important party activists, particularly within the Christian Right. If it took a hard line on the issue, it risked losing the votes of moderate, largely middle-class, Republican and independent women. Ultimately, Dole's weakness among the second group of voters (referred to in the media as "soccer moms") contributed to his defeat, though it is unclear how much of a role the abortion issue actually played. In the 2000 and 2004 Republican conventions, on the other hand, George Bush more strongly committed himself to an anti-abortion (pro-life) position and subsequently benefited from grassroots campaigning and a strong turnout by conservative, born-again Christians.

Years ago, a leading political scientist called the Democrats and the Republicans classic examples of **catchall parties**—that is, parties that try to appeal to a wide range of social classes and groups and, hence, at least until recent years, have had less well-defined policy programs.[2] American parties have until recently articulated policies less clearly than their Western European counterparts, limited as they have been by their diverse constituencies and their relatively weak ideological positions. Although many Western European parties have broadened their constituencies in recent decades (Socialist parties courting middle-class voters, for example), they still tend to have more clearly defined political platforms than their American counterparts. Once a Western European party has achieved a parliamentary majority, its supporters expect it to enact the programs in its platform. In addition, party labels in Europe enable the voters to render a verdict on the performance of a party in control of government and to hold the party accountable at the next election if it performs poorly.

In communist nations, the party has had a still more fundamental role in formulating government policy. In China, Cuba, and Vietnam, for example, Communist Party leaders, rather than the national parliaments or other government bodies, make major policy decisions. Similarly, many of Africa's single-party systems have concentrated policy making in the ruling party. During the late 1980s, Soviet President Mikhail Gorbachev shifted political decision making from the Communist Party to such government institutions as the cabinet and the parliament. That transfer of power was one of the factors that led party hard-liners to attempt the unsuccessful 1991 coup against him. Ironically, the coup's failure not only led to the collapse of the communist regime but also resulted in the temporary banning of the party.

Organizing Government

After national elections in democracies, either a single party or a coalition of parties normally commands a majority in the national legislature. In parliamentary systems, that winning party or coalition chooses the prime minister. Party labels tie various legislators together and enable their leaders to present a coherent program. Although both of the major U.S. political parties have become more ideologically unified in recent years, congressional Democrats and Republicans are still less tightly organized and less likely to vote as a cohesive bloc (especially in the Senate) than are their counterparts in most Western European nations.

Though Americans tend to take pride in Congressional representatives and Senators who don't bow to their party's line, that stress on independence makes it much harder for Congress to get programs passed. Often, major appropriations bills are stalled for months. Faced with the prospect of having government, or a part of it, shut down for lack of funds, Congress has often rushed the bills through at the deadline, sometimes with unnoticed amendments tacked on at the end by proponents of special-interest groups.

THE ORIGINS OF POLITICAL PARTIES

Throughout the world, the growth of parties has been closely linked to the spread of mass political participation. As long as nations were ruled by a small, hereditary elite, there was no need for broadly based political organizations. That situation began to change during Western Europe's nineteenth-century transition from a **hierarchical,** agricultural economy to industrial capitalism. Urbanization and economic development created important new political actors (as they have done more recently in the Third World)—first the middle class and then the industrial working class.

The first European and Latin American parties in the nineteenth century were merely competing aristocratic or upper-middle-class parliamentary factions.[3] As the right to vote was extended to a larger (but still limited) portion of the population, however, parties reached out to the middle class and later to workers (and, eventually, in Latin America to the peasantry). In Great Britain, for example, the Conservative Party represented the interests of the landed aristocracy, and the Whigs (later to become the Liberal Party) were led by the rising class of industrialists. As the franchise was expanded throughout the nineteenth and early twentieth centuries, however, both parties broadened their support. Similarly, in Colombia, the Conservative and Liberal parties—one headed by wealthy, rural landowners and the other by influential merchants—eventually established strong ties to the peasants through **patron–client relations.**

With the achievement of universal male suffrage by the early twentieth century, new types of political parties, known as **mass parties,** emerged in Europe.[4] Unlike their predecessors, which were led by elites seeking popular support, these were led by political outsiders wishing to challenge the established order. Most were socialist parties with close ties to the labor movement, including the French Socialist Party (SFIO) and the British Labour Party. Unlike their more conservative predecessors, they were interested in more than just winning votes.[5] They also wished to introduce their followers to socialism and thereby create a new political culture. Party members were encouraged to become party activists.[6]

During the twentieth century, Western Europe's formerly elitist parties adopted aspects of mass-party structure, including grassroots organizations. At the same time, mass-party organizations and strategies became the models for many of the contemporary parties in Africa, Asia, and Latin America.

In the twentieth century, a new type of political party originated out of **social movements**. These movements are "broad mobilizations of ordinary people [seeking] a particular goal or goals."[7] Generally such social movements represent political outsiders, less powerful groups in society. One thinks of the civil rights movement in the United States, the human rights movement in Latin America, and the environmental movement in Western Europe. In some instances, social movements have begun as anti-system protests and eventually evolved into political parties working within the system or creating a new system. For example, in what was then Czechoslovakia and later split into the Czech Republic and Slovakia, civic protest movements eventually toppled the communist regime and then turned into political parties.[8] Decades earlier, the Gaullist Movement grew into France's largest political party (Box 5-1).

Box 5-1

POLITICAL PARTY LONGEVITY

Even advanced Western democracies may have considerably different political party histories. For example, the U.S. Democratic and Republican parties as well as the British Conservative Party (and the Liberal component of the Liberal Democratic Party) are all at least 150 years old. The British Labour Party was founded at the beginning of the twentieth century. While the British party system has experienced one important change in recent decades (the merger of the Liberal and Social Democratic parties in 1988), other major parties in both countries have enjoyed a considerable longevity.

Such has not been the case with France's major parties. The most successful party at the ballot box in the Fifth Republic (from 1958 to the present) has been a conservative party commonly referred to over the years as the Gaullist or Neo-Gaullist Party because it was formed in 1947 in support of General Charles de Gaulle, the leader of the French resistance in World War II who had served briefly as national president in the interim government following the war. Originally called the Rally of the People of France (RPF), the party's core creed was de Gaulle's opposition to the Fourth Republic's constitutional arrangement (1946–58). The party was dismantled in 1955. Three years later, as the Fourth Republic fell in 1958, the Gaullists formed a party called Union for the

New Republic (UNR) which brought General de Gaulle to the presidency of the new Fifth Republic. Only four years later, however, the UNR merged with the Democratic Union of Labor, a pro-Gaullist, labor union movement, to form the Union for the French Republic–Democratic Union of Labor. Five years after that, in 1967 it changed its name once more to the Union of Democrats for the Fifth Republic (UDR), but soon changed its name again by dropping the word "Fifth" from its title. In 1976, six years after de Gaulle's death, the party was reorganized to become the personal electoral vehicle of former (and future) Prime Minister Jacques Chirac, who subsequently was elected the nation's president in 1995 and 2002. Chirac and his supporters renamed the party the Rally for the Republic (RPR), its sixth name change in less than 30 years. Finally, in the 2002 presidential election, incumbent Chirac united the RPR with a majority of the centrist Union for French Democracy (UDF) and the small Liberal Democracy party to form a new party, the victorious Union for a Presidential Majority (UMP) which soon changed its name to the Union for a Popular Movement (also UMP).

The major leftist party, and foremost rival of the Gaullists and Neo-Gaullists, the French Socialist Party traces its roots back to 1880, with the founding of the

PARTY SYSTEMS

The term *party system* refers to the characteristics of the array of parties operating in a particular country. It indicates the extent of competition between parties and the number of them that have a serious chance of winning elections. The number of competitive parties operating in a particular country fundamentally influences that nation's entire political system. Obviously, countries that are governed continuously by a single party—even if opposition parties are legal—are not usually fully democratic. Conversely, countries that have multiple parties, with none able to garner a majority (or close to it) in the national legislature, are generally less politically stable. Because of the great importance of the number of competitive political parties, descriptions of the Chinese, American, British, or Italian political systems, for example, typically note that they are, respectively, one-party, two-party, two-and-one-half-party, and multiparty systems.

Americans often think of a two-party system as "natural," since we are accustomed to it. If by that we mean that a two-party system is preferable to, say, a multiparty system, the contention is at least debatable. If we mean that having two primary parties

---

French Workers' Party. Only two years later, the party split into a Marxist faction and a more moderate faction. In 1899, several competing socialist and workers' parties consolidated into two parties: the more leftist Socialist Party of France and the more moderate French Socialist Party. Six years later, the two parties merged to become the Unified Socialist Party. In 1920, the more left-wing portion of the party (which, despite its name, was not very unified) broke away to form the French Communist Party. The remaining, more moderate, faction of the party changed its name to the rather cumbersome official title of French Section of the Workers' International (SFIO), though it was commonly known at the Socialist Party. In 1969 the party was reorganized under the leadership of François Mitterand—who later served as national President from 1981 to 1995—and changed its title officially to the Socialist Party.

Are the constant name changes and reorganizations of France's two major parties (and most smaller ones as well) anything more than cosmetic? Why have the major parties in Britain and the U.S. been so much more stable (the two oldest political parties in the world are, respectively, the British Conservative Party and the American Democratic Party)? The answer to the first question is that the constant party reorganizations and name changes in France *are* significant in that they usually indicate either the

emergence of a new movement, a change in a party's programmatic emphasis, a modification of ideology, the emergence of new leadership, or some combination thereof.

Why do French parties, then, change so often in comparison to American and British parties? There is no simple answer, but two factors stand out. First, French political party leaders and voters have historically been more ideologically oriented and more concerned with intellectual distinctions than their more pragmatic English-speaking counterparts. Rather than work out (or fight out) such differences within the party, as Anglo-American parties are prone to do, they are more likely to split or reorganize. This is particularly true of the French left (Communists, Socialists, and others). Second, French parties are sometimes formed or reorganized around the political ambitions of dynamic leaders. This is particularly true of the French right—the Gaullist party was first formed in the 1940s as a political vehicle for General de Gaulle and was reorganized and renamed in the 1970s partly to suit the political ambitions of Jacques Chirac. But even on the left, the Socialists were reorganized and renamed in 1969 partly to serve the political aspirations of Francois Mitterand.

In the 2002 presidential elections, the vote was so fragmented between 11 presidential candidates that no candidate secured as much as 20 percent of the vote.

is the most common arrangement, the notion is simply incorrect. We have seen that, at least until recently, single-party systems were common in Africa, the Middle East, much of Asia, and the now-collapsed communist bloc. At the same time, multiparty systems are more typical in Europe. Indeed, if anything, two-party systems are the exception and are most prevalent in English-speaking nations.

Of course, even the United States has many more than two political parties. Besides the Democrats and the Republicans, American parties include the Green Party, the Libertarian Party, the Socialist Workers Party, and a variety of others. But although so-called third parties in the United States sometimes win at the local level, they are not major players at the national level. Occasionally, however, third-party candidates can play a spoiler's role. Had Ralph Nader not run in the 2000 presidential election as the Green Party candidate, it is likely that most of his votes (including those he won in Florida) would have gone to the Democratic nominee, Al Gore, and that Gore, rather than George Bush, would have won the presidency.

British politics also has been dominated for at least fifty years by two parties, Conservative and Labour, but other parties have attracted a substantial share of the vote, particularly in recent decades. During the 1980s, an electoral alliance between the Liberal and the Social Democratic parties (called simply The Alliance) attracted about one-fourth of the votes in two consecutive national elections, nearly equaling the percentage received by the Labour Party. Subsequently, the two Alliance parties formally merged into the new Liberal Democratic Party, which received 18 and 22 percent of the vote, respectively, in the 2001 and 2005 elections. This suggests that the British system might better be called a **two-and-one-half-party system** (that is, two parties predominate, but a third party presents a significant challenge).

These examples illustrate how difficult it often is to pinpoint precisely whether a particular country has a single-party, a two-party, or a multiparty system. Building on a classification system originally created by the political scientist Jean Blondel, we offer the following categories and measurements:[9]

1. *No-party system:* Either political parties have never developed or they have been banned by a new authoritarian government.
2. *Single-party system:* One party regularly receives more than 65 percent of the vote in national elections.
3. *Two-party system* (including a two-and-one-half-party system such as Britain's): Two major parties regularly divide more than 75 percent of the national vote (but with no single party receiving as much as 65 percent).
4. *Multiparty system:* The two largest parties have a combined total of less than 75 percent of the vote.

No-Party Systems

Although political parties are hallmarks of modern political systems, there remain a number of countries that have never formed political parties with any meaningful following or that have banned previously active political parties. The first group, very limited in number, consists principally of countries with premodern social and economic structures—particularly agricultural societies with low literacy rates—and low levels of political participation. In countries such as Saudi Arabia and, until recently, Afghanistan, political decisions have been made by relatively small, elite bodies (sheikhs, princes, tribal chiefs, or the like) with no need for parties.

Newly installed military governments often have banned political-party activity. In Chile, which had enjoyed one of Latin America's most advanced party systems, the government of General Augusto Pinochet (1973–1990) blamed the country's left-wing parties—the Socialists and the Communists—for the nation's ills. It banned not only those two, but all other parties as well. In recent decades, as democracy has spread in the developing world, military governments and no-party systems have become less common (Chapter 15).

Single-Party Systems

As we have noted, both authoritarian regimes, so common in the Third World, and totalitarian ones have single-party systems. Totalitarian parties, most notably fascist and Marxist-Leninist parties, are mass-membership organizations that seek to exercise total control over society and to inculcate in the population the party's ideological values. Following the revolutions in Russia, China, Vietnam, and Cuba, the communist parties of those countries launched extensive resocialization campaigns to restructure their political cultures (see Chapters 3 and 15). And, at least initially, many activists seemed strongly committed to the party's vision of a new social order.

Because of their capacity to penetrate other social institutions, totalitarian political parties were once considered nearly impossible to dislodge once they had achieved power.[10] In the Soviet Union and Eastern Europe, communist-party functionaries controlled the military, police, factories, state farms, and schools. Yet, ultimately their grip on power weakened. Currently, communist parties retain control in only a few countries, including China, Vietnam, North Korea, and Cuba.

© Reuters NewMedia Inc./CORBIS

A COMMUNIST HOLDOUT North Korean President Kim Jong-Il heads one of the world's last remaining, ruling communist parties. Adhering to an extreme form of Communism, the Kim regime is one of the most insulated and repressive on earth.

A second group of single-party states emerged—following World War II and the subsequent disintegration of Europe's colonial empires—in the newly independent nations of Africa and the Middle East. Like communist parties, many of the Third World's new, ruling parties were organized along **Leninist** lines, with very centralized control. Often, they promoted a nationalistic ideology and tried to resocialize the population to adopt a new political culture. Most of these ruling parties, however, have been too self-serving and corrupt to attract a loyal, mass following. In such countries as the Congo (formerly Zaire) and Syria, power has been maintained primarily through brute force rather than by the spread of revolutionary ideology.

Until recent decades, few African or Middle Eastern countries permitted viable opposition parties to function. A number of Asian governments—including those of Indonesia, Malaysia, Singapore, and Taiwan—also argued that developing countries needed the unifying influence and direction of a single-party system. With the wave of democracy that has swept over the less developed countries since the 1970s (see Chapter 15), however, a growing number of African and Asian nations have permitted fair and honest elections and some have seen a transfer of power from one political party to another.

Particularly when headed by well-intentioned leaders, entrenched ruling parties can sometimes effectively represent a wide spectrum of the population. During the late 1930s, Mexican President Lázaro Cárdenas used the ruling party to integrate previously excluded peasants and workers into the political system. More recently, Tanzanian President Julius Nyerere used his Tanganyika African National Union (TANU) to channel the demands of the country's villagers to the national government. In time, however, the absence of party competition and the passing of idealistic leaders such as Cárdenas and Nyerere has perverted even well-intentioned dominant parties. Indeed, most Third World single-party systems have fallen victim to corruption and the pursuit of special interests.

Two-Party Systems

Two-party and two-and-a-half-party systems are most prevalent in Anglo-American societies, including the United States, Great Britain, Canada, New Zealand, and Australia. However, other countries, such as Austria, Germany, Colombia, Costa Rica, and Uruguay, have had two dominant parties as well (as did Venezuela before those two parties collapsed).

Why do these countries have two dominant parties while so many other democracies have multiparty systems? One important factor influencing the number of parties that can compete effectively is the country's electoral arrangements. We have seen (Chapter 4) that proportional representation more easily permits (but does not guarantee) the development of several competitive political parties, whereas single-member-district systems are more likely to produce two dominant parties. But, usually, the number of viable parties is also rooted in the country's history and political culture. In Anglo-American nations, two-party dominance generally reflects a relatively consensual political culture (Chapter 3). In Latin American countries such as Uruguay and Colombia, with far less political consensus, the two-party system dates to the nineteenth century, when parties representing different segments of the economic elite effectively organized large portions of the population.

Among industrial democracies, two-party systems (such as Great Britain's and New Zealand's) tend to be more stable than multiparty systems because of their greater ability to produce a legislative majority. But in a number of Latin American countries with two-party systems, stability has been elusive. For example, Colombia (long dominated by two parties) has had a turbulent history of political violence.

Just as they are not universally stable, neither are two-party systems always democratic. During its years of minority rule, South Africa had competitive elections, pitting two leading parties against each other. But since only the white minority was allowed to vote for most posts, the two-party system was hardly democratic. Similarly, before Nicaragua's 1979 revolution, the ruling Somoza dictatorship regularly sponsored elections between its own Liberal Party and the Conservatives, a puppet opposition party. The outcomes of those elections, however, were predetermined by the government.

Multiparty Systems

Multiparty systems predominate in Western Europe but also can be found in a number of Latin American and Asian nations, as well as a growing number of African countries. Sometimes they mirror a multiplicity of societal divisions —class, religion, language, race, and ethnicity—that translate into multiple political cleavages. Thus it is not surprising that a country such as Switzerland—with religious differences between Catholics and Protestants, class and ideological divisions, and several spoken languages—has a multiparty system. Yet, some fairly homogeneous nations, such as Sweden, Japan, and Iceland, also have multiple parties.

Thus, social divisions are not the only factors that determine the number of competitive parties. Electoral procedures also play an important role. We have noted that countries that elect parliaments or congresses from single-member districts are less likely to have multiparty legislatures than those using proportional representation (Chapter 4). Single-member-district elections to the U.S. House of Representatives and the British House of Commons discriminate against small parties by denying them legislative representation proportional to their voting strength. (See Box 12-3.) Eventually, such unsatisfactory outcomes tend to discourage supporters of third parties, and thereby restrict their growth. For example, many American voters who might have been tempted to vote for presidential candidate Ralph Nader likely decided against it because they assumed that Nader could not possibly win and, although supporting him might be morally satisfying, it would waste their opportunity to influence the election's outcome.

Proponents of proportional representation argue persuasively that it is a fairer electoral system because it allows smaller parties to be represented in the national legislature with a number of seats proportional to their support from the voters. At the same time, however, because multiparty parliaments make it harder for any single party to achieve a legislative majority, multiparty legislatures tend to be less stable. In parliamentary systems, where the government needs to command a legislative majority to stay in power, the prime minister often must secure the backing of a multiparty coalition. If there are many policy or strategic divisions among the coalition partners, however, the government's life is precarious, because coalition members may withdraw their support at any time. For example, in Italy a succession of unstable parliamentary coalitions produced more than 50 governments during the second half of the twentieth century (although recently government coalitions have become more durable).

Not all multiparty systems are unstable, however. In some countries, the members of the majority coalitions are able to work together for an extended period of time.

Finland, Israel, the Netherlands, Norway, and Switzerland all have been able to produce fairly stable parliamentary majorities with multiparty systems. Indeed, Finland and Switzerland have two of the most fractionalized party systems in the democratic world (that is, the vote is most widely divided among a large number of parties). Yet they are models of political stability. Clearly, they have benefited from political cultures that stress cooperation rather than conflict.

TYPES OF POLITICAL PARTIES

Let us now turn our attention from party systems to the characteristics of individual political parties themselves. Among the many ways to classify political parties, we focus here on two important characteristics: internal organization and ideological message.

Party Organization

Although all major parties have similar goals—to field candidates for elected office, to control the government, and to implement their programs—their internal organizations differ greatly. Some are highly centralized with a top-down command structure, and others are loose federations of regional or local organizations. In the United States, the combined effects of a federal structure (a division of power between the national and state governments), the separation of powers within the federal government itself, and historical and cultural preferences have created highly decentralized parties. As John Bibby has noted, "It is hard to overstate the extent to which American political parties are characterized by decentralized power structures. . . . Within the party organization, the national institutions of the party . . . rarely meddle in nominations and organizational affairs of state parties."[11]

Even at the national level, Democrats and Republicans are organizationally weaker than are most major parties in other industrial democracies. Whereas candidates for national office in Western Europe or Canada are chosen by their party organizations, the United States is one of the few industrialized democracies to select candidates through primary elections. Because they are less beholden to their own party for their posts, American members of Congress are less prone to vote cohesively as a party unit than are most Western European parliamentary delegations.

Which model is more desirable? Many Americans prefer having Senators and congressional representatives who vote their own minds and do not vote with their fellow Democrats or Republicans as a bloc. But critics contend that the parties' diffuse structure makes it difficult to develop coherent governmental programs or to hold either party accountable for its performance in office. It should be noted that in recent years party discipline in Congress has increased. As the conservative wing of the Democratic Party and the centrist wing of the Republic Party have both become smaller, each party has begun to vote more cohesively as a bloc.

Communist parties, both in countries that they have governed and in democratic systems, represent the other end of the organizational spectrum. Following the Leninist principle of democratic centralism, they concentrate policy making and candidate selection power at the top. This extreme centralization has often led to paralysis at lower party levels, whereby officials have hesitated to make even the most mundane decisions on their own. (See Box 5-2.)

==

Box 5-2

VARIETIES OF PARTY ORGANIZATION

Some 70 years ago, the legendary American humorist Will Rogers used to tell his audiences, "I am a member of no organized political party—I'm a Democrat." Although his joke was meant to poke fun at the long-standing Democratic propensity for internal quarreling, it might also have referred to the organizational weaknesses of *both* American parties. Thus, for example, not long ago David Duke, a former Ku Klux Klan leader and known racist, secured the Republican Party's nomination for several state and national posts through local primaries, much to the chagrin of President George Bush, Sr., and other national Republican leaders who were unable to block Duke's nomination.

It is instructive to contrast that looseness of structure with Communist Party organization in the former Soviet Union. Consider the following reaction of a local party official to the failed August 1991 coup against Mikhail Gorbachev by communist hard-liners (Chapter 13). In the Russian city of Klin, only 50 miles outside Moscow, the Communist Party held a previously scheduled lecture on the day that the coup was beginning to unravel. Asked by party members to explain what was happening, local officials waffled: "We had no instructions from Moscow," Igor Muratov, the Klin party leader, later explained. "We could not give our assessment of what was happening."[12]

==

Most Western European parties fall between those two organizational extremes. Those parties are far more centrally controlled and cohesive than American political parties but nowhere nearly as centralized as ruling communist parties.

Party Ideologies: Right Wing through Left Wing

A political party's ideology defines its most fundamental message and underlies the governmental policies that it proposes. Some parties—such as the Swedish Social Democrats, the British Conservatives, and the Chinese Communists—hold fairly well delineated ideological positions. Others—such as the Democrats in the United States and the Mexican PRI—are more ideologically ambiguous, often housing different political factions with conflicting outlooks. Yet others have no explicit ideology at all. Still, most parties, especially in advanced democracies, can be classified according to their ideological perspective.[13]

In Chapter 2, we defined the beliefs and aspirations of the major political ideologies. Here, we classify major political parties according to their ideological leanings and discuss where and when parties in each ideological camp have had electoral success. The party ideologies are listed from right (ultraconservative and conservative) to left (radical).

Neofascist Parties   These ultra-right-wing parties generally stress a militant form of nationalism and the preservation of alleged ethnic purity—views that easily lend themselves to racism. As such, they bear some resemblance to Hitler's Nazi Party and Italy's Fascist Party during World War II, though today's **neofascists** are generally less extreme. In India, the recently governing Bharatiya Janata Party (BJP) identifies Indian nationalism with Hinduism, and branches of the party have encouraged violent attacks against India's Muslim and Sikh minorities. But the party's national leadership has disavowed extremist views and even appeals to Muslim voters for support. In Serbia, Croatia, Romania, and other multiethnic Eastern European countries, a variety of neofascist parties have favored "ethnic cleansing" and have aroused hatred against minority ethnic groups.

In recent decades, the rising number of Third World and Eastern European immigrants to such European countries as Austria, Denmark, France, and Germany has unleashed racist, anti-foreign sentiments among some voters, expressed in growing support for neofascist parties and movements. In France, the National Front's perennial presidential candidate, Jean-Marie Le Pen, has mixed racist criticisms of France's large Islamic, immigrant population (suggesting that they should be shipped home) with anti-Semitic comments (once calling the Nazi Holocaust "a [minor] detail of history"). After Le Pen unexpectedly edged out Socialist Prime Minister Lionel Jospin for second place in the opening round of the 2002 presidential election—thereby advancing into a two-person runoff with incumbent president Jacques Chirac—the Socialists and a number of small leftist parties threw their full support to Chirac, their erstwhile conservative opponent. As moderate conservative and leftist voters joined together to bloc Le Pen, Chirac emerged with 82 percent of the second-round vote.

Elsewhere in Europe, Austria's Freedom Party, another neofascist group, has also built support among voters who blame the country's immigrant population for allegedly increasing crime and taking jobs from native Austrians. The party also opposes Austria's links to the European Union. Over the years, the Freedom Party's charismatic former leader (he left the party in 2005), Jörg Haider, made a number of public statements that appeared to express his sympathy for Nazism and Austria's past links to the Nazis, though he repeatedly has denied it. The party also denies being pro-Nazi, but several of its leading spokespersons have been former members of the Austrian Nazi Party.

In 1999 the Freedom Party finished second in the nation's parliamentary elections, and in early 2000 it entered the ruling government coalition, with Haider taking a seat in the cabinet. Because all well-established Western European parties, from conservatives through communists, strongly reject the ultra-right, neofascists have slim prospects of winning a national election. And, except in Austria, they have been excluded from any ruling coalition. Austria's Freedom Party has gathered significant support from disgruntled voters, and in 1999 it attained 27 percent of the national vote. In the 2002 national elections, however, its share of the vote fell by more than half, plummeting to 10.3 percent. Like other neofascist parties, it appeals particularly to voters who feel threatened by many aspects of Europe's contemporary economic and political life—European integration, globalization, immigration (especially of non-Europeans and non-Christians), and unemployment.

Conservative Parties   Conservative parties are among the oldest parties in Western Europe and Latin America. Although their programs and styles differ from region to region and country to country, they generally share certain beliefs. Those include dedication to such traditional values as patriotism, religion, and family; a desire for stability, coupled with a fear of rapid social change; a high priority on law and order (sometimes even at the expense of civil liberties); support for the free enterprise system; and a commitment to a strong national defense.

But there are also important distinctions among conservative parties in different parts of the world. Latin America's conservative parties generally have represented elite economic interests and have often opposed the full incorporation of workers and peasants into the political system. In some cases, they have been led by traditional, landowning (agricultural) elites who have clung to certain precapitalist norms. In sharply polarized societies with strong leftist unions and political parties, conservatives often have favored authoritarian measures to repress the perceived threat from the left.[14] Thus, facing such challenges, they have supported right-wing dictatorships in such countries as Chile, Uruguay, Brazil, Greece, and Spain. Even the French neo-Gaullist party, which became a very respectable mainstream party, had authoritarian leanings in its early days.[15]

In contrast, conservative parties in stable democracies with relatively consensual political cultures (such as the United States, Sweden, and Great Britain) have been firmly committed to democracy. As the influence of, and perceived threat from, communist or other leftist movements have receded in Latin America and southern Europe, conservative parties in that region have come to embrace democracy.

Some parties—including the Republicans in the United States and, more recently, the British Conservatives—have ardently defended the free enterprise system and opposed most government intervention in the economy. But elsewhere, conservatives have accepted or even initiated substantial government economic planning and comprehensive welfare programs. Indeed, a number of Western European conservative parties, such as France's RPR and Germany's Christian Democrats, have had, at least until recently, economic policies that are quite compatible with those of centrist Democrats in the United States. Instead, many European conservatives are more concerned with political and social agendas featuring nationalism, a strong military, domestic law and order, religion, social stability, and family values.

Since World War II, most Western European nations have been governed at various times either by conservative parties or by socialists. And at least until the 1980s (longer in some nations), most of those conservative governments acquiesced to or supported substantial government economic planning, state ownership of key resources, and welfare measures, many of which were originally introduced by their socialist predecessors. Consequently, the government's role in European economies grew substantially, particularly when compared with the United States and Japan. The 1980s, however, brought a conservative resurgence in much of Europe (as in the United States) and a conservative programmatic shift as many concluded that the state had become too intrusive in their economy, too expensive, and too inefficient. British Prime Minister Margaret Thatcher and U.S. President Ronald Reagan became symbols of that conservative revolution. Resentful of growing budget deficits and higher inflation under earlier governments, the electorate increasingly resisted tax hikes. Consequently, almost all Western governments, even leftist ones, have been forced to cut back on welfare measures and other spending programs.

Socialist governments in Spain, France, and elsewhere reluctantly adopted fiscal policies similar to those advocated by their conservative opponents. Similarly, in the United States, Democrats such as President Bill Clinton embraced the conservative goals of balanced budgets and a scaled-back role for government. And in the past 20 years, in Latin American countries such as Argentina, Chile, and Mexico—where state economic intervention had been quite pronounced—governments led by **populist** parties, once known for their free spending, have also adopted some of the conservatives' anti-statist policies.

Liberal Parties   Liberalism, even more so than conservatism, means different things in different countries and regions. Historically, liberal parties in Europe and Latin America have advocated the separation of church and state, greater equality of opportunity, and the preservation of personal freedom. In Europe, liberal parties were first formed to protect small businesses against the state, and today many still oppose extensive state economic intervention and large government welfare programs. Indeed, many of Western Europe's liberal parties—including Germany's Free Democrats, Italy's Liberals, and the liberal wing of the French UDF—have been pro-business and often forge political alliances with conservative parties. Normally, European and Latin American liberal parties occupy the political center between conservatives on the right and socialists or populists on the left. They generally get their greatest support from middle-class voters, particularly professionals and owners of small businesses.

Liberalism has taken on a different meaning in the United States. From the time of President Franklin Roosevelt's New Deal, the Democratic Party has been identified with government activism and a variety of social welfare programs, including social security. Since the United States, unlike Western Europe or Latin America, has no important socialist or populist parties, and since American labor unions support the Democrats (not the socialists, as in Europe), the Democrats have occupied the left side of the American political spectrum, although their policies would be considered middle-of-the-road in Western Europe. In spite of those differences, however, liberals in both Europe and the U.S. still share a number of important common concerns—most notably their commitment to civil liberties and the rights of the individual. Similarly, liberal American groups such as the American Civil Liberties Union use the judicial system to protect the rights of criminal defendants, minority groups, political dissidents, and others against possible intrusions by the government.

Western European liberal parties have not done well in the past half century. Most have been squeezed out from the left by socialist parties and from the right by conservatives. Hence, they no longer can attract a significant portion of the vote except when they have allied with other parties as Britain's Liberal Party did when it merged with the Social Democratic Party in the 1980s.

In the United States, the Democratic Party, long associated with liberalism, was generally the most powerful political party from the 1930s until the start of the 1980s. For the past few decades, however, fewer and fewer American voters have identified themselves as liberals. Hence, even though the Democrats still controlled one or both houses of Congress for most of the 1970s and 1980s, their presidential candidates generally fared poorly, in large part because voters perceived them as too liberal. In 1996, Bill Clinton became the first Democratic president since Franklin D. Roosevelt to be elected to two full terms. He was able to succeed politically by identifying more closely with his party's moderate wing and avoiding the liberal label (although many Republican conservatives saw him as a liberal wolf in a moderate lamb's clothing).

Socialist Parties   As we noted in Chapter 2, the label "socialist" is sometimes confusing, since it is used to refer to highly democratic parties in Western Europe, to the communist system in the Soviet Union, and to some of the ruling communist parties in Eastern Europe before their fall. We will reserve the terms *"socialist"* and "social democratic" for parties that are firmly committed to democracy and wish to modify, but not erase, capitalism. Generally, **socialist** and **social democratic** labels for political parties can be used interchangeably, though they occasionally denote mild ideological differences. Thus, one of France's major parties is the Socialist Party, and the governing party in Germany as recently as 2005 was the German Social Democratic Party. Socialist parties have governed Sweden, Norway, and Denmark for much of the postwar era. In the past 20 years, socialists or social democrats have also led governments for at least some period of time in a number of other European nations, including Austria, Britain, France, Germany, Greece, Portugal, and Spain. In Latin America, socialist or social democratic parties have played major roles in Chile, Venezuela, Ecuador, and Costa Rica.

During the 1960s and 1970s, some European socialist parties, most notably the French, were divided between Marxist and non-Marxist wings. Both factions claimed to support democracy, and both favored the welfare state and some state ownership of the means of production. The Marxist wings, however, believed in more extensive state intervention and wished to identify the party more directly with the interests of the working class.

By the mid-1980s, however, most of these parties had jettisoned their Marxist factions. For example, the French Socialists, after their first two years in power (1981–1983), moved sharply to the center, abandoned much of their earlier radical rhetoric, and no longer saw state ownership of parts of the economy as a cure-all for the nation's ills. In Spain, the Socialist government experienced an even greater transformation as Prime Minister Felipe González introduced fairly conservative economic policies to combat inflation. Chile's once-radical Socialists currently lead a centrist governing coalition. And, as we will see in Chapter 12, the British Labour Party has regained political power by abandoning many of its previous leftist positions. Stressing economic modernization, efficiency, and "technocratic-administrative capability," socialist parties and governments in much of Western Europe now differ only modestly on economic issues from the region's centrist parties.[16] Socialists in countries such as Spain, however, have been more sympathetic than centrist parties to gay rights, reproductive (abortion) rights, and the right to divorce.

Communist Parties   After the fall of the Soviet Union and its allied communist governments in Eastern Europe, the number of nations governed by communist parties was reduced to a handful, most of them in Asia. China, with more than one billion people and perhaps the world's second-largest economy, is obviously the most important of these (see Chapter 14). Cuba has staggered economically without the support of the Soviet Union, but its charismatic leader, Fidel Castro, retains some influence in the Third World. Other single-party, communist regimes include North Korea, Cambodia (Kampuchea), Vietnam, and Laos.

Outside of the much-reduced communist bloc, communist parties also effectively compete for office in a number of European democracies. At one time, these parties, along with other communist parties throughout the world, faithfully took their lead from the Soviet Union. That began to change in the 1960s and 1970s, when different strains of communism emerged. For example, several communist parties, led by the Italians, followed a new path known as "Eurocommunism." They rejected Soviet-style authoritarianism and embraced (or, in some cases, claimed to embrace) Western democratic values. The Italian Communists, the most democratically oriented of that group, governed many of Italy's major cities. Some of their strongholds, such as Bologna, were widely considered to be the most honestly and efficiently run cities in the country. Winning as much as 34 percent of the national parliamentary vote, the Communists were Italy's second largest party for decades. Since the 1990s, the party has changed its name twice—first to the "Democratic Party of the Left" and then to Democrats of the Left—and has abandoned its communist doctrines, becoming a mildly leftist "clean government" party. As the Christian Democratic and Socialist parties collapsed at the polls under the weight of their own corruption, the former communists became so respectable that in 1996, when an electoral coalition of the Democratic Party of the Left and a number of leftist and centrist parties called "The Olive Tree" won the parliamentary election and gained control of the Italian government, the Milan stock market actually boomed in response to the Olive Tree's reputation for curbing corruption. In the 2006 parliamentary election, the party, now named the Democrats of the Left, helped center-left economist Romano Prodi return to the prime minister's office.

On the other hand, elsewhere in Western Europe, communist parties that were once influential—most notably in France, Greece, Finland, Portugal, and Spain—have lost considerable support in recent decades. The French Communist Party regularly attracted 15 to 20 percent of the vote into the 1980s but is now reduced to less than half of that. Blue-collar workers, who had formed the core of the Communists' support, currently constitute a smaller portion of the workforce and, hence, of the electorate. At the same time, many of today's workers are more affluent—often owning their own homes—leading them to develop middle-class values and to support more moderate political parties.

After the collapse of Eastern European communism in 1989, most of that region's communist parties changed their names and policies, though they are still regularly referred to as "former communist parties." Because they continue to support the welfare state and because they promise full employment, they receive considerable support from workers whose jobs or pensions are threatened by the transition to capitalism. For various lengths of time, so-called reformed communist parties have regained government leadership in Lithuania, Poland, Slovakia, Hungary, Albania, Bulgaria, Moldova, Serbia, and Romania. They have performed better in some countries (introducing economic reforms in Hungary and Poland) than in others, such as Bulgaria and Moldova, where they were known for their corruption and incompetence.

Religious Parties   In many Catholic and Islamic countries, religiously affiliated parties have played an important political role. **Christian Democrats** have governed Germany, Italy, Chile, El Salvador, and a number of other European and Latin American countries. Usually, these parties are linked in some way to the Catholic Church or to Catholic theological doctrine. But in Germany, the party has a Protestant wing as well, and the small Christian Democratic movement emerging in Russia is linked to the Russian Orthodox Church. Religious parties also are influential in Asia and the Middle East. Recent violence between Moslems and Hindus in India was often stirred up by groups aligned with the BJP, a militant Hindu party that moderated its policies when it recently governed the country. In Israel, several small Jewish orthodox parties often hold the balance of power when the nation's largest parties search for partners in forming a governing parliamentary coalition. Sometimes, as with Lebanon's Hezbollah, the links binding parties to religion are very strong, with clerics holding key positions. Other times the linkage is more philosophical, as with the various Christian Democratic parties.

Although most religiously affiliated parties are conservative, others fall all along the ideological spectrum. For example, although some Christian Democratic parties in Latin America are quite conservative, others have influential leftist factions. During the early 1970s, a wing of the Chilean Christian Democrats joined the Marxist coalition

© AP/Wide World Photos

SEEKING SUPPORT Former Israeli Prime Minister Ariel Sharon, right, shakes hands with spiritual leader of the ultra-religious (Jewish) Shas party Rabbi Ovadia Yosef and seeks his party's support. In Israel's multi-party system, governing coalitions need the support of some religious parties.

government of President Salvador Allende. On the other hand, India's Hindu party is highly conservative, and the Islamic parties of the Middle East are difficult to classify ideologically.

PARTIES IN A CHANGING WORLD

Our preceding discussion highlights several important trends in the current role of political parties. In Western Europe and the United States, voter preferences and the political dialogue have swung somewhat toward the right of the ideological spectrum. As we have noted, in these countries the public has become more skeptical of government economic intervention, be it welfare programs in the United States or government control of key productive enterprises in Western Europe.* At the same time,

* France illustrates the extent of government ownership that once existed in many European economies. During the early 1980s, the French government, which had already owned 12 percent of the nation's economy under the conservative governments of the previous decade, increased its share to 16 percent of GNP under the Socialists. In the 1990s, however, that proportion dropped as conservative governments reprivatized parts of the economy.

as we have noted, the relative size of the working class has diminished in these postindustrial societies, and many of the remaining blue-collar workers have acquired middle-class living standards and political attitudes.

These changes have presented real challenges to leftist parties in Western Europe and, to a lesser extent, to the Democrats in the United States. Changes in public opinion and the weakening of the left's electoral base (including organized labor) have often hurt those parties at the polls. Beyond President Clinton's two victories, the Democrats have won only one presidential election since 1972. Although social democratic parties remain a dominant political force in Scandinavia and currently govern Spain and Britain, generally they have been less successful in the rest of Western Europe in recent years.

In response to this challenge, many left-of-center parties now accept a more modest role for government and profess a more middle-of-the-road ideology in an effort to win back disaffected working-class voters and attract greater support from the middle class. Chastened by the Republican congressional triumph of 1994, Bill Clinton set aside his hopes for government-guaranteed health insurance and concentrated instead on such issues as safe streets, education, and welfare reform. Similarly, most European socialist and labor parties have largely abandoned their support for government ownership of parts of the economy and have accepted reductions in the welfare state in the face of budgetary deficits. By moving the Labour Party toward the center, Britain's Tony Blair has led that party to three consecutive victories in national elections after a long period in the political wilderness.

The movement of most major parties in the Western industrial democracies toward the political center has generally reduced ideological and programmatic differences between them. Thus, there are few significant economic policy differences between the French Socialists and the conservative UMP or between the Labour and Conservative parties in Great Britain. Increasingly, elections in the developed world are being decided by voters' perceptions of party competence—deciding which party will be able to govern most effectively—rather than by differences in party ideology.

The biggest losers in this move toward less ideological, centrist politics have been Western Europe's communist parties. As we have seen, they once received an important share of the vote in countries such as Italy, France, Finland, and Spain, where they were the voices of working-class discontent. But as Europe became more prosperous and many workers achieved middle-class lifestyles, class tensions decreased. At the same time, more centrist white-collar workers replaced once-radical, blue-collar workers in the workforce, and the strength of unions declined. All these factors diminished support for the region's communist parties. Their authoritarian and stodgy leadership hurt them as well. Thus, even before the collapse of Soviet communism, Western European communist parties were in decline. The notable exception has been the Italian Communist Party and its successor, the Democrats of the Left. Like the most successful European socialist parties, these parties moderated their ideology, governed efficiently, and picked up middle-class support.

Many political scientists point to a broader trend in Western democratic nations: declining citizen support for political parties in general.[17] That decline, they argue, is reflected in the growing number of citizens who identify themselves as independents and do not support any party. Commenting on the alleged decline of party strength, Kay Lawson and Peter Merkl have difficulty identifying a cause: "We don't know if major parties are failing because they are ideologically out of touch with their electorates, poorly organized, underfinanced, badly led, unaccountable, corrupt, overwhelmed by unethical or fanatical competition, unable to run effectively, or some combination of those factors."[18]

In industrial democracies, an additional causal factor—not mentioned by Lawson and Merkl—may be the rise of postmaterialist values (see Chapter 3). Western political parties have often defined themselves by economic issues, which may be of diminishing interest to postmaterialist voters. As many non-economic issues have moved to the center of the political arena, and as political parties have often proved ill-equipped to handle them, Ronald Inglehart suggested that postmaterialist voters have often turned to feminist groups, environmental organizations, community and religious associations, and other interest groups—the subject of our next chapter. But, contrary to Inglehart's prediction, pooled data from surveys in 59 countries indicate that postmaterialists are actually more likely than their compatriots to join a political party.[19] Russell Dalton maintains that, rather than looking for the causes of decreased *political party* support, we should look to the causes of a broader phenomenon. He points out that for decades citizens of most Western democracies have expressed declining confidence, not just in parties, but in almost all political institutions including the legal system and national legislatures.[20]

Despite these changes, however, many other political scientists insist on the continuing importance of parties in democratic societies. For example, some have argued that, if anything, parties in the United States play an increasingly important role in attracting voters to the polls and in governing the country.[21] And reports of the decline of party affiliations in the U.S. may be exaggerated. While it is true that the percentage of Americans who list themselves as independents (as opposed to Republicans or Democrats) has increased since the early 1950s (from 23 percent in 1952 to 35.2 percent in 1998), that increase took place entirely from 1952 to 1972, and support for the two major parties has remained fairly constant since that time.[22] Pippa Norris's examination of party membership over time across a broad range of nations indicates that the decline in membership has been less uniform, less sharp and, indeed, less certain than many political scientists had maintained.[23]

It is even more difficult to assess or predict trends elsewhere in the world. In much of Africa, Asia, and the Middle East, parties are in their infancy or represent the narrow interests of powerful economic and political actors. Similarly, it is too early to say what kinds of party systems or party loyalties may emerge in Russia and Eastern Europe. The first free elections for the Polish parliament (in 1991) featured more than 50 competing parties, including the Polish Beer Drinkers Party. And the apparent cynicism of many Russians toward their emerging party system has been expressed by a popular joke: When asked what he thought of having a multiparty system, one voter replied, "Wasn't one party bad enough?"

Although new institutions (such as neighborhood associations and interest groups) have emerged in many countries to carry out functions previously reserved for political parties, and although many voters are cynical about parties, political scientists are still impressed by their enduring strength. A recent work by Juan Linz, Hans Daalder, and other leading political scientists concludes that, while support for political parties has eroded in the West (often for reasons that can't be blamed on the parties themselves), parties continue to play a critical function in democratic political systems.[24] Wherever national elections have been held on a continuing basis, political parties have played a fundamental role.

WHERE ON THE WEB?

http://www.politics1.com/parties.htm

A guide to U.S. political parties with links to leaders of the two major parties and party organizations. Information on other American parties is included, down to the smallest and most
obscure.

http://www.politicalresources.net/

A listing of political sites available on the Web, sorted by country, with links to parties and
other institutions.

http://www.gksoft.com/govt/en/parties.html

Further links to political parties throughout the world, sorted by country.

http://home.ican.net/~alexng/can.html

A guide to Canadian political parties and recent elections.

http://www.psr.keele.ac.uk/parties.htm

List of political parties, interest groups, and other social movements; includes links to the home
pages of hundreds of political parties around the world, organized by country.

http://yaleglobal.yale.edu/display.article?id=6240

"Europe's Political Parties Buffeted by Globalization": an article in *Yale Global Online* dealing with
the effects of anti-EU and anti-globalization movements on Europe's political parties.

◆ ◆ ◆

Key Terms and Concepts_____

authoritarian
catchall parties
Christian Democrats
hierarchical
leadership recruitment
Leninist
mass parties
neofascist
no-party regime
party platform
patron–client relations

personalistic party
political aggregation
political party
populist
social democratic
social movements
socialist
statist policy
totalitarian
two-and-one-half-party system

Discussion Questions_____

1. What are the major functions of political parties in a democracy? What are the major arguments that have been made for and against political parties?
2. What evidence supports the idea that the importance of political parties is declining in
   Western industrial democracies? In what ways may postmaterialist values have contributed
   to that decline?
3. What evidence suggests that "reports of the death of political parties have been premature"
   and that parties still play a vital role?

4. Why did left-of-center political parties in Europe, such as the British Labour Party and the Spanish and French Socialist Parties, face declining grassroots support, and how has that decline been related to changes in their countries' workforces? How have those parties adjusted their programs to meet this challenge?

5. What are some factors that explain why the United States and Britain have two-party systems, whereas France, Germany, and most of Western Europe have multiparty systems?

6. Are political parties becoming less popular and less important in the United States and other Western democracies? What is the evidence on both sides of that question?

Notes_____

1. Gabriel Almond, introduction to *The Politics of Developing Areas*, ed. Gabriel Almond and James Coleman (Princeton, NJ: Princeton University Press, 1960).

2. Otto Kirchheimer, "The Transformation of Western European Party Systems," in *Political Parties and Political Development*, ed. Joseph LaPalombara and Myron Weiner (Princeton, NJ: Princeton University Press, 1966).

3. Joseph LaPalombara and Myron Weiner, "The Origin and Development of Political Parties," in LaPalombara and Weiner, *Political Parties*, p. 25.

4. Leon Epstein, *Political Parties in Western Democracies* (New York: Praeger, 1967), pp. 130–166.

5. Maurice Duverger, *Political Parties* (New York: Wiley, 1954).

6. Ibid.

7. Manali Desai, "From Movement to Party to Government," in Jack A. Goldstein, ed., *States, Parties and Social Movements* (Cambridge, England and New York: Cambridge University Press, 2003), p. 171.

8. John K. Glenn, "Parties Out of Movements: Party Emergence in Postcommunist Eastern Europe," in Goldstein, ed., *States, Parties . . .*, pp. 147–169.

9. Jean Blondel, "Types of Party Systems," in *The West European Party System*, ed. Peter Mair (New York: Oxford University Press, 1990).

10. Jeane J. Kirkpatrick, *Dictatorships and Double Standards* (New York: Simon & Schuster, 1982).

11. John Bibby, *Politics, Parties and Elections in America* (Chicago: Nelson Hall, 1987), p. 58.

12. *New York Times*, August 29, 1991.

13. For further discussion of the ideological classification of Western European parties, see Jurg Steiner, *European Democracies* (New York: Longman, 1991), pp. 7–64.

14. Guillermo A. O'Donnell, *Modernization and Bureaucratic-Authoritarianism: Studies in South American Politics* (Berkeley: Institute of International Studies, University of California, 1973); and David Collier, ed., *The New Authoritarianism in Latin America* (Princeton, NJ: Princeton University Press, 1979).

15. Jean Blondel, "The Government of France," in *Introduction to Comparative Government*, ed. Michael Curtis et al. (New York: Harper and Row, 1990), p. 133.

16. Donald Share, "Dilemmas of Social Democracy in the 1980s: The Spanish Socialist Workers Party in Comparative Perspective," *Comparative Political Studies* 21 (October 1988): 429.

17. For a recent study of that phenomenon in the United States, see Martin P. Wattenberg, *The Decline of American Political Parties: 1952–1988* (Cambridge, MA: Harvard University Press, 1990). For evidence that support for political parties is falling in most Western democracies, see Russell J. Dalton, *Citizen Politics*, 3rd ed. (Chatham, NJ: Chatham House, 2002).

18. Kay Lawson and Peter Merkl, "Alternative Organizations: Environmental, Supplementary, Communitarian and Authoritarian," in *When Parties Fail*, ed. Kay Lawson and Peter Merkl (Princeton, NJ: Princeton University Press, 1988), p. 3.

19. Pippa Norris, *Democratic Phoenix: Reinventing Political Activism* (Cambridge, England and New York: Cambridge University Press, 2002), p. 132.

20. Dalton, *Citizen Politics*, pp. 240–246.

21. L. Sandy Maisel, ed., *The Parties Respond: Changes in the American Party System* (Boulder, CO: Westview, 1990); see also Paul Herrnson, *Party Campaigning in the 1980s* (Cambridge: Harvard University Press, 1988).
22. Donald Green, Bradley Palmquist, and Eric Schickler, *Partisan Hearts and Minds: Political Parties and the Social Identities of Voters* (New Haven, CT: Yale University Press, 2002), p. 15.
23. Norris, *Democratic Phoenix*, pp. 218–219.
24. Richard Gunther, José Ramón Montero, and Juan Linz, ed., *Political Parities: Old Concepts and New Challenges* (New York: Oxford University Press, 2002).

For Further Reading _____

Bibby, John. *Politics, Parties and Elections in America.* 4th ed. Belmont, CA: Wadsworth, 2000.

Dalton, Russell J., and Martin P. Wattenberg. *Parties Without Partisans: Political Change in Advanced Industrial Democracies.* Oxford and New York: Oxford University Press, 2000.

Eldersveld, Samuel J., and Hanes Walton, Jr. *Political Parties in American Society.* 2nd ed. Boston: Bedford/St. Martin's, 2000.

Gunther, Richard, José Ramón Montero, and Juan Linz, eds. *Political Parities: Old Concepts and New Challenges.* New York: Oxford University Press, 2002.

Hasan, Zoya, ed. *Parties and Party Politics in India.* New Delhi and New York: Oxford University Press, 2002.

Kaple, Deborah A., ed. *World Encyclopedia of Political Systems and Parties.* 3rd ed. New York: Facts On File, 1999.

Moser, Robert G. *Unexpected Outcomes: Electoral Systems, Political Parties, and Representation in Russia.* Pittsburgh: University of Pittsburgh Press, 2001.

Pempel, T. J., ed. *Uncommon Democracies: The One-Party Dominant Regimes.* Ithaca, NY: Cornell University Press, 1990.

Wattenberg, Martin P. *The Decline of American Political Parties: 1952–1988.* Cambridge, MA: Harvard University Press, 1990.

A General Strike Gets Results   A lone passenger waits for his train as hundreds of commuters board one of the few trains available Tuesday October 10, 1995 at the St. Lazare railway station in Paris. Public workers unions staged a general strike affecting transportation, telephone, power, postal, hospital, and state-owned companies all over France. Unions for more than 4 million workers decided to stage a strike protesting a pay freeze.

© AP/Wide World Photos

6

INTEREST GROUPS

◆ Interest Groups: What They Are and How They Work
◆ The Power of Interest Groups ◆ The Growth of Interest
Groups ◆ How Interest Groups Are Formed ◆ Conclusion:
Interest Groups—A Challenge for Democracy?

Although most Americans know little or nothing about it, there has been a long-standing dispute about lumber between the U.S. and Canada. Since the mid-1970s, Canadian lumber imports have grown from 17 percent of the U.S. market to over 35 percent. Neither the Democrats nor the Republicans have made this trend an issue in their national platforms, and it has not been a major subject of concern in the campaign speeches of candidates for national offices.

Nevertheless, the U.S. political system responded. If voters and parties did not press the federal government on the "problem" of Canadian lumber imports, who did? The answer became clear when two experts in wildlife and forestry policy studied the issue: interest groups made all the difference.

> A small but concentrated softwood lumber industry can successfully lobby their elected officials such as senators and demand protection from foreign competition, despite the fact that such protectionism harms the economic welfare of the nation as a whole. . . . Senators from lumber-producing states, with the support of a number of their colleagues from other states, built sizable coalitions that encompassed a majority of the Senate. The explicit and implicit pressure and demand for action could not easily be ignored by the president.[1]

In May 2002, the U.S. imposed a 27.2 percent tariff on Canadian softwood lumber, making it more expensive for purchase in the U.S. The policy enabled U.S. producers to increase prices, therefore increasing the wealth of lumber companies and their employees.[2] However, their new wealth did not come from Canadian citizens or businesses, but from U.S. citizens building homes and consumers purchasing goods and services from retailers that had to pay more to build their stores and warehouses. Why is it that the relatively small number of people involved in the U.S. lumber industry was able to apply greater influence than the millions of consumers who were harmed by the import restrictions?

Quite simply, organized interests can be more influential than large numbers of unorganized citizens. They use a wide range of techniques to influence members of Congress and to generate votes for friendly legislators. Politicians ignore their power at their peril. If we want to understand the policy process in democracies, we must understand not only voting and parties but also the power of organized interest groups.

It is noteworthy that one of the earliest insights developed in the scientific study of politics had to do with interest groups. Toward the end of the nineteenth century, political scientists increasingly felt that they were missing something by focusing their studies entirely on laws, constitutional rights, and institutions. Although those "formal-legal" studies were (and are) vital, a growing number of political scientists came to understand that the discipline should study political *behavior*. The emphasis on behavior fundamentally changed political science. Instead of studying aspects of government contained in constitutional passages and legislative enactments, political scientists began to analyze the political behavior of citizens and to explore how that behavior affects public policy.

When they emerged from law libraries and shifted their emphasis to the observation of behavior, political scientists immediately discovered something very important: *Organized* political activity is often the critical factor in explaining what government does (and does not do). If we want to understand why some things are changed and others are not, we rarely find the answers by examining the words of the Constitution, or even the results of elections. At least some of the answers have to do with which interests are organized and which interests are not. The interest group thus became a basic subject of political study many decades ago.

The influence of interest groups raises some troubling questions: If some, but not all, people are represented by effectively organized groups, is a system that responds to group influence really democratic? Is such a system fair? Why do some people join groups while others do not? Does the growing power of interest groups threaten the position of political parties? Does it make voting less important? How do interest groups function in nondemocratic systems such as those in China and Egypt, or in democracies such as India's, with social systems far different from our own? These and many related questions help us see that the study of interest groups has become one of the most important, and most controversial, research problems in contemporary political science.

INTEREST GROUPS: WHAT THEY ARE AND HOW THEY WORK

An **interest group** *is an organization that attempts to influence public policy in a specific area of importance to its members.* In contrast to political parties, interest groups do not try to achieve their political objectives by electing their leaders to government office.

Instead, they attempt to persuade elected leaders, administrative officials, judges, and others to make and implement laws and policies in line with their positions. They may be well organized, with strong institutional foundations and professional staffs, or they may be looser arrangements of part-time participants. People establish some organizations to be explicitly political, whereas others are created to achieve religious, economic, or other goals, only occasionally working in the political arena. The term *interest group* thus applies to a diverse array of organizations.*

For example, interest groups in the United States include the Tobacco Institute, the National Rifle Association, the Sierra Club, and the National Association for the Advancement of Colored People (NAACP). The British Medical Association, the Mexican Confederation of Labor, and France's National Union Federation of Agriculturalists (FNSEA) are often in the news in those countries. Although each group is unique, all seek to promote government decisions that advance their interests. (See Box 6-1.)

Kinds of Interest Groups

Interest groups can be classified in several ways. Perhaps the most useful approach is simply to classify them descriptively, on the basis of the interests they pursue. Most fall into one of the following categories.

Labor Unions   Unions such as the United Automobile Workers, the Teamsters, and the Australian Nursing Federation are primarily collective-bargaining units that negotiate contracts for their members with employers. From time to time, however, these organizations apply their energies to the political arena, becoming interest groups by our definition.

---

* Some prefer other terms, such as "factions," "organized interests," "pressure groups," and "special interests." (See the introductory chapter in Allan J. Cigler and Burdett A. Loomis, *Interest Group Politics*, 6th ed. Washington, DC: CQ Press, 2002.)

━━━━━━━━   **Box 6-1**   ━━━━━━━━

The National Rifle Association in the United States

More than four million U.S. citizens are dues-paying members of the National Rifle Association, a powerful and well-known interest group. NRA members receive a publication (*American Rifleman*) and other benefits, including gun insurance and "shooter's liability insurance," but a key NRA activity is participation in electoral campaigns. According to a recent study, the NRA "participates in more than 10,000 campaigns in any given electoral cycle and raises millions of dollars for candidates committed to the goals of the organization."*

Founded in 1871 to promote the "shooting sports," marksmanship, and gun safety, the NRA has become one of the most effective and most controversial U.S. interest groups. The organization promotes gun ownership, shares information about collectible guns, and has a vigorous program regarding gun safety, but it is also prominent in its opposition to virtually any legislation limiting gun ownership. According to the NRA's "Political Victory Fund," in 2004 the organization "was

involved in 265 campaigns for the U.S. House and Senate, winning in 254 of those races. These victories represent the re-election of pro-gun majorities in both the U.S. House and Senate."[3] Earlier that year, the NRA took credit for pressuring Congress to allow the 1994 ban on assault weapons to expire.

The growth of the NRA tells us a great deal about interest groups in general. For one thing, NRA membership has grown tremendously as the U.S. economy grew. More people can afford the "luxury" of contributing to an organization when they have disposable income. However, as shown in the following chart, increases in membership dues created at least a temporary decline in membership, demonstrating that people do take costs into account when they decide to join interest groups.

But the overall pattern of growth shows something else. During the 1990s, gun owners in the United States felt that the Clinton White House was a potential threat to their interests. Many citizens apparently responded to that threat by joining the NRA. In fact, viewed in a longer historical perspective, the overall growth of the NRA, showing a 400-percent increase in membership since the late 1970s, corresponds well to the increased momentum in the United States for stricter gun control. Congress passed the Gun Control Act of 1968 following the assassinations of Robert

---

*Kelly D. Patterson and Matthew M. Singer, "The National Rifle Association in the Face of the Clinton Challenge," in *Interest Group Politics*, 6th ed., ed. Allan J. Cigler and Burdett A. Loomis (Washington, DC: CQ Press, 2002), pp. 55–78. Data for 2006 membership obtained by the authors from the National Rifle Association, Fairfax, Virginia.

In Britain, the British Trades Union Congress (TUC) is directly involved in politics through its powerful role in the Labour Party. In the United States, the Teamsters, the American Federation of County, State, and Municipal Employees (AFSCME), and other unions are always an active presence in elections. In some countries, the impact of unions is less influential. For example, the governments and ruling parties of many African countries have dominated the leadership of most unions, using them as a means of controlling working-class political participation and robbing them of their status as independent interest groups.

Business Organizations   Most of the many kinds of business organizations attempt to influence government from time to time. A few business organizations pursue the interests of business itself (the National Association of Manufacturers, the Chamber of Commerce), although most focus on the special problems of a particular economic sector (such as the Used Car Dealers Association). Business groups sometimes attempt to oppose labor-group demands and often pursue or oppose changes in tax codes or regulations that affect the profitability of their operations. In some Third World nations with powerful economic elites, business groups are linked so closely to

Kennedy and Dr. Martin Luther King, Jr., and opinion polls have shown substantial support for stricter gun laws, especially after incidents such as the assassination attempt on President Reagan in 1981 and the Columbine High School shootings in Colorado in 1999. Although those events may temporarily dampen NRA membership (it dropped to 2.8 million following the Columbine shootings), the general perception that new gun restrictions are likely has made the NRA a larger and possibly more influential organization.

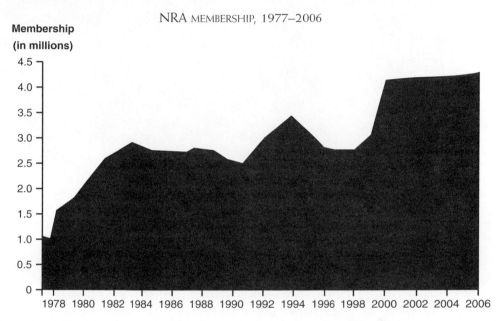

NRA MEMBERSHIP, 1977–2006

Membership (in millions)

SOURCE: Figure derived from Patterson and Singer, 2002; data for 2006 membership obtained by the authors from the National Rifle Association, Fairfax, Virginia.

government, through family ties and friendships, that they exercise a dominant role in policy making. In El Salvador, for example, the "fourteen families," which controlled much of the country's coffee production and export, were long believed to hold veto power over government policy. In other nations, however, with Marxist-oriented regimes, business groups either do not exist or were on the fringes of the policy process (as they were in Nicaragua during the period of Sandinista control).

Gender, Religious, Ethnic, and Age Groups   The feminist movement in the United States has led to the creation of groups such as the National Organization for Women (NOW), which seeks to influence government policies of special concern to women. Similarly, a host of civil rights groups—the NAACP, the Urban League, La Raza Unida—serve as advocates for racial and ethnic minorities. In India, religious and caste groups work closely with the political parties to advocate for their political demands. Interest groups based on age are less common, but the Gray Panthers and the American Association of Retired Persons (AARP) now forcefully advocate for the interests of the elderly in the United States. Similarly, the Children's Defense Fund promotes children's interests.

LABOR LEADERS GET ACCESS TO THE TOP   British Prime Minister Tony Blair, right, shakes hands with labor union leaders from Canada, France, Germany, Italy, Japan, Russia, the United States, and Britain before a meeting. Although its political strength has faded somewhat in the U.S., no elected democratic leader can ignore the power of organized labor.

Communist governments often organize women's or youth organizations that profess to act as interest groups but more frequently are designed to mobilize support for the government. In Cuba, however, the Federation of Cuban Women purportedly helped persuade the government to implement a family code that not only called for the legal equality of the sexes but also required both spouses to share housework equally. The federation's clout was undoubtedly enhanced by the fact that its leader was Fidel Castro's sister-in-law.

Public Interest Groups   Although labor unions and business organizations would have us believe that they are selfless crusaders for the general good, normally they pursue government decisions that specifically benefit their members. A rather different type of interest group is concerned primarily with a vision of fairness and justice for some kind of general public interest. Although it is sometimes difficult to draw the line precisely between private and public interests, public interest groups are distinctive political organizations.

This kind of group is centrally featured in what is probably the most divisive public issue in contemporary U.S. politics: abortion. Organizations favoring or opposing abortion rights—each of which is very committed to strongly held principles—have become important factors in lawmaking and elections at all levels of government.

Other reform groups are formed to fight a particular social problem, such as alcohol-related traffic accidents, in the case of Mothers Against Drunk Driving (MADD). The Sierra Club works to influence government to preserve the environment by supporting such varied steps as recycling, preservation of endangered species, and restrictions on public use of wilderness areas. The Americans for Tax Reform supports a general policy of lower taxes at all levels of government. These organizations are "public interest" groups because they seek the actions and decisions that they feel are justified for the benefit of *all* citizens.

Public interest groups are most prevalent in economically developed countries, where higher levels of education and political awareness, leisure time, and disposable income facilitate their proliferation. But they also exist on a more limited basis in some Third World nations. Citizens in developing nations have begun to organize around environmental issues such as the preservation of rain forests. In Thailand, for example, a Buddhist monk organized farmers to promote environmentally sound use of the land and to work with the government for the preservation of shrinking forest preserves.

Professional Associations and Occupational Groups   Literally hundreds of professions and occupations in industrialized nations are represented by organizations. In the United States, the American Bar Association and the American Medical Association are probably the best known, but other organizations represent electrologists, plumbers, nursing home administrators, hairdressers, podiatrists, and people in many other professions. Farmers have powerful lobbies in the United States as well as in France, Japan, and Argentina. These groups are distinguished by their focus on the special interests of members of an identifiable profession or occupation.

Professional associations work actively to share information—hence the constant parade of conventions in virtually all major cities. Members attending these meetings can go to panel discussions and workshop sessions at which they learn about new techniques or materials relevant to their profession. Professional associations also attempt to influence government, however, particularly with respect to licensing laws and regulations.

These groups are concerned about licensing both because they are naturally interested in maintaining the public's confidence in their respective professions and because they want to keep unqualified people from taking business away from them.* Since effective licensing requirements can be enforced only through governmental action, professional associations exert much of their energy by acting as interest groups.

How Interest Groups Work

Interest groups exploit a wide range of methods in their efforts to influence government. The following approaches are the main ways that interest groups attempt to get what they want.

---

* Some analysts argue that the public would be much better off with unfettered access to these "unqualified" professionals and that, in the name of protecting us against "charlatans," professional associations merely seek to keep competition out and prices up. See Milton Friedman, *Capitalism and Freedom* (Chicago: University of Chicago Press, 1962).

Lobbying Whenever interest groups communicate with governmental officials, they are **lobbying**.* Contact is sometimes informal, as when a legislator or an agency head discusses a policy issue over the phone, through correspondence, or at lunch.

Interest groups also testify before congressional committee hearings, file *amicus curiae*† briefs (documents arguing for or against a particular interpretation of the law) with state and federal courts, submit written reports to administrative agencies, and participate in public hearings of all kinds. All of these activities are important *access opportunities*, providing settings in which interest groups can directly contact decision makers.

Contacts between lobbyists and governmental officials in the U.S. and other established democracies are generally honest, legitimate meetings, despite popular impressions to the contrary. Interest groups lobby primarily by providing information to decision makers, not by purchasing votes. In fact, political scientists specializing in the study of the U.S. Congress often tell of the newly elected representative who, after a year in office, asked, "Where are the lobbyists? I haven't seen one yet." Of course, he had seen and heard dozens of them, but none had tried to bribe him. All the people he met with were simply giving him useful facts and introducing him to interesting points of view—innocent contacts that the freshman representative could not possibly interpret as lobbying.

Legislators, agency officials, and even judges listen to lobbyists because the information they have is often valuable, even though the group providing the information has an axe to grind. For example, when new legislation is considered regarding auto emission standards, one of the groups that Congress and the Environmental Protection Agency (EPA) will turn to for data is the auto industry. Although the interest groups representing the automakers obviously have a stake in the outcome, they also have a great deal of knowledge and experience relevant to the matter at hand. Ultimately, government officials have to decide what weight or credibility they will give that information. Even when the group has a financial stake in the outcome (as with the automakers), the information may still be useful.

Interest groups can exert considerable influence by lobbying. Being in a position to provide critical information is itself a source of power. Good lobbyists are always ready to answer questions and explain the importance of their views. Decision makers often respond to lobbyists' suggestions, incorporating them in compromise solutions that take the groups' positions into account.

In countries where public agencies are not as capable of evaluating private-sector data, interest groups often exercise even more influence than in the United States. Years ago, a leading expert argued that many Italian regulatory agencies relied so heavily on information from the very industrial groups they were supposed to be monitoring that they had become their virtual clients.[4] Similar criticisms are sometimes made about regulators in other countries. However, in some countries, interest groups must work very closely with government to influence policy. A study from the 1990s concluded that French interest groups, particularly "public" interest groups, are dependent

---

* This term derives from the widely observed practice among legislators of discussing major decisions with interested parties in the cloakrooms and lobbies outside the official legislative chamber. Those meeting with legislators in such settings are commonly called *lobbyists*.

† Literally translated, this means "friend of the court."

upon the powerful central French state bureaucracy, although they are frequently able to get government elites to adopt their goals.[5]

Influencing Public Opinion   In democratic systems, it is much easier for an interest group to persuade a legislator or an agency official if public opinion is on its side. Interest groups thus often spend a great deal of time and money attempting to generate support among the public. When they succeed, legislators are less likely to introduce or support legislation opposed by the group. Interest groups in good standing with the public are more effective in influencing government officials.

Interest group efforts to influence public opinion are most common when proposals are under consideration that would hurt group interests. (They are less common when interest groups attempt to obtain something new from government; in these cases, groups prefer to work with legislative committees or with administrative agencies.) For example, you may recall seeing commercials showing an auto executive driving through beautiful national parks while stating how carbon monoxide and other emissions from his company's sport utility vehicles were even lower than federal pollution standards required. A number of recent television advertisements from pharmaceutical companies emphasize their programs that provide free or low-priced prescription drugs to people who cannot afford them. These commercials are certainly aired in hopes of generating increased sales, but the corporations producing them also hope to persuade voters to stop pressuring Congress for even stricter environmental regulation or for price controls. To the extent that a group is successful in creating a favorable image, it reduces public demands on the government to take action against it.

Clearly, influencing public attitudes is most useful in industrial democracies, marked by a relatively high degree of political participation and awareness, and is less relevant in authoritarian or less developed systems. Modern technology, such as computer-controlled telephoning, is exploited effectively by interest groups in the United States, Great Britain, and other advanced nations. Yet, even in a semi-authoritarian society such as Mexico was before the 1990s, one could find newspaper advertisements by business or labor groups making their cases to the public.

Influencing Group Members   Interest groups with large memberships can wield additional power by enlisting the active support of their members. Most interest groups publish some sort of newsletter to communicate with their members, and those publications give them a chance to promote the group's official positions. A noteworthy example of this tactic occurred in 1988, when *The American Rifleman*, published by the National Rifle Association, urged its members to vote against Democratic presidential candidate Michael Dukakis by devoting the entire cover of its October 1988 issue to a single Dukakis statement: "I do not believe in people owning guns." The interest group's effort was doubtlessly successful, and few NRA members voted for Dukakis. The ability to move a huge number of citizens to adopt a particular position can be a great source of influence.

The 2004 presidential campaign in the U.S. featured a number of memorable interest group advertisements designed to mobilize and influence their members. One of the most controversial was designed by the liberal group Moveon.org. It featured video images of German bombers, tanks, and Nazi flags from World War II, comparing Germany's invasion of France and Poland to the U.S. invasion of Iraq. Although this kind of advertisement stimulated a great deal of anger on the part of the interest group's opponents, it probably also helped to mobilize its members.

An organization's efforts to persuade its members often lead to real payoffs, because individuals who are members of organizations are more likely to vote than are unaffiliated people. Government officials realize that the outcomes in close elections are frequently determined by interest group endorsements that influence the voting choices of members.

Making Campaign Contributions   Usually within strict legal limits, interest groups can influence government by contributing to electoral campaigns.* Money is the most typical contribution, but interest groups often supply volunteers and in-kind services to help a candidate in an election.

There are two ways of seeing a connection between campaign contributions and legislative decisions. First, the model of *legislative influence* assumes that a quid pro quo (literally, "something for something") develops between legislators and groups: The legislator promises, explicitly or implicitly, to support or oppose certain bills in exchange for campaign contributions. Contributions can also make a difference as described in the model of *electoral influence*. In this second scenario, candidates have clearly expressed positions on important issues, and interest groups steer their contributions to the candidates whose views would advance group interests. When the campaign money produces electoral success, groups benefit because politicians supporting policies beneficial to the group are in a position to make law.[†]

It is easy to see why campaign contributions from interest groups are a cause of concern in a democracy. If politicians need huge sums of money to buy television time, and if they obtain much of that money from interest groups, they obviously come to depend on interest groups. Such dependence is a source of considerable political power. In a democracy, elected officials are expected to serve their constituents, and yet they are encouraged (some would say "forced") to serve the organized interests they depend on for contributions. As discussed in Chapter 4, many democratic systems have thus made efforts to eliminate the problem by limiting how much money can be spent in campaigns, by requiring that candidates and parties disclose the sources of their funding, and by limiting the amount of money that a single person or organization can contribute.

In other political systems, there may be a much more intimate relationship among parties, candidates, and interest group campaign contributions. For example, for many years in Great Britain, unions automatically checked off a small contribution from the

---

* In the United States, the Bipartisan Campaign Reform Act of 2002, which we will discuss in Chapter 11, has significantly affected interest group contributions to campaigns. Political action committees, or PACs, continue to play a role. PACs are organizations, closely tied to their parent interest groups, set up to funnel money to campaigns. The idea of this and similar laws is to have some separation between lobbying and campaign contributions; for example, the United Auto Workers labor union does not give money to candidates for Congress, but its PAC, the "UAW Voluntary Community Action Program," contributed more than $2 million to such campaigns in 2000. The line between interest groups and their affiliated PACs was blurred considerably when court rulings in the 1970s established that the parent organization could pay for the fund-raising and administrative costs incurred by its PAC. For a good analysis of the history and behavior of PACs in the United States, see M. Margaret Conway, Joanne Connor Green, and Marian Currinder, "Interest Group Money in Elections," in *Interest Group Politics*, 6th ed., ed. Allan J. Cigler and Burdett A. Loomis (Washington, DC: CQ Press, 2002), pp. 117–140.

[†] For a helpful discussion of these two complementary models, see John R. Wright, *Interest Groups and Congress* (New York: Longman, 2003), pp. 146–148.

paychecks of their members, which went to support the Labour Party. Workers could prevent the deduction only if they told their union that they wished to "opt out," a rather uncomfortable request to make. Subsequently, a Conservative-controlled Parliament passed legislation that stipulated that contributions would be deducted only if the union member "opted in." In the Philippines and many Latin American countries, candidates or parties are sometimes so heavily financed by powerful business interests that they become virtual spokespeople for those groups.

Litigation   Court systems are normally designed to try cases involving crimes and disputes between individuals. But interest groups are sometimes able to sue a government official or agency on the grounds that they were harmed by a governmental action (or inaction).* Once in court, the interest group may be able to delay a governmental action it opposes or to obtain more forceful implementation of something it favors. In order to use the courts to influence policy, the group must somehow demonstrate that a law or constitutional provision requires that a governmental official or agency stop or start doing something. Important public policy questions are often addressed when the court hands down a decision. (See Box 6-2.)

Demonstrations and Strikes   Sometimes an interest group can advance its cause or interests by bringing attention to a problem that most people would otherwise overlook. The visual impact of demonstrations, and the fact that they can be covered in a brief television news report make such events particularly popular in developed nations. Media events are also relatively inexpensive to organize. Virtually any demonstrating group can get exposure that would otherwise cost many thousands of dollars. In addition to getting exposure, the demonstration will often "fire up" the group's members, generating internal support that may be lagging.

Strikes are also sometimes used as a political statement, instead of merely a means of demanding higher wages or better working conditions. Workers in Italy, France, and Peru, for example, have often carried out one- or two-day general strikes in which transportation services, electrical power, and much of the nation's commerce grind to a halt. (See Box 6-3.) In Poland, the Solidarity Movement also used strikes and demonstrations effectively in an effort that eventually brought down an entire government.

Demonstrations are most prevalent in political systems that are neither fully democratic (that is, where sectors of society do not have equal access to the political system) nor totalitarian. As long as the Communist Party controlled the mass media in the former Soviet Union and harshly repressed dissent, demonstrations were rare and quickly (often brutally) put down. Now that Russian political activity is less repressed but not yet truly democratic, demonstrations there have become commonplace.

These newer demonstrations range from the more serious and sometimes violent expressions of ethnic politics to less threatening demonstrations, such as smokers

---

* In the United States, Britain, and other countries using the Anglo-American system of jurisprudence, the extent to which a group can do this depends on the law of standing. The familiar phrase *standing to sue* simply means that the party wishing to litigate has a real stake in the matter, not merely an ideological position. Thus, when the Sierra Club sues the U.S. Department of the Interior, it must be able to show that at least one of its members was personally harmed by that agency (or that he or she would be harmed if the challenged agency action were allowed to go forward). The standing doctrine thus limits interest groups' access to the courts, because their concerns will not be heard if they only have an ideological position on the issue.

Box 6-2

THE "DISADVANTAGE THEORY" OF INTEREST GROUP LITIGATION

Achieving an interest group's policy goals through litigation is very different from achieving such goals by lobbying legislators or chief executives. Legislation requires that a majority of the parliament or assembly support the group's position, and both legislators and executives usually have to balance interest group demands against voter preferences and party demands. In most systems, judges enjoy some political independence, although their influence over public policy is usually limited. Still, in some circumstances an interest group may be able to convince a court that a particular governmental action must be changed or preserved, and the resulting decision of the court may produce policy changes the group wants. If a group is politically weak, it may have a greater chance of achieving its goals through litigation than through the legislative and executive branches, where they are outspent and outvoted by larger, more powerful interests.

The famous "disadvantage theory" of interest groups and courts is based on these observations. Initially associated with Richard Courtner, the idea holds that the interest groups that turn to litigation as a strategy for achieving their goals are those groups that "are temporarily, or even permanently, disadvantaged in terms of their abilities to attain successfully their goals in the electoral process. . . . politically 'disadvantaged' groups, [i]f they are to succeed at all in the pursuit of their goals . . . are almost compelled to resort to litigation."[6] Perhaps the best example of interest group behavior illustrating this theory involved the NAACP: During the 1940s and 1950s, this group's efforts to end public school segregation by lobbying

state legislatures failed completely, but a litigation strategy eventually changed public policy dramatically, because the courts provided access denied in other quarters.

However important that example is, researchers are beginning to doubt that the "disadvantage theory" tells the whole story. Recent studies analyzing data on group wealth, goals, and strategies suggest that it is not only "politically disadvantaged" interest groups that use the courts. In fact, profit-seeking groups use litigation more than public interest groups, and groups with better staffs and more financial resources use litigation more than groups with fewer resources.[7] Any interest group with the required financial resources can use litigation to change public policy, sometimes to enforce and secure policy objectives initially won in elected institutions. In such cases, litigation strategies actually reinforce the successes that group power brings through lobbying.

Because the empirical work on interest group litigation undermines the most common understanding of the disadvantage theory, some political scientists have started to think about the problem in different ways. Cary Coglianese concludes that groups suffering a disadvantage are, in fact, the ones most likely to pursue litigation, but the disadvantage that drives them to seek their goals through the courts is *not* a lack of financial or organizational strength. Instead, the groups that file lawsuits to change policy, almost always a long-shot approach, are those groups whose goals are widely unsupported in society and who therefore face an unreceptive political system.[8]

---

protesting the shortage of cigarettes. Of course, in Hungary, Poland, and other Eastern European nations, demonstrations that started as a form of interest group activity by human rights organizations turned into peaceful revolutions that startled the world by toppling totalitarian regimes. In contrast, the massacre of student demonstrators in Beijing's Tiananmen Square in June 1989 revealed the limits of such demonstrations in the most repressive countries.

Demonstrations and other "confrontational" tactics are usually the choice of groups with little confidence that they will succeed through more conventional lobbying efforts. For example, in the American South, African Americans, often disenfranchised and lacking access to the local media, resorted to sit-ins and marches, particularly in the 1950s and 1960s. Similarly, blacks in the townships of South Africa used demonstrations throughout

Box 6-3

INTEREST GROUP TACTICS IN FRANCE

Although interest groups are active in all democratic societies, their methods and objectives vary considerably from country to country. In France, labor unions, business associations, professional organizations, and agricultural groups are officially represented on various government advisory boards.* Advisory councils for the vast public health and retirement system include representatives of labor unions and employers' associations.† That gives those groups an avenue—beyond the familiar U.S. lobbying tactics—for influencing public policy.

Many French interest groups also are more overtly politicized than their American counterparts. Competing farmers' groups and, especially, labor unions are often associated with particular political

parties, and their tactics and objectives often reflect their affiliations.

In October 2005, more than one million people participated in a general strike that affected dozens of French towns. The strike was not prompted by a narrow dispute about an employer's wage rates, but instead was an explicitly political action by organized interest groups. All seven of France's most important trade union confederations took part in the strike, and they were aided by leftist French parties. While the strikers were concerned about wage and pension issues, they were also acting to protest government policies in several areas: an alleged "housing crisis," police mistreatment of immigrants, and what the strikers saw as overly aggressive crackdowns on social protests. In March and April 2006, demonstrations against a proposed change in French labor laws led to a series of severely disruptive demonstrations.

Sometimes, French interest groups use more militant tactics. Farmers, unhappy with government price supports or the challenge of imported agricultural products, have been known to block highway traffic by dumping huge amounts of potatoes or the like on the roads.

*Frank L. Wilson, *Interest-Group Politics in France* (Cambridge, UK: Cambridge University Press, 1987); and William Safran, *The French Polity*, 4th ed. (White Plains, NY: Longman, 1995), pp. 135–160.

†Gary Freeman, "Financial Crisis and Policy Continuity in the Welfare State," in *Developments in French Politics*, rev. ed., ed. Peter Hall, Jack Hayward, and Howard Machin (London: Macmillan, 1994), pp. 188–200.

the 1980s and early 1990s to express their opposition to apartheid legislation before the political process was opened to them. Mexican slum dwellers or peasants, who have been unable to satisfy their demands otherwise, may encamp themselves in front of government agencies either to influence public opinion or to show their resolve to government policy makers. In India, where hunger strikes and sit-ins were used by the legendary leader Mohandas Gandhi to achieve national independence, farmers—as well as language, religious, and caste groups—constantly resort to such tactics. Among U.S. citizens who belong to interest groups seeking government programs to support AIDS research and treatment, those who felt most vulnerable and victimized supported confrontational tactics much more strongly than did activists who did not share such feelings.*

Although demonstrations can be a useful tool for otherwise weak or powerless groups, they also can be counterproductive. Demonstrations may become violent, producing fights and rock throwing. Even demonstrations that remain nonviolent may generate significant opposition to the group. Individuals who would otherwise be sympathetic to the group's cause may begin to see it as lawless or radical. Even though the vast majority of demonstrations are nonviolent, the distinction between demonstration and riot may be lost on much of the general public.

* See M. Kent Jennings and Ellen Ann Anderson, "Support for Confrontational Tactics among AIDS Activists: A Study of Intra-Movement Divisions," *American Journal of Political Science* 40 (May 1996): 311–334.

Corruption   We have suggested that, for the most part, the relationship between interest groups and public officials in industrial democracies is honest. In less developed political systems, however, the roles of bribery and corruption are much more firmly entrenched.

It was widely understood that during Ferdinand Marcos's reign in the Philippines, business groups would not receive favorable government treatment without paying substantial contributions to the president. In Nigeria and the Central African Republic, bribes have been such a prerequisite for dealing with the government or influencing policy that their national leaders have become multimillionaires in societies whose populations are among the poorest in the world. In Western European democracies, corruption is generally less prevalent than in the United States.

As we have seen, interest groups can select one or more of several strategies for influencing the political process. Their choices reflect their character, the degree to which their goals are considered "mainstream," and the kind and amount of resources they command. Interest group behavior is also affected by the nature of the system in which groups operate. Where political power is decentralized in both government structure and party organization (as in the United States), there are many "access points" for interest group influence. One group may find success lobbying Congress, whereas another may work for opposing policies by attempting to influence an executive department. Although the wide range of opportunities for influence makes it possible for many groups to work in the political arena, however, opposing groups can also find access.

A more centralized political system, such as Great Britain's, offers fewer points of access, but the groups that are fortunate enough to "get inside" can expect to have great influence. Thus, decentralized political systems tend to have more numerous and more visible interest groups, whereas centralized systems afford great power to those few interest groups that secure effective linkages.

THE POWER OF INTEREST GROUPS

Why Are Some Groups More Powerful Than Others?

Interest groups operating in the same society are usually subject to the same laws and have access to the same media for communicating with citizens and officials. But it becomes clear on a moment's reflection that some groups are much more powerful than others. Most U.S. politicians safely ignore the Women's Christian Temperance Union, for example, but few British leaders ignore the British Trades Union Congress, and no U.S. senator or representative takes the National Rifle Association or the American Association of Retired Persons lightly. Several factors determine how much power and influence a given interest group enjoys.

Size   All other things being equal, groups with large memberships are more influential than groups with small memberships. A group that officially speaks for a large number of people can influence close elections, and elected officials will therefore listen to the leaders of such groups. A large membership also suggests broad public acceptance for the group's ideas, since there are usually several non-joining supporters for every supportive person who actually belongs to the group. A large size also means that the group has a huge supply of "soldiers" for its work. Letter-writing campaigns, contributions to candidates running for office, and even demonstrations are all more powerful forms of influence when the group can call on many members.

While size is an important factor, other characteristics may more than offset a given group's advantage or disadvantage with respect to size.

Unity   Even large groups can lose much of their effectiveness if their members are divided. A governmental official who wants to be sympathetic to a particular cause or interest may find that a decision demanded by one segment of the group is opposed by another. The safe response is to do nothing. Hence, division within an interest group (or among organizations representing similar interests) leads to a reduction in effective influence.

Groups that can present a united front when pressing their claims are in a much better position. This point was made by a scholar of British politics in a comparison of the power of teachers and doctors. British teachers are represented by a divided array of bickering organizations, whereas doctors have the well-established, cohesive British Medical Association. Although there are more teachers than doctors, government officials regularly consult the B.M.A., whereas teachers' organizations are largely ignored.[9]

Leadership   Effective leaders make a difference. Good leaders persuade the public, communicate effectively with elected officials, generate membership, and hold an organization together. Given the same resources, a group will have less success with a poor leader. This point is frequently made in discussions of the civil rights movement in the United States. During the period in which Dr. Martin Luther King, Jr., led the most important civil rights interest groups, the movement was remarkably successful; but, since his death, even with more members and more money, these groups have had less success. Many suggest that without King's leadership, civil rights groups lost both their unity and much of their capacity to generate support among the general public.

Social Status   A general perception of integrity, professionalism, or prestige is helpful to an interest group. In the United States, the American Bar Association (ABA) is only moderately large (over 400,000 members in 2006) but it has a substantial reservoir of support by virtue of the prestige of the legal profession (despite all of those lawyer jokes).

Hence, when a president nominates a person to a federal judgeship or to fill a vacancy on the Supreme Court, the ABA's rating of that individual is a prominent factor in his or her evaluation by the public, and usually by senators. The ABA is also consulted on many legislative proposals, indicating that elected officials care about the group's opinions and that they are willing to let the public know it. In many Latin American nations, the government has given professional associations of architects, lawyers, and the like the authority to determine who may legally practice the profession. In contrast, the U.S. Used Car Dealers Association does not have much social status, and it has less power as a result (although it often has significant power with respect to state and local policy decisions).

TABLE 6.1   U.S. Citizens Like Some Interest Groups More Than Others

	Percentage Stating that Group is Most Liked	Percentage Stating that Group Is Least Liked	Net Likeability
Environmentalists	24.3	4.4	19.9
Pro-life groups	20.8	4.2	16.6
Pro-choice groups	11.0	4.0	7.0
Labor unions	13.0	6.7	6.3
Nat'l Rifle Association	13.9	14.7	−0.8
Trial lawyers	1.4	11.1	−9.7
Tobacco lobby	1.9	18.3	−16.4
Gay rights groups	1.2	23.0	−21.8

Source: Taken from J. Tobin Grant and Thomas J. Rudolph, "Value Conflict, Group Affect, and the Issue of Campaign Finance," *American Journal of Political Science* 47 (July 2003): 458.

Table 6.1 indicates the rather substantial differences among U.S. interest groups with respect to their reputations among the public. The first column lists the percentage of survey respondents that named that group as their "most liked" interest group, while the second column lists the percentage of survey respondents that named that group as their "least liked" interest group. The third column simply subtracts the "least-liked" percentage from the "most-liked" percentage, thus producing a net "likeability" score. As the data show, interest groups vary tremendously in "likeability," and this factor often makes a big difference in interest group influence.

Wealth   Wealth can contribute to a group's influence in several ways. An interest group with a large treasury, such as the AFL-CIO, can purchase airtime to broadcast "educational" statements and influence public opinion. Wealth can also facilitate access. A wealthy organization can purchase expensive legal services that enhance its participation in government decision making. Wealth does not always produce power for interest groups, but it helps.

Strategic Economic Location   A business group or a labor union may also gain political influence through its control over an important economic resource or its ability to disrupt a vital economic activity. In economies heavily dependent on the export of a small number of crops or minerals, business groups that control those resources (Salvadoran coffee growers or South African diamond-mining corporations, for example) carry considerable political weight in many aspects of a nation's political life. Unions often have substantial influence when they can threaten to disrupt important segments of the economy. During the 1970s, the British coal miners' union wielded great power because of its ability to shut down a vital source of energy. In Peru, the bank workers exercised power far in excess of their numbers by demonstrating their ability to cripple the nation's economy with an extended bank strike.

Geographic Concentration   Some interest groups—such as medical and teacher associations—have members located throughout a political system, whereas others have memberships largely concentrated in a particular area or areas. Geographic dispersion often makes a significant difference with respect to political strength and influence. Groups with members in virtually all areas of the country can work effectively at the national level because they are able to make claims on representatives from virtually all legislative or parliamentary districts. Their influence may be small in any given district, but it is difficult for government to ignore an interest that can generate votes in every area of the country.

In contrast, some interests are geographically concentrated. French wine growers, for example, are primarily found in a few regions. Consumers in the United States are poorly organized compared with the strong union representing the interests of autoworkers, but consumers are obviously spread throughout the country. Thus, when a proposal to protect autoworkers' jobs by restricting imports is considered, the workers often lose. Members of Congress from a few states (including Michigan, Ohio, Wisconsin, and Tennessee) press for such proposals, but most representatives are likely to consider the damage they would do to consumers, since consumers' concerns are present in all districts.

Do Interest Groups Control the System?

One of the most widely recognized images in political science is the "iron triangle." The term is an effort to depict a close relationship among a legislative committee, an administrative agency, and an interest group in a particular policy area (e.g., agriculture, defense procurement).* According to this idea, a group, a committee, and an agency working together develop a powerful and mutually beneficial relationship. Administrators want budget increases from the legislative committees; representatives on those committees want electoral and campaign finance support from the interest groups; and the interest groups want policies favorable to them. Each part of the "triangle" has a strong interest in pleasing the others. Since virtually all important areas of public policy will have their own "iron triangles," and since each one wants to have as much independent power as possible, legislators and administrators in a given "triangle" tend to leave other "triangles" alone to make their own decisions, a favor that they expect will be repaid in kind.[10]

The crucial feature of the "iron triangle" idea is that *policy decisions are dominated by relatively autonomous sets of governmental officials and interest groups, leaving very little role for broader public interests.* This perspective is therefore usually part of a rather negative view of the impact and role of interest groups in the policy process.

A U.S. Supreme Court decision from the 1980s provided a striking illustration of how strong, and how exclusive, the relationships in an "iron triangle" can be. In *Block v. Community Nutrition Institute* (464 U.S. 340, 1984), a group representing the interests of low-income consumers of dairy products tried to get the U.S. Agriculture Department to reconsider one of its rulings, one that would raise the cost of milk. The Court referred to the original arrangement set in place by Congress during the 1930s

---

* Other names for "iron triangles" include "policy whirlpools," "subgovernments," and "triple alliances." Perhaps the first work to use the idea was Ernest Griffith's *Impasse of Democracy* (New York: Harrison-Hilton, 1939). Another often-cited work is J. Leiper Freeman, *The Political Process* (New York: Random House, 1965).

and denied standing to the community group. Justice Sandra Day O'Connor's statement in the majority opinion was remarkable in its frankness:

> [The intent of Congress was to] limit the classes entitled to participate in the development of [milk] market orders. The Act contemplates a cooperative venture among the Secretary, handlers, and producers the principal purposes of which are to raise the price of agricultural products. . . . Nowhere in the Act, however, is there an express provision for participation by consumers in any proceeding (at p. 346).

Advocates of the "iron triangle" concept could never hope to find a more perfect example to make their point. Agricultural policy clearly affects every citizen in one way or another, but Congress had established a "cooperative venture" among dairy producers and the Agriculture Department (overseen by Congressional committees) to make decisions. Consumer interests were not only disregarded—they were authoritatively *excluded* from the process. This is the fundamental reason that "iron triangles" have long been a target of criticism.

Although the idea was a leading political science concept for many years, analysts have recently argued that the "iron triangle" is too simple or perhaps outdated in most policy areas. As discussed in the next section, there has been an explosion in the growth of interest groups, especially "public interest" groups advocating broader interests. As these groups have expanded their power, they have increasingly sought to influence the government officials who previously worked only with the long-time members of the various triangles. These new groups are not always successful, of course (as in the Agriculture Department case), but they have often succeeded in breaking down the exclusive control enjoyed by some groups in earlier decades.

As a result, some political scientists began discussing "issue networks" instead of "iron triangles." The idea is that, though there still may be some relatively stable relationships among interest groups, legislative committees, and administrative agencies in some policy areas, influence is much more fluid, open, and unpredictable than is implied by the "iron triangle" concept. As new groups enter the system, it becomes difficult for any group to dominate public policy in its area of interest, and thus, the "iron triangle" image is less prominent among political scientists as it was in the 1950s.[11] (See Figure 6.1.)

Moreover, some political scientists argue that a close relationship between interest groups and government agencies is not a negative thing at all. In 2004, two researchers studied the impact of interest group influence in 18 developed nations, focusing on the extent to which each country adopted "active labor market policies." These policies are an array of government efforts to help unemployed workers find secure jobs by providing training, subsidized jobs, and unemployment benefits. Although virtually all countries have programs to help the unemployed, there is substantial variation in their quality and effectiveness. According to this study, such policies are more comprehensive in countries in which employer interests are more coordinated in strong interest organizations, and where those organizations are closely integrated into the public policy making process.[12]

The question of interest group control of the political system is thus particularly difficult to resolve. Interest group influence sometimes produces policies opposed by a majority of a nation's citizens, but sometimes that influence is closely allied with the demands of popular movements. In some cases, interest groups form highly exclusive relationships with government bureaus and legislative committees, working to advance their interests in effective "iron triangles," while in other cases they follow an open strategy of

FIGURE 6.1   IRON TRIANGLES AND ISSUE NETWORKS

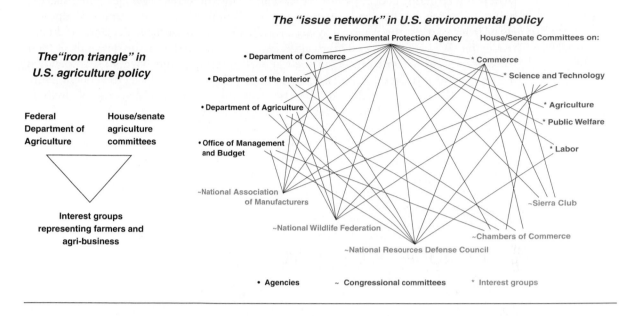

The "iron triangle" in U.S. agriculture policy

Federal Department of Agriculture

House/senate agriculture committees

Interest groups representing farmers and agri-business

The "issue network" in U.S. environmental policy

• Environmental Protection Agency

House/Senate Committees on:

• Department of Commerce

• Department of the Interior

• Department of Agriculture

• Office of Management and Budget

~National Association of Manufacturers

~National Wildlife Federation

~National Resources Defense Council

* Commerce

* Science and Technology

* Agriculture

* Public Welfare

* Labor

~Sierra Club

~Chambers of Commerce

• Agencies   ~ Congressional committees   * Interest groups

mobilizing public opinion. Perhaps the best answer is that the extent to which interest groups control the policy process depends on many factors, including the nature of the system, the visibility of the issue at hand, and the activities of other interest groups.

THE GROWTH OF INTEREST GROUPS

Why have interest groups proliferated in industrial democracies? First, forming an effective organization with dues-paying members and political effectiveness simply takes time. The American labor movement, for example, failed to establish viable organizations for decades, finally succeeding on a grand scale many years after the worst industrial abuses had ended. So, we should expect a steady increase in the number of a nation's interest groups simply because, over time, more will overcome the barriers to organization. Second, a wealthier society can support a larger number of interest groups. When a society becomes affluent, more people have discretionary income, and some people use it to support organizations that pursue causes they care about. The organizations established to protect animal rights, for example, could only have been established in an affluent period; in poorer times, such concerns were secondary for nearly all citizens. Third, people in many countries are increasingly dissatisfied with political parties. As noted in Chapters 4 and 5, political parties seem to be losing support in several nations. As the politics of the abortion issue illustrates, millions of Americans are willing to vote for candidates of either party, as long as the candidate adopts a position on that single issue that is in line with their group's perspective. As political support and energy are directed away from political parties, interest groups become the focal point for political concerns.

The growth of interest groups has worried political scientists for generations.[13] When government decisions are increasingly influenced by organized interests, the ballot box arguably becomes less important. Moreover, as interest groups sap power away from parties, the political system is subject to more difficult demands and controversies. Whereas parties tend to aggregate and then moderate the demands of their supporters in an effort to broaden their appeal, interest groups have no such concern for moderation. In fact, taking extreme positions is often a good way to generate more members. But it is more difficult for the system to respond to an array of divisive, single-minded groups than to a few moderate parties.

Nevertheless, it is also possible to view the growth in the number of interest groups favorably. The proliferation of groups may indicate that more people find political activity and involvement useful and that they have a reasonable expectation that, if they organize properly, the system will listen to them. Without interest groups, many demands go unheard and unheeded, producing unrest that will eventually threaten political order.

How Interest Groups Are Formed

Ironically, to evaluate the ultimate effect of the proliferation of interest groups, we must take a step backward and consider how interest groups *form*. The representativeness of the interest group system is largely a matter of which groups actually become effectively organized and which ones do not, so understanding the formation of interest groups is essential if we are to appreciate the effects of interest groups in the political system.

The Pluralist View

Pluralism is one of the most widely discussed concepts in the study of modern democracies. Its core idea is simple: Pluralists believe that society has not one or two but *many* centers of power. In contrast to Marxism, which sees all political conflict as a struggle between capitalists and workers, pluralists argue that many interests exert influence in a political system and that public policy decisions thus incorporate most of those interests' demands and concerns. The pluralist model is also often used to distinguish industrial democracies from totalitarian societies—Nazi Germany, Maoist China, Iraq under Saddam Hussein—in which political power is highly concentrated and independent interest group or party activity is negligible. David Truman's classic, *The Governmental Process*, remains a foundational work stating the case for pluralism.[14]

Although pluralism is primarily a perspective on how group power is distributed, it also contains an argument regarding interest group *formation*. If political power is divided among a diverse array of interest groups, it must be true that interests naturally and easily become organized. Pluralists argue that virtually any interest can become an effective organized force. Thus, *pluralists claim that whenever a significant number of persons share an objective, they will inevitably organize themselves.* This is the pluralists' answer to the question of how groups form.

The pluralists' straightforward and convincing perspective on interest group formation suggests an optimistic answer to many of the questions raised by the proliferation of interest groups. If virtually every interest in society is represented by effective organizations, then we can be confident that the *array of political organizations* operating in politics at any given time is reasonably representative of the *array of interests in society*. Even if organized group power influences governmental decisions, the system is still fair and balanced, because virtually all interests are effectively represented by organizations, and the largest interests produce the most powerful organizations.

The Elitist View

A very different interpretation has been offered by those who embrace **elite theory**. Instead of an open competition among a wide range of interests, elite theorists see a closed system controlled by a few. They assert that if pluralists were correct about the ability of people with shared interests to form effective organizations, the interests of the poor and racial minorities would have been more effectively advanced than they have been in virtually all developed democracies. Persistent social inequality confirms the weakness of the pluralist vision. *Real* political power is almost entirely in the hands of a **power elite** that represents the interests of only its members, leaving the rest of society and especially the poor relatively powerless.[15]

Elite theory is primarily about how political power is distributed throughout society, but, like pluralism, it derives many of its conclusions from a view of how groups form. Elite theorists accept the premise that everyone has a *legal right* to form organizations, but they insist that a relatively small range of groups actually succeed in getting a stranglehold on the primary centers of political power. In order for an interest to form an organization that will have any real impact, it must adapt itself to be compatible with the elite establishment.

Proponents of elite theory point out that leaders of the largest corporations, the most powerful political officials, and the critically important masters of military institutions all represent a narrow, elite segment of society. Most of these individuals are white males who went to the same schools, belong to the same country clubs, and associate in the same social circles. Far from representing a plurality of interests and perspectives, they are "peas in a pod," supporting essentially the same policies and programs. In short, they share political interests in governmental decisions that preserve the power of the dominant "corporate culture." Thus, instead of seeing government as steered by a plurality of diverse, competing interests, elite theorists contend that the system is dominated either by a single, all-powerful elite class or by a limited number of closely cooperating elites. Groups that exist outside the sphere of the power elite may exert influence over relatively unimportant issues, but the basic direction of social policy is firmly under the control of a narrow range of rather homogeneous interests.

Elite theory leads to a pessimistic interpretation of interest group power in society. As long as elite organizations exert power, society is not very democratic. Elite theorists claim that having the right to vote makes little difference when government action is largely determined by an unrepresentative, essentially closed set of interests. Taken to its logical conclusion, elite theory usually leads to recommendations for radical changes in the nature of society itself, usually by limiting the power of private property. (See Box 6-4.)

The Rational Choice View

Until the mid-1960s, virtually all political scientists adopted either the pluralist or the power elite perspective on interest groups. In 1965, however, a radically different idea was advanced by an economist. In *The Logic of Collective Action*, Mancur Olson, Jr.,

Box 6-4

POLITICAL SCIENCE RESEARCH AND PLURALISM AND ELITE THEORY

Logical arguments and scores of examples can be used to support *both* the pluralist and the elite interpretations of how interest groups are formed and of how power is consequently distributed in society. Elitists can point out that the poor and homeless still inhabit most large cities in developed nations and that their conditions have persisted for generations after pluralists assured us that all interests can be effectively represented by interest groups. In contrast, pluralists note that such organizations as the National Association for the Advancement of Colored People, the Sierra Club, and Mothers Against Drunk Driving are effective interest groups that certainly exist outside the power elite. Which side is right?

The research that has been done to answer this question presents a wonderful illustration of how the scholar's desire to support a conclusion can affect the research process. Robert Dahl, an important advocate of the pluralist perspective in the 1950s, analyzed the political conflicts and movements in a Connecticut city (New Haven) in an effort to determine whether the pluralist idea was valid. Dahl looked at the public policy controversies decided by city hall, considered who were the winners and losers on several decisions, and concluded that some interests win on some issues but later lose on others. This result supported pluralism, he argued, because it proved that no single power elite consistently controlled the government. A *plurality* of groups was engaged in meaningful competition, and no single segment of society had all the effective influence.[16]

In contrast, advocates of elite theory would sometimes "test" their idea by going into a city to ask knowledgeable people, "Who runs things around here?" If the answers from different people included the same names, the researchers would conclude that elite theory is correct. "This is what we expected: Virtually everyone in this town lists the same persons and organizations when asked to identify where the power is. We were right!" Both pluralists and elite theorists were criticized for letting their preconceived notions influence the ways they

designed their research projects. Critics of the pluralists argued that insufficient weight was given to the power of an elite group if the researcher considered only who wins and who loses on issues debated in city hall. The *real* power of the elite could be its ability to keep the truly important questions from even reaching the decision-making arena in the first place.

Since pluralists studied only the decisions made in governmental institutions, they "saw" a world in which power shifted from one interest to another. Elite theorists contend that a positive conclusion was inevitable, given the researchers' approach. Nevertheless, if a powerful elite used its muscle to prevent important issues from reaching the agenda (for example, a major income-redistribution proposal), Dahl would not have seen evidence of that power, thus allowing him to "prove" pluralism. In short, by neglecting **nondecisions**, research proving pluralism was flawed.

Elite theorists have also been criticized. Asking people, "Who runs things around here?" implies that *someone* really is "running things." Posing such a question will certainly get answers, and we should not be surprised that many answers will contain several of the names most familiar to people in the community. Instead of "proving" elite theory, such a result may simply reflect common misperceptions or may merely reflect which personalities make the local equivalent of *People* magazine.

The debate over how interest group power is created and distributed is far from settled. It has become, if anything, more complex and uncertain in the decades since the original lines were drawn. On the one hand, in the United States and in other developed democratic nations, there are more interest groups than ever, as noted earlier, lending possible support to the pluralist way of thinking. On the other hand, social and economic equality seems as far away as ever, a point emphasized by those who claim that a power elite is firmly in control.[18]

reached a startling conclusion: "Rational, self-interested individuals will not act to achieve their common or group interests."[17] This idea rejected *both* pluralism and elitism. It undermined the pluralist faith that people sharing a common interest would automatically form interest groups to pursue common goals, and it undermined the elitist assumption that members of the power elite would work for *their* common interests in ruling society. Olson's idea of **rational choice** infuriated everyone and seemed totally illogical. How could such a claim be made?

Olson's logic is best set out by way of a concrete example. Imagine that a person comes to your door to solicit funds for an interest group called the Citizens' Utility Board (CUB). He explains that CUB will lobby the state Public Service Commission to reduce rates for electricity and natural gas—rates that you agree are too high. He further explains that CUB is working to support a new pricing policy that, if adopted, will save all consumers $350 per year in utility bills. He asks you for a $25 contribution. What do you do?

Pluralists would predict that CUB will succeed in getting new members and contributions if many people are strongly concerned about utility bills. People will see that they have a common interest and will band together to pursue it. That is why the pluralists can be so optimistic about interest groups in general: If an interest is shared by a significant number of citizens, a political organization will pop up somewhere to pursue it. As a result, all important interests will be effectively represented, and the system is therefore healthy and fair.

Elitists would say that the CUB would fail because powerful elite forces will obstruct its formation and exclude it from effective access to the political system.

Olson claimed that both pluralists and elitists miss the fundamental point. Drawing from micro-economics, Olson began by considering what a rational, self-interested person would do when asked to join the group. The man at the door is asking for $25 to help CUB achieve an objective that, if successful, will save each consumer $350 per year. Before contributing, the economically rational individual would ask two questions. First, "Will I get the benefit of the lower utility rates that CUB is working for if you are successful, even if I refuse to help you?" The man at the door will reluctantly admit that noncontributing consumers will pay the same low rates as group supporters.

That leads the rational person to ask a second question: "What difference will *my* $25 make in the lobbying effort?" In response, the man would probably get a bit emotional and claim that "every little bit makes a difference," or words to that effect. But a moment's reflection convinces the rational decision maker that the chances are vanishingly small that a *single* $25 contribution will somehow make the critical difference between success or failure in lobbying the Public Service Commission.

The rational person will thus refuse to help CUB. If the individual makes the contribution, his or her money is certainly gone; yet, there is virtually no chance that giving the money will change utility rates. Since everyone sees the same dismal facts, the solicitor will have a very long day.

Olson emphasizes that this result will occur *even when every person contacted by the man would desperately like the group to achieve its goal.* Even when citizens want the group to succeed, it is in the *individual* interests of potential contributors to keep their money. The rational person thus becomes a **free-rider** on the efforts (if any) of others, and we reach the conclusion that groups cannot form by simply leading people to see their shared interests.[19]

Real-world examples support the rational choice idea. Consider the payment of union dues. If the pluralists were right, we would expect that unions could thrive on voluntary contributions. But unions have to force members to pay. Olson would point out that most union members strongly support the benefits, working conditions, and wages sought by the union, but each member's individual interest is in getting those advantages *while still keeping their money*. Hence, unions must arrange for forced, automatic deductions from paychecks and closed-shop laws to obtain contributions.

As a result, some 90 percent of the auto workers in this country contribute to the collective efforts of the United Auto Workers Union. In contrast, organizations such as the Sierra Club—lacking any way to force supporters of wilderness preservation to contribute funds—exist with contributions from far fewer than 1 percent of environmentally concerned American citizens. Even while acknowledging the importance of the Sierra Club's work, most people who are concerned about wilderness preservation (at least 99 percent of them) have refused to contribute to any environmental group, just as Olson would have predicted.

Olson's idea carries important implications. If interest groups do not form naturally whenever a common interest is shared, and if the size (and strength) of the groups that do exist is not proportional to the magnitude of the interests in society, we cannot reach the happy pluralist conclusion that the array of interest groups working in the system is balanced and representative. Some interests have special advantages, such as labor unions with the ability to deny a union card to anyone refusing to contribute to collective efforts. Other groups have the power to deny contracts and licenses to those who would "let George do it." Those interests form highly influential organizations, even though they may be shared by a relatively small number of citizens. However, people who only share an interest are not so easily organized. The rational choice idea thus suggests a very pessimistic conclusion: Many important interests will not be represented by effective political organizations, and those that are will unbalance the political system in their favor.

Social Movement Theory

Largely in response to the rational choice approach, some social scientists have developed *social movement theory*, which argues that the rational choice perspective is too limited and too narrow in its view of human motivations. Instead of seeing people as soulless "maximizers of utility," advocates of social movement theory emphasize that people may decide to join a political organization because they identify with the social movement it represents. For example, a low-income citizen may be drawn to interest groups that speak for a movement to help the poor; instead of calculating the costs and benefits to himself or herself, the individual will be moved by an emotional identification with the larger movement, and that will often generate contributions. Thus, social movement theory leads to conclusions much closer to those of pluralism than to those drawn from the rational choice perspective; it contends that like-minded people will act collectively, even when a purely *individual* assessment of interests would suggest that one should be a free-rider.[20]

An important illustration of the potential power of social movements is the transnational movement to force governments and international organizations to address the problem of gender violence. One researcher has considered this movement, exploring the organizational power unleashed when people who were otherwise partly divided by race, social status, education, and other factors found themselves sharing the same perspective. When such divisions separate activists, the power of their movement declines, but when an issue emerges that highlights their shared identity, solidarity and policy influence increases. The study of social movements reveals that, at least in some situations, interest group activity is not entirely a matter of rational choices by self-interested individuals.[21]

A Mixed View

Many contemporary political scientists see validity in all four perspectives on the role of interest groups in industrial democracies. Jack Walker, for example, published the results of an extensive study of U.S. interest groups, concluding that there are many different paths to group formation and power. Some form as pluralists would expect, although they are often helped by wealthy benefactors who make major contributions to get groups started.[22] Most political scientists would admit, however, that traditional pluralists are overly optimistic in their expectation that virtually all interests will be represented by an effective organization. Following the elite theorists, it is widely accepted that some groups are more powerful than others and that the most powerful are typically groups pursuing the interests of the large corporations and other members of elite parts of society. Social movement theorists claim that their idea is supported by the numerous and often influential political organizations that gain members by drawing on the power of identification with social movements. Finally, advocates of rational choice thinking point to the fact that groups with the ability to force members to contribute are much more powerful than are interests of the same size that lack this ability.

Each of these interpretations may apply more to some political systems and less to others. A recent study of interest group formation in Russia concluded that citizens are more likely to act in ways that Olson would consider irrational and join social movements when they see a specific person or institution to "blame" for their problems. Where there is no specific attribution of blame, citizens are more likely to suffer in unorganized masses.[23] Our previous discussion suggested that in developing nations (whose populations are less educated, poorly organized, and less politicized), economic wealth or political power or both are often concentrated in a small segment of society. Thus, in these countries, elite theory may be an accurate tool for describing the political power of a small array of interests that exercise a near monopoly of economic and political power. In many African nations, a small Westernized middle class often constitutes a bureaucratic elite that controls the levers of political power.

CONCLUSION: INTEREST GROUPS— A CHALLENGE FOR DEMOCRACY?

However interest groups are ultimately evaluated, it is clear that we cannot begin to understand how government works unless we appreciate their power. The growth of a modern society unleashes a wide range of competing interests, as new industries are developed and as people increasingly begin to affect the lives of others. One way or another, interest groups will form to advance many of these competing interests.

How well the society manages those interests while maintaining some degree of democracy and fairness is one measure of the health of a modern political system. For those reasons, many political scientists feel that the best way to secure a healthy democratic government in the age of interest groups is with strong political parties, as discussed in Chapter 5.

🌐 Where on the Web?

The following World Wide Web addresses are a representative sampling of interest group home pages. Many more groups have a presence on the Web, but here are some of the more interesting Web sites.

http://www.aarp.org

The American Association of Retired Persons is a highly influential interest group advocating policies designed to "shape and enrich the experience of aging."

http://www.smallpropertyowner.com

The American Association of Small Property Owners is committed to legislation and litigation favoring small landlords, property owners, and real estate investors.

http://www.csuchico.edu/~kcfount/index.html

California State University at Chico maintains an excellent list of interest groups, organized by subject matter.

http://www.sec.org.sg

The Singapore Environment Council is an interest group in Singapore dedicated to global environmental concerns.

http://www.ibfan.org/

The International Baby Food Action Network is dedicated to "reducing infant and young children morbidity and mortality."

http://www.commoncause.org

Common Cause is a U.S. interest group focusing on ethical campaigning in the electoral system.

http://www.claremont.org

Claremont is an organization dedicated to "restoring the principles of the American Founding to their rightful, pre-eminent authority."

http://www.moveon.org/

With over 3 million members, Moveon.org claims to "bring real Americans back to the political process." It supports leftist and mostly Democratic Party campaigns and causes in the U.S.

http://progressforamerica.org/

This is the home page for "Progress for America," a conservative interest group in the U.S.

◆ ◆ ◆

Key Terms and Concepts_____

elite theory
free-rider
interest group
lobbying

nondecisions
pluralism
power elite
rational choice

Discussion Questions_____

1. How do political parties and interest groups compare as methods for representing and articulating citizens' interests?
2. Compare the different approaches to understanding how interest groups form. Which is the most valid, and why?

3. The most dramatic change in the politics of interest groups during the last 30 years or so has been the rise of so-called citizen groups or public interest groups. Is the emergence of these groups a good or a bad thing?

4. Compare elitism and pluralism as perspectives on the distribution of organized power. Which theory is more persuasive?

Notes_____

1. Daowei Zhang and David Laband, "From Senators to the President: Solve the Lumber Problem or Else," *Public Choice* 123 (2005): 393–410.

2. A study by an economist at Washington State University concluded that the tariff produced about 100 jobs for the state of Washington, although it led to a slight *decrease* in that state's gross domestic product. See David Holland, "Tariffs on Canadian Lumber Affect Washington State," Washington State E-Newsletter, 2005, http://impact.typepad.com/articles/barriers_to_trade/index.html. As of this writing, the tariff on Canadian lumber remains unsettled, with contradictory rulings by the World Trade Organization and the NAFTA Extraordinary Challenge Committee.

3. Information obtained from the National Rifle Association's Political Victory Fund Web site, http://www.nrapvf.org/About/Default.aspx.

4. Joseph LaPalombara, *Interest Groups in Italian Politics* (Princeton, NJ: Princeton University Press, 1964).

5. See Frank Baumgartner, "Public Interest Groups in France and the United States," *Governance* 9 (January) 1996: 1–22.

6. Richard C. Cortner, "Strategies and Tactics of Litigants in Constitutional Cases," *Journal of Public Law* 17 (1968): 287–307.

7. See Susan M. Olson, "Interest Group Litigation in Federal District Court: Beyond the Political Disadvantage Theory," *Journal of Politics* 52 (August 1990): 854–882; and Kim Scheppele and Jack L. Walker, Jr., "The Litigation Strategies of Interest Groups," in *Mobilizing Interest Groups in America: Patrons, Professions, and Social Movements*, ed. Jack L. Walker, Ann Arbor, MI: University of Michigan Press, 1991, pp. 157–183.

8. Cary Coglianese, "Legal Change at the Crossroads: Revisiting the Political Disadvantage Theory," John F. Kennedy School of Government, Harvard University, Working Paper, n.d., http://www.ksg.harvard.edu/prg/cary/legal.htm.

9. See R. M. Punnett, *British Government and Politics*, 5th ed. (Chicago: Dorsey, 1988).

10. See Jeffrey Berry and Clyde Wilcox, *The Interest Group Society*, 4th ed. (New York: Longman, 2007), chap. 9, for a good overview.

11. The first use of the term *issue networks* is attributed to Hugh Heclo, "Issue Networks and the Executive Establishment," in *The New American Political System*, ed. Anthony S. King (Washington, DC: American Enterprise Institute, 1978), pp. 87–124. Also see John P. Heinz, Edward Laumann, Robert Nelson, and Robert Salisbury, *The Hollow Core* (Cambridge: Harvard University Press, 1993).

12. Cathie Jo Martin and Duane Swank, "Does the Organization of Capital Matter? Employers and Active Labor Market Policy at the National and Firm Levels," *American Political Science Review* 98 (November 2004): 593–611.

13. For example, see E.E. Schattschneider, *The Semi-Sovereign People* (New York: Holt, Rinehart, and Winston, 1960).

14. David Truman, *The Governmental Process* (New York: Knopf, 1956).

15. See C. Wright Mills, *The Power Elite* (New York: Oxford University Press, 1956).

16. See Robert A. Dahl, *Who Governs?* (New Haven: Yale University Press, 1961).

17. See Mancur Olson, Jr., *The Logic of Collective Action* (Cambridge: Harvard University Press, 1965), for an accessible statement of this revolutionary idea.

18. For a more detailed, and controversial, discussion of this problem, see John Manley, "Neo Pluralism: A Class Analysis of Pluralism I and Pluralism II," *American Political Science Review* 77 (1983): 368–383; and the responses by Robert Dahl and Charles Lindblom (384–389). The text discussion follows closely the argument by Peter Bachrach and Morton S. Baratz in "Two Faces of Power," *American Political Science Review* 56 (1962): 947–952.
19. Olson, *The Logic of Collective Action*, chap.1.
20. For a good survey of this perspective, see Jeff Goodwin and James M. Jasper, eds., *The Social Movement Reader: Cases and Concepts* (Malden, MA: Blackwell, 2003).
21. See S. Laurel Weldon, "Inclusion, Solidarity, and Social Movements: The Global Movement Against Gender Violence," *Perspectives on Politics* 4 (March 2006): 55–74.
22. Jack L. Walker, Jr., "The Origins and Maintenance of Interest Groups in America," in *Mobilizing Interest Groups in America: Patrons, Professions, and Social Movements*, ed. Jack L. Walker (Ann Arbor, MI: University of Michigan Press, 1991), pp. 19–40. Walker and David C. King presented the results of a survey attempting to determine the benefits provided by different kinds of groups in "The Provision of Benefits by Interest Groups in the United States," *Journal of Politics* 54 (May 1992): 394–426. This later study helped to demonstrate that no single theory applies to all important organized interests.
23. Debra Javeline, "The Role of Blame in Collective Action: Evidence from Russia," *American Political Science Review* 97 (February 2003): 107–121.

For Further Reading _____

Ainsworth, Scott H. *Analyzing Interest Groups: Group Influence on People and Policies* New York: Norton, 2002.

Balla, Steven J., and John R. Wright. "Interest Groups, Advisory Committees, and Congressional Control of the Bureaucracy." *America Journal of Political Science* 45 (October 2001): 799–812.

Baumgartner, Frank R., and Beth L. Leech. *Basic Interests*. Princeton, NJ: Princeton University Press, 1998.

Berry, Jeffrey. *The New Liberalism: The Rising Power of Citizen Groups*. Washington, DC: Brookings, 1999.

Boehmke, Frederick J. *The Indirect Effect of Direct Legislation: How Institutions Shape Interest Group Systems*. Columbus, OH: Ohio University Press, 2005.

Cigler, Allan J., and Burdett A. Loomis. *Interest Group Politics*, 6th ed. Washington, DC: CQ Press, 2002.

Finkel, Steven E., and Edward N. Muller. "Rational Choice and the Dynamics of Collective Political Action: Evaluating Alternative Models with Panel Data." *American Political Science Review* (March 1998): 37–49.

Grossman, Gene M., and Elhanan Helpman, *Special Interest Politics*. Cambridge, MA: MIT University Press, 2002.

Heaney, Michael T. "Outside the Issue Niche: The Multidimensionality of Interest Group Identity." *American Politics Research* 32 (2004): 611–651.

Heinz, John P., Edward Laumann, Robert Nelson, and Robert Salisbury. *The Hollow Core*. Cambridge: Harvard University Press, 1993.

Herrnson, Paul S., Rondald G. Shaiko, and Clyde Wilcox. *The Interest Group Connection: Electioneering, Lobbying, and Policymaking in Washington*, 2nd ed. Washington, DC: CQ Press, 2005.

Javeline, Debra. "The Role of Blame in Collective Action: Evidence from Russia," *American Political Science Review* 97 (February 2003): 107–121.

Kelly, Christine A. *Tangled Up in Red, White, and Blue: New Social Movements in America*. Lanham, MD: Rowman and Littlefield, 2001.

Lijphart, A. "The Puzzle of Indian Democracy: A Consociational Interpretation." *American Political Science Review* (June 1996): 258–268.

Lohmann, Susanne. "Representative Government and Special Interest Politics: (We Have Met the Enemy and He Is Us)." *Journal of Theoretical Politics* 15 (2003): 299–319.

Lowery, David, and Holly Brasher. *Organized Interests and American Government.* New York: McGraw-Hill, 2004.

Martin, Cathie Jo, and Duane Swank. "Does the Organization of Capital Matter? Employers and Active Labor Market Policy at the National and Firm Levels," *American Political Science Review* 98 (November 2004): 593–611.

Mills, C. Wright. *The Power Elite.* New York: Oxford University Press, 1956.

Morris, Aldon, and Carol McClurg Mueller. *Frontiers in Social Movement Theory.* New Haven: Yale University Press, 1992.

Olson, Mancur. *The Logic of Collective Action.* Cambridge: Harvard University Press, 1965.

———. *The Rise and Decline of Nations.* New Haven: Yale University Press, 1982.

Sheingate, Adam D. *The Rise of the Agricultural Welfare State.* Princeton, NJ: Princeton University Press, 2001.

Truman, David. *The Governmental Process.* New York: Knopf, 1956.

Walker, Jack L., Jr. *Mobilizing Interest Groups in America.* Ann Arbor: University of Michigan Press, 1991.

Warren, Mark. "What Does Corruption Mean in a Democracy?" *American Journal of Political Science* 48 (2004): 328–343.

Weldon, S. Laurel. "Inclusion, Solidarity, and Social Movements: The Global Movement Against Gender Violence," *Perspectives on Politics* 4 (March 2006): 55–74.

Wilson, James Q. *Political Organizations.* New York: Basic Books, 1973.

Zhang, Daowei, and David Laband, "From Senators to the President: Solve the Lumber Problem or Else," *Public Choice* 123 (2005): 393–410.

PART III

POLITICAL INSTITUTIONS

The primary institutions of government—parliaments, presidencies, courts—are perhaps the first things we think about when we attempt to describe or compare governments around the world. Although the design and workings of these institutions vary dramatically, virtually all political systems have some kind of legislative assembly, an executive institution, a system of courts, and an assortment of bureaucratic agencies. The chapters in Part III describe the essential functions that each of these institutions perform. Although their functions are almost universal, we explore the importance of differences in the *design* of governmental institutions: the impact of having a presidential system (like the U.S. and Chile) instead of a parliamentary system (like Great Britain or Israel); the different roles that courts play in making policy; the problems of controlling state bureaucracies; and the issue of limiting executive power. The structure of a political system's institutions has a tremendous influence on the way governments work and on their prospects for stability and democracy.

PARLIAMENTARY DEBATE   Israel's parliament, the Knesset, debates the expansion of Palestinian self-rule.

7

LEGISLATIVE INSTITUTIONS

◆ Lawmaking ◆ Legislatures: Features, Functions, and Structure ◆ Representation ◆ Party Responsibility and Legislative Behavior ◆ The Changing Role of Modern Legislatures

This country has come to feel the same when Congress is in session as when the baby gets hold of a hammer.

—*Will Rogers*

Folks, there's going to be a leetle mite of trouble back in town. Between me and that Legislature-ful of hyena-headed, feist-faced, belly-dragging sons of slackgutted she-wolves. If you know what I mean. Well, I been looking at them and their kind so long, I just figured I'd take me a little trip and see what human folks looked like in the face before I clean forgot.[1]

—*Governor Willie Stark's description of the state legislature in Robert Penn Warren's novel*
All the King's Men

On May 12, 1780, when the British siege of Charleston, South Carolina, succeeded and the town surrendered, American officers were at first permitted to keep their swords. However, the swords were soon demanded by British commanders who were annoyed by the Americans' defiant shouts of "Long Live Congress!"[2]

—*George Will*

It could probably be shown by facts and figures that there is no distinctly American criminal class except Congress.

—*Mark Twain*

Citizens in most democracies have mixed and sometimes heated opinions about their national legislatures. That is probably inevitable, given the contradictory pressures and expectations that these institutions are subject to. They are burdened with the responsibility to make collective decisions, and yet their membership mirrors divisions in society that often seem impossible to resolve. We want legislators to respond to the preferences of citizens in each district or state, but we also want them to act on the basis of all the pertinent scientific information available, even information that ordinary citizens cannot understand. We want them to help the chief executive make good public policy, but we also expect the legislature to obstruct executives who abuse their power.

Much of the study of legislative institutions is devoted to evaluating their behavior and determining the impact of various reforms and structural changes. In some legislatures, particularly the U.S. Congress, fear of excessive lawmaking power led to severe limits ("checks and balances") on the efficiency of the legislative process. Other legislatures are set up in ways that make them highly responsive to winning-party platforms. In parliamentary systems such as Germany's or Japan's, for example, the winning party or party coalition controls both the parliament (the legislature) and the executive branch and can more readily enact its campaign platform. Thus, the design and the operation of legislative institutions often involve basic political questions.

Are legislators supposed to make decisions in accordance with the wishes of others or as their own judgment dictates? What is the connection between legislative and executive institutions and powers? How are legislatures organized? As we will see, the manner in which these and other issues are resolved tells us a great deal about the workings and the nature of a political system.

LAWMAKING

Societies have been subject to law for millennia, but the establishment of specialized institutions to make law is a fairly recent phenomenon. Actually, there are at least two "premodern" methods of creating laws. First, in many traditional societies, laws were given by a supreme being to a prophet, who then brought them to the political system where they became accepted. Second, classical philosophers identified elements of law emanating from nature itself. This notion of "natural law" is based on the assumption that "Nature endowed all beings with the faculty for preserving themselves, seeking good, and avoiding evil."[3] Thomas Jefferson's memorable opening to the American Declaration of Independence is an explicit statement of natural law: All citizens are "created equal" with "unalienable rights" that no persons or legislative institutions created or can take away. The essential element of both divine and natural law is that certain fundamental laws exist independent of *human* lawmaking (which is often termed *positive law* to distinguish it from natural law) and that these more fundamental laws prevail when laws made by people conflict with them.

A body of law that originates in "discoveries" of divine or natural law may be workable in societies that do not change very much. But even relatively underdeveloped nations are now subject to enormous forces of change created by technology, international trade, and political movements. Governments in modern nations must manage complex economic relationships, provide for the expansion and maintenance of essential infrastructure, and respond to an active array of political demands. Thus, virtually all political systems have established legislative institutions.

LEGISLATURES: FEATURES, FUNCTIONS, AND STRUCTURE

What Are Legislatures?

Although legislative institutions vary widely in size, structure, and powers, they share a few basic features. First, legislatures are *multimembered*. Individual legislators may represent provinces, districts, or even ethnic groups, but a legislature is made up of some (usually large) number of them. Second, the members are *formally equal* (although the members of one house may be more powerful than the members of another in cases where a legislature is divided into different houses). Third, legislatures make their decisions by *counting votes*.[4] The Mexican government's executive branch may sometimes resemble a legislature in that it has many officials working there to make decisions, but everyone other than the president is simply an adviser.

Legislative Functions

The primary function of legislatures is to legislate—that is, to *make laws*.* These laws create new restrictions, new rights, new programs, and new tax provisions, and they can repeal or amend existing laws.

Legislative involvement in lawmaking varies across different systems. In some countries (particularly parliamentary systems, discussed below), legislative lawmaking merely *legitimizes* policy choices made by a prime minister, a central committee, a chancellor, or some other chief executive. The U.S. Congress operates in a presidential system, and has more real influence over basic policy decisions than most national legislatures; the more typical parliamentary system arrangement—in Great Britain or Germany, for example—is for a legislature to affirm decisions made by the executive. That act of affirmation, even when the legislature has little realistic opportunity to affect the choice of alternatives, can be very important to the public's general acceptance of the government's laws.

A recent study of legislative influence in Germany and the Netherlands suggests that, when a parliamentary system is ruled by a coalition of several parties, the legislature can play an important role in resolving tensions between the ruling parties in the coalition. Parties in the legislature form a coalition when they have agreed to some policy compromise, enabling the coalition to form a government. However, sometimes a government department minister may want to take steps that reflect his or her own preferences (or those of a faction within his or her party). In these circumstances, "the legislative process provides another important institutional device that coalition partners use to counteract the influence" of these maverick government officials. The study found that when the parties controlling the government were deeply divided, bills drafted by government ministers were more often changed by legislative decisions.[5] Although it is still common for many legislatures to simply affirm policy choices made by a prime minister, the evidence suggests that the legislative role remains an important influence.

In addition to lawmaking, most legislative institutions perform other functions. In both democratic and nondemocratic systems, legislatures *elect* or *appoint* at least some governmental officers. In most European democracies, the parliament elects the nation's executive-branch leaders, the prime minister and cabinet. In addition, legislatures often act in a *judicial capacity*, hearing charges brought against presidents, judges, and individual legislators.

Most legislatures also have the authority to *investigate* governmental operations. The information gathered may be taken into account in new lawmaking, but sometimes the investigative process itself puts pressure on government officials to change their activities, to alter the way a law has been interpreted, or simply to become more efficient. In the United States, legislative investigations have brought considerable information to the public (for example, by publishing the results of important studies of consumer product safety). The relatively loose party control within the U.S. Congress also means

---

* In the United States and other countries following Anglo-American patterns of jurisprudence, laws made by a legislature are called **statutes**, to distinguish them from the laws made by administrative agencies, court decisions, and executive orders. Laws passed by legislatures designate the purposes for which public monies are to be expended and therefore establish the parameters of public policy. Although laws can be made by people or institutions that do not have the basic features of legislatures—as when a tyrant issues edicts or a bureaucrat promulgates rules and regulations—lawmaking is central to the behavior of most legislatures.

that explosive legislative investigations often enable a legislator to make a name for himself or herself by exploiting the resulting media attention. This is more difficult to do in countries such as Great Britain, where party discipline is stronger and the legislative branch's opportunities for independent activity are more limited.

In many countries, legislators perform a more individualized function as well. Citizens or interest groups often feel that they can call on the legislator elected from their district, state, or province to help them with a problem or question. Legislators may find it politically profitable to respond, spending time in **constituent service.** (In especially corrupt systems, such efforts are financially profitable to the legislator.)

Consequently, legislators often act as **ombudsmen,*** helping to determine the meaning of unclear regulations, prompting agencies to process applications more quickly, and seeking changes in official decisions on behalf of affected constituents. These important activities are often vital to the legislator in generating support for reelection. Moreover, in some nations, including Great Britain and Mexico, some legislators have official links to interest groups (such as business associations or labor unions) and may act openly as their advocates in government.

Legislative Structure

Every legislature has several specific structural features designed by constitutions or shaped by age-old traditions. In this section, we discuss three basic structural issues pertinent to virtually all contemporary legislative institutions.

Legislative and Executive Power   Although a few political systems operate without a legislative institution, it is fair to say that all have some kind of executive. The executive is responsible for carrying out and managing the government's programs and laws, as discussed in Chapter 8. How the legislature and the executive work together is one of the most basic issues related to legislative structure and process.

Most political systems can be classified as either **parliamentary systems** or **presidential systems.** In parliamentary systems, the legislature chooses the "head of government"—most often known as the prime minister—and the executive must be an elected member of parliament.[†] To stay in office, he or she must retain the support of the party in parliament that won a majority of seats (or the support of a parliamentary majority created by a *coalition* of parties that agree to work together to support the same prime minister).

Parliamentary systems typically have a separate "head of state," a monarch or some other person with largely symbolic powers. By contrast, in presidential systems, the chief executive is both head of state *and* head of government. He or she is selected independently by the voters and therefore is not accountable to the legislature. (See Figure 7.1.)

It is often argued that the parliamentary system is more consistent with democratic principles. According to supporters of presidential systems, the main advantage of their systems is that they provide greater "checks" on unwise legislatures: A simple legislative

---

* The position of ombudsman was first developed in Scandinavian countries. The person in this position investigates complaints brought by individual citizens regarding government programs, agencies, and policies.

[†] Strictly speaking, the prime minister in a parliamentary system may be *officially* chosen by the president or the monarch, as in Great Britain. But both political expectations and traditional observance demand that the president or monarch "select" the individual elected by the members of the majority party in the House of Commons.

FIGURE 7.1 PARLIAMENTARY AND PRESIDENTIAL SYSTEMS

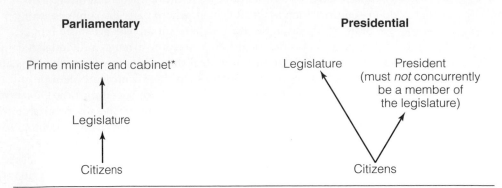

*Together, the prime minister and his or her cabinet are typically called "the Government" in a parliamentary system. In many parliamentary systems, including Great Britain, the prime minister and his or her cabinet must also be current members of Parliament.

NOTE: Arrows indicate paths of political accountability.

majority in a parliamentary system can make any law it wants as long as support can be achieved in one assembly. Parliamentary advocates respond that this is the way it *should* be, that the only thing that should ever "check" the decisions of the parliament is the possibility that the people will vote the other party into power if members of parliament make decisions that the people oppose. That is what democracy is all about! The choice between a parliamentary and a presidential system is thus among the most basic factors in determining how a democratic political system operates. (See Box 7-1.)

Which system produces greater stability? There is considerable disagreement among political scientists regarding the advantages and disadvantages of each system. Some analysts contend that the parliamentary system is more directly responsive to the voters, largely because the voters determine which party has a majority, and that party then controls both the legislative and the executive branches. Such systems are not plagued by the "**dual democratic legitimacy**" of presidential systems (created by the separately elected executives and legislatures), which can lead to gridlock and political frustration.[6]

Experience in Europe and in Latin American countries has led some observers to argue that as a result of their "dual democratic legitimacy," presidential systems have severe shortcomings. In parliamentary systems, voters may have more information about the people governing them, because department heads and other governing officials are almost always established leaders of the majority party. Newly elected presidents appoint their cabinet heads from a far less known array of individuals, drawn from their own inner circles.

But the most important argument against presidential systems is that *they can produce profound instability when a president loses popular support.* Because the chief executive in presidential systems is elected for a fixed term and will normally complete that term (unless a constitutional crisis takes place), presidential systems sometimes produce situations in which the government is led for years by a president with no real political clout, unable to lead effectively. In contrast, prime ministers are forced

Box 7-1

ISRAEL: A HYBRID SYSTEM?

Underlying the two methods used to select the chief executive in almost all democracies are two distinct approaches to the allocation of power. Most nations of the Western Hemisphere intentionally separate executive and legislative powers. Hence, the president is elected directly by the electorate and, at least theoretically, enjoys a national mandate. The legislature cannot remove the executive except through a relatively rare process of impeachment and conviction, not simply as a result of disagreeing with him or her on policy matters.

On the other hand, in a parliamentary form of government—used throughout most of Europe (with the important exception of France)—the powers of the executive and legislative branches are merged rather than separated. The prime minister is elected by the parliament and technically can be removed by parliament at any time.

Israel adopted a hybrid system in 1992, with a prime minister elected directly by the voters. Supporters of this system argued that a separately elected prime minister would command broad public support and have the necessary power to lead the country during times of crisis. However, in March 2001, the Knesset amended the Basic Law to return to a more conventional parliamentary system. The factors that led Israel to abandon its hybrid system reveal a great deal about the differences between parliamentary and presidential democracy.

The rationale for the short-lived system of a directly elected prime minister had to do with what many perceived to be the inappropriately large influence of small parties. When the main parties had virtually equal shares of seats in the Knesset, small parties, often Orthodox religious parties, could determine which of the major parties could form a coalition government and appoint its leader as prime minister. Some reformers believed that a directly elected prime minister system "would 'free' the prime minister from [the]constraining or 'blackmailing' influence of smaller parties."[7]

Ironically, the main impact of the hybrid system was an *increase* in the power of small parties. In parliamentary systems, voters cannot "split" their tickets, voting for one party's candidate for the Knesset and for another party's candidate for chief executive. However, this behavior is very common where the chief executive is separately elected. Referring to the 1996 election, Gregory Mahler reported the impact of the new system on voting choices:

> Probably the single biggest surprise in the election was the significant increase in representation of the smaller parties in the Knesset, and the corresponding decrease in representation for the larger parties. The split-ballot system was in a sense "liberating" for Israeli voters. Many voters who traditionally supported Labor or Likud did so because they saw it as a way to influence the selection of the prime minister, since the leader of the party with the most seats would become prime minister.

Under the new system, a voter's choice for Knesset and prime minister can be from different parties. Many voters did this in the May election: While 50.4 percent of valid votes were cast for the Likud candidate for prime minister, only 25.1 percent of valid votes went to its Knesset list. Similarly, while 49.5 percent of the valid votes were cast for the Labor candidate, only 26.8 percent of valid votes went to its list of candidates for the Knesset.[8]

Why did voters take advantage of the opportunity to split their tickets in such large numbers? Giving voters two ballots (one to elect the prime minister and one to elect a member of the Knesset) allowed voters to select a "mainstream" candidate when voting for prime minister, and then cast a vote for a fringe candidate for the Knesset, thinking that such a vote would do little harm since a more moderate prime minister would be in place. As a result of these and other concerns, in 2001 Israel returned to a more conventional parliamentary system, used for the first time in January 2003. Voters select the members of the Knesset, and that body then selects the prime minister, who must be one of its members.

Israel's short-lived experiment with a hybrid system reflects the conflicting values inherent in the choice between parliamentary and presidential democracies. This experience also shows that the differences between the two systems depends on a great many factors, most importantly the nature of the party system.

to resign if parliamentary support substantially weakens, thereby avoiding this destabilizing condition.[9]

Supporters of presidential systems argue that since the voters directly elect the president, he or she can become a stronger leader than prime ministers in parliamentary systems can be, serving as an effective focal point to hold a nation together during times of great difficulty. Presidential systems are also less likely to have rapid and frequent changes in government as a result of abrupt changes in the balance of power among parties.

The question of which system is superior is not easily answered. The fact that the chief executive in parliamentary systems depends on legislative support more than presidents do in presidential systems presents a difficult question for political scientists. On one hand, presidential systems can enjoy greater stability during shifts in the strength of competing parties, since the president knows he or she can stay in office during a given term regardless of what happens in the legislature. The government is not likely to be replaced very often.

On the other hand, this independence from the legislature can tempt presidents to disregard growing legislative resistance to their policies. If a president overestimates his or her popular support, he or she can take actions that eventually produce disruptive or even violent opposition. In contrast, the legislature in a parliamentary system can remove a prime minister who has strayed significantly from popular demands, by passing a "vote of no confidence" simply on the grounds that his or her policies have become seriously unpopular. Knowing this, prime ministers are less likely to govern in ways that invite rebellious movements. Presidents, in contrast, may be removed only by impeachment, by resignation, or by a constitutional crisis of some kind, remaining in office even when they no longer enjoy political support.[10]

In the final analysis, the nature of a country's party system largely determines which arrangement is better. The existence of a strong two-party system usually produces considerable stability in the legislature, with one party in control for extended periods of time. Such two-party systems may be ideal settings for presidential systems, since the separately elected president can learn to work with the relatively stable group controlling the legislature. However, when a country has a larger number of parties, none of which dominates the system, a separately elected president can lead to serious political problems. In that situation, the president will try to complete his or her term during a period in which the legislature is led by shifting coalitions of small parties, creating uncertainty and rapid changes in political support. Because the president is not accountable to the legislature, a deep chasm can arise between the two elected branches of government.

As one analyst put it, "Even though multi-partyism in itself is not troublesome for democratic stability, the combination of presidentialism and multi-partyism *is* problematic. In world history, only one *multiparty* presidential democracy—Chile—has survived for more than twenty-five years."[11] In short, the fact that the chief executive in a presidential system enjoys political support that is independent of the legislature creates stability and strength when there are two strong parties, but the same arrangement becomes fragile when the legislature is run by shifting coalitions of many small parties.

In which system is the legislature more powerful? On the surface, it would appear that the parliamentary arrangement gives the legislature greater influence. Since the same legislative majority that makes laws and policy also elects the executive, the parliament is hardly likely to select a prime minister who will oppose the majority's policy preferences. The parliament is formally "supreme," and the chief executive will normally be sympathetic to the legislative majority (and vice versa). When parliamentary demands must be satisfied, it is often done by executive compromises. Of course, this supportive relationship runs both ways: In most parliamentary systems, it is more accurate to say that the parliament is supportive of the prime minister, who normally makes most of the policy initiatives.

Thus, both the degree of a system's stability and the relative power of the legislative and executive branches are influenced by factors other than the choice between parliamentary and presidential arrangements. The type of party system that prevails in the legislature, the constitutional powers granted each branch of government, and traditional political practices are also important. In Great Britain, where the prime minister's party regularly holds an absolute parliamentary majority and where party discipline is strong, the prime minister can be confident of getting the House of Commons to pass almost all major bills that he or she and the cabinet propose. Typically, 90 to 95 percent of the prime minister's legislation is adopted—a "batting average" that any American president would envy. Thus, by most estimates the British Parliament (whose most fundamental function is to elect a prime minister) has a much smaller role in policy initiation than does the U.S. Congress.

On the other hand, in countries where no single party holds a parliamentary majority and a coalition of parties elects the prime minister, the chief executive may be weakened by uncertain and shifting legislative support. Under the French Fourth Republic (1946–1958), for example, the legislature dominated the chief executive. Prime ministers had great difficulty getting bills passed and were regularly removed from office by the parliament. Italian prime ministers have been able to count on a surprising degree of relatively stable policy making from their very unstable legislative coalitions only by devoting a great amount of effort to building and maintaining coalitions among parties.*

Presidential systems also vary considerably. The U.S. Constitution provides for a balance of power between the executive and the legislative branches, with the president being able to veto legislation while the Congress enacts laws and sometimes overrides vetoes. In Mexico and most of Latin America, however, both constitutional design and historical practice have produced dominant presidents and very weak legislatures. Presidents can enact many programs through executive decree and generally can dominate the legislature. (For example, a recent study of Argentina found that because legislative candidates are largely selected by "provincial governors and party bosses," legislators cannot develop professional careers or specialized expertise, making the legislature very weak relative to the executive.[12]) In general, legislatures in the developing world, under both parliamentary and presidential systems, are weak and generally do the bidding of the executive.

The Constitution of the French Fifth Republic (1958–present) was designed expressly to strengthen the presidency and weaken the parliament, which had been so dominant in the Fourth Republic. The French Constitution features a dual executive, combining elements of both presidential and parliamentary systems: It has a president (directly elected by the voters) and a prime minister (selected by the president). Both officers have considerable power and dominate a relatively weak legislature.

One or Two Houses   **Bicameralism** (dividing the legislative power into two chambers) is the most common arrangement among the world's legislatures. However, the balance of power between the two chambers varies considerably. The U.S. Congress divides power roughly equally between its two branches. On the other hand, the French

---

* See Carol Mershon, "The Costs of Coalitions: Coalition Theories and Italian Governments," *American Political Science Review* 90 (September 1996): 534–554.

Assembly and the Japanese House of Representatives have considerably more authority than their upper houses. And in Great Britain, the House of Lords, once equal in power with the House of Commons, now can generally do little more than recommend changes to legislation passed by the Commons.*

Bicameral legislatures are popular for two main reasons. First, a second "house" makes it possible for subnational units (states, provinces) to be formally represented. Whenever seats in the legislature are apportioned on the basis of population (as in the U.S. House of Representatives), states, provinces, or other units with smaller populations will have a smaller number of representatives. The citizens of these smaller units may fear that their interests will be ignored in a legislative institution in which seats are allocated to states or provinces on the basis of population. They will be regularly outvoted on policy issues in which their citizens have preferences different from those of citizens in the more populous areas. Thus, seats in the "upper" house are often apportioned in such a way as to moderate those concerns. For example, the U.S. Senate is made up of two senators from each state, regardless of the state's population. A similar allocation of Senate seats by state prevails in Mexico. Hence, citizens in Wyoming have precisely the same voice in the Senate as do citizens in California, although their delegations to the House of Representatives are very different (53 for California, and one for Wyoming). In Germany, each state (*Land*) appoints representatives to the Bundesrat, the parliament's weaker chamber. Representatives from each Land vote as a bloc in accordance with instructions from their state governments.

Some political thinkers (most famously the framers of the U.S. Constitution) advocate bicameralism to make it more difficult to enact ill-considered, dangerous, or unwise legislation. James Madison and his colleagues explicitly feared "mob rule," which they felt would be encouraged by the popularly elected House of Representatives, and they saw the more patrician and politically independent Senate as an essential check needed to maintain stability and order.

Even where there is less fear of democracy itself, however, some people favor bicameralism as a kind of quality control. A genuinely bicameral arrangement means that legislation has two hurdles to clear before becoming law. Requiring passage in the additional house means that bad programs and policy decisions are more likely to be corrected or defeated. But the passage of *any* legislation (even good legislation) is more difficult in a bicameral legislature than in a unicameral arrangement. It is not at all uncommon for a bill to pass the U.S. Senate, for example, only to fail in the House.[†] For those reasons, many political thinkers and citizens have argued that bicameralism is an undemocratic feature: If the "people" are fairly represented in the lower house, how can a system be democratic if it permits the lower house's political choices to be overturned?

One solution is to give the lower house the power to overrule the other body (as in Italy, Japan, and Mexico). Other systems (New Zealand, the U.S. State of Nebraska) have unicameral legislatures largely in response to that concern.

Legislative Committees   The large number of members in most legislatures prevents detailed consideration of legislative proposals when the assembly meets as a whole. To

---

* The House of Lords can delay the passage of non-money bills (those not involving expenditures of government funds) passed by the House of Commons for one session. Lords can suggest changes to a bill involving expenditures, but Commons is free to reject it. In practice, Lords rarely rejects a bill proposed by the cabinet and never rejects a bill fundamental to the prime minister's program.

† However, in Japan and Western Europe, in the event of a split between the two chambers of the parliament, the more powerful lower house can usually override the other—sometimes with a simple majority vote.

work out the "fine print" of a major proposal, virtually all legislative institutions have established committees, each made up of a workable number of legislators who are usually aided by specialized staffs. Although committees were created for these obvious practical reasons, they can have a profound *political* impact.

A key consideration is whether basic policy decisions are made *before* a proposal is assigned to a committee. In the U.S. Congress, bills are usually given to committees as soon as they are introduced. Hearings, discussions, and efforts by interest groups and government agencies to exert political influence take place while the bill is in committee, helping to explain why congressional committees are often called "little legislatures."[13] If a bill fares badly in committee deliberations, its fate can be sealed by negative action or even by inaction. (See Box 7-2.) Normally, the whole House (or Senate) acts only on bills recommended for passage by committee vote. Parliamentary committees in Japan are also quite influential and give opposition parties additional leverage in altering legislation proposed by the government.

In contrast, committees in the British Parliament are authorized to analyze proposed legislation, but they receive bills only after the whole body has made the basic policy decisions. Consequently, British committees are comparably much weaker than their American counterparts. French committees fall somewhere in between.

The strong **committee systems** in the U.S. Congress and the Japanese Diet, among other examples, are also characterized by member *specialization*. It is possible for a particular senator or representative to spend many years on a committee that reflects a special interest or expertise or that is of special importance to his or her district or state. The specialized nature of committees makes it more likely that the whole body will accept a committee's recommendations. Where members do not develop committee specialties—again, as in the British Parliament—the committee's role as a policy-making unit is reduced correspondingly.

The political importance of legislative committees is generally greater when the legislature *decentralizes* political power. Again, the American Congress provides an extreme illustration: The majority party is often unable to enact bills that reflect its platform because committee chairs may not share the party leadership's perspectives (even though the chairs are members of the majority party). For years a majority of

---

Box 7-2

THE POWER OF U.S. CONGRESSIONAL COMMITTEES

Bruce Murphy provides a particularly colorful account of how committees in the U.S. Congress can affect the lawmaking process:

> The key to getting legislation passed by Congress is knowing how to overcome the obstacles built into the law-making process. . . . In the early 1960s, President [John F.] Kennedy was faced with committee chairs who were members of his own party in name only. These men were conservative Southern Democrats who had ascended to the chairmanships of key committees because the historic post-Civil War dominance of the Democratic Party in the

South led to unusually long years in office for senators and representatives from the South. One of these chairs, Judge Howard Smith of the Rules Committee, posed an obstacle to the new president.

> Whenever his committee seemed destined to send liberal legislation to the full House [for passage], Smith's favorite technique was to "go fishin'"—putting the bill in his pocket, driving across the river to his Virginia farm (which did not have a phone), releasing his hunting dogs to keep visitors away—and holding on to the bill to keep it from passing out of committee.[14]

Democratic members of Congress favored reducing the oil-depletion allowance (a tax deduction applying to petroleum extraction), but their efforts were blocked by powerful Democratic committee chairs from Texas and Louisiana (major oil-producing states). The fact that committee power is independent of the majority party's power makes it more difficult to pass legislation, and it expands the range of interests and points of view that must be accommodated.

Gender Quotas   There are fewer women than men in virtually all elected legislatures, regardless of the nature of the political system. However, substantial evidence indicates that legislatures contain a higher percentage of women where proportional representation electoral systems are used than where single-member-district systems are used. As discussed in Chapter 4, PR systems make it possible for a party receiving less than a majority or plurality of votes in a given district to place some of its candidates in the legislature, and this factor apparently explains why PR systems nearly always have a higher proportion of women in their legislative assemblies.[15]

However, the international women's movement and its supporters have been successful in getting a number of countries to adopt several measures designed to increase the number of female candidates elected to legislatures. Some of these measures are not particularly controversial, such as providing for child care facilities in legislative office buildings, creating campaign training programs for women, and giving some financial assistance. The most controversial measure, adopted in at least two dozen countries since 1990, is to create legal quotas for the inclusion of women in national legislatures. Table 7.1 lists the quotas currently in effect in 12 countries, along with the impact of each country's quota shortly after it was enacted. As the table indicates, no country achieved its quota, but all of them experienced an increase in the percentage of women elected to their national legislatures.

TABLE 7.1   STATUTORY GENDER QUOTAS IN SELECTED NATIONAL LEGISLATIVE INSTITUTIONS

Country	Date Quota Enacted	Quota Required	Percent of Women in Legislature *Before* Quota	Percent of Women in Legislature *After* Quota
Argentina	1991	30%	6%	27%
Belgium	1994	33%	18%	23%
Bolivia	1997	30%	11%	12%
Costa Rica	1997	40%	14%	19%
Dominican Republic	1997	25%	12%	16%
Ecuador	1997	20%	4%	15%
France	1999	50%	11%	12%
Mexico	1996	30%	15%	16%
Panama	1997	30%	8%	10%
Venezuela	1998	30%	6%	13%

SOURCE: Pippa Norris, *Building Political Parties: Reforming Legal Regulations and Internal Rules*, 2004, Report Commissioned by the International Institute for Democracy and Electoral Assistance, http://www.idea.int/parties/upload/pippa%20norris%20ready%20for%20wev%20_3_.pdf.

Customs and Norms   Legislatures are an intriguing mixture of conflict and cooperation. Their members normally are drawn from diverse political parties and distinctive regions, and thus the political disagreements of the country are mirrored in the legislature itself. At the same time, at least some large segments of a legislature's membership must work together to produce legislation.

Customs and norms are extremely helpful in maintaining cooperation in legislatures in which individual members have considerable independence. Where decisions are largely made by a central majority party leadership, an individual legislator's behavior is not as critical as it is where each member is given freer rein. In the latter case, the ability to get anything done requires that there be some basis for cooperation, some "rules of the game." In a landmark study of the U.S. Senate, Donald R. Matthews identified several **folkways** that, in the 1950s, firmly controlled each senator's behavior:

> *Apprenticeship*—new members are expected to be "seen and not heard"; *Legislative Work*—one must attend to the often tedious and politically unrewarding details of committee work instead of seeking publicity; *Specialization*—members should focus their attention on matters in a particular field; *Courtesy*—personal attacks are to be avoided, and members should be lavish in praise of other members, . . . ; *Reciprocity*—members should give assistance and political support to colleagues; and *Institutional Patriotism*—members should hold the Senate in high esteem, maintain loyalty to it, and seek to preserve its status.[16]

Students of the U.S. Congress are fond of recounting anecdotes that show how strong those folkways have been. One often-cited instance had to do with a freshman senator who ignored the apprenticeship norm. After several senior senators made brief speeches honoring an elderly senator on his birthday, the freshman made a similar speech. At every mention of his name, the senator being honored grumbled to a colleague, "That son-of-a-bitch, that son-of-a-bitch."[17] It was considered horribly improper for such a junior member to presume to take the floor in this manner.

Legislative norms serve an important function for the institution, but they also benefit members' individual political interests. In an important updating of the Matthews study, Rohde, Ornstein, and Peabody concluded that although apprenticeship and specialization have nearly disappeared (new members are now encouraged to make contributions quickly), norms that help to manage destructive conflict are still in force. The following explanation was given regarding the importance of the courtesy norm:

> Many of the issues with which the Senate deals are controversial. Hard policy choices must be made and there will often be disagreement. . . . While in a given instance of conflict, the proponent of one alternative might gain an advantage by a direct personal attack on the proponent of another alternative, . . . such a course of action could have a devastating effect on the general pattern of activity in the Senate. Personal attacks would encourage [retaliation]. Increased acrimony doubtless would slow the pace of activity. . . . [making] the compromises that are necessary in passing legislation difficult to achieve. While today's *opponent* may become tomorrow's ally relatively easily, it is far more difficult to make an ally of today's *enemy*.[18]

These observers found that the legislative norms that have survived are those that are of "general benefit," such as courtesy, and not those, such as apprenticeship, that primarily benefited a limited group (such as the senior leadership of the 1950s Senate). The Senate's continuing norms act as a restraint on behavior that would otherwise threaten the effectiveness of the institution.

Box 7-3

LEGISLATIVE CUSTOMS AND VIOLENCE

Anyone listening to heated debates in the U.S. Senate is struck by certain rules of etiquette that lead senators to preface a stinging attack on an opponent's position with an extremely polite opening. For example, "I believe that my distinguished friend from [New York, Mississippi] is dead wrong." If he or she opens with "my *very* distinguished colleague," it probably means that the disagreement is more intense.

In other national legislatures, the standards for debate are far less restrained, and in some nations legislative disagreement can get totally out of hand. Recently, a Conservative Canadian MP, incensed by the arguments of a New Democratic Party leader, referred to her as a "slut" (a far cry from "my distinguished colleague"). In an incident in the early 1990s in Taiwan, which has become a genuine democracy after a period of authoritarian, single-party rule, a large number of legislators demonstrated their lack of familiarity with the normal routines of parliamentary debate by breaking into a bench-clearing fist fight that would do any hockey team proud. According to the *Taiwan News*, a prominent legislator recently threatened more than a dozen of his colleagues with violence, producing at least one assault in the legislative chamber.*

*See http://www.etaiwannews.com/Editorial/2001/04/01/ 986092497.htm for the full story.

And, a number of years ago, one Ecuadoran congressman, deeply offended by a personal attack against him on the legislative floor, took out a pistol and started shooting. Fortunately, nobody was hurt as the representatives unceremoniously cowered under their desks. The accompanying photo shows a scene of violence outside the Indian National Assembly.

VIOLENT DEATH AND LEGISLATIVE POLITICS   A scene of violence outside the Legislative Assembly complex in Srinagar, India, in October 2001. Here, civilians are collecting pieces of bodies while paramilitary soldiers stand guard.

Legislative customs also reflect the culture and the traditions of the society at large. (See Box 7-3.) Discussions in the British Parliament are supposedly still influenced by the style of debate (including controlled heckling of the speaker) that evolved at Oxford University hundreds of years ago. Making sense of the behavior in a particular legislature thus often requires an understanding of the unwritten rules that constitute legislative customs.

Electoral System   As discussed in Chapter 4, democracies using the proportional representation system may be very different from those employing the single-member-district system familiar to U.S. voters. Proportional representation makes it possible for a party with a small base of support to get a foothold in the national legislature (since the system grants legislative seats in proportion to each party's share of the popular vote in multimembered legislative districts). Winning a legislative seat in the single-member-district system requires that the candidate receive more votes than any other candidate. Thus, a system using proportional representation would be expected to have a greater diversity of parties than would a single-member-district electoral arrangement.

Evidence suggests that the choice between these two electoral systems affects legislatures. A study of one U.S. state (Illinois) compared the state legislature's ideological diversity before and after Illinois discarded its proportional representation system in 1970. The study is unusual because it is based on a comparison across time, rather than on a comparison of different countries. (It is difficult to draw conclusions about the effect of such factors as electoral laws when making cross-country comparisons, because cultural, economic, and other differences may be responsible for observed differences that appear to be caused by differences in the electoral systems.) The researcher concluded that the ideological diversity of the legislature diminished considerably after the introduction of the single-member-district system.*

A recent study of the German Bundestag suggests that electoral-system factors have another effect on legislators. The importance of constituency service may vary with the type of electoral system under which members of parliament are elected. In Germany, some members of the Bundestag (the lower house) are elected through proportional representation (PR) and the others are elected in single-member districts. The study found that members elected on the basis of voters' choices among *party lists* (the PR system) received appointments to legislative committees that allow them to serve the party platform, whereas members elected under the single-member-district system gravitated to committees that allowed them to work for their geographically based constituencies.[19] Thus, when members get their seats in parliament as a result of voters choosing their *party*, they are less interested in constituent service activities, but those activities become vital for members chosen directly by the voters.

REPRESENTATION

Most of us naturally think of legislators as *representing* the citizens who elected them; most legislators are even given the title of "representative." But legislatures can make laws and perform other basic legislative functions while acting in ways that have little to do with representation. Even when legislators purport to act as representatives, they may "represent" in very different ways.

Three Models of Representation

The Delegate Model   Perhaps the simplest approach to representation is described by the delegate model. A legislator acting in this manner will make decisions largely on the basis of the expressed wishes of constituents, acting as their spokesperson. If a clear majority of a legislator's district favors (or opposes) a particular proposal, the legislator's decision is made. Thus, we would expect a senator from a U.S. farm state or a member of the Canadian Parliament from rural Saskatchewan to favor subsidies for farmers.

Nevertheless, it is difficult for a legislator to act as a delegate when constituents are equally divided (about abortion, for example) or when few voters have expressed views about the issue at hand. Many national issues today, such as international trade policy, are often technical or complex, and voters rarely have clear positions. Acting as a delegate is also difficult when the legislator's own views differ from those of his or her constituents.

* See Greg D. Adams, "Legislative Effects of Single-Member vs. Multi-Member Districts," *American Journal of Political Science* 40, no. 1 (February 1996): 129–144.

The Trustee Model   Should legislators who deeply believe that abortion or capital punishment is morally unacceptable vote against their own principles because their constituents feel differently? In these or other situations, a legislator may make decisions as his or her own judgment dictates, with little regard for the opinions of constituents. Such a legislator acts as a trustee.

Following the **trustee model,** legislators may reason that the voters selected them not only for their specific campaign promises but also for their wisdom and reasoning ability. To make decisions entirely on the basis of what the constituents say, disregarding one's own judgment, would be cheating the constituents out of the best job of representing that the legislator could do. Hence, the trustee acts in accordance with his or her own views of the issues faced in legislative decisions.

The "Politico" Model   Many legislators follow a mixed approach, sometimes called the **politico model.** On some issues and at some times, these legislators will act as delegates; in other situations, they will choose the trustee approach. In both cases they are representing, by some definition, but their behavior is rather different.

Choices among Roles

A legislator's choice of exactly *how* to represent may reflect his or her philosophical position, the political culture of the society, and, of course, the legislator's judgment about the impact that adopting different roles would have on electoral success. For example, if a legislator feels that—by virtue of education, intelligence, or wisdom—he or she is better suited to make public policy choices than is the average citizen, the legislator will naturally tend toward a trustee role. Legislators who see everyone as equally qualified to make judgments will have more sympathy with the delegate model. Different views regarding the basis for government decisions also come into play. Some argue that decisions are largely a matter of scientific study and research, and others emphasize the role of different preferences. The first approach suggests a trustee role, whereas the latter is consistent with the role of delegate.

A recent study of members of the U.S. House of Representatives who have pursued a Senate seat suggests that those who were successful in winning elections adopted more of a delegate role than those who were not. Using an innovative research strategy, Wayne Francis and Lawrence Kenny compared the ideological positions of House members' districts with the ideological positions in the whole state; they found that House members who ran successful statewide campaigns for the Senate usually changed their own ideologies to match the ideological position of the state. Those House members seeking Senate seats who maintained the ideological positions common in their home districts more often failed in the statewide election. This evidence argues that successful U.S. legislators frequently act as delegates, strategically adopting their constituents' policy positions.[20]

PARTY RESPONSIBILITY AND LEGISLATIVE BEHAVIOR

Political parties are critically important in the legislatures of virtually all democracies. Each legislator is usually a member of a party, and all the members from each party form a *caucus,* or *conference,* meeting together from time to time. The relationships

© AP/Wide World Photos

DEBATE IN THE BRITISH HOUSE OF COMMONS   In this image made from television, Members of Parliament attend to a session in the House of Commons, in London, Friday March 11, 2005 during the latest round of debate over the government's controversial anti-terrorism powers.

among legislators who are members of the same party often have a great impact on what happens in the legislature.

As we discussed in Chapter 5, political parties vary greatly according to their internal cohesion and central control. Not surprisingly, then, there are corresponding differences in the amount of power that different parties wield over their national legislators. In Germany and Great Britain, for example, members of the legislature are quite constrained by party discipline; that is to say, each legislator usually votes on important legislation in accordance with the wishes of his or her party's leadership. In other countries, such as the United States and Italy, party leaders have limited influence on the decisions of their members.

The German and British systems are thus said to have **responsible parties**, meaning that the voters can hold the major parties accountable for their performance because the party position is generally supported by all or most of the legislators from that party. Party discipline and responsible parties are highly valued by many political analysts who contrast that arrangement with the relatively undisciplined parties of the United States.

On first impression, the idea of individual legislators being dominated by their parties' leaders may appear unappealing. Most of us disagree with some positions taken by the parties we support, and it would seem natural and even noble for legislators to act contrary to the "party line" whenever their judgment dictates. However, it is well established among most political scientists that the *absence* of party responsibility leads to very negative consequences. Where party leaders have only limited influence over the policy choices of their members in the legislature, it becomes increasingly likely that legislators will be drawn to represent narrow special interests or will be influenced by large campaign contributions. In contrast, if voters and interest groups realize that party responsibility is strong and that therefore most legislators will vote in accordance with the party leadership's wishes, there is less incentive to try to influence individual members. They will vote the party line, regardless of the influence exerted by lobbyists and contributors.

A recent study of several Latin American countries makes a strong case for party discipline in terms of its effect on national budget management. Two political scientists examined the differences among these countries with respect to the extent to which the "personal vote" was important in determining citizens' choices of legislators. Where the party leadership has the power to control nominations, the "personal vote" is low, and it is high where the leadership is weaker. The researchers predicted that where citizens made voting choices on the basis of *candidates* instead of *parties*, the politicians elected to the legislature had less incentive to concern themselves about the national interest in budget stability, instead demanding spending policies that helped their districts even if they were wasteful in terms of the impact on national economic conditions. The findings confirmed their prediction: countries in which the "personal vote" is a major factor tended to have more severe budget deficits than those in which party responsibility was stronger.[21]

Moreover, the proponents of strong party influence contend that such distractions as a legislator's personality, appearance, or personal habits are less important when voters know that the party effectively controls each legislator's votes. Instead, voters will focus on meaningful policy differences that define the competing parties, making their voting choices on the basis of the policies they prefer. When this happens, most political scientists argue that democracy is on stronger ground, because the citizens' votes communicate what they want government to do, not simply how they feel about candidates' personalities and misadventures.

Three kinds of factors affect the extent to which party responsibility is achieved. First, the cohesion of the "party-in-the-electorate" will affect the degree of party discipline in the legislature. The American Democratic Party through most of the twentieth century is perhaps the most often cited example of a party whose divisions among its supporters often translated into divisions among its members elected to Congress. For decades, the Democrats had great electoral success in the American South (partly because of the legacy of the Republican-led Civil War) while maintaining support among most American liberals in other parts of the country. They were often severely divided as a result, and Democratic members of Congress from southern states usually voted *against* the wishes of their party's leadership. Many French and Italian parties are also divided for similar reasons. On the other hand, voters supporting the British Labour Party or the Swedish Socialists are, relatively speaking, much less divided on issues, and the party's members in the Parliament vote with much greater unity and discipline.

Second, legislative rules and practices and national laws regarding political parties may be instituted to increase (or decrease) party control. If party leaders are to enforce discipline, they need to be able to apply sanctions that affect the political success of individual legislators. Whenever party organizations can grant or withdraw committee assignments, campaign funds, and national party support for a member's campaign, party discipline is likely to be high. British parties are able to use those and other sanctions, whereas American parties have much less leverage. Particularly since most U.S. legislators know that they must raise large sums of money *on their own* to compete in a close race, they have little reason to abide by the wishes of party leaders on policy questions. Where a legislator's political success depends more on pleasing a few important constituents or interest groups than on following the party platform, party discipline is diminished.

In the United States, the existence of *primaries* is the greatest factor detracting from party responsibility. A primary election is simply an election in which citizens vote to determine which candidate will be the nominee of their party in the *general election*, which usually takes place some months later. Before primaries were instituted (a century ago), party leaders themselves selected the nominees, and they took each potential nominee's loyalty to the party platform into account when selecting him or her as a candidate. When primaries became the main method of selecting nominees, individuals could simply label themselves "Democrats" or "Republicans" and then seek the nomination by winning in the primary. Having won the nomination through this process, the successful candidate owes little to the party leadership. (Outside the United States, this approach to selecting candidates is very rare.)

Finally, party discipline is often self-imposed, since legislators perceive the propriety of voting in accordance with their parties. The strength of tradition supporting party discipline in Great Britain leads many MPs to place great weight on party loyalty, and it affects their behavior even when the specific sanctions enforcing party discipline may not be so critical.

As noted in Chapters 4 and 5, the power of political parties may be declining in the United States, Great Britain, and other industrialized democracies. The influence of parties on legislative decisions, however, is still quite significant, as party identification continues to be an important determinant of many voters' loyalties.

THE CHANGING ROLE OF MODERN LEGISLATURES

The role of legislative institutions changed considerably in most industrial democracies during the twentieth century. Legislatures were initially seen as the predominant power center in many democratic governments—as suggested, for example, by the fact that the framers of the U.S. Constitution devoted Article I to the Congress (not the presidency). Before the modern era, ideas for government policy often originated in legislatures themselves, and the executive role was correspondingly much less powerful.

Three related factors have diminished the legislative role. First, the growth of bureaucracies—one of the most universal developments of contemporary politics—inevitably displaces some of the role that legislators would otherwise play in initiating policies. Proposals for new programs and changes in existing programs most often originate in the hundreds of agencies set up to administer the modern state. The size of the bureaucracy in most developed nations makes it unavoidable that **policy initiation** shifts away from legislators and to administrators. This tendency is most pronounced in Japan, France, and other countries in which a highly trained and knowledgeable bureaucracy dominates decisions made by the legislature and the executive. Second, modern government is often complicated by the technological nature of many public policy decisions and programs. Legislators are confronted with a dizzying level of detail and with subject matter about which they, as generalists, necessarily know very little. Legislators must allocate their scarce time and energy to matters of high visibility or high concern to their constituents, and thus most policy decisions are made without the knowledge or the direct participation of elected legislators.

Finally, the growing importance of international cooperation, the global economy, and the increasingly complicated nature of international relations in the modern world inevitably amplify the chief executive's importance in most political systems. Chief executives are necessarily the focal points of foreign policy in most countries, and the importance of international events and relationships thus makes legislatures less dominant than in earlier eras. Nevertheless, legislative institutions remain the most straightforward embodiment of democratic principles.

 WHERE ON THE WEB?

http://www.polisci.umn.edu/information/parliaments/index.html

A list of Internet sites for national legislatures around the world.

http://www.house.gov

The home page of the U.S. House of Representatives.

http://www.senate.gov/

The home page of the U.S. Senate.

http://www.parl.gc.ca/common/index.asp?Language=E

The home page of the Canadian Parliament.

http://www.parliament.uk/

The home page of the British Parliament.

http://thomas.loc.gov/home/lawsmade.toc.html

A clear synopsis of the procedural details involved in enacting a bill in the United States.

http://pdba.georgetown.edu/Legislative/legislative.html

The home page of the Legislative Branch Political Database of the Americas, providing basic information on the national legislatures of countries in North, Central, and South America.

http://www.upd.oas.org/lab/democratic/legislativeprocesses.htm

The Organization of American States has assembled information devoted to its program called "Strengthening of Legislative Institutions" on this Web site.

◆ ◆ ◆

Key Terms and Concepts_____

bicameralism

committee systems

constituent service

delegate model

dual democratic legitimacy

folkways

ombudsmen

parliamentary system

policy initiation

politico model

presidential system

responsible parties

statutes

trustee model

Discussion Questions_____

1. What makes legislative institutions distinctive?
2. What are the arguments for and against bicameralism?

3. Under what circumstances can a presidential system be politically less stable than a parliamentary system?

4. What is party responsibility, and why is it important in legislative behavior?

5. What are some different ways that legislators can claim to "represent" their constituents?

Notes_____

1. This monumental American political novel was written in 1946 by Robert Penn Warren (New York: Harcourt Brace Jovanovich). The quotation appears on pp. 145–146. A film based on the book won best picture in 1950, and it was remade in 2006 starring Jude Law, Kate Winslet, and Sean Penn.

2. George Will, *Restoration: Congress, Term Limits, and the Recovery of Deliberative Democracy* (New York: Free Press, 1992), p. 1.

3. Gilman Ostrander, *The Rights of Man in America* (Columbia: University of Missouri Press, 1960), p. 88. For more recent discussions of natural law, see Mark Graham, *Joseph Fuchs on Natural Law* (Washington, D.C.: Georgetown University Press, 2002), and Jean Porter, *Nature as Reason: A Thomistic Theory of the Natural Law* (Grand Rapids, MI: Wm. B. Erdmans Publishing, 2005).

4. See Nelson W. Polsby, "Legislatures," in *Handbook of Political Science*, ed. Fred I. Greenstein and Nelson Polsby (Reading, MA: Addison-Wesley, 1975), pp. 257–319; and the entry for "legislatures" in *The Blackwell Encyclopedia of Legislative Institutions* (Oxford: Blackwell, 1987), pp. 329–333.

5. Lanny Martin and Georg Vanberg, "Coalition Policymaking and Legislative Review," *American Political Science Review* 99 (February 2005), 93–106.

6. Juan J. Linz, "Presidential or Parliamentary Democracy: Does It Make a Difference?" in *The Failure of Presidential Democracy: The Case of Latin America*, ed. Juan Linz and Arturo Valenzuela (Baltimore: Johns Hopkins University Press, 1994), pp. 3–90.

7. Gregory Mahler, "Israel's New Electoral System: Effects on Politics and Policy," *Middle East Review of International Affairs* 1 (July 1997).

8. Ibid.

9. Linz, "Presidential or Parliamentary Democracy: Does It Make a Difference?"

10. Arturo Valenzuela, "Party Politics and the Crisis of Presidentialism in Chile: A Proposal for a Parliamentary Form of Government," in *The Failure of Presidential Democracy: The Case of Latin America*, ed. Juan Linz and Arturo Valenzuela (Baltimore: Johns Hopkins University Press, 1994), p. 141.

11. Scott Mainwaring, "Brazil: Weak Parties, Feckless Democracy," in *Building Democratic Institutions: Party Systems in Latin America*, ed. Scott Mainwaring and Timothy R. Scully (Stanford, CA: Stanford University Press, 1994), p. 392.

12. See Mark P. Jones, Sebastian Saiegh, Pablo T. Spiller, and Mariano Tommasi, "Amateur Legislators–Professional Politicians: The Consequences of Party-Centered Electoral Rules in a Federal System," *American Journal of Political Science* 46 (July 2002): 656–669.

13. Attributed to Woodrow Wilson in *Congressional Government* (Boston: Houghton Mifflin, 1885), p. 57.

14. Bruce Allen Murphy, *Portraits of American Politics* (Boston: Houghton Mifflin, 1991), p. 175.

15. See Andrew Reynolds, "Women in the Legislatures and Executives of the World: Knocking at the Highest Glass Ceiling," *World Politics* 51(1999): 547–572; Lane Kenworthy and Melissa Malami, "Gender Inequality in Political Representation: A Worldwide Comparative Analysis," *Social Forces* 78(1999): 235–269; and Alan Siaroff. 2000, "Women's Representation in Legislatures and Cabinets in Industrial Democracies," *International Political Science Review* 21 (2000): 197–215.

16. Donald R. Matthews, *U.S. Senators and Their World* (New York: Random House, 1960).

17. Ibid., pp. 93–94.

18. David W. Rohde, Norman J. Ornstein, and Robert L. Peabody, "Political Change and Legislative Norms in the U.S. Senate, 1957–1974," in *Studies of Congress*, ed. Glenn R. Parker (Washington, DC: CQ Press, 1985), p. 150.

19. Thomas Stratmann and Martin Baur, "Plurality Rule, Proportional Representation, and the German *Bundestag*: How Incentives to Pork-Barrel Differ Across Electoral Systems," *American Journal of Political Science* 46 (July 2002): 506–514.

20. See Wayne L. Francis and Lawrence W. Kenny, "Position Shifting in Pursuit of Higher Office," *American Journal of Political Science* 40 (August 1996): 768–786.

21. Mark Hallerberg and Patrik Marier, "Executive Authority, the Personal Vote, and Budget Discipline in Latin American and Carribean Countries," *American Journal of Political Science* 48 (July 2004): 571–587.

For Further Reading _____

Bauman, Richard, and Tsvi Kahana. *The Least Examined Branch: The Role of Legislatures in the Constitutional State*. New York: Cambridge University Press, 2006.

Copeland, Gary W., and Samuel Patterson. *Parliaments in the Modern World: Changing Institutions*. Ann Arbor: University of Michigan Press, 1994.

Davidson, Roger H., and Walter J. Oleszek. *Congress and Its Members*. 9th ed. Washington, DC: CQ Press, 2003.

Davidson-Schmich, Louise K. *Becoming Party Politicians: East German State Legislators in the Decade Following Democratization*. South Bend, IN: Notre Dame University Press, 2006.

Dodd, Lawrence C., and Bruce I. Oppenheimer. *Congress Reconsidered*. 8th ed. Washington, DC: CQ Press, 2004.

Doring, Herbert. *Parliaments and Majority Rule in Western Europe*. New York: St. Martin's, 1995.

Jones, Mark P., Sebastian Saiegh, Pablo T. Spiller, and Mariano Tommasi. "Amateur Legislators—Professional Politicians: The Consequences of Party-Centered Electoral Rules in a Federal System." *American Journal of Political Science* 46 (July 2002): 656–669.

Leston-Bandiera, Cristina. *Southern European Parliaments in Democracy*. Oxford, UK: Routledge, 2005.

Loewenberg, Gerhard, D. Roderick Kiewiet, and Peverill Squire, eds. *Legislatures: Comparative Perspectives on Representative Assemblies*. Ann Arbor: University of Michigan Press, 2002.

Londregan, John B. *Legislative Institutions and Ideology in Chile*. New York: Cambridge University Press, 2000.

Muller, Wolfgang C., and Kaare Strom, eds. *Coalition Governments in Western Europe*. Oxford: Oxford University Press, 2000.

Oleszek, Walter J. *Congressional Procedures and Policy Processes*. 6th ed. Washington, DC: CQ Press, 2003.

Pitkin, Hannah F. *The Concept of Representation*. Berkeley and Los Angeles: University of California Press, 1972.

Remington, Thomas F. *Parliaments in Transition: The New Legislative Politics in the Former USSR and Eastern Europe*. Boulder, CO: Westview, 1994.

Schofield, Norman, and Itai Sened, *Multi-Party Democracy: Parties, Elections, and Legislative Politics*. New York: Cambridge University Press, 2006.

Troxel, Tiffany. *Parliamentary Power in Russia, 1994–2001: A New Era*. New York: Palgrave/Macmillan, 2003.

© AFP/Getty Images

8

EXECUTIVE INSTITUTIONS AND POLITICAL LEADERSHIP

◆ The Functions of Executive Institutions ◆ Kinds
of Executive Institutions ◆ Limits on Executive Power
◆ Approaches to Executive Leadership ◆ Conclusion: The
Evolving Challenges of Executive Power

In nearly all political systems, the chief executive officer is the most widely recognized and most powerful governmental figure. Although the importance of legislatures varies greatly across different kinds of governments, the chief executive is prominent in both developed and developing nations. He or she is the focus of media attention, the villain when economies and foreign relations go sour, and the hero when the country experiences success. We even name periods of time in a nation's history after chief executives (the "Thatcher years" in Britain, the "Clinton era" in the U.S.).

It is perhaps therefore ironic that a major theme found in studies of executive institutions is that executive power is limited and constrained in so many ways. Although executives have more authority than individual legislators, and although their actions usually have tremendously greater impact, a typical legislator enjoys greater freedom in decision making. Particularly in modern societies, chief executives are burdened with daunting responsibilities and complicated, frustrating restraints.

This chapter's discussion of the executive is divided into two parts. First, it examines the nature and functions of the executive *institution* in modern political systems. Second, it analyzes the important concept of *leadership*.

THE FUNCTIONS OF EXECUTIVE INSTITUTIONS

Deliberation and action are naturally contrasting processes. Legislative institutions are well designed for deliberation. They provide a setting in which opposing points of view may be expressed and debated, and they usually facilitate detailed consideration of major policy decisions through committee and staff activities. Yet, the same feature that makes them ideally suited to deliberate—the sharing of power among a large number of representatives with diverse perspectives—weakens their abilities to carry out programs and policies. The nearly universal establishment of executive institutions reflects the need to place responsibility for deliberation and policy execution in different institutions. At the same time, there is often considerable tension and competition between a government's executive and legislative branches, because each tends to involve itself in functions that the other considers to be its own.

Identifying the tasks that most naturally fall to executive institutions is helpful in understanding their special nature and how they differ from legislative institutions. All these tasks have one aspect in common: *They are best accomplished under the authority of a coherent, unified institution empowered to act quickly and decisively.*

Diplomacy

It is widely recognized, even by legislators, that **diplomacy** must be primarily under executive control. Although the Mexican parliament may hold debates on trade policy and issues raised at the United Nations, the day-to-day implementation of foreign policy is the responsibility of the Mexican president and his advisers. For one thing, diplomacy often involves negotiation, and it is all but impossible for a multimembered legislature to negotiate with another country. The give-and-take of effective negotiation requires that the decision maker be able to respond quickly and decisively to new demands and concessions from the other side, and legislatures simply cannot work with sufficient coherence or quickness.

Secrecy is a more controversial rationale for the central executive role in diplomacy, but most observers accept it in some measure. The delicate maneuvering of Secretary of State Colin Powell during the months following the September 11, 2001 attacks on the United States was necessarily done behind closed doors as he worked to build a multinational coalition to fight the Taliban and Al Qaeda in Afghanistan. There have been several instances in which American, French, and British executives, among others, have worked to win the release of hostages, and secrecy was critical in each case. In such situations, the other side could never be allowed to know what concessions he may or may not have been ready to make. And sometimes even the idea that negotiations are underway produces a public reaction that destroys the proceedings. Although executive control of diplomacy does not prevent all "leaks," most observers feel that diplomacy would be severely hampered if a multimembered legislature were in charge.

Even when secrecy is not an issue, diplomatic communication is simpler when only executive officials are involved. Summit meetings provide an opportunity for political leaders to explore mutual concerns, and these events often lay the foundation for more formal treaty negotiations. The flexible, personal communication that makes summits productive can take place only among executives and their staffs. Moreover, in case of an international crisis, some single official must be clearly designated as the person to contact.

Emergency Leadership

All countries need **emergency leadership** from time to time, and it is almost always the responsibility of the chief executive to coordinate and manage the governmental response. The executive can act quickly, and he or she is in a position to coordinate governmental activities.

Executives manage relief efforts when earthquakes, floods, or hurricanes occur, but they also take charge when the nation is *critically* threatened. It is during these episodes that we encounter a second justification for the executive's role in emergencies. National security sometimes requires extraordinary actions, some of which might not be acceptable or even legal under normal conditions. Most well known, perhaps, was U.S. President Abraham Lincoln's suspension of some basic constitutional rights during the Civil War. When that kind of emergency action is necessary, only the executive has the legitimacy needed to make critical decisions. In the aftermath of the September 11, 2001 attacks, actions taken to strengthen domestic security by President George W. Bush's attorney general, John Ashcroft, were controversial as well, with many citizens claiming that constitutional protections were weakened. (See Chapter 11 for an extended discussion of President Bush's domestic surveillance initiative, a controversial program that many think is a severe abuse of executive power—and that others see as a necessary and appropriate use of that power).

In the developing world, chief executives often cite real or perceived dangers and emergencies to justify their power. Third World leaders often defend tyrannical powers by pointing to the challenges of economic development and the threat of political instability. The same holds when developing countries are involved in war (Iran and Iraq, for example) or are threatened by outside intervention (Nicaragua).

Box 8-1

THE DILEMMAS OF EXECUTIVE BRANCH SECRECY IN WARTIME: A TRAGIC INCIDENT IN WORLD WAR II

Early in World War II, British intelligence officials successfully developed the capacity to decipher coded communications from German military sources. A Polish mathematician, Marian Rejewski, had employed advanced mathematics as early as 1932 to break code from Enigma, the name the Allies gave to the early German code machine, and he shared this information with the British in the years leading up to the war's outbreak in 1939. The British thus had access to German communications, obtaining information about where U-Boats were deployed, German invasion plans, and, eventually, Luftwaffe bombing targets.

Prime Minister Winston Churchill was keenly interested in the information obtained from the German code system. However, he was also aware that he could never permit the Germans to learn that the British had succeeded in breaking it. If German officials realized that the British had succeeded in gaining access to top secret German military communications, they would change their code, and it would then be worthless to the British. The dilemma was stark: Churchill desperately wanted continued access to the intelligence, but he could not take actions that revealed to the Germans that he had broken their codes.

The British worked out methods to conceal that they had broken the code while still acting on the secrets they had obtained. For example, when they learned where some German submarines or supply ships were headed, they were careful not to use air strikes against them unless they could do something to make the Germans believe that the British had learned about the location of the German ships through some method other than intercepting coded messages. Sometimes, Churchill ordered British scout planes to fly in areas where German observers would see them, creating the impression that it was a lucky sighting by one of these planes that led to the sinking of German ships by British air strikes.

The most controversial decision that Churchill made regarding the German codes had to do with the German bombing of the town of Coventry in November 1940. Frederick Winterbotham, in a 1974 book entitled *The Ultra Secret*, reported that Churchill had knowledge of the German bombing raid on Coventry some 48 hours before the attack occurred. There was certainly time to evacuate much of the city and to take measures to avert the bombing. However, doing so would have alerted the Germans that their

© AP/Wide World Photos

Coventry Cathedral lies in ruins November 16, 1940, after the Nazi bombing attack of November 14 on Coventry, England. The entire roof was brought down in heaps of debris, foreground, by the high explosives.

codes had been broken. According to Winterbotham's account, Churchill refused to alert the city. The bombings took place, killing more than 1,200 people and destroying over 4,000 homes.

Some historians (see the books by Peter Calvocoressi and Ronald Lewin, noted below) argue that the German communication that the British had intercepted was not as clear about Coventry being a target as has been often claimed. There may have been some doubt in Churchill's mind about whether Coventry was really the target, and thus it may have been this doubt that prevented him from ordering an evacuation. However, it is clear that Churchill placed a very high priority on preventing the Germans from learning that his intelligence service had broken their codes, and it is quite possible that he withheld information that could have minimized the loss of life from some attacks. On the other hand, most historians conclude that the British success in keeping Germany from learning about their success in code breaking may have shortened the war by as much as a year. But the dilemma created by the need for secrecy has rarely been as excruciating as it was in this case.

See Frederick Winterbotham, *The Ultra Secret*, New York: HarperCollins, 1974; Peter Calvocoressi, *Top Secret Ultra*, New York: Pantheon Books, 1980; and Ronald Lewin, *Ultra Goes to War*, New York: McGraw-Hill, 1978, for more about this famous example of military secrecy.

Budget Formulation

A government budget has been called a set of "goals with price tags attached."[1] In most countries, **budget formulation,** or at least a budget proposal, is an executive responsibility, and for very good reasons. Legislators represent specific states, provinces, or constituencies and often develop close ties with a few groups or interests. Strictly speaking, it would not be *rational* for a legislator to consider the benefits and the costs of a spending decision from a national perspective. When a particular expenditure is targeted for his or her state or district, that legislator's judgment will be driven by a key fact: *His or her constituents will receive virtually all of the benefit created by the expenditure while paying only a small portion of the costs* (since those are divided among the whole nation's taxpayers). Because all legislators face these same facts, it is not realistic to expect them to pursue fiscal responsibility in budget decisions.

The need for executive responsibility for the budget proposal became all too clear in the United States during the early years of the twentieth century. Before 1921, the budget of the United States was simply a patchwork quilt of unrelated acts of Congress that authorized expenditures and established tax rates. The budget process was uncoordinated and ultimately irresponsible. It was as though a family decided to let the husband buy the car, the wife buy the house, and the children buy the food and the furniture—all working with no information about what the others were spending. Even members of the U.S. Congress agreed that the central control of budget preparation was needed, and the Budget Act of 1921 was passed, creating a new executive power.*

Control of Military Forces

In many, but not all, countries the chief executive is the person primarily in charge of the armed forces. Chief executives are rarely empowered to direct the military on their own—the British cabinet usually must support the prime minister's decisions to commit the armed forces, for example. And, after the 1973 War Powers Act was adopted, the U.S. Congress was empowered to cut off funding for military activities that extend beyond a 60-day period. Nevertheless, the chief executive has a central role in control of military forces virtually everywhere. There can be no ambiguity regarding the authority to act if a situation demands a military response, or even if the threat of a response is important.

Investing the chief executive with supreme authority over the military is important for domestic reasons as well. In less politically developed nations, military leaders have frequently seized government power through **coups d'état.** When the troops' first loyalty is to their officers, military leaders can often displace the civilian government on the grounds that national security demands it. In some cases, a chief executive's very attempt to assert control over the military leads to his or her overthrow by a military coup. (See Box 8-2.)

Chief Administrator

Most chief executives also are **chief administrators;** they have primary responsibility for managing the agencies that implement government programs and laws. Some central authority must be in charge of staffing, accounting for, planning, and coordinating

---

* It should be noted, however, that the U.S. president's budget proposal still must be enacted by Congress; the president simply proposes a comprehensive budget.

Box 8-2

THE MILITARY AND THE CHIEF EXECUTIVE IN HAITI

Haiti illustrates the way in which chief executives in weak political systems are often toppled by their military establishments. In 1986, President Jean-Claude Duvalier (1971–1986) was ousted from power by a popular uprising that brought to an end a corrupt and repressive dictatorship begun by Duvalier's father, François (1957–1971). In the absence of a strong political order to replace the old dictatorships, however, chief executives have been at the mercy of the military. During the four years following Duvalier's fall, the country experienced a series of military coups and an abortive election. Finally, in 1990, Father Jean-Bertrand Aristide won a landslide victory to become Haiti's first democratically elected president in an election that was widely perceived as relatively fair and open.

Yet, despite Aristide's tremendous support among the Haitian masses, the military ousted him in September 1991, less than one year after he had taken office. A major element contributing to his removal was his plan to create a Palace Guard that he would control directly giving him independence from the military. Following his ouster, Aristide was in exile in the U.S. Thousands of Haitians were killed under the subsequent military rule, and over 40,000 Haitians attempting to leave by boat were rescued at sea by the U.S. Coast Guard. The United States and the Organization of American States placed an embargo on trade with Haiti in an attempt to bring the president back.

In September 1994, the U.S. led a multinational force to restore Haiti to a democratic government. Haiti's military leaders agreed to step down, and, by October 15, Aristide had been restored to power. Following elections in 1995, Rene Preval was elected (Aristide was constitutionally barred from running for re-election), and Haiti had its first democratic transition between two elected presidents.

However, the political situation did not remain settled very long. Elections in 2000 returned Aristide to office, although it is estimated that only some five percent of Haitians went to the ballot box. With severe economic deterioration, political instability and violence mounted, and in 2004 a rebel group advanced on the capital. Aristide resigned and left the country, and the Chief Justice of the Haitian Supreme Court became president. Relatively peaceful elections took place in February 2006, and Rene Preval won a close victory.

Developments in the next several years will indicate whether or not Haiti has made real progress toward political stability. Its troubled and violent recent past shows, among other things, that chief executives in weak, unsettled governments can be quickly undermined by military rule. (For more information on Haiti's government and politics, see Robert I. Rotberg, *Haiti's Turmoil: Politics and Policy under Aristide and Clinton*, Cambridge, MA: World Peace Foundation, 2003, and Paul Farmer, *Uses of Haiti*, Monroe, ME: Common Courage Press, 2006.)

---

the activities of many diverse agencies. Legislatures are ill suited to those tasks for the same reasons that they cannot effectively direct diplomacy or overall budget formulation: Sound management requires a comprehensive, coherent authoritative voice that multi-membered legislatures do not have.

Moreover, their managerial duties inevitably give chief executives opportunities to change policies. When appointing officials to direct agencies, a chief executive selects individuals who share his or her policy preferences and who can act on those preferences in setting agency priorities. Every new American president, for example, appoints hundreds of high-ranking federal officials. Even when the powers and duties of executive-branch agencies are established by legislation, there are usually numerous opportunities for interpretation, prioritizing, and setting new initiatives within the framework of that legislation. The executive can therefore shape policy by making key appointments to the bureaucracy.

In Great Britain and in several other European nations, the chief executive has greater control of appointment power than in the United States, where the independently elected Congress must approve many important appointments. In part, that is because executive and legislative power typically is merged in most other democracies (the prime minister is elected or confirmed by the parliament) and the notions of separation of powers and checks and balances are not well developed. Also, in Third World nations, with typically weak legislatures, the executive has a fairly free hand in making appointments.

Although the specific features of executive powers to manage administrative agencies vary across different systems, the main point is that those powers inevitably give the executive opportunities to shape policy. The strongest executives exploit those opportunities to the fullest, applying their powers to advance their political preferences and to secure their continued support. It is simply not possible to grant a chief executive comprehensive authority to manage without also giving him or her at least some power to affect policy itself.

Policy Initiation

Although legislative action establishes government policy in most systems, the chief executive in nearly all systems plays a prominent role in initiating policy. In Great Britain, all important policies are initiated by the prime minister and the cabinet. A similar relationship exists in other parliamentary democracies, such as Germany and Canada. In Third World countries, legislatures tend to be thoroughly dominated by the executive branch. Even the U.S. president, who often faces a Congress dominated by the opposing party, is called the *chief legislator,* since most bills that become laws begin as presidential proposals.

Symbolic Leadership

Chief executives also act as **symbolic leaders** of their countries, a role that transcends their specific powers and functions. In times of crisis, it is easier to look to a specific human being as leader than to look to a committee or an assembly.

Charles de Gaulle galvanized the French and forestalled national disintegration in 1958 when France was rocked by a constitutional crisis and unrest in Algeria, and Winston Churchill effectively motivated and unified the British during World War II, as did Franklin D. Roosevelt in the United States during the Great Depression and through all but the last months of the same war. In each instance, those countries needed strong leaders to rally the loyalty and energy of their citizens, and their chief executives led them as no other public figures could have. More recently, Third World leaders such as Ghana's Kwame Nkrumah and South Africa's Nelson Mandela have become symbols to their people of the struggle against colonialism and racist domination.

KINDS OF EXECUTIVE INSTITUTIONS

Although each country's chief executive is unique in some respects, all can be usefully classified on the basis of two characteristics: the way in which they are selected and their relationship to the legislature. These factors have a great bearing on how powerful the executive is and on how he or she performs executive functions.

Hereditary Monarchies

There are only some three dozen countries that currently have hereditary monarchs, and in many of those the monarchy has only a ceremonial or a symbolic role. All hereditary monarchs draw, to some degree, on **traditional authority.** Because they are selected on the basis of their parents' identities, there is usually little doubt about which person succeeds the current monarch. This is one of the benefits of the hereditary monarch system: the clear line of succession means that violent clashes over leadership can be avoided when a reigning monarch dies.

Although the hereditary monarch was the most typical chief executive in pre-modern times, monarchy has largely been eclipsed by more democratic types of executives. Modern political life involves widespread public involvement and participation, and—although that does not always make democracy inevitable—the chief executive must increasingly be seen as legitimate in ways that hereditary monarchs cannot be. Political history is thus filled with rejections of monarchy, including not only the American, French, and Russian revolutions but also the fall of the German Kaiser and the Shah of Iran.

Surviving hereditary monarchies are typically required to share power with legislative assemblies. Classic monarchies assumed power over all government functions, including lawmaking and even judging, but that simple arrangement has all but vanished. In Great Britain, Belgium, the Netherlands, Sweden, and Norway, essentially all the monarch's powers have been lost, making them largely ceremonial positions. Monarchs have maintained substantial political authority in only a few countries, most notably in Morocco, Jordan, Saudi Arabia, and Kuwait.

Directly Elected Chief Executives

The presidents of Mexico, Colombia, the Philippines, the United States, and France are examples of directly elected chief executives. This method of selection creates a potentially very powerful institution, because the executive is then normally the only official chosen by the entire nation's electorate. (In fact, the French president is sometimes referred to as an "elected monarch" to underscore the tremendous powers he enjoys.) No individual legislator or judge can claim the legitimacy accorded to a directly elected chief executive.

Chief Executives in Parliamentary Systems

As noted in the previous chapter, the parliamentary system is the most common form of democratic government. The chief executive in such a system is elected not by the citizens but by the members of the legislature. Since the same parliamentary majority that selects its leader as prime minister is also able (by definition) to enact legislative proposals, parliamentary chief executives may be far less constrained by legislative preferences. However, as we discussed in Chapter 7, a chief executive in a parliamentary system sitting atop a shifting and uncertain multiparty coalition in the legislature can be less secure than an independently elected chief executive who has to enact policy through a separate legislative branch.*

Nondemocratic Executive Institutions

Executives tend to be strong in industrialized democracies because the executive office in such systems is at the center of a tremendous array of public programs and institutions and because these executives are highly visible in the mass media. Executive power is also dominant in developing societies, but for different reasons. Sometimes an executive

---

* Of course, other factors—such as culture, a candidate's personality, and foreign policy events—are also involved in determining how often the executive office changes hands. Israel has one of the most fractionalized party systems in the democratic world, but it has had only eight prime ministers. Israeli coalitions tend to stay together longer partly because of the perceived threat from the country's neighbors.

WORKING FOR COMPROMISE   Israeli Prime Minister and leader of the newly formed Kadima Party Ariel Sharon arrives for a meeting of his party at the Knesset, or Israel's Parliament, in Jerusalem, Monday November 28, 2005.

is the national leader of an all-powerful ruling party (such as Fidel Castro in Cuba). In other instances, he or she secures power by controlling the country's military forces. As we have seen, chief executives may be former heroes of wars for independence or revolution (Vietnam's Ho Chi Minh or China's Mao Zedong) or may have power and prestige by virtue of a religious position (most notably, Ayatollah Khomeini, who founded an Islamic state in Iran in 1979 and ruled there until his death ten years later). In many of these cases, the individual is more of a national leader than a true executive, perhaps performing the function of symbolic leadership but otherwise having little to do with essential executive functions, which may be performed by other, less visible members of the executive establishment.

Moreover, legislative and judicial institutions are often less influential in nondemocratic and developing nations. They generally have less legitimacy, and many of them have been changed so often that they have not become an established part of the government. The executive, by contrast, is able to apply force and to personify the traditions and values of the dominant culture. Some twenty nations have no legislative assemblies at all, and many others have notoriously weak legislatures. The executive is thus dominant in these systems because the other institutions of government are weak and undeveloped. In the Third World, government power is primarily *executive* power.

LIMITS ON EXECUTIVE POWER

Despite the substantial authority that they hold, executives in most countries—particularly executives in democratic systems—face limits on their power. In a leading study of the U.S. presidency, Richard Neustadt concluded that, even with all the president's legal and political powers, presidential power is simply the "power to persuade."[2] President

Harry Truman certainly understood this when he chuckled over the likely experiences of his successor, General Dwight Eisenhower: "He'll sit here," Truman would remark (tapping his desk for emphasis), "and he'll say, 'Do this! Do that!' *And nothing will happen. Poor Ike*—It won't be a bit like the Army. He'll find it very frustrating."[3] Chief executives in other nations have doubtless had the same experience. Having achieved the most sought-after position in their countries, they often conclude that their powers are nothing like what they imagined. In the Philippines, President Corazón Aquino was elected president with the help of a peaceful popular uprising. Her courage in the wake of her husband's assassination and her commitment to democracy and nonviolence made her a hero throughout the world. Once in office, however, she was virtually powerless against the entrenched influence of the military, opposition political cliques, and business and landowning interests.

Of course, some executives are more powerful than others, but the phenomenon of limited executive power is nearly universal. Why is the power of modern executives so often a limited commodity?

Term Limits

The length and number of terms for many chief executives are restricted by constitutions or basic laws. The Twenty-Second Amendment to the U.S. Constitution (ratified on March 1, 1951) limits the president to two four-year terms. Many Latin American nations—including Mexico, Venezuela, El Salvador, Uruguay, and Chile—limit their presidents to one term. Near the end of that term limit, the incumbent often sees his or her influence diminish somewhat, since the power to reward and punish supporters is coming to an end. (This is often termed the "lame duck" period.) The French president may serve two long (seven-year) terms, making that position potentially more powerful.

Sources of Power as Limits

To maintain authority, executives are often required to make certain choices. An executive whose power is based on personal charisma, for example, finds it necessary to spend precious time and energy reinforcing the public's favorable perceptions. An executive whose authority is based primarily on citizens' respect for the law must avoid even the appearance of acting illegally, yet he or she will often find that those very laws restrict policy choices. The same point could be made about executives who draw their power from tradition or a sense of representativeness; they must continuously monitor the extent to which their actions erode the favorable perceptions that made their positions possible. Even a dictator holding power exclusively through military coercion avoids making choices that disturb the armed forces.

Examples abound of executives who lost power by exceeding these limits. While much of the world is familiar with controversies about U.S. presidents being accused of abusing their powers (Richard Nixon, Ronald Reagan, Bill Clinton, and George W. Bush can all be placed in this category), it is not only or even primarily an American phenomenon. In 2006, Thailand's Prime Minister Thaksin Shinawatra was in serious trouble despite having won a landslide election in 2005. He was accused of corruption, abuse of power, tax evasion, censoring the media, and other crimes. In the last decade, top executive officials have been in serious legal and political trouble in Kuwait, South Korea, Spain, Italy, South Africa, and Mexico.

During the 1980s, Mikhail Gorbachev's policies of *glasnost* (openness) and *perestroika* (social and economic restructuring) in the last years of the Soviet Union ultimately undermined the authority of the Communist Party (which he also headed), leaving him virtually no basis of authority when living standards began to decline.

Thus, although most political executives have several sources of authority, maintaining power requires that they act in a prescribed manner. In effect, their powers come with strings attached, and the most successful executives recognize that fact.

Governmental Institutions as Limits

A key characteristic of developed political systems is *institutional complexity*. Although most chief executives have formal authority over an array of institutions, the impression that one gets from looking at the "organizational chart"—that the executive's command is extensive and profound—is often misleading. Legislatures, agencies, courts, and commissions make modern, effective government possible, but they also check and constrain executive power.

For one thing, many government institutions have their own missions and often their own clientele interests. Legislators represent constituents or sub-national units, and agencies are often associated with distinct groups (such as farmers, labor unions, business). Executives encounter resistance when they make policy choices that undermine the interests represented by those institutions.

Even where the executive's legal authority is clear, government institutions typically have many opportunities to delay or obstruct executive wishes. Moreover, as we discuss in Chapter 10, government agencies normally develop "standard operating procedures" that become rigid over time. Executive directives that require a departure from bureaucratic routines often cause conflict and a breakdown of coordination.

In short, the wide range of institutions that a chief executive supervises constitutes only partly controllable forces that must be accommodated to make and implement policy. They are in place—with their established ways of operating and their associated interests—long before a particular executive assumes office. He or she cannot treat those institutions as "blank slates" on which new programs and policy changes can be written. Even authoritarian political leaders usually have to pay heed to powerful institutions such as the military, organized business groups, established party leaders, and the clergy.

In developing political systems, the chief executive typically deals with a smaller number of much weaker institutions. Legislatures, courts, and bureaucratic agencies usually exist, but they are normally much less influential, and citizens accord them much less respect as institutions. In a sense, chief executives in developing systems enjoy a greater latitude and freedom of decision than do their counterparts in the developed world. At the same time, the absence of effective governmental institutions limits the range and effect of what executives can accomplish. In short, when compared with their counterparts in developed nations, Third World executives are frequently stronger figures in weaker governments.

The Mass Media and Executive Power

Newspapers, radio, and television can serve as tools of executive power, and they can also severely limit it. As noted in Chapter 4, when the mass media are under the control of the government, they can be used to shape public sentiments and set the political agenda in ways helpful to those in power. Lenin, always an astute organizer and motivator of people, realized that a national newspaper could be a central tool in creating and maintaining support. The paper he established for Soviet citizens, *Pravda,* means "truth," although it was always far more concerned with ideological instruction than with accuracy. The Nazis in Germany—along with Marxist governments in China, North Korea, Cuba, and elsewhere—similarly have used the mass media as a force for strengthening the power of the political leadership.

In contrast, when the mass media are controlled by a diverse range of voices, executives are often forced to take "press reaction" into account when making choices. For example, in early 1993, President Clinton's first choice to be his attorney general, Zoë Baird, withdrew her name from consideration after the media informed the public that she had employed illegal aliens as household workers. With a controlled press, such information would not have been revealed, and the executive's candidate would have been approved. In 2003, British Prime Minister Tony Blair felt the impact of the media when a government expert on weapons, David Kelly, apparently killed himself after he was named as the source of a BBC story reporting that British analysis of weapons of mass destruction in Iraq had been intentionally distorted. The story, and the resulting suicide, considerably undermined Blair's effective authority.

The explosion of Internet technology and an army of "bloggers" in many countries has made it increasingly difficult for any monopoly control of information to be secure. Chief executives cannot assume that their secrets will remain undercover when so many people have the ability to share information with millions of citizens almost

© AP/Wide World Photos

THE SHOT SEEN ROUND THE WORLD   Nguyen Ngoc Loan, then National Police Chief in South Vietnam, is shown executing a prisoner suspected of being a Viet Cong collaborator in 1968. The visual impact of this photo, among many others, reduced U.S. popular support for the war effort.

instantly. As a result, media management has become a critically important skill for modern chief executives.

APPROACHES TO EXECUTIVE LEADERSHIP

The basic executive functions can be performed in widely different ways. Adolf Hitler, Franklin Roosevelt, Margaret Thatcher, Charles de Gaulle, and Saddam Hussein all performed at least many of the tasks of political executives, and all left a mark on history. Yet, as leaders, they had little in common. Every chief executive is unique, of course, and each faces distinctive problems and challenges, making it difficult to generalize. Nevertheless, we can identify some important factors that affect the ways in which executives operate; understanding these factors may help us make sense of the differences among executive leadership.

The *political culture* of the country, the *personality* of the individual, and *the way in which the executive attained power* are central influences on the nature of executive leadership. The prevailing ideology also may be critical in determining how a chief executive performs. The following categories describe approaches to leadership, but it should be noted that actual executives often exhibit aspects of several approaches or change from one to another during their tenure in office.

Sociologist Max Weber (1864–1920) discussed three kinds of authority in his classic work translated and published in English in 1947.* Although he focused primarily on leadership in organizations, the first three types of authority we discuss here—charismatic, rational-legal, and traditional—are drawn from his pioneering analysis of leadership, and they fully apply to chief executives in political systems.

Charismatic Authority

Historians, sociologists, psychologists, and others have long recognized that some people are able to exert considerable influence over others by virtue of their personal magnetism. In popular parlance, we refer to such people as *charismatic*. They command respect, and even adulation, sometimes moving followers to make great sacrifices. The key point is that **charismatic authority** flows not from the legal basis of one's power but from an individual's personal "gifts."**

Charismatic leaders often come to power as a result of heroism in revolution, or through an ability to inspire citizens in war or during some other crisis. Some were among history's most brutal and repressive tyrants; others earned worldwide admiration for their pursuit of noble ideals; still others remain both admired and condemned. Adolf Hitler and Benito Mussolini were charismatic figures, as were Franklin D. Roosevelt, Winston Churchill, Juan Perón (Argentina), and Gamal Abdel Nasser (Egypt). Each of those leaders persuaded large numbers of downtrodden people to believe in a better future.

Charismatic leaders require more than an opportunity created by depression or war; they must also have a special personal appeal. For example, Huey Long, the infamous

---

* See Max Weber, *The Theory of Social and Economic Organization,* trans. A. M. Parsons and Talcott Parsons (New York: Free Press, 1947).

** The term *charisma* comes from the Greek word for "divine gift."

Box 8-3

HUEY LONG

In his biography of Huey Long, the noted historian T. Harry Williams gives us this picture of Long's ability to generate and use charisma, even though he had to gain support among both the Protestants of northern Louisiana and the Catholics of the south:

Throughout the day in every small town Long would begin by saying: "When I was a boy, I would get up at six o'clock in the morning on Sunday, and I would hitch our old horse up to the buggy and I would take my Catholic grandparents to mass. I would bring them home, and at ten o'clock I would hitch the old horse up again, and I would take my Baptist grandparents to church." The effect of the anecdote on the audiences was obvious, and on the way back to Baton Rouge that night the local leader said admiringly, "Why, Huey, you've been holding out on us. I didn't know you had any Catholic grandparents." "Don't be a damn fool," replied Huey. "We didn't even have a horse."[4]

---

governor of and senator from Louisiana in the 1920s and 1930s, was the object of unprecedented praise and affection on the part of many poor, uneducated residents of that state (as well as many wealthier citizens), in part because his style and personality were so appealing to them. (See Box 8-3.)

In many cases, charismatic leadership is related to *ideology*; indeed, any ideology that contains a low tolerance for political diversity (such as fascism and Leninism) provides a fertile ground for charismatic leaders. Such ideologies buttress a leader's ability to inspire the masses by focusing their energies on alleged threats to the nation (such as racial minorities, foreign powers, class enemies).

The problems of charismatic leadership stem from its foundation in the personal qualities of the leader. When one's authority derives from the personal regard in which he or she is held, and not from law or the limits of established institutions, the person's power may become dangerous. Indeed, part of the attractiveness of many charismatic leaders comes from their image as fighters—they are seen as being in combat with a selfish upper class, a hated ethnic group, or a hostile foreign power. Such leaders may even increase their personal appeal by creating new powers to wield against opposing forces.

Leaders whose claim to power is based primarily on their charismatic leadership often produce unstable conditions, particularly in nations with weak political institutions and little or no democratic traditions. The leader may be able to manipulate the adoration of the masses, who are often convinced that their support is justified by the executive's great wisdom or even supernatural talents. Replacing the executive in these situations is often very challenging. Term limits or constitutional restraints may be only limp impediments when a charismatic leader wants to stay in power.

Thus, the historical record of chief executives who rely primarily on charismatic leadership is mixed. As one would expect, when they are successful, charismatic leaders are extremely effective in performing the symbolic leadership function, and, in some instances, the unifying force of such leaders is precisely what a country needs. For example, Charles de Gaulle helped unify the French Resistance in World War II and brought the country together during the late 1950s when France was on the brink of civil war. And John Kennedy influenced the attitudes of many Americans toward race, laying the foundation for civil rights legislation after his assassination. Charismatic leaders are often less successful in handling other executive functions. For example,

Kennedy was far less successful as chief legislator than was his decidedly *un*charismatic successor, Lyndon Johnson. Many charismatic leaders have performed poorly in financial management, in diplomacy, or in controlling the armed forces. Their failures occur because the personal quality that got them power—their ability to inspire the masses—has nothing to do with other needed leadership skills.

Traditional Leadership

In his discussion of different kinds of authority, Weber identified another distinctive kind of authority: traditional authority. People often give allegiance to leaders because the institutional positions they occupy are established in the traditions of the culture. The most common illustrations are the British monarchy and the Japanese emperorship. Great Britain's monarchy is the world's oldest continuous line of succession and is imbued with a tremendous sense of tradition. In many Third World peasant communities, councils of village elders may enjoy similar authority passed on from generation to generation.

Tradition is also a source of power for elected executives. Although the British monarch has virtually no power today, the prime minister claims authority and status by virtue of the long traditions associated with that office. A widely accepted perception that some power or prerogative is an established tradition adds to the executive's ability to lead. The force of tradition in this sense is apparent when executives attempt to wield power in nontraditional ways—they quickly find out that the executive's position is much more secure when operating within traditions than when trying to establish new ones.

For example, U.S. President Franklin Roosevelt defied tradition when he proposed to "pack" the Supreme Court with justices who would be favorable to his economic wishes. Although the Constitution clearly does not prohibit having more than nine justices, the resulting public furor made it evident that *tradition* was a powerful force. Nevertheless, it is fair to conclude that the importance of traditional authority diminished in the turbulent twentieth century, and most executive leaders must draw on other sources of power.

Rational-Legal Authority

Weber identified another kind of authority, which is based on the acceptance of established law. Executives make use of legal authority by making decisions and taking actions within the scope of authority granted to their positions under law. Where this kind of authority exists, people obey the executive because they accept his or her power under law.

Rational-legal authority can be a significant component of executive leadership where the people see the legal foundations of the government as legitimate and established. Leaders who come to power through a revolution or coup must rely on something else—charismatic authority, perhaps, or military force—since there is no widely recognized legal framework to lend legitimacy to their executive actions. The problem with legal authority is the opposite of the problem with charisma.

Sometimes, executives must "bend" the law to maintain national security or lead the country through a crisis. If an executive's authority is based on nothing other than the people's acceptance of law, he or she may lack support when leadership requires steps of questionable legality. Thus, even in systems in which the force of law is strong, the most effective executives are able to draw on some other source of authority.

Representative Authority

The authority for some instances of executive leadership derives from the perception that the incumbent is representative of some legitimate power, usually the "people" or the "majority." This authority is distinct from the authority of a charismatic personality, tradition, or even law. In democratic systems, executives justify certain policy choices on the basis of **representative authority,** asserting that the majority elected them to make those choices. The presidents of France and the United States, for example, can make such a claim. In contrast, many analysts felt that Mikhail Gorbachev, former president of the then–Soviet Union, made a critical error when he asked the constitutional assembly, established in March 1989, to elect him president, rather than choosing to run for the post in a genuinely national election. Winning a popular election would have given Gorbachev greater legitimacy when making difficult decisions about the decaying economy.* The need to establish representative authority is even more essential in countries with strong democratic principles. In those nations, representative authority is a key ingredient in making executive actions legitimate.

Representative leadership is thus difficult to achieve if the process through which leaders are chosen is not seen as fair and open. Until the end of apartheid, the leader in South Africa could claim little or no representative authority over the majority of citizens. (For blacks, his authority was doubtless coercive.) Representative authority is rarely adequate as an exclusive basis for executive power, however, for the same reasons that legal authority is rarely enough. Executives are sometimes appointed, and sometimes even elected executives win with less than a majority of the vote. President Clinton, for example, won in 1992 and 1996 with 44 percent and 49 percent of the vote, respectively, because of the presence of a third-party candidate, Ross Perot. And George W. Bush won in 2000 even though his opponent, then Vice President Al Gore, Jr., received more of the popular vote.

Most executives occasionally face the necessity of making policy choices that are contrary to the wishes of the people who elected them (as when Franklin Roosevelt, who ran in 1940 on a peace platform, led the United States into World War II). In such cases, a chief executive would be powerless if authority rested solely on the perception that all executive power derives from the principle of representation.

Coercive Authority

The power to use force is an inescapable part of executive leadership. Effective executives generate support for their actions by staying within the law, through the attractiveness of their personalities, by embodying their countries' traditions, or by emphasizing how they are representing the people; but the possibility of force is always present. The significance of that possibility varies tremendously, of course. When charismatic leaders lose their charisma, they may use police or military force to demand the obedience that their personalities previously earned them.

---

* In fact, when Gorbachev eventually did run for the presidency in a popular election in 1996, he received only 1 percent of the vote.

In deeply divided countries, large segments of the population often reject the legal foundations and traditions that are held in high esteem by other parts of society. Both of these problems are common to the developing world. For example, General Augusto Pinochet (former president of Chile), President Hafez Assad (Syria), and the emir of Kuwait were not elected in competitive elections and have represented only a part of the population. Executives in such countries are thus unable to lead effectively by appealing to traditional, representative, or legal authority, and even their charismatic qualities may not be recognized in many quarters. In such cases, **coercive authority** becomes essential to executive leadership. (See Box 8-4.)

Box 8-4

LEADERSHIP, AUTHORITY, AND ZIMBABWE'S PRESIDENT ROBERT MUGABE

In 1965, following decades as a British colony, Rhodesia won its independence. The country's name was changed to Zimbabwe, and one of the leaders of the independence movement, Robert Mugabe, became the leader. His leadership style became a dangerous combination of coercive and charismatic authority, producing severe difficulties and instabilities.

Rhodesia had become a net exporter of agricultural produce and was one of the more economically successful African states during the 1950s and 1960s. It did not give equal rights to its black citizens, however, leading to considerable unrest that fueled much of the independence movement. After the nation achieved independence, the racial inequalities largely remained.

© AP/Wide World Photos

LEADERSHIP IN ZIMBABWE   President Robert Mugabe addresses supporters of his ZANU-PF party, during an election rally in Bindura, Tuesday March 29, 2005.

(Continued)

Box 8-4

LEADERSHIP, AUTHORITY, AND ZIMBABWE'S PRESIDENT ROBERT MUGABE (*Continued*)

By the 1980s, Mugabe pursued violent policies that strengthened his power. Military forces massacred thousands of Ndebele civilians, brutally hacking them to death. By the late 1980s, he suppressed Zimbabwe's free press and he had several opposition party leaders imprisoned. Mugabe also allegedly rigged national elections, making it impossible to vote him out of office. He is now one of the world's longest serving chief executives.

Presumably to correct a long-standing injustice, Mugabe recently embarked on a program of confiscating farms owned by non-black descendants of the original European colonists. Some 95 percent of Zimbabwe's white-owned farms have been taken from their owners and claimed for the black majority. Most reports suggest that the lands have been given to Mugabe's supporters, thus strengthening his political position.

Although the injustices in Zimbabwe were and are real, it is also clear that President Mugabe has sought to increase his power through his policies. He appears as a savior to many poor blacks, who see him as a crusader for basic fairness, and he is able to reward influential individuals who may otherwise support someone else. But per capita Gross Domestic Product in Zimbabwe is only some $1900, and the national GDP lost 4 percent of its value in 2005.

Between 1999 and 2003, the economy contracted by nearly 30 percent.

Mugabe's brutal hold on power continues. On his birthday in 2006 (February 21), a small protest march of a few hundred members of a group called "National Constitutional Assembly" demonstrated against his policies. After Mugabe's police force suppressed the march, 70 of the demonstrators were arrested, most of whom remained in jail for some time. A week earlier, more than 400 people were arrested in demonstrations against economic conditions, including many women carrying infants. In March, eight people were arrested and charged with being part of a plot to assassinate Mugabe. The economic hardships have worsened, as Zimbabwe has the world's highest inflation rate, severe food shortages, and crushing unemployment.*

The case of Zimbabwe under Mugabe demonstrates how charisma and unlimited access to military coercion can produce a strong president but an unstable society.

(See Martin Meredith, *Our Votes, Our Guns: Robert Mugabe and the Tragedy of Zimbabwe* [New York: Public Affairs, 2002].)

*Information on the 2006 incidents was taken from a CNN story, http://edition.cnn.com/2006/WORLD/africa/02/21/mugabe.zimbabwe.reut/index.html.

In modern political life, a single foundation for executive leadership is normally too limited and too vulnerable to change to enable an executive to operate effectively. In practice, most executives combine several kinds of authority. The actual mix will depend on the leader's personal qualities and on the nature and homogeneity of the country's political culture.

CONCLUSION: THE EVOLVING CHALLENGES OF EXECUTIVE POWER

The central role of the chief executive is virtually universal among political systems. Although specific executive institutions vary considerably—and although cultural, legal, and even religious traditions create different approaches to leadership—the need to have unified control of the execution of laws, diplomacy, and emergency management has made it impossible for governments to function without executive power.

The challenges of the modern world (greater use of technology, more deadly weapons of mass destruction, more immediate communication, and extensive interdependence) will make the executive's role even more important in the future. Understanding how executive power is wielded, and how it is limited, will remain fundamental political issues.

 WHERE ON THE WEB?

The best way to locate Web sites that focus on executive institutions is to search under specific country or person headings. For example, to find information about the French president, search for links pertaining to French government; to find information about Tony Blair, search under Government—United Kingdom. The following sites include a few good examples of general sources.

http://www.whitehouse.gov
The official home page of the U.S. White House offers information about White House documents, history, and tours.

http://www.pm.gov.uk/output/Page1.asp
The official home page of the British Prime Minister, this site includes current news, biographical information, and a guide to current legislation.

http://www.kremlin.ru/eng/
The official home page of the Russian President.

http://www.geocities.com/CapitolHill/5557
Lists the full history of Australian prime ministers since 1901.

http://www.thepresidency.org/
The home page for The Center for the Study of the Presidency, located in Washington, DC.

http://www.chileangovernment.cl/images/stories/docs/ bacheletbiography.pdf
The official biography of new Chilean President Michelle Bachelet Jeria.

http://presidencia.gob.mx/en/
The English-language version of the home page of the Mexican president.

http://www.kremlin.ru/eng/
The English-language version of the home page of the president of the Russian Federation.

http://www.sweden.gov.se/sb/d/577
The English-language version of the home page of Sweden's prime minister.

❖ ❖ ❖

Key Terms and Concepts_____

budget formulation	emergency leadership
charismatic authority	rational-legal authority
chief administrators	representative authority
coercive authority	symbolic leaders
coups d'état	traditional authority
diplomacy	

Discussion Questions_____

1. Which governmental functions are most closely associated with executive institutions? Why are they normally seen as within the executive's domain?
2. Discuss some of the limits on the power of chief executives.
3. What are the differences among charismatic, rational-legal, and traditional authority?
4. What kind of executive leadership is best suited to democracy, and why?

Notes_____

1. Aaron Wildavsky, *The Politics of the Budgetary Process*, 4th ed. (Boston: Little, Brown, 1984), p. 2.
2. Richard E. Neustadt, *Presidential Power: The Politics of Leadership from FDR to Carter* (New York: Wiley, 1980).
3. Ibid., p. 9.
4. T. Harry Williams, *Huey Long* (New York: Bantam, 1970), p. 1.

For Further Reading _____

Anderson, Christopher J., André Blais, Shaun Bowler, Todd Donovan, and Ola Listhaug. *Losers' Consent: Elections and Democratic Legitimacy*. Oxford: Oxford University Press, 2005.

Barber, James D. *Presidential Character: Predicting Performance in the White House*. 4th ed. Englewood Cliffs, NJ: Prentice Hall, 1992.

Beckett, Francis. *The 20 British Prime Ministers of the Twentieth Century*. London: Haus Publishing, 2006.

Canes-Wrone, Candice, and Kenneth W. Schotts. "The Conditional Nature of Presidential Responsiveness to Public Opinion." *American Journal of Political Science* 48 (October 2004): 690–706.

Chalaby, Jean K. *The DeGaulle Presidency and the Media: Statism and Public Communications*. London: Palgrave Macmillan, 2002.

Colaresi, Michael. "When Doves Cry: International Rivalry, Unreciprocated Cooperation, and Leadership Turnover." *American Journal of Political Science* 48 (July 2004): 555–570.

Fishman, Ethan M. *The Prudential Presidency: An Aristotelian Approach to Presidential Leadership*. Westport, CT: Praeger, 2001.

Hallerberg, Mark, and Patrik Marier. "Executive Authority, the Personal Vote, and Budget Discipline in Latin American and Caribbean Countries." *American Journal of Political Science* 48 (July 2004): 571–587.

Herbst, Jeffrey. *States and Power in Africa: Comparative Lessons in Authority and Control*. Princeton, NJ: Princeton University Press, 2000.

Jones, Charles O. *Passages to the Presidency: From Campaigning to Governing*. Washington, DC: Brookings, 1998.

Martin, Lanny. "The Government Agenda in Parliamentary Democracie." *American Journal of Political Science* 48 (2004): 445–461.

Mayer, Kenneth R. *With the Stroke of a Pen: Executive Orders and Presidential Power*. Princeton, NJ: Princeton University Press, 2001.

Meredith, Martin. *Our Votes, Our Guns: Robert Mugabe and the Tragedy of Zimbabwe*. New York: Public Affairs, 2002.

Moore, Reese T. *European Leaders: A Bibliography with Indexes*. Huntington, NY: Nova Science Publishers, 2001.

Mughan, Anthony. *Media and the Presidentialization of Parliamentary Democracy*. New York: Palgrave, 2000.

Neustadt, Richard E. *Presidential Power and the Modern Presidents: The Politics of Leadership from Roosevelt to Reagan*. New York: Free Press, 1991.

Nielson, Daniel L. "Supplying Trade Reform: Political Institutions and Liberalization in Middle-Income Presidential Democracies." *American Journal of Political Science* 47 (July 2003): 470–491.

Opfell, Olga S. *Women Prime Ministers and Presidents*. Jefferson, NC: McFarland, 1993.

Polsby, Nelson W., and Aaron Wildavsky. *Presidential Elections: Strategies and Structures of American Politics*. 11th ed. Lanham, MD: Rowman and Littlefield, 2003.

Rudalevige, Andrew. *Managing the President's Program: Presidential Leadership and Legislative Policy Formulation*. Princeton, NJ: Princeton University Press, 2002.

Schlesinger, Arthur M. *The Imperial Presidency*. Mariner Books Edition. New York: Houghton-Mifflin, 2004.

Williams, T. Harry. *Huey Long*. New York: Bantam, 1970.

THE BEGINNING OF A SUPREME COURT CASE   Yaser Esam Hamdi, whose case led to the Supreme Court ruling that Americans held in this nation as "enemy combatants" must be able to contest their detention, was captured in Afghanistan in late 2001 as a suspected Taliban fighter. Hamdi is shown here being led away by a Northern Alliance soldier (R) after his capture December 1, 2001.

© Reuters /Landov

9

JUDICIAL INSTITUTIONS

◆ Judicial Functions ◆ Justice and the Political System
◆ Kinds of Law ◆ Judicial Institutions: Structure and
Design ◆ Judicial Decisions and Public Policy
◆ Perspectives on Judicial Policy Making

In 2001, a U.S. citizen named Yaser Esam Hamdi was captured on a battlefield in Afghanistan following a combat operation. He claimed that he was not fighting against U.S. forces and was in the country to help with relief efforts. He further claimed that he was simply trying to escape the country when he was captured. Hamdi was taken to the U.S. base in Guantanamo Bay, Cuba, and held there until officials found out that he was a U.S. citizen. He was then kept in solitary confinement in a Navy brig in Charleston, South Carolina. Classified as an "enemy combatant," Hamdi was held without a hearing or an opportunity to see a lawyer.

In June 2004, the U.S. Supreme Court announced its ruling in *Hamdi v. Rumsfeld* (542 U.S. 507). The government's position was that since Hamdi was captured in an active combat zone, he was properly classified as an enemy soldier taken on the field of battle. The Fourth Circuit Court of Appeals agreed, and concluded that "no factual inquiry or evidentiary hearing allowing Hamdi to be heard or to rebut the Government's assertions was necessary or proper." Supporters of the government position argued that, if there is a Constitutional requirement to give a hearing and access to a lawyer to Hamdi, it would be necessary to do so for every prisoner taken on the field of battle in every war. Hamdi was not being charged with a crime, according to this view; he was merely being held to prevent his returning to active combat against the U.S.

Hamdi's position was that the Constitution guaranteed all U.S. citizens a right to due process, in particular a right to a meaningful hearing and legal representation, before they can be held in jail. If the government could avoid respecting his due process rights merely by classifying him as an enemy combatant, the government could conceivably do this whenever it wanted to deny a person a right to a hearing before incarcerating him or her indefinitely.

The case presented some tremendously difficult questions, and the Supreme Court's divided opinion reflected the tension between conflicting objectives. In his dissent, Justice Clarence Thomas argued that the Court was not in a position to question the judgment of the armed forces regarding the continued imprisonment of Hamdi and those taken in similar circumstances:

> The Executive Branch, acting pursuant to the powers vested in the President by the Constitution and with explicit congressional approval, has determined that Yaser Hamdi is an enemy combatant and should be detained. This detention falls squarely within the Federal Government's war powers, and we lack the expertise and capacity to second-guess that decision.

Justice Antonin Scalia, also dissenting, took the opposite approach:

> Where the Government accuses a citizen of waging war against it, our constitutional tradition has been to prosecute him in federal court for treason or some other crime. Where the exigencies of war prevent that, the Constitution's Suspension Clause, Art. I, Section 9, cl. 2, allows Congress to relax the usual protections temporarily. Absent suspension, however, the Executive's assertion of military exigency has not been thought sufficient to permit detention without charge.

Scalia and Thomas both grounded their views in Constitutional provisions, but they reached completely different conclusions. Scalia explained that the Due Process clause was designed because the authors and ratifiers of the Fifth and Fourteenth Amendments did not trust the government to incarcerate only those citizens that should be incarcerated, and therefore the government must afford citizens a right to a public trial to protest their innocence. If Hamdi is dangerous and if he fought against the U.S., argued Scalia, then the government should prosecute him for treason, and the ensuing trial will constitute Hamdi's right to due process. Thomas argued that the Constitution's grant of power to the president as Commander in Chief essentially authorizes him to act freely in setting policies for enemy combatants.

The court majority reached a compromise, holding that the government must give "enemy combatants" a hearing, but that the normal rules of evidence would not be required (the government would be allowed to rely on "hearsay," for example, in making its case against the person being imprisoned, and the burden of proof would be on the "enemy combatant," not on the government). Thomas thought the ruling improperly restricted the government; Scalia argued that the hearing procedures afforded inadequate protection to the rights of citizens.

In the *Hamdi* decision, a public policy question that had been, and continues to be, the subject of intense debate among citizens and their representatives was resolved by judges. How that could occur and the difference it makes for government are two of the questions we will address in this chapter.

The judiciary is perhaps the most controversial and most confusing of the major branches of modern governments. Legislatures and executives are expected to make and enforce policies; to authorize public expenditures for roads, schools, and social programs; to enact standards for worker and consumer safety; and to maintain national security, among many other things. The judiciary's functions and decisions are fundamentally different. Its decisions are—at least to a significant degree—based on judgments regarding *justice* and the *meaning of law,* not simply judgments about which of several alternative policies is most cost effective or most desirable.

Judicial Functions

As noted in Chapter 1, rule adjudication is a basic function of government. Narrowly speaking, it involves the application of rules to individual cases. Nevertheless, the functions of courts in modern governments go far beyond the resolution of a private conflict between individuals or the application of law to particular individuals accused of crimes. Judicial decisions have an effect on the whole society, not only on those in the courtroom.

Of course, the primary function of judicial institutions is to *resolve conflict.* In a comprehensive, cross-national study, a noted scholar found that the practice of locating a disinterested third party to broker the resolution of a conflict between two people is so basic that "we can discover almost no society that fails to employ it."[1] Sometimes, courts resolve conflict between two people regarding an alleged injury or contractual obligation. Courts also resolve conflicts of a higher order, as when they interpret constitutional provisions. Where they are perceived as trusted, nonpartisan institutions, courts typically have considerable power to resolve conflicts that citizens would not resolve on their own. (See Box 9-1)

For that reason, judicial institutions can also help to *maintain social control.* To the extent that judicial authority is well established and stable, most citizens feel an obligation to comply with judicial decisions. (See Box 9-2.) Judicial institutions thus also perform the function of *legitimizing the regime.* When a court rules that a disputed legislative

Box 9-1

THE COURTS, SCHOOLS, DRUGS, AND STUDENT PRIVACY

One of the most controversial aspects of the "war on drugs" in the United States is the increasingly common practice of drug testing. A number of private corporations routinely test their employees and applicants for present and past drug use, and some public school systems have initiated policies of drug testing for some students.

The issue of illegal drugs highlights a conflict between two important social goals: the elimination of damaging controlled substances, and the preservation of privacy. It was perhaps inevitable that the issue of drug testing would reach the agenda of judicial institutions in the United States. In Tecumseh, Oklahoma, the local school district adopted a policy of requiring all students engaged in extracurricular activities to take a urinalysis drug test before participating in such activities, and to submit to random drug testing thereafter. Two students, Lindsay Earls and Daniel James, were told that they must submit to the tests before they could participate in the show choir, the marching band, the Academic Team, and the National Honor Society, and they objected to the drug testing as an unconstitutional violation of their privacy.

A previous decision by the Supreme Court held that schools could insist on random drug testing for students participating in *athletic* activities, largely because rigorous physical activity could create special problems for students engaging in drug use. However, in June 2002, the Court extended that idea to *all* extracurricular activities.* Although the Constitution does not *require* drug testing in schools, the majority concluded that it does not prohibit it, and that the school can require any student electing to participate in extracurricular activities to subject himself or herself to drug testing without obtaining a warrant and without any basis for suspecting the student of drug use.

Four justices dissented, arguing that student privacy requires that there be some individualized suspicion that a student is using illegal drugs before he or she can be forced to submit to urinalysis.

*The case was *Board of Education of Independent School District No. 92 v. Earls et al.* Argued March 19, 2002—Decided June 27, 2002.

or executive action is in accordance with law—or constitutional—most citizens accept the result, giving greater support to the government. For example, the court system in Germany has been particularly important in legitimizing the profound governmental transitions that occurred in the process of integrating East and West. The dramatic changes in South Africa's political system brought about by the end of apartheid and the introduction of genuine universal suffrage were also legitimized with the aid of that country's court system.

Judicial institutions also frequently perform the function of *protecting minority rights.* Particularly in democracies, where legislatures and executives are responsive to majority will, courts may have a unique ability to hear and respond to the interests of those who, by virtue of their small numbers, cannot succeed in lobbying other branches of government. Finally, judicial institutions are often involved in *making public policy,* since some judicial decisions shape policy choices made by executives and legislatures.

This list of functions emphasizes that judicial institutions often affect the functions and activities of other branches of the government, and yet judicial decisions involve a distinctive process that sets them apart. We evaluate legislative and executive decisions by the degree to which they promote the public interest, but we evaluate judicial decisions by whether or not they are *just.* Judicial decisions involve different standards, and judges operate in distinctive institutions that have a very different claim to legitimacy. The fact that courts are so different from electoral institutions

Box 9-2

THE COURTS AND SOCIAL CONTROL:
THE CRISIS IN COLOMBIA

The nation of Colombia has experienced severe political instability for many years. Well-armed rebel groups control parts of the country, and the influx of drug money has fueled considerable violence. According to Human Rights Watch, a Washington, DC–based organization focusing on violations of human rights throughout the world, there were at least 92 documented "massacres" in Colombia during the first ten months of

© AP/Wide World Photos

DRUG VIOLENCE IN COLOMBIA   Anti-riot police officers clash with protesters in Florencia, the capital of the Southern Department of Caqueta, in Colombia, in 1996. The peasants in this coca-growing region responded with violence to a U.S.–backed campaign to target the drug trade at its source, by wiping out the shrub used to process cocaine. Drug-related violence in Colombia continues to be a serious issue.

while making their own contributions to policy is the main reason that questions about the proper role of courts in the political process remain confusing and divisive.

JUSTICE AND THE POLITICAL SYSTEM

The Concept of Justice

Nearly everything we can say about **justice** is culturally bound. Cultures vary tremendously with respect to concepts of "just" punishment, for instance. As discussed in Chapter 1, there is no universally accepted list of human rights. Consequently, it is difficult to say exactly what justice means in the abstract, although there is nearly universal agreement that it includes three things.

2001 (the office of the Public Advocate in Colombia defines a "massacre" as the killing of three or more people at the same place and time), and the violence has only escalated in subsequent years.

In February 2005, at least eight people, all residents of the "Peace Community of San Jose de Apartadó," were brutally killed. Those who were murdered included four children. On the night of February 25, 2006, members of the FARC (Fuerzas Armadas Revolucionarias de Colombia, or Revolutionary Armed Forces of Colombia) stopped a bus in the state of Caquetá. They opened fire on the bus and then set it on fire with the passengers aboard. They killed nine people and injured at least that many more. Two days later, the same group shot and killed nine town council members. In March 2006, the same group killed at least 20 civilians in attacks using gas canister bombs.*

The courts in Colombia have not been very successful in maintaining social order. In May 2005, the Colombian Attorney General shut down an investigation of a general who had been implicated in a 1997 massacre of 49 civilians in the town of Mapiripan, despite the fact that both military and civilian courts had ordered the Attorney General to investigate.

These and many other incidents demonstrate that the courts in Colombia have been largely ineffective in dealing with problems of violence and terrorism. Victims are reluctant to bring charges, both because they fear for their lives and because the courts have

rarely convicted or punished those accused of massacres. This leads to widespread efforts at vigilante justice, contributing to a spiraling pattern of breakdowns in social control.

For courts to deal effectively with these problems, it is important that judges and witnesses feel safe to do their jobs. One of the steps Colombia has taken to achieve a sense of safety is the creation of "faceless judges" and secret testimony from witnesses. According to a report submitted to the United Nations in 1996, "testimony presented by a secret witness is admissible before a regional court. Only the judicial official and the agent of the Public Ministry know the identity of the witness and they are obliged to keep it anonymous until the personal security of the witness is guaranteed.†

Most legal scholars have long condemned secret trials and secret testimony because such procedures often produce injustice. However, the threats against Colombian judges and witnesses are very real. In the late 1980s, Consuelo Sánchez, then the youngest judge in Colombia, signed a warrant for the arrest of Pablo Escobar, then the most notorious drug lord in Colombia. She immediately received a death threat, and the Colombian government sent her to the United States with a diplomatic post. After a dozen years, the Colombian government withdrew her post, claiming that she would be reasonably safe in her native country.

Ms. Sánchez applied for asylum to remain in the United States.

---

*See the extended coverage of instability and judicial system weaknesses in Columbia at the Web site of Human Rights Watch, www.hrw.org.

†See also the Web site for a Madison, Wisconsin-based group active in working for justice in Columbia: www.columbiasupport.net.

Perhaps the most widely accepted element of justice is the notion that law must be fairly applied. If the law states that a person should lose his or her hand as punishment for stealing (as it does in Saudi Arabia and some other Islamic nations), it would be unjust for that penalty to be applied only to people from a particular region or ethnic group. If the law states that all property will be taxed at the same rate, it would be unjust for an influential citizen to pay at a lower rate. If the law grants voting rights only to those who own land, it would be unjust for a person who owns the necessary land to be denied the right to vote because, for example, the individual is a member of a hated ethnic group. And if the law states that all young men and women must perform military service (as in Israel), it is unjust for a court to allow some to escape the draft because of family connections.

Of course, few of us would find that simple principle of justice (equal application of the law) adequate. It describes only a part of what justice means. If justice is nothing more than consistent application of the law, what do we do about the possibility that the law *itself* is unjust? The example about voting and land ownership illustrates such a case. Even if judges apply that law in a just manner (that is, with consistency), most people would find it unjust to grant voting rights on the basis of land ownership. Similarly, many of us would question the justice of laws, no matter how consistently applied, that deny certain legal rights to *all* females or to *all* members of a racial minority. The problem is that cultural and historical differences across societies make it impossible to identify many universally accepted concepts of justice. Considerable agreement exists, however, about the more basic principle, that—regardless of the substance of the law—*justice demands that the law be consistently applied.*

A second widely accepted principle is the idea that *the severity of punishment should correspond to the severity of the crime.* Although cultures vary radically with respect to the kinds of punishment they find acceptable, nearly all have a range of punishments that vary in severity to correspond to a range of crimes. Thus, although a number of nations deem capital punishment an appropriate penalty for murder, none finds it just to apply that penalty to traffic violations or to underage drinking.

Third, it is almost universally accepted that justice demands *an accurate application of punishment.* Whatever the law, and whatever the punishment, the innocent should not be penalized. Thus, nearly all cultures have created some kind of fact-finding process, or trial, to determine whether a person who is accused of a crime is guilty. Widely accepted judicial values preclude punishing a person for something he or she did not do.

These basic aspects of justice account for the distinctiveness of judicial institutions in most political systems.* It takes specialized institutions to produce fair and accurate decisions about individual guilt. The legitimacy of the political system itself is enhanced when citizens perceive judicial institutions as operating in accordance with standards of justice; the regime becomes illegitimate in the eyes of most citizens when judicial institutions appear unfair, "rigged," or helpful only to a certain part of the population.

Two Systems of Justice

The actual workings of judicial institutions are significantly affected by the system of justice under which they operate. Although each country has its own special features, most have either an *adversarial* or an *inquisitorial* system. The systems vary with regard to the role of judges, the importance of lawyers, and the approach to fact-finding, although both systems are designed to evaluate evidence and apply the law fairly and accurately.

The Adversarial System   Anglo-American law operates under the **adversarial system.** The judge is supposed to be impartial, representing neither party but standing for the interests of the justice system. He or she is relatively passive as the **plaintiff** and the **defendant** present evidence, examine witnesses, and make legal arguments.

The adversarial process typically includes provision for a **grand jury** to make preliminary decisions in criminal cases, since the judge is essentially neutral. The prosecutor, who is formally distinct from the judge, first presents evidence to a grand jury

---

* Of course, we often use the terms *just* and *unjust* in a different way. We may say, for example, that it is unjust for a poor family to go without medical care or that it is unjust for wealthy people to be taxed at a higher rate than poorer ones. Such statements reflect views of what is in the public interest, rather than legal norms, and they are therefore usually discussed in the explicitly political institutions of government.

in an effort to establish that a person should be formally charged (indicted) for a crime. If the grand jury issues an indictment (a formal accusation) and the case goes before the court, the judge's role is limited. Although he or she retains the power to decide which laws are applicable and how they should be understood by the jury, the judge has little power to introduce evidence or to question witnesses. The judicial decision itself thus critically depends on the positions articulated by contending prosecution and defense attorneys.

The Inquisitorial System   Among industrial democracies, France has the best-known **inquisitorial system**, the most striking feature of which is the active role played by the judge. French magistrates fully examine the evidence in a criminal case, discussing the allegations with the defendant and the witnesses. Judges can also supervise the gathering of additional information.

Thus, cases normally come to the trial stage only when the judge is convinced that the accused is guilty. The trial provides an opportunity for the accused to dispute facts publicly, but new evidence or arguments are not usually presented. It is rare for a criminal case that is brought to trial to end in anything other than conviction.[2]

The Systems Compared   No consensus exists regarding which of these two systems is superior. In democratic societies, both systems usually are acceptably fair and accurate, although serious miscarriages of justice have occurred in both systems. There are some important practical differences between the systems, however.

The adversarial system depends critically on the skill and experience of lawyers. If defendants are unable to obtain effective legal representation, their positions will not be articulated well. Since the judge assumes a largely passive role, facts and arguments that should be presented will probably not become part of the record. This problem is especially significant for poorer citizens, although most systems now provide for publicly funded legal assistance for the poor. But before 1963 in the United States, the state's experienced prosecuting attorney usually would be opposed by an unrepresented defendant. The unfairness of that situation led to the famous *Gideon v. Wainwright* decision, requiring the provision, at state expense, of a public defender so that the poor could receive legal representation.[3] Even so, poor criminal defendants are frequently represented today by overworked and underprepared public defenders, whereas Mafia dons, former professional athletes, or corrupt officials hire the best attorneys available.

The inquisitorial system is far less affected by differences in skill and experience among the lawyers representing defendants. Nevertheless, it requires the existence of a highly skilled and scrupulously independent judge. If French judges were widely perceived as politically motivated or ignorant of the law, the system would certainly not have the legitimacy that it has. The established tradition of selecting judges through a special training academy is thus a basic adjunct to the French inquisitorial system of justice.

KINDS OF LAW

Law is one of the most widely used terms in political analysis. Understanding the law requires first that we appreciate the different kinds of law that exist. Laws vary with respect to origin, status, and subject matter.

Natural and Positive Law

Philosophers, judges, and politicians have argued about the existence and content of natural law for millennia, and such arguments will doubtless continue as long as people discuss justice and government. In simple terms, **natural law** is a moral or ethical standard grounded either in nature itself (how things *should* be according to some view of a natural order) or in theology (what the Divine has dictated). Natural law exists apart from **positive law,** the body of laws devised by humans. Some legal and moral philosophers have devoted great energies to discovering principles of natural law. Among the most important are Aristotle, Cicero, Thomas Aquinas, the Stoics, Locke, and Rousseau.

Aside from the realm of philosophy, natural law emerges most often in rhetoric as people debate political movements or issues. For example, following John Locke's writings, the American revolutionaries contended that several British laws governing them were invalid because they violated *rights under natural law.* Thomas Jefferson invoked natural law in the Declaration of Independence so that the radical action the colonists were taking would not appear to be simply arbitrary or selfish. Essentially, he argued that the laws enacted by the British King and Parliament were unjust when held against the standard created by the view of natural law that he advocated.

Today, many people argue similarly that natural law demands the rejection of positive laws authorizing prison terms for political dissidents or members of particular religions. People on both sides of the abortion debate in the United States claim that natural law requires changes in positive law; some of those opposing abortion rights argue that natural law protects the right of the unborn, whereas many supporters of abortion rights assert the existence of a natural law right of privacy that prohibits legislators from enacting restrictions on abortions. The idea of natural law is enormously important in political philosophy, but its most common role is as an element in political debate.

Basic Law

The idea that some body of law is supreme exists in many political systems. **Basic law** may exist in a written constitution, in a religious document, or even in time-honored traditions. The key feature of basic law is that when other laws contradict it, basic law is assumed to be controlling. Basic law thus serves as a set of standards that limit which laws legislatures, agencies, or executives can enact.

The U.S. Constitution is perhaps the most well-known example of basic law, primarily because questions about the *constitutionality* of other laws are so often raised in disputes brought to court (see Chapter 11). Its first ten amendments itemize specific actions that the Congress and the president cannot take, thereby establishing important civil rights. Although the British constitution is unwritten, the strong traditions in that system limit the kinds of laws Parliament can pass, and thus those traditions serve as a kind of basic law. (See Box 9-3.) In Iran, all legislation must conform to Islamic law as expressed in the Quran.

An inevitable problem arises when basic law appears to conflict with other laws: Someone or some institution must decide whether a conflict actually exists. For example, when a U.S. community passes a gun-control ordinance, a sharp debate erupts between proponents of the restriction and those who feel it violates the Second Amendment. Courts generally resolve the dispute, creating a potential threat to democratic accountability, as we discuss later in this chapter and in Chapter 11. But if no

Box 9-3

DO BILLS OF RIGHTS MATTER?

The idea of a "bill of rights" is perhaps the most commonly discussed example of basic law, but it is arguable that its existence makes little difference in the actual workings of a political system. A study in the *American Political Science Review* evaluated the actual effects of bills of rights on the political process. The author, Charles Epp of the University of Kansas, noted that "nearly every new constitution or constitutional revision adopted since 1945 (almost 60 by rough count) contains a bill of rights" (p. 765). To address the question of whether the adoption of a bill of rights has any impact, Epp studied the Canadian system, which adopted the "Canadian Charter of Rights and Freedoms" in 1982. He was therefore able to compare the system before and after the adoption of its bill of rights.

What difference are bills of rights *supposed* to make? Epp points out that supporters of such charters argue that they increase the emphasis on rights in the political culture and thus increase the tendency of courts to intervene in policy actions by the legislative and executive branches. Evidence does indicate that the Canadian Supreme Court has placed greater emphasis on civil liberties and rights cases in recent years, that it

has been more likely to support rights claims, and that a greater proportion of its cases involves disputes between individuals and government. However, Epp found that most of these changes in judicial behavior have been a function of the development of a more complete "support structure" for legal mobilization, including steady growth in the size of the legal community and expanded government programs to finance rights litigation and advocacy.[4]

The Canadian experience thus suggests that, at most, the adoption of a bill of rights is but one among many factors that can lead to greater limits on government power in the area of individual rights and freedoms.

Nevertheless, the idea of a bill of rights has considerable support in most democracies. In a May 1995 poll, over three-fourths of British citizens supported the idea of a written constitution and a bill of rights. After the signing of the European Charter of Fundamental Rights, a comprehensive bill of rights covering the European Union, they finally have one. However, there may yet be conflicts to be resolved between this Charter and British law.

---

judicial body is capable of overriding the legislative institution that makes regular law, basic law may lose most of its importance. In such instances, the parliament simply passes the law it wants, along with a resolution stating that the law does not violate basic law. The impact of basic law thus varies from one political system to another.*

Statutory Law

Laws passed by the legislature or a parliament make up a nation's **statutory law**. These laws include proscriptions of criminal acts, the establishment of tax obligations, the creation of regulatory powers, and many other matters. In addition to the texts of statutes themselves, statutory law exists in **statutory interpretation**. The application of statutes, even specific ones, is often unclear. In deciding cases, courts often issue interpretations of the provisions contained in statutes, and those interpretations become part of the law. Following the concept of *stare decisis* (Latin for "let the decision stand"), as most legal systems around the world do, the interpretations are written down and serve as guides for subsequent applications. In a very real sense, the meaning of statutes is derived *both* from their original texts *and* from judges' interpretations of them.

---

* In Canada, interpreting basic law was previously a legislative task, although since 1982 the judiciary has assumed this role under the Canadian Charter of Rights and Freedoms.

For example, in 2006, the U.S. Supreme Court had to interpret Congress's intentions in writing the Controlled Substances Act, a law passed in 1970. The citizens of Oregon, through a state referendum, had passed the Oregon Death with Dignity Act in 1994, which permitted licensed physicians to dispense a lethal dose of drugs on request by a terminally ill patient. The Bush Administration argued that, despite the Oregon law, physicians dispensing drugs for suicide could be prosecuted under the Federal Controlled Substances Act, because that act limited the use of controlled substances to "legitimate medical purposes." The state of Oregon argued that the Controlled Substances Act did not give the federal government power to interfere with a state's power to legalize physician-assisted suicide, because Congress never intended for the Act to apply to such practices (only to the problem of illegal sales of controlled substances).

The Court, in a 6-3 decision, interpreted the scope of the Controlled Substances Act in the way that the state of Oregon did: "we conclude the CSA's prescription requirement does not . . . bar [the] dispensing [of] controlled substances for assisted suicide in the face of a state medical regime permitting such conduct." Hence, the "law" defining the legality of physician-assisted suicide is not a matter of simply looking at the words of a statute, but must be understood by considering the statute *and* its interpretation by the Supreme Court.*

Common Law

Even with their accumulated interpretations, basic and statutory law cannot cover all situations that confront courts. **Common law** is a distinct kind of law that also guides judicial decisions. Specifically, the term derives from the evolution of the British legal system. After the time of William the Conqueror (the eleventh century), judges were appointed and authorized to rule "in the King's name." Without a comprehensive, detailed statutory code, the judges applied principles of fairness that had become established in different areas in Great Britain. They did not accept all customary practices, however, and, after generations, a set of principles that were applied uniformly throughout the land became known as common law.[5]

In the U.S. and British systems, perhaps the best illustration of common law is the law governing *torts*: "What limits a person's freedom to hurt another person? When does law say I cannot threaten someone with a blow? When can't I strike the blow? When may I not publicly insult another (libel and slander)? When may I not do careless things that injure other people (negligence)?"[6] Those and similar questions have been answered throughout much of British and American history by the precedents of common law. Traditional practices and concepts of fairness, as applied by generations of judges, delineated what constituted wrongful acts in those and many other contexts.

As a practical matter, when lawyers want to find out for their clients whether a particular activity is legal under common law, they consult the decisions in previous court cases that indicate the meaning of the common law. Instead of looking at the laws made by legislatures (statutes), the lawyer must consider the "judge-made" common law to find the answer. The concept of *stare decisis* applies to matters of common law just as it applies to questions of statutory interpretation, and thus, a lawyer can argue that a previous decision involving facts similar to those faced by his client should guide the

* See *Gonzales, Attorney General,* et al. *v. Oregon,* et al. Supreme Court of the United States, Case No. 04-623, Argued October 5, 2005, Decided January 17, 2006.

judge's ruling. The opposing lawyer will search for precedents that suggest a different conclusion, and the judge (or jury) has to decide which precedent applies.

Of course, statutory law can displace common law by specifying certain interpretations. For example, the common law on nuisance behavior is, in many U.S. states, supplemented by statutory definitions. Statutory law often incorporates principles that first appeared as precepts of common law.

Civil and Criminal Law

A distinction between civil and criminal law is found in nearly all political systems. When two individuals have a dispute, the state may or may not be concerned. If the dispute is primarily between the private parties, it is a matter for **civil law**. Examples include disputes regarding slander, the location of property lines, and liability for accident damage. One party sues another for compensation, and the court is asked to decide which party has the valid claim.

Criminal law has to do with actions that the state has defined as offenses against the state. If a person robs a bank, for example, it is not up to the bank to sue the thief. The state will prosecute the violator under criminal statutes. The rationale is that the thief not only injured the bank but also threatened the security of the society at large. In some cases, the same action can result in *both* civil and criminal litigation. In what are surely the most widely publicized trials in decades, O. J. Simpson had to defend himself in both civil and criminal courts against allegations that he murdered his wife and her friend. He was found not guilty in criminal court in 1995, but a jury in a civil trial found him liable for the victims' deaths a year later. Some people felt that it was unfair for Simpson to have to defend himself twice from the same accusation, but the state only prosecuted him once (the criminal trial). The civil action involved private parties attempting to gain compensation.

Most societies have broadened the range of conduct regulated by criminal statutes, creating the possibility of criminal convictions for actions previously settled as civil disputes under common law. This trend has great practical import, since the victim does not have to take legal action for punishment to occur when the act in question is criminal. Civil rights laws, for example, made certain acts of discrimination or harassment criminal offenses, whereas previously the injured party would have needed to institute a civil suit for relief.

Judicial Institutions: Structure and Design

We can best appreciate the distinctiveness of judicial institutions by contrasting the kinds of decisions they make with those made by legislative and executive institutions. To illustrate, consider the difference between a *legislative* question about taxation (Should we raise the property tax rate?) and a *judicial* question about taxation (Is Jane Doe guilty of tax evasion?). The answer to the first question is a matter of our views of good public policy: the need for more revenue, the predicted impact of higher taxes on economic growth or on different income groups, and so forth. The answer to the second question has to do with individual justice: what a particular person did or did not do, when, and why.

In most systems, citizens believe that these two kinds of decisions must be made in different kinds of institutions using different procedures. For example, consider the problem of a *biased decision maker*. It is perfectly appropriate for a Canadian member of Parliament to have come to a firm position about a national farm bill before debating the issue in the legislative chambers. Nobody expects an Irish, Italian, American, or German legislator to be impartial when he or she participates in deliberations; in fact, the legislator would not be a very good representative if he or she had *no* pre-announced positions.

However, we would find it profoundly unjust for a judge to enter the courtroom after having publicly announced his or her "position" about Jane Doe's tax return. We would also consider it unfair if the judge's decision had been affected by Doe's partisan affiliation or the judge's party's attitude toward her. Pre-announced positions and external influences are fine when officials make legislative or policy decisions, but they constitute a miscarriage of justice when purely judicial decisions are at stake.

The difference between the standards applying to legislative and judicial decisions is the reason that judges and courts are given different powers and separate institutions and the reason that they are (usually) selected through a different process. Judges are even made to appear distinctive. In Western cultures, for example, judges frequently wear robes, elaborate wigs, and other striking apparel, and we often address them in ways that underscore their unique position. In African tribal societies, judges may sit on a distinctive throne when rendering decisions. Judicial decision making is a special kind of governmental action, and most political systems make great efforts to establish and preserve its legitimacy. The way judges are selected, the structure of the judiciary, and the power of the judiciary over the other parts of government are three central questions about judicial institutions that we examine here.

Selection and Tenure of Judges

Judges can be chosen by appointment or by election and can serve fixed or indefinite (life) terms. Whereas U.S. Supreme Court judges serve for life (or until voluntary retirement), members of the French Constitutional Council serve fixed nine-year terms. Judges in some countries may be removed only after a finding of illegal conduct in office; in other systems, judges may be removed as easily as cabinet officers.

Judicial behavior is significantly affected by the choices made among these alternatives. Rules governing the selection and tenure of judges usually represent a compromise between two incompatible values: *political accountability* and *judicial independence.* Democratic values require accountability to the people, but, as noted earlier, judicial decisions are usually supposed to follow standards of fairness and objectivity. Thus, democratic systems typically expect their judges to be both politically accountable *and* politically detached—responsive to public will and yet insulated from it. Systems for selecting judges are shaped by those often irreconcilable goals.

In some countries, judges are selected through a process that begins with their formal education. For example, French judges are selected only from among those who choose to enter the National Center for Judicial Studies for four years after completing their legal training. In the United States, judges may be elected (most states) or appointed (federal courts), but there are no strict guidelines regarding their education (although, in practice, a law degree is required). In contrast, Japanese judges must first pass a National Bar Examination to enter the Legal Training and Research Institute

(Shihou Kenshuu Sho), and only about 1,000 of the more than 20,000 candidates who take the exam each year actually pass it. After two years of training, graduates of the institute must choose among three career options: attorney, prosecutor, or judge. There is virtually no movement between these career paths in Japan.[7] Employing yet another approach to selecting judges, those who serve on Swiss courts are elected by the two chambers of the National Assembly.[8]

Most processes for selecting judges contain features that try to minimize the extent to which either independence or accountability is compromised. Perhaps the most explicit attempt to achieve both accountability and independence in the United States is the **Missouri Plan,** an arrangement adopted by that state in 1940. Under this system, the state governor selects a judge from a set of nominees submitted by an independent nominating commission. The commission is made up of lawyers, former judges, community leaders, and citizens. Supporters contend that the Missouri Plan ensures that only qualified, competent judges will be nominated, since the nominating commission has the time and the expertise to select the best candidates. At the same time, accountability is secured because the commission is designed to be somewhat representative and because the plan usually provides for the rejection of nominees (or the recall of appointed judges) by popular referendum. Since the governor is an elected official, further accountability is introduced into the process through his or her participation.

Where judges are elected by citizens, as in 31 U.S. states, the elections are usually officially nonpartisan (that is, the candidates cannot run as members of a political party). Candidates must also satisfy certain qualifications. The election system thus is expected to establish some responsiveness to the public, but safeguards are in place to minimize explicitly partisan political influence.

However, a recent study of U.S. state judges suggests that even non-partisan elections affect the decisions that judges make. Using data on criminal sentences from over 22,000 cases in Pennsylvania, two political scientists found that "elected judges will become more punitive" as their re-election time approaches. Voters generally are more concerned about cases in which convicted criminals receive light sentences than cases in which judges hand down overly severe sentences. Because most judges are motivated to win re-election, they apparently make sentencing decisions that reflect voters' demands. The data from this 2004 study indicate that, due to their perception that voters prefer judges that are "tough on crime," Pennsylvania judges handed down an additional 1,800 to 2,700 years of incarceration in 22,000 cases."[9] Similarly, a 2002 study found that, despite the existence of laws designed to protect judicial independence, political pressures in Argentina led judges to refrain from issuing rulings against government actions until the last months of a weakening regime. The courts there are reluctant to rule contrary to the wishes of the government while the administration is still strong. Finally, a 2001 study of Japan found that judges who support the government on "sensitive" policy questions tend to do better in their careers.[10] In short, while appointed judgeships may seem completely removed from popular control, the voters have an important indirect influence. Presidents, prime ministers, and others who appoint judges make appointments that reflect their ideological positions, and they often influence the activities of those already serving.

The independence of judges depends on the extent to which removal is possible, as well as on the manner in which they are selected. Since both prosecutors and politicians may want to influence a judge's decisions, effective judicial independence requires that judges must be protected from these improper influences. The simplest

---
Box 9-4

An Extreme Case of Judicial Independence

It is possible that judicial independence can get out of hand. In most Western nations, citizens cannot sue judges or hold them personally liable for making incorrect or even illegal decisions. The rationale for that is simple: Judges are supposed to make their decisions on the basis of the facts and the law pertaining to a case, not on the basis of a concern for their own financial interests. A 1978 U.S. Supreme Court case tested that principle.

The mother of a 15-year-old girl petitioned an Indiana federal judge to have her daughter surgically sterilized. Although the girl had been making adequate progress in school, she had allegedly become sexually active. Apparently fearing the consequences, her mother told the judge that the girl was "somewhat" retarded and asked him to order her sterilization. Without any

hearing, and acting without any legal power, the judge issued a court order.

Under the order, the hospital officials told the girl that she was being taken to the hospital for an appendectomy, where the sterilization procedure was performed. When she subsequently found out why she could not bear children, she sued the judge, and her case ultimately was brought before the U.S. Supreme Court. Three justices felt that the judge's decision was so far beyond his legal authority that it should be considered outside the limits of his role and thus that he should be liable for damages. Nevertheless, the Court's majority ruled that the judge was "immune from damages liability even if his approval of the petition was in error." See *Stump v. Sparkman*, 435 U.S. 349 (1978).

---

way to achieve this protection is by granting judges permanent tenure and by limiting the extent to which their salaries can be reduced (as in the case of U.S. federal judges). French prosecutors and judges are lodged in the same ministry, although the separateness of their positions is recognized. In other cases, special commissions are established to supervise judges. The purpose of all these provisions is to minimize the likelihood that judges will feel the necessity to make certain decisions to preserve their jobs or salaries. (See Box 9-4.)

Hierarchy in Judicial Institutions

Hierarchy is a nearly universal feature of judicial institutions. Virtually all political systems have multiple units of the judiciary, and some courts are explicitly subordinate to others. In the U.S. federal court system, for example, 94 district courts constitute the first level, 13 circuit courts of appeal represent the second level, and the Supreme Court stands at the top. That basic three-layer judicial system has been widely adopted, although the relative sizes of the layers vary widely across countries.*

The most important difference among levels is between the lowest court and all others. **Trial courts** are where cases are heard for the first time, and in adversarial systems they are where facts are introduced and discussed. Higher courts, known as **appellate courts,** normally do not consider new factual evidence bearing on cases but reserve their time to evaluate the application of the law in the lower court (or courts). Appellate courts attempt to determine whether the trial court applied appropriate law and whether its interpretations were correct. Appellate courts are far less numerous than

---

* In France, the lower courts are the *Tribunaux de Premiere Instance;* in Germany, they are the *Landsgerichte;* and in Great Britain, the corresponding units are the county and the crown courts. The national supreme court of Germany is the *Bundesgerichtshof;* in Switzerland it is the *Swiss Federal Tribunal;* and in France it is the *Court of Cassation.*

trial courts, since most trials are not appealed. The hierarchy of judicial institutions has two important benefits. First, it provides for an effective check on incompetent, irresponsible, arbitrary, or corrupt judicial decisions. If a trial court improperly considers or excludes evidence, or if a judge or a prosecutor fails to follow legally required procedures, the appeals court may reverse the decision or call for a new trial. Even when errors are made in good faith, an appeal can lead to their correction. Second, a system of appellate courts creates the possibility of *uniform* interpretation of the law. Without a system of superior appellate courts, new interpretations of law would apply only in the districts in which trial courts devised them. When the highest appellate court interprets the law, the law has the same meaning throughout the system.

Judicial Review

The concept of basic law, discussed earlier, implies that ordinary or statutory law must not abridge certain basic principles. However, citizens, politicians, and scholars almost never agree about claims regarding a conflict between statutory law and basic law. Whether or not a given law (or executive action) actually violates basic law can be a matter of great controversy, and therefore some institutional power must be available to issue an authoritative judgment.

In some systems, the courts have that power. **Judicial review** has been defined as "the power . . . to hold unconstitutional and hence unenforceable any law that [is deemed] . . . to be in conflict with the Basic Law."[11]

Courts have the power of judicial review in the U.S., Italy, Canada, Germany, Japan, India, the Republic of Ireland, Australia, and Norway, among some two dozen other countries. In France, the nine-member Constitutional Council can overturn parliamentary legislation as well as decrees made by the prime minister or the president, but its powers are somewhat limited and sometimes subject to presidential pressures.[12]

Although one often speaks of the "Anglo-American legal system" to indicate an approach to courts and law that has been partially adopted in a number of countries, the United States and Britain follow very different approaches to judicial review. The concept of **parliamentary supremacy** is firmly established in Britain. Where there are disagreements regarding whether or not a given Act of Parliament violates basic rights or well-established practices, Parliament itself has the power to decide the issue. The British Parliament is thus legally free to enact any statute it wants.

Many U.S. citizens would be uncomfortable with such a system. For example, the Bill of Rights is a set of statements prohibiting Congress from taking certain actions— if Congress itself could decide whether or not a law it wants to enact is forbidden by the Constitution, most Americans would say that the Constitution would have no real impact. Congress would do what it wants and then pass a law saying it was constitutional. Advocates of parliamentary supremacy argue that the U.S. system frustrates democratic government and that in the absence of a court empowered to overturn Acts of Parliament, the British Parliament is effectively held in check by the electoral system and competition among political parties.

Judicial review in some countries—Germany and India, for example—leads to less court involvement in public policy than in the United States but constrains the legislature more than in Britain. As one analyst put it, although courts in these systems rarely issue rulings that overturn major policy decisions, they do insist that legislative actions be "reasonable" and "nonarbitrary."[13]

Judicial Decisions and Public Policy

As we stressed at the start of this chapter, the types of decisions they make is what distinguishes judicial institutions from executive and legislative institutions. Whereas democratic values require that policy makers be influenced by citizens, vote totals, parties, and interest groups, our concept of justice requires that judges be insulated from political influence so that their actions will be free from prejudice or partisanship.

In most political systems, citizens agree on the need for an independent judiciary in cases that have no significant impact on policy, such as most criminal trials. The winds of public opinion should not influence an appellate court's decision about whether or not to uphold a murder conviction. But when judicial decisions involve policy—those affecting school integration, pollution, or abortion, for example—the question of judicial independence becomes far more controversial.

How Judicial "Policy Making" Occurs

Many judicial decisions involve more than a determination of the facts; they also raise questions of legal interpretation. The precise meaning of the law is often uncertain, either because circumstances arise that were not foreseen when the constitutional provision or law was written or because policy makers deliberately avoided the politically painful process of spelling out particular applications of the law. When judges "fill in the details," they make their own interpretations, and those interpretations often include important policy choices.

Consider the following example: Before 1970, U.S. states could terminate benefits to welfare recipients as soon as the state welfare department decided that the recipient no longer satisfied the eligibility requirements. Following state statutes, the agency would send a letter to the recipient explaining that benefits had been terminated and that the recipient could request a hearing to dispute the agency's decision. No benefits would be paid while the hearing was pending, however.

In accordance with applicable state law, benefits to several welfare recipients in New York were terminated. The recipients appealed to federal court, claiming that the State of New York had violated the due process clause of the U.S. Constitution. The clause, included in the Fourteenth Amendment, states that no person may be deprived of "life, liberty, or property" without due process of law. Claiming that welfare benefits are property, the plaintiffs argued that they could not be terminated unless and until the state gave recipients an opportunity for an oral hearing *before* the termination of benefits. Only in this way would the state be respecting the right to due process before depriving anyone of property.

The state interpreted the due process clause differently. It argued that the clause did not require the state to give the welfare recipient a hearing whenever the state concluded that he or she was no longer eligible for benefits. After all, the recipient was not being put in jail or being subjected to a fine. The Supreme Court agreed with the welfare recipients, overturning the New York law.*

The Supreme Court's decision fundamentally altered the day-to-day administration of welfare policy throughout the country. A dissenting justice (Hugo Black) contended that the decision would require states to hire more lawyers and to devote

---

* The landmark case was *Goldberg v. Kelly*, 397 U.S. 254, 1970.

more of the money allocated for public welfare to litigation expenses. Moreover, he suggested, the new arrangement could make welfare caseworkers reluctant to approve borderline welfare applications, since it would now be more costly and time-consuming to terminate benefits awarded in error. Whether for good or ill, the way in which welfare policy is implemented in a number of states was significantly affected by the Supreme Court's interpretation of fewer than a dozen words of the Constitution.

Judicial decisions can also change or make policy when no constitutional or basic law issues are at stake. For example, beginning in the 1930s, U.S. federal law has established that employees have the right to bargain collectively with their employers, and that employers are guilty of an "unfair labor practice" when they refuse to bargain with a legally constituted union. In the 1940s, a group of "newsboys" (that rather old-fashioned term was used in the case) sought to bargain collectively with the Hearst Corporation. Hearst refused, claiming that the "newsboys" were not "employees" within the meaning of the law. At that point, federal law did not specify what the term *employee* meant; it only stated that employees had certain labor rights. In a very controversial decision, the Supreme Court held that the newsboys were employees, and that, consequently, the Hearst Corporation was guilty of an unfair labor practice.* The Court thereby affected the development of national labor policy by resolving this specific dispute between several dozen sellers of newspapers and one corporation.

The point here is that judicial policy making is *inevitable*. Courts cannot limit the impact of their judgments to the parties before them. The interpretation of law changes policies and programs, sometimes altering decisions previously considered to be political or even managerial matters. How we evaluate the reality of judicial policy making is a subject of continuing controversy.

PERSPECTIVES ON JUDICIAL POLICY MAKING

Judicial Restraint

The idea of **judicial restraint** is that courts should accept the decisions of legislative, executive, and administrative officials except when those decisions are *clearly* contrary to basic law or inconsistent with other legal guidelines. Challenges to the constitutional acceptability of a law should be evaluated according to the intentions of those who drafted the constitution or the law in question. Thus, judges should overturn a piece of legislation only if it is clearly in violation of explicit constitutional provisions.

For example, in the welfare rights case we described, judicial restraint would demand that courts interpret the Constitution narrowly so that the New York law could be upheld. The drafters of the due process clause surely did not have welfare benefits in mind when they wrote it; the clause was intended to require a fair trial before a person is punished (by forfeiting life, liberty, or property) for violating the law. Advocates of judicial restraint would therefore argue that the court "made up" law when it forced New York to provide an oral hearing to welfare recipients before termination of benefits. If policy is to be changed in this way, it is legislators, not the courts, who should make the change.

---

* See *National Labor Relations Board v. Hearst*, 322 U.S. 111 (1944).

An important rationale for this position is that courts lack democratic legitimacy as policy makers. In democratic systems, legislatures and elected executives are legitimate policy makers because they were supposedly selected by the voters on the basis of their announced policy positions. If they make policy choices that the people oppose, the voters will elect different legislators or executives in the next election. Judges making policy are not subject to those critical democratic safeguards.

Other reasons have been offered in support of judicial restraint. The process of judicial decision making itself arguably makes courts poor policy-making bodies. Courts can take into account only the information brought to them, and the cases that come their way may be exceptional and unrepresentative of the broader context in which the policy change will be implemented. In contrast, legislators and executives, along with administrative agencies, can gather information extensively, and they can make policy on the basis of the typical, not the extraordinary, cases.[14]

Even in European judicial systems, where judicial review is far less prominent than in the United States, judicial policy making is controversial. Politicians and judges in Italy, France, and Germany continue to disagree about the propriety of an active judicial role. Some argue that "where a gap in the [law] exists, the judge should imagine what the legislature would do. [Others] specify that the judge should imagine what he [or she] would do if he [or she] were the legislature."[15]

Judicial Activism

One of the most common responses to the judicial restraint idea is the notion that courts have a special ability to represent minority political interests, and that these interests will never obtain adequate representation from institutions that naturally respond to majorities of voters. Proponents of **judicial activism** thus argue that some minority interests are permanently excluded from effective participation. Judicial policy making may effectively represent those interests when the other parts of the political system seem closed to them.

For example, the policy of desegregating U.S. public schools was initiated by a judicial decision (*Brown v. Board of Education of Topeka*, 347 U.S. 500, 1954). Efforts to achieve that result had repeatedly failed in legislative action at both the state and the federal levels. In a sense, the courts provided political representation to voices left unheeded by the other policy-making institutions of the system.* If strict doctrines of judicial restraint meant that courts could not engage in policy making, courts would not be able to enhance representation in this way.

Advocates of judicial restraint quickly point out that although judicial activism sometimes produces good policies, it is, as a process, inconsistent with democracy because judges are not elected. However, at least one political scientist has recently argued that courts should be active in policy decisions even though they are not politically accountable and even though they cannot be politically neutral. According to this view, "there is nothing wrong with a political court or with political motives in constitutional adjudication."[16] The tension between advocates of activism and restraint guarantee that this issue will remain unresolved for generations. (See Box 9-5.)

---

* The idea that courts may generally represent the interests of those who are "politically disadvantaged" in their abilities to exert influence elsewhere in the political system is discussed in Chapter 6.

Box 9-5

THE COURTS AS POLICY MAKERS: A DEBATE

The late John Hart Ely was among the most prominent legal scholars in U.S. history. His *Democracy and Distrust— A Theory of Judicial Review* (1980) is the most frequently cited book about law published in the 20th century. He died in 2003.

A portrait by Alonzo Chappel of Chief Justice John Marshall, who headed the U.S. Supreme Court from 1801 to 1835.

Whether or not courts should be engaged in policy making continues to be a topic of heated argument among legal scholars, political theorists, and politicians. Two well-known U.S. contemporary legal writers reflect opposite perspectives on the issue in striking terms.

Robert Bork, a former judge on the U.S. Court of Appeals who the Senate refused to confirm when President Reagan nominated him for the Supreme Court in 1987, is perhaps the most famous contemporary advocate of judicial restraint. In a case involving whether the due process clause protects the right of people to engage in homosexual conduct in private, Judge Bork described the role of the court in policy making in the following way:

> [This court is] asked to protect from regulation a form of behavior never before protected and

indeed traditionally condemned. If the revolution in sexual mores that the [petitioner] proclaims is to arrive, it must arrive through the moral choices of the people and their elected representatives, not through the ukase of this court. . . . The Constitution creates specific rights. A court that refuses to create a new constitutional right to protect homosexual conduct does not thereby destroy established rights that are solidly based in constitutional text and history.[17]

Bork's way of thinking—one that emphasizes that judges must be careful to follow the plain meaning of the words in the Constitution and in statutes—is often termed "strict constructionism." Perhaps the first person to use this phrase in describing how judges

(Continued)

Box 9-5

THE COURTS AS POLICY MAKERS:
A DEBATE (Continued)

© AP/Wide World Photos

Former President Gerald Ford, left, introduces Supreme Court Associate Justice nominee Robert Bork, Tuesday September 15, 1987, as the Senate Judiciary Committee began confirmation hearings on the nomination on Capitol Hill. Ford praised Bork as being "uniquely qualified" for the post. At right is Sen. Robert Dole, R-KS, who also made a statement on Bork.

should interpret law was Chief Justice John Marshall, in 1824:

> What do gentlemen mean by a "strict construction"? If they contend only against that enlarged construction, which would extend words beyond their natural and obvious import, we . . . should not controvert the principle. . . . As men whose intentions require no concealment generally employ the words which most directly and aptly express the ideas they intend to convey, the enlightened patriots who framed our Constitution, and the people who adopted it, must be understood to have employed words in their natural sense, and to have intended what they have said. (*Gibbons v. Ogden*, 9 Wheat. 1, 1824).

The late John Ely, also a leading legal scholar (by one count, he is the fourth most cited legal scholar of all time), saw a broader role for judicial decision making than Marshall or Bork. Arguing that the elected institutions of government do not function perfectly to represent all of society's interests, Ely suggested that judicial policy making may fill in some important gaps:

> It is an appropriate function of the [Supreme] Court to keep the machinery of democratic government running as it should, to make sure the channels of political participation and communication are kept open. The Court should also concern itself with what majorities do to minorities, particularly [in the case of] laws "directed at" religious, national, and racial minorities and those infected by prejudice against them.[18]

Ely claimed that if courts allow themselves to infuse their own ideas into the interpretation of constitutional provisions, they can engage in judicial policy making that will be "representation enhancing." Thus, they would secure minority rights that would be demolished by the unchecked activities of other parts of the political system, and which would be unaddressed if courts simply applied the intentions of those writing laws and constitutions in centuries gone by. To make the system work, claimed Ely, courts must be able to go beyond "strict constructionism," interpreting constitutional provisions not in a neutral or objective sense (which he and many others feel is impossible anyway), but by interpreting them to the advantage of groups and citizens who have little political influence in the elected branches of government.

The debate over judicial activism is a sticky problem for many political systems, but particularly for the United States, as we will see in Chapter 11.

Judicial Policy Making as a Stabilizing Force

Abrupt changes in policy can be destabilizing in any society. When legislatures create new rights or obligations, they radically affect personal, economic, and other kinds of interests. Lawmakers may attempt major transformations of policies in various areas, and although the changes may be ultimately wise, they may threaten the stability of the system. A third perspective thus approves of judicial policy making because of its potentially moderating influence on changes emerging from legislatures and executives.

In practice, judicial policy making may provide for more gradual changes in policy. Historians suggest, for example, that when the U.S. Supreme Court struck down numerous aspects of President Franklin Roosevelt's New Deal legislation in the 1930s, its decisions had the effect of making the greatly expanded federal regulation of the marketplace a more gradual development. If the Court had had no power to make policy, the country would have been subjected to radical shifts in economic policy literally overnight, with possibly severe impacts on political stability.

Hence, the judicial role in policy making is a mixed blessing, even in democratic systems. The necessity for judicial institutions, and their inevitable involvement in legal and constitutional interpretation, suggests that the role of courts in the political process will continue to be challenging and controversial as modern governments address contemporary problems.

 ## Where on the Web?

http://www.conseil-constitutionnel.fr/langues/anglais/ang4.htm
The home page for the French Constitutional Council.

http://curia.eu.int/en/index.htm
The home page for the Court of Justice of the European Communities.

http://www.law.cornell.edu/supct/justices/fullcourt.html
Photos of current U.S. Supreme Court justices, along with opinions and articles written by them.

http://www.findlaw.com/casecode/supreme.html
A reference service providing links to all decisions of the U.S. Supreme Court.

http://www.stf.gov.br/
The home page for the Supreme Federal Tribunal of Brazil.

http://www.supcourt.ru/EN/supreme.htm
The home page for the Supreme Court of the Russian Federation (includes English version).

http://www.worldlawdirect.com/
A commercial law site designed to provide answers to thousands of questions about law and courts around the world.

http://www.legal500.com/index.php
The official Web site of the "Legal 500 Series," a resource for commercial lawyers worldwide.

◆ ◆ ◆

Key Terms and Concepts_____

adversarial system
appellate courts
basic law
civil law
common law
criminal law

defendant
grand jury
inquisitorial system
judicial activism
judicial restraint
judicial review

justice

Missouri Plan

natural law

parliamentary supremacy

plaintiff

positive law

statutory interpretation

statutory law

trial courts

Discussion Questions_____

1. Why is the selection of judges often so controversial? What conflicting goals are involved?
2. What is natural law?
3. How do courts become involved in public policy making?
4. What is the difference between the inquisitorial and adversarial systems of justice?

Notes_____

1. The functions of judicial institutions are discussed in detail in Martin Shapiro, *Courts: A Comparative and Political Analysis* (Chicago: University of Chicago Press, 1981). Some of the text's discussion is adapted from this source.
2. See Henry J. Abraham, *The Judicial Process*, 4th ed. (New York: Oxford University Press, 1980), pp. 105–107; and Shapiro, *Courts*, pp. 133ff.
3. 373 U.S. 335 (1963).
4. Charles R. Epp, "Do Bills of Rights Matter? The Canadian Charter of Rights and Freedoms," *American Political Science Review* 90 (December 1996): 765–779.
5. Lief H. Carter, *Reason in Law* (Boston: Little, Brown, 1979), p. 110.
6. Ibid., p. 111.
7. See Sabrina Shizue McKenna, "Proposal for Judicial Reform in Japan: An Overview," *Asian-Pacific Law and Policy Journal* 2 (Spring 2001).
8. See Henry J. Abraham, *The Judicial Process*, 5th ed. (New York: Oxford University Press, 1986).
9. See Gregory A. Huber and Sanford C. Gordon, "Accountability and Coercion: Is Justice Blind When It Runs for Office?" *American Journal of Political Science* 48 (April 2004): 247–263.
10. See Gretchen Helmke, "The Logic of Strategic Defection: Court–Executive Relations in Argentina Under Dictatorship and Democracy," *American Political Science Review* 96 (June 2002): 291–303; and J. Mark Ramseyer and Eric B. Rasmusen, "Why Are Japanese Judges So Conservative in Politically Charged Cases?" *American Political Science Review* 95 (June 2001): 331–344.
11. Henry J. Abraham, *The Judicial Process* (New York: Oxford University Press, 1962), p. 251.
12. See William Safran, *The French Polity* (New York: Longman, 1991), pp. 178–182.
13. K. L. Bhatia, *Judicial Review and Judicial Activism: A Comparative Study of India and Germany from an Indian Perspective* (New Delhi: Deep and Deep Publications, 1997).
14. See David Horowitz, *The Courts and Social Policy* (Washington, DC: Brookings, 1977).
15. Shapiro, *Courts*, p. 146.
16. See Terri Jennings Peretti, *In Defense of a Political Court* (Princeton, NJ: Princeton University Press, 1999), p. 73.
17. *Dronenburg v. Zech*, 741 F. 2d 1388 (1984), pp. 1396–1397. Quoted in Archibald Cox, *The Court and the Constitution* (Boston: Houghton Mifflin, 1987), p. 331.
18. John Hart Ely, *Democracy and Distrust* (Cambridge: Harvard University Press, 1980), p. 76.

For Further Reading_____

Bhatia, K. L. *Judicial Review and Judicial Activism: A Comparative Study of India and Germany from an Indian Perspective.* New Delhi: Deep and Deep Publications, 1997.

Buurca, Graainne, and J. H. H. Weiler. *The European Court of Justice.* Oxford: Oxford University Press, 2002.

Cardozo, Benjamin. *The Nature of the Judicial Process.* New Haven: Yale University Press, 1921.

Carter, Lief H. *Reason in Law.* 7th ed. New York: Longman, 2004.

Cox, Archibald. *The Role of the Supreme Court in American Government.* London: Oxford University Press, 1976.

Dean, Meryll. *Japanese Legal System: Text, Cases, and Materials.* 2nd ed. London: Cavendish Publishing, 2003.

Dworkin, Ronald. *Sovereign Virtue: The Theory and Practice of Equality.* Cambridge, MA: Harvard University Press, 2002.

Dworkin, Ronald. *Taking Rights Seriously.* Cambridge: Harvard University Press, 1978.

Ely, John Hart. *Democracy and Distrust.* Cambridge: Harvard University Press, 1980.

Hart, H. L. A. *The Concept of Law.* 2nd ed. New York: Oxford University Press, 1997.

Helmke, Gretchen. "The Logic of Strategic Defection: Court–Executive Relations in Argentina Under Dictatorship and Democracy." *American Political Science Review* 96 (June 2002): 291–303.

Hesse, Joachim Jens, and Nevil Johnson. *Constitutional Policy and Change in Europe.* New York: Oxford University Press, 1995.

Holland, Kenneth M., ed. *Judicial Activism in Comparative Perspective.* New York: St. Martin's, 1991.

Huber, Gregory A., and Sanford C. Gordon. "Accountability and Coercion: Is Justice Blind When It Runs for Office?" *American Journal of Political Science* 48 (April 2004): 247–263.

Kritzer, Herbert. *Legal Systems of the World: A Political, Social, and Cultural Encyclopedia.* Santa Barbara, CA: ABC-CLIO, 2002.

Menski, Werner F. *Comparative Law in a Global Context: The Legal Systems of Asia and Africa,* 2nd ed. New York: Cambridge University Press, 2006.

Ramseyer, J. Mark, and Eric B. Rasmusen. "Why Are Japanese Judges So Conservative in Politically Charged Cases?" *American Political Science Review* 95 (June 2001): 331–344.

Svensson, Marina. *Debating Human Rights in China: A Conceptual and Political History.* Lanham, MD: Rowman and Littlefield, 2002.

Tushnet, Mark, ed. *Arguing Marbury v. Madison,* Palo Alto, CA: Stanford University Press, 2005.

PAPERWORK AND BUREAUCRACY   An official working for the Revenue Department in the Indian state of Karnataka retrieves a bundle of documents. After 2004, the office computerized its land records and banned paper records in an effort to increase the accuracy and accessibility of documentary information.

10

BUREAUCRATIC INSTITUTIONS

◆ What Is Bureaucracy? ◆ Bureaucratic Functions
◆ The Growth of Bureaucracy ◆ Bureaucracy Evaluated
◆ Bureaucracy and Democracy ◆ Can Bureaucracy
Be Improved? ◆ Bureaucracy in Political Life

On August 29, 2005, a devastating hurricane made landfall in Louisiana, Mississippi, and Alabama. Katrina's winds, coupled with sea surges and levee failures, caused unprecedented damage, particularly to the city of New Orleans. Local, state, and federal officials were involved in evacuation and rescue efforts and agencies at all levels of government worked extensively to provide food, shelter, medical care, and transportation for thousands of evacuees.

A barrage of criticism followed the governmental response to Katrina. Thousands of people were homeless for months, shelters were overcrowded and dangerous, security for businesses was poor, and all efforts appeared uncoordinated. While some complaints were directed at New Orleans Mayor Ray Nagin, Louisiana Governor Kathleen Blanco, and President George Bush, the Federal Emergency Management Agency (FEMA) was the target of the most heated attacks.

FEMA was established in 1979 by President Jimmy Carter. It was elevated to cabinet status by President Bill Clinton in 1993 and incorporated into the Department of Homeland Security by President George W. Bush in 2003. In 1989, following another hurricane (Hugo), Senator Ernest Hollings (Democrat, South Carolina) opined that

© AP/Wide World Photos

BUREAUCRATIC FAILURE?   Hurricane Katrina devastated New Orleans, leaving thousands homeless and destroying roads, businesses, and infrastructure. Bureaucracies at the federal, state, and local levels were severely criticized for delays and ineffectiveness in their responses.

FEMA was staffed by "the sorriest bunch of bureaucratic jackasses I've ever known." Representative Norm Mineta (Democrat, California) said that "FEMA could screw up a two-car parade." Following the Katrina disaster in 2005, Senator Trent Lott (Republican, Mississippi) specifically scolded FEMA's director Michael Browne: "If he doesn't solve a couple of problems that we've got right now, he ain't going to be able to hold the job, because what I'm going to do to him ain't going to be pretty." Senator Susan Collins (Republican, Maine) concluded that "governments at all levels failed," and expressed her concerns about the government's ability to handle a terrorist attack:

> If our system did such a poor job when there was no enemy, how would the federal, state and local governments have coped with a terrorist attack that provided no advance warning and that was intent on causing as much death and destruction as possible?[1]

Although many factors were involved in the unsatisfactory response to the Katrina disaster, there is widespread agreement that the results would have been far better if the bureaucratic institutions involved had been better organized and more efficiently managed.*

The problem of *bureaucracy* figures strongly in the problem of emergency management, as it does in most major governmental activities. In this case, public policy goals that virtually all citizens shared still required a complex arrangement of administrators to disburse money, design and enforce safety requirements, and make thousands of intricate decisions. Bureaucratic realities inevitably became part of the nation's response to its most costly natural disaster.

At a broader level, the nature and the behavior of bureaucratic institutions affect politics and government in all countries. We often think that the primary issues in government have to do with policy *making;* that is why we focus so much attention on elections and on executive and legislative institutions. Nevertheless, the workings of the **bureaucracy** often make the difference between success and failure, efficiency and waste, and even life and death.

Bureaucratic power is important in all countries. In nations with constantly shifting legislative coalitions and weak chief executives, the bureaucracy may be the primary decision-making body, largely because it is the only part of the government with experience in getting things done. Sometimes, bureaucracy dominates because leaders diminish the importance of other political institutions. During the 1960s and 1970s, military leaders seized power in several of the more economically developed countries of Latin America (Brazil, Argentina, Chile, Uruguay). The generals who took office had a bureaucratic approach to government that they had acquired in military administration, and they often blamed many of their countries' problems on political parties, elected officials, and the democratic process itself. They essentially disregarded legislatures and strengthened the hand of civilian "technocrats" (bureaucrats with economic or other technical training).[2]

Some democratic governments have delegated far greater authority to their bureaucracies than does the United States. The power of high-ranking bureaucrats in Great Britain is so widely recognized that a popular television sitcom titled *Yes, Prime*

---

* See Sandra K. Schneider, "Administrative Breakdowns in the Governmental Response to Hurricane Katrina," *Public Administration Review* 65 (September/October 2005): 515–517.

Minister spoofed a fictitious prime minister who was repeatedly manipulated by senior civil servants. France's very centralized and powerful national bureaucracy predates the French Revolution and provided efficiency and stability during a period (1945–1958) when the nation's prime minister and cabinet changed on the average of once every six months. The French Fifth Republic (1958–present) brought far greater political stability. Many of the most critical policy decisions are made by the president or the prime minister in concert with high-ranking technocrats, particularly those in the planning commissions.

In short, bureaucratic power exerts great influence in virtually all political systems. In the United States, bureaucrats make more than 80 laws (in the form of administrative regulations) for each law passed by Congress.[3] Those rules establish the level of emissions that will be tolerated from coal-burning power plants, a wide range of safety requirements, and other matters that involve basic policy choices. They decide where and how roads will be built, they approve and deny requests for public welfare, and they write and evaluate environmental impact statements. Regardless of culture or form of government, bureaucracy is a fact of modern political life. In this chapter, we study what a bureaucracy is, why it tends to grow in modern societies, why it is so often criticized, and how its power challenges democratic values.

WHAT IS BUREAUCRACY?

Although we often use the term *bureaucracy* as a pejorative ("He's just a mindless bureaucrat" or "She's going to give us some bureaucratic resistance"), the term actually refers to a distinctive form of organization.

The famous German sociologist Max Weber (we discussed his classic ideas about leadership in Chapter 8) set forth the concept of the bureaucracy in 1922. His work was an attempt to describe what he believed to be the basic features of a form of organization that would eventually exist in all modern societies. In fact, Weber argued that bureaucracy was an essential part of modern life. He identified several core principles of this new form of organization:[4]

1. Bureaucratic workers operate within **fixed jurisdictions** and are responsible for specific tasks. This enables bureaucrats to develop expertise in particular areas, and it also makes bureaucracy accountable, by establishing which individuals are responsible for which concerns.

2. Bureaucrats exercise authority within a firm system of **hierarchy.** Subordinates are clearly under the control of their superiors, a fact known by subordinate and superior alike. In a well-ordered bureaucracy, this strengthens accountability, because each bureaucrat knows which person he or she is expected to obey.

3. Bureaucracy operates on the basis of *written rules.* Consistency of treatment and efficiency are improved when bureaucrats are required to keep detailed official records of their actions and when specific rules apply to specific cases. Without a system of written rules, two welfare claimants with identical circumstances would receive different treatment, for example. Written rules ensure that the

IT'S A 300 PAGE GOVERNMENT QUESTIONNAIRE ABOUT CUTTING BACK ON BUREAUCRACY!

www.CartoonStock.com

This cartoon satirizes bureaucracy in the U.S., but bureaucracies in virtually all political systems could have been the target of the cartoonist.

workings of bureaucracy do not depend on the personality or opinions of individual bureaucrats.

4. Bureaucrats assume their positions through *expert training.* Thus, bureaucrats should not normally be appointed on the basis of political **patronage** or through nepotism.

Weber's model was an ideal that the bureaucracies of even the most modern nations fail to achieve fully. In virtually all countries, including the United States, patronage and personal connections play a role in some bureaucratic appointments. Thus, in both Chicago and Mexico City, membership or active participation in the political party in power may be necessary to hold certain bureaucratic posts.

A 2006 study of bureaucracy in Ethiopia concluded that it is particularly difficult for a political system to maintain Weber's bureaucratic neutrality when ethnic or religious conflict is severe.[5] Where there is no shared national identity or uniform political culture, it is virtually impossible for a nation's bureaucracy to embody the traditional bureaucratic values of objectivity and consistency or professionalism. In such settings, the political leadership uses the bureaucracy to its own ends, ignoring the disenfranchised and creating a spoils system that undermines bureaucratic efficiency.

Yet, Weber's model is worth considering for three reasons. First, even though bureaucratic principles are not perfectly realized anywhere, they are achieved to some degree everywhere. Second, Weber's model identifies those characteristics of bureaucracies that can make them effective agents of public policy. Finally, we suggest that the very characteristics that Weber enumerated may have both negative and positive consequences. Indeed, scholars, bureaucrats, and politicians alike in various countries differ about how fully governmental bureaucracies *should* match the Weberian ideal.

Who Are the Bureaucrats?

In defining which people are bureaucrats, it is necessary to distinguish between theory and practice. We usually refer to all government officials who are not elected to a legislature or to a chief executive's post, and who are not judges or soldiers, as bureaucrats. For our purposes in this text, we define the term more narrowly in accordance with Weber's usage:

> **Bureaucrats** *are public officials who acquire their positions on the basis of their qualifications and skills and who are primarily responsible for the implementation of public policy.*[6]

The degree of professionalization within actual bureaucracies varies greatly. Perhaps the most decidedly professional national bureaucracy is the French civil service. In France, most senior civil servants are recruited from the Ecole Nationale d'Administration (ENA), a highly competitive and prestigious institution of higher learning. In general, recruitment and promotion in the French civil service are closely tied to professional skills.[7] Although the U.S. bureaucracy is not as highly professionalized as the French—largely because of the absence of a national training institution dedicated to producing a corps of career bureaucrats—the use of entrance and promotional examinations ensures some level of professional skill.

British bureaucrats have a somewhat different reputation. Although they are also highly respected for their integrity and dedication, they are often criticized for elitism and lack of technical expertise. Senior civil servants often come from upper-class backgrounds and may benefit from having the proper connections in the "old boys'" network. Many have been educated at Oxford or Cambridge, but they tend to be generalists with a nontechnical education and are consequently less qualified than their French or German counterparts to deal with the economic and technical problems of a modern, complex society.

In communist political systems, government bureaucrats are often recruited and promoted on the basis of their commitment to the regime's ideology rather than on the basis of their technical expertise. Following the Cuban Revolution, for example, agricultural production suffered because managers of state farms (officials in the Ministry of Agriculture and bureaucrats in the agrarian reform agency) were often selected on the basis of their commitment to the revolution, even if they knew nothing about farming. In both the Chinese and the Mexican bureaucracies, young administrators wishing to advance up the organizational ladder must attach themselves to a more powerful patron within their ministry or agency. As that patron advances up the bureaucratic ladder, he or she will bring lower-ranking "clients" up as well.

Thus, in everyday parlance, the term *bureaucrat* applies to a rather wide variety of people in different systems. But, using Weber's approach, the most "bureaucratic" bureaucrat is one who fits the ideal of being appointed on the basis of expertise and training, despite the fact that, in practice, many bureaucrats are selected on other grounds. As discussed later in the chapter, scholars and politicians have long debated whether bureaucrats should be neutral experts or people chosen for partisan reasons by an elected leader; the former may be more expert, but the latter are more likely to represent the political values of the citizenry. This tension between the values of competence and representativeness exists in virtually all bureaucracies.

Bureaucratic Functions

Although the tasks assigned to bureaucrats vary widely, even among developed democratic nations, there are certain universal bureaucratic functions. The distinguishing features of those tasks are their technical nature and the level of detail they involve.

Revenue Collection

No viable political system can govern without tax revenues, and a regular, established process for collecting taxes is a key element of effective government. A specialized agency for tax collection is typically found in all developed systems, democratic or otherwise.

National Defense

In most countries, a significant proportion of modern government spending is devoted to national defense. In addition to the members of the armed forces, this function requires a considerable "army" of bureaucrats. Civilians employed by the U.S. Department of Defense currently number nearly 675,000, for example, and those employees are essential to the procurement of supplies and weapons systems and general management.

Service Delivery

Many services cannot be provided effectively by private means. Public health services, road construction, national park and forest management—among many other services—would not be performed as well, or would not be as widely available, if government agencies did not provide them. The magnitude of bureaucratic service delivery varies considerably, however, across systems. In Canada, New Zealand, Germany, and France, for example, bureaucracies provide a more extensive array of public services than in the United States.

Income Maintenance and Redistribution

Governments in modern industrial societies, capitalist and socialist alike, have established agencies to administer a wide variety of "safety net" programs designed to help people in financial difficulty. Bureaucrats are essential in this area because the policies require that each applicant's eligibility be determined case by case and because most programs attempt to provide follow-up help to the recipients of government assistance.

Regulation

Most societies seek to regulate individuals and businesses to ensure the safety of consumer products and the workplace, to restrict the use of public lands, to protect the environment, and to maintain the fairness of competition in the marketplace, among many other purposes. Although some people believe that regulation is excessive in modern societies, almost everyone believes that some level of regulation is needed, and regulatory agencies are established for that purpose.

Research

The market provides only things that people will buy, and basic research is not easily packaged as a consumer product. When societies want to engage in large-scale scientific work, bureaucrats often play important roles. Private universities and even corporations also make contributions to scientific knowledge, but much of the most important basic research—such as space exploration and advanced work in nuclear physics—is managed by bureaucrats.

Specialized Governmental Functions

Nearly all governments also provide a national currency and postal services, with specialized bureaucratic agencies for each.

Management of State Enterprises

In most countries, even capitalist ones, some economic activities are publicly owned. These include the Tennessee Valley Authority (TVA) and most municipal bus systems in the United States; the computer, steel, and chemical industries in France; the petroleum industry in Mexico; the railroads and electric power in most of the world's nations; and the majority of industrial and commercial enterprises in China. Administration of those enterprises is an important part of bureaucratic activity.

THE GROWTH OF BUREAUCRACY

Bureaucracies expand as modern societies develop. Legislatures generally remain at a given size (although their staffs usually constitute growing bureaucracies in their own right), and societies usually do not increase the number of their chief executives. Bureaucratic agencies multiply and expand, however, suggesting that growth itself is possibly a universal characteristic of bureaucracy.

Figure 10.1 shows the growth of bureaucracy in the United States over six decades. Federal employment has increased slowly since the 1950s, but growth has been rapid at state and local levels. Not only are there more bureaucrats today, but their activities also consume a greater proportion of the nation's gross national product (GNP), and they constitute a larger proportion of the workforce than in previous decades. Contrary to what one might have expected, there was a slight increase in federal employment during the years of the Reagan administration and a slight decrease during the Clinton years.

Why Does Bureaucracy Grow?

Two kinds of answers to the growth-of-bureaucracy question are given most often. The first reflects our growing *need* for bureaucracy: We need more bureaucrats and agencies as scientific and technological advances make government activity increasingly necessary. As societies become industrialized, the tasks of monitoring and controlling pollution, regulating the safety of the workplace, and ensuring that consumer products are not harmful become more important and more difficult. Advances in science and industrial development eventually require government involvement as research expenses outstrip the resources of private organizations.

FIGURE 10.1   GROWTH OF U.S. BUREAUCRACY

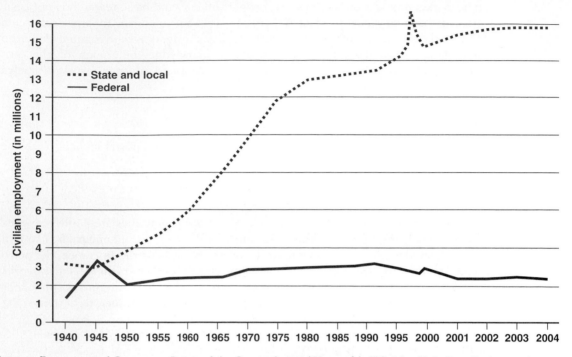

SOURCE: Department of Commerce, Bureau of the Census, *Statistical History of the U.S.* (New York: Basic Books, 1976), p. 1100; *Statistical Abstract of the U.S.* (Washington, DC: U.S. Government Printing Office, 1996), pp. 319, 346; data for 1997–2005 from the U.S. Census.

Industrial growth creates bureaucratic expansion in another way as well. When most of a society's people are concerned about their next meals, they have limited interest in broad social issues such as conservation or environmental protection. As people become more affluent, however, they often find that they care about a great range of social values. It is no coincidence that Americans and Europeans began to care deeply about protecting endangered species, ensuring the safety of workers and consumers, and wilderness preservation only after their societies became generally affluent.* Bureaucracies grow in response, as policies are made to address these concerns and agencies are established to implement them.

However, bureaucracies have also grown rapidly in developing nations, even with their lower levels of industrialization and economic modernization. For example, the devastating spread of AIDS in Eastern and Central Africa has forced governments in those regions to expand their public health bureaucracies.

Political pressures are a second reason for the growth of bureaucracies. In industrial democracies, interest groups demand regulations and services that require the creation of new agencies. In the U.S., organized labor was largely responsible for the

* See the discussion of post-materialism in Chapter 3.

establishment of the National Labor Relations Board and the laws it implements, and environmental interest groups successfully demanded the establishment of the Environmental Protection Agency. Indeed, in the United States almost all government agencies enjoy the support of at least a few influential interest groups.

In developing nations, bureaucracies sometimes emerge as the result of international as well as domestic political pressures. In Latin America, where farmland is generally concentrated in the hands of a small percentage of the rural population, pressures developed in the 1960s for reforms that would redistribute some land from large estates or uncultivated public property to poor farmers. In Peru, Colombia, Venezuela, Chile, and elsewhere, peasants organized federations, invaded large estates, and sometimes joined revolutionary movements to protest rural conditions. President John Kennedy, worried by the specter of the Cuban Revolution, launched a major foreign aid program for Latin America, called the Alliance for Progress. Under its terms, the United States promised economic assistance to nations that implemented land redistribution and other reforms. Anxious to maintain U.S. aid, virtually every country in the region passed reform legislation and created agrarian reform agencies. In time, only a few of those nations actually redistributed much land, but the reform bureaucracies remained, regardless of how much (or how little) change they actually administered.

Political pressures of a different nature have also contributed to the expansion of Third World bureaucracies. (See Box 10-1.) Often, educational systems in developing nations have expanded more rapidly than have employment opportunities in the modern sector of the economy. Hence, these nations are often faced with a large number of high school or university graduates who have no prospect for employment in the private sector. Left unattended, this group of skilled people might become a source of political unrest. Consequently, many governments prefer to hire them into the government bureaucracy, even if useful work cannot be found for them in the private sector. The visitor to a ministry of education or agriculture in Latin America will often see three bureaucrats doing the work of one.[8]

Box 10-1

THIRD-WORLD BUREAUCRACIES

Although bureaucracies are necessary components of any political system, they can become burdensome if they do not maintain proper professional standards. The governments of many developing countries overstaff their bureaucracies in order to reward political supporters and create employment for university and high school graduates facing a difficult job market. During the 1980s, Africa's public sector employed half the region's nonagricultural wage earners (many of whom worked in the bureaucracy). But a World Bank study of one West African country concluded that 6,000 of the 6,800 headquarters staff at two government ministries were redundant.[9]

While doing research at Ecuador's Ministry of Agriculture, one of this book's authors observed a ministry employee (whom we shall call "Mr. Sandoval") spending most of the day staring out the window or reading a book. Toward the end of the day, the office receptionist brought in a small group of peasants who wanted the ministry's help in a land dispute. When the nervous group leader had trouble getting his words out, the receptionist snapped at him, "Hurry up! Mr. Sandoval is a very busy man!" Not only do bloated bureaucracies create a drain on government expenditures, they also often justify their existence by turning out a vast array of regulations that stymie private businesses, large and small, and periodically force citizens of all kinds to spend hours on end getting unnecessary documents or permissions.

BUREAUCRACY EVALUATED

As noted earlier, the term *bureaucracy* often carries a negative connotation. Fortunately, real bureaucracies are not necessarily ineffective, unresponsive, or evil. Even in the United States, where bureaucracy regularly serves as a target of criticism during political campaigns, most people have fairly positive feelings about government agencies.* In a now-classic study, one researcher found that strong majorities of respondents considered government workers to be competent, efficient, and even friendly.[10] More systematic evaluations suggest a more balanced view: Bureaucracies have a great positive potential for *efficiency*, but they are almost universally plagued by *rigidity* and *resistance to innovation*.

Positive Qualities of Bureaucracy: Efficiency and Responsibility

It may seem odd to speak of bureaucracy as efficient and responsible, but for many important functions of government, bureaucratic organization is the only way to approach acceptable levels of efficiency and responsibility. Before governments instituted bureaucracies, tasks were randomly assigned to amateurs who held positions on the basis of their friendship with a monarch or a politician. It was impossible to determine which person was responsible for which decision, and there was little specialized training. In contrast, core bureaucratic principles—clear lines of specialization and the strict application of written rules—enable the modern Internal Revenue Service, for example, to process millions of tax returns quickly and, generally, with considerable accuracy. A less "bureaucratic" arrangement would simply not work.

A Persistent Bureaucratic Problem: Rigidity and Resistance to Change

The most discussed, and probably most common, problem of bureaucracy has to do with rigidity. Bureaucracy is slow to adapt to new programs, conditions, or special concerns. It is not usually known for its encouragement of innovation. The problem of bureaucratic rigidity does *not*, however, stem from the personal characteristics of individual bureaucrats. According to Charles Goodsell's popular book on U.S. bureaucracy, "bureaucrats are no less flexible, tolerant, and creative than other people—perhaps they are a little more so."[11] If the problem is not caused by individuals, it must reflect deeper causes *inherent* in the nature of bureaucracy, and we should expect bureaucracy to resist change regardless of which people are in charge. Generations of study have identified three reasons that bureaucracies tend to resist change.

Rules and Routines   First, the same **routines**—written rules and procedures—-that make possible the efficient processing of typical cases and decisions also make it difficult for bureaucracy to make adjustments or modifications when a special case arises. The mere existence of bureaucratic rules often tempts officials to try to fit

---

* A new study of "bureaucracy bashing" in U.S. elections found that the negative comments made by politicians have actually harmed bureaucratic effectiveness by creating low morale, hampering the recruitment of talented personnel, and "fostering an environment of distrust." See R. Sam Garrett, James A. Thurber, A. Lee Fritschler, and David H. Rosenbloom, "Assessing the Impact of Bureaucracy Bashing by Electoral Campaigns," *Public Administration Review* 66 (March/April 2006): 228–241.

unique cases into established categories when an innovative response would better serve the public. Although these rules and routines make bureaucracy more efficient *when they are appropriate,* some cases require unique solutions, and bureaucrats often try to solve them by applying established routines. (But see Box 10-2.)

Communication Problems   A second reason for bureaucratic inflexibility has to do with the fixed jurisdictions in which bureaucrats work. Communication is made difficult when each person's responsibilities are rigidly set. Bureaucrats have fixed jurisdictions and specialized responsibilities so that they can become experts in a narrow range of tasks and so that it will be clear who is responsible for which jobs, as discussed earlier. Those are important advantages to a bureaucracy. Nevertheless, some problems require discussion and cooperation among subordinates in different units. If bureaucrats feel that they can work only on problems assigned to them by their departmental supervisors, new solutions requiring joint operations with subordinates in other departments may be slow in coming.

Change and Bureaucratic Power   Bureaucracy also inhibits innovation because major changes in policies and operations often threaten the power position of specific managers. If a particular bureaucrat is in charge of, say, a snow-removal unit, he or she enjoys certain personal advantages (such as power, prestige, and control of a large budget). Those advantages would lead the bureaucrat to resist innovations that change his or her position. An innovative move to provide snow-removal service through contract work by private businesses may be a good idea, but it will be resisted if it leads to changes in the power positions of important bureaucrats.

Evidence from the former Soviet Union, China, and the developing world suggests that average citizens in those countries face far greater problems with bureaucratic rigidity than do citizens in other countries. One of the authors of this text recalls receiving a notice in the mail, while he was living in Ecuador, telling him that a package had arrived from a family friend in the United States. Knowing that the parcel contained about $30 worth of English-language paperbacks and other items hard to come by in Quito, he headed for the post office naively believing that all he needed to do to retrieve his package was to show his slip of paper and perhaps pay a small fee. Two days later—after having passed through five government offices scattered around town, paid three minor taxes totaling $12, secured the requisite importer's license for $7, and had at least nine documents stamped—he returned to the post office to claim his package. He left feeling far more fortunate than the Ecuadoran woman in front of him on "the last line." She was solemnly informed by the postal clerk that she had underpaid one of her tax payments by 3 sucres (worth $.02 in U.S. currency) and would have to go back across town to straighten out that tax. The postal clerk was unswayed by the woman's explanation that she had merely paid what the bureaucrat at one of the tax windows had told her to pay.

BUREAUCRACY AND DEMOCRACY

Nothing in Weber's list of bureaucratic principles mentions "government by the people." Instead, bureaucracy is "government by experts obeying their superiors." Decisions are made on the basis of training, analysis, and authority, not on the basis of opinion polls or votes. The realization that an establishment of bureaucrats makes

Box 10-2

A CASE OF BUREAUCRATIC IMPROVISATION

Bureaucrats are called many things, but they are rarely considered experts at improvising. As discussed in this chapter, government organizations have strong tendencies toward rigid adherence to standard operating procedures and routines, and often that tendency is valuable in making bureaucracies predictable and dependable. However, when government encounters a situation demanding an innovative or flexible response, *sometimes* bureaucracies can rise to the task.

The state of Israel faced a tremendous and sudden challenge to its ability to provide decent housing in the 1990s. The former Soviet Union opened the doors to free Jewish emigration in 1988 after years of severe restrictions, and thousands of these citizens planned to relocate to Israel. By 1998, more than 800,000 Russian Jews had immigrated to Israel, increasing Israel's population by 15 percent.

Among the many problems that this huge influx of people caused (imagine moving all the residents of a city the size of Indianapolis suddenly into an already populated country the size of Delaware) was an impending housing shortage. Two specialists in public management who recently studied Israel's experience noted that "it was clear that [the new immigrants] would soon overwhelm the existing housing stock," and "the Ministry of Housing was thus left with the mission of providing the immigrants with a permanent roof in a very short space of time without adequate means." For a variety of reasons, the government concluded that it could not slow down the immigrants' arrival, nor could it set up temporary tent housing.

The bureaucracy responded by improvising and cutting red tape. The Housing Ministry supported an act of the Knesset that allowed housing proposals for two hundred or more units to be approved through a streamlined process. The new arrangement gave power to six "District Housing Commissions," each of which was empowered to change existing land-use regulations, grant building contracts, and authorize building plans.

The improvising paid off. It cut construction time in half, "increased by a magnitude of four the rate of housing construction, and produced an adequate supply of housing for immigrants."* According to the authors, Israel's housing policy innovations show that bureaucracies can be innovative if the right conditions are in place. Specifically, bureaucracies need flexible and mentally agile personnel, and a culture that supports flexible solutions. (They argued that the cultures in Germany, France, the Netherlands, Britain, and Australia are not very supportive of bureaucratic innovation, but that those in Italy, Spain, the United States, and Israel are.) Finally, they suggested that an "unpredictable and rapidly changing" set of problems can induce bureaucracies to depart from their standard procedures.

*See Ira Sharkansky and Yair Zalmanovitch, "Improvisation in Public Administration and Policy Making in Israel," *Public Administration Review* 60 (July–August 2000): 321–329.

A CRISIS FOR THE HOUSING MINISTRY Israel's Ministry of Housing faced a serious problem as hundreds of thousands of Russian Jews entered the country during the 1990s. This photograph shows the tent and drying laundry of a family of immigrants waiting for more substantial housing opportunities.

© David H. Wells/CORBIS

Box 10-3

THE U.S. ENVIRONMENTAL PROTECTION AGENCY
RESISTS POLITICAL CONTROL

During the 1980s, President Ronald Reagan was convinced that the Environmental Protection Agency had long engaged in excessive regulation, and he wanted to reduce its activity and change its orientation. The conflict between Reagan and the EPA provides a particularly apt illustration of the problem of bureaucratic resistance to political control, since it involved a chief executive with strong popular support and a large bureaucracy with a definite sense of its own priorities and mission. A 1995 study suggests that despite Reagan's best efforts, the EPA effectively blocked his strategy of changing the agency's orientation.[12]

Reagan did several things to reshape the EPA. First, he campaigned on a platform that included support for deregulation, including environmental deregulation, helping to undermine the general public acceptance of EPA initiatives. Second, Reagan's first budget proposal included a major reduction for the agency, "including a 50 percent reduction in research and development, and 35 percent reductions in abatement, control, and compliance expenditures."[13] Third, unlike his predecessors, Reagan broke with tradition and appointed EPA administrators who were publicly hostile to certain missions of the EPA. Most notably, Anne Gorsuch

(later Gorsuch-Burford), who was appointed and confirmed as EPA administrator in May 1981, was outspoken in her criticism of EPA enforcement activities. In short, Reagan used all the tools of the modern presidency to alter the orientation of EPA activities: He rallied public opinion, he altered budget numbers, and he used his appointment power aggressively.

Who won the war? According to Ringquist's recent study, the EPA won a clear victory: "[Reagan's] strategy produced only short-term rewards, and in the long run produced an outcome in opposition to the President's expressed policy preferences."[14]

The agency used several characteristics of bureaucracy to its advantage. For one thing, the enforcement of environmental regulations is so complex and detailed that agency personnel were able to maintain a strong enforcement presence by using less visible actions to achieve their ends. Second, the EPA could rely on linkages with citizen groups and its supportive clientele to help in the achievement of its objectives, but this case demonstrates that even a popular president's multifaceted effort at political control can be ineffective in changing bureaucratic behavior.

---

most laws and decides most legal cases makes many people wonder whether a system with a large bureaucracy can really be democratic. (See Box 10-3.)

There is evidence that bureaucrats themselves are aware of the inconsistency between the guiding principles of bureaucratic activity and the ideals of democracy. According to a recent study of bureaucrats in Seoul, South Korea, many government officials regard basic elements of democracy as incompatible with bureaucracy.[15]

Why Bureaucracy Resists Democratic Control

The Bureaucrat's Information Advantage Many administrative actions, decisions, and policies are based on scientific data, careful and elaborate studies, and highly technical issues. When a political leader questions a bureaucratic decision, he or she is usually in a poor position to evaluate whether or not the answer given by the bureaucrat is sound. The politician is a generalist; he or she knows a little about a great many issues. In contrast, the bureaucrat is usually a specialist with detailed knowledge of subject matter that may be highly technical. It is often difficult for the politician to make sense of the answers given by bureaucrats. (See Box 10-3.) A recent study suggests that there is a basic trade-off between the extent to which a bureaucracy develops useful expertise and the extent to which it remains politically dependent on elected legislators.[16] When legislators need an agency to acquire a broad range of expertise, they generally grant it a great deal of administrative independence, thus making political control more difficult.

Iron Triangles, Sloppy Hexagons, and Issue Networks   Even more important than their information advantage is the power that bureaucrats may enjoy as a result of their relationship with influential interest groups and legislative committees. The significance of this relationship is suggested by the **iron triangles** idea, as discussed in Chapter 6. Essentially, the term was coined to describe a close connection among bureaucratic agencies, interest groups, and legislative committees in specific policy areas. Interests outside the triangle are, according to the theory, typically powerless to force policy actions opposed by those inside it, and are powerless to resist what the insiders want.

Where the iron triangle concept is an accurate picture of how policy decisions are made, serious questions are raised about bureaucratic power. As discussed in Chapter 7, *reciprocity* is a common norm in democratic legislatures, suggesting that legislators often find it useful to support one member's proposals in return for that member's support on another matter. Legislative reciprocity can thus heighten the autonomy of iron triangles, since the whole legislature may be willing to permit one committee to act in accordance with its fellow triangle participants (so that the members of that committee will be tolerant in return). Taken to its logical conclusion, the iron triangle concept implies that by allying themselves carefully with influential interests, bureaucratic agencies can insulate themselves from all but the friendliest control by the legislature.[17]

In developed countries, the explosion of interest groups during the past few decades has challenged the autonomy of the triangles. Environmental groups bring their interests to bear on, say, highway policy decisions that were previously made with the nearly exclusive involvement of a narrow range of actors. Consumer groups, feminist groups, and others similarly make demands that "invade" iron triangles. One political scientist suggested the term *big sloppy hexagons* to designate the more typical arrangement.[18] And, as we noted in Chapter 6, many analysts contend that the idea of an "issue network" more accurately describes the patterns of interaction among interest groups, bureaucrats, and legislative committees, because the term suggests the open, fluid, and diverse interactions that take place among the participants in most policy areas.[19] The situation is less predictable, with a wider range of interests involved, than when the iron triangle accurately described bureaucratic politics.

Nevertheless, the rise of issue networks and the erosion of iron triangles does *not* mean that bureaucrats are unable to use interest group power to increase their independence. The declining autonomy of the triangles simply means that bureaucrats must work harder to manage their interest group and legislative supporters, and there are few indications that they are unable to do so. Bureaucratic power continues to be an issue in contemporary democracies, and bureau and interest group alliances are still an important reason for that power.

Can Bureaucracy Be Made Compatible with Democracy?

The reality of bureaucratic power can arguably be accommodated within democratic principles in several ways. Considering them helps us appreciate the long-standing tension that has existed between bureaucracy and democracy.

The Politics/Administration Dichotomy   One approach is to deny the existence of the problem by invoking the *politics/administration dichotomy*. This is the simple idea that policies are made by politicians and that bureaucrats merely carry out, or administer, those policies. If bureaucratic power is applied only to the mundane tasks of implementing the policy choices made by political leaders, then we can be made to feel much more comfortable about the existence of bureaucratic power. Perhaps you have heard that "there is no Democratic or Republican way to pick up the garbage"; that sentiment is an expression of the politics/administration dichotomy. It suggests that bureaucrats make decisions on the basis of objective managerial considerations while steering clear of political matters. To the extent that this is true, the reality of bureaucratic power need not threaten democracy.

Nevertheless, this dichotomy cannot resolve our concerns about bureaucratic power in a democracy. As mentioned earlier, the vast majority of decisions—even many decisions involving basic policy choices—are actually made by bureaucrats. It is not enough, therefore, simply to assert the principle of the politics/administration dichotomy (see Box 10-4).

Technical Responsibility   Carl Friedrich, an important figure in political science from the first half of the twentieth century, suggested a second approach to the problem of bureaucratic power in a famous 1946 essay.[20] He began by admitting that bureaucrats make basic policy choices and, moreover, that they make so many of them, involving so much technical knowledge, that it is impossible for politicians to oversee bureaucrats effectively. Instead of concluding that democratic values are hopelessly lost, however, Friedrich suggested that bureaucrats are effectively controlled and made to act responsibly by *the force of their own standards and sense of professionalism*. He called that force **technical responsibility.**

The idea is simple. Bureaucrats normally feel the force of the standards used to evaluate performance in their respective fields. An environmental engineer considering a new pollution standard may not be effectively controlled by public opinion (since the public is not able to evaluate the decision independently), but the bureaucrat's desire to maintain his or her professional standing leads to generally sound and responsible decisions.

Friedrich's argument has merit. On a day-to-day basis, bureaucrats make more decisions on the basis of what sound professional practice demands than on the basis of public preferences. Yet, it takes little imagination to think of cases in which bureaucrats make decisions opposed by the public but nonetheless sound in technical terms. As one of Friedrich's critics pointed out, "Many a burglar has been positively hated for his technical skill."[21] Professional standards and technical responsibility may make bureaucrats skillful, but if they are doing things that the people do not want, their professionalism in doing them does not make their actions democratic.

An Expanded Role for Citizens   Other approaches emphasize changing bureaucratic procedures, especially those having to do with **citizen participation**. It is often suggested that bureaucrats will be more innovative, flexible, and responsive to public needs if they are forced to listen to the public as they make decisions. Many governments therefore require that public hearings be held before new bureaucratic rules and regulations are passed into law. The bureaucrats are not normally required to abide by the wishes expressed at those hearings, but at least they are exposed to the complaints and ideas presented. Evidence suggests that public hearings lead bureaucrats

---

Box 10-4

THE "REPRESENTATIVE BUREAUCRACY?"

Democracies of all types claim that their legislatures, executive institutions, and possibly even their courts represent the interests, preferences, and demands of the people, but there have always been difficulties in setting up *bureaucracies* to be representative. As Ken Meier noted in his classic *American Political Science Review* essay, President Andrew Jackson was an early U.S. proponent of the **representative bureaucracy** idea, arguing that "any position in the government was so easily mastered that no training was needed," and that therefore the bureaucracy could be staffed by political allies of the party that won the most recent election.[22] The bureaucracy would then be likely to behave in ways that represent the majority of citizens, since it would be staffed by people who share the values of the politicians that won the election.

The most common complaint about politically representative bureaucracy is that it undermines the neutral competence that professionalism requires. If bureaucrats seek to please the politicians who appointed them, they cannot be expected to be fair, consistent, and professional, according to this view. On the other hand, bureaucrats who are driven *exclusively* by their sense of professional standards may become insensitive to the values of citizens. As discussed in the section on "technical responsibility," the conflict between representation and professionalism as bureaucratic principles has been a perplexing issue for generations.

Political scientists have attempted to shed light on the problem in recent years by empirical investigation. In a 1998 study, three researchers studied the staffing and behavior of the Farmers Home Administration (FmHA) to determine if an ethnically representative workforce led to policy outputs (in terms of loan approvals) that were fairer to minorities. The data confirmed the authors' hypothesis: the more representative the bureaucratic office, the greater the "likelihood that . . . officials will make loan decisions favoring minority applicants."[23] The next year, Meier and two associates analyzed some 350 local school districts over a period of six years, measuring the degree to which the staff of each district was representative of the population it served, in terms of ethnicity. They also measured the percentage of students who achieved passing grades on state-required competency exams in each district. The findings demonstrated that "both minority and non-minority students perform better in the presence of a representative bureaucracy."[24]

Finally, in 2006, Meier and Laurence J. O'Toole, Jr. reported an empirical study that compared the influence of bureaucrats and the influence of politicians, again using a school district setting. They compared the impact of bureaucratic representativeness and the impact of the representativeness of elected politicians on the educational success of ethnic minority students. They found that having a representative *bureaucracy* had more than four times the impact of having a representative *political leadership*. The clear implication is that "the influence of the bureaucracy trumps that of elected political leaders."[25]

At least in these specialized contexts, the evidence is clear that bureaucrats act differently when they are ethnically representative of the citizens they serve. In itself, this finding undermines the claim that a highly objective, neutral professionalism drives bureaucratic behavior, or that bureaucrats simply follow the directives they receive from politicians. Incorporating this realization into our understanding of democratic government remains a challenge, however. When a bureaucrat's own values lead him or her to implement and make policy in ways that work against the preferences of political leaders (and the voters who elected them), it becomes difficult to determine which interests or citizens the representative bureaucrat is representing.

---

to consider problems from different perspectives as they encounter factors that had not occurred to them before such hearings and that the hearings thereby affect actual decisions.[26]

In Cuba, elected representatives to local, regional, and even national legislative bodies (called organs of *Poder Popular*, or "popular power") meet periodically with their constituents to hear complaints about the performance of the state bureaucracy. Indeed, in a society where opposition to governmental policy is not tolerated, these sessions not only are aimed at discovering instances of bureaucratic incompetence or malfeasance but also serve as a pressure valve because they are the only real political complaint citizens may publicly lodge.

Unfortunately, most public hearings required by law in most developed or developing countries have little effect. The general public is normally not able to explore the highly technical issues involved in most bureaucratic decisions, and people's concerns are often met with such statements as: "Oh, we have considered that, and your idea cannot be adopted because of. . . ." Moreover, many ideas at public hearings are contradictory (as when hunters and animal rights advocates press for opposite changes in a compromise about hunting regulations). Thus, although it is difficult to be against the idea of citizen participation, the ability of participation to remove concerns about bureaucracy in a democracy is limited.

Strengthened Political Supervision   This last approach has been used since bureaucracy was first established: Adopt reforms that enable elected officials to oversee bureaucracy more effectively. As mentioned earlier, the technical nature of many bureaucratic decisions, coupled with the vast number of bureaucrats and programs, normally makes it impossible for politicians to exert rigorous control. Nevertheless, steps can be taken to strengthen political supervision, thus improving the surveillance and monitoring of bureaucratic activity by both legislatures and chief executives.

Reorganizing the bureaucracy may also strengthen the hand of politicians in dealing with bureaucrats. Usually, reorganizing (that is, taking programs and officials from one agency and giving them to another or to a new agency) is advocated as an efficiency measure. Much duplication and waste are eliminated through effective reorganization. Nevertheless, reorganization can also help to disrupt the iron triangles that inevitably develop and that make bureaucrats so difficult to control. During the final years of the Soviet Union, Mikhail Gorbachev made great efforts at reorganization, largely in an attempt to counter the tremendous power of the Soviet bureaucracy. Richard Nixon initiated a failing attempt at a fundamental reorganization in the early 1970s, for much the same reason.

In conclusion, none of the methods of reconciling bureaucracy with democracy seems entirely satisfying. Even with technical responsibility, citizen participation, and strengthened political supervision, bureaucrats will inevitably have tremendous power in all modern societies. Dealing with this problem is an enduring challenge for all modern political leaders, democratic or otherwise.

CAN BUREAUCRACY BE IMPROVED?

Almost everyone agrees that governments must have bureaucracies, and yet almost everyone also feels that bureaucracies cause serious problems. Since bureaucracies cannot be eliminated, two sets of ideas have been advanced to improve them, to make them more adaptable and more easily controlled.

Make Bureaucracy Less "Bureaucratic"

Studies of business administration during the past 30 or 40 years suggest that organizations can become more adaptable if certain bureaucratic features are changed. For example, instead of maintaining the rigid lines of authority that lock people in fixed jurisdictions, many businesses have found it useful to give employees wider, more flexible job assignments. These arrangements allow workers to develop working relationships with many different people in the organization, not simply with people in the same official unit. Workers acquire a deeper interest in their tasks, since they are given a greater range of responsibility and more room for creativity. These organizations find it much easier to innovate and to adapt to changing circumstances.

The public sectors in many industrial democracies have also moved toward less "bureaucratic" bureaucracies. Although the basic bureaucratic rules are still observed to a large extent, the value of flexible organizational structure has made many public organizations more adaptable. For example, many federal agencies in the United States have adopted *flextime* scheduling, allowing workers to decide which hours during the week they will work. Workers who are given broader and more flexible jurisdictions are likely to bring more creative energy to their jobs.

Make Bureaucracy Smaller

Many people are becoming convinced that the best way to avoid the problems created by bureaucracy is to make it smaller, removing powers previously entrusted to bureaucrats and giving them to the private sector. In China, Deng Xiaoping called for sharp reductions in the bureaucracy during the 1980s. Although some of the reduction was associated with the transfer of economic activities (most notably, farming) to the private sector, bureaucratic cutbacks were an end in themselves. Clearly, Gorbachev had similar objectives in the former Soviet Union, although bureaucratic resistance stifled most of his efforts. In all communist societies, when state policy determines the prices and production of virtually all goods and services, bureaucratic shortcomings resonate throughout society. Taking some powers away from bureaucrats (and giving them to individuals making self-interested decisions in the marketplace) is one way to avoid bureaucratic problems.

Reducing the size of the vast state bureaucracies has become a high priority for many Latin American nations as well. Here, governments may be motivated as much by economic necessity as by the search for greater efficiency. Argentina, Mexico, and Brazil, for example, are saddled with huge budget deficits and vast external debts. To reduce those deficits and to secure refinancing of their debt from the International Monetary Fund (IMF) and from foreign banks, their recently elected governments have been forced to reduce the size of their bureaucracies.

In the United States, for similar reasons, some states, counties, and cities have "contracted out" for many public services previously handled by bureaucrats. When public officials decide how garbage is collected or how streets are cleaned, for example, it is argued that they have no incentive to be innovative or particularly efficient. Critics of *public* service delivery thus charge that this approach is inherently wasteful.[27] Greater efficiency would be attained if governments opened bidding among private firms for contracts to perform those services. Fewer bureaucrats would be employed, and fewer dollars would be spent.

However, the contracting approach remains controversial. Government loses some measure of control when public services are not provided directly by public servants. Some people question how diligent private contractors can be in seeing that services are provided *equitably* when they have such an incentive to maintain *efficiency*. (For example, private garbage crews working on a city contract may not serve hard-to-reach or poor sections of town as often as they serve well-to-do areas.) Attempts to privatize prisons have been particularly controversial. In any event, even if contracting out proves to be workable, it is not applicable to many bureaucratic functions.

BUREAUCRACY IN POLITICAL LIFE

What role does bureaucracy play in government and in our view of politics? Bureaucracy is obviously necessary. And if the work of government is going to be done with any measure of efficiency, consistency, and reliability, it will have to be done by organizations operating to a large degree in accordance with the principles of bureaucracy. It is worth noting that no modern system—regardless of culture, history, or ideological foundation—has been able to function effectively without a bureaucracy.* Although the necessity for bureaucracy is best understood in the context of carrying out government policy, it is also well established that bureaucrats do more than implement the decisions of others. The nature of their jobs brings bureaucrats into close contact with those they serve and regulate. That fact, coupled with their technical expertise, makes bureaucrats a powerful force contributing to public policy.

Bureaucracy, a necessary part of government, seems destined to resist control, making it a continuing source of tension in modern government. If the advantages of bureaucratic administration are to be maintained while controlling it and making it more adaptable, political leaders must approach the problem from a number of perspectives. Reforms calling for an enlarged citizen role, reorganization, strengthened political controls, and enhanced professionalism are all ways to enable political leaders to harness the power of bureaucracy without making it unable to perform its tasks. Understanding the benefits and the dangers of bureaucracy is vital for all modern political leaders.

 ## WHERE ON THE WEB?

Most Web sites pertinent to bureaucratic institutions are subject-matter specific. For example, sites are devoted to the U.S. Environmental Protection Agency, the British Department of Transport, and thousands of other agencies and bureaucracies around the world. Several universities also have sites devoted to their graduate programs in Public Administration. Following are a few illustrative sites as well as some general ones.

http://www.lafollette.wisc.edu

The home page of the Robert LaFollette Institute of Public Affairs at the University of Wisconsin, a leading graduate program providing training in public administration and policy studies.

http://www.uncc.edu/stwalker/sica/

The Comparative and International Administration Section of the American Society for Public Administration.

---

* To some extent, China's Great Proletarian Cultural Revolution (particularly in the late 1960s) was an attempt to do without a bureaucracy. The effort failed miserably, as discussed in Chapter 14. During the first decade of the Cuban Revolution (1959–1969), Fidel Castro tried to run the country through a combination of revolutionary exhortation and personal charisma, with little bureaucratic control. Here, too, the attempt was an economic and political failure, though not nearly as disastrous as China's.

http://www.opm.gov/

The home page of the U.S. Office of Personnel Management, with information about human resource administration in the federal government.

http://www.iiasiisa.be/egpa/agacc.htm

The home page for the European Group of Public Administration, the purpose of which is "to strengthen contacts and exchanges among European specialists in Public Administration, both scholars and practitioners."

http://www.geocities.com/gov_pubad/international.html

"Cynthia's International Public Administration Page," a set of links to important information about bureaucracies in a wide range of countries and about public administration research activities.

◆ ◆ ◆

Key Terms and Concepts_____

bureaucracy
bureaucrats
citizen participation
fixed jurisdictions
hierarchy

iron triangles
patronage
representative bureaucracy
routines
technical responsibility

Discussion Questions_____

1. What are the features that make bureaucratic institutions distinctive?
2. What accounts for the tendency of bureaucracies to become rigid and resistant to innovation?
3. Why do governments need bureaucracy?
4. Why does bureaucracy resist democratic control, and what can be done about it?

Notes_____

1. The remarks by Senators Hollings and Mineta were quoted in an article by Jerry Ellig in *The Hill, The Newspaper for and about the U.S. Congress,* March 22, 2006. The quotations from Senators Lott and Collins were taken from a BBC report, http://news.bbc.co.uk/1/hi/world/americas/4222272.stm.
2. Guillermo O'Donnell, "Reflections on the Patterns of Change in the Bureaucratic Authoritarian State," *Latin American Research Review* (Winter 1978): 3–38.
3. Quoted from a statement by U.S. Representative S. Levitas of Georgia, in John Sheridan, "Can Congress Control the Regulators?" *Industry Week* (March 29, 1976): 25–26.
4. This discussion is drawn from *Max Weber: Essays in Sociology,* ed. H. Gerth and C. Wright Mills (New York: Oxford University Press, 1946).
5. See Berhanu Mengistu and Elizabeth Vogel, "Bureaucratic Neutrality among Competing Bureaucratic Values in an Ethnic Federalism: The Case of Ethiopia," *Public Administration Review* 66 (March/April 2006): 205–217.
6. A number of political appointees are usually named to top posts in the bureaucracy when a new chief executive assumes office in most developed democracies, but this group is normally a small percentage of all bureaucrats. It should be noted, however, that in some local and state governments in the United States, a far higher proportion of positions are allocated

through patronage. Nevertheless, an important Supreme Court case (*Rutan et al. v. Republican Party of Illinois,* 110 S. Ct. 2729, 1990) made it unconstitutional to require partisan affiliation as a condition for obtaining a state job.

7. Ezra N. Suleiman, *Politics, Power and Bureaucracy in France* (Princeton, NJ: Princeton University Press, 1974).

8. Similar observations were made during the Depression in the United States about the Works Progress Administration (WPA), created by the Roosevelt administration to build public works and hire the unemployed. In both cases, however, it is possible that the social or political benefits to society of reducing unemployment may have outweighed the costs of inefficiencies.

9. Richard Sandbrook, *The Politics of Africa's Economic Recovery* (New York: Cambridge University Press, 1993), p. 43.

10. Charles Goodsell, *The Case for Bureaucracy,* 2nd ed. (Chatham, NJ: Chatham House, 1985).

11. Goodsell, p. 103.

12. Evan J. Ringquist, "Political Control and Policy Impact in EPA's Office of Water Quality," *American Journal of Political Science* 39 (May 1995): 336–363.

13. Ibid., p. 345.

14. Ibid., p. 359.

15. Sung-Don Hwang, *Bureaucracy v. Democracy in the Minds of Bureaucrats* (New York: Peter Lang, 2000).

16. Kathleen Bawn, "Political Control versus Expertise: Congressional Choices about Administrative Procedures," *American Political Science Review* 89 (March 1995): 62–73.

17. Several classic books include discussions relevant to this problem. See J. Leiper Freeman, *The Political Process,* rev. ed. (New York: Rand McNally, 1965); and Emmette S. Redford, *Democracy in the Administrative State* (New York: Oxford University Press, 1969).

18. Charles O. Jones, "American Politics and the Organization of Energy Decision-Making," *Annual Review of Energy* 4 (1979): 99–121.

19. Hugh Heclo, quoted in Richard J. Stillman, *Public Administration: Concepts and Cases* (Boston: Houghton Mifflin, 1992), p. 426. See also Heclo's "Issue Networks and the Executive Establishment," in *The New American Political System,* ed. Anthony King (Washington, DC: American Enterprise Institute, 1978), pp. 87–124.

20. The essay was titled "Public Policy and the Nature of Administrative Responsibility." It has been reprinted many times, but it first appeared in *Public Policy* 1 (1940): 3–24.

21. See the essay written in response to Friedrich's (note 19): Herman Finer, "Administrative Responsibility in Democratic Government," *Public Administration Review* 1 (Summer 1941): 335–350.

22. Kenneth J. Meier, Robert D. Wrinkle, and J. L. Polinaro, "Representative Bureaucracy and Distributional Equity. Addressing the Hard Question," *Journal of Politics* 61 (November, 1999): 1025.

23. Sally Coleman Selden, Jeffrey L. Brudney, and J. Edward Kellough, "Bureaucracy as a Representative Institution: Toward a Reconciliation of Bureaucratic Government and Democratic Theory," *American Journal of Political Science* 42 (July 1998): 717.

24. Kenneth J. Meier, Robert D. Wrinkle, and J. L. Polinard, "Representative Bureaucracy and Distributional Equity: Addressing the Hard Question," *Journal of Politics* 61 (November 1999): 1025–1039.

25. Kenneth J. Meier and Laurence J. O'Toole, Jr. "Political Control versus Bureaucratic Values: Reframing the Debate," *Public Administration Review* 66 (March/April 2006): 187.

26. See William T. Gormley, Jr., "The Representation Revolution: Reforming State Regulation through Public Representation," *Administration and Society* 18 (1986): 179–196. Other views of citizen participation are presented in D. Stephen Cupps, "Emerging Problems of Citizen Participation," *Public Administration Review* 37 (1976): 478–487; and Richard L. Cole and David A. Caputo, "The Public Hearing as an Effective Citizen Participation Mechanism,"

American Political Science Review 78 (1984): 404–416. A more recent, and rather negative, appraisal is provided by Marissa Golden, "Interest Groups in the Rule-Making Process: Who Participates? Whose Voices Get Heard?" in *Public Management Reform and Innovation: Research, Theory, and Application*, ed. H. George Frederickson and Jocelyn Johnston (Tuscaloosa: University of Alabama Press, 1999), pp. 285–311.

27. See E. S. Savas, *Privatizing the Public Sector* (Chatham, NJ: Chatham House, 1982), for the most well known statement supporting this movement.

For Further Reading _____

Allison, Graham, and Philip Zelikow, *Essence of Decision*. 2nd ed. New York: Longman, 1999.

du Gay, Paul. *In Praise of Bureaucracy*. London: Sage, 2000.

El-Ayouty, Yassin, Kevin J. Ford, and Mark Davies, eds. *Government Ethics and Law Enforcement: Toward Global Guidelines*. Westport, CT: Praeger, 2000.

Frederickson, H. George, and Jocelyn M. Johnston, eds. *Public Management Reform and Innovation: Research, Theory, and Application*. Tuscaloosa: University of Alabama Press, 1999.

Frederickson, H. George, and Kevin B. Smit. *Public Administration Theory Primer*. Boulder, CO: Westview Press, 2003.

Goodsell, Charles. *The Case for Bureaucracy: A Public Administration Polemic*. 4th ed. Chatham, NJ: Chatham House, 2003.

Gortner, Harold F., Carolyn Ball, and Kenneth L. Nichols. *Organization Theory: A Public and Non Profit Perspective*. Belmont, CA: Thomson-Wadsworth, 2007.

Hall, Daniel E. *Administrative Law: Bureaucracy in a Democracy*. 3rd ed. Englewood Cliffs, NJ: Prentice Hall, 2006.

Heady, Ferrel. *Public Administration: A Comparative Perspective*. 6th ed. Boca Raton, FL: CRC Publishers, 2001.

Henry, Nicholas. *Public Administration and Public Affairs*. 10th ed. Englewood Cliffs, NJ: Prentice Hall, 2007.

Hwang, Sung-Don. *Bureaucracy v. Democracy in the Minds of Bureaucrats*. New York: Peter Lang, 2000.

Jreisat, Jamil. *Comparative Public Administration and Policy*. Boulder, CO: Westview Press, 2002.

Klingner, Donald E., and John Nalbandian. *Public Personnel Management: Contexts and Strategies*. 5th ed. Englewood Cliffs, NJ: Prentice-Hall, 2003.

Mayne, John, and Eduardo Zapico-Goni, eds. *Monitoring Performance in the Public Sector: Future Directions from International Experience*. London: Transaction Publishers, 1997.

Mouritzen, Poul Erik, and James H. Svara. *Leadership at the Apex: Politicians and Administrators in Western Local Governments*. Pittsburgh: University of Pittsburgh Press, 2002.

Ostrom, Vincent. *The Intellectual Crisis in American Public Administration*. 2nd ed. Tuscaloosa, AL: Alabama University Press, 1989.

Pollitt, Christopher, and Geert Bouckaert. *Public Management Reform: A Comparative Analysis*. Oxford: Oxford University Press, 2000.

Rohr, John. A. *Founding Republics in France and America*. Lawrence: University Press of Kansas, 2000.

Savas, E. S. *Privatizing the Public Sector*. Chatham, NJ: Chatham House, 1982.

Shafritz, Jay M., Albert C. Hyde, and Sandra J. Parkes. *Classics of Public Administration*. 5th ed. Stamford, CT: Wadsworth, 2003.

Weber, Max. "Bureaucracy." In *From Max Weber: Essays in Sociology*, translated and edited by H. H. Gerth and C. Wright Mills. New York: Oxford University Press, 1946.

PART IV

POLITICS IN SELECTED NATIONS

Several of this text's earlier chapters focus on the political system's underlying functions or processes, such as political socialization or voting. Others examine critical institutions, including political parties and legislatures. In Chapters 11 through 16, we will shift our attention from particular functions or institutions to a more integrated analysis of politics in individual nations or regions. We will look at five nations to examine how the components of their political systems interact in each country. In addition, Chapter 15 focuses on political and socioeconomic development in Africa, Asia, Latin America, and the Middle East. Here are some representative questions posed in this section: How has Great Britain's historical development influenced its political culture? How does the great concentration of power in the hands of Russia's president affect that country's chances for consolidating democracy? How long will China be able to reconcile a free-market economy with a Leninist political system?

The countries discussed here—the United States, Great Britain, Russia (and its predecessor, the Soviet Union), China, and Mexico—represent a range of political and economic systems. Their governments share certain objectives, including the desire to protect national interests and to maintain themselves in power. But these countries also illustrate how differently governments operate, how divergent are their policy objectives, and how greatly their effectiveness varies.

Some of those differences are best explained by analyzing the issues discussed earlier in the text. For example, we can understand a great deal about a nation's political and economic systems by knowing whether it is democratic or authoritarian, Marxist or capitalist. But each country's political practices are also products of its unique culture and history. By focusing on the interplay of historical influences, social characteristics, economic forces, political beliefs and behavior, and governmental institutions within each nation, we further our understanding of politics in a changing world.

SOME CRITICAL APPROACHES AND ISSUES

In the coming chapters, we revisit some of the concerns of our earlier chapters, including the influence of political culture, voting systems, political parties, interest groups, and institutional structures. But we also examine the historical forces that have shaped each country's contemporary political values, behavior, and institutions. Although a nation's history may not predetermine its present, no country can escape its past. Great Britain's tradition of gradual and peaceful change; the birth of the United States as a "land of new settlement," free of a feudal past; China's historical struggle for stability; Russia's tradition of autocratic Czarist rule; and Mexico's economic and social problems have all left their indelible marks on the contemporary political systems in those countries.

The wave of democracy that swept over Eastern Europe and parts of the Third World in the closing decades of the twentieth century has put to rest many doubts about democracy's viability in non-Western nations. To be sure, democracy remains too tenuous in many countries to inspire confidence that it will become firmly established. Still, the reality and the rhetoric of democracy clearly have been in the ascendancy in recent years. Hence, a central concern in all our case studies will be the strength of democracy or the potential for its emergence.

Finally, our case studies will focus on a critical area of contemporary government activity: economic policy. All five nations have mounted considerable debates regarding the state's proper role in the economy. In the past, Russia's and China's command economies assigned the state a dominant economic role. Great Britain and Mexico established more mixed economies, with the nature of state intervention varying considerably. Of the nations discussed here, the United States has allowed the least state economic intervention. But during the 1980s and 1990s most of the countries in our study reduced statism considerably. Time will tell how permanent a pattern that change will be and what its consequences will entail.

GREAT BRITAIN AND THE UNITED STATES: DEVELOPED DEMOCRACIES

Both the United States and Great Britain are long-established industrial democracies. Both nations enjoy a high level of political freedom, a plurality of interest groups, competitive elections, and protected civil liberties. And all have advanced industrial economies guided primarily by market (capitalist) principles.

At the same time, however, important differences distinguish the two nations. Great Britain's political system has developed gradually over many centuries. Its political institutions have been emulated by other democracies and aspiring democracies throughout the world. Yet, it also maintains preindustrial traditions—a monarchy, a somewhat rigid class system—that seem inconsistent with the values of a modern democracy.

The United States, on the other hand, is still a relatively new nation whose democratic practices and public policy grew less from ancient traditions than from dramatic events such as the American Revolution, the Civil War, and the Great Depression. Its many opportunities for people of all social classes have shaped its political culture and policies. But so has its record of racial discrimination and division.

RUSSIA AND CHINA: PAST AND PRESENT COMMUNIST GIANTS

Until recently, the Soviet Union and China were the world's preeminent communist states. In both nations, Marxist-Leninist ideology established the political and economic agenda, and Communist Party leaders made critical political decisions with few external constraints. Their "command economies" featured state ownership and centralized planning.

Beginning in the late 1970s in China and a decade later in the USSR, however, both systems began to change. In the Soviet Union, Mikhail Gorbachev's reforms failed to save the established political and economic systems. Instead, they contributed to the collapse of the Soviet Union and the fall of Central/Eastern European communism. In contrast, China's leaders have decentralized and privatized the economic system well beyond Gorbachev's program of *perestroika* ("restructuring"). The country has established a dynamic capitalist economy, though one with a significant, remaining state sector and continued state regulation. The result has been phenomenal economic growth and a continuously growing private sphere. At the same time, however, China's ruling elite has resisted pressures for democratic reform.

Our case studies reveal significant similarities and important differences between the rise and decline of Marxism–Leninism in Russia and the modification of communism in China. Despite the collapse of Soviet communism in 1991, Russia still has not completed a transition to democracy, and of late has been reverting to a more authoritarian form of governance. China's economy now emphasizes a mixture of Marxist planning and free-market activity. But despite the country's economic boom, corruption, growing inequality, environmental degradation, and political decay are contributing to growing political protest and unrest. While not yet at a level that threatens the political system, popular discontent may do just that in the coming decades.

MEXICO: A DEVELOPING NATION

Among the dozens of countries in Africa, Asia, and Latin America, none truly represents the developing world. We have focused on Mexico because it is not only a modernizing, democratizing nation, but also a neighbor of the U.S., one of this country's leading trading partners, and home to one of Latin America's most intriguing political histories.

During the nineteenth century, Mexico suffered from severe economic inequalities, an exclusionary political system, political instability, and foreign domination. As a consequence, the country erupted in revolution in 1910, the first mass insurgency of the twentieth century. To address their country's political and economic problems, Mexico's revolutionary leaders created a more stable, more inclusive, and more effective political system. At the same time, however, the system was also authoritarian and corrupt. The 2000 Mexican presidential election brought full electoral democracy to Mexico as the PRI, the ruling party, was swept out of office after 71 years in power. Yet the failures of the current government, coupled with high levels of inequality, ongoing (if reduced) corruption, and sluggish economic growth almost brought the left-leaning PRD to power in the 2006 election.

11

U.S. GOVERNMENT: THE DILEMMAS OF DEMOCRACY

◆ The Founding Period ◆ Governmental Institutions
◆ Participation in U.S. Politics ◆ U.S. Politics: Prospects
and Challenges

The study of American government inevitably confronts a basic paradox: *Americans have extensive popular control over their governmental institutions, but the fragmented power of those institutions often makes them unresponsive to majority demands.* The system reflects the ideal of democracy in its history and in its political culture, but its constitution and institutions actually weaken the immediate influence that public preferences have over governmental decisions.

Politicians, citizens, and scholars have been divided for generations over how democratic the U.S. system is and how democratic it should be. Some argue that the system's fragmentation frustrates efforts to enact needed progressive policies. The independently elected president often vetoes congressional actions, or the actions are sometimes held unconstitutional by the Supreme Court. Presidential initiatives often fail in Congress, even when the president enjoys considerable popular backing. Fragmented power thus frustrates majority rule. Others claim that fragmented power ensures the protection of minority rights; pure majority rule would threaten them. Still others point out that the extra time it takes to get the fragmented system to act allows for a careful, searching analysis of policy alternatives.

As the world looks for appropriate models of democracy to guide the formation of new governments in Europe, Latin America, and elsewhere, the U.S. arrangement appears to many as a mixed bag. Although we are well aware that democracy can be undermined by tyrants and the force of arms, the U.S. experience suggests that democracy also may be compromised by the way government institutions are designed. Despite a long tradition of open, competitive elections, U.S. voter turnout is relatively low, particularly among the poor.[1] Moreover, despite notable successes, there is a widespread perception that the U.S. system has failed to achieve social and economic equality and to sustain a strong, competitive industrial base.[2] Those and other problems arguably stem from the fragmented nature of U.S. government. Citizens and leaders cannot make long-term, coordinated policies when decisions can be blocked or checked in so many ways, and voters often feel that their choices have no meaning when victorious candidates are unable to enact their platforms. The study of U.S. government thus raises fundamental questions about the nature of democracy itself.

THE FOUNDING PERIOD

Every political system reflects both its unique historical and cultural foundations *and* the political ideas that shaped its institutions. That is particularly apparent in the case of U.S. government. Things would be different if James Madison, Thomas Jefferson, Alexander Hamilton, and a few others had never lived, but the government they crafted would have been profoundly different if they had tried to apply their ideas in some other cultural setting.

Key Cultural Features at the Founding

Many Americans living in 1787 had recently emigrated from Europe, and many others were children or grandchildren of immigrants. They had vivid memories of the European experience. People recalled that in most European nations at that time, the poor did not own their own land but worked for a landlord, and businessmen had to purchase permission from a guild or a government official before starting an enterprise.

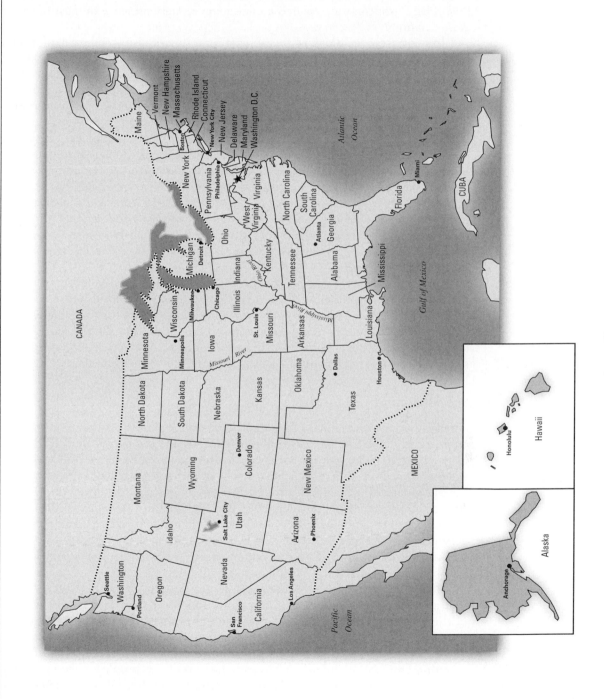

Most Europeans lived in the same villages in which they and their parents were born.* Recurring European wars created a continuing military presence in most of the immigrants' nations.

In contrast, even many of the poorest rural Americans owned small plots of land, and there were few restrictions on those who wanted to set up shops or factories. Early Americans were accustomed to moving around to find new opportunities and jobs, and the abundance of arable land and natural resources encouraged them to do so. Physical separation from Europe isolated them from the threats that made military authority so pervasive in the lives of ordinary French, British, or German citizens.

Those factors had a great impact on the attitudes of most Americans toward politics and government. Some of them had left Europe specifically to escape restricted opportunities, and others sought religious freedom or cheap land. Of course, some people came as slaves, and women were certainly second-class citizens. Thus, we cannot claim that the newly independent British colonies constituted a fully free or democratic society. Nevertheless, the salient features of American society—poor farmers with claims to their own land, no requirements for "royal licenses" to start businesses, extensive geographic mobility, the absence of a large standing army—created the beginnings of a unique political culture.

In the absence of restrictive social institutions, Americans developed a sense of personal initiative, a freedom to experiment, and a faith in individualism that stood in contrast to the predominant cultural outlook in Europe.[3] When they became accustomed to the lack of arbitrary official constraints on their lives, they did not want them reinstated. They consequently did not arrange their affairs around a set of governmental or social institutions, preferring instead to confront the "challenges of the frontier."[4]

Early American Political Thought

The system's governmental institutions were designed in this cultural setting. But the culture did not create the system by itself. Two specific events shaped the political ideas of the founding period. One was the Revolutionary War and the **Declaration of Independence** in 1776, and the other was the governmental experience *after* the Revolutionary War leading up to the ratification of the Constitution in 1789. Many Americans assume that the Declaration and the Constitution reflected the same ideas and sentiments, but they were written more than a decade apart, and they embody very different ways of thinking. The first strengthened the democratic spirit, whereas the second gave impetus to the notion that government power would have to be checked and divided.

As every U.S. schoolchild learns, the Declaration of Independence proclaimed that all men were "created equal," that governmental power derives from the consent of the governed, and that people have the right to abolish government that does not answer to them. As a famous historian said nearly a century ago, "This was a complete and sweeping repudiation of the English political system, which recognized the right of monarchy and aristocracy to thwart the will of the people."[5] The successful war effort that followed vindicated those who had faith in the ability of common citizens

---

* Even as late as 1870, for example, 95 percent of the people living in Bavaria had been born there. See Karl Deutsch, Jorge Dominguez, and Hugh Heclo, *Comparative Government: Politics of Industrialized and Developing Nations* (Boston: Houghton Mifflin, 1981), p. 22.

to work together to change society. The American Revolution affirmed the value of democracy that the Declaration of Independence pronounced.

Nevertheless, the following decade of government under the **Articles of Confederation** led many to *fear* democracy. Leading citizens expected that democratic government would permit the great mass of poor citizens to attack property rights. Their fears were heightened by **Shays's Rebellion** in Massachusetts in 1786. When farm mortgages were about to be foreclosed, Daniel Shays, a veteran of the Revolutionary War, led an assault on a Massachusetts courthouse with a mob of more than a thousand men armed with pitchforks and barrel staves. The independent states under the Articles of Confederation refused to contribute money to fund a military effort to secure order, thus requiring Massachusetts to put down the insurrection with its militia. The rebellion, along with smaller incidents in other areas, had a great impact on the framers of the Constitution:

> Shays's Rebellion, that heroic and desperate act by a handful of farmers, is surely the dom-
> inant symbol of the period and in many ways the *real source of the Constitution*. It was the
> frightening, triggering event that caused a particular selection of delegates to be appointed
> by their legislatures, induced them to spend a hot summer at an uncertain task in
> Philadelphia, and provided the context for their work and its later reception. . . . The need
> to protect property and contain democracy could hardly be made more compelling.[6]

Although the Declaration of Independence and the Revolution breathed life into the idea of democracy, the unrest during the 1780s made some of the framers anxious about it. These conflicting pressures are apparent when we compare the Declaration of Independence and the Constitution: The former document is a genuine and fervent appeal to the democratic spirit, whereas the latter is cautious and fearful of popular government.

The Politics of the U.S. Constitution

The Constitution was a collection of great compromises. It reflected democratic values in its effort to accommodate broad political participation, but it included features designed to limit the power of majority rule. Some of the framers felt that if laws could be passed by a single legislative chamber directly representing the people—without any check applied by a separately elected upper chamber or a separately elected chief executive—perhaps the poor (the majority) would demand laws that would destroy the liberties of the wealthy (the minority). Generations of critics have claimed that the U.S. Constitution was designed to obstruct such efforts and that it is therefore profoundly undemocratic.[7]

Some are less severe in their interpretations. For example, George Carey argues that the framers put **checks and balances** into the Constitution not to frustrate the majority but to prevent arbitrary, lawless officials from abusing their powers. Although he admits that the framers were concerned about majority tyranny, Carey argues that they were confident that the nature of American society itself would prevent such problems. In the *Federalist Papers* (especially numbers 10 and 51), James Madison explained that the "multiplicity of interests" in the "**extended Republic**" of all thirteen states would make it practically impossible for a single, narrow interest to dominate.

> In the extended Republic of the United States, and among the great variety of interests,
> parties, and sects which it embraces, a coalition of a majority of the whole society could
> seldom take place on any other principles than those of justice and the general good.[8]

According to Carey, since the *great diversity of interests in the society will itself moderate majority power*, it is likely that the checks and balances in the Constitution were put there simply to restrain tyrannical officials, not to stifle the majority. Perhaps the framers were not so undemocratic after all.[9]

The debate over the extent to which the U.S. Constitution is, or was intended to be, democratic has raged for more than two centuries, and the controversy will continue as the world moves ever closer to democratic principles. Even if we cannot resolve the ultimate question of whether the Constitution is genuinely democratic, however, it clearly was designed to create a more deliberate, more fragmented, more cumbersome governing process. Whether that is, on balance, helpful or damaging to the political system remains a basic political science question.

GOVERNMENTAL INSTITUTIONS

Both the promise and the frustrations of democracy are reflected in the structure of U.S. institutions. Imperfectly democratic, often politically inefficient, and certainly unwieldy, these institutions have been the target of numerous reform efforts.

Congress

Although the U.S. Congress performs all the functions identified as basic to legislative institutions in Chapter 7, it remains a highly distinctive legislature.

Bicameralism   Most of the world's legislatures are **bicameral** (that is, they have two houses), but upper houses are typically rather weak. In the United States, both chambers must approve legislation in identical form if it is to become law. A bill supported by the majority of the people's representatives in the House will fail if 51 senators oppose it.

In addition to the simple fact of having two houses, the special nature of bicameralism in the U.S. Congress makes it arguably undemocratic in other ways. (See Box 11-1.) Consider the *differences* between the House and the Senate. To be eligible for election to the Senate, a person must be 30 years old; the requirement is only age 25 for the House. Citizens elect senators for six-year terms; members of the House serve two-year terms. And until the Seventeenth Amendment was ratified in 1913, *state legislatures elected each state's senators*, whereas citizens elected House members in districts of roughly equal sizes.

Those differences have great political importance. Many of the framers were concerned that the House, made up of younger citizens elected directly by the people for short terms, would adopt ill-conceived, insufficiently considered legislation, driven by the whims of public opinion and the demands of the uneducated. Senators would act as a needed restraint. With six-year terms, senators could afford to make decisions that were unpopular at the moment. They would also be older, and, most important, state legislatures would elect them, making it likely that senators would be among the most educated, most accomplished citizens in each state. For those who feared that the House would reflect the demands of the unruly mob, the Senate provided reassurance: no House decisions could become law unless they were also approved by the restrained, experienced, and judicious members of the upper house.

As noted in Chapter 7, the other reason for the two-chamber structure of the U.S. Congress had to do with state power. If all legislative power were lodged in a single

Box 11-1

THE FILIBUSTER AND THE "NUCLEAR OPTION"

The filibuster is among the most notorious and most colorful features that distinguish the House and the Senate. The Senate, in keeping with its image as a grand deliberative body, has had a tradition of few limits on debate. The filibuster is both a feature of that tradition and a way to protect the power of Senate minorities. Formally, it is a consequence of Rule XXII of the Senate's Standing Rules. The rule states that during a debate on a particular measure, 16 senators can demand a vote on a motion to end debate. Upon the submission of such a petition, the presiding officer must

© AP/Wide World Photos

Sen. Strom Thurmond of South Carolina, then a Democrat, gestures while testifying before the House Judiciary Subcommittee on Capitol Hill against proposed civil rights legislation in February 1957.

> submit to the Senate by a yea-and-nay vote the question: "Is it the sense of the Senate that the debate shall be brought to a close?" And if that question shall be decided in the affirmative by three-fifths of the Senators duly chosen and sworn . . . said measure, motion, or other matter pending before the Senate, shall be the unfinished business to the exclusion of all other business until disposed of.

What is the political impact of this obscure provision? Note that the rule states that the vote to end debate (actually to limit it for one final hour) must pass by a *three-fifths* vote. Consider what you could do if you were one of, say, 43 senators opposing a proposed bill supported by the other 57. You know that it will be enacted if a vote is taken. When someone makes a motion to stop debate, your group of senators votes no, and even though your group constitutes a minority, debate must continue because the motion was not supported by three-fifths of the Senate. The filibuster is broken when a few senators opposing the bill are persuaded to change their minds, perhaps in return for a favor on another bill or as a result of a change being made in the bill under consideration.

The filibuster thus gives power to a legislative minority. Lacking the votes to pass or block proposals, 41 senators can force the majority to make adjustments. Senator Strom Thurmond, then a Democrat from South Carolina, set the all-time filibuster record in 1957, speaking on the Civil Rights Act for 24 hours and 18 minutes. (The Civil Rights Act eventually passed, but not until 1964.) The filibuster also figured prominently in the defeat of President Clinton's health care plan in 1993. Like other features of the U.S. Congress, the filibuster dilutes majority rule.

However, a 2004 study found that the filibuster may be less obstructive of majority rule than is often thought.

Gregory Wawro and Eric Schickler examined the filibuster and the threat of filibusters in recent Senate debates over tariff legislation and found that "narrow majorities were quite successful in legislating."*

The greatest change in the use and power of the filibuster in recent years occurred in 2005. Democrats had used filibusters to prevent the Senate from voting on motions to confirm several of President George W. Bush's nominees to the federal Courts of Appeals. Anticipating that there would be upcoming opportunities to appoint justices to the Supreme Court, the issue became increasingly heated on both sides. Democrats knew that, with 55 Republican Senators, they were unlikely to be able to block any of Bush's nominees, and several Democrats therefore stated that they would support the use of a filibuster (thereby requiring 60 senators to support a motion to stop debate) whenever Bush nominated an "extremist" judge. Democrats in the Senate were under tremendous pressure from interest groups supporting them to take whatever steps were necessary to prevent the appointment of new justices that would lead to a reversal of *Roe v. Wade*, the landmark abortion case.

*Gregory Wawro and Eric Schickler, "Where's the Pivot: Obstruction and Lawmaking in the Pre-Cloture Senate," *American Journal of Political Science* 48 (October 2004): 758–774.

(Continued)

Box 11-1

THE FILIBUSTER AND THE "NUCLEAR OPTION"
(Continued)

Filibusters have rarely been used to block judicial appointments. Republicans argued that using this method to block virtually all Bush nominees would create a precedent under which all future nominees would effectively need 60 votes in order to gain confirmation. Thus, the Republican leadership introduced the idea of the "nuclear option" (sometimes called the "constitutional option"), which would have ended the filibuster of judicial appointments.

Here's how it would work: Senators anticipating that they are in a minority regarding a judicial appointment would invoke Rule XXII, meaning that 60 votes would be required before the appointment could be confirmed. A senator favoring the nominee would raise a "point of order" claiming that the filibuster is not permissible in cases of judicial appointments, and the presiding officer would rule in favor of the point of order. A debate would ensue on the point of order when the minority side appealed the ruling, and the majority would move to table the appeal. The motion to table would win, only requiring 51 votes, setting a precedent

that would block filibusters of judicial appointments in the future.

The fallout from such a scenario would be difficult to predict, but it could lead to a removal of the filibuster from other senate decisions when a new majority seeks retaliation. Because so many senators feel strongly that the filibuster is a worthy tool that promotes helpful compromise and moderation, a bipartisan group (the "gang of 14") crafted a way to stop the impasse. Democrats in this group pledged to vote in favor of closing debate (thereby allowing the confirmation vote to go forward), except in "extraordinary circumstances." In return, Republicans pledged not to support the "nuclear option."

The impasse was avoided, and the Bush nominees were confirmed. Later, following the death of Chief Justice William Rehnquist and the retirement of Sandra Day O'Connor, the Bush nominees for their vacancies were also confirmed (Chief Justice Roberts and Associate Justice Alito). As long as the "gang of 14" is able to maintain the commitments of its members, it appears that the filibuster will survive.

House of Representatives, with seats allocated on the basis of state population, small states would be dominated and possibly exploited by large states. But each state has two senators, regardless of population, giving the states equal power in that chamber. That arrangement, the **Connecticut Compromise**, was essential in obtaining the support of small states for ratification of the Constitution.

Congressional Committees   Committees perform limited functions in some legislatures, assembling information and hammering out language. British committees, for example, do not typically take it upon themselves to make basic choices about policy, and if they did, the House of Commons would not feel bound by their decisions. But much of the real deliberation that occurs in the U.S. Congress takes place in its committees. They investigate agencies, demand reports and studies, and debate major policy issues. In most instances, the whole chamber approves only bills recommended for passage by the appropriate committee.

The power of committees in the U.S. Congress reflects, in part, the relative weakness of political parties. When party discipline is strong, committee leaders are likely to be loyal to the party platform, and committees exert less independent influence. If party leaders in the U.S. system could deny a member the right to run for reelection under his or her party's label, and if party leaders could control most campaign spending (as they can in some other systems), committee chairs would naturally be inclined to support and oppose legislative proposals in accordance with the wishes of party leadership. But, to an extent unequaled elsewhere, candidates for the U.S. Congress are chosen in **primaries,** preliminary elections in which voters select each party's nominees. Primaries take away a basic power otherwise enjoyed by party leaders, enabling candidates to achieve political success without having to please party leaders.

Not only do U.S. party leaders lack those powers, but also the tradition of the *seniority system* in Congress actually increases the independence of committee chairs. The seniority system is the practice of electing the committee member from the majority party with the longest period of consecutive service to be the chair. When the system was firmly in place, a committee chair could act in ways that showed complete disregard for the party's expressed policy goals, knowing that his or her political position was secured through the continued respect for the seniority system. Reforms passed during the 1970s weakened the seniority system—making it easier to elect chairs who are less senior but more loyal to the majority party's platform—but it still amplifies committee independence to some degree. The position of committee chair brings prestige and provides members with opportunities to secure constituent benefits.[10] The relative independence of committees enables legislative factions that would be outvoted on the floor to use committee leadership positions to affect policy choices. They can often "write their preferences into law" with little input from the membership outside the committee.[11]

Political Parties in Congress   Although a British citizen would find the absence of party discipline in the U.S. Congress striking, the parties do have considerable influence, and there are strong indications that party discipline increased considerably during the 1990s. From the mid-1950s through the mid-1980s, a majority of one party's members voted against a majority of the other party's members on less than half of the recorded floor votes, both in the House and in the Senate. On most votes, it was very common for a member to disregard his or her party's "line." As recently as 1982, "the House voted along party lines just 36 percent of the time, and the Senate just 43 percent."[12] However, by 1995, about 70 percent of floor votes involved one party largely voting against the other. "In the Senate, 73 of the first 100 votes divided among party lines, and on 56 of those, the Republicans did not have a single defector."[13]

Figure 11.1 shows the substantial increase in "party-line voting" that has taken place since the early 1980s. Votes identified as "party-line votes" are those on which a majority of Democrats voted one way and a majority of Republicans voted the opposite way. The figure shows that party unity became very high in 1995, in both the House and the Senate, but that it has diminished somewhat since then, although it remains higher than in the 1970s and 1980s.

Party labels have become more meaningful and more influential in Congress for several reasons, but perhaps most important is the recent ascendance of the Republican Party in the South. For most of the twentieth century, the states of the former Confederacy elected Democrats to Congress, even though the South was (and is) rather more conservative than the rest of the country. As discussed in Chapter 3, party identification is largely handed down from generation to generation, and the South's Democratic loyalties were forged during the Republican-led Civil War. Thus, the Democrats in the Congress were made up of liberals from the other regions of the country and conservatives from the South. These differing attitudes severely degraded party discipline, since Southern Democrats would regularly vote on many issues with Republicans. During the last 30 years or so, that pattern has changed dramatically.

FIGURE 11.1   PARTY UNITY: PERCENTAGE OF VOTES IN CONGRESS IN WHICH A MAJORITY
OF ONE PARTY OPPOSED A MAJORITY OF THE OTHER PARTY

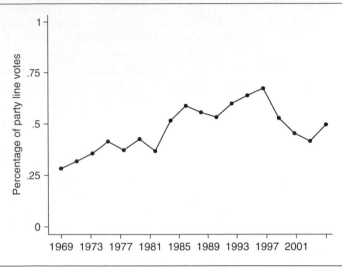

As recently as 1952, 54 percent of the Democrats in the House of Representatives were from Southern states, while only 8 percent of the Republicans were Southerners. By 1994, 33 percent of Republicans were southerners, and in 2005 this number grew to 37.5 percent. The number of Democrats in the House who were from the South continued to drop: only 25 percent of House Democrats represented these states in 2005.

Those numbers indicate that a major partisan realignment has taken place in the South, and that it has persisted and deepened over time. Large numbers of Southern voters changed their party loyalties. (Contemporary Southern politicians often quip, "Whenever a good old boy's great-granny passes on, he feels it's safe to become a Republican!") The remaining Democrats in Congress, increasingly from the coastal states, the upper Midwest, and the northeast, are more consistently liberal, making it possible for the Republicans to portray themselves as a clear alternative, and both parties thus have become more coherent and unified with regard to the platforms they advocate.

Despite the influence of parties, many members of Congress still stray from their parties' platforms on occasion. Campaign contributions arguably influence their votes on pending legislation. Concerns about the effect of contributions led to the enactment of the Bipartisan Campaign Reform Act of 2002, which limited so-called "soft money" and paid issue advertisements by groups in an effort to minimize the influence of money in congressional and other federal elections. (See Box 11-2.) Reformers argue that if members of Congress were forced to adopt their parties' lines, campaign contributions from interest groups could not sway them.

Incumbency and Political Competition   One of the most hotly debated questions regarding Congress in the 1990s has to do with the power of **incumbency advantage**. In recent years, fewer than 15 percent of the seats in the House have been **marginal seats** (that is, seats won by less than 55 percent of the popular vote). Most elections have been landslides for the incumbents.[14] In 2004, 97.8 percent of House incumbents won

Box 11-2

POLITICAL ACTION COMMITTEES (PACS), THE BIPARTISAN CAMPAIGN REFORM ACT OF 2002 "527" ORGANIZATIONS, AND FREEDOM OF SPEECH

The role of **political action committees (PACs)** and the money they contribute are controversial elements in contemporary U.S. politics. Campaign contributions from corporations and unions triggered heated debate for generations, and the development of PACs actually emerged from an effort to control them.* From the early 1900s, corporations had been prohibited by law from contributing to electoral campaigns, although labor unions could contribute freely. However, during World War II, Congress passed legislation that banned union contributions, and the ban was restated in the Taft-Hartley Act of 1947. PACs later emerged as a way for unions (and corporations) to make contributions indirectly, by setting up legally separate entities for "political education." The Federal Election Campaign Act of 1971 formalized the status of PACs and prompted dramatic growth in their numbers. The law contained an amendment, that affirmed the legality of PAC operations, as long as PAC funds were not obtained through membership dues or commercial transactions.

Union leaders did not expect that corporate interests would also take advantage of this law, but they were profoundly mistaken. By 1976, for example, 433 corporations had formed PACs; by 1992, there were 1,930 corporate PACs. According to the Federal Election Commission, a total of 4,499 PACs contributed some $604 million in the 1999–2000 election cycle. PACs can contribute only $5,000 to a single candidate in a given election, but they can give an unlimited amount to all campaigns combined. Those limits are left unchanged in the Bipartisan Campaign Reform Act (BCRA) of 2002.

However, the Act was designed to diminish the influence of money in federal elections by banning "soft money" contributions and by restricting "electioneering" ads paid for by unions, corporations, and PACs *that use the names or pictures of candidates during the weeks preceding an election.*

What is "soft" money? During the 1980s and 1990s, this term came to mean contributions to national parties or the parties' congressional and senatorial election committees, in contrast to the "hard" money contributed directly to campaigns. (In the 2000 and 2002 election cycles, soft money contributions to the Democratic and Republican parties totaled well over $200 million each.) The term derives from the fact that "soft" money contributions were exempt from the limits applying to direct contributions to campaigns because they were to be used for "party building" instead of campaigning.

However, the advocates of the BCRA argued that, in practice, soft money contributions were used almost entirely for purchasing campaign ads that merely *claimed* to be "public education" or party-building efforts. As long as the ads did not specifically urge the viewer to vote for or against a particular candidate, and as long as the hard-money funded campaign organizations did not coordinate with soft money contributors to direct advertisements funded with soft money, no laws were broken. Given that it was difficult to prove "coordination," and that advertisements could effectively be used to sway voters without explicitly asking viewers to vote for or against a candidate, reformers argued that soft money contributions were merely a way to circumvent the limits on hard money.†

If soft money contributions were really being used to advance campaigns, candidates would presumably do things in office to please the organizations that made those contributions. Reformers argued that it was not adequate to limit hard money contributions and to require disclosure of those contributions. The BCRA thus prohibited parties from accepting soft money contributions after November 6, 2002.

There is an interesting loophole, however, in the BCRA. The most commonly heard number during the 2004 presidential election was "527," the label given to groups who were exempt from the soft money contribution ban. These organizations are essentially PACs, but they are exempt from regulation. According to the IRS, a "527" group (the name comes from the pertinent section of the IRS code) is an organization that is created to receive and disburse funds to influence or attempt to influence the nomination, election, appointment or defeat of candidates for public office. Although "527s" are required to make regular reports to the IRS regarding

---

*The following discussion is drawn from John R. Wright, *Interest Groups and Congress* (Boston: Allyn & Bacon, 1996), pp. 116–122.

†See Jonathan Krasno and Kenneth Goldstein, "The Facts About Television Advertising and the McCain-Feingold Bill," *P.S.: Political Science and Politics* (June 2002): 207–212.

(*Continued*)

Box 11-2

POLITICAL ACTION COMMITTEES (PACS), THE BIPARTISAN CAMPAIGN REFORM ACT OF 2002 "527" ORGANIZATIONS, AND FREEDOM OF SPEECH (*Continued*)

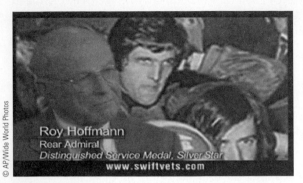

Retired Adm. Roy Hoffmann, head of the Swift Boat group, is seen in an anti-John Kerry ad released Thursday August 5, 2004.

This image from video shows a scene from a television ad by the on-line political action group MoveOn.org on January 17, 2003. Alluding to the famous 1964 Lyndon B. Johnson presidential campaign ad, the group wanted to convince Americans that President George W. Bush's policies would lead to nuclear war.

their funding and expenditures, they are exempt from regulation by the Federal Election Commission.

During the 2004 presidential election, a number of "527s" ran paid advertisements that attacked both President Bush and Senator Kerry. Television advertisements by the Swiftboat Veterans for Truth were controversial testimonials by Vietnam Veterans claiming that Senator Kerry had misrepresented the facts about his war record. MoveOn.org, a left-leaning "527," ran ads attacking President Bush, claiming that he had lied about weapons of mass destruction in Iraq. (See photos above).

One of the problems with "527s" is the fact that parties and campaigns are not able to control their activities. Both the Democratic and Republican parties attempted to distance themselves from at least some of the most extreme messages sent by the "527s" supporting them

(although it is likely that both parties welcomed the support that they produced among some parts of their respective bases.) As of this writing, efforts are underway to place restrictions on the campaign-related activities of these organizations. (See Table 11.1.)

Another major controversy regarding the BCRA has to do with its constitutionality. It bars unions, corporations, and nonprofit organizations (including "527s") from buying issue ads within sixty days of a general election or thirty days before a primary, *if those ads refer by name to any candidate for federal office.* This issue

re-election, and nearly every Senate incumbent won as well. For some observers, the decline in electoral competition is a disturbing trend. Voter turnout is low when elections are essentially uncontested, and voters begin to see their legislators as professional insiders, dedicated only to the advancement of their own permanent careers. (See Figure 11.2.)

Why has this change occurred? Some argue that the federal bureaucracy provides a huge array of opportunities for incumbents to help constituents (for example, by

TABLE 11.1 OVERVIEW OF FEDERAL 527 POLITICAL ORGANIZATIONS, 2002 AND 2004 ELECTION CYCLES

Federal 527 Organizations	2002 Election Cycle		2004 Election Cycle			
	No. of Groups	Total Receipts In 2002	No. of Groups	Organized after BCRA No.	Organized after BCRA Percent	Total Receipts in 2004
Democratic-Oriented Organizations	28 (plus 26 leadership PACs)	$107,200,590	59	41	69%	$321,185,549
Republican-Oriented Organizations	14 (plus 20 leadership PACs)	$43,686,999	21	9	43%	$83,922,290
Total	42 (plus 46 leadership PACs)	$150,887,589	80	50	63%	$405,107,839

SOURCE: Steve Weissman and Ruth Hassan, "BCRA and 527 Groups," Campaign Finance Institute (March 8, 2005).

NOTE: Leadership PACs are committees established and controlled by officeholders. Prior to BCRA, these PACs could raise and spend soft money.

was addressed in *McConnell v. FEC*, decided in December 2003. The court majority upheld the restrictions in the BCRA, concluding that the government's interest in preventing "actual or apparent corruption of federal candidates and officeholders" justifies the contribution limits. Moreover, the BCRA's provisions that prohibit candidates and officeholders from raising soft money to promote and attack federal candidates is "a valid anti-circumvention provision," necessary to make sure that the overall objective of the Act is met. Justice Scalia wrote an emotional dissent:

This is a sad day for the freedom of speech. Who could have imagined that the same Court which,

within the past four years, has sternly disapproved of restrictions upon such inconsequential forms of expression as virtual child pornography, . . . tobacco advertising, . . . dissemination of illegally intercepted communications, . . . and sexually explicit cable programming, . . . would smile with favor upon a law that cuts to the heart of what the First Amendment is meant to protect: the right to criticize the government (*McConnell v. FEC*, Scalia, dissenting).

The problems of regulating campaign communications without restricting constitutional guarantees of free speech will ensure that this issue will be a central difficulty in U.S. politics for some time to come.

seeking funding for special projects, or obtaining exceptions to regulations). Only incumbents can profit politically from doing those things, whereas challengers have to try to get votes on the basis of their policy views.[15] The vigorous policy debates that effective challenges would produce are thus lost as incumbents gain support by effectively handling the bureaucracy, not by taking positions on the issues.

The increasingly sophisticated *gerrymandering* of district boundaries by both parties has been the major factor producing the scarcity of competitive districts in recent years.

FIGURE 11.2   DECLINE IN NUMBER OF COMPETITIVE INCUMBENT HOUSE RACES

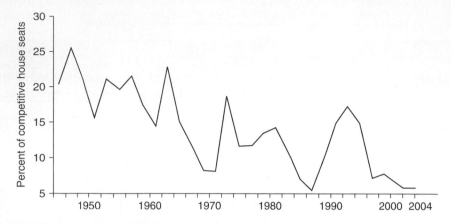

SOURCE: David W. Brady and Jeremy C. Pope, "Congress: Still in the Balance." *Hoover Digest* (Fall 2004) and data compiled by the authors.

Because all states (except Iowa) have procedures for drawing district boundaries that make districts "safe" for one or the other party, it is now extremely difficult for an incumbent to be unseated. In 2005, voters in Ohio and California considered proposals to institute non-partisan arrangements for drawing district lines, but both referenda failed.

The movement for **term limits** is largely a response to the power enjoyed by incumbents in Congress. If legislators were limited to, say, 12 years in office, they would not devote so much of their time to constituent matters, interest groups would not have such an incentive to use campaign dollars to develop relationships with legislators, and issues would become more important in elections, according to term limit advocates. Opponents of term limits argue that legislators gain essential skills only after they have had considerable legislative experience. An often-mentioned danger of term limits is that legislators facing a certain end to their congressional careers would, from their first days in office, try to curry favor with special interests so that they would have secure future positions. However the term-limit idea is resolved, the fact that it is seriously advocated reflects real concern about Congress.[16]

The Midterm Elections of 1994, 1998, and 2002: A New Pattern in U.S. Politics?   For nearly half a century, from 1954 through 1995, the House of Representatives was controlled by the Democratic Party. The Senate was also in Democratic hands during most of that period. The 1994 congressional elections produced a historic change. The Republicans won a net gain of over 50 seats in the House of Representatives, giving them a 236–199 majority, and they took over the Senate with a 53–47 edge. The 1996 elections trimmed the GOP's majority in the House a bit, but the Republicans actually won a net gain of 2 Senate seats. The fact that they were able to maintain control of Congress during a presidential election in which a Democrat won the White House indicated that Republican control of Congress would be secure for some time.

However, in 1998, the Democrats gained five seats in the House and four in the Senate. *That was the first time since 1934 that the party controlling the White House actually gained seats in the House of Representatives in a mid-term election.* In 2000, the Republicans won the White House, but, contrary to the normal "coattails" effect, the Republicans suffered a net loss of three seats in the House.

In the 2002 mid-term election, the 1998 result was repeated, this time to the benefit of the Republicans. The party in the White House *again* gained seats in the House of Representatives. The Republicans gained 6 seats, increasing their majority to 229–205 (there is one independent who votes with the Democrats), and they also gained two seats in the Senate. There was little consensus among analysts who tried to explain the result, but most observers pointed to the effectiveness of President Bush as a campaigner, the poor campaign strategies of the Democrats, and the lingering effect of the September 11, 2001, terrorist attacks.

These recent elections have challenged conclusions drawn from generations of political science research. The notion that the party winning the White House would lose seats in the House of Representatives in the "midterm" election two years later is perhaps the most reliable prediction that has been made about U.S. elections. The classic explanation is referred to as "surge and decline."

Simply put, the "surge and decline" theory holds that the higher voter turnout during presidential elections is made up of strong party identifiers plus a large number of voters with weak party identification. For whatever reason (economic conditions, war or other crisis, scandals), the political "winds" during a given presidential election favor one party or the other, and it is the voters with *weak partisan loyalty* that are most swayed by those factors. They vote for the presidential candidate who wins with the benefit of these favorable short-term forces, and, while they are in the ballot box, they also vote for the candidate running for the House from that same party. Two years later (during the mid-term election), the weak partisan voters stay home, leaving the House election entirely in the hands of the strong party identifiers. Without the boost that the weak partisan voters produced when the presidential election was taking place, the president's party loses some close House seats, thus producing the pattern repeated in every mid-term election between 1936 and 1994.

Some political scientists now reject the "surge and decline" theory. In a recent article in the *American Political Science Review,* two analysts argue that a substantial number of voters support House candidates from the party that wins the presidency during a presidential election because they favor what that party stands for during the campaign, but that, two years later, many of the same voters become disturbed by the actions of the president's party, and thus come to prefer the other party's candidates. In 1998 and 2002, the "swing" voters became more supportive of the party controlling the White House (the Democratic Party in 1998, and the Republican Party in 2002), for reasons that were perhaps unique to those elections. The Clinton impeachment controversy apparently convinced some voters that the Republicans in Congress were reckless, leading to Democratic gains in 1998, and international security threats in 2002 strengthened support for Republicans during that election. The party holding the presidency should still be expected to lose congressional seats in future mid-term elections, but the results from 1998 and 2002 demonstrate that extraordinary circumstances can produce a very different outcome.[17]

Congress: An Antique Political Institution?   For generations, critics of the U.S. Congress have argued that its decentralization of power impedes effective policy making. Congress is good at reflecting narrow, localized concerns, but it fails to act in response to broad policy demands made by national majorities. Yet some see value in the fact that Congress represents narrow, particularistic, local interests instead of broad, national-majority preferences. Perhaps Congress—by representing interests that are overlooked in the national view taken by the president—gives voice to interests that would otherwise go unheard. Following the majority rule principle, those interests *should* be ignored, and disregarding them would certainly make it easier to enact legislation such as meaningful deficit reduction. But Congress arguably performs a helpful role by representing the diverse interests that make up U.S. political life, even if doing so makes the institution less efficient.

Scholars studying Congress consider those and other ideas when they grapple with the realization that the U.S. Congress is typically considered to be the world's most important legislative body while also chronically in need of fundamental reform. Congress has more political independence from the executive than other legislatures, thus giving it more prominence than the "rubber-stamp" bodies in some democracies, but its internal divisions and the absence of consistent party responsibility make it frequently unable to act on broad majority demands. This paradox of congressional strength and weakness is why the institution remains such a fascinating subject for political research.

The Presidency

John F. Kennedy described the modern presidency in the following way:

> The American Presidency is a formidable, exposed, and somewhat mysterious institution. It is formidable because it represents the point of ultimate decision in the American political system. It is exposed because decisions cannot take place in a vacuum: the Presidency is the center of the play of pressure, interest, and idea in the nation; and the presidential office is the vortex into which all the elements of national decision are irresistibly drawn. And it is mysterious because the essence of ultimate decision remains impenetrable to the observer—often, indeed, to the decider himself.[18]

That statement captures the sense of puzzlement that strikes most observers of the presidency. The U.S. political system looks to the president for leadership, granting the office a level of attention denied to other institutions, but it also severely limits the president's power.

Presidential Powers　U.S. presidents have the basic powers generally associated with political executives: They serve as the chief diplomat, the commander of the armed forces, the nation's symbolic leader, the leader in times of emergency and crisis, and the most important source of policy proposals. Their powers are tremendous. As discussed in Chapter 8, however, chief executives in democratic systems typically have *limited* power, and the U.S. president—sometimes called the most powerful person on earth—faces particularly severe and complex limits.

A full inventory of presidential powers includes both those with origins in the Constitution and those that have evolved through history. The Constitution at least implies that the president will conduct foreign relations, and it is explicit regarding his power to command the armed forces and serve as chief of state. Other powers derive from the essential nature of the position itself and from the way incumbents have operated within it. These include the president's leadership of his party and his role as symbolic leader of the nation.

Strong presidents use their unique political position to shape the nation's agenda: Lyndon Johnson focused national attention on the plight of the poor in the 1960s, leading to dramatic legislative enactments; in the 1980s, Ronald Reagan effectively highlighted the issues of deregulation and of renewed military preparedness. In contrast, many observers faulted George H. W. Bush for failing to emphasize any theme or purpose during his single term (1989–1993). Bill Clinton's first term (1993–1997) was marked largely by his failure to gain passage of his central policy initiative, national health reform, and his second term by scandal and impeachment. George W. Bush's presidency will be marked largely by his leadership in the nation's response to the terrorist attacks of September 11, 2001, and his controversial decision to invade Iraq in 2003.

By many historical accounts, the most important president was the only great president to serve but a single complete term, Abraham Lincoln.* The Civil War presented Lincoln with basic choices that would alter forever the nature and the stature of the presidency. If he had looked to Congress to set the direction of the war effort, and if he had been content to operate within the limits of his office, the presidency would have remained a relatively weak institution. Instead, Lincoln responded to the national emergency by crafting an expansive vision of leadership. He ignored Congress when he felt it necessary to do so, writing the Emancipation Proclamation without any observance of checks and balances. He ordered restrictions on the mail, blockades of ports, and other actions—all without congressional approval. Largely as a result of those kinds of actions, Lincoln's presidency established much of the foundation for the enormous powers of the modern institution.

Franklin Roosevelt assumed the presidency in 1933, during a very different kind of crisis, the Great Depression. He responded by broadening the reach of government in economic and business affairs, thus initiating the modern welfare state. He also brought the presidency into closer personal contact with citizens, forging a bond that assumed almost mythical proportions. The larger governmental role that Roosevelt demanded required changes in constitutional doctrine: among other things, the Supreme Court eventually accepted the idea that Congress could delegate lawmaking power to administrative agencies.

Limits on the Presidency   U.S. presidents appear to be forced continually to assert their power, to struggle for the authority to act. The most important limit on their power is, of course, the fact that the president is elected independently of the Congress. Unlike British prime ministers, U.S. presidents cannot assume that the same popular vote that put them in office will ensure the passage of their legislative proposals. President George W. Bush's failure to gain passage of his Social Security reform proposals in 2005 illustrates how a president can be defeated, even when he has been elected recently and when the Congress is controlled by his party.

Of course, in the U.S. system, the president and the majority of Congress may be of different parties, a situation that occurred for all but 12 years between 1961 and 2000. This phenomenon of "divided government" is currently a subject of intense scrutiny by political scientists. The traditional view is that divided government produces near paralysis. Yet, historical research reveals that many important policy innovations have been enacted during periods of divided government. Effective presidents

---

* Lincoln had begun his second term one month before he was assassinated.

Box 11-3

THE IMPEACHMENT OF WILLIAM JEFFERSON CLINTON

In the first two months of 1999, Bill Clinton became the first elected president of the United States to be impeached by the House of Representatives. (Andrew Johnson, also impeached and acquitted, had not been elected, but became president after Abraham Lincoln was assassinated.) Clinton's primary place in history will doubtlessly be marked by those events.

The charges against Clinton are well known. He was sued in a sexual harassment case by a former Arkansas state employee, Paula Jones. As is typical in

CLINTON ON TRIAL   As specified by the Constitution, the chief justice of the Supreme Court (William Rehnquist) presides over the Senate trial of impeached President William Jefferson Clinton in January 1999. The only other U.S. president to have been impeached was Andrew Johnson, in 1868. The Senate failed to remove Clinton from office.

---

can work with a Congress dominated by the other party about as well as they can work with a Congress led by their own party.[19]

Bill Clinton's impeachment in 1999 (see Box 11-3) suggests both the limits on presidential power and the ways in which a popular president can survive under tremendous criticism. Most observers contend that the strong economy during that period, coupled with Clinton's great popularity in certain parts of the electorate, enabled him to escape conviction in the Senate. However, by most accounts, his record of legislative successes is weak.

Besides being limited by the nature of institutions and parties, presidential power is also limited because political conflict in the United States does not fit a clear ideological pattern. Instead of representing one dominant majority, presidents must work to balance a large array of diverse interests. When they can command a united majority of society's political energies, they have a much freer hand, even within the checks and balances that limit their authority.

The Institutional Presidency   Analysts and politicians agreed years ago that "the president needs help," and the *institutional presidency* is the term used to indicate the

sexual harassment cases, there were no reliable eyewitnesses to the alleged conduct, and so the complaining party (Jones) sought to demonstrate a pattern of behavior to strengthen her claim. Jones's attorneys had discovered that President Clinton had had a sexual relationship with a young subordinate in the White House, and they sought testimony about that relationship to use in their litigation. Under oath, Clinton denied having a sexual relationship with the subordinate, Monica Lewinsky. When forensic evidence proved that there had been a sexual relationship, a movement in Congress began to impeach President Clinton for the crimes of perjury and obstruction of justice.

The House of Representatives narrowly voted to approve two Articles of Impeachment, but the Senate acquitted Clinton. (Article I failed to pass on a vote of 45 voting guilty and 55 voting not guilty; Article II failed on a vote of 50 guilty and 50 not guilty.)

The fallout from the Clinton impeachment is difficult to judge. One thing that changed very quickly, however, was the law regarding independent counsel prosecutions of elected federal officials. Enacted in the aftermath of the Nixon Watergate scandals, the independent counsel law created an arrangement under which the attorney general was required to appoint an independent counsel to investigate allegations about federal elected officials. The idea was that political appointees in the Justice Department could not be assumed to be adequately independent of the White House or of partisan politics, which was certainly the case during the Nixon years. However, many analysts criticized the independent counsel arrangement, arguing that it created an office with an unlimited budget and purview to prosecute a single individual, and that there were no checks on the counsel's behavior.

In virtually all cases, independent counsels were attacked by their targets as being on "witch-hunts" and being partisan. President Reagan's supporters argued along those lines in the 1980s, and President Clinton and his supporters did so in the case of Kenneth Starr during the 1990s. The independent counsel law expired in 2000, and Congress decided not to reenact it. Congress or the president's Justice Department will be expected to pursue such investigations in the future.

The other consequences are much more difficult to judge. Most commentators have referred to a substantial erosion of trust in elected leaders as the main effect of the Clinton years. His supporters became cynical about the law and the partisan nature of ostensibly objective investigations. Clinton's opponents argue that he diminished respect for the office of the president both by his own actions and by his supporters' frequent claim that previous presidents behaved much as he had.

The one thing everyone can agree on is that the Clinton years were a fascinating chapter in U.S. political history.

extensive system of supporting institutions surrounding the chief executive. Most important, the **president's cabinet,** which traditionally consists of the heads of major departments and others of similar status selected by the president to be in the group, has existed since Washington's time, and most presidents get useful advice from these individuals. But presidential cabinets rarely function as genuine policy-making bodies. Presidents typically select cabinet secretaries to please important interest groups or to repay political favors. Once in power, these officials gain independent support from important constituencies, and they usually come to identify with the goals of the departments they manage.

This tendency toward independence on the part of cabinet officials has long been recognized, as suggested by the famous remark by Charles Dawes (Calvin Coolidge's vice president) that "the members of the Cabinet are the President's natural enemies."[20] Similarly, President Lyndon Johnson complained, "When I looked out at the heads of the departments, I realized that while all had been appointed by me, not a single one was really mine. I could never fully depend on them to put my priorities first. . . . ."[21] Although hearing a diverse array of voices can be helpful to a president, the independence of many cabinet members makes the cabinet less useful than most presidents expected when they assumed office. Presidents thus usually have an informal group of close advisers, often called the "kitchen cabinet," who remain close to the president and share ideas on policies and political strategy.

The vast workings of the executive branch demand a much larger institutional establishment than the cabinet. In 1939, Franklin Roosevelt created the Executive Office of the President (EOP), an umbrella term for a group of organizations including the Office of Management and Budget, the Council of Economic Advisers, and the National Security Council. These units coordinate policy making and maintain contact between the president and dozens of administrative agencies.

The large executive establishment thus performs two somewhat contradictory functions. Some people are chosen to *secure political support* from interests who, because of the weak partisan identification and discipline in U.S. politics, would otherwise oppose the administration. The units of the EOP, in contrast, are intended to *centralize presidential control.*

Presidential Character   Social scientists are often drawn to conclusions about economic and social "forces" that can be measured and predicted. However, the U.S. presidency provides an excellent context for illustrating that individuals make a difference. Although constitutional features, economic conditions, and changes in partisan alignment, among many other things, affect presidential actions and choices, it is clear that the nature of the person in the office also has great impact. This is the basis for the study of **presidential "character."**[22]

There is a wide consensus that the 43 men who have served as U.S. presidents constitute a varied lot. Some brought a strong ideological fervor to the office, acting aggressively to change the direction of government policies and programs, challenging Congress and the courts. Others were content to manage the status quo. Some enjoyed the office, relishing its challenges with enthusiasm, whereas others developed a siege mentality, focusing on perceived threats.

When James Barber explored the backgrounds and actions of several twentieth-century presidents in an effort to discover the nature of their personalities, he argued convincingly that much of U.S. history has been shaped by differences in the characters of the men who have served as president. Franklin Roosevelt's "active-positive" personality gave him strength as a leader and helped him reach for his optimistic vision in designing a new role for government. In great contrast, Barber classified Richard Nixon as an "active-negative" president, claiming that his personality led him to devote an unusual amount of energy to defeating and eluding "enemies." If presidents' personalities had been different, their presidencies would have been different.[23]

Table 11.2 lists the results of four recent efforts to assemble "ratings" of the U.S. presidents based on surveys. The first three are surveys of scholars, and the fourth is a 2005 survey of U.S. citizens. Although one would expect that the political ideology of the raters would influence their choices, it is remarkable that there is so much agreement among the scholars' rankings. Washington, Lincoln, and Franklin Roosevelt are the three most highly ranked presidents in each scholarly survey, and Buchanan, Andrew Johnson, and Harding are consistently ranked very low. There is considerable disagreement regarding recent presidents, however, with Reagan ranking in the "near great" category in two of the scholars' surveys, and first by the public opinion poll, but in the "low average" rating in Schlesinger's study. (Historians are reluctant to render a

TABLE 11.2 SCHOLARLY AND PUBLIC RANKINGS OF U.S. PRESIDENTS

President	RANKING BY SCHOLARS			PUBLIC OPINION	
	Schlesinger	Federalist Society	Wall Street Journal 2005	Gallop Poll 2005***	
Lincoln	1	2	2	3	**The Top Three**
Washington	2	1	1	7	Washington
F. D. Roosevelt	3	3	3	4	
Jefferson	4	4	4	11	
Jackson	5	6	10		
T. Roosevelt	6	5	5	10	
Wilson	7	11	11		Lincoln
Truman	8	7	7	9	
Polk	9	10	9		
Eisenhower	10	9	8	13	
J. Adams	11	13	13		
Kennedy	12	18	15	5	F. Roosevelt
Cleveland	13	12	12		
L. Johnson	14	17	18		
Monroe	15	16	16		
McKinley	16	14	14		**The Worst**
Madison	17	15	17		
J.Q. Adams	18	20	25		Pierce Buchanan
B. Harrison	19	27	30		
Clinton	20	24	22	2	
Van Buren	21	23	27		
Taft	22	19	20		
Hayes	23	22	24		
G.H.W. Bush	24	21	21	12	A. Johnson Grant
Reagan	25	8	6	1	
Arthur	26	26	26		
Carter	27	30	34	8	
Ford	28	28	28		
Taylor	29	31	33		
Coolidge	30	25	23		Harding Hoover
Fillmore	31	35	36		
Tyler	32	34	35		
Pierce	33	37T	38		
Grant	34	32	29		
Hoover	35	29	31		
Nixon	36	33	32	14	Nixon
A. Johnson	37	36	37		
Buchanan	38	39	40		
Harding	39	37T	39		
Garfield	*	*	*		
W.H. Harrison	*	*	*		
George W. Bush	**	**	**	6	

* Garfield and W.H. Harrison were omitted from the scholars' surveys because they served such short terms.

** George W. Bush was only included in the Gallup public opinion poll.

*** The Gallup poll asked the respondents the following question: "Who do you regard as the greatest United States president?" The presidents are ranked on the basis of the percentage of the sample that indicated each president as "greatest." Only 14 presidents received mentions from at least one percent of the sample; therefore the other presidents were not ranked in this poll.

SOURCES: The Schlesinger survey was based on the responses of 32 presidential historians in the 1990s and was obtained from a feature in *The New York Times Magazine*, "The Ultimate Approval Rating," December 15, 1996, pp. 46–49. The Federalist Society survey was based on responses from 78 scholars said to represent a "politically balanced" group selected by Akhil Reed Amar (Yale), Alan Brinkley (Columbia), Steven G. Calabresi (Northwestern), James W. Ceaser (Virginia), Forrest McDonald (Alabama), and Steven Skowronek (Yale). It was obtained as published in the *Wall Street Journal's* "Opinion Journal," November 16, 2000. The 2005 *Wall Street Journal* ranking was drawn from a survey of "130 prominent professors of history, law, political science, and economics" in February and March of 2005, and is available at http://www.opinionjournal.com/extra/?id=110007243. Finally, the Gallup poll was based on a survey of 1,008 U.S. adults taken in February 2005. The full study is available at http://www.pollingreport.com/wh-hstry.htm.

judgment about a president's place in history while he is still in office, and thus George W. Bush is not included in the scholars' rankings.)

Careful study of the U.S. presidency reveals much about the political system as a whole. Presidents are given great responsibilities and important powers, but the checks and balances of the system and the absence of coherent partisan or ideological divisions among citizens often deny presidents the power to implement the platform that got them elected. The great presidents are those who are able to transcend those constraints, forging support in a system not inclined to grant it.

The Judicial System

If a single institution had to be selected to illustrate the distinctiveness of government in the United States, most observers would choose the judiciary. It is both powerful and politically unaccountable, and it further fragments the policy-making power of the system.

Organization   The U.S. judiciary consists of state courts (including the various municipal courts that states create) and federal courts. Each state has a system of trial and appellate courts, although each state's arrangement is unique in some respects. State courts hear cases dealing with state law (most criminal matters are issues of state law), and federal courts deal with cases pertaining to acts of Congress, administrative rules, and constitutional provisions. Each state has at least one of the 94 federal *district courts*. Appeals from the district courts and from the agencies are heard by the 13 *U.S. Courts of Appeals,* located in geographic regions known as "circuits." The single *Supreme Court* hears appeals from the appeals courts and from state supreme courts. It decides about 140 cases per year.

The Evolution of Judicial Power   When it began operating in 1790, the Supreme Court had a rather limited and uncertain status. It received no important cases during its first few years, and it did not attempt to overturn presidential or congressional acts. However, the Court's power was greatly expanded as a result of **Marbury v. Madison,** the 1803 case regarding a minor government job that became the "rib of the Constitution."[24] President Thomas Jefferson and Secretary of State James Madison refused to grant a commission for a judgeship to William Marbury, who had been promised the job during the last days of the Adams administration. The previous secretary of state, John Marshall, had neglected to send the commission. Jefferson decided to take advantage of Marshall's oversight and give the job to a supporter of his own party. Marbury petitioned the Supreme Court to force the president to give him his commission.

Many people expected that the Court would approve Marbury's request. (After all, the chief justice was none other than John Marshall, the former secretary of state who wanted Marbury to have the commission in the first place!) But there was a legal problem: The jurisdiction of the Supreme Court as defined by the Constitution did not include the power to act in response to that kind of request; instead, an *act of Congress* (The Judiciary Act of 1789) created that power.

If Marshall had tried to force Jefferson to give Marbury the job, Jefferson might have ignored him, and a precedent would have been set establishing that the Court's pronouncements carry little weight. Instead, Marshall held that it was *unconstitutional* for Congress to alter the jurisdiction of the Court, since its jurisdiction was set forth in the Constitution, and thus the Court was powerless to act on Marbury's petition. Although Marbury *should* get the job, he argued, the Court could not hear his petition. Thus, the Court did not force Jefferson to give the job to Marbury. In accepting *Marbury v. Madison,* however, Jefferson helped to solidify the notion that the Supreme Court has the power to decide whether a law is "constitutional."*

Despite its importance, it would be wrong to assume that this case was the exclusive source of the Supreme Court's power. Americans have always been unusually reverent about the "law." (The Declaration of Independence is, after all, a rather legalistic document, particularly when compared with, say, the Communist Manifesto as a revolutionary statement.) In other countries, people are less willing to accept policy decisions by judges.[25] As a noted judge and legal scholar explained: "Struggles over power that in Europe call out regiments of troops, in America call out battalions of lawyers."[26]

U.S. voters have demonstrated their widespread acceptance of judicial independence in policy making on several occasions. During the 1930s, Franklin Roosevelt enjoyed tremendous support for his innovative policies both in Congress and among voters, but several features of his recovery plan were held unconstitutional by the Supreme Court in 1935 and 1936. Roosevelt severely criticized the "nine old men" on the Court, and then he introduced a plan to create new positions on the Court to "ease the workload" for the elderly judges—a plan that would have brought the size of the Supreme Court to 15.[27] The plan failed:

> The Court-packing plan was defeated despite the President's landslide victory at the polls only a few months earlier and despite the overwhelming popular support for New Deal legislation. Although much of the opposition was partisan, the resistance to the Court packing plan ran much deeper. At its source lay the American people's well-nigh religious attachment to constitutionalism and the Supreme Court, including their intuitive realization that packing the Court in order to reverse the course of its decisions would not only destroy its independence but erode the essence of constitutionalism. . . .[28]

In the early 1970s, judicial authority was challenged in a very different way. Richard Nixon stated that he would "ignore" an order by a federal district court to submit tapes of conversations that had taken place in his office. The judge requested the tapes because they could show evidence that Nixon directed subordinates to obstruct an investigation of a burglary committed by members of his campaign staff (the **Watergate** affair). When the matter of the tapes first came to light, public opinion was largely on the president's side—much of the evidence that he had committed a crime was uncorroborated and ambiguous.[29] Nixon's assault on the judiciary changed things dramatically, however. Not only did he ignore the order, but he also fired a special prosecutor who would not obey him. Although Nixon changed his mind within 72 hours, his support plummeted, and eventually he was forced to resign.

The Watergate affair demonstrates the peculiar importance of the independence of the judicial system in the United States. Archibald Cox noted that a Scandinavian legal scholar was astonished by this episode: "'It is unthinkable,' he said, 'that the courts of any country should issue an order to its Chief of State.' "[30] In the United States, the idea is not at all unthinkable, and voters have shown that they will not support a president who disregards judicial power.

---

* Although most analysts accept this conclusion, it should be noted that some argue along other lines. For example, see Robert L. Clinton's *Marbury v. Madison and Judicial Review* (Lawrence: University of Kansas Press, 1989).

The Court and Policy Making   As noted in Chapter 9, judicial decisions often make public policy. Adjudication involves interpreting statutes and constitutional provisions in particular contexts, and such interpretations inevitably resolve policy issues. For example, if the Constitution prohibits "cruel and unusual" punishment, and if housing a prisoner without proper space or sanitary facilities is interpreted as "cruel and unusual," then the effect of that judgment is to "make" prison management policy.

In that and many other areas, the Supreme Court has made decisions that would otherwise be made in legislative and executive institutions. Some of its policy choices simply dictate what the "political" branches of government *cannot* do (they cannot outlaw flag burning, for example), whereas others (such as the prison cases) require governments to take positive action. The status of the Constitution in U.S. society, coupled with the entrenched principle of judicial review, makes judicial involvement in policy making a fact of political life.

Nevertheless, judicial power over policy making is limited. For example, presidents and the Congress can diminish the impact of Court opinions by reducing enforcement efforts. The "power of the purse" is often manipulated to give greater or lesser weight to judicial policy making, as when Congress decided to release previously withheld federal funding from racially imbalanced school systems. Ambiguous or divided judicial opinions also leave legislators and executives uncertain about what is legal.*

Most analysts thus have a balanced view of the Court's actual impact on policy making. In a famous study from the 1950s, Robert Dahl began with the assumption that the Supreme Court *could* conceivably act against the wishes of democratic majorities whenever it wanted. He was interested in determining how often that occurred. After an extensive study of numerous cases over several decades, Dahl concluded that the Court is most likely to alter public policy when majority preferences are vague and divided and that, on most issues, judicial decisions eventually reflect public demands.

The reason that judicial policy making is not as out of touch with majorities as some have feared has to do with the selection of federal judges. Presidents appoint justices who reflect their views (and the views of the voters electing them). Since the typical president gets to select two or three Supreme Court justices in a four-year term (along with hundreds of appointments to lower courts), the judiciary's political complexion will not remain contrary to popular demands for long periods. Still, within limits, the judiciary is important in policy making.[31]

The Politics of Appointments to the Supreme Court   The Supreme Court's policymaking role makes Court appointments a very political matter. The process is quite simple: The president selects a nominee and submits the person's name to the Senate for its "advice and consent." Since 1925, nearly all nominees have testified before the Senate Judiciary Committee, answering legal questions as well as questions about their background and their positions on controversial issues. Of the nearly 150 men and 2 women who have been nominated to serve as justices on the Supreme Court, all but 28 have been confirmed by the Senate.

The process reflects both the power and the constraints faced by presidents. Their choices have been accepted some 80 percent of the time, allowing them to shape the

---

* For good examples, see *Regents of the University of California v. Bakke*, 438 U.S. 265 (1978), *Bush v. Gore*, 531 U.S. 98 (2000), or *Grutter v. Bollinger* (2003).

direction of the Court, often for a long time to come. Of course, the fact that appointments to the Court are effectively for life (justices serve "during good behavior") means that those appointed to the Court can develop views that are very different from their previously held positions that led to their nominations. After President Dwight Eisenhower appointed Chief Justice Earl Warren, who became one of the most liberal justices of the twentieth century, Eisenhower declared that his appointment was "one of the two biggest mistakes I made."[32] In his uniquely colorful way, Harry Truman complained about having appointed Tom C. Clark to the Supreme Court: "It isn't so much that he's a *bad* man, it's just that he's such a dumb son of a bitch. He's about the dumbest man I think I've ever run across."[33] Presidents have only an imperfect power to shape the Court's political orientation.

The Bureaucracy

As in all industrialized nations, bureaucracy has become a major feature of government in the United States. Over 16 million Americans work for administrative agencies, not counting those in the military. The U.S. bureaucracy mirrors the distinctive political traits that are apparent in the rest of the government. The same distrust of central authority that led to checks and balances within and between legislative and executive institutions has also produced a fragmented, decentralized bureaucracy.

U.S. bureaucratic institutions are deliberately arranged to maximize control by forces both inside and outside government. In countries with cultures less hostile to bureaucratic management or with strong party systems, bureaucracies are given greater latitude to make and implement policy. The majority party in such systems has the power to enact its platform, and the bureaucracy is often left free to carry it out. The U.S. bureaucracy, however, is subject to demands not only from the majority party but also from powerful individual legislators and their committees, most of which have power to affect agency funding and authority.

Ironically, the problem is magnified by the fact that the bureaucracy is often left with vague directions. Congress delegates authority to an agency to solve some problem, but when agency officials take concrete action, a legislative committee or an interest group may vigorously oppose it. The "benzene case" from the 1980s is a good example of this syndrome.* Congress had debated two very different approaches to regulating benzene (a toxic substance) in factories. One approach was to restrict exposure so that all known risks would be eliminated; the other approach was to impose only those limits deemed to be "cost-effective." Committee hearing records revealed that some members of Congress supported each approach. No bill that satisfied only one side could be passed.

What did Congress do? It delegated power to an agency to decide the issue. The Occupational Safety and Health Administration (OSHA) thus not only had the traditional duties of implementing but also had to make a basic value judgment. When the agency made up its mind (it adopted the more restrictive approach), interests opposing the decision then sued, and the agency lost. This pattern—vague mandates coupled with the need to satisfy conflicting influences—is repeated continually in the U.S. bureaucracy.

It is thus inevitable that bureaucracy in the United States is frequently the subject of severe criticism. The idea that bureaucratic agencies are "captured" by those they serve

---

* See *Industrial Union Department, AFL-CIO v. American Petroleum Institute,* 448 U.S. 607 (1980).

or regulate is a familiar refrain. The bureaucracy is also criticized for being wasteful, especially when policies and programs work at cross-purposes. Many complain that the bureaucracy is "out of control," noting that bureaucrats make too many basic decisions.

Some, perhaps most, criticism of the U.S. bureaucracy reflects a generalized frustration with the intractable nature of social problems. The bureaucracy may simply be a scapegoat for problems that have little to do with the efficiency or professionalism of administrative operations. The U.S. bureaucracy is expected to behave in accordance with traditional norms of efficiency and expert management and at the same time to be open to diverse and contradictory political directions. It is ordered to plan for the future from one uncertain budget to another. The fragmented power of U.S. government produces a bureaucracy that is highly open to public involvement and scrutiny but often is unable to act in a coordinated, authoritative manner.

PARTICIPATION IN U.S. POLITICS

Political Parties and Elections

Although elections and parties remain the two most dominant elements of political participation in America, studies regularly reveal a long-term decline in voter turnout and partisan attachment. These trends shape the character of modern politics in the United States.

Voter Turnout   Figure 11.3 is a graph of the percentage of voter turnout in presidential and midterm elections since 1790. After a dramatic increase during the 1830s, turnout declined around the end of the nineteenth century and remained at a lower level despite some fluctuations. About 62 percent of the eligible population voted in the 1952 presidential election, only 50 percent voted in 1988, about 55 percent in 1992, 49 percent in 1996, and 55.5 percent in 2004.*

Three factors have contributed to declines in voter turnout. First, the dip in turnout between the 1968 and 1972 elections reflected the Twenty-Sixth Amendment's lowering of the voting age to eighteen, since it added a large group of citizens to the potential voting pool who do not regularly vote. Second, since the early 1960s, the proportion of voters who feel that government can effectively solve their problems has declined. The Vietnam War convinced many voters that their government could not be trusted, that it would not pursue the public interest, and that it would not always achieve its purposes. Government policies also fell short of expectations in domestic affairs. Although many citizens felt increased confidence in government as a result of experiences during the Great Depression of the 1930s, the War on Poverty initiated in the 1960s has not been as successful.[34] In addition, intense media coverage of scandals has made many citizens cynical about politics.

Finally, declining party identification leads to lower voter turnout. One study concluded that one-fifth of the decline in turnout has been caused by declining partisanship.[35] When people feel a strong attachment to a party, they are more likely to vote, even if the issues and candidates in a given election may not interest them. Without strong partisan loyalty, many voters stay home.

---

* Some argue that simple turnout figures may give a distorted picture of the extent of U.S. political participation because the U.S. uses the electoral process for more offices and more kinds of decisions than do other democracies. When all of these elections are taken into account, U.S. voter turnout appears stronger.

FIGURE 11.3   Voter Turnout in U.S. Elections

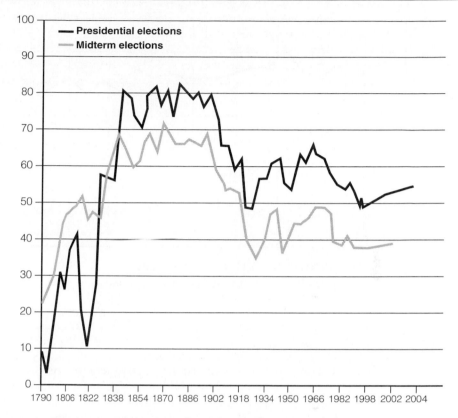

SOURCES: Harold W. Stanley and Richard G. Niemi, *Vital Statistics on American Politics*, 2nd ed. (Washington, DC: CQ Press, 1990), p. 78; *Statistical Abstract of the U.S.* (Washington, DC: U.S. Government Printing Office, 1996 and 2001); and the U.S. Census Bureau, *Statistical Abstract of the United States*, 2006, table 407, "Participation in Elections for President and U.S. Representatives: 1932 to 2004."

Political Parties in the United States   The authors of a leading text about U.S. political parties described U.S. political parties in the following way:

> . . . [b]y the standards of the parties of the other democracies, . . . the American political parties cut an unimpressive figure. They lack the hierarchical control and efficiency, the unified setting of priorities and strategy, and the central responsibility we associate with large contemporary organizations and often find in parties in other nations.[36]

Remarkably, that assessment echoed a famous analysis from 1950:

> Alternatives between the parties are defined so badly that it is often difficult to determine what the election has decided even in the broadest terms.[37]

U.S. parties have long been a disappointment to political scientists and others who have looked to them as tools that would make democracy work better, *if only they were better organized and more responsible.* The two major U.S. parties still fall short of the responsible party model, but they are becoming more meaningful as symbolic labels

FIGURE 11.4 PARTY IDENTIFICATION, 1952–2004

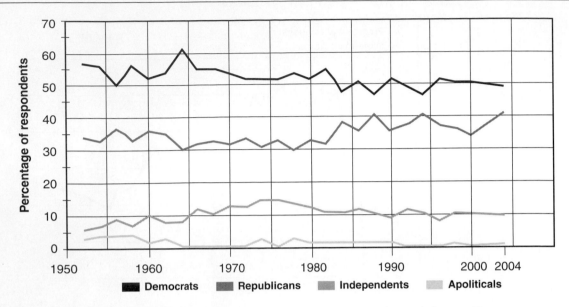

SOURCE: National Election Studies. University of Michigan (http://www.electionstudies.org/). Reprinted by permission.

and more effective as organizers of political energy. As discussed earlier, one of the largest obstacles to partisan coherence—the persistent division of the Democratic Party into southern conservatives and liberals from other parts of the country—is quickly being removed, enabling the parties to become more focused on a roughly consistent pair of opposing messages. Still, political parties in the United States are less disciplined and less responsible than their counterparts in Great Britain, Israel, Germany, and many other modern democracies.

Moreover, the decline of party identification in the United States in recent years suggests that the parties' clearer distinctiveness has not produced a corresponding increase in party identification among the voters. Figure 11.4 indicates the number of U.S. voters who have claimed to identify with the two major parties since 1952. A perceptible decline in identification coincides with the increased incidence of "ticket splitting": In recent elections, more than half of all voters report voting for presidential and congressional candidates of different parties, whereas only 30 percent did so during the 1950s.

The deterioration of party identification has many causes, including the dissatisfaction that many voters feel regarding public institutions in general. As discussed in Chapter 4, the advent of postmaterialism also inhibits strong partisanship. As environmental issues, abortion rights, and other non-economic controversies dominate political life, more people are confused about which party to support. Both the wealthy suburbanite who supports the Republicans on tax issues but supports the Democrats on abortion and pollution control *and* the lower-income voter who agrees with conservative Republicans regarding prayer in the public schools but embraces Democratic positions on health policy are likely to be torn between the two major parties. Since there are many more such confused voters now than in previous decades, this pattern may contribute to declining partisanship.

The impact of the media also facilitates a decline in partisanship. When television amplifies the importance of a candidate's personal qualities (positive or negative), the party label becomes less important. Finally, interest groups increasingly provide outlets for energies that would otherwise be devoted to political parties, particularly for people who are drawn to "single-issue" politics involving, say, abortion or gun control.

It would be wrong, however, to conclude that U.S. parties are not important. Party identification remains the most important influence on voting choice, and party organizations, despite their weaknesses, still play a pivotal role in selecting candidates. Perhaps the best assessment is that the U.S. parties will continue to exert an influence but that they will share that influence with other organizations, particularly with interest groups.[38] Given the nature of the U.S. political system, we should not expect that the parties will ever become the "governing instruments" that the advocates of party responsibility envision.[39]

Interest-Group Activity   Political organizations have long been a part of U.S. politics, and, perhaps surprisingly, many political scientists had a positive view of interest groups during the first half of the last century (although many others criticized their impact). Some saw interest groups as providing ways for people to indicate the *intensity* of their preferences (compared with voting, which indicates only their *direction*). Most analysts now view interest groups in the United States more critically.

A basic reason for the growing concern about interest groups has to do with how they operate. As discussed earlier, the most distinctive political feature of U.S. institutions is the extent to which they fragment governmental authority. Interest groups exist in all modern democracies, and even in the developing world, but the fragmentation of power in U.S. government gives them great opportunities to affect public policy.

Interest groups in the United States take advantage of the arrangement of Congress by developing close connections with committees and committee staff and by providing campaign funds that central party leadership cannot command. In a sense, interest group power is both a cause and a consequence of weak partisanship; interest groups divert members of Congress from party platforms, and they provide a way for citizens who have lost faith in parties to express their demands. U.S. interest groups also exert considerable influence in courts, exploiting the policy-making opportunities that exist there. Interest groups that are effective in other political arenas compound their power by taking action in the judicial branch.[40]

Most observers are no longer confident that the interest group system is representative of the country as a whole. Whereas everyone has the right to vote, some people have the added benefit of effective political organizations acting on their behalf. Most citizens do not. If public policy depends to a significant degree on the balance of *organized* forces, then those who are not represented by effective organizations are at a disadvantage.[41]

Beyond the problem of representation, others argue that the growing power of interest groups makes it increasingly difficult for Congress or the president to craft and implement coherent or comprehensive programs. Interest group influence is apparent in agriculture policy, education policy, transportation policy, and many other areas. U.S. interest groups will continue to create severe difficulties for government in the years to come; their existence reflects the openness of American society, but their influence may obstruct necessary policy making.

U.S. POLITICS: PROSPECTS AND CHALLENGES

The United States currently faces profound challenges that will severely test its political system. Perhaps Americans will have to construct new, less fragmented governmental institutions in order to provide for the sustained, coordinated public authority needed to solve the system's social, economic, and foreign policy problems. Or perhaps another inspirational president will emerge, who, like Lincoln or Roosevelt, will transcend narrow political divisions and mobilize support for necessary public decisions. In any case, the system faces several basic problems.

Box 11-4

DOMESTIC SURVEILLANCE, THE BUSH ADMINISTRATION, AND THE WAR ON TERROR

On December 15, 2005, *The New York Times* printed a story that disclosed the existence of a highly classified surveillance program operated by the Bush Administration. The *Times* reported that Bush had signed an order in 2002 authorizing the National Security Agency to "eavesdrop on Americans and others inside the United States to search for evidence of terrorist activity without the court-appointed warrants ordinarily required. . . ." Within a few days, five members of the Senate Judiciary Committee, a group including both Democrats and Republicans, demanded an investigation. The Republican chairman of the committee, Arlen Specter, immediately stated that the program was "clearly and categorically wrong."

The dispute over the NSA wiretapping program is an excellent illustration of the conflict between presidential power and constitutional restraints, particularly during a time of war. Senator Russ Feingold (Democrat, Wisconsin) called on the Senate to censure President Bush, claiming that he had undermined the most fundamental protections against tyranny and abuse contained in the constitution: "I tell you, he's President George Bush, not King George Bush. This is not the system of government we have and that we fought for."

Feingold and a few other senators continued their attacks, claiming that if the president is allowed to spy on Americans without court orders, there are effectively no limits to what the government can do to gather information. Bush's critics were especially disturbed by the program in light of the fact that the Foreign Intelligence Surveillance Act, signed into law in 1978, established a special court to streamline the process of obtaining judicial authorization for domestic wiretapping. The NSA program did not even make use of the FISA court process.

President Bush and his defenders responded by arguing that the attacks on September 11, 2001, would not have been possible without frequent communications between terrorists on U.S. soil (some of whom may have been citizens) and Al-Queda members in other nations. The NSA program, according to the Bush administration, was only designed to eavesdrop on phone calls in which one party was suspected of terrorist involvement, and a large majority of Americans were convinced that the program was necessary.

The administration pointed to two legal justifications for the program. First, when Congress passed the "Authorization to Use Military Force" on September 14, 2001, it empowered the president to "use all necessary and appropriate force" to retaliate and eliminate those responsible for the terrorist attacks on September 11. The president contended that this authorization included not only the power to send soldiers, planes, and ships to attack terrorists, but also to engage in electronic surveillance, interruption of financial transactions, and other means to destroy the enemy. The second argument was simply that Article II of the Constitution, by designating the president "commander in chief" of the armed forces and by giving him authority over foreign affairs, implicitly authorizes the president to order the surveillance.

The Impact of International Terrorism

The attacks on the World Trade Center and the Pentagon on September 11, 2001, made U.S. citizens feel vulnerable and threatened in ways that had not been experienced in six decades. The fact that the threat was not produced directly by an enemy state or army severely complicated the nation's response in two ways. The United States had to deal with the possibility of infiltration in not only its system of airline transportation but also its systems for mail, computer communications, power plants, and other things important in everyday life. The nature of that threat led to controversial proposals to strengthen the power of the FBI and other agencies to gather and keep information on citizens and immigrants (see Box 11.4), and to streamline judicial proceedings to prevent possibly dangerous suspects from

---

A key issue in the debate is the contrast between government surveillance for *gathering foreign intelligence* and government surveillance for *criminal prosecution*. This distinction was discussed in a 1980 case, *United States v. Truong Dinh Hung*, 629 F.2d 908. That court held that the Constitutional requirement of a warrant was different when the government sought foreign intelligence: "the Executive Branch should be excused from securing a warrant only when 'the object of the search or the surveillance is a foreign power, its agents or collaborators,' and 'the surveillance is conducted primarily for foreign intelligence reasons." Critics of the NSA program point out that this case dealt with surveillance carried out *before* the FISA process was in place, and that the FISA law limits the president's power, forcing him to seek at least a FISA court order before engaging in surveillance on U.S. soil.

Beyond the realm of constitutional law, the controversy over the NSA wiretapping program raises important questions about the impact of international terrorism on the U.S. government. It is certainly not the first time that these concerns have been raised. In 1963, political scientist Harry Howe Ransom wrote a book entitled *Can American Democracy Survive Cold War?*, an examination of the conflict between government's need for spying, secrecy, and counter-intelligence activities, and the democratic principles of openness and public accountability.* The situation has become substantially more difficult since then. Advances in electronic communications and computing that have taken place in recent decades, and the special nature of the war on terrorism, make the line between legitimate governmental needs and governmental abuse of freedom especially difficult to draw.

Some observers consider the current controversy over the NSA wiretapping program as just another example of a pattern of executive encroachments on constitutionally protected freedoms during times of war. As noted above, Abraham Lincoln undermined the most basic of our constitutional rights. On September 24, 1862, he proclaimed that "the Writ of *Habeas Corpus* is suspended in respect to all persons arrested, or who are now, or hereafter during the rebellion shall be, imprisoned in any fort, camp, arsenal, military prison, or other place of confinement by any military authority or by the sentence of any Court Martial or Military Commission." (A Writ of *"Habeas Corpus"* essentially demands that a person being held in custody be brought to court so that an impartial tribunal can determine whether or not the person is being lawfully imprisoned.) In 1917 and 1918, President Woodrow Wilson got Congress to pass the Espionage and Sedition Acts, which made it a federal crime to publicly criticize the draft or the president.

It may be argued that the historical record provides a bit of comfort in that these egregious violations of constitutional rights did not endure after the wars that led presidents to take such steps had ended. On the other hand, the war on terrorism is not likely to end with a surrender ceremony and a peace treaty, if indeed it ever completely ends at all. In light of the long-term nature of the conflict, the advanced technology employed by both terrorists and governments, and the huge stakes involved, it is probable that the current conflict between presidential war powers and constitutional rights will remain a difficult problem for U.S. democracy.

*Harry Howe Ransom, *Can American Democracy Survive Cold War?* (New York: Doubleday, 1963).

engaging in terrorist attacks. How the nation balances its need for security with the principles of due process and individual privacy will be a major challenge for years to come.

Of course, the most controversial action taken by the U.S. government was the invasion of Iraq in 2003. Although Saddam Hussein's regime fell relatively quickly, the creation of a stable democratic government has proved difficult. The war in Iraq has had profound effects, increasing partisan discord in U.S. elections and complicating diplomatic relations with U.S. allies, particularly those in Europe. Politics and government in the U.S. will be affected for decades both by the continuing dangers of terrorism and the Iraq war.

Economic Transformation and the Global Economy

The economic transformation facing the United States at the beginning of the twenty-first century presents a serious challenge to the political system. As unskilled jobs are "exported" to Mexico, Korea, and Malaysia, among many other places, the U.S. industrial base is threatened, and some jobs are lost. In recent years, General Motors, Sears, and IBM announced immediate and planned layoffs of tens of thousands of workers, devastating many communities. The aerospace industry—a leading export industry—is threatened as well.

Many analysts contend that a major coordinated public response is necessary to ease the difficulties caused by these changes. To keep the manufacturing activities that remain, U.S. industry must successfully compete with companies in Japan, Germany, and elsewhere that did not exist as competitors a generation ago. Successful competition may require investment in basic research, in urban infrastructure, and in education. Unlike the original movement of society from agriculture to industry, current economic changes will not be gradual or relatively self-managing.[42]

Immigration Policy

In 2006, upwards of 8 million illegal aliens were in the U.S., the vast majority of whom came from Mexico in search of jobs and economic opportunity. Immigration policy has become an extremely divisive problem, touching on a great many issues and raising difficult questions:

1. Does an unsecured border with Mexico constitute a threat to national security and an opportunity for terrorists to infiltrate the U.S.?
2. Is it appropriate, fair, or humane to condemn illegal immigrants as felons (this was proposed in a bill introduced in Congress in March 2006), when they are simply seeking employment in jobs that U.S. citizens will not take?
3. What are the costs that taxpayers must bear to provide health, educational, and other services to illegal aliens and their families?
4. Does the presence of illegal aliens in the U.S. economy drive down the wages of U.S. workers?
5. Can the U.S. economy survive without the labor of illegal aliens?

Americans are bitterly divided over immigration policy. Some favor building a wall to prevent people from entering the country illegally, and an organization of private citizens has worked in several states that border Mexico to apprehend and report illegal immigrants. Others feel that a crackdown on illegal immigrants is a kind of thinly-disguised prejudice against persons of Hispanic origin. In response to a proposal to make it a felony to enter the country illegally, Senator Hillary Clinton expressed the outrage that many citizens felt in comments she made on March 22, 2006: "This bill would literally criminalize the Good Samaritan and probably even Jesus himself."

President Bush proposed a plan that received some support from moderate politicians from both parties, but it is stalled in Congress as of this writing. His plan would increase funding for the Border Patrol, making it possible to prevent more illegal aliens from entering the country, but it would also create a "temporary worker program" that would allow illegal aliens working in the U.S. to remain in the country and continue to work after paying a small fine. Some critics call this part of the plan "amnesty," claiming that it will only encourage people to enter the country illegally, while others feel that it is too punitive.

Hundreds of thousands of people, including both U.S. citizens and illegal aliens, demonstrated in New York, Los Angeles, and several other cities in March and April 2006 to protest congressional proposals to further criminalize people entering the country illegally. However, public opinion polls suggest that any solution to the problem will be difficult politically. A poll by NBC News and the *Wall Street Journal* reported in March 2006 that 56 percent of Americans are opposed to any plan that would grant temporary-work status to people who have entered the country illegally. Nearly two-thirds of the respondents favor using "whatever steps are necessary" to prevent immigrants from entering the country illegally, including the use of military forces.*

The debate over immigration will be a critical challenge for the U.S. in the years to come. It involves legal, ethical, diplomatic, and economic questions, and it is profoundly divisive.

Race Relations

The status and condition of African Americans has been the most consistently difficult and controversial problem faced by U.S. government. The issue was divisive at the Constitutional Convention, when it was decided to count slaves as three-fifths of a person for the purpose of determining state population. Slavery was, of course, the root of the Civil War. And, in the twentieth century, debates over civil rights divided Americans deeply.

As divisive and difficult as race relations were, the issues posed in the 1950s and 1960s were arguably less difficult for the system than the issues faced today. Thirty-five years ago, the major civil rights controversies were about official restrictions on African American voting rights and laws that required African Americans to eat only at segregated restaurants. Although progress in those areas was difficult, it mainly required changing laws and providing security to protect those who would exercise their rights.

* The NBC/WSJ poll, along with other results on immigration-related polls, may be found at http://www. pollingreport.com/immigration.htm.

We can now say that African Americans enjoy the same legal rights to vote, travel, attend college, and pursue careers that other Americans have had for generations. Nevertheless, the National Urban League issued a report in 2005 that found severe remaining inequalities. The "inequality index," a measure incorporating data on housing, wealth, education, and civic engagement, was only 73 percent, indicating the average disparity between blacks and whites. The average African American household income in 2004 was only 64.5 percent of the average white household income ($30,134 compared with $46,697 for whites).[43] It is clear that African Americans have not shared equally in the general prosperity of American society. Not only are income levels and wealth far below average levels, but African Americans also experience other problems more deeply. African Americans are much more likely to be victims of crime than other Americans (murder is the leading cause of death for young African American males), and in many states more male African Americans are in prison or on parole than in college.

These problems challenge the political system profoundly. The civil rights movement of a generation ago emphasized the need to *remove discriminatory practices*, whereas current problems of race relations are more controversial. In 1996, California voters ratified the California Civil Rights Initiative, which outlawed racial and gender preferences in state government and state higher education. As several studies predicted, the end of racial preferences produced a significant decline in the number of African Americans, at leading University of California campuses in 1997. In 2003, two important Supreme Court cases addressed the use of racial factors in admissions to institutions of higher education (*Grutter v. Bollinger,* and *Gratz v. Bollinger*), both arising from practices at the University of Michigan. In the *Grutter* ruling, five members of the Supreme Court upheld the affirmative action policy at the Law School, but in the *Gratz* case, six justices voted to hold the policy used by the undergraduate college unconstitutional.* The mixed signals coming from these cases will ensure that the legal status of racial preferences will remain unsettled for years.

The Status of Women

Although U.S. women are legally protected from most forms of discrimination, their status remains a major political issue. Interest groups such as the National Organization for Women (NOW) demand federal laws to establish national child care facilities and insist that employers be more flexible in accommodating workers' family responsibilities.

Thus, as with African Americans, the solutions to the concerns of women in the United States go beyond the repeal of discriminatory laws. They require decisions that confront basic moral concerns (such as abortion) and others that involve elaborate government regulation of the workplace. These problems are a major challenge for the political system, and they will not be resolved easily or quickly.

Health Care

It is estimated that Americans spend nearly 20 percent of their gross domestic product on health care. Part of that increase reflects quality improvements, and part reflects

---

* See *Gratz v. Bollinger,* 539 U.S. 244, and *Grutter v. Bollinger,* 539 U.S. 306, decided June 23, 2003.

the fact that the population has become older, but many believe that the skyrocketing costs will require some kind of governmental response. The failure of the Clinton health care proposal in 1994 suggests that a centralized governmental arrangement is not politically realistic in the near future, but this issue is likely to remain a major concern. Beginning in 2006, the Bush Administration's plan adding prescription drug coverage to the Medicare program went into effect, providing financial help to older Americans facing increasingly expensive pharmaceuticals. However, the cost and complexity of the program made it controversial and unpopular in many quarters, illustrating the difficulties involved in facing the larger challenge of providing health care generally.

Changes in the International System

The first half of the twentieth century saw the United States thrust into a leadership role in international relations. From an essentially isolationist posture that predominated in the 1800s, the United States became one of the two main forces in the bipolar world that emerged at the end of World War II. The United States devoted a large proportion of its productive capacity to fighting wars to contain the power of its major competitor, the Soviet Union, and to fostering nuclear deterrence. The cold war shaped foreign and even domestic policies.

The cold war ended in 1991 with the official demise of the Soviet Union. The United States responded by announcing major reductions in nuclear and conventional forces and plans for deeper reductions in the future. East–West conflict no longer defines the international system, which is increasingly marked by more complex ethnic and cultural clashes. Economic competition will almost certainly be the primary issue in foreign policy, and adversarial relations will be more complex and subtle as the world becomes more interdependent.

The problem of international terrorism thus struck at a time when the fundamental feature of the international system was no longer the "bipolar" competition that existed during the cold war years. Although that change has made many nations more flexible in their diplomacy (in that they no longer have to consider how their actions and statements affect the balance of power between two hegemonic states), it also makes diplomacy more complicated. There is greater emphasis on international law and organization than in recent years. How the United States will pursue its interests in international affairs in this changing environment will consume a great deal of the energies of our presidents.

The Future of American Democracy

The United States has faced enormous challenges throughout its history. Industrialization, the Civil War, foreign military threats, and the specter of nuclear holocaust presented the system with problems that required enormous and costly responses. For the most part, the challenges were met successfully. But the new challenges may actually be more threatening, possibly requiring fundamental changes in the system itself.

Still, democracy in the United States has been among the world's greatest successes, regardless of how success is measured. Even now, leaders in the fledgling democracies of Eastern Europe look to the United States—not to Great Britain,

Germany, or Japan—as the model to emulate. Whether that success has resulted from the special U.S. institutions, or despite them, will remain a basic question in the study of U.S. government.

 WHERE ON THE WEB?

http://www.fec.gov/sitemap.shtml
The home page of the Federal Election Commission.

http://www.americanpresidents.org/survey/historians/
C-Span site providing "life portraits" of all American Presidents.

http://www.270towin.com/
A fascinating site allowing the viewer to enter assumptions about the states that each party's presidential candidate will win in a presidential election, showing the resulting electoral vote totals. The site also includes a map of the states won by each party in recent elections.

http://www.cfinst.org/studies/vital/index.html
Home page of the Campaign Finance Institute.

http://www.pbs.org/newshour/impeachment/
The Public Broadcasting System's Web site containing documents and commentary on the impeachment of President Bill Clinton.

http://www.house.gov
The home page of the U.S. House of Representatives; includes weekly updates and links to members' pages.

http://www.senate.gov
The home page of the U.S. Senate; includes weekly updates and links to members' pages.

http://www.whitehouse.gov
The home page of the White House, containing presidential speeches and other materials relevant to the presidency.

http://www.supremecourtus.gov
The home page of the Supreme Court.

http://www.fjc.gov
The Federal Judicial Center's homepage. Created in 1967 as a separate organization within the Federal Judiciary System, the Federal Judicial Center is intended to "further the development and adoption of improved judicial administration."

http://www.multied.com/elections
Contains electoral vote results for all U.S. presidential elections from 1789 to the present.

http://www.democrats.org/
The home page of the U.S. Democratic Party.

http://www.rnc.org
The home page of the U.S. Republican Party.

http://www.cnn.com/ALLPOLITICS/
The Cable News Network's page devoted to daily and recent political news, focusing on national events.

http://clerk.house.gov/index.html

Site for the Office of the Clerk, U.S. House of Representatives, containing a wealth of historical information.

http://www.lib.umich.edu/govdocs/legishis.html

The University of Michigan's document center on the U.S. Congress.

http://thomas.loc.gov/links/

A list of Web resources for Congress, designed by the Library of Congress.

http://www.campaignline.com/

The online version of "Campaigns and Elections," a commercial site with information about predicting elections.

http://www.c-span.org/questions/senate.asp

A C-SPAN site set up to provide answers to frequently asked questions about Congressional procedure, elections, and many other subjects.

http://www.ou.edu/special/albertctr/cachome.html

The site for the Carl Albert Center for congressional research.

http://www.apsanet.org/~lss/

The Legislative Studies Section of the American Political Science Association.

http://www.mrdata.net/Impeach/articles.htm

A collection of documents and materials on the Clinton impeachment.

http://www.270towin.com/

An interactive site that permits the user to determine which party wins the presidency after guessing which candidate wins each U.S. state's electoral votes.

http://people-press.org/dataarchive/

The home page for the Pew Research Center for the People and the Press. It includes the full text of a wide range of public opinion reports.

http://www.presidentelect.org/

A fascinating site showing the electoral college results for all U.S. presidential elections, along with supplementary information.

http://www.hmdc.harvard.edu/ROAD/

Judged the "Best Political Science Research Website" by the American Political Science Association, the Harvard "Record of American Democracy," or ROAD, contains a tremendous amount of information.

http://www.uselectionatlas.org/USPRESIDENT/

An updated Web site with data and maps indicating the results of presidential elections from 1789 to the present.

http://www.ropercenter.uconn.edu/

The home page of the Roper Center for Public Opinion Research. Includes data on Presidential approval ratings from Franklin Roosevelt to George W. Bush.

http://www.americanpresidents.org/survey/historians/

The C-Span Survey of Presidential Leadership.

http://www.presidentsusa.net/presidentialrankings.html

A set of links to information about comparing U.S. presidents.

http://www.zogby.com/

The home page of Zogby International, a highly regarded polling organization.

http://www.politicalmoneyline.com/

A nonpartisan site that lists campaign contributions to U.S. political campaigns.

http://www.opensecrets.org/

The home page of the Center for Responsive Politics. The site includes a great deal of data regarding the influence of money in U.S. elections.

◆ ◆ ◆

Key Terms and Concepts_____

Articles of Confederation	political action committees
bicameral	(PACs)
checks and balances	presidential "character"
Connecticut Compromise	president's cabinet
Declaration of Independence	primaries
"extended Republic"	Shays's Rebellion
incumbency advantage	term limits
Marbury v. Madison	Watergate
marginal seats	

Discussion Questions_____

1. In what respects was the Founding period ambivalent about democracy? How did that ambivalence shape the Constitution?
2. What is distinctive about the U.S. Congress, and how does it participate in policy making?
3. How is the power of the presidency limited in practice?
4. Does the Supreme Court's role in policy making make the system more or less democratic?
5. Why has voter participation been low in recent U.S. elections?

Notes_____

1. According to one observer, the American poor see government as "distant, incomprehensible, and inaccessible." See Jennifer Nedelsky, *Private Property and the Limits of American Constitutionalism* (Chicago: University of Chicago Press, 1991), p. 215.
2. See, for example, John Manley, "Neo-Pluralism: A Class Analysis of Pluralism I and Pluralism II," *American Political Science Review* 77 (1983): 368–383. Also see the symposium on Inequality and American Democracy in *PS: Political Science and Politics* 39 (January 2006).
3. Louis Hartz, *The Liberal Tradition in America* (New York: Harcourt, Brace, 1955).
4. Samuel P. Huntington, *Political Order in Changing Societies* (New Haven: Yale University Press, 1968), pp. 125–126.
5. James A. Smith, *The Spirit of American Government*, quoted in *The Case against the Constitution*, ed. John Manley and Kenneth Dolbeare (Armonk, NY: Sharpe, 1987), p. 4.
6. Kenneth M. Dolbeare and Linda Medcalf, "The Dark Side of the Constitution," in Manley and Dolbeare, *The Case against the Constitution*, p. 127.
7. For example, consider Robert Dahl's assessment: "Madison's nicely contrived system of constitutional checks" prevented the poor from having "anything like equal control over government policy." More recently, John Manley echoed that view: "[the framers] saw inequality,

heard popular demands to change it, and acted to block these demands." See Robert Dahl, *A Preface to Democratic Theory* (Chicago: University of Chicago Press, 1956); and John Manley, "Class and Pluralism in America," in Manley and Dolbeare, *The Case against the Constitution.*

8. James Madison, Federalist 51, in *The Federalist Papers* (New York: Modern Library, 1937), pp. 340–341. See the provocative discussion of this concept in George W. Carey, "Separation of Powers and the Madisonian Model: A Reply to the Critics," *American Political Science Review* 72 (March 1978): 151–164.

9. See also Pauline Maier, Lance Banning, *The Sacred Fire of Liberty: James Madison and the Founding of the Federal Republic* (Ithaca, NY: Cornell University Press, 1995. For a recent and spirited attack on the democracy of the U.S. system, see Robert A. Dahl, *How Democratic is the American Constitution?* New Haven, CT: Yale University Press, 2002.

10. David E. Price, "Congressional Committees in the Policy Process," in *Congress Reconsidered*, 3rd ed., ed. Lawrence C. Dodd and Bruce I. Oppenheimer (Washington, DC: CQ Press, 1985), p. 167.

11. Ibid., p. 163.

12. See the *Congressional Quarterly Almanac* (Washington, DC: Congressional Quarterly, 1995), p. C8.

13. Ibid.

14. See Robert S. Erikson and Gerald C. Wright, "Voters, Candidates, and Issues in Congressional Elections," in *Congress Reconsidered*, 6th ed., Lawrence C. Dodd and Bruce I. Oppenheimer, eds. (Washington, DC: CQ Press, 1997), pp. 143–144.

15. Morris Fiorina, *Congress: Keystone of the Washington Establishment*, 2nd ed. (New Haven: Yale University Press, 1989).

16. A former opponent of term limits, the conservative columnist George Will makes a persuasive case for them. See *Restoration* (New York: Free Press, 1992). For a good statement opposing term limits, see Morris Fiorina, *Divided Government*, 2nd ed. (Boston: Allyn & Bacon, 1996).

17. Walter R. Mebane, Jr., and Jasjeet S. Sekhon, "Coordination and Policy Moderation at Midterm," *American Political Science Review* 96 (March 2002): 141–157.

18. John F. Kennedy, foreword to *Decision-Making in the White House*, by Theodore C. Sorensen (New York: Columbia University Press, 1963).

19. See Fiorina, *Divided Government*; and David Mayhew, *Divided We Govern* (New Haven: Yale University Press, 1991).

20. Quoted in Richard Neustadt, *Presidential Power: The Politics of Leadership from FDR to Carter* (New York: Wiley, 1980), p. 31. See also John Bibby, *Governing by Consent* (Washington, DC: CQ Press, 1992), pp. 496–500.

21. Doris Kerns, *Lyndon Johnson and the American Dream* (New York: Harper and Row, 1976), p. 253.

22. James David Barber, *The Presidential Character* (Englewood Cliffs, NJ: Prentice Hall, 1972).

23. Ibid.

24. Glendon Schubert, *Constitutional Politics* (New York: Holt, Rinehart, and Winston, 1960), p. 178.

25. Louis Hartz, *The Liberal Tradition in America* (New York: Harcourt, Brace and World, 1955).

26. Robert H. Jackson, *The Struggle for Judicial Supremacy* (New York: Vintage Books, 1941), p. xi.

27. Archibald Cox, *The Court and the Constitution* (Boston: Houghton Mifflin, 1987), p. 149.

28. Ibid., pp. 149–150.

29. Archibald Cox, *The Role of the Supreme Court in American Government* (New York: Oxford University Press, 1976), p. 8.

30. Ibid., p. 4.

31. See Robert A. Dahl, "Decision-Making in a Democracy: The Supreme Court as a National Policy-Maker," *Journal of Public Law* 6 (Fall 1957): 279–295. Also see Jonathan D. Casper, "The Supreme Court and National Policy Making," *American Political Science Review* 70 (1976): 50–63.

32. Elmo Richardson, *The Presidency of Dwight D. Eisenhower* (Lawrence, KS: Regent's Press, 1979), p. 108.

33. Merle Miller, *Plain Speaking: An Oral Biography of Harry S Truman* (New York: Berkeley, 1973), pp. 225–226, quoted in *The Challenge of Democracy*, 2nd ed. by Kenneth Janda, Jeffrey Berry, and Jerry Goldman (Boston: Houghton Mifflin, 1989), pp. 497–498.

34. Paul R. Abramson and John H. Aldrich, "The Decline of Electoral Participation in America," *American Political Science Review* 76 (September 1982): 502–521.

35. John Aldrich, David Rohde, Gary Miller, and Charles Ostrom, *American Government: People, Institutions, and Policies* (Boston: Houghton Mifflin, 1986), p. 290.

36. Paul Allen Beck and Frank J. Sorauf, *Party Politics in America*, 7th ed. (New York: Harper-Collins, 1992), p. 112.

37. Committee on Political Parties, American Political Science Association, "Toward a More Responsive Two-Party System," *American Political Science Review* 44 (1950): 2.

38. Beck and Sorauf, *Party Politics in America*, p. 469.

39. Mayhew, *Divided We Govern*, p. 199.

40. See Susan Olson, "Interest Group Litigation in Federal District Court: Beyond the Political Disadvantage Theory," *Journal of Politics* 52 (1990): 854–882.

41. For example, see D. Stephen Cupps, "Emerging Problems of Citizen Participation," *Public Administration Review* 37 (1977): 478–487; and Marcus Ethridge, "Collective Action, Public Policy, and Class Conflict," *Western Political Quarterly* 40 (1987): 575–592.

42. See Lester C. Thurow, *The Zero-Sum Solution* (New York: Simon & Schuster, 1985), for a compelling statement that new economic vitality will require a stronger governmental role.

43. See Lee A. Daniels, ed., *The State of Black America 2006*, Washington, DC: National Urban League/Publications Unit, 2006. Data on household income taken from U.S. Census Bureau Web page: http://www.census.gov/prod/2005pubs/p60-229.pdf.

For Further Reading _____

Abramson, Paul R., John H. Aldrich, and David W. Rohde. *Change and Continuity in the 2000 and 2002 Elections*. Washington, DC: CQ Press, 2003.

Adler, E. Scott. *Why Congressional Elections Fail*. Chicago: University of Chicago Press, 2002.

Adler, E. Scott, and John S. Lapinski, eds. *The Macropolitics of Congress*. Princeton, NJ: Princeton University Press, 2006.

Barone, Michael, and Richard E. Cohen. *The Almanac of American Politics, 2006*. Chicago: University of Chicago Press, 2005.

Beard, Charles A. *An Economic Interpretation of the Constitution*. New York: Macmillan, 1913.

Belsky, Martin H. *The Rehnquist Court: A Retrospective*. New York: Oxford University Press, 2002.

Bennett, Robert W. *Taming the Electoral College*. Palo Alto, CA.: Stanford University Press, 2006.

Black, Amy E. *From Inspiration to Legislation: How an Idea Becomes a Bill*. Upper Saddle River, NJ: Prentice-Hall, 2007.

Brader, Ted. *Campaigning for Hearts and Minds: How Emotional Appeals in Political Ads Work*. Chicago: University of Chicago Press, 2006.

Campbell, Colton C., and Paul S. Herrnson. *War Stories from Capitol Hill*. Upper Saddle River, NJ: Prentice-Hall, 2004.

Campbell, Tom. *Separation of Powers in Practice*. Palo Alto, CA: Stanford University Press, 2004.

Cohen, Jeffrey, Richard Fleisher, and Paul Kantor. *American Political Parties: Decline or Resurgence?* Washington, DC: CQ Press, 2001.

Conway, M. Margaret. *Political Participation in the United States*. 3rd ed. Washington, DC: CQ Press, 2000.

Cook, Timothy E. *Governing with the News*. 2nd ed. Chicago: University of Chicago Press, 2005.

Dunn, Charles W. *The Scarlet Thread of Scandal: Morality and the American Presidency*. Lanham, MD: Rowman and Littlefield, 2001.

Dunn, Charles W. *Seven Laws of Presidential Leadership*. Upper Saddle River, NJ: Prentice-Hall, 2007.

Epstein, Lee, Jeffrey A. Segal, Harold J. Spaeth, and Thomas G. Walker. *The Supreme Court Compendium*. 3rd ed. Washington, DC: CQ Press, 2002.

Fenno, Richard F. *Going Home: Black Representatives and Their Constituents*. Chicago: University of Chicago Press, 2003.

Finkelman, Paul, and Melvin I. Urofsky, *Landmark Decisions of the United States Supreme Court*. Washington, DC: CQ Press, 2002.

Fiorina, Morris P. *Congress: Keystone of the Washington Establishment*. 2nd ed. New Haven: Yale University Press, 1989.

Fiorina, Morris P., Samuel J. Abrams, and Jeremy C. Pope, *Culture War? The Myth of a Polarized America*. New York: Pearson Longman, 2005.

Flanigan, William H., and Nancy H. Zingale. *Political Behavior of the American Electorate*. 11th ed. Washington, DC: CQ Press, 2005.

Hamilton, Alexander, John Jay, and James Madison. *The Federalist Papers*. New York: Modern Library, 1937.

Hershey, Marjorie Handon, and Paul Allen Beck. *Party Politics in America*. 11th ed. New York: Longman, 2004.

Hockin, Thomas A. *The American Nightmare: Politics and the Fragile World Trade Organization*. Lanham, MD: Lexington Books, 2003.

Holbrook, Thomas. *Do Campaigns Matter?* Thousand Oaks, CA: Sage, 1996.

Jacobson, Gary C. *The Politics of Congressional Elections*. 6th ed. New York: Longman, 2003.

Manley, John F., and Kenneth M. Dolbeare, eds. *The Case against the Constitution*. Armonk, NY: Sharpe, 1987.

Manza, Jeff, Fay L. Cook, and Benjamin I. Page. *Navigating Public Opinion: Polls, Policy, and the Future of American Democracy*. New York: Oxford University Press, 2002.

Mayhew, David. *Divided We Govern*. New Haven: Yale University Press, 1991.

Mayhew, David. *Electoral Realignments*. New Haven: Yale University Press, 2004.

Miller, Mark C., and Jeb Barnes, eds. *Making Policy, Making Law: An Inter-branch Perspective*. Chicago: University of Chicago Press, 2004.

Neustadt, Richard E. *Presidential Power and the Modern Presidents: The Politics of Leadership from Roosevelt to Reagan*. New York: Free Press, 1991.

Posner, Richard A. *An Affair of State: The Investigation, Impeachment, and Trial of President Clinton*. Cambridge: Harvard University Press, 1999.

Rozell, Mark J., and Clyde Wilcox, eds. *The Clinton Scandal and the Future of American Government*. Chicago: University of Chicago Press, 2000.

Schier, Steven E. *You Call This an Election? America's Peculiar Democracy*. Chicago: University of Chicago Press, 2003.

Skowronek, Stephen. *The Politics Presidents Make: Leadership from John Adams to George Bush*. Cambridge: Harvard University Press, 1993.

Sunstein, Cass R. *Designing Democracy: What Constitutions Do*. New York: Oxford University Press, 2000.

Sunstein, Cass R., and Richard Epstein. *The Vote: Bush, Gore, and the Supreme Court*. Chicago: University of Chicago Press, 2001.

Troy, Tevi. *Intellectuals and the American Presidency: Philosophers, Jesters, or Technicians?* Lanham, MD: Rowman and Littlefield, 2002.

Wand, Jonathan, et al. "The Butterfly Did It: The Aberrant Vote for Buchanan in Palm Beach County, Florida." *American Political Science Review* 95 (December 2001): 793–810.

Watson, Bradley C. S. *Courts and the Culture Wars*. Lanham, MD: Lexington Books, 2002.

Whitney, Gleaves. *American Presidents: Their Farewell Messages to the Nation, 1796–2001*. Lanham, MD: Lexington Books, 2002.

© Tim Graham/CORBIS

12

GREAT BRITAIN: A TRADITIONAL DEMOCRACY

◆ The Relevance of British Politics ◆ Contemporary British Society and Political Culture ◆ Political Parties and Voting ◆ Interest Groups ◆ The Structure of Government ◆ Public Policy and the British Economy ◆ Great Britain in the Twenty-First Century

In 1649, King Charles I was beheaded following the defeat of his Royalist troops in the English Civil War (1642–1648). One central issue in that conflict had been this simple, yet crucial, question: "Should the monarch's power be absolute or should **Parliament**, the nation's legislature, impose limits on royal rule?" Although Charles's defeat temporarily replaced the monarchy with a republic, it did not immediately establish democracy. Oliver Cromwell, commander of the victorious parliamentary army, soon imposed a military dictatorship.

Following Cromwell's death, the monarchy was restored, but the struggle between Parliament and the crown continued until 1688. Dissatisfied with King James II, the legislature removed him from office and replaced him with his son-in-law and daughter, William and Mary. Known as the **Glorious Revolution,** that event firmly established parliamentary dominance, whereas elsewhere in Europe royalty still based their authority on divine right. At the same time, it closed one of Britain's* most turbulent epochs, ushering in an extended period of relative stability that has lasted until today.

THE RELEVANCE OF BRITISH POLITICS

Britain is intrinsically fascinating to many Americans. It is, after all, the source of many of our own cultural and political traditions. But Britain is also important to political scientists, since it has been a model of democratic pluralism and political stability. Even without a written human rights act (until 1998), it maintained considerable personal freedoms and civil liberties. British political institutions—competitive party elections, parliamentary representation, and cabinet government—have been models for democratic governments throughout the world. The country's record of gradual and relatively peaceful political change contrasts with the civil war and bitter conflict that have afflicted so many other nations, including the United States. We will suggest, however, that evolutionary change and the durability of the country's historic values have also contributed to political, economic, and social rigidities.

The Origins of British Democracy: Great Britain a Model of Stability

Although Britain's government has evolved substantially since the Glorious Revolution, its constitutional order has remained in place for more than 300 years. In contrast, France has had some 20 different constitutions since 1789 and has experienced five republics, two empires, and three monarchies.[1] Similarly, a number of other European countries (such as Germany, Italy, and Russia) and many Third World nations have been racked by internal upheavals and dictatorships.

This is not to suggest that Britain has been free of domestic violence, even in modern times. Turbulent labor strife persisted from the nineteenth century through the 1930s, and in recent decades the conflict over Northern Ireland's fate convulsed that region. The Irish Republican Army (IRA), drawn from the minority Catholic population, fought for the North's unification with the Irish Republic, whereas Protestant unionists were determined to keep it part of the United Kingdom of Great Britain and

---

* The names "Great Britain" and "Britain" are used interchangeably throughout this chapter.

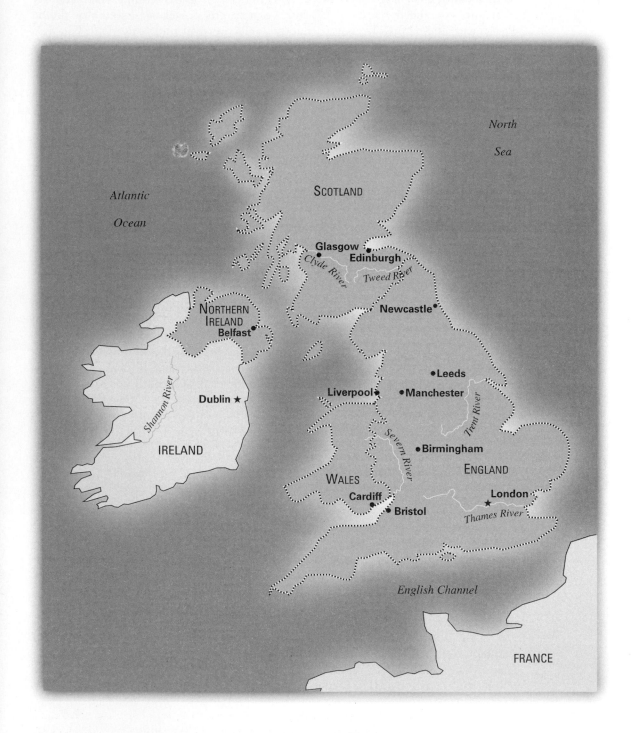

A TENUOUS PEACE   Despite a 1998 peace accord and the IRA's disarmament, ongoing tensions could still derail the process. Here, Belfast Catholics face police in a 2005 confrontation over an earlier Protestant march.

Ireland (the country's official title). A settlement was finally reached (discussed later in this chapter), but was subsequently suspended.

The Slow March to Democracy

Although the growth of parliamentary power enhanced popular sovereignty, as of the nineteenth century the British political system was still far from democratic, and Parliament remained very unrepresentative. The House of Commons, an elected body, shared power equally with the House of Lords, whose members at that time had all inherited their seats and served for life. Even the House of Commons was elected by a very small portion of the population (male property owners), often through corrupt electoral practices.

The landmark Reform Act of 1832 redrew electoral districts and modestly expanded the size of the electorate, from 5 percent of the adult population to 7 percent. Indeed, it was not until 1884 that **suffrage** was extended to most adult males. Women did not receive the right to vote until 1918, and even then the franchise was limited to women older than 30 whose husbands owned property. Finally, a decade later, all women over the age of 21 received the franchise with no property qualifications.

Well into the twentieth century, British electoral practices retained other elitist elements. Until 1949, for example, businesspeople who lived in one parliamentary district and owned an enterprise in another were allowed to vote for representatives in both. The same double vote existed for university graduates, who were able to cast

| Box 12-1 |

DEVOLUTION AND REFORMING
THE HOUSE OF LORDS

Perhaps the most significant innovations that Prime Minister Tony Blair has introduced involve constitutional reform, fundamental changes in the way that Britain is governed. The most important of those reforms, to date, may be **devolution**, the transfer of some power from the British central government to several regional governments. Beginning in 1997, the nation's Parliament transferred considerable authority over local matters to the Scottish Parliament and Welsh Assembly. Many citizens in Scotland and, to a lesser extent, Wales had felt dominated by London (and the English) for generations. The two regions felt particularly aggrieved during the most recent period of Conservative Party rule (1979–1997) and to some extent this constitutional reform was Blair's reward to two regions that had regularly produced strong Labour pluralities and offered little support to the Conservatives. Transfer of some powers to the Scottish Parliament and the far weaker Welsh Assembly took place after each region had approved devolution in separate referendums—the Scots by a solid majority and the Welsh by a paper-thin margin.[2] And, in that same year, the people of London and other large cities were allowed to elect their own mayors directly for the first time in decades.

The second major constitutional reform, not yet complete, has involved a dramatic restructuring of the House of Lords. Of less immediate political consequence than devolution, reform of Lords still has great symbolic importance as an indication of the ongoing, gradual diminution of aristocratic privilege. Early in the twentieth century, the House of Lords was stripped of its ability to block any legislation involving fiscal allocations passed by the House of Commons. Since 1949, it has been able to delay non-money bills for only one year.

At the close of the twentieth century, Lords was composed of 759 peers who had inherited their seats and 477 "life peers," distinguished figures appointed for life through the Prime Minister's recommendation (a practice dating to 1958) but unable at death to pass on their seats to their heirs. Though it periodically suggests valuable amendments to legislation sent to it by Commons, the House of Lords has long been an obvious anachronism, a legislative body, however limited its powers, that was unelected and largely hereditary. Roll-call analysis of the 2000 parliamentary session revealed that nearly 100 peers (about 1 in 12) failed to appear for a single vote.

ballots in their home district as well as for the **Member of Parliament (MP)** who represented their university.[3]

Moreover, only in 1911 did the Parliament Act give the House of Commons (the elected national legislature) legislative supremacy. Thereafter, the House of Lords could delay but not defeat bills passed by Commons. The number of bills proposed by the government (cabinet) that are rejected by the House of Lords is quite limited but varies considerably. Under the current Prime Minister, Tony Blair, for example, it has ranged from only two bills in 2000–2001 to 88 in 2002–2003. Constitutional reforms enacted by the current Labour Party government have converted Lords from a body whose members primarily inherited their seats into a largely appointed body. (See Box 12-1.) The dominance of Commons over Lords is now so strong that, although technically the words *Parliament* and *parliamentary* refer to both houses, they are used primarily to mean the House of Commons.*

* Thus, when we refer to "parliamentary elections," or "a vote in Parliament," we normally are referring exclusively to the House of Commons.

Some of the appointed peers are distinguished figures in areas such as the arts, while many others are former politicians or statesmen who seem to have little time for their obligations at Lords. As of 2005, 192 of the appointed Lords had previously sat in the House of Commons.[4] The former Prime Minister, Lady Margaret Thatcher, who was present for only 25 percent of the votes, explained through a spokesperson that "she has lots of commitments elsewhere . . . but she tries to get to the House whenever she can." He added, "I think she works hard enough for Britain." Andrew Lloyd-Weber, the theater composer and tycoon, voted only once out of 186 votes. Lord Attenborough, the noted film director, participated in 15 percent of the votes. Typically in the 2004–2005 session about half of the peers were present on any given day. Even among those peers who do attend sessions, a number—particularly elderly peers—are occasionally seen dozing through the debate.

Fearful that the Blair government might abolish all hereditary peerages, the Conservative Party leadership in Lords went behind the backs of their party's leadership in the House of Commons to work out a deal with the Labour government. Under the terms of a 1999 agreement, only 92 of the 759 hereditary peers were allowed to maintain their seats in the House of Lords. All hereditary peers were required to submit a *75-word* essay explaining their reasons for wanting to continue in Lords and their major past achievements. Based on those essays, their fellow peers chose the 92 "elected hereditary peers" (i.e., they were elected by other Lords). Lord Onslow's essay read in its entirety: "It would be as vainglorious to proclaim a personal manifesto [that is, an essay stating his reasons for wanting to stay] as it would be arrogant to list any permanent achievements." He was elected.

But this is only a temporary resolution, with a final legislation still to be hammered out regarding how members of the House of Lords are to be selected in the future. Since 1999, Parliament has voted on a series of proposals, ranging from having all House of Lords peers appointed (Blair's preference), to having all of them elected by the public (backed by the Conservatives and many Labour Members of Parliament), with various combinations of election and appointment in between. For now, no proposal has passed the House of Commons. The combination of removing most of the inherited peers and Prime Minister Blair's appointment of several hundred lifetime peers has already changed the House of Lords' political orientation. In early 1999, prior to reform, 41 percent of the peers identified themselves as Conservatives and only 15 percent as Labourites. By late 2001, only 34 percent were Conservatives and 28 percent identified with Labour.[5]

The Strengths and Weaknesses of Gradual Change

In contrast to other **industrial democracies**, Britain's contemporary political institutions cannot be traced to a single event such as the French Revolution or the ratification of the U.S. Constitution. Instead, British democracy has been fashioned by gradual, **evolutionary change**, lacking the drama of major upheavals. Moreover, the British have no written constitution but instead their "unwritten constitution" is a combination of their parliamentary legislation, statutes, legal practices, and political customs.

For many years, Britain was considered a model pluralist democracy. Its parliamentary form of government was copied in flourishing democracies such as Canada, Australia, and New Zealand and was adopted less successfully in many former British colonies in Africa and Asia. The country's history of gradual change fostered an atmosphere of political openness and tolerance. It also enshrined institutions and customs—the monarch's coronation, the changing of the guard at Buckingham Palace—that bind the population together (and also provide the pomp and circumstance that attracts millions of foreign tourists annually). That unifying cultural heritage provides an enviable foundation for democratic government.

At the same time, however, the very traditions and practices that have created national unity and stability also have frequently become barriers to progress. That is to say that although peaceful, evolutionary change has an obvious value, it also has inhibited the modernization of British institutions and beliefs. For example, the country's rather rigid class structure has, in the recent past, restricted educational opportunities and limited upward social mobility (movement up the social or class ladder) for much of the population.

Britain was the home of the Industrial Revolution in the eighteenth and early nineteenth centuries, but many of the aristocracy's cultural values subsequently contributed to the country's economic stagnation. The upper-class preference for a career in finance, law, or journalism rather than industry gave industrial entrepreneurship a diminished status. Interestingly, most of the inventors and businessmen who initiated the Industrial Revolution were from "nonestablishment" religions—not Church of England—and were not "well born." Similarly, from Victorian times until quite recently, industrialists were often more interested in demonstrating their social standing than in improving productivity and keeping up with foreign competition. These factors contributed to the country's decline from being the world's leading economic power in the nineteenth century to second-class status today, behind the United States, Germany, Japan, France, and others.[6] Only in the past ten years or so has Britain once again achieved one of Europe's fastest economic growth rates.

CONTEMPORARY BRITISH SOCIETY AND POLITICAL CULTURE

> Against the envy of less happier lands; This blessed plot, this earth, this realm, this England.
>
> *—Shakespeare, Richard II*

In our discussion of political culture (Chapter 3), we noted that people in different countries feel differing degrees of satisfaction or dissatisfaction with their own political institutions and their fellow citizens. The gratification that Shakespeare expressed in being English is still shared by many of his countrymen. A number of years ago, a Gallup poll revealed that 80 percent of all Britons were proud of being British. More recent opinion surveys have indicated that national pride is higher in Britain than in many other Western European nations.[7] In part, that pride rightly reflects the strengths of British society. It is a very safe country, with homicide and overall crime rates less than one-fourth that of the United States and a police force that normally patrols the streets unarmed. Most Britons, quite accurately, view their fellow citizens as generally trustworthy, friendly, and polite.

A part of the country's stability and political success can be attributed to its rather well developed sense of national unity. As we noted in Chapter 3, Great Britain is often considered a model consensual political culture, most of whose citizens are in substantial agreement about their political goals and practices. A political consensus is more easily fostered in a society that is not deeply divided socially. When London had to endure repeated bombings during World War II, foreign observers were impressed by the sense of national purpose that united citizens of all backgrounds. Londoners seemed to exhibit a similar sense of common purpose after the 2005 terrorist bombings. Over time, Britain has been split by fewer ethnic, racial, religious, and geographic differences than have nations such as the United States, South Africa, Russia, and Belgium. Yet, important divisions do exist within British society, and some have notable political and economic consequences.

Sources of National Unity

In our discussion of political development (Chapter 15), we will suggest that nations with many religions, languages, ethnicities, or racial groups generally have had more tumultuous political systems than have countries with more **homogeneous societies** (societies that are more uniform in social composition). That may help us to understand Britain's relatively peaceful development and the sources of its political strength.

As an island nation, its people have always felt distinct from the other European nations across the English Channel on "the Continent." At times, that distinction has contributed to a false sense of superiority. Legend has it that several decades ago, when dense fog cut off all sea and air traffic across the English Channel, one British newspaper ran a headline declaring the "Continent Isolated." Compared with other Western European populations, the British people are still far less committed to merging with the rest of Western Europe and more skeptical of the **European Union (EU)**. Thus, for example, Britain is one of the only EU nations to have so far refused to adopt the Euro, the common European currency now being used in most of Western Europe. Although such insular attitudes have created problems for the British in the past—for example, their economy was hurt by their initial refusal to join the European Economic Community (now the European Union)—they did contribute to a consensus within the British Isles.

Almost 85 percent of Britons come from England, with most living in southern England, in close proximity to London. Furthermore, the population is overwhelmingly urban, with about two-thirds of the population of England and Wales found in seven metropolitan areas.[8] Not only does one person in six live in greater London, but most of the country's political, economic, and cultural elites reside in or near the capital. In many ways, then, most Britons have similar lifestyles, read the same newspapers, and relate to the same political symbols.

Sources of Internal Division

Even though the extent of homogeneity and consensus in Great Britain is impressive, important social differences also exist.

The Role of Social Class   In the absence of rural-urban conflicts or strong ethnic, racial or religious divisions, the greatest predictor of British political behavior and attitudes has been **social class**. Blue-collar workers, the poor, and those with limited educations are more prone to vote for the Labour Party. White-collar workers, professionals, businesspeople, people with more education, and the middle and upper classes in general are more likely to support the Conservative Party (also known as the **Tories**). Though there is a link in most industrial democracies between class background and party preference, historically the connection has been particularly strong in Britain.[9] Since the 1970s, that correlation has weakened as more British workers vote Conservative and more middle-class voters support Labour. Still, social class remains the best predictor of a person's electoral preference.

Historically, the nation's political leaders have been drawn disproportionately from the upper class. Aristocratic families (those with inherited titles bestowed by the crown) dominated the political system until the late nineteenth century. The rise of the Liberal Party in the late nineteenth century and the Labour Party in the early twentieth opened greater opportunities for politicians of middle- and working-class backgrounds. Moreover, since the 1970s, prime ministers of all three major parties have generally had middle-class origins.

It is within the Conservative Party that upper-class dominance has been most pronounced. Until the 1970s, all Tory prime ministers were drawn from the aristocracy or other segments of the upper class. Since that time, access to party leadership has opened up with Prime Ministers Heath (1970–1974) and Thatcher (1979–1990) having middle-class origins and John Major (1990–1997) coming from a working-class family. Even so, most Conservative MPs (Members of Parliament, i.e., the House of Commons) today still come from the upper or upper-middle classes.

British class distinctions have been reinforced by distinct educational tracks for different groups. At the top of the educational system are the country's most exclusive, private, boarding schools, called (confusingly for Americans) **public schools**.* The most famous of these—including Eton, Harrow, Winchester, Rugby, and Westminster—are hundreds of years old. Because of these schools' high cost and elitist orientation, their students are overwhelmingly well-to-do. Although less than 5 percent of the British population attends public schools, their graduates dominate the top ranks of the Conservative Party, the civil service, and high finance. In a recent Parliament, for example, nearly two-thirds of all Conservative MPs (and almost 40 percent of the entire Parliament) had graduated from these exclusive schools.[10]

Not surprisingly, the British are highly aware of the role of class. Moreover, unlike Americans, they believe that there are fundamental conflicts between the interests of the middle class and those of the working class. In a 1996 public opinion poll, Britons were asked whether "a person's social class [at birth] affects their chances in life" a lot or a little. Sixty percent of the respondents answered "a lot." More strikingly, when asked in another poll if there was "a class struggle in Britain" [presumably of a nonviolent nature], a surprising 81 percent of all Britons answered "yes."[11]

Yet, despite the country's well-known and keenly felt class divisions, the British have been less sharply divided politically by class *antagonisms* than the French or the Italians, for example. Consequently, whereas the communist parties in France and Italy once attracted a quarter or more of the votes (reflecting substantial working-class discontent with socioeconomic conditions), the British Communist Party has never received much support to speak of.

Two factors have kept British class hostilities in check. First, historically the upper class was more receptive than its counterparts elsewhere in Europe to social programs benefiting the working class and the poor. Indeed, in the late nineteenth century the Conservative Party introduced many of the country's earliest social reform programs. The Conservatives remained receptive to government welfare programs after World War II when the newly elected Labour government introduced a wide range of social programs in the **"welfare state"** (discussed later in the chapter). Although those measures were originally introduced by Labour Party socialists, the Tories continued to fund and support most of them after they returned to power in the 1950s. Only since

---

* Most British students attend secondary schools run by their local government. These have had various names, including "grammar schools" and "comprehensives," but they are *never* called "public schools."

Box 12-2

KNOWING YOUR PLACE

In recent decades, while the influence of class on British society has diminished considerably and the country has become more of a meritocracy (a society in which advancement is based on merit rather than social status), old habits and attitudes die hard for many. Thus, Prince Charles undoubtedly spoke for many upper-class Britons and for some in the middle class when he recently wrote that people should know their place in society and not aspire excessively to move up the occupational or social ladder.

In a 2004 court case, Elaine Day, a former staff member in the prince's household, charged that she had been dismissed from her job when she complained about unwelcome sexual advances by an aide to the prince. She also noted that when she had previously asked the prince whether secretaries such as

herself had opportunities for promotion, he reacted angrily in a memo that was presented to the court. "What is wrong with people these days?" he wrote. "Why do they all seem to think they are qualified to do things far above their capabilities? This is all [the result of] a child-centered education which admits no failures. People all seem to think they can be pop stars, high court judges or. . . . heads of state without ever putting in the necessary work or having the natural ability." This from a man whose primary qualification for his position in the royal family was his birth. The memo, said Ms. Day, was in keeping with the prince's belief that "everyone should know their place." When asked about the memo by the press, the prince admitted that he had some "fiendishly old-fashioned views."[12]

the 1970s have Conservative governments (most notably Margaret Thatcher's) criticized and pared down the welfare state.

The upper classes' more conciliatory outlook contributed to a second factor that reduced class tensions over the years: the average citizens' admiration for the **aristocracy** and widespread deference to the upper classes. Even today, despite the royal family's frequent missteps reported in great detail by the mass media, the British public retains tremendous affection for the queen (and maintains a somewhat morbid interest in royal scandals). Meanwhile, at least some prominent members of the royal family maintain a class-based view of society (see Box 12-2).

Regional Divisions   Regional differences are another important source of political division in Britain. Despite having belonged to the United Kingdom for hundreds of years, many Scots and Welsh remain resentful of English political and economic domination. Not long ago, for example, a number of English-owned vacation homes on Wales's north coast were burned down by angry nationalists. More peaceful alienation in Scotland peaked in the 1970s when the Scottish National Party, committed to the creation of an independent Scottish state, attained 30 percent of the region's vote. In Wales, the nationalist **Plaid Cymru** party also has attracted some support. Although the majority of Scots and Welsh wish to remain within the United Kingdom, economic and cultural tensions remain.[13] Following 1997 referendums in which both the Scots and the Welsh voted to establish their own regional parliaments, the new Labour party government established such legislatures.

A far more vexing challenge to the country's unity has come from Northern Ireland. Responding to clashes between Catholics and Protestants and to terrorist activities by the Irish Republican Army, the British stationed between 10,000 and 15,000 troops in the region in an attempt to keep the peace. Between 1969 and 2001, about 3,500 people died, and more than 25,000 were wounded. If a similar percentage of Americans had died in civil unrest, it would translate to more than 500,000 deaths.[14] At the same time, the British authorities' efforts to establish order provoked numerous violations of the residents' civil liberties, particularly those of Catholics. Periodically, IRA terrorism extended into England, resulting in many bombings, disruptions of public transport, and several attempts on the lives of Prime Ministers Thatcher and Major.[15] After difficult and protracted negotiations, in 1998 both sides (along with the British and Irish governments) signed the "Good Friday" peace accord, creating a joint Catholic–Protestant government in the north. Despite several false starts, at least two extended breakdowns, and growing Protestant unhappiness with the outcome, the accord has so far brought the troubled region an extended period of *relative* peace. But for several years home rule was suspended due to IRA violations of the peace agreement. However, in mid-2005 the IRA announced that it was giving up the armed struggle and would disarm. As of this writing, the major Protestant (Unionist) parties remain suspicious of the IRA's intentions and a final, negotiated peace has yet to be achieved. Bloody riots by Protestant extremists in 2005 suggested their discontent over the apparent loss of Protestant dominance.

Racial Divisions   Until the 1950s, Britain's population was overwhelmingly white. Since then, however, there has been a large influx of immigrants from India, Pakistan, Bangladesh, the Caribbean, Hong Kong, and Africa. By 1989, the country had approximately 2.5 million immigrants, mostly from former British colonies. Although nonwhites still constitute only a bit more than 5 percent of the population, they tend to be concentrated in a fairly small number of urban, industrial areas. Religious differences (a majority of the immigrants are Muslim, Hindu, or Sikh), competition for jobs, and racism have contributed to ongoing social tensions, including periodic urban race riots since the 1980s, most recently in a number of northern English cities in 2001. In recent years, the National Front and the British National Party—two neofascist political parties expressing and fomenting racist backlash within the white working class—have received growing electoral support in a small number of localities, and their activists aggravated the 2001 race riots in the North. Both the NF and the BNP, however, have far less voter support than do comparable neofascist parties in France, Austria, and Germany. The rise of Islamic extremism among some Muslims (including the children of immigrants), most notably the 2005 terrorist attacks on London's buses and subways, has increased tensions and produced a government commitment to raise surveillance of Islamic extremist groups.

POLITICAL PARTIES AND VOTING

Political party organizations dominate politics more thoroughly in Britain than in the United States for three important reasons. First, Britain has no primary elections. Hence, local party organizations (controlled by party activists), not the voters, select candidates for the House of Commons. Second, British voters get to vote for only one office in the national government: their representative in the House of Commons. The party with a parliamentary majority then selects its leader as prime minister. Thus, the executive branch and the legislative branch are controlled by the same party, and the electorate has no opportunity for ticket splitting. Finally, party delegations within

TABLE 12.1 SELECTED NATIONAL ELECTION RESULTS, 1951–2005
(PERCENTAGE OF THE VOTE)

Year	Conservatives	Labour	Liberal/Alliance/Liberal Democratic
1951	48.0	48.8	2.5*
1983	42.4	27.6	25.4[†]
1987	42.3	30.8	22.6[†]
1992	41.9	34.4	17.8[‡]
1997	30.7	43.2	17.2[‡]
2001	31.7	40.7	18.3[‡]
2005	32.2	35.2	22.0[‡]

*Liberal Party.

[†]Alliance of Liberals and Social Democrats.

[‡]Since 1992, the leading third party has been the Liberal Democratic Party.

SOURCE: Gillian Peele, *Governing the UK* (Malden, MA: Blackwell Publishing, 2004), p. 81; The British Council <.britishcouncil.org/governance-expertise-election2005.htm>

Parliament usually vote as a unified bloc, with MPs voting as their party leaders urge them to. As a consequence, Conservatives, Labour, and Social Democrats speak to the public with a more unified and more clearly defined message than do Democrats or Republicans in the United States.

A Two-and-a-Half-Party System

Great Britain has a party system dominated by two giants, but with a third party getting a significant share of the vote. Since the decline of the Liberal Party in the 1920s, most seats in Parliament have been won either by the Conservative Party or the Labour Party. But, unlike smaller parties in the United States, Britain's "third party" attracts an important share of the popular vote and wins a number of parliamentary seats. Two-party dominance peaked in the 1950s when the combined Conservative and Labour party votes accounted for between 93 and 97 percent of the total (see Table 12.1). In the past two decades, however, that share has dropped to only 67 to 77 percent, with the lowest total in 2005.

The first substantial postwar challenge to the two-party system was mounted in the 1980s, when the Liberal Party joined with the Social Democratic Party in an electoral "Alliance." Although it was able to gain about one-fourth of the popular vote in the 1983 and 1987 parliamentary elections, the Alliance ended up with less than 4 percent of the seats in Parliament (see Box 12-3 and Table 12.2). After the merger of the Alliance's two partners in 1988, the new Liberal Democratic Party won as much as 22 percent of the vote in the 2005 election, but its share of MPs still falls far short of that figure.

The prospects for British third parties are severely hampered by the country's electoral system. Because British MPs (like U.S. congressional representatives) are elected from several hundred single-member districts, a political party may win a substantial proportion of the nation's vote and yet have little to show for it in Parliament if it does not win many individual districts. That proved to be the Alliance's downfall. Although it attracted approximately one-fourth of the national vote in the 1980s, it repeatedly

Table 12.2   Results of the 1983, 1987, 2001, and 2005 National Elections

	1983	1987	2001	2005
Conservatives				
Percentage of the vote received	42.4	42.3	31.7	34.2
Percentage of seats won	61.1	57.8	24.4	30.5
Labour				
Percentage of the vote received	27.6	30.8	40.7	35.5
Percentage of seats won	32.1	35.2	60.8	55.1
Alliance (1983 and 1987) or Liberal Democrats (2001 and 2005)				
Percentage of the vote received	25.4	22.6	18.3	22.0
Percentage of seats won	3.5	3.4	7.6	9.6

Source: Philip Norton, *The British Polity*, 3rd ed. (New York: Longman, 1994), p. 83; The British Council, britishcouncil.org/governance-expertise-election2005.htm; The United Kingdom Parliament Web site, parliament.uk/directories/hcio/stateparties.cfm.

finished second to the Conservatives in southern English districts and second to Labour in northern England, Scotland, and Wales. Consequently, although it polled almost as many votes as the Labour Party in the 1983 election (25.4 percent), it received only one-ninth as many seats (3.5 percent) in the House of Commons (Table 12.2). In the wake of the 1987 election, the Social Democrats collapsed, and the Liberal Democratic Party was formed a year later (originally with a slightly different name). The underrepresentation suffered by the Liberal Democrats in 1997 through 2005 was almost as severe. (See Box 12-3.) It should be noted that, similarly, it is possible for a

---

Box 12-3

PARTIES AND THE ELECTORAL SYSTEM

Whereas the United States and Britain have two dominant parties, most of the world's democracies have multiparty systems. In countries such as Italy and France, for example, ten parties or more often win representation in the Parliament. Rarely in France (and never in Italy) does any single party have a majority in the legislature. Even in Germany, with fewer parties, the governing parties have often needed the support of the smaller Free Democratic Party or the Green Party to secure a legislative majority.

Most Western European nations select their parliaments through **proportional representation**, an electoral system that enhances the prospects of candidates from smaller parties (Chapter 4). In place of many single-member districts, members of the Parliament are elected from larger districts having multiple representatives. Voters choose between lists of candidates presented by each party. When the votes are tallied, each party attains a percentage of seats in the Parliament proportional to its share of the total vote. Had Great Britain used proportional representation, the Liberal–Social Democratic Alliance and its successor, the Liberal Democrats, would have received about 20 percent of the seats in the House of Commons in the last four elections. Instead, they had to settle for 3 to 10 percent (Table 12.2). Although Tony Blair originally promised to hold a referendum on whether to change Britain's electoral system to proportional representation, his government has failed to do so since such a change would inevitably cost Labour (and the Conservatives) seats in the House of Commons.

British party to win the most votes and not receive the most seats in Parliament (just as a U.S. presidential candidate can win the most votes and lose the election in the electoral college). That has happened on two occasions in the postwar period: 1951 and 1974.

The Conservative Party (the Tories)

The Conservatives are Britain's oldest and most successful political party. Formally organized in the 1830s, the party began as the voice of the British aristocracy and landed gentry. Over the years, however, it has become a broadly based party with electoral support from a wide range of voters.

The Conservatives continue to receive their most intense backing from upper-class and middle-class voters. Ever since universal suffrage was established in the early decades of the twentieth century, however, they have also attracted a significant segment of the working-class vote, without which they could never win at the polls. For example, Margaret Thatcher and John Major led the party to four successive electoral victories (in 1979, 1983, 1987, and 1992) by sweeping the most economically dynamic parts of the country (London and the rest of southern England) and winning over one-third of the working-class vote.

In the past, the Tories, like conservative parties elsewhere, have defended the status quo. In the tradition of Edmund Burke (Chapter 2), the party has insisted that change should be gradual so as not to undermine "the existing fabric of society." Whereas the Labour Party initiated bold new programs over the years, the Conservative position was more reactive until the 1980s.[16] Closely linked to the business community, the party favors limited taxation and lower government expenditures than Labour does, but supports a strong national defense.

At the same time, however, for decades Conservative Party leaders believed that government had an obligation to protect the less privileged members of society. Consequently, in the decades after World War II, various Conservative administrations accepted and supported an array of government welfare programs. For years, the economic policies of Conservative and Labour governments differed only modestly, as Tory leaders from the late 1940s until the 1970s supported "caring capitalism," which accepted the welfare state.[17]

That situation changed dramatically in the mid-1970s, when Margaret Thatcher assumed the party's leadership. In her years as prime minister (1979–1990), the "Iron Lady," as she was called, launched a major assault on big government. Conservatives stridently defended free enterprise and the values of the market system.[18] In 1992, two years after Thatcher's resignation as Prime Minister, her successor, John Major, led the Conservatives to an unprecedented fourth consecutive victory.

Thus, by the start of the 1990s, the Tories seemed to have established themselves as the country's dominant political party. Soon, however, their strength evaporated. By 1997, the popularity of Major's government had sunk to record lows and Tony Blair had reinvigorated the Labour Party, producing a resounding Labour victory in that year's parliamentary election. Since then, Prime Minister Blair, a master politician, has outflanked the Conservatives on many issues. As a consequence, the Tories have been reduced to bickering internally over Britain's role in Europe and other issues with little vote-drawing power. Recently traditionalist factions within the party have battled modernizers (libertarians) over issues such as immigration and gay rights. The party

© AP/Wide World Photos

A CHALLENGING ALLIANCE   Tony Blair meets with President Bush to discuss the war in Iraq. Blair's government has been the most ardent supporter of U.S. policy in the region, a position that has begun to erode Blair's popularity at home.

is also divided between Eurosceptics, those who are opposed to further British integration into the European Union, and those who are more open to integration.

Meanwhile, Labour has stolen the reputation for efficiency and economic management that once carried the Conservatives to victory. The Tories, looking out of date and out of touch, suffered another devastating defeat in the 2001 parliamentary election. As Labour has repositioned itself as Britain's middle-of-the-road party, the Tories have not yet figured out what they want to say to the electorate. By the 2005 election the party gained a number of seats and helped narrow the Labour Party lead considerably (Tables 12.1 and 12.2). But this was more a function of a decline in Tony Blair's popularity (partly attributable to public unhappiness over British involvement in Iraq) than it was to an improvement in Conservatives' standing with voters. Although they have changed their party's leader following each of their last three electoral defeats, none of these changes has reinvigorated their popularity to date.

The Labour Party

The Labour Party was founded in 1900 from an alliance of socialist organizations and labor unions. Within two decades, it had become the country's second-largest party, and in 1923 it headed a short-lived government. As its name implies, the party has been closely linked to the nation's trade-union movement and receives its most important electoral support from workers. Unions have provided a large share of the party's financial resources and until recently played a significant role in selecting its parliamentary leader. But though many Labour MPs have entered politics from the union movement, the party's top leadership has come largely from the middle class, particularly teachers, university professors, and other professionals. Like all British parties, Labour draws votes across class lines, although not as successfully as the Conservatives until recently.

When Labour came to power in 1945, it created an extensive state welfare system and **nationalized** important sectors of the economy, including the railroads, coal mines, and steel.* Until the mid-1990s, the Labour Party continued to favor many socialist programs. For example, one of the most controversial sections in its charter endorsed government "ownership of the means of production" (major industries, transport, and so forth).[19]

Always controversial, government ownership of major firms had lost significant voter support by the 1970s. As the Thatcher administration reprivatized British Aerospace, Jaguar, British Petroleum, the telephone system, and other enterprises, many average citizens purchased stock in those firms. Recognizing that Labour's socialist positions were hurting it at the polls, Tony Blair persuaded the party organization in the mid-1990s to end its support for extensive state ownership.

Labour's other important policy objective in the postwar era was creating the welfare state: an array of government programs related to health care, retirement pension, unemployment compensation, and public housing. This element of Labour Party doctrine remained quite popular, and succeeding governments—Labour and Conservative alike—maintained it until the Thatcher era. Proponents of the welfare state note that it has contributed to a lower infant mortality rate, a longer life span (credited to the government-run national health program of free, universal care), and a safety net for the needy. Opponents charge that it has overtaxed the nation and stifled economic growth. Today, Labour still defends the remaining components of the welfare state, especially the national health service, but the party no longer wishes to expand it. In fact, Prime Minister Blair during three terms in office has restored few of the programs that his Conservative predecessors had eliminated.

Blair's first budget featured a tax cut for business and differed only marginally from John Major's. Indeed, under Blair, "**New Labour,**" as it now calls itself, has abandoned most of its socialist positions and has become a middle-of-the-road party. On issues such as taxes and fighting crime it has stolen the Conservatives' thunder. Now its policies are designed to win the support of centrist, middle-class voters and business by championing improved cooperation between the public and the private sectors and greater efficiency in both. One of Blair's most symbolically important changes was the renunciation of Labour's long-standing commitment to government ownership of a portion of the economy. More broadly, New Labour has shed the image of a party of big government by promising not to raise taxes and to improve public services by making them more efficient rather than by increasing government spending.

What was most remarkable about Labour's new position is that it accepted many of the free-market reforms introduced by the Thatcher government. But, the Blair government has distanced itself from a hard ideological stance in favor of a more pragmatic approach. Unlike Thatcherites, who were instinctively against most government programs, or the traditional Labour Party, which was instinctively for them, Blair's position has been that "what matters is what works."[20] Indeed, the Blair government has a commitment to policies that are shown to work better by social science research, rather than ideology. At the same time, it has looked more carefully at public policies in the United States and Europe to see what ideas are worth borrowing.[21]

---

* The term *nationalization* (as well as the verb, to *nationalize*) refers to the transfer of an industry or a company from private to state ownership.

Although Blair's centrist policies have alienated many of the old Labour Party militants (particularly leftists and trade unionists), so far they have been very popular with the voting public, including the middle class. Indeed, the decision to reform the party was based on the realization that the size of the working class (Labour's traditional voting base) was shrinking and the ranks of the middle class and white-collar workers (traditionally more likely to vote for the Tories) were growing. In order to win, Blair's team concluded, New Labour had to become a "catchall party" winning support from a broad array of voters. The strategy worked! In 1997, nearly one-third of all professionals and managers and nearly one-half of all skilled white-collar workers voted for New Labour, a substantial gain over prior elections (the 2001 and, to a much lesser extent, 2005 election results were similar).[22] Thus, Blair has led Labour to three consecutive victories, something that the party had never been able to do before. But the 2005 victory came with the party attracting only 35.5 percent of the vote, a record low for a winning party in modern times. Weakened by his pursuit of the Iraq war and a growing reputation for being "too slick," Blair has promised to step down as Prime Minister before the next election and hand power to the Labour Party leader who succeeds him.

In foreign policy, Blair has also pursued a centrist position, becoming the most articulate and forceful defender of the U.S. War on Terrorism, including the wars in Afghanistan and Iraq. Indeed, since the September 11 World Trade Center attack, so active has Blair been in supporting U.S. foreign policy that Europeans sometimes jokingly referred to him as the United States' second Secretary of State. The 2005 terrorist attacks on London's public transport system have brought Britain even closer to the U.S. in the war on terrorism.

It is worth noting that New Labour still remains well to the left of the Conservatives on social issues. For example, far more Labour MPs than their Tory counterparts are female, Black, Asian, or gay, and the party has been more sympathetic to those groups' interests than have the Conservatives. Indeed, Labour's 1997 parliamentary victory doubled the number of women in Parliament from 60 to 120 by establishing gender quotas for Labour parliamentary candidates.[23]

The Liberal Democratic Party

Great Britain's leading third party, the Liberal Democratic Party, was founded in 1988. Originally called the Social and Liberal Democrats, it took its present name the following year. With a policy position to the left of the Conservatives and to the right of Labour, the Liberal Democrats originally presented themselves as a centrist alternative to the two major parties, though that distinction, at least for now, has disappeared since the 1990s when Labour moved toward the center. Indeed, since 1997, on issues such as public health, taxes, civil liberties, and the war on Iraq, the Liberal Democrats have taken a position to the left of Labour. Thus, the party not only was the only one to strongly oppose the war in Iraq but it has been highly critical of some of Blair's anti-terrorism measures, which it views as unnecessarily violating individual civil liberties.

The foundation for this new party was laid in the 1980s through the electoral alliance between the Liberal and the Social Democratic parties. Once one of the country's two major parties (in the nineteenth and early twentieth centuries), the Liberals were passed in the 1920s by the rising Labour Party. Reduced to insignificance after World War II, the Liberals later staged a modest comeback. By the early 1970s, they were receiving almost 20 percent of the vote. The Social Democrats, on the other hand, were not founded until 1981, when 27 Labour MPs and one Conservative defected from their respective parties seeking a more moderate alternative. In the 1983 and 1987 general elections, the Liberals and the Social Democrats both endorsed a single slate of parliamentary candidates (half from each party) called the Alliance.

Following their disappointing showing in the 1987 election, the Alliance partners decided to merge into a single party that soon came to be known as the Liberal Democratic Party. In recent parliamentary elections, the Liberal Democrats have attracted around 20 percent of the vote, maintaining its position as Britain's leading third party. Its support is greatest among middle-class professionals and managers and is somewhat weaker among blue-collar workers. As we have seen (Box 12-3 and Table 12.2), the Liberal Democrats (like the Alliance) are unable to win a portion of parliamentary seats commensurate with their electoral strength.

INTEREST GROUPS

Interest groups play an important role in the British political process. Two have been particularly influential. The Trades Union Congress (TUC), roughly equivalent to the American AFL-CIO, represents more than eighty of the nation's largest unions and is an integral part of the Labour Party. During the 1970s, the TUC and other labor unions exercised a considerable amount of political influence. Indeed, the high level of strikes and labor strife under Conservative Prime Minister Heath (1970–1974) and Labour Prime Minister Callaghan (1976–1979) helped bring their respective governments down.

But organized labor's influence declined sharply under Margaret Thatcher. Her government passed a number of bills weakening trade unions, and, in a critical confrontation, it defeated a bitter and prolonged strike by the powerful miners' union against the state-owned coal mines. During Thatcher's eleven years in office, union membership nationwide declined from 12 million to 10 million. The shift in the country's economy away from industry and toward the service sector has further weakened the labor movement (as it has in the United States) and by 2002, union membership was down to 7.7 million. At the same time, the number of days lost to strikes nationwide declined by almost 90 percent from 1981 to 2000.[24] More recently, Tony Blair's organizational reform of the Labour Party has eroded the unions' political influence in the party they helped found.

A second important national interest group is the "CBI, the Voice of Business." Formerly known as the Confederation of British Industry (CBI), it is the country's most influential business organization, representing three-fourths of the nation's large and medium-sized manufacturers. Unlike the TUC, the CBI is not officially linked to any party, but it has had a close relationship with the Conservatives and usually receives a sympathetic hearing from that party's leaders. And unlike the TUC (which has provided major financial support to the Labour Party), the CBI itself gives no funds to the Conservatives. But many individual members of the confederation (including most of the nation's largest corporations) contribute heavily to the Tory coffers.

From the early 1980s until 1997, the influence of all interest groups declined appreciably as the Thatcher and Major Conservative governments relied less on their input.[25] Ironically, under Blair's New Labour government consultation between the government and the CBI has increased, as Blair seeks to woo business support. But the CBI will undoubtedly stay more sympathetic to the Tories.

In addition to lobbying, many interest groups are officially represented on government advisory and supervisory boards. But, although British interest groups often have been influential at the administrative and bureaucratic level, their leverage in Parliament has been more limited. Because each party's parliamentary delegation typically votes as a fairly solid bloc, interest groups do not have the opportunity to sway individual legislators as they do in the United States. Furthermore, British campaign funding is channeled through the national political party organizations. So, again unlike the United States, it is difficult for a British interest group to win an individual legislator's support through campaign contributions. Ultimately, to gain their political objectives, interest groups must win the support of the leadership of the cabinet and the governing party's leaders.

The Structure of Government

Britain's government structure is far more centralized—and hence more simplified—than U.S. government. There is no state government, and the powers of local government are far more circumscribed than they are in the United States. In short, political power in Britain, as in most European democracies, is highly concentrated at the national level. Within the national government, authority is concentrated as well. There is no separation of powers and, hence, nothing comparable to the struggles in the United States between Congress and the president. Under a parliamentary system (which merges the legislative and executive branches), voters also have few electoral choices for national office. Whereas the U.S. voter selects a number of candidates for the national government—a member of the House of Representatives, two senators, the president, and the vice president—British voters elect only one: their representative to the House of Commons (their MP).

Parliament

Following each general election, it is the task of the House of Commons to select a prime minister. In many ways, this is the most important function Parliament performs during its term in office. Normally, however, its choice is obvious, once the voters have spoken. As long as one party has won a majority of the seats in the House of Commons, its leader is assured of becoming the prime minister. And only once in the last 60 years (in 1974) has no party been able to win that majority. In that situation, the final outcome is more ambiguous, since a prospective new prime minister would have to gain the additional support of a party (or parties) other than his or her own, or would have to form a minority government.

The prime minister's government (including the cabinet) serves only as long as it can command Parliament's confidence and support. Any time that it feels the government has performed unsatisfactorily, the House of Commons may express "no confidence" in the prime minister by a simple majority vote. Following such an outcome, the prime minister must resign or have the monarch call for new elections. Unlike impeachment of a U.S. president, ousting a prime minister requires no trial by the legislative branch. Moreover, a **vote of no confidence** requires no suspicion of illegal activity and no violation of the oath of office.

On the surface, then, this process appears to place British prime ministers on extremely thin ice, subject to the whims of Parliament. In actuality, however, they can normally rest secure in the knowledge that they have a firm grip on power until the next election. As long as their party has a parliamentary majority, they need only maintain the confidence of their own supporters. Since majority MPs have no incentive to vote their own party out of power, only one prime minister in more than half a century, James Callaghan, has lost a no-confidence vote (in 1979). But several times in recent decades MPs from the majority party have become so dissatisfied with the prime minister's performance that he or she has felt compelled to resign. In 1963, for example, following a sex scandal and possible breach of national security in his cabinet, Prime Minister Harold Macmillan resigned (though he himself was uninvolved in the scandal), claiming ill health. More recently, Margaret Thatcher resigned in 1990 after it became clear that she no longer had sufficient support among her Conservative MPs.

Besides serving as a watchdog over the prime minister and the cabinet, Parliament's most critical function is to consider legislation. Yet, its legislative powers are startlingly limited, compared with those of the U.S. Congress. All bills of any national importance are introduced into Parliament by the cabinet. Because the governing party normally has a majority in the House of Commons, and because British parties vote largely as a bloc, rarely does a bill introduced by the cabinet meet defeat. In recent decades, **party discipline** (voting as instructed by the party leadership) has diminished somewhat, and more government bills than previously have been defeated in Parliament. The number of votes lost by the prime minister (far less than 10 percent), however, remains rather small compared with the legislative record of U.S. presidents who, like Bill Clinton and the senior George Bush, have often faced an opposition majority in at least one house of Congress.

Unlike Congress, then, Parliament's primary function is not so much to design legislation as to review it. Although proposed government legislation is rarely defeated, it is sometimes altered or even withdrawn if it faces sufficient parliamentary opposition. Parliament also performs a watchdog function by regularly subjecting the prime minister and the cabinet to intensive questioning. These obligatory "question sessions" are closely followed by the media and force government ministers to defend their policies before the aggressive challenge of opposition-party MPs.

The Cabinet

The cabinet is the ultimate decision-making body in British politics. Heading that body and selecting its other members is the prime minister, the "first among [ministerial] equals." The number of full ministers is normally 20 to 25. They, in turn, are assisted by about 60 to 70 noncabinet and junior ministers. All ministers are chosen from either the House of Commons or, far less frequently, the House of Lords. Thus, whereas the U.S. Constitution prohibits individuals from simultaneously holding posts in the executive and legislative branches, British political tradition *requires* cabinet members to sit in both.

Except for the few **coalition governments**, when more than one party joins together to form a majority (during World War II, for example), ministers are selected exclusively from the prime minister's party. They usually come from the party's most respected parliamentary members and normally represent the party's major factions.

Appointment to the cabinet is the crowning achievement of an MP's political career. Ministers serve at the pleasure of the prime minister, however, and can be removed at any time.

The cabinet meets regularly to discuss government policy and consider potential legislation. It is here that the country's most important political decisions are made. The prime minister sets the agenda and sums up the discussion and policy decisions at the close of each meeting. Rarely is there a formal vote. Prime ministerial styles vary greatly. Whereas most leaders try to reach a consensus, others do not hesitate to impose their policies on the cabinet, even if theirs is a minority position. It was said of Margaret Thatcher that she summed up the conclusions of the meeting even before discussion began. John Major had a far more conciliatory style and sought cabinet consensus, while Tony Blair, though not as openly aggressive as Thatcher, has dominated cabinet meetings and reduced their influence on policy.

Once the prime minister has announced a decision, all cabinet members are collectively responsible for the policy and must quiet any qualms that they have. In the past, ministers who could not abide by that decision had no recourse other than to resign. Since that would undoubtedly hurt their careers as party leaders, resignations based on open policy differences have been extremely rare, though Robin Cook, Leader of the House of Commons, former Foreign Secretary and one of Labour's leading figures, resigned from the Cabinet after Tony Blair's decision to take the country into the war in Iraq. In recent times, extensive media coverage and the resulting news leaks often pierce the veil of secrecy over cabinet meetings, and internal policy differences are more easily known.

Although strong-willed prime ministers have overridden their cabinets and imposed their position, no prime minister can afford to oppose his or her colleagues consistently. Thus, Margaret Thatcher's frequent disregard of opposing views from other Conservative Party leaders and factions eventually contributed to her loss of leadership.

The Bureaucracy

The modern British civil service dates to 1854, when open competition replaced patronage as the basis for recruitment. Whereas new administrations in the United States appoint their supporters to thousands of high-ranking bureaucratic positions, British governments are much more constrained. All but the very top ministry positions are reserved for nonpartisan career civil servants. Since the highest-ranking civil servants (the "mandarins") normally have more experience and expertise in their fields than do the ministers and secretaries under whom they serve, they are in a position to exercise considerable influence. Indeed, in British popular culture (including a recent television sitcom), ranking mandarins are often seen as manipulating and controlling the ministers whom they serve.

In fact, the notion of an "unelected dictatorship" (of bureaucrats) is exaggerated.[26] The civil service is generally admired for its dedication and fairness. For the most part, it has done an admirable job of serving both Conservative and Labour governments impartially. But critics on both the left (radical Labourites) and the right (Thatcherites) have complained that entrenched civil servants often oppose policies that seriously threaten the status quo and, consequently, may drag their heels in implementing change.

Others argue that, however well motivated they may be, senior civil servants—who are drawn primarily from the upper middle class and are often educated at elite schools—are out of touch with much of society. They observe that people of working-class origins (constituting over half the nation's population) hold only 5 percent of the three thousand senior bureaucratic positions. At the same time, not long ago a government study noted that 72 percent of those entering the civil service had attended Oxford or Cambridge universities, and 48 percent had graduated from what the British call public schools (elitist private institutions that educate only 5 percent of the population).[27]

The Judiciary

Although U.S. criminal and civil law are derived in large part from British law, the two judicial systems differ fundamentally in regard to the courts' political role. As we saw in our discussion of U.S. politics (Chapter 11), the Supreme Court's political power derives from its capacity to overturn congressional legislation and executive actions by declaring them unconstitutional. The British court system has no comparable power. If the judicial branch rules that Parliament or the government has acted contrary to established constitutional norms (recalling that Great Britain has constitutional traditions but no written constitution), Parliament needs only pass a new law making its intentions explicit on the matter. Under the doctrine of parliamentary sovereignty, that new law would automatically be constitutional and not subject to reversal by the courts. But if the courts overrule an unpopular or embarrassing government practice, Parliament may be reluctant to reestablish that behavior.[28]

Britain's membership in the European Union (EU)—formerly the European Community (EC)—adds another level of authority to the judicial system. The 1972 European Communities Act stated that EC law takes precedence over any member nation's domestic law . Thus, for example, the EU's Court of Justice may rule that British environmental regulations conflict with rules enacted through EU treaties. That ruling would be binding on British courts, and the British law would be struck down. In 1998 the British Parliament passed the **Human Rights Act.** The bill incorporated the European Convention on Human Rights (of the EU), giving the country its first written Bill of Rights since the late seventeenth century. At the time, civil liberties advocates hailed this as a major step forward. However, in 2005, following the terrorist attacks and attempted attacks on the London mass transit system, Blair announced new security regulations, some of which appear to contradict the European Convention and his own Human Rights Act. He declared that he would ask Parliament to amend the Act if necessary.

PUBLIC POLICY AND THE BRITISH ECONOMY

The government first began to manage the country's economy actively in the 1930s as it attempted to counter the effects of the worldwide economic depression. World War II, which brought severe shortages and extensive German bombing of London and other British cities, inflicted further suffering. At war's end, in response to the nation's prolonged period of deprivation, the newly elected Labour Government greatly enhanced the state's role in rebuilding the economy and protecting the public's welfare. Although the Conservative opposition at that time and Tory governments in the following decades were more cautious than Labour about state economic intervention, they still supported an activist government working for the general good. Thus, from the late 1940s until 1979, Britain's national government (like its counterparts in most of Western Europe) intervened far more intensely in the economy and enacted more welfare measures than the U.S. government did.

The Establishment of the Welfare State (1945–1951)

The postwar Labour Government introduced an array of programs revolutionizing the state's role in society. The new national health care system offered tax-funded medical care for all. To remedy the country's severe housing shortage, the state funded a network of **council housing,** low-income public housing administered by local government.

The government expanded unemployment compensation and retirement pensions to create a "safety net" for the needy. In all, the Labour Government created a welfare state to provide the population with "cradle to grave" security. In addition, it nationalized a number of basic industries, including coal mining, iron, and steel—believing that those industries would better serve the national interest under state ownership.

The Postwar Settlement

When the Conservatives returned to power in 1951, they reversed some aspects of Labour's economic policy but maintained many others. For example, they reprivatized (returned to private ownership) the iron and steel industries. But during the next 28 years, Conservative and Labour governments alike retained and enlarged the national health care system and other fundamental elements of the welfare state. Public housing was greatly expanded, ultimately providing shelter for *one-third* of the country's population. Still, haunted by memories of the great depression, Conservative and Labour administrations alike pursued full-employment policies. For example, when major private firms faced bankruptcy, the government often stepped in with loans and stock purchases, or, when necessary, it took them over to keep them running.

Political scientists argue that during that period an unofficial and unspoken compact existed between the Conservative Party and the business community on one side, and the Labour Party and the trade unions on the other. Labour moderated its impulse for additional socialist reform, and the Conservatives accepted existing welfare programs that provided for the working class. That compact, referred to as the **postwar settlement,** remained in place until the late 1970s.[29] For much of that period, the nation enjoyed moderate economic growth, low inflation, and unemployment levels that rarely reached 3 percent.[30]

The Collapse of the Postwar Settlement

Thus, in the mid-1960s, the British government could truthfully tell its people that they'd "never had it so good." The nation's standard of living was higher than it had ever been before. Beneath the surface, however, serious economic problems loomed. Britain's postwar growth and industrial productivity trailed well behind those of Japan, the United States, and most of Western Europe. One by one, Germany, France, the Netherlands, Norway, Sweden, Denmark, and others passed the British in per capita income (GNP per capita). Britain became less competitive in the world market. Once among the world's leading producers of automobiles, motorcycles, and ships, it lost a large portion of those industries when it could no longer compete with countries such as Japan, Germany, and the United States. Burdened by budget deficits and crippling trade deficits (exporting less than it imported), the country accumulated a large foreign debt. By the 1970s, the economy had reached a crisis.

The reasons for Britain's economic slide were complex and subject to debate. Conservative and Labour analysts offered differing explanations and conflicting solutions. As real wages (the purchasing power of people's wages) stagnated or fell, the Labour Party became more radical, and unions became more militant. At the same time, power in the Conservative Party shifted from its once-dominant centrist faction to the right. The consensus of the postwar settlement was breaking down. As inflation soared above 20 percent in the mid-1970s, labor–management conflict intensified, with both sides struggling to keep up with rising prices. During the 1970s, the country lost more days to strikes than in the preceding 25 years combined.

In the winter of 1979, six weeks of strikes cut off garbage collection, heating-oil delivery, and hospital service. That "winter of discontent," as it was known, turned public opinion against the Labour Government and helped produce a Conservative victory in the 1979 national election.

The Thatcher Revolution

When Margaret Thatcher, the newly elected Conservative prime minister, took office, she revolutionized British politics much as her friend and admirer, President Ronald Reagan, did shortly afterward in the United States. Both countries, like most industrial democracies at that time, faced stagnant economic growth, high inflation, and budget deficits.

Prime Minister Thatcher, like President Reagan, was determined to reduce the role of government in the economy and to remove what both believed were unnecessary shackles on the free-enterprise system. Thatcher's tight-fisted fiscal policies initially drove the country into a recession. Unemployment rates nearly tripled, to more than 12 percent—the highest rate since the Great Depression of the 1920s and 1930s. At the same time, however, the administration rejected a basic element of the postwar settlement. Believing that it would only lead to greater budget deficits and continued inflation, the government refused to bail out ailing industries or employ other traditional methods to combat unemployment.

Looking at the country's long-term economic slide, the administration concluded that the solution was less government rather than more. It tried to create an "enterprise culture" in which citizens would look to the free market and not government for economic solutions. At the same time, Thatcher and her successor, John Major, reprivatized a wide range of government-owned enterprises—including the telephone, electricity, natural gas, and water systems—putting their shares up for sale on the stock market. Much of the vast network of public housing was privatized as well when tenants were given the opportunity to buy their apartments or houses from the state (at favorable prices) if they wished. On the other hand, in the face of public opposition, both Thatcher and Major refrained from major assaults on state welfare plans including dismantling the national health service.

How successful was **Thatcherism?** The answer depends on whom you ask. Conservative Party and private-sector supporters insist that she cured Britain of its excessive dependence on state-sponsored economic solutions. By reducing taxes and promoting an "enterprise culture," her government encouraged the growth of thousands of new companies, particularly in the nation's south. Supporters note that by the mid-1990s, Britain had one of the fastest-growing economies in Western Europe (although there had been sharp ups and downs under both Thatcher and Major). In many cases (though not all), privatized firms have performed more efficiently than they had under state control.

Many critics of Thatcherism in the Labour Party, the unions, and even her own party conceded a number of those accomplishments but contended that too frequently they came at an unnecessarily high cost. Although unemployment rates declined from their peaks of the mid-1980s, they remained much higher than they had been before Thatcher. Much of the north—once Great Britain's industrial heartland—failed to share in the economic revival.

But no matter how history eventually judges the Conservative revolution, for now the champions of reduced government have won the day. In Britain, as in the United States and much of the world, the role of government has been significantly scaled back and is unlikely to return to former levels in the foreseeable future. Although many voters viewed the Thatcher revolution as too heartless or too extreme, most were more suspicious of the Labour Party's commitment to greater government intervention. Hence, the Conservatives won four consecutive national elections.

Realizing this change in public attitudes, Tony Blair has led the Labour Party away from socialist or big-government solutions. His "New Labour" government (1997–) has renounced the party's previous support of government ownership of major industries, has kept a lid on taxes, and has left untouched most of the Thatcher policy changes, accepting them as necessary. Much of the current Labour Party program—including improving technical and scientific education (to help private enterprise compete), lowering business taxes, and fighting crime—is quite acceptable to centrist and moderately conservative voters. Thus, the Blair government has done as much to confirm the Conservative revolution as to challenge it.

GREAT BRITAIN IN THE TWENTY-FIRST CENTURY

Despite its impressive history of democracy and stability, Britain did not fare particularly well economically for much of the twentieth century. In recent times, the governments of Margaret Thatcher and John Major stimulated private-sector investment and opened up new opportunities for entrepreneurial talent. But it is too early to know whether they turned around Britain's weak economic record. Progress was sometimes uneven as periods of improved growth alternated with economic downturns.

Tony Blair is trying to introduce his own brand of efficiency and cooperation between the public and private sectors. Britain has modernized and become more competitive in recent decades. In fact, once having had one of the slowest growing economies in Western Europe, since the mid-1990s Britain has enjoyed the most rapid economic growth in the region.

Changing social attitudes and wider educational opportunities have opened up the country's confining class system somewhat. Wealthy, self-made businesspeople are more numerous and more socially accepted within the "old money" elite. The "old boys" network of aristocrats and other public school graduates no longer dominates Conservative Party leadership. The restructuring of the economy since the 1960s has diminished the size of the working class, while the middle class (particularly white-collar workers, professionals and salaried managers) has grown. For all those reasons, there is now a weaker correlation between an individual's class origins and his or her party preference. Many workers have become homeowners, including those who bought their council housing units in the 1980s. Initially at least, many of them considered themselves more middle-class and were more likely to vote for the Conservative Party than when they were renters.

At the same time, however, since the late 1990s, as the number of public service professionals has grown substantially (including teachers, civil servants, health care professionals, and social workers), middle-class support for the Labour Party has increased.[31]

Yet, social class still divides society more sharply in Britain than in the United States, Japan, or most of Western Europe. Even with the social changes just mentioned, opportunities for upward social mobility remain more limited than in other industrial democracies. Indeed, a 1992 survey of top positions in business, the professions, and the arts by the *Economist*, a respected periodical, found that graduates of public schools and Oxford or Cambridge still dominated those posts and that there had been less change than previously believed.[32] More recent research (2002) by the University of Essex indicated that opportunities for upward social mobility were actually declining, after a period of greater fluidity, and that children of the working class faced the greatest obstacles.[33] Thus, young men and women whose parents can afford to send them to public schools still start life with tremendous advantages over the rest of society. And even with the weakened correlation between class origin and political preference, "class remains the single most important social factor underlying the vote."[34]

A BRIGHT PAST AND FUTURE   Students at Eton, Britain's most elite "public school," line up for a ceremony marking the school's 550th anniversary. Many of Eton's privileged graduates go on to successful careers in business or politics.

© Homer Sykes / Alamy

As it moves into the twenty-first century, Britain will also have to decide whether it is willing to shed its traditional insularity and become an active, economically competitive part of Western Europe. While the European Union moves, somewhat haltingly, toward greater economic unification and a single currency, Britain has dragged its heels more than any other EU member. Whereas the Labour Party once was the most suspicious of European economic unity, now it is the nationalist wing of the Conservative Party that balks at taking orders from "[foreign] EU bureaucrats in Brussels."*

 WHERE ON THE WEB?

http://politics.guardian.co.uk/
Multiple links on British politics to and through the *Guardian*, one of Britain's most respected newspapers.

http://www.keele.ac.uk/depts/por/
Keele University (UK) guide to British Politics, especially elections and parties.

http://news.bbc.co.uk/1/hi/uk_politics
Links to the British Broadcasting Company (BBC), a government-owned but scrupulously independent television and radio network.

http://classweb.gmu.edu/chauss/cponline/britain.htm
Politics in Britain: Links to a major British newspaper, government agencies, political parties.

http://www.economist.com/index.html
A leading British news analysis magazine, *The Economist*.

◆ ◆ ◆

Key Terms and Concepts_____

aristocracy	Parliament
coalition government	party discipline
council housing	Plaid Cymru
devolution	postwar settlement
European Union (EU)	proportional representation
evolutionary change	public schools
Glorious Revolution	social class
homogeneous societies	suffrage
Human Rights Act	Thatcherism
industrial democracies	Tories
Member of Parliament (MP)	vote of no confidence
nationalization	welfare state
New Labour	

* The EU is headquartered primarily in Brussels, Belgium.

Discussion Questions_____

1. In what ways has British democracy served as a model for democratic government in other parts of the world?
2. Discuss the effects of class divisions on British society and British politics. What is the relationship between the British educational system and its class system? Given the historically significant role that class differences have played in Britain, why have class hostilities—as expressed in political divisions—been less sharp there than in countries such as France and Italy?
3. How does the British parliamentary election system discriminate against "third parties"? Specifically, how have the parties in the Alliance during the 1980s and the contemporary Liberal Democrats been weakened by Britain's single-member-district parliamentary elections? What are the relative advantages and disadvantages of single-member-district elections as compared with proportional representation?
4. Ten years ago, the Conservative Party won its fourth consecutive national election and many wondered when the Labour Party would ever regain political power. Now Labour has won three consecutive victories and the Conservatives seem to be in disarray. What turned things around for both parties?
5. What have been the major political changes introduced by Tony Blair's "New Labour" government?

Notes_____

1. Jean Blondel, "The Government of France," in *Introduction to Comparative Politics*, by Michael Curtis et al. (New York: Harper and Row, 1990), pp. 105–109.
2. Michael O'Neill (ed.), *Devolution and British Politics* (Essex, England: Pearson-Longman, 2004).
3. Richard Rose, *Politics in England* (Boston: Little, Brown, 1974), pp. 42–43.
4. The UK Parliament Web site, parliament.uk/faq/faq1,cfm, August 2005.
5. Gillian Peele, *Governing the UK* (Malden, MA: Blackwell Publishing, 2004), p. 81.
6. Paul V. Warwick, *Culture, Structure, or Choice? Essays in the Interpretation of the British Experience* (New York: Agathon, 1990).
7. Philip Norton, *The British Polity*, 3rd ed. (New York: Longman, 1994), p. 32.
8. R. M. Punnett, *British Government and Politics* (Prospect Heights, IL: Waveland, 1988), pp. 4–7.
9. Robert R. Alford, *Party and Society* (Chicago: Rand McNally, 1963).
10. Derived from Norton, *British Polity*, p. 269.
11. R. Jowell, S. Witherspoon, and L. Brook, *British Social Attitudes, the Fifth Report*, 1988–1989 ed. (London: Gower, 1988), p. 227.
12. *The New York Times* (November 19, 2004).
13. Geoffrey Smith and Nelson Polsby, *British Government and Its Discontents* (New York: Basic Books, 1981), chap. 2.
14. BBC Web site, BBC.com.
15. For early analysis of the problems of Northern Ireland, see Kevin Boyle and Tom Hadden, "Options for Northern Ireland," in *Developments in British Politics 2*, ed. Henry Drucker et al. (London: Macmillan, 1986); Brendan O'Leary, "Northern Ireland and the Anglo-Irish Agreement," in *Developments in British Politics*, ed. Patrick Dunleavy et al. (New York: St. Martin's, 1990). A more recent account by a major player in the peace negotiations is Marjorie Mowlam, *The Struggle for Peace, Politics and the People* (London: Hodder & Stoughton, 2002).
16. Max Beloff and Gillian Peele, *The Government of the UK* (New York: Norton, 1985), p. 177.
17. Peter Dorey, *Policy Making in Britain* (London: Sage, 2005), p. 270.
18. For a discussion of Margaret Thatcher's enormous impact on contemporary British politics, see Peter Jenkins, *Mrs. Thatcher's Revolution* (Cambridge: Harvard University Press, 1988).

19. Beloff and Peele, *Government of the UK*, p. 185.
20. Peele, *Governing the UK*, p. 90.
21. Dorey, *Policy Making in Europe*, pp. 278–280.
22. BBC/NOP exit poll cited in Dennis Kavanagh, *British Politics: Continuities and Change*, 4th ed. (Oxford and New York: Oxford University Press, 2000), p. 128.
23. Bill Jones and Dennis Kavanagh, *British Politics Today*, 7th ed. (Manchester, England, and New York: Manchester University Press, 2003), p. 95; Pippa Norris, "Gender and Contemporary British Politics," in *British Politics Today* (Malden, MA: Blackwell Publishers, 2002), ed. Colin Hay, pp. 38–41.
24. Peele, *Governing the UK*, pp. 349–350.
25. Neil J. Mitchell, "The Decentralization of Business in Britain," *Journal of Politics* 52, no. 2 (May 1990): 622–637.
26. Norton, *British Polity*, pp. 202–206.
27. Michael Curtis, "The Government of Great Britain," in Curtis et al., *Introduction to Comparative Politics*, p. 77.
28. Philip Norton, *The British Polity*, 2nd ed. (New York: Longman, 1991), pp. 343–345.
29. "Britain," in *European Politics in Transition*, by Mark Kesselman et al. (Lexington, MA: Heath, 1987).
30. Ian Budge, David McKay, et al., *The Changing British Political System: Into the 1990s*, 2nd ed. (New York: Longman, 1988), p. 7.
31. Ivor Crewe, "Parties and Electors," in *The Developing British Political System*, 3rd ed., ed. Ian Budge and David McKay (New York: Longman, 1993), pp. 101–104.
32. "The Ascent of British Man," *Economist*, December 19, 1992, p. 21.
33. Cited in Jones and Kavanagh, *British Politics Today*, pp. 19–20.
34. Crewe, "Parties and Electors," p. 102.

For Further Reading _____

Bartle, John and Anthony King, eds. *Britain at the Polls, 2005.* Washington, DC: CQ Press, 2005.

Breitenbach, Esther, Alice Brown, and Fiona Mackay, eds. *The Changing Politics of Gender Equality in Britain.* New York: Palgrave, 2002.

Dorey, Peter. *Policy Making in Britain.* London: Sage, 2005.

Jones, Bill, and Dennis Kavanagh, *British Politics Today.* 7th ed. Manchester, UK, and New York: Manchester University Press, 2003.

Morrison, John. *Reforming Britain: New Labor, New Constitution.* London and New York: Pearson Education, 2001.

Mullard, Maurice. *New Labour, New Thinking: The Politics, Economics and Social Policy of the Blair Government.* Huntington, NY: Nova Science Publishers, 2000.

Peele, Gillian. *Governing the UK.* Malden, MA: Blackwell Publishing, 2004.

Seldon, Anthony, ed. *The Blair Effect.* London: Little, Brown, 2001.

Walters, Simon. *Tory Wars: Conservatives in Crisis.* London: Politicos, 2001.

FALLEN HEROES   Tourists stroll Moscow's famed Gorky Park amid statues of former
Soviet Communist leaders toppled by angry crowds.

13

RUSSIA: THE STRUGGLE FOR DEMOCRACY

◆ The Relevance of the Russian Experience ◆ The Growth of an Authoritarian Political Culture ◆ The Russian Revolution and Its Aftermath ◆ From Totalitarian to Authoritarian Rule ◆ Crisis in the Soviet Economy ◆ The Gorbachev Era: Reforming Soviet Society ◆ Ethnic Unrest and the Breakdown of Control from the Center ◆ The Birth of a New Russia ◆The Growth of Russia's Multiparty System ◆ Political Parties: From Too Few to Too Many and Perhaps Back ◆ The Structure of Government: A Centralized Presidential System ◆ Restructuring the Economy ◆ Russia Begins the Twenty-First Century: The Putin Presidency ◆ Putin and the Creation of an All-Powerful Presidency ◆ The Challenge of a Dual Transition ◆ The Political Challenge ◆ The Economic Challenge ◆ An Uncertain Future

The transition from authoritarian government to democracy is always difficult and fraught with danger, particularly in a country having no prior democratic experience. The conversion of a state-controlled (communist or command) economy to a free-market economy is no less demanding. Rather than bringing about rising living standards, Russia's transition to capitalism brought its people enormous suffering for a decade or more. Small wonder that for countries such as Russia, simultaneously experiencing a political *and* an economic transition has presented a particularly formidable set of challenges. By the first decade of the twenty-first century, Russia's transition to capitalism—however imperfect—seems relatively secure. At the same time, under the leadership of President Vladimir Putin the country appears to be backing away from democracy and returning somewhat toward to its authoritarian past.

The collapse of the Soviet Union's communist dictatorship and its centrally controlled, "command" economy was years in the making. So, to understand Russia's current **"dual transition,"** we must first examine the political and economic systems of the USSR (Union of Soviet Socialist Republics), a country that at the close of 1991 disintegrated into 15 nations, including Russia. We must also understand both communism's accomplishments and its failures in order to better comprehend not only why the Soviet Union collapsed but also why many Russians today remain nostalgic for some aspects of the old communist order.

The Relevance of The Russian Experience

Few events influenced the twentieth century as intensely as the Russian Revolution of 1917, and none has affected contemporary world politics more profoundly than the recent disintegration of the Soviet empire. The collapse of the Soviet Union ended the cold war, which had dominated international relations and U.S. foreign policy in the second half of the twentieth century. At the same time, it undercut the previously substantial influence of Marxist-Leninist ideology in much of Africa, Asia, and Latin America. The Soviet experience demonstrates that even seemingly entrenched authoritarian systems can collapse. But subsequent developments in Russia have also highlighted the difficulty of establishing a postcommunist order.

To understand the decay of the USSR as well as the many difficulties now facing Russia, we must first explore the roots and development of the old communist system. We will see that although communism initially had some important accomplishments, those gains were achieved at a frightfully high cost. Furthermore, by the 1970s, the old order had begun to run out of steam. What will emerge in the new Russia is still unclear. So far, however, political and economic changes have been far more contentious and more difficult than anticipated.

Although there have been important advances toward a market economy, the country's initial progress toward political democracy (including relatively free and fair elections and greater freedom of speech, press, and religion), has been undercut by Vladimir Putin's administration. Government and the economy are deeply infiltrated by the Russian mafia, a powerful array of organized crime syndicates. Political corruption is widespread, and much of the country outside the largest cities is controlled by political bosses. During the 1990s relations between the president and the Parliament were

often contentious, reaching their depths in 1993 when parliamentary opponents of then-President Boris Yeltsin seized the parliamentary building, causing the president to order army troops to shell it. Since that time, relations between those two branches of government have been greatly tilted in favor of the president. Although independent newspapers and journals freely criticized government officials during the Yeltsin administration, Putin's government has regained tight control over the nation's television networks. And, while independent newspapers persist, there has been a troubling increase in the arrest or harassment of journalists who criticize the government. Meanwhile, state power has been overly centralized in the national government and the hands of the president.

Of greater concern to the average Russian, the transition from a state-dominated economy to the free market created horrendous conditions for nearly a decade, with the Gross National Product (GNP) shrinking by some 40 percent in the 1990s and living standards falling correspondingly. Life expectancy has declined significantly as the result of spiraling infant mortality rates and the deterioration of the health care system. Only since 1999 has the economy stopped its disastrous descent and begun to grow. But, although the economy has grown strongly since then, it has yet to recover all of its losses and it is too early to be certain if it has turned the corner.

These events demonstrate the difficulty of creating a pluralist democracy in a traditionally authoritarian society and the challenge of introducing capitalism into a society so long dominated by communist norms.

The Growth of An Authoritarian Political Culture

Just as the origins of British democracy can be traced to the Magna Carta and other seminal historical events, so too do the roots of Russian authoritarianism lie in the country's prerevolutionary past. In the early thirteenth century, Mongol invaders conquered Russia. More than two centuries of Mongol rule (1236–1480) enhanced the existing tradition of royal **absolutism**. Moreover, until the reign of Czar Peter the Great (1682–1725), the country had little contact with Western Europe and remained isolated from the liberalizing cultural and political influences of the Protestant Reformation and the Renaissance.[1] Although royal absolutism ended in Western Europe during the eighteenth and nineteenth centuries, the powers of Russia's czars remained relatively unchecked.

The Russian Revolution and Its Aftermath

The Decline and Fall of the Czarist Regime

The modern state in the Soviet Union, as in the United States and France, was born of revolution. During the nineteenth century, various groups challenged the repressive czarist government as a series of poor military efforts, from the Crimean War (1853–1856) until World War I, undermined the regime's legitimacy.[2] Finally, the suffering brought on by World War I helped topple the system. In March 1917, food riots erupted in Petrograd, the nation's capital at the time (now St. Petersburg). When mutinous troops joined the uprising, the old regime fell with hardly a fight.

The Transition to Bolshevik Rule

The moderate, provisional government that replaced Czar Nicholas was soon challenged by the **Bolsheviks** (Communists), headed by Vladimir Lenin. As in many modern revolutions, power shifted from political moderates to the radicals.[3] On October 25, 1917, Lenin, promising to end Russian involvement in the war, sparked an uprising in Petrograd, seizing control of the capital and then the nation.

Lenin and Marxist-Leninist Ideology

The Bolsheviks' victory brought them to power in an unexpected locale for a Marxist regime. As we saw in Chapter 2, Marx had expected communist revolutions to take place in more industrialized societies when the oppressed **proletariat** (working class) had developed sufficient class consciousness to rise up against capitalist exploitation. But Russia was among the least industrialized nations in Europe, with a comparatively small and inexperienced working class.

From Lenin's perspective, then, the Russian proletariat had yet to develop sufficient political consciousness to act in its own best interests. Consequently, he argued, the communists—who had the necessary appreciation of Marxist principles and an understanding of the mass's "true interests"—needed to organize a **vanguard party** to lead the masses (see Chapter 2). Whereas Marx had called for a transitional "dictatorship of the proletariat" followed by a "withering away" of the state, Lenin stressed an all-powerful state dominated by a vanguard Communist Party. Thus, Marx's utopian vision of socialist society was translated in practice into an authoritarian system. By 1921, Lenin had banned all opposition parties; placed labor unions, peasant organizations, and other interest groups under Communist Party control; and forced the press, literature, and the arts to follow the party line.

Three years later Lenin died, having only begun to create a communist state. Subsequently, he assumed mythic proportions in Soviet society. Millions of citizens, young and old, regularly visited his birthplace or viewed his body in Moscow's Red Square, and under Soviet Communism his bust graced all government buildings. Even after the fall of communism, many Russians still revere him.

Stalinism and the Totalitarian State

Following Lenin's death, power passed to the Communist Party's general secretary, Joseph Stalin, who established one of the world's most totalitarian regimes. It was marked by extreme glorification of the national leader, state intervention in virtually every significant aspect of public life, and the regularized use of state terror against the population.

Stalin transformed private agriculture into state-dominated collective farms. "By forced **collectivization** of agriculture Stalin put the regime in control of grain, drove millions of peasants off the land and into factories, and sent to labor camps millions of . . . kulaks [more affluent peasants]."[4] The resulting disruptions caused severe famine and millions of deaths. The all-powerful vanguard party and the state became the motors for rapid economic modernization, strident nationalism, and militarism.

Stalin concentrated all political power in his own hands, enforced by his dreaded secret police. Over the years, millions of ordinary citizens (an estimated 5 percent of the population) and many political leaders were sent to prison or to a network of slave-labor camps known as the **gulag**, where nearly a million of them perished.

From Totalitarian to Authoritarian Rule

Nikita Khrushchev and De-Stalinization

After Stalin died (1953), Soviet leaders resolved to deny such absolute power and hero worship (**cult of personality**) to any future leader. Although the party secretary remained the most potent figure in the political system, a new collective decision-making process required him to consult with the **Politburo** (the party's elite leadership council) and, to a lesser extent, the larger **Central Committee** (the body that elects the party leader). Moreover, although restraints on political dissent continued, systematic repression ceased being fundamental tools of state policy.[5]

In 1956, Nikita Khrushchev, the first secretary of the Communist Party, shocked the Twentieth Party Congress with a historic speech denouncing Stalin's crimes. Although the speech was officially secret, its content became widely known and symbolized the process of de-Stalinization. At the same time, millions of political prisoners were released from the gulag, and individual freedoms increased. Khrushchev's reforms were limited and many were rolled back by his successors. Still, he ended the worst excesses of Stalinism and opened up greater possibilities for subsequent change. His "secret speech" inspired a younger generation of future reformers, including Mikhail Gorbachev, whom later analysts dubbed "children of the Twentieth Party Congress."[6]

Leonid Brezhnev and the Period of Stagnation

Nikita Khrushchev was ousted from power in 1964 and was succeeded by Leonid Brezhnev, who led the country for 18 years (1964–1982). Brezhnev's administration was far less innovative and less tolerant of dissent. The primary features of post-Stalinist politics endured: collective decision making, efforts to improve mass living standards, and increased input from scientific and technical experts. But the Brezhnev regime was obsessed with political stability and, consequently, was unwilling to risk policy innovations. As the Soviet economy began to decay in the 1970s and corruption increased, many government leaders recognized the need for change; but, mindful of how Khrushchev's reform efforts had alienated his fellow party leaders, Brezhnev refused to rock the boat. Subsequently, the Brezhnev years came to be known as "the period of stagnation." Following his death in 1982, his two elderly successors died in office relatively quickly—Yuri Andropov (1982–1984) and Konstantin Chernenko (1984–1985).

Mikhail Gorbachev and the Origins of *Perestroika*

When Mikhail Gorbachev assumed the leadership of the Soviet Communist Party in 1985, he was the nation's youngest and best-educated leader since Lenin. The country he now led had changed substantially in the previous decades. For all its faults and brutality, the communist system had modernized an erstwhile underdeveloped nation. Once populated primarily by scarcely educated peasants, Russia had urbanized and industrialized considerably, with millions of high school and university graduates. The communist system also had provided Russians with the basic necessities of life: free (if mediocre) medical care, cheap (if inadequate) housing, and guaranteed employment.

By the late 1970s, however, that system had fallen victim to both its accomplishments and its failures. It had produced an educated population with a greatly expanded middle class. But increased contacts with the West and greater intellectual freedom led many Soviet professionals and intellectuals to chafe under the limitations of Soviet life—its poor-quality consumer goods, its inefficiencies and long lines, and its lack of political freedom. Gorbachev and his colleagues understood their discontent and recognized the necessity for change. So the new leader committed himself to greater openness and candor (*glasnost*) about the country's problems to allow restructuring or modernization of society (*perestroika*).

CRISIS IN THE SOVIET ECONOMY

The push for *perestroika* was motivated principally by the need to remedy the economy's increasingly poor performance. Thus, before discussing the Gorbachev era, we turn our attention to the economy he inherited, noting both its accomplishments and its failures.

A Command Economy

Like all communist nations, the Soviet Union had a state-controlled **command economy**. The centrally planned system maximized the government's capacity to shape and control major economic decisions. From the 1920s until the late 1980s, virtually all the country's productive resources—factories, farms, transport, communications, and commerce— were state-owned and controlled. Unlike free-market economies, Soviet production decisions, wages, and prices were dictated by government planners, rather than by the market forces of supply and demand.

Economic Accomplishments

Despite its more obvious weaknesses, the Soviet planned economy had a number of important accomplishments, at least in the first half-century or so of communist rule (1917–1967). The government turned an underdeveloped nation into a major industrial-military power in but a few decades. Western estimates of Soviet economic performance indicate that from 1928 to 1955, the GNP grew at an impressive average annual rate of roughly 5 percent.[7] "Entire industries were created, along with millions of jobs that drew peasants away from the countryside and into higher-paying jobs and higher living standards."[8] Although growth rates slowed after the 1950s, they still compared very well with those of major industrial democracies. According to the CIA, the total rate of Soviet economic growth from 1950 to the mid-1980s was 50 percent higher than in the United States.* Soviet living standards continued to improve into the early 1970s as consumers received many benefits previously denied them.[9]

The planned economy brought the Soviet population economic security, low unemployment, and a high level of equality.[10] Government subsidies provided consumers with basic foods and other necessities at very low and fairly unchanging prices. As Marshall

* Of course, the Soviet economy was starting from a much lower base point.

Goldman notes, the state offered the people protection from "the three evils of capitalism": unemployment, inequality, and inflation.

In the post-Stalinist era, with terror no longer the centerpiece of government control, those economic benefits were crucial for political stability. In effect, a tacit bargain was established between the government and the people in which the state provided economic security and improved living standards and, in turn, the population accepted communist political control.[11]

Economic Weaknesses

By the early 1970s, however, the country's impressive economic growth rate had begun to slow. Per capita income, which had grown at an average annual rate of 5.9 percent from 1966 to 1970, increased by only 2.1 percent in the five years preceding Gorbachev (1980–1985).[12] Although the command economy had jump-started industrialization, it failed to advance the country into the next stage of development. Industry and agriculture still used obsolete and wasteful production methods. Even after the collapse of communism, Russia's economy has continued to stagger under that legacy.

There were many reasons for the country's economic stagnation. In the absence of price signals, state planners had little basis for ascertaining what consumers wanted or for determining how to allocate resources. Because factory managers were rewarded for meeting government production quotas regardless of production efficiency or product quality, most consumer goods were of very poor quality. Furthermore, since workers enjoyed substantial job security but had little opportunity for economic advancement, the system discouraged hard work. As a popular saying put it, "They pretend to pay us and we pretend to work." As long as the Soviet people had limited educations and were only a generation removed from the wretched poverty of the countryside, they appreciated and supported a system that had given them secure employment, cheap food and housing, free medical care, and rising living standards. By the 1970s and 1980s, however, a far more educated population, including a large middle class, wanted more than the basic necessities of life. Many wanted the improved consumer goods and the freedoms that Westerners enjoyed.

At the same time, the government faced a fiscal crisis. The arms race with the United States and the Soviet war in Afghanistan augmented an already bloated military budget. The cost of foreign aid added to the budget deficit. And far too much was being spent on consumer subsidies designed to pacify the Soviet public. One government spokesman noted, "The state pays four rubles, eighty kopecks [cents] for a kilogram of meat and sells it [to consumers] for one ruble, eighty kopecks."[13] When Gorbachev took office in 1985, the national government's budget deficit was three times higher (as a percentage of GNP) than that of the United States.

THE GORBACHEV ERA: REFORMING SOVIET SOCIETY

Mikhail Gorbachev's reforms had two major dimensions. *Perestroika* involved restructuring national institutions, with special emphasis on economic reform. *Glasnost* promised greater freedom of expression in the mass media, the arts, and general political discourse. Yet, beyond a vague commitment to change, Gorbachev failed to offer clearly conceived final goals or a plan for getting there. Critics used an old Russian adage to describe *pere-stroika*: "If you don't know where you are going, any road will take you there."[14]

The Flowering of Political Reform

Ironically, the accomplishment that earned Gorbachev the greatest acclaim in the West—increased political freedom—was initially conceived, not as an end in itself, but as a vehicle for achieving economic change. Little in his record suggests that he was committed to pluralist democracy. Indeed, until his last year in office he resisted reform pressures to end the Communist Party's monopoly on power and to legalize opposition parties.

Why, then, did Gorbachev commit himself to *glasnost?* Jerry Hough suggested that only by offering middle-class bureaucrats, scientists, and technicians greater freedom of expression and increased contact with the West could Gorbachev have hoped to win their badly needed support for economic change.[15] Another explanation is that he knew that his attempts to decentralize the economy and reduce the party's political dominance would meet stiff resistance from the **nomenklatura**, the nation's large bureaucratic elite (discussed later), who stood to lose power and privilege. By allowing the media to expose the failures of the system, he might weaken the powerful conservative opposition.

Finally, "a bit of democracy would . . . disarm the suspicions of the West, allowing him to divert resources from the cold war and to attract foreign investment."[16] Gorbachev's key advisors had enough exposure abroad to know that Soviet economic modernization would require improved trade and communications with the capitalist world. Soviet scientists and administrators had to be plugged more directly into the information revolution.

But whatever were Gorbachev's original motivations, the political changes during his reign were nothing short of breathtaking. The country's most acclaimed dissident, Nobel Laureate Andrei Sakharov, was released from internal exile and subsequently elected to the national parliament. Virtually all political prisoners were freed. Long-taboo subjects—from airplane crashes to nuclear accidents, from street crime to government corruption—were now discussed openly on national television and in the press. In Moscow and Leningrad, independent newspapers and magazines criticized government policy. Religious freedom was restored. And, at least in the large cities, people lost their fear of freely expressing themselves to each other. In the words of one analyst, "Society . . . learned to talk to itself."[17] Though the USSR was not yet a democracy, the vestiges of authoritarianism were quickly receding.

Foreign policy reforms were equally dramatic. Gorbachev extricated the country from its bloody involvement in Afghanistan. The cold war came to an end. Military expenditures were curtailed. And when the people of Eastern Europe rose up against their communist governments in 1989, the USSR decided not to intervene militarily. Ironically, however, as Gorbachev's popularity abroad soared, it declined at home. His inability to improve the economy led most Soviet citizens to blame him for their declining living standard, as well as for a growing sense of chaos.

The Limits of Economic Reform

Glasnost was introduced as a vehicle for economic modernization, but instead, political change hurtled forward while economic reform proceeded at a snail's pace. The administration knew the economy needed repair but seemed to have little idea of how to do it. "Behind Gorbachev's ringing call . . . [for radical reform] stood a vague, incomplete set of generalities of little use in constructing actual reform legislation."[18]

At the start, instead of restructuring the command economy, Gorbachev tried to make the existing system more efficient. Ministries were reorganized, new quality standards were imposed, and a major campaign was mounted against alcohol consumption (a severe social problem and a contributor to poor performance in the workplace). But little came of those efforts. Ministerial reorganization only added new layers of bureaucratic red tape. Quality control standards had to be abandoned when factories had most of their output rejected. The anti-alcohol campaign provoked popular resentment, a torrent of anti-Gorbachev jokes, and a boom in moonshine whiskey.

One of President Gorbachev's few successful economic reforms was the legalization of small private enterprise for the first time since the 1920s. Larger private firms soon emerged, some legal, others not. They included restaurants, nightclubs, taxis, banks, auto dealers, computer importers, small construction firms, and black market merchants selling smuggled goods from the West—all offering services that were inadequately provided by the state. By 1991, 5.6 million people earned at least a portion of their income from the private sector.

A Worsening Economic Crisis

It soon became apparent that, rather than curing the nation's stagnant economy, *perestroika* had thrown it into reverse. The GNP, which had grown sluggishly in the mid-1980s, began to decline. By the Soviet Union's last year (1991), the economy was in a free fall, with GNP dropping some 15 percent and industrial production in chaos. Lines in state stores lengthened, and consumer goods became even scarcer. Inflation, previously nonexistent in this controlled economy, surged.

A fundamental problem, initially not well understood in the West, was that the transition from a command economy to a free-market system, no matter how intelligently pursued, is inevitably terribly painful. Previously, workers had been retained regardless of the need for their labor in order to guarantee full employment; companies continued operating regardless of their profitability. As one Soviet economist had observed cynically, "Our unemployment is [really] the highest in the world. But, unfortunately, all our 'unemployed' get paid."[19] Finally, state subsidies kept consumer prices artificially low. For example, from the 1960s to the start of the 1990s, bread prices never increased. The subsidized price of bread was so low that many farmers fed bread instead of grain to their livestock because it was cheaper.

Of course, that was all very inefficient. Consequently, foreign economic advisers and reform-oriented Soviet economists advocated economic adjustment policies that would phase out consumer subsidies, close many unprofitable firms, and privatize major portions of the state sector. Only by laying off unneeded workers, forcing factories to show a profit, and compelling producers to compete for consumers, they insisted, would production *eventually* become more efficient, profitability increase, and the quality and array of consumer goods improve.

For nearly two years, however, the government vacillated. Since freeing prices would sharply raise the cost of food and other necessities, the administration naturally hesitated to risk further popular discontent. The Parliament, still dominated by old-line communists, showed even less enthusiasm for market reforms. Finally, the still-influential state bureaucracy, fighting to hold onto its power, derailed reform wherever it could.

Although Soviet workers and consumers told pollsters that they favored a rapid conversion to a market economy, most were unwilling to suffer the initial consequences. For example, in 1991 a spokesman for striking coal miners insisted that Gorbachev should resign because he had only taken halfway measures in reforming the economy. But, when asked about the impending termination of government subsidies for consumer goods (a necessary ingredient of reform), he voiced his adamant opposition.

As the political system became less repressive and the state's power to direct economic decisions declined, sufficient free-market incentives were not created to replace the decaying controls from on high. Simply put, Gorbachev removed the stick from the Soviet economy and failed to replace it with a carrot. The result was a series of bottlenecks in which factories acted out of misguided self-interest and failed to coordinate their activities.

Marshall Goldman has suggested that one of Gorbachev's key errors was to introduce political freedom *before* he had pushed through necessary, but painful, economic reforms.[20] For example, because farmers were no longer forced to sell their harvest at state-determined prices, many chose to store their crops in anticipation of rising prices. Worried consumers took to hoarding, thereby adding to the shortages. As the economy deteriorated, miners and industrial workers exacerbated the decline by exercising their newfound ability to strike.

ETHNIC UNREST AND THE BREAKDOWN OF CONTROL FROM THE CENTER

Together with the economy, ethnic conflict was *perestroika*'s Achilles' heel. The removal of political repression unleashed nationalist tensions and calls for national independence long suppressed by the czarist and Soviet governments.

The drive for secession was strongest in the Baltic states, whose populations had experienced independence between the world wars. With the USSR's highest educational levels and most advanced economies, Estonia, Latvia, and Lithuania identified more strongly with Western Europe than with other Soviet republics. Independence movements were also strong in Moldavia, Georgia, Ukraine, and Armenia. One factor that led communist hard-liners to attempt an armed coup against Gorbachev in 1991 was their desire to prevent the disintegration of the Soviet empire. Ironically, soon after that coup failed, the USSR dissolved, and all 15 of its republics became independent nations.

THE BIRTH OF A NEW RUSSIA

Of course, by far the largest of the former Soviet republics was Russia, which had accounted for two-thirds of the USSR's land area and more than half its population. Boris Yeltsin—who had criticized Gorbachev for the slow pace of economic and political reform—had resigned his high-ranking position in the Soviet Communist Party and was then expelled from the party. After being elected president of the Russian republic in June 1991 in the first free election of a Russian leader, Yeltsin saved Gorbachev from an anti-reformist military coup two months later. But, he then helped force the breakup of the Soviet Union, making him the president of an independent Russia. For the rest of the 1990s, he presided over Russia's difficult and often chaotic transition to capitalism and democracy. Yeltsin himself showed both authoritarian and democratic tendencies. He could be strong and decisive in times of crisis (such as the 1991 coup attempt and his 1993 armed confrontation with the Parliament) but at other times was often hobbled by indecision, poor health, and alcoholism.

THE GROWTH OF RUSSIA'S MULTIPARTY SYSTEM

With Gorbachev's legalization of competing parties in 1990 and the subsequent collapse of the Soviet system, Russia was transformed from single-party rule to a multiparty system. Although the last election for the Russian Republic's Parliament had permitted independent opposition candidates, the government did not allow political parties other than the Communist Party. By the time of Russia's first postcommunist national election in 1995, however, the country had 262 legally registered parties. More than 40 of them fielded candidates for that year's parliamentary elections, of which nearly 10 had significant support.

Under the Russian Constitution of 1993, a new national Parliament was established. Voters cast two ballots to select the 450 deputies in the **State Duma**, the dominant parliamentary chamber. Until now, one vote has been for a single representative from the voter's district (1 of 225), and the other has been for a party list of candidates. The 225 party-list seats have then been distributed proportionately to all the political parties that have received at least 5 percent of the national vote, and the remaining Duma seats have been awarded to the winners in each of the 225 districts.

In 2005, however, Parliament approved President Putin's proposal to eliminate the 225 single-member districts in the next election and elect all 450 Duma members from the party lists. In order for a party to win any proportional representative seats from its party list, it will need to receive 7 percent of the vote. While such a change seems reasonable at first glance (many democracies have parliaments elected solely through proportional representation), Putin's intent seems clear. In the 2003 Duma election only four parties received even 5 percent of the vote. Some half dozen were able to gain seats in the Duma only through single-member-district elections. The new rules will eliminate small parties from Parliament and exclude some of Putin's harshest critics from the parties favoring democratic reform. Other legislation makes it harder for parties to register and to receive government campaign funding.

What follows is a discussion of Russia's transition from a single-party system (until 1990) to multiparty competition and, most recently, back to single-party dominance.

POLITICAL PARTIES: FROM TOO FEW TO TOO MANY AND PERHAPS BACK

The Soviet Union's Only Party

A fundamental requisite of democratic government is free and fair competition between at least two political parties, each capable of winning a national election at some time. Under the Soviet Union, of course, such contestation was absent. From the time of the 1917 revolution until shortly before the collapse of the USSR, the Communist Party, had a monopoly of power as "the leading and guiding force of Soviet society." Not only did the Communist Party Politburo, and to a lesser extent the Central Committee, make all major policy, but also all important government officials were drawn from the upper echelons of the party.

At its peak in the late 1980s, about 19 million people—about 10 percent of the adult population—belonged to the Communist Party. In all walks of life—in every factory, collective farm, laboratory, and university faculty—one found party members and party cells. Reasons for joining the party included some mix of ideological commitment and opportunism. Membership frequently was a prerequisite for preferred employment and facilitated access to housing and other scarce consumer goods. Surveys of Russian emigrants suggest that by the 1980s, personal advancement was a more common motive for joining than political or moral objectives.[21] Still, its large and diverse membership allowed the party to penetrate virtually every aspect of Soviet life.

Communist Party control over society was reinforced by the *nomenklatura* system, the party's power to control political and bureaucratic appointments. The term referred to a vast list of positions within the Soviet state bureaucracy, the military, state-owned enterprises, labor unions, the media, cultural organizations, and professional groups. Appointment to all those posts required party consent. But "although *nomenklatura* implies only Party approval or confirmation of personnel decisions, in fact the Party often [took] the initiative in filling positions on the list."[22] In common Soviet political discourse, *nomenklatura* also referred to the thousands of bureaucrats who held those posts, constituting a tremendously powerful and privileged power elite. So great was their control that even after the collapse of communism, they continue to exert considerable influence in Russia's state bureaucracy and remaining state-owned enterprises. Many of them now control important components of the new private sector.

The Development of a Fragmented Multiparty System

Although democracy requires a competitive party system, it tends to function poorly when there are *too many* parties. Under those circumstances, it is difficult for any party or even a coalition of political parties to achieve a workable majority in the national Parliament. Since 1991, Russia has been cursed with an excess of political parties, many of which have been highly unstable, often forming for a period of time to further the interests of an important political figure or group and then dissolving before the next election. Indeed, hundreds of political parties have sought or achieved legal status in the past dozen years, and 58 of them were legally registered as of early 2001.[23]

Approximately 30 political parties or coalitions fielded candidates in the 2003 parliamentary elections, with about a dozen of them winning at least one seat. As Table 13.1 indicates, until the 2003 parliamentary election no party came close to winning a governing majority (226 seats). In the most recent election, however, the pro-Putin United Russia Party won nearly half the seats in the Duma, which, with support from a number of other deputies, has made Putin the first Russian president to command a secure working majority in the Parliament. Since that time a significant number of other deputies have allied with United Russia, giving the administration 305 seats (of 450) in the Duma, not only guaranteeing Putin a majority on almost any vote but giving him enough support to amend the constitution. There are still a number of

---

TABLE 13.1   RUSSIA'S PARLIAMENTARY ELECTION RESULTS: 1995–2003

Political Party	Percentage of the Party List Votes (Total Number of Duma Seats)		
	1995	1999	2003
Authoritarian Parties			
Communists	22.3% (147)	24.3% (113)	12.8% (51)
Liberal Democrats	11.2% (51)	6.1% (17)	11.7% (37)
Motherland (Rodina)			9.2% (37)
Center Parties			
United Russia (Unity)*	_____	23.3% (72)	38.0% (221)
Our Home Is Russia	10.1% (55)	1.2% (7)	_____
Democratic Reformist Parties			
Yabloko	6.9% (45)	6.1% (20)	4.4% (4)
Union of Right Forces		8.5% (29)	4.0% (3)

*United Russia was created before the 2003 election through the merger of Unity and Fatherland–All Russia.

SOURCE: *IDC, Russian Parliamentary Election Results, 1995:* http://idc.cis.lead.org/observer/Russia-95/elec-res.html; 1999: http://www.rferl.org/elections/russia99results/; 2003; wikipedia.ort/wiki/Russian_legislative_election%2V_2003.

---

small parties and independents (the latter elected in single-member districts), but they no longer can exert political leverage.

Russian parties run the ideological gamut from communist to fascist. In between can be found others classified as nationalist, ultranationalist, liberal (reformist), social democratic, centrist, religious, regional, and "single-issue" (including feminist, agrarian, military, and environmental). But, as Table 13.1 shows, the leading vote-getters in Russia's three last parliamentary elections can be placed into three broad categories[24]: authoritarian, centrist, and democratic reformist.

Authoritarian (Antidemocratic) Parties   Since their country's transition to an electoral democracy, roughly one-third of all Russian voters have voted for two to three parties that, whatever their current rhetoric, reject democracy—particularly the Communist Party and the neofascist Liberal Democratic Party (briefly known as the Zhirinovsky Bloc). In 2003, they were joined by Motherland, an ultra-nationalist party with communist leanings. The communists, in particular, repeatedly clashed with the government of Boris Yeltsin and, to lesser extent, with Vladimir Putin. Since United Russia gained control of the Duma in 2003 and Putin was overwhelmingly reelected president in 2004, these parties, especially the Liberal Democrats and part of Motherland, have supported many of the president's initiatives. While the party's strength declined in the 1999 Duma elections, it rebounded in 2003 and probably took votes away from the communists.

Unlike reformed communist parties that have staged comebacks in other Eastern European countries (including Lithuania, Hungary, and Poland) after altering their names and ideologies, the Russian Communist Party has changed neither. Since many of the party's most capable leaders (including Yeltsin and many of Russia's current leaders) abandoned it in the late 1980s or the early 1990s, the party has been led by lukewarm reformers and *nomenklatura* hacks who rejected Gorbachev's reforms and now only reluc-tantly accept (or claim to accept) elements of democracy and the free market. Until recently, the party has attempted to slow the privatization of Russian industry and farm-land, tried to slow the pace of free-market reforms, and has opposed closer Russian ties to the West.

Still, with close to one-fourth of the party-list votes in the 1995 and 1999 Duma elections, the Communist Party remained the country's leading vote-getter. Only in 2003 did United Russia pass the Communists as the largest party in the Duma. Furthermore, it has finished second in the country's three presidential elections and its leader, Gennady Zyuganov, had been considered a serious threat to defeat President Yeltsin in 1996 (Table 13.2). Its support in the 2004 presidential election, however, was less than half its total in the previous two elections. And its poor showing in the 2003 Duma election was influenced partly by the surprise showing of Motherland (or Homeland), a highly nationalistic party with a socialist domestic program, and by the electoral rebound of the Liberal Democrats. It is widely believed that the Kremlin sponsored Motherland (Rodina) in order to siphon off votes from the Communist Party. Since the election, Motherland has split as a major faction supported Putin.

Who are the voters who have continued to give the communists roughly one-eighth to one-third of the vote? They come disproportionately from elderly voters, those without high school degrees, and the poor, groups particularly undermined by the economic decay of the 1990s. Senior voters not only have seen the value of

---

TABLE 13.2   Russia's Presidential Election Results: 1996–2004

1996 Presidential Elections

	First Round	Second Round
Boris Yeltsin (independent, incumbent)[*]	35.3%	53.8%
Gennady Zyuganov (Communist Party)	32.0%	40.3%
Alexander Lebed (independent)	14.5%	—
Gregory Yavlinski (Yabloko)	7.3%	
Vladimir Zhirinovsky (Liberal Democrats)	5.7%	

2000 Presidential Election

Vladimir Putin (independent, incumbent)[*]	52.9%
Gennady Zyuganov (Communist Party)	29.2%
Gregory Yavlinski (Yabloko)	5.8%
Others, invalid votes, and "against all"	12.1%

2004 Presidential Election

Vladimir Putin (independent, incumbent)[*]	71.9%
Nikolai Kharitonov (Communist Party)	13.8%
Others, invalid votes, and "against all"	14.3%

[*]Yeltsin and Putin officially ran as independents but were backed by various political parties that had been formed largely for the express purpose of supporting them, most notably United Russia, now the country's dominant party and firmly under President Putin's control.

Sources: http://www.geocities.com/CapitolHill/2568/e_rpe96r.html; http://www.rferl.org/elections/russia00report/; http://www.electionguide.org/resultsum/russia_pres04.htm.

their pensions evaporate but also are in greater need of the economic safety net that communism provided. They are least equipped to prosper in the emerging capitalist economy.

Rural voters are among the nation's poorest population and also have depended on government subsidies. Given the party's disproportionate share of older Russians and its relative weakness among younger voters, most analysts have expected the Communist Party vote to decline over time as many of its voters pass away. The results of the most recent Duma and presidential elections suggest that this process may finally have begun.

The Liberal Democratic Party is largely the personal political vehicle of its leader, Vladimir Zhirinovsky. It came out of nowhere to win the most votes in the 1993 parliamentary elections and placed second in 1995. Perhaps the most outrageous major political figure in Russia, Zhirinovsky, among other things, has called for dropping neutron bombs on the Baltic states and advocated waging nuclear war against Germany. His speeches have often been laced with racist and anti-Semitic slurs.

Like other extreme nationalist groups, the party appeals to Russian patriotism and to those who regret the country's loss of superpower status. Russians have historically been distrustful of the West, and many now feel that their culture is being polluted by crass commercialism, from McDonald's to the limousines of the nouveau riche. Finally, its extreme positions on law and order also attract voters. Zhirinovsky, for example, once pledged to lower the spiraling crime rate by summarily executing 100,000 criminals. Though its support fell in the 1999 parliamentary election, the Liberal Democratic party rebounded in 2003, finishing slightly behind the second-place Communists.

Centrist Parties   Most of Russia's major centrist (middle-of-the road) parties have been outgrowths of the personal ambitions of the country's most influential government officials. Consequently, their fortunes have risen and fallen with those of their leaders. Our Home Is Russia, for example, was little more than an electoral machine for President Yeltsin and later, former Prime Minister Chernomyrdin. As Table 13.1 indicates, its fortunes declined (from 10.1 percent of the national vote in 1995 to 1.2 percent in 1999) as both men lost political power. Unity was formed in 1999 by politicians allied with then–Prime Minister Vladimir Putin, who rode his popularity to a strong showing in that year's parliamentary election. Fatherland All Russia was established by supporters of former Prime Minister Yevgeny Primakov (once considered the front-runner in the 2000 presidential election) and Moscow Mayor Yuri Luzhkov. Neither of those leading centrist parties in 1999 had even existed in 1995 (Table 13.1).

By the 2003 parliamentary election Fatherland had merged with Putin's Unity party (even though its leaders had been political enemies) to form United Russia, the party that now dominates the Duma. With the additional support of friendly parties, President Putin can now count on over two-thirds of the votes in Parliament. It is clearly Putin's intention that United Russia remain the dominant political party beyond his presidency. The party has generally avoided discussion of ideological issues and primarily presents itself as the party of order and stability, and, most important, the party of Vladimir Putin. Interestingly, many of the leading centrist politicians began their careers as government officials in the days of communist rule (Yeltsin) or as officials in the KGB security apparatus (Putin, Primakov). Perhaps for that reason, their commitment to democracy has at times mixed with antidemocratic behavior (such as manipulation of the media), most notably under Putin.

Democratic Reformists   Generally led either by the most ardent economic reformers in the Yeltsin government (former Prime Ministers Sergei Kiriyenko and Yegor Gaidar of the Unity of Right Forces) or by outside intellectuals (Gregory Yavlinski of Yobloko), these parties most forcefully support rapid free-market reforms and liberal democracy. Many of their leaders either have received graduate degrees from the West or have established links with leading Western universities such as Harvard. Sophisticated, urbane, and strongly committed to both free markets and a free society, they are highly regarded by Western politicians and specialists on Russia. But, they have never attracted support from a large share of the electorate. As Table 13.1 indicates, neither reformist party received as much as 10 percent of the vote. Russian voters tend to fear the fast track toward free enterprise that ardent reformists favor. The media, mostly biased in favor of Putin's 2000 presidential campaign, as it had favored Presidential Yeltsin four years earlier, degraded the race by accusing the leading reformist candidate, Gregory Yavlinski, of being a "tool of foreigners, homosexuals, and Jews." Democratic reformists have their greatest support among younger, more educated voters and residents of Moscow and St. Petersburg. By the 2003 Duma elections, however, neither party received as much as 5 percent of the party list vote, depriving them of any proportional representation seats (i.e., they won none of those 225 seats and were only able to win a few seats in single-member districts). With the elimination of single-member districts in the next Duma election and a 7 percent minimum for party list seats, these democratic reformist parties are likely to lose all parliamentary representation.

Though Russian parties appear ideologically diverse, those differences are becoming overshadowed by the personal ambitions of their leaders. Moreover, they tend to be weakly organized, with poorly articulated programs and ideologies, thereby intensifying the problems of effective governance. Only the Communist Party has had a large membership with an extensive grassroots structure (though both are declining). For most parties, statistics on their own membership are notoriously unreliable and generally dishonest, but officially the communists claimed 500,000 members, considerably fewer than the roughly 11 million members at the time of the Soviet Union's 1991 collapse. But since their support comes disproportionately from the elderly, that figure has fallen along with the party's vote count in national elections. Other parties have a tough time attracting dues-paying members, since noncommunist Russians tend to be distrustful of all political parties. Yabloko is believed to be the only party with honest and accurate membership figures. Remarkably, its 5,000 members once made it Russia's third-largest party (in terms of membership, not votes).

Further evidence of many parties' weakness is the frequency with which they come and go. As previously noted, they are often created solely to further the political interests of a particular leader or set of leaders and fade from the scene when those leaders do. For example, after finishing the 1995 Duma elections with the third-largest number of total seats, Our Home Is Russia faded into insignificance as Prime Minister Chernomyrdin left the scene. Conversely, two centrist parties—Unity (pro-Putin) and Fatherland All Russia (originally anti-Putin)—and one democratic reformist party (Unity of Right Forces) had not existed in the 1995 election but emerged with the Duma's second-, third-, and fourth-largest parliamentary delegations in 1999, behind only the communists (Table 13.1). Indeed, Unity, which finished second, had been formed a scant two months before the election! While United Russia has recently emerged as the leading party, it has yet to establish a strong organizational base independent of President Putin.

In recent years, a strong party—probably too strong—has finally emerged in the form of Putin's United Russia. Few believe that Putin plans to eliminate free elections or ban opposition parties. Nor is it clear that the Russian people would accept such actions if he tried. However, some observers believe that the president is trying to build a party that will dominate Russian politics for the foreseeable future.

THE STRUCTURE OF GOVERNMENT: A CENTRALIZED PRESIDENTIAL SYSTEM

The Russian constitution of 1993 created a national government with some elements of a presidential system (such as that of the United States) and some of a parliamentary system (such as Britain's). The president is directly elected to a four-year term, with a limit of two terms in office. He or she, in turn, appoints a prime minister subject to the approval of the Duma (the more powerful house of Parliament). At the same time, Russia maintains a federal system that, at least in theory, offers a degree of local control to its still-heterogeneous population.

In actuality, however, the new constitution culminated a period of intense contestations between the legislative and executive branches, and shifted political power firmly into the hands of the president. In the years since, Presidents Boris Yeltsin (1991–1999) and Vladimir Putin (2000–) have often circumvented the Parliament. So, too, throughout their two presidencies considerable local and regional political power has been transferred to the national government.

Parliament and the President: The Executive and the Legislative Branches Battle for Power

The Soviet Parliament, known as the **Supreme Soviet**, was quite powerless before 1989. Meeting for only one week annually, it endorsed the government's legislative package without dissent.[25] In 1988, however, constitutional reforms restructured the national legislature, giving it greater independence and responsibility. New parliamentary structures were created at the national and republic levels. The following year, several hundred dissident candidates were victorious in the national election and open parliamentary debate began to build.

Following the dissolution of the USSR, the Russian Republic's Parliament (as opposed to the now-defunct Soviet Parliament) was automatically transformed into that newly independent nation's legislature. Until then, it had worked rather smoothly with the Republic's President Yeltsin. That cooperation, however, derived from having a common enemy (Mikhail Gorbachev) and a common goal (removing Russia from the USSR). Once the Soviet Union collapsed, the consensus quickly collapsed. Although the communist system had fallen, more than 85 percent of the deputies in the Russian Supreme Soviet were Communist Party representatives who had been elected while the party still dominated Soviet politics. Most had little in common with the president's team of economic reformers, and few shared their objectives.[26]

Soon, conflict between the two branches of government intensified, centering on both institutional and programmatic issues. Like Soviet President Gorbachev before him,

Yeltsin created an enormously strong presidency, free of significant constitutional constraint by the legislature.[27] Not surprisingly, Parliament became increasingly restive.

Russia's mounting economic crisis added to the tension. After the collapse of Soviet communism, Yeltsin and his chief economic planner, Yegor Gaidar, favored so-called economic **shock therapy**, which involved speedy **privatization** of state enterprises, rapid conversion to a market economy, sweeping cuts in government expenditures, currency devaluation, and the slashing of trade barriers.[28] Quickly, however, the Gaidar team faced growing opposition from the Parliament and the state bureaucracy, many of whom feared voter reaction to the economic suffering inevitably associated with the early stages of shock therapy.

From 1992 to 1993, conflict between the branches of government shifted to two questions: the nature of a new constitution and the possibility of early parliamentary or presidential elections. Yeltsin was able to stave off efforts to impeach him (though barely) and forced the legislature to back down in several important confrontations.

At the same time, however, Parliament removed Yeltsin's authority to rule by decree, forced several key ministers and presidential aides from office, and placed roadblocks in the path of economic reform. Finally, faced with the prospect of government paralysis, the two sides agreed to hold a national referendum in April 1993, asking voters to express their level of confidence in Yeltsin and his policies and to determine whether there should be early elections. Of those voting (almost two-thirds of eligible voters), 59 percent supported the president, 53 percent supported his economic and social program, 67 percent favored early parliamentary elections, and slightly over half voted against an early presidential election.[29] By voting its confidence in Yeltsin and his reforms—however narrowly—and by supporting early elections only for Parliament, the Russian public seemed to accept economic restructuring in spite of its pain.

But the referendum failed to bring political peace. As conflict intensified, each side challenged the other's legitimacy. Yeltsin dismissed Vice President Alexander Rutskoi (one of his leading opponents), dissolved the Parliament, and scheduled new, year-end legislative elections. In response, a parliamentary majority determined that the president had acted unconstitutionally (which he most certainly had) and had thereby lost his authority to govern. Parliamentary leaders swore in Rutskoi as the new president and barricaded themselves in the White House, Russia's massive Parliament building. When armed supporters of this rebellion tried to seize Moscow's city hall and a nearby television station, pro-Yeltsin army troops shelled the White House and captured it at a cost of almost two hundred lives.

President Yeltsin had beaten back his communist and nationalist opponents, but it was hard to determine which side had more recklessly undermined the constitution and violated basic democratic principles. By ordering a bloody attack on the nation's Parliament, Yeltsin lost considerable moral standing. Still, with the 1993 constitution greatly enhancing the president's authority, both President Yeltsin and President Putin have dominated the legislative branch ever since.

RESTRUCTURING THE ECONOMY

The worst is over.

—*Boris Yeltsin: October 1992, October 1993, April 1994, July 1997*[30]

Shock Therapy versus Gradualism

Year after year, Boris Yeltsin's economic team tried to turn around the collapsing, post-communist economy. Each time, President Yeltsin tried to reassure the public that the dizzying economic decline, which had begun in the late 1980s, would finally be stopped and that "the worst is over." Each time, his reassurances proved worthless. Indeed, during the 1990s the economy shrank in every year but two (1997 and 1999), sometimes declining as much as 13 or 14 percent in a single year. Overall, from 1990 to 1998, the country's GNP fell by a total of 40 to 50 percent.

Following the collapse of the Soviet Union, many distinguished Western economists flocked to Moscow to advise the new Russian government. With the budget deficit out of control (equaling 30 percent of the country's gross domestic product (GDP), production declining, and inflation skyrocketing, some type of economic restructuring and stabilization was clearly needed.[31] The International Monetary Fund (IMF), most foreign advisers, and Yeltsin's leading economic planners all agreed that such reforms needed to include privatizing state enterprises, freeing prices (allowing goods to be sold for their free market value), liberalizing trade (removing tariffs and other barriers to imports), and sharply reducing the budget deficit.[32]

For a year, Yeltsin's economic team and foreign advisors debated whether these reforms should be introduced rapidly or more gradually. While there was evidence that shock therapy (a rapid and dramatic reform) was generally more effective in reducing inflation and trade deficits, it is also extremely painful in the short run as consumers would have to pay the full value of consumer goods that the government had formerly sold to them at deep discounts.[33] Because free trade would allow superior-quality foreign goods to enter the country, terminating government subsidies to inefficient industries would cause many factories to shut down, putting their employees out of work. In a number of countries these economic consequences had led to political unrest.

Shock Therapy and Continuing Economic Decline

At the start of 1992, the leading proponent of shock therapy, Prime Minister Yegor Gaidar, initiated that process by freeing prices on most consumer goods. With government subsidies and price controls removed, *prices jumped 345 percent in the month of January alone*.[34] By late 1993, 81,000 of the country's 196,000 state enterprises had been privatized, including factories that employed 20 percent of the industrial workforce and most retail stores.[35] Millions of Russians became shareholders in the largest industrial firms through a process of government vouchers.[36] By early 1996, some 120,000 state firms had been privatized. The private sector accounted for more than half the nation's GNP and about two-thirds of its industrial output.[37] No other former communist country has privatized so extensively or so rapidly.

Still, those reforms did not end the economy's free fall dating back to the Gorbachev era. In fact, in many ways things got worse. During the next few years, industrial production dropped more sharply than it had in the United States during the Great Depression.[38] In 1992, the year shock therapy was introduced, *prices rose by 2,520 percent*.[39] It is estimated that 90 percent of the population saw their lifetime savings become worthless.[40] Not until 1994–1995 did the annual inflation rate drop below 300 percent. From 1990 to early 1993, the average Russian's real wage (what his or her wages could purchase) fell by more than 40 percent.[41] High inflation continued through most of the 1990s. Thus, an item that cost 100 rubles in 1990 would cost 1,270,000 rubles by 1998.[42] The greatest victims of rampant inflation were the elderly, reduced to poverty as their meager pensions lost half their value.[43]

Furthermore, a very disturbing trend has continued from the Soviet era: Infant mortality has risen sharply, and life expectancy has declined to Third World levels. During the first half of the 1990s, life expectancy for male Russians, which had been declining slowly since the 1960s, fell astonishingly from 63.8 years to 57.3. After recovering ground from 1995 to 1998 (reaching 61.3), male life expectancy fell back again to 58 in 2002.[44] Today, Russia's male life expectancy ranks in the lowest 25 percent of all nations—behind such countries as Vietnam and Nicaragua. Indeed, outside of Africa—where many nations have been devastated by AIDS—life expectancy for Russian men is among the lowest in the world. Women's life expectancy has also fallen somewhat, but at 72.2 is an astounding 13 years higher than the men's average (the largest gender gap in the world).

It was not until 1997 that government policies finally brought inflation under control (to a mere 15 percent) and the economy grew ever so slightly. Unfortunately, that brief recovery was aborted in 1998 when many Asian economies were hit with a major financial crisis. The nation's currency, the ruble, lost two-thirds of its value (relative to the dollar) in only one year, economic output declined a disastrous 5 percent and inflation jumped back to 86 percent in 1998.[45] By the end of that year, about 35 percent of the population lived below the poverty line, up from just 12 percent in 1991.[46] Obviously, the transition to a market economy was far more difficult than President Yeltsin's advisers had anticipated.

Vladimir Putin and New Economic Growth (1999–2005)

Since 1999 Russia has finally reversed more than a decade of economic decline. The recovery from the severe 1998 economic crisis came far more quickly that anyone had predicted. Inflation, which had jumped to 86 percent in 1999, dropped the following year to 21 percent and has ranged from 11 to 22 percent since that time.[47] While still high by U.S. standards, these figures are an immense improvement over the 2,500 percent inflation rate for 1992 or even the 86 percent rate of 1999.

Furthermore, after a decade of falling production, the Russian economy has grown for six straight years (1999–2004) by rates of 5 to 10 percent annually, its fastest growth in a generation.[48] While this is obviously good news, it may be less impressive than it appears at first glance. Much of the economic surge has been created by the huge jump in petroleum prices, Russia's primary export. But the profits from soaring oil prices largely benefit state companies or those owned by the wealthy **oligarchs** (a term used to refer to a small number of multimillionaires who control much of the Russian economy). Most of the population has seen far more limited gains. Also, oil prices are volatile and past price booms have usually been followed by substantial declines. Sharp drops in world petroleum prices hurt the economy during both Gorbachev's and Yeltsin's administrations and could be a threat once again.

No doubt the economic turnaround has contributed significantly to President Putin's high popularity ratings and his landslide victory in the 2004 elections. His party has done particularly well with female voters, with women far more likely than men to vote for it in the 2003 parliamentary elections. In fact, the economic recovery had begun before Putin was appointed prime minister or assumed the presidency and resulted from higher oil prices and the 1998 decision to devalue the ruble (Russia's currency).

That is not to say that Putin's government doesn't deserve any credit for the improved economic climate. Perhaps more than anything, Putin ended a decade of weak government and vacillating state policy with a new period of stability.[49] Property rights were strengthened so that businessmen could think of their firm's long-term prospects, rather than always seeking a quick profit. Both business and the public agreed that the weak state existing under Yeltsin had to be strengthened so that it could carry out such basic functions as protection of public safety and collection of needed taxes. As a result of increased tax revenues combined with declining government expenditures, years of huge budget deficits under Yeltsin and the Soviet government that preceded him were turned into surpluses nearly every year of Putin's administration.

Still, the Russian economy suffers from a number of fundamental flaws. The bureaucracy is too powerful and too corrupt. Control of the economy remains in the hands of a small number of corrupt multimillionaires whose monopolistic holdings exempt them from the discipline of the free market. And too few Russians have benefited from the economic recovery.

Obstacles to Economic Reform

Even the most competent Russian leaders would have encountered tremendous obstacles in transforming the economy. Eastern Europe's experience has demonstrated that the transition from a command economy to the free market is very difficult anywhere. (Only the Czechs and Hungarians have managed the change relatively smoothly.) It is particularly hard in Russia, which had experienced communist rule for a far longer

© AP/Wide World Photos

A DIFFERENT TONY SOPRANO   Vyacheslav Ivankov and his wife head to court (2005). A Moscow jury acquitted Ivankov, an alleged Russian mafia leader, in two 1992 killings, and freed him.

period of time than its neighbors had. But the privatization process has also been rife with corruption, with many of the old communist *nomenklatura* using their positions as industrial managers to become wealthy capitalists. In a society where people were raised to value equality, there has been a tremendous rise in inequality. As we have seen, the number of Russians living in poverty grew sharply in the 1990s. But increased inequality, not declining GNP, accounts for most of that poverty. Today the poorest 40 percent of the population earns a substantially lower share of the national income than they did in 1991. Amid the nation's growing impoverishment, the new super-rich class of financiers and speculators ostentatiously flaunt their foreign luxury cars and European high-fashion clothing.

At the same time, corruption has become pervasive in Russian life, emanating primarily from the powerful crime mafia that has filled the gap left by a declining state. As one observer noted, "The market economy in Russia is lawless, like the 'Wild West,' and organized crime controls the distribution of commodities."[50] Thus, a 1994 government report claimed that three-quarters of all Russian businesses paid 10 to 20 percent of their income to the mafia as protection money. Such payments drive up business costs and contribute significantly to inflation.[51] In the late 1990s Russia's minister of internal affairs estimated that "40 percent of the country's private businesses and an even higher proportion of state enterprises were controlled by organized crime."[52]

As a consequence of these problems, many observers feel that Russia has failed to create a healthy capitalist economy. Russians themselves seem to long for the time when the state offered them greater economic security than they now enjoy. One opinion poll, for example, indicated that 72 percent of the population believed that the state should provide a job to anyone who needs it. Roughly 50 percent favored some state control over prices and over private business.[53] Similarly, an exit poll of more than seven thousand voters conducted during the 1996 presidential election showed that 58 percent believed that the state should own large industrial enterprises, 26 percent felt that the firms' workers should own them, and only 12 percent favored private ownership.[54]

To be sure, Russia's economic decline began during the last years of communism (1988–1991), and the economy has actually begun to improve in the past few years. But such facts offer little consolation to the elderly pensioners, single-parent families, farmers, and others whose living standards have eroded so greatly.

RUSSIA BEGINS THE TWENTY-FIRST CENTURY: THE PUTIN PRESIDENCY

As Boris Yeltsin's health and popularity deteriorated, he resigned from office at the end of 1999 and turned over the presidency to his prime minister, Vladimir Putin. Three months later, Putin was elected to a full term, defeating Gennadi Zyuganov, again the Communist Party challenger, by a margin of 53 percent to 29 percent (see Table 13.2). Thus, Putin avoided a second-round runoff and far outperformed his mentor, Yeltsin, who had attained only 35 percent of the vote in the first round of the 1996 presidential election, edging Zyuganov by a mere 3 percentage points.

Vladimir Putin's popularity stemmed largely from his record as a resolute prime minister, particularly his hardline military policies aimed at crushing the Chechen secessionist movement in Southern Russia. In many ways, Putin has seemed to be everything Boris Yeltsin was not, at least during the latter's second term in office. Whereas

Yeltsin had been inconsistent—constantly changing his prime minister and his economic policies—emotional, in fragile health, and unpredictable, Putin is none of those things. Taking office at the age of 48, he is one of the country's youngest national leaders. A black belt in karate, he is bright, healthy, confident, and consistent. Indeed, after several decades of economic chaos and political uncertainty, Vladimir Putin seems to be exactly what the Russian voters want. As one Russian voter said, "He's someone you don't have to be ashamed of. He's the first normal person to head Russia."[55] His approval ratings in national polls have hovered around the impressive level of 70 to 80 percent during most of his administration (except for a dip in early 2005) and he was overwhelmingly reelected in 2004.

Given Putin's very high approval rate at the time and his government's domination of television (the major source of news for most Russians), there was never any doubt that he would easily be reelected. Indeed, so many of his potential opponents had dropped out of the race that his main problem was insuring sufficient opposition to give his reelection some legitimacy. It is rumored that some candidates were induced to stay in the race in return for favors by the Kremlin. Sergey Mironov, speaker of the upper house of Parliament and presidential candidate of the virtually unknown Party of Russia's Rebirth-Party of Life, didn't sound like an enthusiastic opponent when he said, "We all want Vladimir Putin to be the next president." Indeed, the president's reelection was so assured that he essentially failed to campaign and made only one campaign speech.

There is much about President Putin that disturbs Russian human rights groups and other proponents of democracy. Following his graduation from law school, Putin began his career in the KGB, the Soviet Union's dreaded internal security and international espionage service. In 1998, President Yeltsin appointed him chief of Russia's post-KGB domestic security agency, the Federal Security Service (FSB). Since assuming the presidency, Putin has raised concerns about his commitment to democracy because of his closed operating style, his promotion of many former KGB colleagues to prominent posts in government, and his efforts to concentrate power in the central government, particularly in the president's hands. Thus, one Western analyst warned (perhaps excessively stridently), "Now, with the political ascendancy of Vladimir Putin, [the] banality of evil has reached the summit of power in the Kremlin—a situation that should cause more concern to U.S. policymakers than it apparently does."[56]

Having first established his political popularity (while serving as Boris Yeltsin's prime minister) by ruthlessly repressing the Islamic-based Chechen rebellion, Putin as president has continued an iron-fisted policy in that region, grossly violating international human rights standards. At the same time, the government has also taken over Russia's independent television networks. A number of journalists who had written exposés or criticisms of the government have been jailed or harassed. And Aleksander Nikitin, an environmentalist who helped a Japanese TV crew photograph Russian naval vessels illegally dumping wasted nuclear fuel at sea, was arrested and charged with treason. Said Nikitin of Putin and the president's longtime colleague who had orchestrated his arrest, "There is no such thing as an ex-KGB agent, just as there is no such thing as an ex–German shepherd." More recently, Putin has initiated a number of measures to concentrate even greater power in the president's hands and to increase national government control over Russia's autonomous regions. None of that bodes well for democracy.

Putin's defenders concede that he has a questionable background and sometimes exhibits authoritarian tendencies. But they argue that such tendencies are common among Russia's political leaders, many of whom had been politically socialized and trained under the old Soviet system. U.S. policymakers generally have been impressed by his efforts to establish closer relations with the West. They also insist that the Russian state had become so weakened under Boris Yeltsin that Putin had to restore some of its authority, including its ability to collect taxes. Pointing to his positive qualities, they argue that although the president has tried to intensify his own powers, he has also introduced an important new criminal procedural code that limits the authority of government prosecutors and substantially increases the rights of defendants, giving them, among other things, the right to a jury trial. Until 2001 Russia still used the old Soviet criminal code, which, among other things assumed that a defendant was guilty until proven innocent. Under the new code, introduced by Putin's administration, defendants are considered innocent until proven guilty. The results so far have been limited. In courts where judges still decide the cases, the conviction rate has been lowered minimally from 99 percent to 95 percent. However, in those areas where trial by jury has been introduced, conviction rates have fallen to 85 percent (still very high when compared to the U.S. rate of about 60 percent).[57]

For the most part, President Putin has remained very popular among ordinary Russians, as his administration has produced steady economic growth (after more than a decade of decline), strong leadership, and a revival of nationalism. Early in his administration he received high praise from President George W. Bush and other Western leaders. Following the September 11, 2001, attacks on the United States, he was one of the first foreign leaders to pledge full support to the United States in its war on terrorism. Since that time, his increasingly authoritarian behavior and his increasingly nationalist foreign policy have diminished his standing in the West somewhat. Thus, for example, many outside observers were shocked when, in his April 25, 2005, State of the Nation address, he called the collapse of the Soviet Union "the greatest political catastrophe of the last century."[58] Equally disturbing was his blatant intervention on behalf of Viktor Yanukovich, a pro-Russian presidential candidate in Ukraine, and his support of Yanukovich's blatantly fraudulent electoral victory (a policy that backfired when popular demonstrations forced new elections, which were won by the candidate whom Putin had opposed). At the same time, however, Putin has tried to maintain close ties to the West and has backed international efforts such as the Kyoto Accord limiting greenhouse emissions so as to control global warming. Putin has also supported Russia's continued economic transformation to capitalism. For all of those reasons, the governments of most Western democracies have tended to overlook his antidemocratic behavior and his brutal repression of the Chechen rebellion.

PUTIN AND THE CREATION OF AN ALL-POWERFUL PRESIDENCY

When Vladimir Putin came to office, he inherited a powerful presidency based on Boris Yeltsin's 1993 Constitution. But Yeltsin's capacity to fully wield that power had been limited by his ill health, declining popularity (he left office with a 2 percent approval rating), and his frequent negotiations and compromises between different factions (clans) supporting him. Putin has none of these restraints. Consequently, he has concentrated political power in his own hands in a manner unmatched since the days of the Soviet Union.

Centralizing State Power

Not long after taking office, Putin made clear his support for "**vertical power**" that concentrates control and lodges the country's destiny in the hand of its supreme leader (the president).[59] At other times, he has spoken of creating a "guided democracy." Like his predecessor, Putin has frequently used the president's power to issue laws by decree, without parliamentary approval. But he also has expanded presidential power in a number of new ways.

One of the president's goals has been to transfer the powers of local and regional governments to Moscow and, ultimately, the presidency. Soon after being elected to his first full term (2000), Putin pushed a tax reform bill through Parliament that shifted tax revenue from local and regional governments to the federal government and, effectively, the president. At the same time, he issued a presidential decree dividing the country into seven federal districts, each headed by a presidential Envoy who would allow Putin to manage the country's regional and national-minority republics. Subsequently, he had the Duma empower him to remove elected regional leaders if the courts (generally subservient to the president) decide that they have violated federal law more than once. He also restructured the Federation Council—the upper house of Parliament originally created to give local officials a say in national policy—by removing regional governors and making membership in the entire Council subject to presidential appointment. In 2004, Parliament approved Putin's plan to end the election of regional governors once their current terms end and to have all future governors nominated by the president. With that authority he will remove the last independent force in national politics.[60] Most recently (November 2005), the Duma overwhelming passed the first draft of President Putin's bill extending government control over NGOs (non-governmental organizations such as environmental groups) and charities operating in Russia, thereby greatly weakening one of the few remaining independent voices in civil society. Under the legislation, international NGOs such as Greenpeace, Amnesty International, and the Ford Foundation will no longer be able to operate inside Russia, while Russian NGOs—many of them active in areas such as public health and human rights—would be subject to government regulation.

Putin's critics have been particularly troubled by his frequent appointment to key administrative posts of men drafted from the security services (including many former colleagues from the KGB) and the military, institutions not known for their democratic political culture. Indeed, their influence is greater than it had been under Gorbachev's Soviet Union. As of late 2003:

> Five of the seven heads of Russia's macrofederal districts [were] military or security officers, as [were] . . . 25 percent of the Russian political elite as a whole, representing a sixfold increase in military and security representation . . . since the late Soviet period. . . . Two-thirds of Putin's presidential staff [had] backgrounds in the security services.[61]

Putin, the Television Media and the Oligarchy

Another very troublesome manifestation of Putin's authoritarian tendencies has been his war with independent (privately owned) television networks. Two events particularly aroused his ire over media coverage. Only months after he took office, the Kursk, a Russian nuclear submarine, sunk while on maneuvers, killing all 118 sailors on board. The media criticized the government's secrecy regarding the cause of the accident, its

REVIEWING THE TROOPS IN CHECHNYA   President Vladimir Putin stands with Russian soldiers following an awards ceremony near Grozny, Chechnya. First as Prime Minister and then as President, Putin won popularity at home and condemnation from human rights groups abroad for his policies aimed at crushing the secessionist rebellion in Chechnya at all costs.

failure to ask for international help, its rather inept handling of the rescue attempt, and the president's apparent initial detachment from the rescue. The second, and ongoing, source of irritation to Putin were the periodic media revelations of military incompetence and brutality in the anti-secessionist war in Chechnya.

Soon after winning the 2000 presidential election, Putin made it clear that he would not be as tolerant of media criticism nor as conscious of press freedom as Yeltsin had been. Although Yeltsin had manipulated the media, especially during his presidential campaign and when he was under attack, he generally accepted media criticism. On the other hand, while claiming to respect the need for a free press, Putin clearly was distrustful of an independent mass media. In his first annual address to the Russian Parliament, the president charged that "sometimes [the media] turn into means of mass disinformation and tools of struggle against the state."[62]

The president's primary initial target was Media-MOST, the country's largest privately owned media conglomerate and, most important, its NTV television network. Owned by billionaire oligarch Vladimir Gusinsky, Media-MOST had, since 1993, given the public independent news coverage, sometimes critical of the government. During the first Chechen war (1994–1996), for example, its reporters had eluded Russian troops to report on army human rights violations and inefficiency. Still, when Boris Yeltsin faced a serious electoral challenge from the Communist Party's Gennady Zyuganov in the 1996 presidential race, NTV, like all the oligarchically controlled news media, blatantly slanted its news coverage in the president's favor. But Gusinsky subsequently had a falling out with Yeltsin and failed to back Putin in the 2000 presidential race.

Starting just two months after his election, Putin's government initiated a series of police raids into Gusinsky's businesses, with employees sometimes intimidated at gunpoint. Gusinsky himself was placed under house arrest. A month later he agreed to sell Media-MOST to Gazprom—the national natural gas monopoly that is 40 percent government owned—in return for his freedom. Shortly afterwards, Gusinsky fled the country. When the staff of NTV refused to change their critical position toward the government, Gazprom security men raided the network headquarters and ousted those journalists and employees not willing to toe the government's line. A number of independent journalists who left NTV took over and expanded another network, TV-6. Supported from abroad by exiled tycoons Boris Berezovsky and Gusinsky, they presented professional and balanced news coverage. The government, however, used legal maneuvers to have the courts declare TV-6 insolvent. Soon afterward the station closed its doors, only to be reopened by new management acceptable to the government.

Boris Berezovsky is another media oligarch ousted by President Putin. Under President Yeltsin, Berezovsky had become one of the nation's most powerful men. As part of Yeltsin's inner circle, he had led a group of tycoons who had financed the president's reelection campaign in 1996. Beyond holding positions in government, he was also Yeltsin's personal financial advisor and helped funnel substantial funds to the president's pocket. In addition to his private holdings—which included a major airline and much of the country's aluminum industry—Berezovsky was given minority ownership and operating control of ORT, the government's largest television network. While he had been an important force supporting Putin's 2000 presidential campaign, he soon irritated the new president by criticizing his handling of the Kursk submarine disaster. With the prospect of criminal charges for fraud and money laundering hanging over him, Berezovsky fled to England where he was granted political asylum. Soon ORT, like NTV, was faithfully following the government line. Such events have a broader whirlpool effect as journalists in privately owned media (including the press) increasingly have engaged in self-censorship to avoid angering Putin or his advisors.[63]

Although these were the most dramatic assaults on media freedom, under Putin a number of journalists have been detained and in some cases found it prudent to leave the country. In 2003, one study disclosed that 20 journalists had been assassinated that year and there had been 120 physical attacks on newspapers or their journalists.[64] To be sure, many of those assassinations were ordered by the mafia or by local officials independent of the Kremlin, but the courts and police have rarely brought the perpetrators to justice. A number of independent news outlets continue to operate. But 90 percent of Russians get their news from television, and the government controls all stations with a national viewership. When asked, some 80 percent of all Russians who were polled claimed that they considered freedom of the press to be important. Yet, most of those respondents were relatively indifferent to the government's assaults on NTV and TV-6. Perhaps because the most powerful media owners being pushed aside were leading members of the widely hated capitalist oligarchy, most Russians failed to see the struggle as linked to press freedom.[65]

Putin against the Oligarchy

Vladimir Putin has not merely attacked the leading media barons, he has done battle with oligarchs in other economic activities, targeting those who wielded particular political power under Boris Yeltsin, or have tried to exercise independent political

---

Box 13-1

THE OLIGARCHY: RUSSIA'S NEW CAPITALIST TYCOONS

In the first years after the collapse of the Soviet system, President Yeltsin and his reformist advisors, such as Prime Minister Yegor Gaidar, looked for ways to quickly privatize much of the economy still in the hands of the state. One solution was to distribute vouchers to the general population and to workers in factories set for privatization. In many cases, workers acquired 49 percent of the stock in their company, while the former government managers received 51 percent and effective control. The vouchers given to the general public could later be traded for company stocks. While millions of Russians did trade at least a part of their vouchers for stocks, the majority did not. Having lived their lives under communism, most had no understanding of the potential value of their vouchers and they willingly sold them to speculators for a small fraction of their potential worth. Armed with these vouchers and ties to the Kremlin, and aided by healthy bribes, these budding entrepreneurs were able to purchase state firms at perhaps 10 percent of their real value, thereby emerging as a new class of super tycoons generally known as the oligarchs.

The oligarchs emerged largely from two areas. The first were directors of the country's major companies under the Soviet system; that is, they were members of the Communist *nomenklatura* who quickly jumped ship in 1992 and turned themselves into so-called *nomenklatura* capitalists. The second, dominant group consisted of outsiders, including university professors, gangsters, and businessmen who had operated in the Soviet black market before private enterprise was allowed. For example, one future billionaire started his business career in pre-*perestroika* times illegally selling bibles (Alexander Smolensky). Another used his own car as a taxi (Vladimir Gusinski). After President

Gorbachev allowed limited private enterprise, they and other aspiring capitalists began legal businesses in areas such as computer imports, auto imports, and banking. When the Russian economy was largely privatized in the early to mid-1990s, these men used their capital and other finances secured from their own banks to acquire control (at highly discounted prices) of some of Russia's largest companies, particularly in natural resources such as oil, gas and metals.[66] Thus, for example, in 1995, Mikhail Khodorkovsky and his associates bought Yukos, Russia's second-largest oil company, for $159 million, perhaps 5 percent of its real worth.

All told, by some estimates Russia's 10 to 30 richest oligarchs controlled almost half of Russia's gross domestic product by the late 1990s. More cautious assessments in 2004 suggested that the combined wealth of the nation's 36 richest tycoons ($110 billion) equals one-quarter of the country's GDP. Similarly, the oligarchy in general is reputed to have owned 85 percent of the value of Russia's largest private companies. In 1997, right before the financial collapse of 1998, *Forbes* magazine included five Russians in its list of billionaires worldwide. By 2006, 33 Russians made the *Forbes* listing of the world's 793 billionaires, the third highest number for any nation (though Russia ranked about 62nd in per capita national income).[67]

Some oligarchs established close links with President Yeltsin, and a number of them were largely responsible for his reelection in 1996 by bankrolling his campaign and giving him nearly exclusive campaign coverage on their television networks. They initially hoped to have a similar relationship with Vladimir Putin and supported his 2000 presidential campaign. But, as we will see, he soon turned against a number of them.

---

influence under Putin, or have criticized the president.[68] Early on, the president demoted two powerful figures in Gazprom (the natural gas monopoly) including Viktor Chernomyrdin, who had served several times as Yeltsin's prime minister. Among the most famous oligarchs—along with Berezovsky and Gusinski—whom Putin toppled was Mikhail Khodorkovsky, then Russia's wealthiest man, with an estimated worth of some 15 billion dollars. A number of other tycoons have decided to flee the country. In October 2003, Khodorkovsky was arrested on charges of tax evasion, fraud, embezzlement and theft. Nearly two years later, he and his business partner were convicted and sentenced to nine-year jail terms. (See Box 13-1) Once again

Putin's target had little public support, with one poll showing that only 4 percent of all Russians considered Khodorkovsky to be innocent.

In truth, Putin's war on the oligarchs could be justified on a number of grounds. Almost all of them had acquired most of their wealth through bribery, fraud, and insider connections. They are widely despised because they amassed vast wealth during the 1990s at a time when most Russians saw their standard of living drop precipitously. Russians also resent the fact that Boris Yeltsin was so beholden to several oligarchs who had inordinate influence in determining government policy. Moreover, while the government has had great difficulty balancing the budget, oligarchs have evaded billions of dollars in taxes. The arrest or threatened arrest of several oligarchs on charges of tax evasion produced a rapid rise in tax payments, both by oligarchically controlled firms and the private sector generally.

But there is also good reason to suspect Putin's motives. The attack on the oligarchy has narrowly targeted only those who had criticized him or supported opposition political forces. Mikhail Khodorkovsky, for example, had funded the election campaigns of many Duma deputies who were, thus, somewhat beholden to him. It was estimated that some 100 of the deputies (one fourth of the Duma) had drawn significant campaign contributions from him and were in his debt. Putin has indicated to the oligarchs that if they don't involve themselves in politics they will not be bothered by his administration. Khodorkovsky, who mistakenly thought of himself as untouchable, not only involved himself but funded opposition candidates and speculated about running for president in 2008. At the same time, however, a number of new oligarchs have emerged under the patronage of the Putin administration who have heeded the president's warnings to stay out of politics.[69] Nor has the government cracked down on the Russian mafia, a major economic actor, perhaps because many mafia tycoons are the president's former colleagues in the KGB. "Shareholder abuse and corporate looting" continue and are tolerated by the government.[70]

Thus, while Putin's attacks on key oligarchs have been widely applauded in Russia and bolstered the president's popularity, his main purpose seems to be asserting the power of the central government rather than cleaning up Russian capitalism. The administration felt that control of Russia's most important exports—oil and natural gas—should be in the hands of the state rather than private firms. Thus, as part of the settlement of its billions of dollars of unpaid taxes, Khodorkovsky's firm, Yukos, Russia's second largest oil company, was taken over by the state-controlled natural gas company, Gazprom. Finally, while most of Russia's oligarchs have not been challenged economically, Putin has taken away their political power and made them subservient to the state rather than the other way around.

THE CHALLENGE OF A DUAL TRANSITION

Much has changed in Russia since 1990. The country has aspects of an electoral democracy, regularly holding free (though no longer fair) competitive elections. But it is still not a liberal democracy (with guaranteed civil liberties) and has moved further from that goal in recent years. It lacks adequate safeguards for civil liberties and a free press (media), and its citizens' attitudes toward democracy are somewhat ambivalent. It has created a primarily capitalist economy, but large portions of that economy are controlled by organized crime or by political insiders with questionable connections to the government.

Major political and economic transitions are never easy, nor are their outcomes certain. Although the demise of Soviet communism was understandably hailed in the West, there is no guarantee that Russia will develop into a democratic nation with a free-market economy. We know that the initial euphoria that followed the overthrow of tyrannies in Iran, Ethiopia, and Nicaragua was soon dispelled by the difficulties of development. Might the same thing happen in Russia?

Throughout the 1990s, the Russian people endured a tremendous decline in their living standards (one that began in the last years of the Soviet Union). Since 1999 Russia has experienced nearly seven consecutive years of economic growth, with some improvement in standards of living. Other problems more clearly persist into the twenty-first century: soaring crime rates, rampant government corruption, a tremendous decline in the country's influence and prestige, and the virtual collapse of the social welfare safety net that previously afforded citizens some protection from poverty. That there were few riots and little political turmoil (with the obvious exception of the Chechen rebellion) is a testament to the people's forbearance and, perhaps, to their willingness to work within the democratic system.

THE POLITICAL CHALLENGE

In 2001, Michael McFaul listed the following weaknesses of contemporary Russian democracy: **superpresidentialism**; a weak political party system; weak **civil society**; an insufficiently independent press and electronic media; an ineffective state; frequent absence of the rule of law; and a weak democratic political culture.[71] These weaknesses have greatly worsened since then.

Superpresidentialism

As we have seen, the 1993 political and military standoff between President Yeltsin and his opponents in the Russian Parliament culminated in a new constitution that gave the president enormous powers and eliminated effective checks and balances. From that time onward, the Duma exercised little restraint on the president. By the time of his reelection in 1996, however, Yeltsin's health was too poor for him to fully wield his presidential powers. Moreover, he was sympathetic to some political competition and tended to be influenced by a number of competing "clans" or power groups.

Vladimir Putin, on the other hand, has taken presidential power to new heights, particularly since the 2003 Duma elections gave him full control of the legislature. As he has received authority to nominate regional governors and members of the upper house of Parliament, and has tamed the oligarchs and largely controlled the media, Putin has concentrated more power in the hands of one man and one office than the country has seen for decades.

A Weak Political Party System

Strong political parties are necessary for a vibrant democracy, for they serve as a vehicle for conveying demands and other inputs from average citizens to the government. Russia has managed to develop a competitive party system more quickly than have many new democracies in other parts of the world, but its political parties suffer from several major faults. And, as we have seen, votes are divided among too many parties to produce an effective parliamentary majority.

Except for the Communist Party, political parties generally have lacked grassroots support and organization and have tended to come and go, often serving as little more than electoral machines for a particular strongman such as Yeltsin or Putin. For many Russians, the Soviet Communist Party gave parties a bad name. "After quitting the Party in 1990, [Boris] Yeltsin vowed never to join another party again, and many in Russia sympathized with his pledge."[72] Like his predecessor, President Putin is officially not a party member, although the country's dominant party, United Russia, clearly exists to advance his interests. Indeed, it has become the overwhelmingly dominant party and may remain so after Putin's presidency has ended.

Weak and Manipulated Mass Media

During the final years of *glasnost* and in the early years of President Yeltsin's administration, a free mass media, willing to criticize the government and expose its failures, emerged for the first time. But that media independence has diminished greatly since the mid-1990s as ownership of network television has became concentrated in the hands of the government and a few private conglomerates. These private media oligarchies shamelessly slanted their coverage of the 1996 and 2000 presidential elections in favor of Yeltsin and Putin. Since then, as we have seen, Putin's government has taken over all the major television networks and re-instituted periodic government intimidation or censorship of radio and newspaper journalists. While still freer than in pre-*glasnost* Soviet days, the media has become much more tightly controlled than it was ten years ago. Finally, a small, but increasing, number of journalists have been arrested or, more often, threatened or censored in recent years for criticizing the government.

Weak Civil Society

An important ingredient of a democratic political system is a strong civil society: a comprehensive network of groups such as labor unions, business associations, church groups, and the like that can influence the political system but are independent of government control. In the USSR, society was organized extensively—women's groups, youth groups, sports leagues—but those organizations were controlled by the government. Russian society, as compared to the former communist nations of Central Europe, has been slow to develop civil society. Thus, for example, when the Soviet Union collapsed, few strong and independent labor unions were formed to replace the old government-controlled unions. Workers who try to organize strong unions are often harassed.

An Ineffective State

Given the Soviet government's tremendous power and the current concentration of political authority in the Russian president's hands, we might have assumed that today's Russian state would be a potent force. But such is not the case. To be sure, the president is quite powerful relative to other branches of government, and the government frequently arbitrarily intervenes in its citizens' lives. But, all too frequently, the state is unable to perform basic governmental tasks. Faced with new challenges such as creating an efficient market economy, combating organized crime, and containing ethnic rebellion (Chechnya), the state apparatus has yet to find effective tools for action. Public confidence in political institutions such as Parliament or the presidency remains very low, even though President Putin himself is very popular.[73] The military has been in shambles, unable, despite its indiscriminate use of force, to terminate the rebellion in Chechnya or to handle large hostage situations. The police have been inept in their fight against a rising tide of crime. And, a crumbling government health system is helpless in the face of serious tuberculosis and HIV epidemics. Recently, the World Health Organization (WHO), citing the unresponsiveness and injustices of Russia's medical care system, ranked that system 130th in the world out of some 160 nations![74]

President Putin's goal has been to create a stronger, more effective state. In some ways he has done so, but his approach has been detrimental to democracy. State power has been overly centralized in the central government and within it, the presidency. But it is not at all clear that the state is any more efficient or effective. Putin has concentrated power in the hands of a huge government bureaucracy and a clique of former intelligence officers (KGB or FSB), neither of whom has a particularly good understanding of democracy or capitalism.

Inadequate Rule of Law

An important element in democratic government is a judicial system that acts independently of the executive and legislative branches and that treats its citizens fairly. Russian courts have been deficient in both respects, though in recent years the rights of most criminal defendants have improved somewhat. But, local criminal courts and the police are seriously underfunded and, consequently, do not function properly. In the major cities, many police have links to organized crime. Many mafia leaders (especially those with KGB backgrounds) are protected by the government. Prison conditions remain wretched.

Failure to Create a Democratic Political Culture

A variety of surveys conducted after the fall of Soviet communism suggested that many Russians lacked cultural values believed necessary for a consolidated liberal democracy, such as respect for civil liberties—including those of unpopular minorities—and a commitment to protect and expand political freedom even when doing so carries some risk to social stability. Thus, public opinion polls have indicated that many Russians favor a strong leader who can maintain social stability more than they value democracy (see Box 13-2). Critics of these studies argue that the Russian people's commitment to core democratic values is stronger than many had expected and that responses to a particular question may present an unfairly negative image of the nation's cultural values.

Not surprisingly, sharply falling living standards in the 1990s, rampant government corruption and incompetence, and the upsurge in crime since the fall of communism have soured many Russians on the Western model of liberal democracy that has become the international gold standard. Whereas 70 percent of the population in the early 1990s favored "Western type democracy," by 1998 that proportion was down to 20 percent.[75] To be sure, other surveys show that support for a more general notion of democracy (not necessarily identical to the Western model) remains high. Yet, when asked "What kind of political system, in your opinion, would be most appropriate for Russia?" almost one-half (47 percent) of all respondents preferred the Soviet political system *as it existed before perestroika*, only 12 percent chose "the Western type of

---

Box 13-2

PUBLIC OPINION TOWARD DEMOCRACY

Depending on when the questions are asked and how they are phrased, Russian opinion polls show considerable public ambivalence toward democracy and confusion about its meaning. Various polls have revealed that most Russians say they support democracy. For example, one survey early in Putin's administration showed 64 percent of Russians stating that they support the idea of democracy, while only 18 percent were against it. Yet 24 percent believed that democracy is "a bad way to govern Russia." By fairly overwhelming margins (87 percent) respondents said that freedom to elect their own leaders, freedom to have one's own convictions, and freedom of expression were very important to them. Nearly as many (81 percent) said that freedom of the press, radio, and television was also important to them (though 14 percent said it wasn't).[76]

Yet, such pro-democratic sentiments often don't square with public reactions to actual events. For the most part, public opinion has been rather indifferent to President Putin's many power grabs. When asked about specific moves that Putin has taken recently to control opposition voices—the elimination of gubernatorial elections and of single-member-district elections for the Duma—Russians split down the middle, with almost half approving and a roughly equal number disapproving.[77] Despite his enormous expansion of presidential power, Putin's approval ratings have hovered around 70 percent.

Although most Russians voice support for democracy, they have diverse understandings of what that concept means. While for some it includes free elections and civil liberties, others identify it with equality or personal security. Consequently, they express some rather astounding opinions about their political

leaders. When asked in 2004 which of Russia's current political leaders were most democratic, the two most popular choices were Putin (despite his having reduced democratic rule considerably) and neo-fascist Vladimir Zhirinovsky (possibly the least democratic of Russia's leading politicians). Both men were selected twice as often as either Irina Khakamada or Grigory Yavlinsky, the two presidential candidates most committed to democratic reform. Similarly, when respondents were asked to name the most democratic of Russia's political leaders during the past century, Putin received by far the most votes (29 percent), and Brezhnev (the longtime Communist leader) was next. Mikhail Gorbachev and Boris Yeltsin, who were in actuality far more democratic, trailed behind. Moreover, though a majority of Russians say they support democracy, only 25 percent of them had a positive opinion of democratic leaders and parties, while 51 percent were indifferent or couldn't answer and 14 percent had a negative opinion.[78]

Vladimir Putin's extraordinary level of support despite his often undemocratic behavior suggests that Russians place their highest priority on stability, security, and order, not Western-style democracy. That is understandable in light of Russia's enormous level of crime (including one of the world's highest murder rates) and its abundant government and private-sector corruption. Nor is there necessarily any contradiction between supporting both order and democracy. But given Russia's authoritarian history and its disrespect for the rights of defendants, support for strengthening the security forces and other "law-and-order" beliefs are often coupled with indifference to civil liberties.

---

democracy," and only 11 percent favored "the political system that exists [in Russia] today."[79] As the economy improved over the ensuing six years (1998–2004), approval ratings for Russia's "present system of government" rose (despite Putin's restrictions on democracy during the end of that period), but only in 2004 did that rating equal the approval rating for the pre-*perestroika* (hardline communist) era.[80]

Given these attitudes, it shouldn't be surprising that antidemocratic parties (especially the Communist and Liberal Democratic parties) have secured a substantial share of the vote in all three parliamentary elections since the fall of communism, whereas the parties most committed to democracy (most recently Yabloko and Unity of Right Forces) have done quite poorly.

The War in Chechnya

Located in the Caucasus in Russia's southern tier, the predominantly Muslim repub-lic of Chechnya has been fighting for independence since 1994 (although, in fact, the Chechens have been battling for independence, on and off, since tsarist rule in the nineteenth century). In the first Chechen war, the Russian army was so inept and demoralized that Russian public opinion turned increasingly against the war. Faced with a mounting opposition at home, his dwindling popularity as presidential elec-tions approached, and the military's inability to defeat the rebellion, President Yeltsin signed a peace agreement in 1996 that effectively gave the rebels control of Chechnya, though the region's final status was not to be officially decided until 2001. In 1999, however, the second Chechen war began after a series of explosions in apartment houses in the cities of Moscow, Volgodonsk, and Buinaksk, killing a total of 300 people. The bombings were blamed on Chechen terrorists, and most Russians accept that explanation. Some government critics, however, suspect the government itself set the bombs in order to mobilize public opinion behind a new war with Chechnya.

Under the direction of then-Prime Minister Putin, the Russian assault was far more intense and well organized than previously. Chechnya faced intensive bombing and the capital city of Grozny was reduced to rubble. On the ground, thousands of civil-ians were killed or forced to flee the region, and the Russian army committed numer-ous human rights violations. In time, the army was able to gain relative control of the Republic (at least during daylight hours). But, Russian troops remain tied down in an apparently unending struggle to control the region. At the same time, the rebels have resorted to terrorism to continue their struggle. Islamic extremists from abroad have also joined the rebels, some of them associated with al-Qaeda.

Repeatedly Russia has been rocked by serious terrorist attacks. For example, in October 2002, 41 Chechen militants seized a theater in suburban Moscow, taking some 900 hostages and threatening to blow up the building unless Russian forces withdrew from Chechnya within a week. On the third day of the siege, Russian spe-cial forces stormed the theater after releasing an opiate gas (designed to put the mili-tants to sleep) that ended up killing 128 of the hostages. In the worst terrorist action of all, Chechen militants seized a school in the town of Beslan (near Chechnya) and held hostage some 1,200 people whom they threatened to kill unless Russian forces with-drew from Chechnya. When Russian forces stormed the building, 336 hostages were killed in the gun battle, including parents (there for opening day ceremonies), teachers, and children (half the victims). As with the Moscow theater rescue, subsequent inves-tigations indicated that Russian security forces had totally botched their operation. A number of other terrorist attacks of a smaller magnitude have also occurred.

Whereas the first Chechen war became highly unpopular in Russia, the terrorist attacks have caused most Russians to support this war. Indeed, Prime Minister Yeltsin's vigorous response to the 1999 apartment house bombings strengthened his presiden-tial candidacy in 2000, and his hard line in the war has contributed to his ongoing popularity and his landslide reelection in 2004. But while the Russians have established substantial (but not complete) control over Chechnya, they still must expend enor-mous resources occupying the region. And terrorist attacks are likely to continue. At the same time, the ongoing war has given Putin license to muzzle the press at home. It has also led to greater Russian chauvinism and increased racial prejudice against darker-skinned people from the country's southern tier. In the words of one analyst, "the impact of the Chechen conflict on Russia's politics . . . cannot be overestimated. It has generated, through the demonization of the Chechen people, a wave of racism in other parts of the [Russian] federation."[81]

For several reasons—fear of encouraging other secessionist movements, determination to retain Chechnya's oil wealth, and the region's strategic location for a petroleum pipeline—Russia is unlikely to leave Chechnya for the foreseeable future. But it is equally unlikely to quell the rebellion and its accompanying terrorism. Meanwhile, the battle continues to erode the quality of Russian democracy.

THE ECONOMIC CHALLENGE

The privatization of the Russian economy and the growth of the private sector have been sweeping and are likely irreversible. After a decade of calamitous decline, the economy has enjoyed robust growth since 1999. Inflation has been brought down from the astronomical levels of the early- to mid-1990s. But, serious weaknesses and concerns remain. We have noted the precarious nature of recent growth since it is built, in large part, on soaring oil prices, which may well come down in the future.

Moreover, even with the recent economic expansion and substantial improvements in real wages, the national standard of living has yet to recover to its level prior to *perestroika*. Income inequality, which rose enormously in the early 1990s, has not declined since that time. As of 2002 the richest 20 percent of the population earned 40 percent of the nation's income (up from 30 percent in 1991), while the poorest 20 percent of all Russians earned only 6.4 percent. At the same time, per capita income in Moscow is more than three times the national average. That distribution of income is more unequal than Western Europe's and more closely resembles the profile of a developing, nation.[82] As we have seen, life expectancy for men has declined to shocking levels, medical care has greatly deteriorated, and the population is growing smaller.

The manner in which privatization took place has harmed the transition to capitalism. One of the strengths of the free market is that it fosters competition between business enterprises. In Russia, however, state monopolies were sold to oligarchs as private monopolies. Just as the old state monopolies had been managed inefficiently, the new private ones, not burdened with competition, are similarly poorly run. Small wonder that in a 2003 survey, "77 percent of Russians believed that the results of the country's privatization process should be fully or partially revised."[83] Corruption is also rife as businessmen often have to pay off the mafia as well as government officials. According to one respected survey, in 2005 Russians will pay government officials $3 billion in bribes while businesses will pay $316 billion, more than twice the size of the national budget. A 2005 World Bank study found that 78 percent of all Russian businesses pay bribes to government officials. At the same time, nearly $600 million is paid to university administrators, deans, and professors by students entering university (such bribes are virtually obligatory for admission). Others report having to pay small bribes to get the results of lab tests at hospitals.[84]

Putin's crackdown on certain oligarchs for fraud and tax evasion could have contributed to greater honesty in the business world had it been fairly applied. But, tycoons were only prosecuted if they had meddled in politics and antagonized the

Putin administration. Those who were prosecuted were treated arbitrarily, with no regard for their civil liberties. As a result, one of the fallouts from the war on selected oligarchs has been a loss of confidence by potential investors, scaring off the very investment that the government so greatly desires.

AN UNCERTAIN FUTURE

In late 2004, Freedom House (a research institute dedicated to furthering democracy) issued its highly respected annual report on democracy throughout the world. For the first time in years, Russia's rating was lowered from "partly free" to "not free."[85] This does not mean that the country has regressed to Soviet-style authoritarianism. There is still some criticism of the government in the mass media (excepting most television channels). Independent think-tanks and pro-democratic politicians speak out against government excesses. Despite an understandable cynicism about politics, a higher percentage of Russians vote in their presidential elections than Americans do. Votes seem to have been counted relatively fairly for at least the first three parliamentary elections and to a lesser extent in the three presidential races. Until 2003, all the major candidates had accepted the outcomes of national elections and supported their legitimacy. And the level of civil liberties, though not what it should be, is clearly higher than in Soviet days.

Still, as the latest Freedom House rankings indicate, under President Putin Russia has moved away from democracy, rather than toward it. Despite his denials, there are some who believe that Putin will have his supporters in the Duma revise the current two-term limit on the presidency so as to allow him a third term in 2008. Alternatively, he and his advisors may simply want to handpick his successor. What is clear is that United Russia has achieved a level of dominance in national politics not seen since the fall of communism and that Putin and his inner circle wish to keep it that way. Thus, even if it is unlikely that Putin would or could impose a one-party system, it appears that his government is trying to reproduce the political order that prevailed in Mexico until recently (see Chapter 16). Opposition parties were allowed to run for office, but the ruling party won all significant elections, most notably the presidency, for some 70 years.

 WHERE ON THE WEB?

russiavotes.org/
University of Strathclyde (Britain) site on Russia; provides information on Russian elections and democracy.

themoscowtimes.com/
The *Moscow Times* Web site, a useful English-language newspaper.

http://english.mn.ru/english/
Another Russian newspaper in English, *The Moscow News*.

http://www.ru/
Russia on the Net.

◆ ◆ ◆

Key Terms and Concepts_____

absolutism
Bolsheviks
Central Committee
civil society
collectivization
command economy
cult of personality
dual transition
Duma (State Duma)
glasnost
gulag

nomenklatura
oligarch (oligarchy)
perestroika
Politburo
privatization
proletariat
shock therapy
superpresidentialism
Supreme Soviet
vanguard party
vertical power

Discussion Questions_____

1. What is a command economy? What were the major accomplishments and failures of the Soviet Union's command economy?
2. What factors caused Mikhail Gorbachev to introduce his policies of *glasnost* and *perestroika*?
3. What were the major accomplishments and failures of those policies?
4. Discuss the development of Russia's multiparty system since the early 1990s. What are the major weaknesses of the current political party system?
5. Discuss the role of the president in Russian national politics. What changes have taken place in that role under Presidents Yeltsin and Putin?
6. What are the major political, economic, and social problems still facing Russia in its transition to democracy and capitalism?
7. Discuss the ways Russia's oligarchs accumulated their wealth. What has been the nature of President Putin's struggle with the oligarchs?

Notes_____

1. D. Richard Little, *Governing the Soviet Union* (New York: Longman, 1989).
2. Frederick C. Barghoorn and Thomas F. Remington, *Politics in the USSR* (Boston: Little, Brown, 1986), chap. 1.
3. Crane Brinton, *The Anatomy of Revolution* (New York: Vintage, 1965).
4. Barghoorn and Remington, *Politics in the USSR*, p. 16.
5. Peter Hauslohner, "Politics Before Gorbachev: De-Stalinization and the Roots of Reform," in *Inside Gorbachev's Russia*, ed. Seweryn Bialer (Boulder, CO: Westview, 1989).
6. Dusko Doder and Louise Branson, *Gorbachev: Heretic in the Kremlin* (New York: Penguin, 1990), pp. 23–24.
7. Abraham Bergson, *The Real National Income of Soviet Russia Since 1928* (Cambridge: Harvard University Press, 1961), p. 261.
8. Ed A. Hewett, *Reforming the Soviet Economy: Equality versus Efficiency* (Washington, DC: Brookings, 1988), p. 38.
9. Ibid.
10. "Soviet Economic Performance: Strengths and Weaknesses," in Hewett, *Reforming the Soviet Economy*.
11. Timothy Colton, *The Dilemma of Reform in the Soviet Union* (New York: Council on Foreign Relations, 1986); "Bureaucratic Conservatism and the Post-Stalinist Settlement," in Kesselman et al., *European Politics in Transition* (Lexington, MA: Heath, 1987).
12. Hewett, *Reforming the Soviet Economy*, p. 52.

13. Jerry F. Hough, *Opening Up the Soviet Economy* (Washington, DC: Brookings, 1988), p.13.

14. Jim Leitzel, *Russian Economic Reform* (New York: Routledge, 1995), p. 1.

15. Hough, *Opening Up the Soviet Economy*, pp. 43–44.

16. *New York Times*, February 3, 1991, p. 1.

17. Ben Eklof, *Soviet Briefing* (Boulder, CO: Westview, 1989), pp. 42–45.

18. Hewett, *Reforming the Soviet Economy*, p. 304.

19. Hedrick Smith, *The New Russians* (New York: Random House, 1990), p. 185.

20. We are indebted to Marshall Goldman for a number of the insights and examples in this section, which he offered at a lecture at the University of Wisconsin, Milwaukee, in March 1991.

21. Donna Bahry and Brian Silver, "Public Perceptions and the Dilemmas of Party Reform in the USSR" (paper presented at the annual meeting of the American Political Science Association, Atlanta, September 1989), p. 13.

22. Donald Barry and Carol Barner-Barry, *Contemporary Soviet Politics* (Englewood Cliffs, NJ: Prentice Hall, 1991), p. 137.

23. *The New York Times*, February 8, 2001.

24. For an excellent summary of the ideological spectrum of Russian political parties, see http://128.172.170.24/rus/rusparty.htm. Although the site is now a few years old and some of the parties listed have disappeared, its descriptions of party ideologies are still valid. A similar classification of Russian parties by ideology appears in M. Steven Fish, "The Advent of Multipartyism in Russia, 1993–95," *Post-Soviet Affairs* 11, no. 4 (1995): 348–353.

25. Jeffrey W. Hahn, "Introduction: Analyzing Parliamentary Development in Russia," in *Democratization in Russia: The Development of Legislative Institutions*, ed. Jeffrey W. Hahn (Armonk, NY: Sharpe, 1996), pp. 3–26.

26. Lilia Shevtsova, "Parliament and the Political Crisis: 1991–1993," in Hahn, *Democratization in Russia*, pp. 30–31. On the percentage of Communist Party members, see David Lane and Cameron Ross, "From Soviet Government to Presidential Rule," in *Russia in Transition*, ed. David Lane (London: Longman, 1995), p. 5.

27. John P. Willerton, "Yeltsin and the Russian Presidency," in *Developments in Russian and Post-Soviet Politics*, ed. Stephen White, Alex Pravda, and Zvi Gitelman (London: Macmillan, 1994), pp. 25–56.

28. Marshall I. Goldman, *Lost Opportunity: Why Economic Reforms in Russia Have Not Worked* (New York: Norton, 1994), pp. 160–189; and Alan Smith, introduction to *Challenges for Russian Economic Reform*, ed. Alan Smith (Washington, DC: Brookings, 1995), pp. 5–9.

29. Lilia Shevtsova, "Russia's Post-Communist Politics: Revolution or Continuity?" in *The New Russia: Troubled Transformation*, ed. Gail W. Lapidus, (Boulder, CO: Westview, 1995), pp. 20–21; and Thomas F. Remington, "Ménage à Trois: The End of Soviet Parliamentarianism," in Hahn, *Democratization in Russia*, p. 108.

30. John Lowenhardt, *The Reincarnation of Russia: Struggling with the Legacy of Communism* (Durham, NC: Duke University Press, 1995), p. 110. We added the 1997 reference.

31. Anders Aslund, *How Russia Became a Market Economy* (Washington, DC: Brookings, 1995), p. 275. GDP (gross domestic product) is a measure similar to GNP but excludes earnings from abroad.

32. Alan Smith, "The Economic Challenge Facing Russia," in Smith, *Challenges for Russian Economic Reform*, pp. 1–20.

33. Josef C. Brada, "The Transformation from Communism to Capitalism: How Far? How Fast?" *Post-Soviet Affairs* 9, no. 2 (1993): 87–110; Anders Aslund, *Economic Transformation in Russia* (New York: St. Martin's, 1994); and Jeffrey D. Sachs and W. T. Woo, "Reform in China and Russia," *Economic Policy* 18 (April 1994): 101–145.

34. Abraham Shama, "Inside Russia's True Economy," *Foreign Policy* 103 (Summer 1996): 112.

35. *New York Times*, November 11, 1993.

36. Stephen White, *After Gorbachev* (Cambridge, England: Cambridge University Press, 1993), p. 277; and Michael Kaser, "Privatization in the CIS," in Smith, *Challenges for Russian Economic Reform*, p. 141. Thus, Russia now has more stockholders than does the United States.

37. Shama, "Inside Russia's True Economy," p. 112; and *The New York Times*, January 28, 1996, and June 16, 1996.
38. *The New York Times*, June 19, 1994.
39. Aslund, *How Russia Became a Market Economy*, p. 275; Goldman, *Lost Opportunity*, pp. 106–107, 109, claims a slightly lower rate of inflation.
40. Allen C. Lynch, *How Russia Is Not Ruled* (Cambridge, UK: Cambridge University Press, 2005), p. 94.
41. Peter Rutland, "The Economy: The Rocky Road from Plan to Market," in White et al., *Developments in Russian and Post-Soviet Politics*, p. 154.
42. Marshall Goldman, "Render Onto Caesar: Putin and the Oligarchs," *Current History* 102 (October 2003), pp. 320–326.
43. *The New York Times*, September 25, 1993.
44. *The New York Times*, August 2, 1995; *Radio Free Europe* (July 5, 2000), "Russia: Life Expectancy Declining," http://www.rferl.org/nca/features; and Francis C. Notzon et al., "Causes of Declining Life Expectancy in Russia, *JAMA (Journal of the American Medical Association)* 279, no. 10 (March 11, 1998): 793–800; Waller, *Russian Politics Today*, p. 231.
45. Stephen White, Alex Pravda, and Zvi Gitelman, eds., *Developments in Russian Politics* 5 (Durham, NC: Duke University Press, 2001), p. 183.
46. Yoshiko M. Herrera, "Russian Economic Reform, 1991–1999," in *Russian Politics: Challenges of Democratization*, ed. Zoltan Barany and Robert G. Moser (Cambridge, UK, and New York: Cambridge University Press, 2001), p. 161.
47. WorldWide Tax and Finance Site, worldwide-tax.com/russia/rus_inflation.asp.
48. Index Mundi, "Russia Economy Profile," indexmundi.com/russia/economy_profile.html.
49. William Thompson, "The Russian Economy under Vladimir Putin," in *Russian Politics Under Putin*, ed. Cameron Ross (Manchester, UK, and New York: Manchester University Press, 2004), pp. 114–132.
50. Leitzel, *Russian Economic Reform*, p. 41.
51. *The New York Times*, January 30, 1994.
52. Donald D. Barry, *Russian Politics: The Post-Soviet Phase* (New York: Peter Lang, 2002), p. 1.
53. *The New York Times*, April 20, 1993.
54. Poll conducted by Mitofsky in cooperation with CESSI Ltd. and quoted in *The New York Times*, June 18, 1996.
55. "Putin's Dubious Allure: 'He's Not Making Things Worse,'" *The New York Times* (March 9, 2004).
56. Amy Knight, "The Two Worlds of Vladimir Putin," *The Wilson Quarterly* (Spring 2000).
57. Mark Kramer, "Out of Communism: Reforming the Russian Legal System, *Current History* 102 (October 2003): 327–332.
58. CBC News (May 31, 2005), cbc.co/news/background/russia/timeline.html.
59. Waller, *Russian Politics Today*, p. 33.
60. Allen C. Lynch, *How Russia Is Not Ruled*, pp. 160–161.
61. Ibid., p. 161; Olga Kryshtanovskaya and Stephen White, "Putin's Militocracy," *Post-Soviet Affairs* 19, no. 4 (October-December, 2003): 289–306.
62. Marsha Lipman and Michael McFaul, "Putin and the Media," in *Putin's Russia*, ed. Dale R. Herspring, p. 70.
63. Laura Belin "Politics and the Mass Media under Putin," in Ross (ed.), *Russian Politics Under Putin*, pp. 133–150.
64. Marsha Lipman and Michael McFaul, "Putin and the Media," in *Putin's Russia*, ed. Dale R. Herspring, pp. 70–71; Waller, *Russian Politics Today*, p. 221.
65. Ibid., pp. 77–78.
66. Peter Rutland, "Putin and the Oligarchs," in *Putin's Russia*, ed. Dale R. Herspring (Lanham, MD: Rowman & Littlefield Publishers, Inc., 2003), pp. 133–152.
67. Goldman, "Render Unto Caesar"; Michael Waller, *Russian Politics Today* (Manchester, UK, and New York: Manchester University Press, 2005), p. 196; "World's richest men live in

Moscow and New York," *Pravda* (Moscow) http://english.pravda.ru/society/stories/13-03-2006/77185-billionaires-0

68. Laszlo Csaba, "Russia's Political Economy," in *Toward an Understanding of Russia: New European Perspectives*, ed. Janusz Bugajski (New York: Council on Foreign Relations, 2002), p. 31.

69. Anatoly M. Khazanov, "What Went Wrong? Post-Communist Transformations in Comparative Perspective," in *Restructuring Post-Communist Russia*, ed. Yitzhak Brundy et al. (Cambridge, England: Cambridge University Press, 2004), p. 49.

70. Marshall Goldman, "The Russian Transition to the Market: Success or Failure?" in Brundy et al. (ed.), *Restructuring Post-Communist Russia*, pp. 132–133.

71. Michael McFaul, *Russia's Unfinished Revolution: From Gorbachev to Putin* (Ithaca, NY, and London: Cornell University Press, 2001), pp. 309–337. McFaul also mentions some other weaknesses, which we have omitted.

72. Ibid., p. 315.

73. Neil Robinson, *Russia: A State of Uncertainty.* (London and New York: Routledge, 2002), p. 166.

74. Judith Shapiro, "Health and Health Care Policy," in White, Pravda, and Gitelman, *Developments in Russian Politics 5*, p. 193.

75. Barry, *Russian Politics*, p. 172.

76. Timothy J. Colton and Michael McFaul, "Putin and Democratization," in *Putin's Russia*, pp. 20–22.

77. Russia Votes, "Opinions About Electoral Reform," http://www.russiavotes.org/Duma_reform_cur.htm.

78. Public Opinion Foundation (Russia), http://bd.english.fom.ru/report/cat/societas/society_power/democracy/.

79. McFaul, *Russia's Unfinished Revolution*, p. 333.

80. Russia Votes Web site (visited August 2005) from New Russian Barometers, http://www.russiavotes.org/.

81. Waller, *Russian Politics Today*, p. 80.

82. Lynch, *How Russia Is Not Ruled*, p. 100.

83. Waller, *Russian Politics Today*, p. 208.

84. *The New York Times* (August 13, 2005).

85. Arch Puddington and Aili Piano, "The 2004 Freedom House Survey," *Journal of Democracy* 16, no. 1 (January 2005): 103–108.

For Further Reading _____

Barry, Donald D. *Russian Politics: The Post-Soviet Phase.* New York: Peter Lang, 2002.

Brudny, Yitzhak, Jonathan Frankel, and Stefani Hoffman, eds. *Restructuring Post-Communist Russia.* Cambridge, UK: Cambridge University Press, 2004.

Handelman, Stephen. *Comrade Criminal: Russia's New Mafia.* New Haven: Yale University Press, 1995.

Herspring, Dale R., ed. *Putin's Russia: Past Imperfect, Future Uncertain* Lanham, MD: Rowman & Littlefield Publishers, 2003.

Lynch, Allen C. *How Russia Is Not Ruled.* Cambridge, UK: Cambridge University Press, 2005.

McFaul, Michael. *Russia's Unfinished Revolution: From Gorbachev to Putin.* Ithaca, NY, and London: Cornell University Press, 2001.

Ross, Cameron. *Russian Politics Under Putin.* Manchester, UK, and New York: Manchester University Press, 2004.

Waller, Michael. *Russian Politics Today.* Manchester, UK, and New York: Manchester University Press, 2005.

White, Stephen, Alex Pravda, and Zvi Gitelman, eds. *Developments in Russian Politics 5.* Durham, NC: Duke University Press, 2001.

© Reuters NewMedia Inc./CORBIS

14

CHINA: SEARCHING FOR A NEW VISION

◆ The Relevance of Chinese Politics ◆ China's Imperial Legacy ◆ The Chinese Revolution and Its Origins ◆ China under Mao (1949–1976) ◆ Deng Xiaoping (1978–1997), Jiang Zemin (1995–2002), Hu Jintao (2002–) and the Post-Maoist Era ◆ Reforming the Chinese Economy ◆ China's Political System: The Communist Party ◆ The Structure of Government ◆ Problems of Political Reform ◆ Sources of Discontent ◆ Obstacles to Democratic Change ◆ China's Uncertain Future

Study Chairman Mao's writings, follow his teachings and act according to his instructions. Mao Zedong's thought is Marxism-Leninism of the era in which [capitalist] imperialism is heading for total collapse and socialism [communism] is advancing to worldwide victory.[1]

—Chinese government directive in the 1960s

To get rich is glorious![2]

—Communist Party Leader Deng Xiaoping in the 1980s

The strident and confident words of the first quotation above introduced a volume of quotations from the then-revered leader of China's Communist Party, Mao Zedong.* Known in the West as "the little red book," it was one of the most widely read volumes on earth during the 1960s—required reading for literate Chinese. All communist governments have turned to Marxist doctrine as a source of legitimacy, but none more so than Mao's China.

Mao's message was clear. China, he argued, was an underdeveloped nation threatened by Western imperialism and internal class conflict. Only through struggle and commitment to communist ideology could China vanquish poverty, elitism, and imperialism. "Without a party built on the Marxist-Leninist theory and . . . style," he wrote, "it is impossible to lead the working class and the broad masses of the people in defeating imperialism and its running dogs." Today, those dreams lie largely in tatters as the Chinese economy has virtually abandoned Marxist practices in favor of the free market. Thousands of Chinese have become millionaires, including eight who made *Forbes* magazine's 2006 listing of the world's 793 *billionaires* (up from two in 2005). Rather than despising the rich, government leaders now encourage people to emulate them. The Communist Party continues to dominate politics but has little mass following.

THE RELEVANCE OF CHINESE POLITICS

With 1.3 billion people, China contains over one-fifth of the human race, far exceeding the combined populations of the United States, Great Britain, Russia, and Mexico. This chapter will discuss the enormous capacity of Mao's totalitarian system for implementing political and economic change. But it will also note the enormous human suffering that Maoism inflicted on the Chinese people and will trace the causes of that system's demise. Like the Soviet Union before its collapse, China features an authoritarian political culture, a dominant Marxist ideology, and an all-powerful ruling party.

The differences between these two communist giants, however, even before the breakdown of the USSR, were as important as their similarities. During the Maoist era (1949–1976), China's government and Communist Party tried to inculcate Marxist ideology in its population to a greater extent than the Soviet regime had. Conversely, whereas Mikhail Gorbachev's attempts to reform the Soviet command economy failed miserably, China's reforms since 1978—creating a mixed communist/free-enterprise economic structure—have produced the world's fastest-growing economy.

---

* In China, as in much of East Asia, a person's family name precedes his or her given name. Thus, Mao Zedong and President Hu Jintao are called Chairman Mao and President Hu.

RUSSIA

Lake
Baikal

KAZAKHSTAN

HEILONGJIANG

MONGOLIA

KYRGYZSTAN

XINJIANG UYGUR

JILIN

NEI MONGOL
(Inner Mongolia)

Shenyang

Tarim River

LIAONING

N. KOREA

NINGXIA
HUI

Beijing

Tianjin

HEBEI

S. KOREA

SHANXI

SHANDONG

Yellow
Sea

QINGHAI

Yanan

Huang Ho

JIANGSU

GANSU

Xi'an

HENAN

XIZANG
(Tibet)

SHAANXI

Nanjing

Shanghai

NEPAL

SICHUAN

HUBEI

Yangtze River

Wuhan

ANHUI

ZHEJIANG

Chengdu

INDIA

BHUTAN

Chongqing

JIANGXI

East
China
Sea

BANGLADESH

HUNAN

Fuzhou

GUIZHOU

FUJIAN

YUNNAN

GUANGXI ZHUANG

GUANGDONG

TAIWAN

MYANMAR
(BURMA)

Guangzhou
(Canton)

HONG KONG

HAINAN

LAOS

THAILAND

PHILIPPINES

VIETNAM

CAMBODIA

From the late 1950s through the mid-1970s, China was among the most ideologically driven of all communist nations. The radical campaigns of the Cultural Revolution (1966–1976)—which elevated Mao Zedong to the level of a demigod and turned his ideology into a virtual state religion—caused enormous destruction and countless deaths. But the moral certainty and fanaticism that characterized Mao's rule declined soon after his death. Under the leadership of **Deng Xiaoping** (1978–1997) and then Jiang Zemin (1995–2002),* China moved decisively away from Maoist orthodoxy. In the past 25 years, the government has introduced free-market economic reforms that are much more sweeping and far more successful than anything attempted by President Gorbachev during the last years of the USSR (Chapter 13). Today, by some measures China has the world's second-largest economy (as measured by parity purchasing power) and may surpass the United States as the world's largest by the year 2050.[3] Even before its recent entry into the World Trade Organization (WTO), it was one of the United States' largest trading partners, and its role in the world economy will certainly continue to grow. Consequently, not only has China been a model for market reform in the world's remaining communist countries, but its rapid growth also has been the envy of almost all developing nations.

But those economic reforms have been unaccompanied by corresponding political reforms and freedoms, as happened in the Soviet Union under *glasnost*. In the spring of 1989, students in a number of Chinese universities staged protests, with considerable non-student support, demanding more honest and more responsive government.

Week after week in Beijing (the nation's capital), they organized massive rallies in **Tiananmen Square,** the very spot where Mao Zedong had exhorted his revolutionary shock troops four decades earlier. On June 4, 1989, army tanks rolled into the square, killing several hundred student demonstrators and making Tiananmen a symbol of government repression throughout the world. China's leaders, so recently hailed in the West for their economic reforms, were reviled for their repressive politics. Since that time, political repression has eased considerably and individual freedoms "to buy what [people] want, enjoy private lives, speak more openly, and even to travel abroad. . . ." have expanded.[4] But basic civil liberties still are lacking and the authority of the Communist Party remains absolute.

China scholars have long argued that the country's unique history and political culture are not easily compared with those of other communist countries or other developing nations. Consequently, we must first examine China's historical and cultural legacies to better understand its images of itself and of the outside world.

CHINA'S IMPERIAL LEGACY

China, argued one leading historian, is a "nation imprisoned by her history."[5] Those traditions are particularly relevant to its modern politics. Some two hundred years before the birth of Christ, the Qin dynasty first unified the country's feudal kingdoms into an empire. Subsequent dynasties fell to military insurrections or peasant uprisings, some of which

---

* Although Deng remained the nation's paramount leader until his death in 1997, in his final years his advanced age and his failing health meant that authority was already passing to other top officials, particularly Chinese Communist Party (CCP) general secretary and national President Jiang Zemin. Hence the overlap of two years in their authority (1995–1997). Jiang actually served eight years (1989–1997) prior to Deng's death as CCP secretary, national president, and heir apparent.

lasted up to one hundred years and caused the deaths of millions.[6] Even today, the legacy of China's violent past—which lasted well into the twentieth century—is the widespread conviction of many citizens that centralized, authoritarian rule is necessary to avert serious disorder. Like modern Maoism, traditional Confucian morality stressed social order and harmony, including "the values of the group at the expense of the individual."[7]

The overthrow of the imperial regime early in the twentieth century and the communist victory decades later fundamentally transformed Chinese society. Yet, the country's history of bloody uprisings and its search for harmony through some form of authoritarian rule continue to loom large in its contemporary political consciousness.

THE CHINESE REVOLUTION AND ITS ORIGINS

Foreign Domination and the Collapse of the Empire

For centuries, Chinese leaders saw their nation as "the Middle Kingdom," the cultural center of the earth. The country's culture and technology had filled Marco Polo and other Western travelers with awe. Starting in the nineteenth century, however, China began to experience increasing military and economic threats from abroad. Although never formally colonized, China suffered from Western and Japanese economic domination that weakened its political sovereignty as well.[8]

Foreign domination was accompanied by internal upheavals. The Taiping Rebellion (1850–1865), a huge peasant uprising, nearly toppled the imperial regime before the revolt was crushed at the cost of some 20 million lives. By the time Japan attacked China at the close of the nineteenth century, segments of the elite had lost faith in the government and looked, instead, to Western models of modernization.[9] The emperors' inability to protect the country from foreign exploitation undermined their legitimacy and contributed to the demise of the two-thousand-year-old imperial order. In 1911–1912, an uprising led by dissident military officers and provincial government officials toppled the old regime.

Warlords and Civil War (1912–1928)

For nearly two decades after the empire fell, civil war raged between nationalist reformers and the armies of regional strongmen known as **warlords**.[10] During that time, two political parties were born that soon dominated Chinese politics. The first, the **Nationalist Party**, or **Kuomintang (Guomindang) (KMT)**, was led by a mix of Western-oriented intellectuals, military officers, businessmen, and rural landlords. After years of struggle, General Chiang Kai-shek's KMT army defeated the most important warlords in 1928 and established a new central government.

Meanwhile, in 1921 a small group of Marxist intellectuals had formed the Chinese Communist Party (CCP). Although the party grew to nearly 60 thousand members in six years, its growth was limited by its orthodox Marxist belief that only the working class could be the agent of revolution. The fact was that in China, an overwhelmingly rural society at that time, industrial workers constituted less than 1 percent of the population.[11] Convinced that the country was not yet ready for a communist revolution, the fledgling CCP allied with the Kuomintang against the warlords.

On the eve of the KMT's victory, however, Chiang Kai-shek turned against the communists and decimated them. From 1927 to 1930, Chiang's "White Terror" killed many thousands of Communist Party members and sympathizers, effectively destroying the party's urban base.[12]

The Revolution Begins (1928–1936)

Its disastrous alliance with the KMT forced the communists to rethink their strategy. One party faction, headed by **Mao Zedong,** decided to organize beyond the working class and reach out to the peasants, who made up about 85 percent of China's population. In the years that followed, Mao and his followers built a rural guerrilla army, the **People's Liberation Army (PLA),** operating out of communist-controlled regions.

Soon they governed some six million people in south-central China.[13] Still no match for Chiang's more powerful army, however, the communists retreated northward in 1934. Fewer than 10 percent of the 100 thousand PLA soldiers and political activists who started that "**Long March**" north survived the arduous 6,000-mile trek, "an odyssey perhaps unequaled in modern times."[14]

The Development of Maoist Revolutionary Thought

Despite the tremendous loss of men associated with it, the Long March itself and the subsequent experience governing "liberated regions" in the northwest taught the communist leadership important organizational lessons that later turned the tide of victory in their favor.[15] To win peasant support, they introduced greater economic and political equality in a society traditionally rife with inequalities of wealth, education, and gender. As the PLA eventually overcame great odds to defeat better-armed KMT armies, Mao Zedong became convinced that—properly organized and ideologically inspired—the masses (peasants and workers) could overcome any obstacles, no matter how daunting.

The Anti-Japanese War (1937–1945)

Japan's military occupation of northern China in 1931 was the turning point in the Chinese civil war. Because the KMT government was unable to mount an effective resistance against the Japanese during the war, it lost its legitimacy, just as its predecessor, the imperial government, had fallen when it had failed to turn back foreign aggressors. During World War II, the communists and the KMT reached a truce and renewed their former alliance, this time to join in a struggle against the Japanese. The PLA's superior military tactics enabled them to expand the area they controlled considerably. By the war's end, the communists governed liberated zones with a combined population of 130 million people. The Communist Party grew from 20 thousand members in 1935 to 1.2 million in 1945, and PLA troops and militias grew to 3.4 million men.

The Communist Victory (1945–1949)

Following the end of World War II and the Japanese defeat, the civil war between the Communist and Nationalist armies resumed. But, having failed to defend China adequately or to win the peasants' loyalty, the KMT had lost its political mandate. By 1949, after a series of losses, its army and its loyalists fled the mainland to the island of Taiwan. On October 1, Mao Zedong founded the People's Republic of China. "Our nation," he declared to a cheering throng in Tiananmen Square, "will never again be an insulted nation. We have stood up."

Mao's Version of Marxist-Leninist Ideology

Like many other revolutionaries who achieved power after a prolonged struggle—including Lenin, Fidel Castro, and Ho Chi Minh—Mao Zedong was far more ideologically committed than his successors were to be, strongly believing in the power of Marxism to mobilize the Chinese masses.[16]

We have previously noted several features of Maoist thought: the central role of the peasantry, a strong egalitarian commitment, and a glorification of class struggle. But Mao also insisted that class struggle did not end with the victory of the revolutionary forces. Even after it has seized power, he argued, a Marxist regime must be ever vigilant against the families of former capitalists and landlords still residing in China, against Western imperialism, and even against corrupt cadres (party and government officials) within the Communist Party and government bureaucracy itself.[17]

Those alleged ongoing threats were used to justify recurrent mass mobilization campaigns. Mao felt these crusades were needed to maintain the people's ideological commitment and to ensure the revolution's purity. But, at the very least, the ongoing mass mobilization campaigns disrupted people's lives and hurt the economy. At their worst, as in the Great Leap Forward and the Cultural Revolution, they caused millions of deaths. Not until the late 1970s were Deng Xiaoping and the new CCP leadership able to moderate the role of ideology in society.

China Under Mao (1949–1976)

Establishing the Basis of Communist Society (1949–1956)

The early years of communist rule established the fundamental components of the new society. Acknowledging the peasants' central role in the CCP victory, the government's first priority was redistribution of farmland. Before the revolution, less than 10 percent of China's rural population owned over half the agricultural land. In just a few years, those farms were taken from the landlords and distributed to more than 300 million landless peasants.[18] In the cities, private businesses were absorbed by the state. The end of decades of civil war and the creation of centralized political authority facilitated economic recovery. Coupled with more equitable distribution of resources, economic growth improved the living standards of most Chinese.

Political institutions were patterned on the Soviet model. Party authority was absolute, and perceived enemies of the revolution were brutally repressed. But for many uneducated peasants who had joined the PLA or the CCP, the new political system offered opportunities for upward mobility that were previously unimaginable. New conditions of social peace, greater equality, land reform, and improved living standards all earned the new regime considerable popular support.

The Great Leap Forward (1958–1961)

Although the Chinese economy grew impressively in the early years of communist rule (1949–1956), Mao Zedong feared that the Soviet-style economic development model in place was inappropriate for China's impoverished rural society. That model emphasized capital investment and the development of heavy industry. But since China had little investment capital and vast human labor resources, Mao sought to maximize Chinese self-sufficiency and to draw on the country's primary resource—the numbers and energy of its people. As we have noted, he believed that, if properly inspired, the Chinese masses could make tremendous progress in a short period of time.[19]

Thus, for example, when the **Great Leap Forward** campaign was launched in 1958, the government called on the people to gather scrap iron on their farms and streets for use in backyard steel furnaces. But the most radical changes took place in the countryside, where agricultural units were consolidated into large **communes**. Peasants were no longer allowed to own private farm plots or animals, and rural life was collectivized.[20]

Although it may have promoted short-term production spurts, the longer-term effects of the Great Leap Forward were catastrophic. In the cities, production speedups caused machinery breakdowns, production bottlenecks, and subsequent declines in output. In rural areas, the effects of Mao's radical policies were more disastrous. The communes were unpopular and far too large to manage effectively. Because of ill-conceived production and harvesting decisions by central planners, much of the harvest failed to reach the market, and vast amounts of food rotted in the fields or were consumed by birds, insects, and rodents. From 1959 to 1962, those planning errors (sometimes compounded by bad weather) devastated production. As a result, up to 25 million people died of hunger and malnutrition.[21]

The Reds-versus-Experts Debate (1959–1965)

Mao's failed radical campaigns generated sharp divisions among party leaders regarding a proper strategy for reinvigorating economic development. The conflict pitted more pragmatic party leaders (whom China specialists have labeled the **Expert faction**) against ultraradicals headed by Mao and PLA leader Lin Biao (referred to as the **Red faction**).

Led by China's president, Liu Shaoqi, and his ally Deng Xiaoping, the pragmatists ended the Great Leap's most radical and disastrous components. By 1962, peasants were again permitted to cultivate private plots. Justifying private farming by appealing to efficiency rather than ideology, Deng Xiaoping exemplified the Expert faction's pragmatic attitude when he declared, "It doesn't matter whether the cat is black or white as long as it catches mice" (that is to say, "Satisfactory results matter more than the correct ideology"). Similarly, these leaders felt that state-owned enterprises should be managed by the most competent experts, not necessarily by those most committed to Maoist ideology.

Although the Expert faction had helped restore economic growth, its pragmatic approach troubled Mao and his radical allies. They felt that the communist governments of the USSR and Eastern Europe had lost contact with the masses when they had come under the control of bureaucratic elites. The Expert faction's pragmatic policies, they feared, would produce the same outcome in China as technically trained experts took the place of radical revolutionaries fully committed to egalitarian principles. In one form or another, conflict between more ideologically driven leaders and more pragmatic ones became an ongoing feature of Chinese politics from that time until the early 1990s.

The Cultural Revolution (1966–1976)

As the pragmatists extended their influence in the CCP, Mao turned to more radical groups for support: specifically, the military and the nation's youth. In August 1966, he launched the Great Proletarian Cultural Revolution—or, simply, the **Cultural Revolution**—seeking to root out party and government cadres who were allegedly subverting the revolution ("capitalist roaders") and to destroy all Western or capitalist influences in China's cultural life. Toward that purpose, Mao exhorted Chinese youth to organize into militant units called **Red Guards** to attack cadres, teachers, artists, and intellectuals who were not sufficiently revolutionary.[22]

Thus, the Cultural Revolution was fought at two levels. Within the party elite, Liu Shaoqi, Deng Xiaoping, and other moderates were arrested, attacked, and humiliated (Liu died while in custody, and Deng's son was partially paralyzed when he fell or was thrown from a window). More than 70 percent of the party's Central Committee members were purged from their posts.[23] At the mass level, Red Guards ran rampant, arresting, beating, and killing alleged reactionaries. At times, peasants, workers and even contending military units were swept into the street battles, totally disrupting daily life. By 1967, the nation had sunk into chaos, and the military had to be called in to restore order. Within two years, the Red Guards were disbanded and the worst excesses of the Cultural Revolution were terminated. But thought control and intimidation continued until Mao's death in 1976.

The tragedy of the Cultural Revolution illustrates how seemingly benign objectives (keeping government officials in touch with the people and guaranteeing equality) can lead to vast human suffering when pursued fanatically in a totalitarian setting. Deng Xiaoping later claimed that nearly three million Chinese fell victim to political persecution during those years.[24] The number of people killed will never be known. Estimates vary wildly, ranging from half a million to 20 million, with most scholars supporting figures at the lower end of that spectrum.[25] Intellectuals, professionals, and technicians—the Red Guards' prime targets—were traumatized for years to come. The economy suffered tremendously. Eventually, the Red Guards themselves became the campaign's victims. Often unable to settle back into a normal life, they came to be feared by Mao as a disruptive force, and many of them were sent off for years of "reeducation" in the countryside.

The Death of Mao and the Struggle for Succession (1976–1981)

In 1976, a political earthquake hit China with the death of its two most important leaders: **Zhou Enlai,** its premier (prime minister) since 1954; and Communist Party Chairman Mao Zedong, the revolution's "great helmsman" since 1935. Although Mao and his revolutionary line retained substantial popular support, the excesses of the Great Leap Forward and the Cultural Revolution had seriously weakened the regime's legitimacy. Once a widely admired hero, by the time of his death 20 years later Mao had spent much of the regime's political capital.

So, only one month after Mao Zedong died, his successor, Hua Guofeng, ordered the arrest of Mao's widow, Jiang Qing, and three other leaders of the CCP's most radical faction. The "Gang of Four," as they were labeled, were accused of responsibility for the worst excesses of the Cultural Revolution and were later brought to trial.

With those four serving as convenient scapegoats for Mao's horrors, their arrest signaled to the Chinese people that the Cultural Revolution was over.

DENG XIAOPING (1978–1997), JIANG ZEMIN (1995–2002), HU JINTAO (2002–), AND THE POST-MAOIST ERA

Hua Guofeng was soon outmaneuvered by Deng Xiaoping in the battle for national leadership. Deng, the consummate pragmatist and political survivor, had twice come back from political purgatory to outlive or outmaneuver his Red-faction opponents. By 1981, his supporters had ousted Hua from his positions as premier and party leader. Choosing not to hold either of the top political posts himself, Deng installed his two lieutenants, Zhao Ziyang and Hu Yaobang, as chairman of the Communist Party and premier, respectively, while he retained control of the military and was the most powerful leader from behind the scenes.

From 1976 to 1985, the most radical political officials were removed from the center of power. A 1981 pronouncement by the Communist Party Central Committee called the Cultural Revolution "the most severe setback [to] . . . the party, the state and the people since the founding of the People's Republic." Leadership conflicts between left and right factions continued under Deng. But with the Maoist radicals vanquished, even CCP leftists conceded the necessity of departing from Marxist economic dogma. Consequently, the party's leadership debate during the 1980s and much of the 1990s often pitted those who favored more rapid market-oriented economic reform (or, less frequently, political liberalization) against those who wished to move more slowly.[26]

Deng, Jiang, and the Process of Reform: China and Russia Compared

During the 1980s, Deng Xiaoping and his team instituted economic changes that were far more sweeping than those later introduced in the USSR by Mikhail Gorbachev. After Deng's death in 1997, Jiang Zemin further embedded those reforms and expanded them. Unlike Gorbachev's reforms in the Soviet Union, however, the changes have been limited to the economic arena, with far less emphasis on political change.

As we observed in Chapter 13, Gorbachev's most important innovations came in the political sphere: competitive elections, the end to the Communist Party's monopoly on power, open debate in the legislature, a freer mass media, and the opening of "political space" for public discussion. On the other hand, Soviet *economic* reform before the collapse of communism was far more restricted and was generally ineffective or even catastrophic. In China, the locus of reform was reversed. Economic innovations have been far-reaching and mostly quite successful. Political reforms, however, have been far more restrained and sometimes have been rolled back (as in the three years following the repression of the student democracy movement).

REFORMING THE CHINESE ECONOMY

What prompted the Chinese leadership to embark on a program of major economic change in the 1980s? As in the Soviet Union, the early decades of communist rule had brought the country impressive economic growth. Between 1952 and 1975, even with the major setbacks of the Great Leap Forward and the Cultural Revolution, the economy grew at an impressive annual pace of 8.2 percent and industry expanded at 11.5 percent per year.[27] Those rates far exceeded the norms in other developing nations.[28] Even after factoring in population growth, per capita GNP doubled. The combination of rapid economic growth, more equitable income distribution, better health care, and increased literacy in that period benefited the masses of Chinese peasants and laborers considerably.

Despite such gains, however, the People's Republic remained a very poor country, with much of the population still ill-housed and malnourished. Moreover, as in the Soviet Union (Chapter 13), the command economy proved more effective in the earliest stages of economic growth than at a later point. By the late 1970s, the country's leaders could scarcely fail to notice that some of their capitalist neighbors were developing far more rapidly than China was and were offering their citizens much higher living standards. Once praised for outpacing India and most of Asia, China in the 1970s was criticized for lagging far behind its old adversaries Taiwan, South Korea, and Hong Kong.

In response, starting in 1978, the Chinese leadership introduced economic changes so dramatic and far-reaching that a leading scholar, Harry Harding, has described them as "China's Second Revolution." Economic modernization replaced class struggle and political mobilization as the centerpiece of government policy. The People's Republic pursued economic and cultural contacts with both the West and the booming capitalist nations of East Asia that it had once scorned. Free-market mechanisms and private ownership replaced centralized state control in major sectors of the economy. We will examine the impact of those changes in three critical areas: agriculture, commerce and industry, and foreign economic relations.

The Second Revolution in Agriculture

Initially, Deng Xiaoping's most significant reforms affected agriculture, where most of the population was employed. CCP moderates had long argued that peasants are more productive when they control their own private plots of land, whereas Maoist radicals favored collectivized agriculture. During the Great Leap Forward and again during the Cultural Revolution, private farming was prohibited, and peasants were forced into less-efficient collective farms.

In 1978, however, the government announced its **responsibility system**, giving peasants control over their own family plots.[29] Within seven years, private family plots had largely replaced collective farm communes. Peasants were permitted to lease land, hire farm labor, and sell a portion of their crop directly to consumers at free-market prices once they had sold their crop quota to the state. Thus, farmers were given strong economic incentives, previously lacking, to boost agricultural production.

The results of "unleashing the entrepreneurial talents of China's peasants" were impressive. From 1980 to 1984, the value of agricultural output increased by approximately 40 percent.[30] Urban consumers enjoyed a wider variety of foods from which to choose. Greater output and higher crop prices produced a remarkable 12 percent annual increase in rural living standards.[31] Formerly scarce consumer items such as televisions and bicycles now dotted the countryside, particularly in areas closest to urban markets. Although the rate of agricultural growth tapered off considerably after the late 1980s, rural per capita income in 1999 was still *15 times higher* than it had been in 1978.[32] For all those reasons, some economists credit Deng's rural reforms with the greatest short-term improvement in human living standards ever achieved anywhere.

Deng's decision to introduce rural economic reform first was masterful. Not only did it greatly benefit a large segment of the populace (after all, China's population was about three-fourths rural at the time), but introducing privatization and market incentives was far easier in farming than in the urban, industrial sector. And, when the government cracked down on the urban democracy movement in 1989, peasants—who had gained so much from Deng's reforms—remained silent and apparently uninterested.

Since the late 1980s, however, rural economic growth has lagged substantially behind urban development, and the gap between urban and rural living standards is now as wide as ever. As peasants have become aware of that restored inequality, as they have been burdened with high taxes, and as they have become fed up with the abuses of local Communist Party bosses, rural protests have increased substantially.

Commercial and Industrial Reforms

Seeking to reduce urban unemployment and to offer consumer services not adequately provided by the state, government reforms introduced in the 1980s permitted small private businesses to operate for the first time since the start of the Cultural Revolution.

© AP/Wide World Photos

SPREADING WORKER PROTEST   More than 1,000 employees and retirees protested recently in front of the Yunnan Fabric Company in Kunming, demanding pension payments. The incident was one of thousands of protests across China each year in which employees have accused their employers of delaying or denying salary and pension payments.

By 1990, some 25 million people were employed in the urban private sector (shops, restaurants and the like). Although that number still constituted only a small percentage of the population, it fostered a more consumer-oriented culture. Dress and hairstyles that would have been prohibited in the Cultural Revolution became commonplace in China's cities. State enterprises such as department stores, which previously enjoyed a monopoly, now faced stiff competition from private stores, forcing many of them to extend store hours and improve service. During the 1990s, the country's urban housing stock was sold to its residents at low prices.

Although private businesses were at first confined to small family operations, since the 1980s, the government has allowed ever-larger manufacturing enterprises in the private sector, some employing hundreds of workers or more. In addition, workers in smaller state enterprises were encouraged to assume control of their factories and manage them as cooperatives. By the start of the twenty-first century, those cooperatives (called **collectives**) together with other newly created collective industries in China's villages accounted for almost 40 percent of the nation's industrial output. Privately owned firms now contribute more than 30 percent. That has left **state-owned enterprises** (**SOEs**)—which not long before had produced almost 90 percent of China's industrial output—producing less than one-third of the national total (and falling).[33]

But whereas the state sector's share of industrial *production* fell sharply, its share of the industrial *labor force* declined only slightly, from 78 percent of the workforce in 1977 to 65 percent in 1996.[34] Periodically, the government announces plans to privatize most of the remaining large state industries and to introduce more free-market practices in those firms that aren't privatized. But such reforms are politically very difficult, since new private-sector owners would undoubtedly dismiss a large portion of the former state enterprises' bloated workforce. Consequently, reforms have come very slowly. Today there are still more than 60 thousand SOEs remaining in the country, most of which are fairly inefficient and about one-half of which regularly lose money.[35]

Although economic reform has been enormously successful in many ways, it also has brought a number of undesirable consequences—occasional inflation, unemployment, and popular discontent. For example, in the 1980s and early 1990s the elimination of government price controls (which had kept prices below their free-market value) unleashed higher inflation rates and spurred discontent among urban consumers. Although tighter government spending policies brought inflation down sharply in the first years of the 1990s, it spiked again in 1994 at almost 25 percent annually.[36]

Another pernicious effect of economic change has been an enormous growth in corruption. Although private firms are an ever-growing force in the economy, businessmen must still depend on government officials to secure vital licenses, permits, and supplies. That has opened vast new opportunities for bribery, allowing many cadres or their children (these widely despised, corrupt, adult children are disparagingly known as **princelings**—little princes) to use their political positions for personal enrichment.[37] Corruption within the state and private sector has been a growing problem for decades and probably has done more to undermine popular support for the regime than any other factor.[38] In 1997, the Communist Party announced that during the previous five years it had investigated more than 725,000 charges of criminal conduct within its own ranks—undoubtedly only a small portion of those who were actually guilty—and, as a consequence, had expelled 121,000 members and detained 37,000 people on criminal charges.[39] Periodically, the party stages major show trials of corrupt government officials and businessmen, handing down harsh punishments that occasionally include executions. In one recent, high-profile case, the deputy mayor of Beijing committed suicide. But most people view these trials as symbolic, barely hitting the tip of the iceberg, and very rarely affecting top CCP officials or their children. In fact, few cases are brought to trial at any level. In 2004, for example, almost 171,000 government and party officials were caught in corruption scandals, but fewer than 5,000 (less than 3 percent) faced criminal prosecution.[40]

A third unpopular by-product of rapid economic growth has been increasing inequality, including broad income gaps between the developed coast and the country's interior, and between China's urban and rural populations. To be sure, the gap between rural and urban incomes narrowed considerably in the early years of economic reform (1978–1984).[41] Whereas city residents earned only a bit over one-and-one-half times as much as did peasants in 1984 (China's smallest urban-rural gap ever), by 2002 they were earning more than three (3.1) times as much, higher than it had been at the start of rural reform in 1978.[42] That doesn't mean that peasant incomes have declined since the mid-1980s. On the contrary, they have continued to improve, but urban incomes have increased much more rapidly. Nationwide, the richest 10 percent of the Chinese population earned 32 percent of the nation's income in 2002, up from 30.8 percent in 1995.[43] Since then, income inequalities have intensified further. New gated communities, with names like Orange County, Sun City, and Manhattan Gardens, are being built to accommodate the newly rich business class. Their huge homes, modeled after upscale suburban residences in the U.S., sell for anywhere between $500,000 and $1.5 million, 250 to 750 times the annual salary of a typical Chinese worker.[44] While such income gaps are not extreme by international standards, they are unsettling to a population unaccustomed to them.

As a consequence of the growing urban-rural gap, millions of peasants have been moving to the cities in search of jobs and a better life. But migration has exceeded the urban areas' capacities to absorb additional labor, and many unskilled migrants have joined a new, homeless, urban underclass. China's "floating population" of surplus labor (as these semi-illegal migrants are called) is estimated to include about 150 million people.[45] The growth of this new underclass has increased crime and other urban social ills. While it was technically illegal to move to the cities without government permission, the authorities generally ignored that regulation for many years and recently removed that restriction. Officials see these migrants, who drive down urban labor costs, as necessary for further economic expansion. They are frequently exploited and often are not paid the wages due them.

China's poor farmers were the major supporters of Mao's revolution and were the major beneficiaries of Deng's post-1978 economic reforms. Yet, as the urban-rural income gap reasserts itself and farmers chafe under corruption, government regulations, and high taxes, increasing numbers of rural protest demonstrations and riots suggest that the government is less able to count on peasant support.

Foreign Economic Ties

During the height of the Cultural Revolution, China isolated itself from the outside world and denounced Western and Soviet influences. Under Deng Xiaoping's **open-door policy** since the 1980s, however, cultural, trade, and investment ties to the West and to the overseas Chinese community in Asia have flourished. For example, the government opened special economic zones (SEZ) for foreign investment, primarily on

China's southeast coast. It invested heavily in the infrastructure there and offered multinational companies preferred treatment to bring in advanced foreign technology and expand manufactured exports. Today, China is the world's largest exporter of manufactured goods. Deng's successor, Jiang Zemin, widened the opening to the outside world as China entered the World Trade Organization (WTO). Membership opens up new opportunities for exports and for foreign investment at home. At the same time, however, it carries heavy risks, because local products will have to compete much more vigorously with imported goods. Inevitably, many inefficient Chinese firms, especially SOEs, will go out of business, adding to the country's growing urban unemployment.

Between 1979 and 1991, total foreign direct investment (FDI) in China averaged $2.16 billion annually. But from 1992 to 1996, FDI exploded to more than $40 billion per year, making China the largest recipient of foreign investment in the developing world.[46] And by 2002, China passed the United States as the world's leading recipient of FDI, reaching $100 billion that year. That investment has brought enormous prosperity to China's coastal cities and has contributed to an expanding middle class and skilled working class. But, as we have noted, living standards in the country's interior, particularly its rural villages, have lagged far behind.

CHINA'S POLITICAL SYSTEM: THE COMMUNIST PARTY

Turning our attention from China's economy to its political system, we will first examine the fundamental organisms of that nation's politics: the Communist Party and the government. Formal political institutions often have an ambiguous role in revolutionary societies. That was particularly true under Mao because of his inherent suspicion of the state and party bureaucracies. The Cultural Revolution's assault on party and state cadres was so savage that by the late 1960s, both political institutions were on the verge of collapse.

Although the constitution states that the Chinese Communist Party is subject to state authority, in fact the party has always been the principal policy maker. All the important government, military, and societal leaders (such as union heads) are party members and accept strict party discipline. The leader of the party, its general secretary—previously called the party chairman under Mao—has been among the country's most powerful leaders. Indeed, he has been *top* leader both before and after the years 1978–1997 (when Deng Xiaoping ruled from behind the scenes).

Party Membership

As we have seen, CCP membership expanded greatly from the start of the Japanese occupation through the end of World War II, and continued to grow after the PLA's victory. At the Communist Party's Fifth Congress (1945)—the last one held before the communists took power—national membership was 1,211,148. By the Sixth Congress (1956), it had risen to 10,734,384. Today, there are more than 66 million party members, constituting about 5 percent of China's total population. Fewer than one in five party members are women, who are underrepresented at all levels of the party. For party members coming out of the peasantry and urban poor, membership often opened previously unimaginable opportunities.

Party membership was a valuable asset but also a major commitment. Under Mao, members not only were expected to participate constantly in political activities but also were required to engage in "criticism–self-criticism" sessions that probed the depths of their revolutionary commitment. Those found wanting might be publicly disgraced. Today, the terms of membership are less demanding and the level of ideological scrutiny is far lower, but some members are still expelled periodically for corruption or lack of adequate commitment. Indeed, the party claims to have expelled 124,000 members for corruption between 1997 and 2002. In a few cases of extensive corruption, punishment can be extremely harsh. Thus, for example, in 2000, the vice-chairman of the National People's Congress was convicted of corruption and executed.[47] But these prosecutions still affect a small portion of those who are corrupt.

As in the Soviet Union, people's reasons for joining the party typically involved some mix of idealism and opportunism. Given the sharply diminished level of Chinese support for Marxism–Leninism in the last 15 years or more, there is evidence that the proportion of party members who have joined primarily for personal advancement has risen sharply. (See Box 14-1).

Party Structure

The CCP's structure was modeled after that of the Soviet Communist Party and is similarly hierarchical. Party authority is exerted from the national level down through provincial and local units. The principles of "democratic centralism" demand that party policies initially be discussed widely at all levels, but once the party's leaders have announced their positions, they must be obeyed without challenge. In fact, the primary purpose of local party discussions has been to legitimize leadership policies and give the rank-and-file a *feeling* of participation.

The most important components of the party are the National Party Congress, the Secretariat, the Central Committee, the Politburo, and the Standing Committee of the Politburo. The general secretary (party leader), currently Hu Jintao, is now limited to two five-year terms.

The National Party Congress met very infrequently under Mao Zedong, coming together only twice during the communists' first 20 years in power (in 1956 and 1969). Since the early 1970s, it has met more regularly but still gathers only once every five years for a few days. Some 4,000 delegates attended the last Congress in 2002. Although it is nominally the party's supreme authority, its very brief and infrequent meetings do little more than ratify decisions made by the CCP leadership. In fact, the major function of the National Party Congress is to "elect" the Central Committee, which it does by ratifying the choices of the party leaders.

Between party congresses (that is, most of the time), the Central Committee serves as the official authority in the party. Essentially, however, it merely endorses the choices given to its members. While its debates in recent years have been a bit more lively, it only meets once per year and, like the party congress, ratifies leadership decisions. Recently composed of 170 to 200 full-time and 100 to 150 part-time members, the Central Committee represents the party elite, including military officials and leaders of "mass organizations" representing women, youth, peasants, and workers. In recent years, it has become more educated and, hence, less representative of the general population. The number of Committee members who had graduated from college rose from 55 percent in 1982 to 98.6 percent in 2002. Over half now have degrees in science, engineering, management, or finance, giving them a very technocratic orientation.[48]

Box 14-1

CAPITALISTS CAN NOW BE COMMUNISTS

Because China's huge Communist Party has been the guiding force in national politics since 1949, two fundamental issues have been what requirements a person must satisfy to qualify for membership in the CCP and what types of people are eligible to join the party.

As long as the party was guided by Maoist ideology, the answers were relatively clear-cut. A party member had to believe in the ideological principles of "Marxism–Leninism, Mao Zedong Thought," which included a belief in ongoing class struggle and a strong commitment to societal equality. Membership was encouraged from the formerly "oppressed masses"— namely, the working class and the peasantry—and, next, from committed professionals and bureaucrats (Mao himself had been a librarian).

In the years since Deng Xiaoping's ascendancy in the late 1970s, those standards have changed appreciably. Income differences and other inequalities that Mao so abhorred have become acceptable and, indeed, are even encouraged by government policies. Economic growth in China's coastal cities, spurred by a rising private sector, has created huge gaps between standards of living in those cities and those of the rest of the country, particularly the rural interior. With the opportunities offered by an expanding private sector and with Deng's declaration that "to get rich is glorious," a new class of wealthy business entrepreneurs and middle-class professionals has developed. Mao's exhortations to the Chinese people to sacrifice everything for the good of the whole (and the revolution) have

been forgotten as the Communist Party legitimizes itself by preaching "happiness through consumption."[49] Although China was once among the world's most egalitarian societies, its income distribution today is not only more unequal than in much of Europe and Asia but also worse than in the United States (one of the most unequal industrialized nations).

As one American journalist observed, "In practice there is little these days that is communist about China, a country where laid-off workers hunt for jobs, yuppies buy stocks and houses, and since last year, private businessmen have been recruited as party members."[50] As a result of those changes and as a consequence of the mass disillusionment brought about by the 1989 Tiananmen Square massacre and subsequent government repression, few people in China today believe in communist ideology. Indeed, in one survey, Communist Party members were asked whether they were proud to be party members. A surprising 43 percent said they weren't.[51] More surprisingly, most independent analysts doubt that many Communist Party members believe in Marxism–Leninism, either. Most of the more than 60 million party members join out of opportunism—that is, for the material advantages and prestige it brings. In one survey of 800 graduating university students *who belonged to the Communist Party or Communist Youth League,* only 38 (under 5 percent) stated that they believed in communism.[52] Even at the higher ranks of the party and the government, China's leaders seem to espouse communism merely

---

The Communist Party and the People's Liberation Army have long been closely linked, and the military has been well represented in the Central Committee, and the Politburo. At the same time, however, the party's Central Military Commission (CMC) governs the military and ensures civilian control over the armed forces. The PLA's political influence peaked in the late 1960s, receded under Deng, and slightly rebounded under Jiang Zemin. On the one hand, military involvement in politics has generally diminished over the past decades because of the growing professionalism of the officers' corps. On the other hand, because Jiang's power base was more limited than either Mao's or Deng's, he was particularly dependent on the military's support, causing the armed forces' political influence to grow somewhat.[53] Jiang was also the first CMC chair who had not formerly been an army general.

At the top of China's power structure sit the CCP's Politburo (currently consisting of 24 members including alternates) and its Standing Committee—now a subgroup of nine members—which carries out day-to-day operations and consists of the party's most powerful figures. Both the Politburo and the party itself are led by the general secretary.

© Keren Su/CORBIS

AN ECONOMIC GIANT   As one of the world's largest and fastest growing cities, prosperous Shanghai, with its impressive skyline, has become a symbol of China's economic growth.

for the sake of keeping themselves in power. Many top political leaders send their children to study or live in the West. Thus, in place of Marxism, the CCP now seeks support as the protector of stability and nationalism.

In the summer of 2001, Jiang Zemin and the Politburo opened party membership to private-sector entrepreneurs (businessmen), the very group that Mao and other traditional communists had seen as the enemies of the peasantry and the working class.

Until the 1980s, the Politburo was an aging group whose members often traced their communist credentials to the early days of the Revolutionary War. Five of the 28 members elected in 1982 were more than 80 years old, and the entire group averaged 72 years of age. Once entrenched in power, however, Deng Xiaoping, himself then approaching 80, pushed for a younger party leadership. By 1987, the average age of Politburo members was eight years younger than it had been in 1982. Today, in addition to being younger, Politburo members are more educated than their predecessors, more likely to have a technocratic background, and less likely to have come out of the military.[54]

Yet, under Deng's reign, this transfer of power to a younger generation was more apparent than real. China's aged leaders, particularly Deng and a small group of party elders (mostly over 80 years old), retained their power from behind the scenes, even after their formal retirement, and younger party leaders still depended on them for support.

Deng's death in 1997—after years of infirmity—finally allowed the transfer of political power from Deng's "second generation" of revolutionary leadership (after Mao's) to a **"third generation"** composed of "younger men" primarily in their sixties or even early seventies. Jiang Zemin, who had been named as Deng's eventual successor eight years earlier, became China's paramount leader.

Not long after Deng's death, Jiang's supporters enforced a party rule requiring the CCP's "core leaders" (those under consideration for appointment to the Politburo) to retire at the age of 70 and mandated that Politburo members already in their seventies retire at the next party congress (held that year and then every five years). At the 1997 Fifteenth Party Congress, six of the seven "core leaders"—many of them potential challengers to Jiang—who were more than 70 years old *did* resign (some quite reluctantly). Jiang, however, the last of the seven, did not retire because his comrades allegedly begged him not to. He subsequently did retire, however, at the next party congress in 2002 (at age 76) and transferred his last powers (control of the military) to the new general secretary in 2004. This was the first transfer of power other than through death in Communist China's history.

As we have seen with the Politburo, other important party organisms have experienced a very gradual shift toward younger figures. For example, Central Committee members at the 1997 party congress were significantly younger than their predecessors, averaging 55.9 years of age.[55] When Vice President Hu Jintao succeeded Jiang as CCP general secretary at the 2002 party congress, he assumed the leadership of the party at the relatively tender age (by Chinese standards) of 60. The Premier and most of China's top communist officials are of a similar age, with the Politburo installed at the 2002 Party Congress averaging 61 years of age. Retirement for all Politburo members is now fixed at 70 years.[56] Informally it is also understood that the party general secretary should be limited to two (five-year) terms and should also retire by the age of 70.[57] Thus, at the Sixteenth Congress, over half the members of the previous Politburo were forced to retire because of the new age limits, producing the biggest turnover in that body during the past 25 years.

THE STRUCTURE OF GOVERNMENT

China's government primarily administers policies initiated by the Communist Party, but the impact of the government's vast bureaucracy on day-to-day life is enormous. The state affects vast areas of public activity, controlling a substantial (though declining) portion of the economy and many functions reserved for the private sphere in pluralist democracies. During the Maoist period, Premier Zhou Enlai, the leading government official, provided the administrative skills that Mao lacked. He helped to keep the government together and to return society to a degree of normality after the chaos of the Cultural Revolution.

Under Deng Xiaoping, the influence of China's premiers (prime ministers) often matched that of the party general secretary, and both figures (along with the nation's president) were beholden to Deng, who held nominally less-powerful positions. Jiang Zemin, of course, was both general secretary of the CCP and president of the nation. Although he had to negotiate and, to some degree, share power with other important party figures, there was no Deng-like figure behind the scenes pulling the strings of power. Since Deng's death, the premier has again become less powerful than the party general secretary.

The National People's Congress (NPC)

The NPC is China's legislature, whose primary function is to legitimize rather than evaluate legislation proposed by the national leadership. Since the 1980s, however,

NPC sessions have sometimes featured policy debates, and the government's legislative proposals occasionally have been amended. Shortly after the post-Tiananmen political crackdown ended (1992), nearly one-third of the NPC's nearly 3,000 deputies either abstained from voting or voted against the government's controversial proposal to build the massive, environmentally destructive Three Gorges hydroelectric dam.[58] In 1998, 45 percent of NPC delegates would not vote for a government report on corruption (either abstaining or voting against the report). Negative votes of 20 to 30 percent on the government's draft legislation have become common. Since its members (elected every five years) include some deputies who are not party members, the NPC offers the leaders a somewhat broader perspective on issues. In recent years a small number of its members have spoken out against government proposals and it has exercised growing influence, sometimes convincing the leadership to amend its policies.

The State Council and the Premier

The national government's major executive body is the State Council, whose members direct the national government's ministries and commissions. Its most important concern is economic administration, but it also plays an important role in such areas as education, science, technology, and foreign affairs. In 1998, the Council was reduced in size (the number of Ministries and bureaucrats was cut back), reflecting the state's diminished role in the economy. As of 2005 it had 35 members. Most ministers also sit on the CCP's Central Committee, reflecting the substantial overlap between government and party leadership. Because of its large size, the State Council carries out most of its work in a smaller Standing Committee. At the State Council's head is the premier, who plays a pivotal role in policy making, especially economic policy. A recent premier, Zhu Rongji, for example, was given much of the credit for restoring China's economic growth after the Asian financial crisis of 1998 and for maintaining a low level of inflation. Usually, the premier is the second- or third-highest-ranking leader of the Communist Party.

Elections: The NPC and Local Officials

During the Maoist era, elections of government officials were essentially meaningless. Popular "elections" (with no choice) took place only at the village or local level for representatives to the "basic-level" People's Congress. Those representatives then elected the legislature for the administrative level immediately above them: Basic-level delegates elected their county or city congress; they, in turn, elected their provincial representatives; and finally, the various provincial congresses elected the National People's Congress (NPC).

In 1979, the government introduced several very modest gestures toward greater political openness. Voters now elect township-level and county congresses directly and can often choose between more than one candidate in local races. Legislation in 1987 and 1998 extended that right so that today rural villages, townships, and counties directly select their officials in competitive elections. In many villages, very likely the majority, villagers still do not have a real choice. But in other rural communities there are genuinely competitive elections. These officials make fundamental decisions on local budgets, taxes, and village development.[59] Sometimes these village leaders have challenged the authority of the local Communist Party secretaries, who officially outrank them and who are not elected. National and provincial legislatures are still elected indirectly. And city dwellers still do not elect their local officials.

The Judicial System

The Chinese legal system differs greatly from the U.S. system in that it includes two components: a formal court system and "extrajudicial" structures through which a defendant's neighbors, co-workers, or other peers exert social pressure on the defendant. During the more radical periods of Chinese politics—most notably, from the Great Leap Forward through the Cultural Revolution (1958–1976)—extrajudicial structures were dominant. During more moderate periods, the formal system has prevailed.[60]

In both periods, however, the courts have been subordinated to the Communist Party, and there has been no process of judicial review. At the same time, the defense lawyers' role has not been to defend their clients but rather to "safeguard the interests of the state."[61] In this arena as well, there has been some progress since Deng's ascendancy, which continued during the Jiang Zemin years. Chinese intellectuals, dissidents, and businesspeople have begun to bring suit against CCP organizations and government officials for defamation of character, abuse of power, and other violations. Although such suitors generally lose and sometimes suffer retribution, in some high-profile cases they have caused government officials to back down.[62]

A recent study found that prison conditions in China vary considerably from place to place depending on decisions made by the relevant provincial government.[63] Punishment in the penal system is still generally very harsh and the system has aroused much international criticism. Western news media have exposed instances of Chinese exports (or, frequently, exports of multinational corporations manufacturing in China) made by prisoners under inhumane work conditions. Many crimes—including rape, robbery of substantial sums, bribing of certain government personnel, damaging of state property, embezzlement, tax evasion, and distribution of pornography—are potentially punishable by death. Not only does China lead the world in *legal* executions, but for a number of years *its total (5,000 to 10,000 in 2001) has exceeded that of all other nations combined.* Several years ago, reports exposed certain prison officials who had been harvesting the organs of executed prisoners to sell for transplants abroad. Prison authorities claimed that the prisoners had consented to the harvesting beforehand.

A variety of legal reforms since the mid-1990s have expanded the rights of defendants, allowed defense lawyers greater independence from the state, abolished the crime of counterrevolutionary activity, and, since 1996, established the principle that defendants are considered innocent until convicted. Despite those and other reforms in the criminal code, however, 99 percent of all criminal defendants are still found guilty.[64] Thus, any improvement in a criminal defendant's rights has come at the pre-trial stage (i.e., the decision on whether or not to bring charges). Confessions are often coerced out of criminal defendants through torture, and witnesses supporting the defendant are frequently barred from testifying. One recent account details how a prisoner was tortured into admitting to have murdered a woman whom, in fact, he had never met. The judge refused to allow him to recant his confession, and he was convicted and sentenced to death. Two years later, while the defendant was on death row, a serial killer confessed to several murders, including that one, and provided information that only the killer could have known. The police tried to remove that murder from the serial killer's confession and to continue with the other defendant's execution. The man was saved only when a police official subsequently joked about the incident to a reporter.[65]

PROBLEMS OF POLITICAL REFORM

Discussions of transformations in the communist world often have overstated the linkages between economic reform and political reform. Some argue that a market economy cannot develop effectively without a parallel loosening of state political controls. In theory, reducing state control over the economy and over people's lives at the workplace, creating a larger and more independent private sector, and increasing the size of the middle class should eventually create strong pressures for democratic change. Yet, dramatic economic changes in China so far have produced only limited political liberalization.

Since Deng introduced his first comprehensive economic reforms, contending factions in the CCP elite have debated the nature and the pace of economic and political change. During the 1980s, reformers such as Hu Yaobang (party general secretary from 1981 to 1987) and, especially, Zhao Ziyang (premier from 1980 to 1987 and party general secretary from 1987 to 1989) favored economic modernization and greater political freedoms, although not democracy. On the other hand, conservatives* such as Li Peng (premier from 1987 to 1998 and subsequently head of the national congress) remained skeptical about far-reaching economic or political reforms.

Though conceding the need to reduce centralized economic planning, conservatives have warned of the dangers they see as inherent in a transition toward the free market (including greater corruption and inflation). More important, they see no reason to link economic liberalization (reduction of state economic controls) to political reform. In earlier years, they pointed to the "economic miracles" that had taken place in Taiwan, South Korea, and Singapore under the direction of right-wing authoritarian governments.† During the decade that followed Mao's death, political repression lessened, and the Chinese people enjoyed a more relaxed political atmosphere, particularly when compared with the terror of the Cultural Revolution. People have been spared the constant barrage of political indoctrination that had characterized the Maoist era. Dissident intellectuals such as astrophysicist Fang Lizhi spoke for a budding human rights movement. At least in the cities, average citizens have expressed themselves more freely in private conversations. And, in contrast to the all-encompassing cultural indoctrination of the Maoist era, popular culture—partly imported from Hong Kong and Taiwan—now includes rock music, independent art, and literature.[66] In general, citizens who wish to avoid politics are now relatively free to select a lifestyle of their own choosing. At the same time, however, the government has severely persecuted many members of the nation's Tibetan and Muslim minorities believed to support secessionist movements. And in recent years, it has imprisoned thousands of members of the **Falun Gong**, a spiritual sect stressing meditation and exercises, with hundreds allegedly dying while in police custody.

Thus, despite some progress, China has not achieved a degree of political openness comparable to that of the USSR under *glasnost*. Ironically, because of the great

---

* The use of the terms *radical*, *liberal*, and *conservative* in the context of Chinese communism can be confusing to Americans. Whereas "radicals" in the Maoist era were those who supported Marxist orthodoxy, in the 1980s radical reformers (and liberals) were those who wanted to move away from mainstream Marxism. "Conservative" in today's China describes those who wish to maintain traditional Marxist ideas (just as conservatives everywhere tend to favor maintaining the status quo).

† Ironically, just as China's hard-liners were admiring Taiwan and South Korea for having fashioned dramatic economic growth and equitable distribution under authoritarian rule, those nations started their transition toward greater democracy.

success of their economic reforms, Chinese leaders were not under the same pressures as Gorbachev was to open up the political system. Nor did Deng face the challenge from ethnic minorities that weakened the Soviet system, since 93 percent of the Chinese population is of the same ethnicity: Han (although ethnic unrest has been a factor in the more remote regions of the country).[67]

The Chinese press, despite being somewhat more open to critical discussion than previously, is not nearly as independent as the Russian media became under Gorbachev. Indeed, censorship and periodic arrests of journalists have increased since Hu Jintao assumed power in 2002. As Nicholas Kristof recently observed, "China now imprisons more journalists than any other country."[68] Obviously, the long prison terms to which some journalists have been sentenced have led their colleagues to practice self-censorship. In 2006, after the government had shut down Freezing Point, an influential news journal, a group of former high party and press officials denounced the closure, suggesting divisions within the party regarding censorship. To be sure, the mass political executions and other gross excesses of the Maoist era have come to an end, but the state continues to jail and torture political prisoners selectively.

Despite a relaxation of repression since the early 1990s, there has been no real movement toward democracy. Instead, the government has permitted some **political liberalization,** a general (but not universal) loosening of authoritarian controls and repression. The party now allows people greater freedom to choose their own lifestyles and to speak their minds in personal conversations. Indeed, as the state's economic role has receded, it has lost some of its power to control people's personal lives. The constant campaigns and indoctrination of the Maoist era are long gone. Kenneth Lieberthal, a noted expert on Chinese politics, describes the present system as "fragmented authoritarianism" (indicating that some cracks in the system have opened it up somewhat), and Harry Harding calls it "consultative authoritarianism."[69]

SOURCES OF DISCONTENT

The Problems and Limits of Economic Reform

Although China's economic transformation since the late 1970s has been nothing short of astonishing, the Western media have often exaggerated the scope of reform and underestimated the problems that it has produced. For example, some analysts have argued that Chinese leaders were leading their nation inexorably away from centralized planning toward a market economy.

In fact, even today the state continues to own important portions of the economy and to tightly regulate other parts. The ongoing conflict between the conservative and liberal factions of the Communist Party caused government policy under Deng Xiaoping to swing back and forth from left to right. At times, further change was slowed or even stopped as conservatives in the party leadership defended aspects of a centrally planned economy (though nobody in recent years has proposed *reversing* the market reforms). Although the Western media often viewed Deng as a liberal, in truth he actually tried to balance the two factions, often siding with the conservatives on political matters (cracking down on dissidents) to win their support for liberal economic measures.

Economic policy debates continued under Jiang Zemin, but policy swings were less dramatic. In part, that is because the conservatives have largely lost the battle and accepted the transition to a more market-driven economy. In part, it is because Jiang was much more cautious than Deng had been about innovating change. The current president and CCP leader, Hu Jintao, has slowly continued the process of market reforms (indeed, his daughter is married to a rich Chinese businessman) but has taken an increasingly hard line against political reform and has cracked down on dissent.

The West's admiration and worry about China's economic miracle since the 1980s is quite understandable. From 1980 to 1986, the Chinese economy grew at the astonishing rate of 10.5 percent annually, the highest of any major nation in the world (only South Korea at 8.2 percent was close) and ahead of all other developing nations. After a mild slowdown in 1989 and 1990, annual GNP growth surpassed 12 percent in 1992–1994 and then averaged about 8 percent through 2004. In all, China's GNP quadrupled from 1978 to 2004. As we have noted, using one measuring rod of national output (PPP) it is now the world's second-largest economy.[70] The country's standard of living has increased correspondingly, though it remains low by U.S. standards.

This tremendous economic expansion, however, has produced a number of problems. In the late 1980s and early 1990s, an overheated economy brought serious inflation for the first time since the creation of the People's Republic. Although the 1988 and 1989 annual inflation rates of 20 to 30 percent were not high by Third World standards, they provoked panic buying among Chinese consumers accustomed to constant prices in the previous decades.[71] Inflation has been under control since 1996 but could surge if the economy again overheats. The government has announced its intentions of slowing down growth from its 2004 level of 9 percent in order to reduce inefficient investments and economic bottlenecks.

Perhaps the most enduring and despised negative side effect of market reform and rapid economic growth, however, has been increased government corruption. As foreign corporations and China's own private sector have rapidly expanded their activities, private firms still depend on the state for many critical inputs. A new class of influence peddlers has developed, composed of people whose political clout can cut through bureaucratic red tape to secure needed licenses, credit, parts, and raw materials for the right price. Often, these intermediaries are cadres who are the children of more powerful party and government officials.[72] During the 1980s, Deng Xiaoping's son, known to be a very rich man, became a national symbol of such hated corruption. The widespread perception of official malfeasance has undermined the government's legitimacy and battered the image of honesty that the Communist Party had established under Mao.* A recent opinion survey revealed that "corruption remains the most important source of public discontent with the regime," with 71 percent of respondents expressing dissatisfaction with the integrity of public officials and only 4 percent claiming they were satisfied.[73]

The Causes of the Student Democracy Movement

Discontent over several of these issues helped spawn the country's most powerful and threatening protest movement since the revolution, the student democracy movement of 1989. That huge movement threatened to topple the communist government or at least dramatically change its character. Ultimately, the breadth of the democracy movement and its eventual brutal repression dramatically altered China's image in the

---

* Not only is corruption pervasive in China today, but also the public's perception of the problem is somewhat exaggerated by the fact that some normal business practices are considered illegitimate by Chinese who are unaccustomed to a market economy. For example, many Chinese feel that it is corrupt for any businessperson to make very large profits.

world and has influenced the course of Chinese political attitudes until today. In some ways, it is quite surprising that a major protest movement of that type should have erupted when it did. During the preceding decade, China's standard of living had doubled, agricultural production had soared, and consumer goods had become far more available. At the same time, political regimentation had eased. Still, as Martin King Whyte has noted, many urban Chinese felt that reform had not gone far enough, and others believed it had gone too far.[74]

The government's open-door policy to the outside world had been designed to bring the country into the modern technological age. But as Chinese governments had discovered as far back as the early nineteenth century, it is impossible to import foreign technology and know-how without also exposing the population to new cultural and political values, some of which may be threatening to the ruling elite. As thousands of young Chinese studied in Western European and American universities; as foreign tourists and businesspeople poured into China; as foreign films, literature, and radio broadcasts became more widely available, Chinese students, professionals, entrepreneurs, and intellectuals could hardly fail to be influenced by foreign ideas. Many were impressed by Western-style democracy, and others looked enviously at Mikhail Gorbachev's policies of *glasnost* and *perestroika* in the Soviet Union.

The initial cause of the student demonstrations was dissatisfaction over living conditions and job prospects. Upon graduation, "most [students] could look forward to lives earning modest and largely fixed salaries in jobs not of their choosing, under less-educated supervisors who often did not appreciate their talents. . . ."[75] As their protest expanded, however, the students' goals reached far beyond their personal well-being. Though not necessarily favoring Western-style democracy, student leaders and their supporters desired a more open society—including greater freedom of speech, more independent mass media, and reduced political repression. Interviews of student activists suggested that most of them were primarily interested in reforming the system from within rather than overturning it. Some political leaders, most notably CCP General Secretary Zhao Ziyang, favored dialogue with the students.

But government hard-liners became increasingly anxious as they saw student protesters joined by large numbers of workers, government bureaucrats, and intellectuals. Protests spread to dozens of Chinese cities, and demands widened. As the base of dissent grew, marches in Beijing drew as many as one million people, many of them moved by resentment over nonideological issues such as inflation and government corruption.

When Deng finally threw his support to the hard-liners, martial law was declared, and troops were brought to the capital to clear Tiananmen Square and break up the demonstration. On June 4, 1989, the PLA brutally ended the democracy movement, killing hundreds of young people who were encamped in the square. In the city of Chengdu, hundreds more died in clashes between protesters and police.

The Aftermath of Tiananmen Square

The crushing of the democracy movement led to a broader crackdown on political dissent and the purge of several high-ranking party and government reformers. CCP General Secretary Zhao Ziyang was stripped of power and replaced by Jiang Zemin, who later also served as the nation's president. Throughout society, political controls were tightened. Several thousand student and worker activists were arrested in the months following the Tiananmen massacre; many of them sentenced to long jail terms.

Once again, as in 1983 and 1987, there was a substantial upsurge in ideological indoctrination. In short, much of the progress away from totalitarian politics during the 1980s was, at least temporarily, rolled back.

But the post-Tiananmen crackdown was relatively short-lived. Pro-reform government officials at the local and provincial levels successfully resisted many conservative economic efforts and by 1992, the forces of economic reform returned in full force. The degree of political repression after Tiananmen, although substantial, was far lower than in the Maoist era. Since 1992, many freedoms have been restored and individual rights, at least outside the political arena, are now more respected than they had been before the student democracy movement. Today, young Chinese can surf the Internet (although with government censorship), listen to Western rock or their favorite Taiwanese singers, and aspire to be rich businessmen. At the same time, most of them consciously avoid politics.

OBSTACLES TO DEMOCRATIC CHANGE

At the height of the massive demonstrations in 1989, with hundreds of thousands of workers and students protesting and the first government troops unwilling to use force against them, some analysts speculated that the communist regime was on the verge of collapse. In fact, it was not nearly as vulnerable as the communist governments of Eastern Europe proved to be when they fell from power later that year or when the Soviet regime itself collapsed in 1991. Today, few believe that the Chinese communist regime will collapse in the foreseeable future. How has the Chinese government managed to maintain one of the few remaining communist states (along with Cuba, North Korea, and Vietnam)?

Some experts on democratic transitions have argued that China's political culture, like that of many other Asian nations, is not as hospitable to democracy as are Western cultures.[76] China's Confucian culture, those critics argue, emphasizes hierarchy, harmony, order, and subordination of the people to their rulers. All of these would be challenged by the turmoil that would likely accompany a transition to democracy. Cultural explanations also point out that democracy was slow in coming to other Confucian nations, such as South Korea and Taiwan, even after they had achieved high income and educational levels. Even student leaders in the 1989 demonstrations had a vision of good government that was quite different from Western ideals of democracy.[77]

A related historical argument contends that China has no democratic tradition to build upon and has been cut off from democratic change outside its borders. Ironically, survey research suggests traditional Confucian values appear to have a greater impact in the political culture of communist China than they do in Taiwan or Hong Kong.[78]

Although cultural and historical explanations such as those no doubt have some validity, they fail to address the fact that values and traditions can change. Even if it is true that Confucian values slowed the transitions to democracy in South Korea and Taiwan (and many would dispute that), those countries *have* created a more democratic political culture and now have successfully made the transition to democratic government.

China's social structure, rather than its culture or history, may offer a more useful explanation for the regime's ability to resist democratic forces. Unlike the former USSR, Eastern Europe, South Korea, or Taiwan, China is still populated primarily by peasants. Historically, peasants throughout the world have been less supportive of democracy than have the middle and working classes.[79] In China, the student-led democracy movement was confined to the cities and never spread to rural regions, where 75 percent of the Chinese people resided at that time. It is hard to know how the Chinese peasantry felt about the protest, but Western journalists who traveled to rural communities during the pro-democracy demonstrations found villagers generally indifferent. Few of them understood the protesters' demands, since their only information came from government radio and television. Despite China's many political mobilization campaigns, most peasants remained passive until the 1990s. Indeed, the ebbs and flows of past political campaigns and the violence and deaths often associated with them have made many peasants wary of independent political activity.

Of course, the Tiananmen protests came at the end of a decade in which the peasants had been the major beneficiaries of Deng Xiaoping's economic reforms. Rural living standards, although still very low by Western criteria, have more than tripled since resumption of private farming began in the early 1980s. Not surprisingly, then, the students' concerns about media freedom and job opportunities and the workers' anger over corruption and inflation carried less weight in China's peasant villages (although peasant resentment over corrupt local officials later became a major source of discontent).

Even today, with China's rural population still representing about 60 percent of the national total, as long as the government maintains the support of the rural population, its strength will be formidable. But, in the last two decades, peasant discontent has clearly increased. In their book *Chinese Village, Socialist State*, several noted scholars argued that, despite their economic gains in the 1980s, many Chinese peasants were unhappy about ongoing government intervention in their lives and about the state's imposition of low prices for their crops.[80] Since the early 1990s, rural unrest has spread as peasants have demonstrated against corrupt or repressive local government and CCP officials and have been angered by the government's one-child policy (see Box 14-2). At times, villages have seized government buildings, held officials hostage, and blocked roads. In other instances, peasants have elected noncommunist village officials who have challenged local (unelected) party bosses. Should peasant unrest eventually become sufficiently widespread, it would pose a major threat to the regime.

In urban areas, the situation is also complex. The government has crushed all student and worker resistance, but has done so at a heavy cost to its own legitimacy. The mood in the cities, particularly among young people, seems to be one of resignation. Young Chinese today are much more critical of Marxism than they were before the Tiananmen Square crackdown. Whereas then they may have hoped to reform communism, now they seem to have lost any faith in it. Nor is cynicism limited to China's youth. A few years ago, even several high-ranking Chinese government officials (some as high up as the ministerial level) privately told a *New York Times* correspondent that they had no faith in communism. (See Boxes 14-1 and 14-3.) Disillusionment is surely even more widespread at the middle and lower levels of government and the party.

As in the countryside, urban protests have been on the rise in recent years. Some of the largest have been motivated by workers' discontent over losing their jobs with state-owned enterprises (government companies). For example, in 2002, tens of thousands of laid-off workers protested in the city of Daqing when a state-owned petroleum company failed to pay them their promised severance pay. Protests by terminated workers have spread, particularly in the country's northeast, home to some of the country's most outdated industrial plants.[81] Other workers have mounted large-scale demonstrations after being evicted to make room for urban development projects (often by government officials who have been bribed by urban developers). Yet other

Box 14-2

CHINA'S ONE-CHILD POLICY AND THE GENDER GAP

One important source of discontent in the countryside has been the government's so-called "**one-child**" **policy**. Despite China's huge population, during the first three decades of the communist regime government officials then insisted that population growth added to the nation's strength. By 1979, however, China's population neared one billion, almost twice what it had been in 1949. Government officials concluded that lowering population growth was imperative. A new policy was introduced limiting families in cities and some rural areas to a single child. In other rural regions family size was to be limited to two children. Families that did not adhere to those limits would lose government benefits or might be forced to have abortions. Government propaganda has stressed the patriotic need to adhere to these controls, and enforcement has been carried out by neighborhood watch groups (consisting primarily of elderly women).

The policy has helped reduce fertility rates from 5.8 births per woman to 1.9 and has cut annual population growth from 2.7 percent to less than 1 percent. The greatest drops have been in the cities, where many families have accepted the idea of one-child families, which enables parents to concentrate their educational and other spending on their only child. In rural areas, however, where children are considered an important economic asset (to help farm the land and support their parents in their old age), the policy has provoked considerable resistance. Still, even there birth rates also have declined (though not as dramatically). Given the huge strain that China's rapid economic growth has put on its (and the world's) natural resources and on the environment, the ecological benefits of limiting population growth are very significant.

At the same time, however, the policy also has had unfortunate social consequences. Because Chinese culture traditionally has valued sons more than daughters, especially in rural areas, a substantial number of families have made sure that one child would be male. This means that many expectant mothers, whose medical tests have revealed that they are pregnant with girls, have chosen to have abortions. Many others have engaged in female infanticide or abandonment of daughters. Orphanages, for example, have far more girls than boys. And because of the large number of female babies killed shortly after birth, the ratio of boys to girls—normally 106 to 100—has reached 117 to 100. During the 1990s, the number of recorded female births was more than 6 percent below what it would normally be.[82] To be sure, not all of this can be blamed on government policy. Female infanticide was common in China long before the 1949 revolution, as families with limited resources for additional children wanted to make sure their offspring would be male. And in India, without comparable government pressures, female infanticide and selective abortions have also sharply increased because of cultural preferences for boys. Still, there is little doubt that the compulsory nature of China's program has added to the problem.

In recent years, China's leaders have become concerned about these unanticipated negative results, particularly the bitterness that population control has caused in the countryside. Also of concern is the prospect of some 30 million men being unable to find mates two to three decades from now and a rapidly growing elderly population having to be supported by a decreasing urban work force. Consequently, leading government officials have recently made pronouncements about the worth of women. More importantly, the government has begun to relax its one-child policy and has made it illegal for medical providers to tell parents the sex of their expected child.

---

protests have erupted in neighborhoods that had been exposed to industrial pollution. Recently, as many as 15,000 protesters in a Shanghai suburb hurled rocks at police in extended demonstrations demanding the shutdown of a pharmaceutical plant, which residents blame for polluting the atmosphere. These protesters had been inspired by riots three months earlier in a city only 50 miles away, where 10 thousand demonstrators had overrun police (killing several of them) and forced at least the temporary shutdown of a pesticide plant.[83] Occasionally, demonstrators may actually be successful, persuading higher-ranking government officials to curtail an unpopular local project

---

Box 14-3

THE GLORIFICATION OF WEALTH

Only a generation ago, China, perhaps more than any nation on earth, decried class differences and viewed wealth as a vice. In the aftermath of the Tiananmen Square massacre, a new generation of urban youth, many of them the children of Red Guards, worship personal success and the accumulation of wealth. The number of private autos in China has tripled in the last five years. "Despite general contempt for the ruling regime . . . some young Chinese . . . pay lip service to official ideology as a means of getting ahead." But the most successful youth are those who have become entrepreneurs in the growing private sector (often the children of government or party cadres). They "can be seen shopping for upmarket clothing . . . in the exclusive boutiques of Beijing and Shanghai" or buying "diamond or sapphire brooches and rings at $1,000 or more"—more than an average annual urban wage.[84]

---

or remove a corrupt local official. But most protests fail and the government harshly represses any movement that challenges Communist Party hegemony, such as attempts to form labor unions independent of party control.

In fact, almost all of these large protests have been aimed at specific local officials or particular complaints. There is currently little disposition to challenge communism or the regime itself. That brings us to a final explanation for the communist regime's longevity, the success of the country's economic reforms. Communist regimes fell in the Soviet Union and Eastern Europe after their economies had begun to decay (see Chapter 13). Mikhail Gorbachev's halfway reform measures in the USSR only accelerated the problem. By contrast, China's population has generally enjoyed an unparalleled increase in its standard of living during the past two decades. Although that growth has not been without its problems—most notably growing inequality and occasional inflation—the fact that most Chinese are living better than their parents could have ever imagined has made them less predisposed to challenge the political system.

Still, while citizen protests have remained very localized and as of yet pose no threat to the government, they are becoming more frequent. In the last decade, peasants have demonstrated—sometimes violently—against corrupt and arbitrary local communist officials, high taxes, failure to receive the government's promised price for their crops, confiscation of their land, pollution by power plants, and harsh birth-control policies. For example, many local village and party officials have been known to confiscate villagers' land and then sell it (for personal profit) to private developers. Farmers who resist may be subjected to police intimidation. Such land seizures have spawned many of the recent peasant protests. This sprawl of factories, housing, and shopping centers has reduced significantly the area of China's arable land, posing a threat, not only to farmers, but to the country's food supply (a particular problem since only one-fourth of China's territory is arable). Peasants are particularly upset that their tax rate is considerably higher than that of city dwellers although their incomes are much lower.

According to government reports, in 1993 there were 1.5 million cases of rural protests. Most of these involved one or two people, but 830 of them included more than 500 participants and 78 involved more than 1,000 protesters. In two months of 1997 alone, widespread rural anti-tax riots involved half a million people.[85] Some of these became quite violent. Thus, for example, during one year in the early 1990s rural demonstrations led to the injury of 8,200 government officials and the deaths of 560 policemen. Since that time, rates of rural protest increased sharply. Looking only at large-scale demonstrations, another government study indicated that there had been about 10,000 protests in 1994 (urban and rural), but that figure had risen to 74,000 a decade later.[86] Sometimes local officials impose illegal taxes (bound for their own pockets), pocket some of the taxes, or refuse to distribute tax refunds. Protesters sometimes succeed in removing such officials or in getting some financial satisfaction. In early 2005, responding to rural discontent, the national government promised a small reduction in rural taxes.

Occasionally, local Communist Party officials have even been put on trial for police violence committed against demonstrators. But, in general, the protesters' complaints have not been satisfied. A 2005 protest in the village of Dongzhou aimed to prevent the construction of a new coal-fired electric power plant. Here, as in previous instances, farmers had seen their land confiscated, with little compensation. Police opened fire on several hundred villagers, many armed with homemade bombs, killing perhaps 30 protesters. Subsequently, when news of the incident seeped out, the government imposed a news blackout and both bribed and threatened witnesses in the village not to reveal to outsiders what had happened.[87]

CHINA'S UNCERTAIN FUTURE

Soon after the Tiananmen massacre, Western diplomats and Chinese democracy activists both widely predicted that communist rule would crumble within three or four years. But, in recent years, even the party's harshest critics have been hard put to offer a convincing reason why it could not muddle through into the foreseeable future.[88]

Of course, history is full of surprises. Nobody could have predicted in 1986 that the Communist Party would lose control of the USSR in five years, and few would have predicted in 1995 that the same would happen to PRI dominance in Mexico (Chapters 13 and 17). China's policy lurches and internal unrest since the 1950s have exceeded those of either the Soviet Union or Mexico. Yet, because of the combination of economic, social, and cultural factors just discussed, no credible challenge to the CCP has yet emerged. As we have observed, few Chinese—not even CCP officials—believe in Marxism-Leninism anymore. And many people look upon the ruling party as a self-serving, corrupt machine. Yet, Chinese civil society—the network of organized groups in society that are independent of government control—remains extremely weak, and there has not been much disposition to challenge the nation's powerful military and internal security forces.

More recently, those China experts who expected Deng Xiaoping's death to bring about fierce internal struggles between contending leaders were equally mistaken, underestimating the strength both of his successor, Jiang Zemin, and of the communist regime. At the Sixteenth Party Congress in 2002, the party carried out its most orderly transfer of power ever (the first not brought about by the death of the former leader), as Hu Jintao succeeded Jiang as general secretary. The following year Hu replaced Jiang as president. Until 2004, Jiang continued to exercise considerable power, both because he had hand picked a majority of the Standing Committee of the Politburo and because he continued to chair the powerful Central Military Committee, the position that Deng Xiaoping had used for decades as his power base. But, in September of 2004, Jiang resigned from that post as well, turning it over to Hu and completing the transfer of power. China's leaders are now less divided into rival factions than in past years. The new leadership, however, will have to deal with a number of underlying economic, political, and social problems that, if left unsolved, may eventually undermine the present political system.

Probably the regime's two most pressing socioeconomic challenges in the near future are maintaining the country's high rate of economic growth and combating the growing economic inequality that the growth model has produced in recent years. It is totally unlikely that China can maintain for long the same growth rate that it has enjoyed for the past decade (between 7 and 15 percent annually). As any rapidly expanding economy grows from a small base into a larger one, the *rate* of growth inevitably slows down. No country has maintained annual growth rates of 7 percent or more indefinitely. In the best case, China will have to settle for steady growth at a slower rate.

Moreover, there are major flaws in China's economy that will inevitably retard future growth. Andrew Nathan, a leading scholar of Chinese politics, recently wrote cynically about that country's high economic growth rate:

> Twelve percent growth has brought goods to the market, construction cranes to the streets. . . . The numbers are real. . . . but much of what they measure is fake. Some state enterprises consist of waste piles of spoiled goods surrounded by subsidized workers on a permanent break, but the output, jobs and cigarettes [smoked on break] increase their respective national numbers.[89]

China's state-owned enterprises (SOEs), which generated 80 percent of the country's GDP at the start of Deng's reforms, only produced about 17 percent by 2003. But they still employed half of the urban workforce and controlled over half of the nation's industrial assets. Most of them are very inefficient and almost half of them are money-losing operations that stay alive only through government subsidies. As of 1990, those subsidies accounted for *one-third of the national government's budget!*[90] At the same time, the government has severely damaged the private banking system by forcing banks to make loans to unprofitable SOEs, loans that everyone knows are unrecoverable. Should the Chinese economy slow down, the large number of unrecoverable loans could set off a banking crisis. Now that China has entered the World Trade Organization and will have to sharply reduce its tariffs and other restrictions on imports, the inefficient SOEs will become even bigger money losers as they are unable to compete with imported goods or begin to export. Current subsidy levels, much less additional subsidies necessitated by WTO membership, are not sustainable in the long term. If the government begins to reduce its subsidies, as it probably will be forced to, many SOEs will have to shut down, laying off substantial numbers of workers. They would be added to an officially estimated 20 million workers already unemployed as of 2000.[91] In fact, the real number today may be as high as 100 million. From 1995 to 2003 alone, 55 million workers were laid off in a country that had previously guaranteed them lifetime employment (know as "the iron rice bowl").[92]

Even if China is able to maintain vigorous growth, it will still face the problem of increasing inequality. In most cases, income inequality grows in industrializing nations during their early to middle stages of development. In China, this has been a particular problem because of the government's great emphasis on equality during the Maoist era. Income gaps have been particularly wide between cities and rural areas, and between coastal China and the interior of the country. People living in villages, especially in the country's interior, have often felt left behind. In a recent poll of residents of Beijing, a city with income levels well above the national average, respondents were asked whether they felt "satisfied," "so-so," or "dissatisfied" about government performance in eight critical areas—including controlling inflation, job security, housing, and medical care. The area of government performance that drew by far the most neg-ative evaluations was its record in "minimizing the gap between rich and poor." More than 60 percent responded that they were either "very dissatisfied" (16.7 percent) or somewhat dissatisfied (44 percent).[93] One must assume that the level of popular dis-satisfaction is considerably higher in the nation's poorer regions. In short, a future eco-nomic slowdown, rising industrial unemployment (caused either by privatization or by the closing of inefficient SOEs), layoffs caused by import competition through the WTO, and greater regional inequality could turn the relatively localized worker and peasant protests into a broader political movement.

Both President Hu Jintao and his premier, Wen Jiabao (who holds direct respon-sibility for the economy), have indicated that reducing inequality and eradicating poverty, especially in the countryside, were among their highest priorities. Both men, unlike their predecessors, had spent substantial parts of their careers in the poorer, Western provinces of the country. Consequently, the Chinese press trumpeted their commitment to reducing poverty. Rejecting the relatively secluded style of China's past leaders, they have often toured various parts of the country making populist speeches promising reforms for the poor, better health care for SARS (severe acute respiratory syndrome) and AIDS victims, and reduced perks for political leaders. Sometimes they have intervened on behalf of supplicants, securing back pay for indi-vidual workers who have not been paid for their labor. In 2005 the government announced new, long-term policies for agriculture designed to raise rural incomes. These included "funding for agricultural research and technology, protecting farmland against illegal confiscation, supporting irrigation and environmental projects, and directing more investment and credit toward the countryside."[94]

The following year, mindful of the spreading peasant discontent, the national gov-ernment announced a major program to expand rural benefits in the areas of educa-tion, health care, and welfare. The program promises to include free education for many rural students (who must now pay school fees) and higher farm subsidies. It should be noted that the government's share of health care costs had fallen from 36 percent in the 1980s to 15 percent by 2000, leaving the burden of costs on the shoul-ders of poor peasants.[95] Left unresolved, at least for now, is one of the reforms most desired by villagers, giving them the right to buy or sell land and taking the land out of the control of village officials. Much of the recent rural unrest came from peasants who had been forced by local party or government officials to sell their land at modest prices to developers, who then make large profits.

But in spite of their public pronouncements and isolated interventions, to date the national government has instituted only limited changes to achieve its stated goal of greater social justice. Many of the plans are vague and long-term, and Hu has proven to be very cautious, not the bold reformer that many had hoped for. It is not clear how com-mitted he really is to economic reform and whether he is ready to take on the serious opposition to reform within China's powerful bureaucracy. A test of government inten-tions will be how well it carries out the rural development programs announced in 2006.

Party leaders have made efforts to make government agencies report more hon-estly on problems such as potential epidemics. Following an early official coverup of the country's 2003 SARS outbreak (a disease that causes death in some 10 percent of those infected and that spread from China, raising fears of a worldwide epidemic), Hu purged several high-ranking health ministry officials and China became more forth-coming about the disease's spread. But, "while both Hu and Wen had called for honest reporting about SARS and its impact, other directives were sent out to make sure the media was not able . . . to gain greater press freedom."[96] The regime has been more forthcoming about the more recent outbreak of bird flu (including about ten human deaths).

At the same time, Hu's government seems to have intensified efforts to control corruption among local officials, though it is not clear how effective that campaign has been.[97] The press, once prohibited from exposing corruption, has been encouraged to do so since the 1990s. But only in rare cases it is allowed to expose officials at higher levels. Contradictory government signals to the press make it difficult for journalists to determine what the boundary lines are. At the 2003 meeting of the National People's Congress, the government announced that in the previous five years it had investigated 207,103 cases of corruption. Once again, however, prosecutions rarely reached the upper levels of government.

Most analysts believe that, however sincere or insincere are the government's campaigns, corruption continues to rise. Because Hu Jintao presented himself as a reformer when he assumed leadership of the Communist Party, many Chinese intellectuals and social scientists saw him as a possible Chinese counterpart to Mikhail Gorbachev who might expand civil liberties. But, while China's level of personal freedom remains far higher than it was prior to 1990, Hu has actually imposed stricter limits on the press, free speech, and independent political analysis than had existed for the past 10 to 15 years. Since taking office, he has tightened controls on the media, NGOs, university Internet sites, and independent think-tanks. In a 2004 speech to the Communist Party Central Committee, he warned that "hostile forces" were trying to undermine the party by "using the banner of political reform to promote Western bourgeois parliamentary democracy, human rights and freedom of the press." While Hu has talked about improving "intra-party democracy" (more free exchange of ideas between communist officials), he has made it clear that, like his predecessors, he is firmly opposed to relaxing the Communist Party's firm grip on power. Noting that openness had led to the collapse of Soviet communism, he insisted that the media not "provide a channel for incorrect ideological points of view." On other occasions he has praised the North Korean political system, among the most repressive on earth. Human rights experts note that arrests of intellectual dissidents, labor and peasant activists, and "Internet freethinkers" have increased in recent years.

Following the mass uprisings that toppled authoritarian regimes in Georgia (2003) and Ukraine (2004)—both former Soviet republics—the Chinese leadership became particularly worried about the possibility of a popular unrest. In 2004 and 2005, censorship was tightened, including on Web sites and blogs.[98] Books previously permitted that discussed economic disparities in the country were pulled from bookstore shelves. The activities of foreign and domestic NGOs operating in China (in areas such as the environment, legal aid, and education) have been restricted. Dozens of writers, journalists, and artists—including a Chinese researcher for *The New York Times*—have been arrested and in some cases sentenced to jail sentences of 10 years or more. At least one attorney who tried to represent jailed political dissidents was disbarred. Political controls over universities have also intensified.

One example of the mixed signals that the government has sent out about political reform is the issue of accountability among government officials. Under President Hu's administration, Chinese citizens have been encouraged to petition the national government regarding abuses by local or provincial (but not national) officials. Between 2003 and 2004 the number of such citizen complaints rose 46 percent in 2003 and another 100 percent in 2004. Although some officials were disciplined or even arrested, the party leadership decided to put the brakes on this process. Consequently Hu issued new regulations that make it easier for accused local officials to punish those who lodge complaints against them. Indeed, even before that backtracking, a survey by the Chinese Academy of Social Sciences revealed that only 1 out of 5,000 people who lodged complaints felt that they had gotten any results.[99]

Historically, an emerging middle class and bourgeoisie (the business class) have been in the forefront of transitions to democracy. Most recently, the spread of advanced education and the growth of the middle class have contributed to democratic pressures in Mexico and Russia (Chapters 13 and 17). In contrast, so far at least, the crushing of the 1989 democracy movement in China and the repressive period that followed led university students and young professionals to withdraw from politics and political protest. Today, young people generally seem more interested in making money than in campaigning for political reform. But that may change (Box 14-4)! As the economy modernizes further and expands, the number of educated and skilled workers and professionals available to organize and participate in a future democracy movement will expand correspondingly. Someday, they may follow in the footsteps of prodemocracy movements elsewhere.

Box 14-4

CHINA'S COMMUNICATIONS REVOLUTION

One of the greatest potential challenges facing communist rule in the future is China's electronic communications revolution. As of early 2005, the country had 350 million cell phone users, more than any other country in the world. At the same time there were some 100 million Internet users (up from only 17 million in 2000), with the number growing about 30 percent annually. The government is well aware of the potential dangers these can pose in terms of the ability of any future opposition-group supporters to quickly contact each other via cell phones or for citizens to acquire information via the Web. Search engines that are approved by the government must accept certain limits. Thus, Google, Internet Explorer, and others had to agree to block search words such as "freedom" and "democracy." The government is believed to have about 50 thousand people policing the Internet.

Recent anti-Japanese demonstrations illustrate the potential danger. Students and other young people demonstrated in Shanghai in support of government criticism of Japan and China's objections to Japanese permanent membership in the U.N. Security Council. Japan is still widely disliked in China for its atrocities in World War II and its refusal to apologize for them. What bothered the government was not the subject of the protests, which it supported, but rather the fact that they were expanding spontaneously and had become violent. Moreover, using text messages, instant messaging, and the Internet, grassroots organizers mobilized large numbers of protesters and sent banned photos of protest violence, while the government was unable to identify the movement's leaders. Ironically, the Shanghai police sent out text messages telling people to stop protesting.

At an earlier point the Falun Gong, a banned spiritual group, had used cell phones to organize their demonstrations, including one in which about 10 thousand demonstrators surrounded the Communist Party headquarters in silent protest. Ultimately, the government security forces have screening devices that can be used to intercept cell phone and e-mail messages containing key words and then trace them back to the sender. But in the recent Shanghai demonstrations government screening was able to stop one communications medium (the Internet), but not another (cell phone text messaging). In recent years, there has been increased censorship of the Internet along with closings of many Web discussion groups. But the anti-Japanese and the Falun Gong protests suggest that as the communications revolution expands, the authorities will find it increasingly difficult to control would-be demonstrators.[100]

WHERE ON THE WEB?

http://www.library.utoronto.ca/east/chinese_politics.htm

An extensive guide to articles and Web sites on Chinese politics provided by the University of Toronto East Asia Library.

http://www.asianinfo.org/asianinfo/china/politics.htm

Brief background information and links on Chinese politics.

http://www-sul.stanford.edu/depts/asrg/poli_sci.htm

A bibliography of books and other sources of information on twentieth-century Chinese politics.

http://www.hrw.org/asia/china.php

Home page for information on human rights in China and Tibet published by Human Rights Watch, a highly respected and objective group.

Key Terms and Concepts

collectives

communes

Cultural Revolution

Deng Xiaoping

Expert faction

Falun Gong

Great Leap Forward

Kuomintang (Guomindang)
    KMT

Long March

Mao Zedong

Nationalist Party
    (Kuomintang, KMT)

one-child policy

open-door policy

People's Liberation Army (PLA)

political liberalization

princelings

Red faction

Red Guards

Reds versus Experts

responsibility system

SOEs (state-owned enterprises)

third generation

Tiananmen Square

warlords

Zhou Enlai

Discussion Questions

1. What was new and distinct about Mao Zedong's interpretation and application of Marxism-Leninism (communism) in China? How has China's application of communist principles changed since the death of Mao?

2. What have been the major accomplishments of the economic reforms instituted under the leadership of Deng Xiaoping and Jiang Zemin? What are some of the major social and political problems that arose out of those reforms?

3. Describe the role that the Communist Party plays in Chinese politics. How have the party's membership and role changed over time?

4. Since the end of the 1970s, China has moved from a communist (command) economy to a largely free-market (capitalist) one. Describe the main features of that conversion. What are the potential political consequences of that change?

5. China stands today as the last major nation with a political system dominated by its Communist Party. What are the prospects for a transition to democracy in that country?

Specifically, what are the major factors that might drive China toward democracy, and what are the major obstacles to such a transition?

6. How is China's one-child policy enforced? What have been the positive and negative consequences of the policy?

Notes_____

1. Drawn from Lin Piao's inscription and preface to the second edition of *Quotations from Chairman Mao Tse-tung* (Peking: Foreign Language Press, 1966). Since 1979, most contemporary English-language writings on China use the pinyin system of transcribing Chinese characters into Roman letters. Thus, *Lin Piao, Mao Tse-tung*, and *Peking* (using the pre-1979 Wade-Giles method) are now spelled *Lin Biao, Mao Zedong*, and *Beijing*. For footnote citations, we reproduce whatever spelling was used in the original work. Almost all names in the text are in the pinyin system.

2. Widely cited quotation from Deng Xiaoping, China's paramount leader from the late 1970s to the mid-to-late 1990s.

3. Using unadjusted GNP figures, China's economy is smaller than that of Japan (and the U.S.). But a newer method of calculating national income adjusts each country's raw GNP to reflect what it can actually purchase domestically. This statistical adjustment creates a GNP measured by PPP, or *parity purchasing power*. With that method of calculation, China's economy is larger than Japan's. PPP is widely considered to offer a more accurate picture of a nation's GNP.

4. Orville Shell quoted in *China's Transition*, by Andrew J. Nathan (New York: Columbia University Press, 1997), p. 227.

5. John K. Fairbank, *China: The People's Middle Kingdom and the U.S.A.* (Cambridge, MA: Belknap Press of Harvard University Press, 1967), pp. 3–4.

6. Alan Liu, *How China Is Ruled* (Englewood Cliffs, NJ: Prentice Hall, 1986), pp. 7–8.

7. Suzanne Ogden, *China's Unresolved Issues* (Englewood Cliffs, NJ: Prentice Hall, 1989), pp. 16–20.

8. James R. Townsend and Brantly Womack, *Politics in China* (Boston: Little, Brown, 1986), p. 46.

9. Maurice Meisner, *Mao's China and After* (New York: Free Press, 1987), pp. 10–11.

10. Liu, *How China Is Ruled*, p. 18.

11. Meisner, *Mao's China and After*, pp. 5, 25, 28.

12. Ibid., p. 27.

13. Ibid., p. 32.

14. Edgar Snow, *Red Star over China* (New York: Random House, 1938), p. 177.

15. Two decades later, Premier Zhou Enlai and other Chinese government leaders still looked to the Long March as their decisive struggle. See Edgar Snow, *Red China Today* (New York: Vintage, 1970), pp. 111–112.

16. A leading work on Maoist ideology is Franz Schurmann, *Ideology and Organization in Communist China* (Berkeley and Los Angeles: University of California Press, 1968).

17. A *cadre* is "almost any individual with [political] authority over other adults." James D. Seymour, *China: The Politics of Revolutionary Reintegration* (New York: Crowell, 1998), p. 117.

18. James Wang, *Contemporary Chinese Politics* (Englewood Cliffs, NJ: Prentice Hall, 1989), p. 13. Many landlords were jailed or condemned to death by peasant tribunals.

19. Townsend and Womack, *Politics in China*, pp. 119–120.

20. For an account of the Great Leap Forward, see Roderick MacFarquhar, *The Origins of the Cultural Revolution*, vol. 2, *The Great Leap Forward (1958–60)* (New York: Columbia University Press, 1983).

21. Harry Harding, *China's Second Revolution* (Washington, DC: Brookings 1987), p. 12; Ogden, *China's Unresolved Issues*, pp. 46–50; and Nicholas Lardy, *Agriculture in China's Modern Economic Development* (Cambridge, England: Cambridge University Press, 1983).

22. There is a vast literature on the Cultural Revolution. Some important works are Liang Heng and Judith Shapiro, *Son of the Revolution* (New York: Vintage Books, 1983); K. S. Karol, *The Second Chinese Revolution* (New York: Hill and Wang, 1974); Jean Esmein, *The Chinese Cultural Revolution* (New York: Anchor Books, 1973); and Lowell Dittmer, *Liu Shao-ch'i and the Chinese Cultural Revolution* (Berkeley and Los Angeles: University of California Press, 1974).

23. Richard Baum and Louise Bennett, eds., *China in Ferment* (Englewood Cliffs, NJ: Prentice Hall, 1971), p. 2.

24. Fox Butterfield, *China: Alive in the Bitter Sea* (New York: Times Books, 1982), p. 349.

25. Harding, *China's Second Revolution*, p. 12, offers the lower estimate; the higher figure comes from Liu, *How China Is Ruled*, p. 48.

26. Wang, *Contemporary Chinese Politics*, pp. 48–73; and Harding, *China's Second Revolution*, pp. 77–95.

27. Harding, *China's Second Revolution*, pp. 30–31. Data in this section are all drawn from Harding.

28. Stephen White et al., *Communist and Postcommunist Political Systems* (New York: St. Martin's, 1990), p. 322; and Harding, *China's Second Revolution*, p. 30.

29. Nicholas Lardy, "Agricultural Reforms in China," *Journal of International Affairs* (Winter 1986): 91–104. The responsibility system was not actually implemented until 1980.

30. Harding, *China's Second Revolution*, p. 106.

31. Marc Blecher, "The Reorganization of the Countryside," in *Reforming the Revolution*, ed. Robert Benewick and Paul Wingrove (Chicago: Dorsey, 1988), p. 100.

32. The World Bank Group, *Transition Newsletter* (February–March 2001), pp. 13–14. http://worldbank.org/transitionnewsletter/febmarch2001/pgs13-14.htm.

33. June Teufel Dreyer, *China's Political System: Modernization and Tradition*, 3rd ed. (New York: Addison Wesley Longman, 2000), p. 149.

34. Nicholas R. Lardy, "The Challenge of Economic Reform and Social Stability," in *China under Jiang Zemin*, ed. Hung-mao Tien and Yun-han Chu (Boulder, CO: Lynne Rienner Publishers, 2000), p. 138.

35. Willy Wo-Lap Lam, *The Era of Jiang Zemin* (Upper Saddle River, NJ: Prentice Hall, 1999), p. 291.

36. Dreyer, *China's Political System*, p. 155.

37. On government corruption, see Andrew Wedeman, "Corruption in Politics," in *China Review: 1996*, ed. Maurice Brosseau (Hong Kong: Chinese University Press, 1997), pp. 61–94.

38. Mixin Pei, "Racing against Time: Institutional Decay and Renewal in China," in *China Briefing: The Contradictions of Change*, ed. William A. Joseph (Armonk, NY: Sharpe, 1997), pp. 11–50.

39. Richard Baum, "Jiang Takes Command: The Fifteenth National Party Congress and Beyond," in *China under Jiang Zemin*, p. 30, n. 20.

40. Mixin Pei, "The Dark Side of China's Rise," in *Foreign Policy* (March/April, 2006), www.foreignpolicy.com.

41. Guonan Ma, "Income Distribution in the 1980s," in *China's Quiet Revolution: New Interactions between State and Society*, ed. David S. G. Goodman and Beverley Hooper (New York: St. Martin's, 1994), pp. 20–26.

42. *English People's Daily* (February 26, 2004, english.peopledaily.com.cn; The World Bank Group, *Transition Newsletter* (February–March 2001); and *China's Retreat from Equality*, ed. Carl Riskin, Zhao Renwei, and Li Shi (Armonk, NY: Sharpe, 2001), chaps. 1 and 2.

43. *English People's Daily*, ibid.

44. *The New York Times* (February 3, 2003).

45. *The New York Times* (June 28, 2005).

46. "Survey: China," *Economist*, March 8–14, 1997, p. 10; and Jan S. Prybla, "All That Glitters? The Foreign Investment Boom," *Current History* 94, no. 593 (September 1995): 275.

47. *The Economist: Country Briefings* (February 9, 2004), economist.com/countries/China.

48. Tony Saich, *Governance and Politics of China*, 2nd ed. (New York: Palgrave, 2004), p. 99.

49. Jeffrey N. Wasserstrom, "China's Brave New World," *Current History* 102, no. 665 (September 2003): 267.

50. *The New York Times*, May 2, 2002.

51. Yiu-chung Wong, *From Deng Xiaoping to Jiang Zemin* (Lanham, MD: University Press of America, 2005), p. 273.

52. Stanley Rosen, "The State of Youth/Youth and the State in Early 21st-Century China," in *State and Society in 21st-Century China*, ed. Peter Hays Gries and Stanley Rosen (New York and London: Routledge Curzon, 2004), p. 242.

53. Ellis Joffe, "The People's Liberation Army and Politics: After the Fifteenth Party Congress," in Tien and Chu, *China under Jiang Zemin*, pp. 99–134.

54. Ibid., pp. 88–89.

55. Shiping Zheng, "China's Leadership After the 15th Party Congress: Changes and Implications," in *Transitions Toward Post-Deng China*, ed. Xiaobo Hu and Gang Lin (Singapore: Singapore University Press, 2001), p. 125.

56. Yongnian Zheng, "The 16th National Congress of the Communist Party," in *Leadership in a Changing China*, ed. Weixing Chen and Yang Zhong (New York: Palgrave Macmillan, 2005), pp. 16–17.

57. Gang Lin, "Leadership Transition, Intra-Party Democracy and Institution Building in China," in ibid., pp. 38–70.

58. Merle Goldman, "Is Democracy Possible?" *Current History* 94, no. 593 (September 1995): 259. For a more negative assessment of the NPC, see Barrett L. McCormick, "China's Leninist Parliament and the Public Sphere," in *China after Socialism*, ed. Barrett L. McCormick and Jonathan Unger (Armonk, NY: Sharpe, 1996), pp. 29–53.

59. Emerson M. S. Niou, "An Introduction to the Electoral System Used in Chinese Villages," in *Contemporary China: Approaching the 21st Century*, ed. Rebecca McGinnis (Bethesda: University of Maryland Press, 2000), p. 93; Youxing Lang, "Crafting Village Democracy in China," in *Leadership*, ed. Chen and Zhong, pp. 105–130.

60. Wang, *Contemporary Chinese Politics*, pp. 133–135.

61. Ibid., p. 137.

62. McCormick, "Conclusion," in McCormick and Unger, *China after Socialism*, pp. 260–261.

63. James Seymour and Richard Anderson, *New Ghosts, Old Ghosts: Prisons and Labour Reform Camps in China* (Armonk, NY: Sharpe, 1998).

64. Dreyer, *China's Political System*, pp. 179–184.

65. *New York Times*, "Deep Flaws, and Little Justice, in China's Court System." September 21, 2005.

66. Geremie Barmé, "Soft Porn, Packaged Dissent and Nationalism: Notes on Chinese Culture in the 1990s," *Current History* 93, no. 584 (September 1994).

67. Graeme Gill, "The Political Dynamics of Reform: Learning from the Soviet Experience," in McCormick and Unger, *China after Socialism*, p. 65.

68. Nicholas Kristof, "A Clampdown in China," *The New York Times* (May 17, 2005).

69. Harding, *China's Second Revolution*, p. 128.

70. See endnote 3 for a definition of PPP. *CIA Factbook* (July 28, 2005) http://www.cia.gov/cia/publications/factbook/geos/ch.html; Bruce Reynolds, "The Chinese Economy in 1988," in *China Briefing, 1989*, ed. Anthony Kane (Boulder, CO: Westview, 1989), pp. 28–29; Dreyer, *China's Political System*, p. 155; and Asian Development Bank Report (April 19, 2002), http://www.adb.org/Documents/News/2002/nr2002041.asp. As noted earlier, China was obviously starting from a much lower base than a developed nation and, despite its rapid growth, remains a far poorer country than any industrial democracy. Still, by the end of the twentieth century, it had developed the world's second-largest economy.

71. Reynolds, "The Chinese Economy," pp. 33–34; and Dwight H. Perkins, "The Prospects for China's Economic Reforms," in *China Briefing, 1990*, ed. Anthony Kane (Boulder, CO: Westview, 1990), p. 25.

72. Liang Heng and Judith Shapiro, *After the Nightmare: Inside China Today* (New York: Collier, 1986), pp. 130–148, offers an excellent personalized account of an encounter with the corrupt daughter of a government cadre.

73. Pei, "Racing against Time," p. 18.

74. Martin King Whyte, "Social Sources of the Student Demonstrations," in Kane, *China Briefing,* 1989, pp. 25–46.

75. Ibid., p. 50.

76. See, for example, Samuel Huntington, *The Clash of Civilizations and the Remaking of World Order* (New York: Simon & Schuster, 1996).

77. Joseph Esherick and Jeffrey Wasserstrom, "Acting Out Democracy: Political Theater in China," *Journal of Asian Studies* 46 (November 1990): 835–865.

78. Manion, "Politics in China," pp. 435–436.

79. Barrington Moore, *The Social Origins of Dictatorship and Democracy* (Boston: Beacon Press, 1967); and D. Rueschemeyer, E. Huber Stevens, and J. Stevens, *Capitalist Development and Democracy* (Chicago: University of Chicago: 1992).

80. Edward Friedman, Paul G. Pickowicz, and Mark Selden, *Chinese Village, Socialist State* (New Haven: Yale University Press, 1991).

81. Timothy B. Weston, "The Iron Man Weeps," in Gries and Rosen, *State and Society,* pp. 67–86.

82. Melanie Manion, "Politics in China," in *Comparative Politics Today,* ed. Gabriel Almond et al. (New York: Pearson Longman, 2006), 451–454.

83. "Riots in Shanghai Suburb as Pollution Protest Heats UP," *The New York Times* (July 19, 2005).

84. Beverley Hooper, "Chinese Youth: The Nineties Generation," *Current History* 90, no. 557 (September 1991): p. 258.

85. Joseph Fewsmith, "The Government of China," in *Introduction to Comparative Government,* 5th ed. (New York: Pearson Longman, 2006), p. 492.

86. *The New York Times* (July 19, 2005, and August 23, 2005); Patricia Thornton, "Comrades and Collectives," in Gries and Rosen, *State and Society,* pp. 87–104.

87. *The New York Times* (December 14, 2005, and December 17, 2005).

88. Lam, *The Era of Jiang Zemin,* p. 289.

89. Nathan, *China's Transition,* p. 218.

90. Dreyer, *China's Political System,* p. 149.

91. Michael Bonnin, "Perspectives on Social Stability After the Fifteenth Congress," in Tien and Chu, *China under Jiang Zemin,* p. 155.

92. Weston, "The Iron Man Weeps," in Gries and Rosen, *State and Society,* p. 69.

93. Jie Chen and Yang Zhong, "Are Chinese Still Interested in Politics," in Hu and Lin, *Transitions Toward Post-Deng China,* p. 158.

94. Manfred Elstrom, "The Meaning of China's New Agricultural Policy," China Elections and Governance Web site (April 2005), chinaelections.org.

95. Mixin Pei, "The Dark Side of China's Rise."

96. *Ibid.* p. 89 and pp. 334–335.

97. Saich, *Governance and Politics of China,* p. 331.

98. Yongding, "China's Color-Coded Crackdown," *Foreign Policy* Web site (posted October 2005), www.foreignpolicy.com.

99. *Washington Post* (April 24, 2005), *The New York Times* (December 31, 2004).

100. "A Hundred Cell Phones Bloom, and Chinese Take to the Streets," *The New York Times* (April 25, 2005).

For Further Reading _____

Dreyer, June Teufel. *China's Political System: Modernization and Tradition.* 3rd ed. New York: Addison Wesley Longman, 2000.

Gries, Peter Hays, and Stanley Rosen, eds. *State and Society in Twenty-First Century China.* New York and London: Routledge Curzon, 2004.

Lam, Willy Wo-Lap. *The Era of Jiang Zemin.* Upper Saddle River, NJ: Prentice Hall, 1999.

Liang Heng and Judith Shapiro. *Son of the Revolution*. New York: Vintage Books, 1983.

Pei, Minxin. *China's Trapped Transition: The Limits of Developmental Autocracy*. Cambridge, MA: Harvard University Press, 2006.

Saich, Tony. *Governance and Politics of China*, 2nd ed. New York: Palgrave, 2004.

Starr, John Bryan. *Understanding China*. New York: Hill and Wang, 2001.

Tien, Hung-mao, and Yun-han Chu, eds. *China under Jiang Zemin*. Boulder, CO: Lynne Rienner Publishers, 2000.

© AP/Wide World Photos

15

THE POLITICS
OF DEVELOPING NATIONS

◆ Economic and Social Underdevelopment ◆ Political
Underdevelopment and Development ◆ Theories
of Underdevelopment and Development ◆ Sources
of Political Conflict ◆ Problems of Political
Participation ◆ Women in Third World Society
and Politics ◆ Third World Political Institutions
◆ Military Intervention ◆ Strong States, Weak States
◆ Recent Developments and Future Trends

Although the governing of nations is always difficult, political leaders in the **Third World** face a particularly daunting task.* Recent headlines suggest the magnitude of that challenge: Famine plagues North Korea and Niger; long-standing rebellions and civil wars in Sudan, Congo, and Somalia kill more than three million people; economic inequality grows in Mexico and much of Latin America; Sunni Muslims bomb Shi'ite civilians in Iraq; political repression continues in Myanmar (Burma), Saudi Arabia, and many other Third World regimes.

The more than 120 African, Asian, Latin American, and Middle Eastern nations that compose the developing world are a disparate group. An elite few, including the Bahamas, Singapore, and Hong Kong, have per capita incomes that approach or equal those of such developed nations as Spain and New Zealand. Others, including Trinidad-Tobago and Costa Rica, have relatively stable and effective political systems. But all of them, even the most stable and affluent, share *some* important elements of social, economic, or political underdevelopment, including substantial illiteracy (Saudi Arabia), particular economic vulnerability (a drop in coffee prices, for example, can damage the Kenyan economy), sharp social and economic inequalities (Brazil), political corruption (Nigeria and South Korea), and authoritarian government (Singapore and Malaysia). In most **less developed countries (LDCs)**, several factors, such as poverty, illiteracy, ethnic conflict, foreign intervention, and sharp class divisions, combine to produce political instability, government repression, or both.

What accounts for the Third World's political and economic underdevelopment? No single answer suffices. This chapter will evaluate the general phenomenon of political and socioeconomic development in Africa, Asia, Latin America and the Caribbean, and the Middle East. To begin our analysis, we define and examine two distinct, but closely related, phenomena: socioeconomic underdevelopment and political underdevelopment.

ECONOMIC AND SOCIAL UNDERDEVELOPMENT

Upon first visiting the developing world, most outsiders are shocked by its enormous poverty: many people living in shacks, beggars in the street, inadequate infrastructures, to name a few visible signs. Table 15.1 presents basic economic indicators for two highly-developed nations (the United States and Japan), one high-income, Third World economy (Hong Kong), two middle-income Latin American nations (Mexico and Brazil), two Asian giants (China and India, with 40 percent of the world's population between them), and two poor African countries (Egypt and Nigeria).

Column 1 indicates each country's per capita income (adjusted for PPP).[1] Clearly there are broad differences among the Third World economies. Hong Kong—like Singapore, South Korea, and Taiwan—is a **newly industrialized country**[†] **(NIC)** whose per capita income is now comparable to that of advanced industrialized nations,

---

* The term *Third World* refers to the politically and economically less-developed nations of Africa, Asia, Latin America, and the Middle East. It was coined to differentiate them from the world's industrial democracies (First World) and from communist countries (Second World). Although the origins of this title are now dated because of the collapse of the Second World, the term is still commonly used interchangeably with *developing world* and *less developed countries (LDCs)*.

[†] Hong Kong is not an independent country, but rather a semi-autonomous part of China. But its capitalist economy is separate from China's and treated as such in UN statistics.

TABLE 15.1   MEASURES OF ECONOMIC DEVELOPMENT

Country	Per Capita Income (PPP)	Share of the Poorest 20%	Share of the Richest 20%	Ratio of Richest 20% to Poorest 20%
United States	$35,750	5.4%	45.8%	8.4
Japan	$26,940	10.6	35.7	3.4
Hong Kong	$26,910	5.3	50.7	9.7
Mexico	$ 8,970	3.1	59.1	19.3
Brazil	$ 7,770	2.0	64.4	31.5
China	$ 4,510	4.7	50.0	10.7
Egypt	$ 3,810	8.6	43.6	5.1
India	$ 2,670	8.9	41.6	4.7
Nigeria	$ 860	4.4	55.7	12.8

SOURCE: United Nations Development Programme (UNDP), *Human Development Report 2004 Cultural Liberty in Today's Diverse World:* Human Development Indicators—Tables 13 and 14, http://www.undp.org/.

but which continues to demonstrate aspects of political and social underdevelopment. Most Third World nations, however, have average annual incomes that are only one-third (Mexico) to one-fortieth (Nigeria) that of the U.S.

A country's per capita income gives us some measure of its standard of living, but not a full image. A second important factor is the way in which that income is distributed. Two countries may have the same average incomes, but if income is more heavily concentrated in the first country, it will have more people living in poverty.

Columns 2 and 3 of Table 15.1 indicate what percentage of each country's total income is earned by the richest 20 percent of the population and by the poorest 20 percent. Thus, for example, in Brazil the richest 20 percent of the population earns almost two-thirds of the country's annual income (64.4 percent), while the poorest 20 percent of the population earns a mere 2.0 percent. Column 4 indicates the ratio of average incomes within the richest 20 percent of the population to that of the poorest 20 percent. Thus, for example, the richest 20 percent of Brazil's population earns 31.5 times as much as does the poorest 20 percent. By contrast, in Egypt the richest 20 percent of the population earns only 5.1 times as much as the poorest segment. So, although Brazil has an *average* annual income more than double Egypt's, the poorest segment of Egypt's population is actually better off than their Brazilian counterparts since they earn more than four times as high a *share* of national income.

Although highly developed nations generally tend to have more equal income distributions than poorer countries do, Table 15.1 reveals considerable variation within each group. To be sure, Japan has perhaps the world's most equal income distribution and Brazil has one of the most unequal. At the same time, however, the United States (with one of the highest concentrations of income among developed countries) has greater income inequality than either Egypt or India.

Although per capita income and income distribution data are important indicators of a country's economic level, they don't necessarily tell us all we need to know about the population's living standards, including their health and education. So, while more

TABLE 15.2　Indicators of Social Development

	Human Development Index (rank)	Life Expectancy (years)	Adult Literacy (percent)	Real Income Rank (PPP) Minus HDI Rank
Canada	.943 (4)	79.3	99.0	+5
United States	.939 (8)	77.0	99.0	−4
South Korea	.888 (28)	75.4	97.9	+9
Argentina	.853 (34)	74.1	97.0	+14
Cuba	.809 (52)	76.7	96.9	+39
Mexico	.802 (53)	73.3	90.5	+5
Brazil	.775 (72)	68.0	86.4	−9
Saudi Arabia	.768 (77)	72.1	77.9	−33
China	.745 (94)	70.9	90.9	+5
Egypt	.653 (120)	68.6	55.6	−12
India	.595 (127)	63.7	61.3	−10
Nigeria	.466 (151)	51.6	66.8	+15
Ethiopia	.359 (170)	45.5	41.5	−1

Source: United Nations Development Programme (UNDP), *Human Development Report 2004:Cultural Liberty in Today's Diverse World:* Human Development Indicators—Table 1, http://www.undp.org/.

affluent countries tend to have better health care and more schools, Table 15.2 indicates that countries that make concerted efforts in the areas of education and health care may achieve better social conditions for their citizens than do other, richer, countries that neglect these areas. The **Human Development Index (HDI)**, as calculated by the United Nations Development Program, is widely perceived by scholars as the best indicator of a population's well being. The HDI is a composite index based on a country's per capita income, average life expectancy, literacy rate, and educational level. Statistics for all of these factors are combined into a single index, which, in theory, can range from a high of 1.000 to a low of 0.000. The countries in Table 15.2 are listed in order of their HDI scores, from a high of .943 in Canada to a low of .359 in Ethiopia (column 1). The second number in column 1, in parentheses, indicates each country's HDI ranking among nearly 200 countries in the world. Thus, Canada has the world's fourth-highest HDI score (Norway is first), the United States ranks eighth, and Ethiopia ranks 170th. Columns 2 and 3, respectively, indicate each country's average life expectancy and literacy rate.

Perhaps the most interesting statistic in the table is to be found in column 4. It compares a country's world ranking in per capita income with its ranking for HDI. Since HDI scores usually correlate with per capita income, we would normally expect a country with, say, the fiftieth highest per capita income in the world to rank about fiftieth on HDI. In column 4, each country's HDI *ranking* is subtracted from its per capita income ranking. Thus, for example, if country A had the fourth highest per capita income in the world and the twelfth highest HDI, its score in column 4 would be a negative score of −8 (4 − 12 = −8), the negative sign indicating that its HDI ranking was lower than its per capita income ranking and that, in a sense, it has under-achieved in educating its population and raising their life expectancy (an indication of health care and nutrition). If country B ranked 70th in the world in per capita income and 50th in HDI, its score in column 4 (70 − 50 = 20) would be +20. This would indicate that, although the citizens of country B were less educated, less literate, and less long-lived than those of country A (i.e., its HDI score ranked much lower), country B and its government had performed much *better* in those areas than one would have expected based on its per capita income—i.e., it had "overachieved."

Not surprisingly, the table indicates that the richest countries (Canada and the United States) have the highest life expectancy and adult literacy rates and, consequently, the highest HDI scores, whereas very poor countries, such as India, Nigeria, and Ethiopia, ranked lowest on these dimensions. At the same time, however, several countries had higher HDI scores than their per capita income would have predicted, while other countries underachieved. For example, even though Cuba's per capita income (not shown in this table) is only about half of Argentina's or Saudi Arabia's, its life expectancy is higher than in either of those two countries and its adult literacy rate is considerably higher than Saudi Arabia's. Indeed, Cuba was the greatest "overachiever" (+39) among the countries in this table. Its unexpectedly high HDI score reflects its government's strong emphasis on public health and educational programs. On the other hand, Saudi Arabia's very poor performance (−33) indicates that its government has not used its enormous petroleum wealth effectively to raise health and educational levels. Thus, despite having a per capita income almost three times as high as China's (again, not shown in the table), the Saudi literacy rate is considerably lower. That educational underachievement is partially linked to Saudi Arabia's limited educational opportunities for women. Nigeria and Argentina was also overachievers, while Egypt, India, and, to a lesser extent, the U.S. were underachievers (that is, they had lower HDI rankings than their income levels would have predicted).

Although economic modernization and growth in a developing nation eventually raise living standards, the early-to-middle stages of that growth frequently create new pockets of poverty by raising the country's level of economic inequality. Years ago, economist Simon Kuznets observed that in the middle stages of economic development, income inequality actually tends to increase. The so-called **Kuznets effect** also reveals that inequality eventually tends to decline in the more advanced stages of economic growth.[2] Since growing income gaps in society tend to generate class tensions, not surprisingly many countries, such as Brazil, Mexico, and Peru, at the middle level of development are more prone to political unrest.[3] (See Figure 15.1.)

Several factors underlie the high rates of inequality in many LDCs. On the one hand, per capita incomes in the most economically developed cities tend to be as much as four or five times greater than in rural areas. Within the countryside itself, particularly in much of Latin America and parts of Asia, land ownership is highly concentrated. That combination of urban-rural income inequality and disparities in rural land ownership helps keep the rural poor at the bottom of the income ladder. It also helps drive the dramatic migration from countryside to city that has taken place in so many developing nations. As some Third World cities have doubled their populations in little more than a decade, sprawling slum neighborhoods have developed, usually lacking adequate sanitation or water facilities. Nigeria's population was only 16 percent urban in 1970 but is expected to reach 40 percent by 2010.[4] That creates further layers of inequality—between the urban population as a whole and the rural poor, and in the cities between the middle class and skilled working class, on the one hand, and

Figure 15.1   The "Kuznets Effect:" Economic Development and Income Distribution

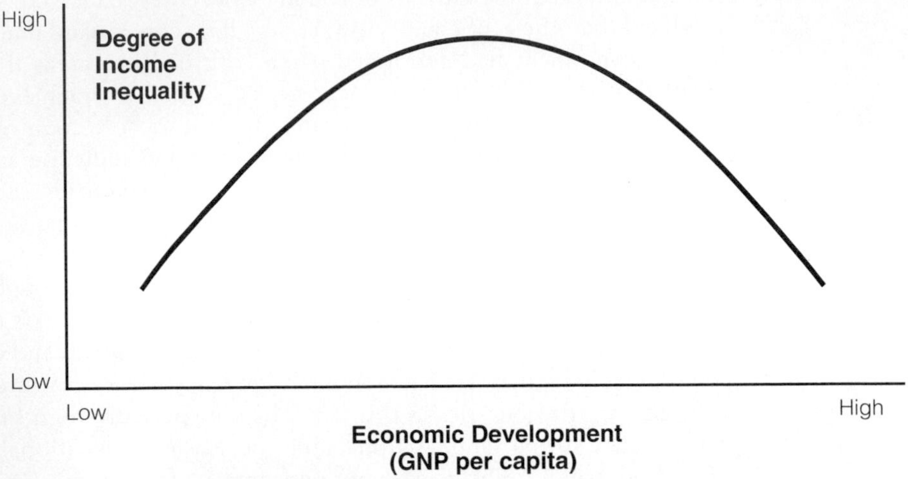

High

**Degree of
Income
Inequality**

Low

Low   High

**Economic Development
(GNP per capita)**

unskilled or semi-employed inhabitants of squatter communities on the other. In China, the growing economic gap between the country's major cities and the countryside has induced more than 100 million peasants to migrate to the cities in the last decade or so, with another 50 million expected to do so in the coming decade.

Although the Kuznets curve shown in Figure 15.1 suggests a *general* pattern of growing inequality associated with early economic growth, the policies of *individual* governments can alter that relationship significantly. Nations such as Taiwan, South Korea, Costa Rica, and Cuba, with very different economic and political systems, have achieved more equitable income distributions through redistribution of farmland from landlords to peasants, mass education, and welfare programs. Some countries, such as Brazil and Mexico, have attained impressive economic growth with poor income distribution, while others have accomplished more equitable economic distribution but slow growth (Cuba, for example). Unfortunately, many countries, such as Zimbabwe, Peru, and Namibia, have both high inequality and low growth. Only a few, such as Indonesia, South Korea, and Taiwan, have achieved both high growth and relative income equality.[5]

Over the past 40 years or so, the developing world has generally made impressive gains in health and education, but serious shortfalls remain and in some regions there has been backsliding. On the one hand, between the early 1970s and the end of the twentieth century, Third World infant mortality rates—the proportion of infants who die in the first year of life—fell by an impressive 40 percent. That decline and other health improvements lifted life expectancy from 53.4 years in 1960 to 64.6 years in 2003. At the same time, however, since 1990 the AIDS pandemic in sub-Saharan Africa has reduced life expectancy in a dozen countries (sometimes drastically), including Botswana, South Africa, and Zimbabwe.[6] Moreover, despite lowered infant mortality, each *hour* an average of 1,200 children die in the developing world, an annual mortality toll that is 36 times greater than the 300,000 people killed in the Asian tsunami of 2004. And 2.5 billion people (40 percent of the world's population) currently live on less than $2 per day.[7]

POLITICAL UNDERDEVELOPMENT AND DEVELOPMENT

Of course, underdevelopment also has a political component. Defining it, however, has been elusive at times, and some leading scholars have questioned the value of the term **political underdevelopment** itself.[8] With those caveats in mind, let us consider some definitions and characteristics of political underdevelopment and development.

Fundamental Definitions

Nations suffering from low political development—most notably in Africa, Asia, and the Middle East—often have created their current government institutions—such as parliaments or the bureaucracy—only recently. Thus, those institutions have not been around long enough to have acquired their own traditions, nor has much of the population yet developed emotional attachments to them or respect for them. If they perform poorly or are corrupt, their **legitimacy** is weakened further.

Second, in developed countries, most political participation takes place "within the system"—that is, within regularized and legal channels such as elections or lobbying. In contrast, political activity in many LDCs is often nonlegal or even violent. For example, the conflicting needs and interests of different ethnic groups may be solved peacefully through existing political institutions or, if those institutions cannot resolve them, they may erupt into violence.[9] More politically advanced Third World counties, such as Costa Rica and the Bahamas, have achieved reform relatively peacefully through interest group politics, negotiation, and legislation. By contrast, where within-system solutions have failed, as in Congo or Indonesia, ethnic tensions have provoked bloody conflict.

Finally, less developed governments often lack the capacity to govern effectively. They may have great difficulty collecting necessary taxes, responding effectively to emergencies, or maintaining order. During the 1970s, Nigeria and Mexico, major petroleum exporters, accumulated considerable wealth from their petroleum exports and appeared on the verge of an economic takeoff. But excessive external borrowing, wasteful spending, ineffective administration, and corruption all caused their governments to squander many of their opportunities and to plunge the countries into extended economic declines.

Democracy and Development

Before the late 1980s, most political scientists stressed two goals of political development: achieving political stability and establishing effective governments. More important, they often implicitly suggested that achieving stability was the first priority, and other goals—such as democracy, social justice, and equity—would have to follow later.[10] Some observers questioned whether democracy was yet attainable in Third World settings or even desirable at that time. In recent years, however, troubled by the numerous instances of government repression in the LDCs, a growing number of analysts have concluded that democracy and social equity must be integral parts of political development.[11]

Beyond the prima facie moral argument that *all* societies, no matter how poor, should be protected from state repression and should be free to choose their own political leaders, most experts now agree that although democracy does not guarantee that a nation's political system will be stable or efficient, in the long run those goals may be unattainable without some level of democracy.

Other Manifestations of Political Underdevelopment

Let us now turn our attention to a number of political conditions that, although they do not *define* political underdevelopment, are common characteristics of LDCs. Like economic resources, political influence in the developing world tends to be unequally distributed. Power is often concentrated in the hands of particular ethnic minorities or economic and political elites. Furthermore, government policies generally favor the urban upper and middle classes and, to a lesser extent, unionized blue-collar workers at the expense of the rural poor and unorganized urban workers, who together usually constitute the majority of the population.

Although the number of Third World **electoral democracies** (countries with free and fair contested elections, but without extensive civil liberties) has grown substantially since the 1970s, today most developing nations still lack the fundamental standards of **liberal democracy** (countries with substantial civil liberties as well as free and fair elections). Despite gains in recent decades, most LDCs still lack genuinely contested elections, free speech, an open media, and respect for civil liberties. In Africa, the Middle East, and much of Asia, military or single-party rule is still the norm. Elsewhere, in such countries as El Salvador and Guatemala, even when contested elections do take place, the military, security forces, or armed vigilantes have often intimidated certain candidates and parties. Few nations in Africa, Asia, or the Middle East enjoy a free press, as their governments generally control the airwaves. Prominent human rights monitoring groups, including Amnesty International and Human Rights Watch, have cited countries such as Syria, Turkey, Sudan, Myanmar, North Korea, and Colombia in the recent past for their imprisonment and torture of political dissidents and for their murder of real or imagined government opponents.

During the 1970s, as many as 30 thousand young Argentineans died in prison or disappeared as a result of the military government's "dirty war" against the left. The Khmer Rouge regime was responsible for the deaths of more than one million Cambodians. Since the 1980s, human rights conditions have improved in Latin America and in parts of Asia. A substantial number of African and Middle Eastern nations, however, continue to be victimized by political repression.[12]

Given the unrepresentative and repressive quality of many Third World governments, it is easy to understand why they often lack legitimacy. Citizens view their government with apathy or hostility. In a number of LDCs, popular unrest has challenged the government, often at great risk to the protestors: student protests against government repression in Myanmar, demonstrations against government corruption and repression in Kenya, Egypt, and Zaire, student clashes with police in Thailand. In parts of India, corruption is so pervasive that poor mothers in run-down maternity wards often have to bribe the nurse and doctor—handing over as much as one week's wages—to be allowed to see or hold their own baby.[13] The most intense forms of popular discontent have led to revolutionary movements or civil war in nations such as Sudan, Congo, Nicaragua, Angola, Afghanistan, and Pakistan.

The types of grievances that lead to violence are varied. Latin America's guerrilla struggles have been rooted in class conflict. Revolutionary movements in Cuba,

Nicaragua, El Salvador, Peru, and Colombia have brought disenchanted students and intellectuals together with peasants and the urban poor. The primary sources of their discontent have been inequitable land and income distribution, poverty, rising prices, state corruption, and government repression. Violent conflict in Africa and parts of Asia, on the other hand, is more frequently tied to ethnic or regional hostilities, with class divisions playing a secondary role. Secessionist movements in Eritrea and Tigre fought for decades before gaining independence or greater autonomy from Ethiopia.

The toll from these conflicts has been staggering. From 1981 to 1991, some 75 thousand died in El Salvador. In the Angolan civil war, over half a million perished either from the fighting or from war-related starvation. In Nigeria, Ethiopia, Congo, Sudan, Mozambique, Guatemala, Indonesia, India, Cambodia, and Lebanon, staggering numbers of citizens—sometimes in the hundreds of thousands or even millions—have died directly or indirectly from ethnic or class conflict. Recently, attacks by pro-government militia in Sudan have led to tens of thousands of deaths in the Darfur region.

Because governments in the developing world so frequently lack legitimacy or effective links to the people, many are extremely vulnerable. Often, the armed forces seize power, seeking to establish political stability, to replace an ineffective or corrupt leader, to pursue a particular development program, or, most commonly, simply to protect the military's own institutional interests. All too often, however, these military regimes have turned out to be more corrupt, more repressive, and less efficient than the civilian governments they had replaced.

Before examining manifestations of political underdevelopment in greater detail, we will consider the ways in which social scientists have tried to explain the *causes* of underdevelopment and the pathways that they have prescribed for change.

THEORIES OF UNDERDEVELOPMENT AND DEVELOPMENT

Having described the differences between developed nations and the LDCs, we must now ask why it is that some countries have developed their political and economic systems while others are still struggling. Over the years, analysts have offered two distinct explanations. The first insists that political and economic development are driven primarily by *domestic* factors (within the Third World), most notably changes in the country's cultural values. The second approach emphasizes the effects of *international* trade and investment, suggesting that *external* exploitation is the primary cause of Third World underdevelopment. These approaches are called, respectively, *modernization theory* and *dependency theory*.[14]

Modernization Theory and the Importance of Cultural Values

In the decades after World War II, as the demise of European colonialism produced a host of newly independent nations in Africa and Asia, Western social scientists formulated an understanding of development and underdevelopment known as **modernization theory**.[15]

Despite the tremendous array of problems facing the Third World, modernization theorists were initially relatively optimistic about its prospects for development. They

expected that most LDCs could follow a path of economic and political modernization roughly parallel to that which had earlier been traveled by Western industrial
democracies. The LDCs merely needed to promote modern cultural values and to
create appropriate economic and political institutions. Transforming the culture of
developing nations was considered the key to modernization.

Drawing on the theories of seminal sociologists such as Max Weber and Talcott
Parsons, the theory distinguished between clusters of traditional versus modern
values.[16] Modern societies, it claimed, were more prone than traditional ones to judge
people by universal standards (that is, to evaluate them according to their own ability
rather than their family or ethnic origins), to believe in the possibility and desirability
of change, to be concerned with social and political issues beyond the scope of family
or village, and to believe that one should try to influence the political system.[17]

But how can a society with traditional values acquire modern ones? In large part, the
argument ran, modern values emerge as a natural by-product of socioeconomic change,
particularly urbanization and industrialization. When people leave their farms for factory
jobs in the cities, they commonly become literate and are exposed to new ideas and
experiences. Education and the mass media were also seen as key agents of change.

Thus, modernization theory focused on the *diffusion* of modern ideas both from the
developed world to the developing world and, within the Third World, from city to
countryside. Western foreign aid, trade, and institutions such as the Peace Corps could
help speed the process. Thus, modernization was envisioned, in part, as a process of
getting developing nations to think and act "more like us." "As time goes on," Marion
Levy predicted, "they and we will increasingly resemble one another. . . . The more
highly modernized societies become, the more they resemble one another."[18]

Along with modern values, LDCs need to develop more specialized and more complex political and economic institutions. They need to develop trained bureaucracies in
which promotions are determined by merit, rather than by connections, and decisions
are based on universally applied standards. A modern legal system is needed. And political parties have to channel popular demands and aspirations to the government.

In time, many of the early assumptions of modernization theory had to be modified. Initially, it had been too optimistic in its view of political and socioeconomic
change, assuming that modernizing countries could simultaneously and relatively
smoothly achieve economic growth, greater equality, democracy, stability, and greater
national autonomy. As Samuel Huntington has noted, the theorists erroneously
assumed that "all good things go together."[19] Eventually, a more sophisticated and pessimistic form of modernization theory emerged, asserting that change is often a
painful and disruptive process involving difficult choices. Indeed, although modernity
is associated with political stability, the painful transition from **traditional society** to
modern society, said Huntington, is often profoundly destabilizing.[20] In countries
such as South Korea and Brazil, modernization was initially advanced by authoritarian
governments rather than by democracy.[21]

Dependency Theory

Beginning in the 1950s, a number of social scientists, primarily in Latin America and
the United States, raised more fundamental objections to modernization theory.
Under the banner of **dependency theory**, they challenged most of its fundamental
assumptions.

To begin with, they rejected the notion that LDCs could follow the same path to development as Western nations had. When Great Britain became the world's first industrial power, they noted, it had faced no external competition. In today's world, nations trying to industrialize have to compete against well-established industrial giants. In addition, argued Theotonio Dos Santos, LDCs have to borrow financial capital and must purchase advanced technology from the developed world, thereby making them dependent on external economic forces and ultimately weakening their growth.[22]

Whereas modernization theorists generally saw Western influence in the Third World as beneficial, so-called *dependencistas* insisted that it was Western colonialism that had turned Africa and Asia into poorly paid sources of cheap food and raw materials for the colonial powers. And long after Third World nations had achieved political independence, they remained economically and politically dependent on the developed world. Production and export of manufactured goods—the most profitable economic activities—were allegedly confined to the highly industrialized democracies, called "**the core**." Third World nations ("the periphery") were largely relegated to the production and export of food and raw materials, condemned to trade for industrial imports on unfavorable terms.[23]

In the political realm, dependency theorists insisted that Third World economic elites, backed by the economic and military power of the "core nations," maintained a political system that benefited the few at the expense of the majority. Dependency theory was obviously an attractive model for Third World scholars, suggesting that underdevelopment was not the fault of the LDCs but, rather, the result of foreign exploitation. But in U.S. universities, as well, dependency theory challenged and sometimes displaced modernization theory as the major scholarly explanation of underdevelopment.

But just as early modernization theory had been overly optimistic about the prospects for simultaneous economic and political development, early dependency theory proved to be excessively pessimistic. When *dependencistas* proposed solutions to the Third World's problems, they were often very vague or unpromising.

Despite that bleak prognosis, however, nations such as Brazil and Mexico began to enjoy substantial industrial growth. In his more sophisticated version of dependency theory, Fernando Henrique Cardoso rejected the contention that all Third World countries were condemned to underdevelopment. Drawing heavily from the experience of his native Brazil, Cardoso contended that the active intervention of the state and the linking of domestic firms with multinational corporations could allow some LDCs to industrialize and enjoy considerable economic growth. He referred to this process as "associated-dependent development."

Cardoso noted that countries such as Brazil, Colombia, and Mexico could industrialize while remaining dependent on multinationals in the "core" for investment, credit, and technology. Nevertheless, he and other critics viewed that kind of development as undesirable in a number of ways. Growth was led by heavily mechanized companies that did not hire sufficient local labor and produced more profitable— hence more expensive—goods that benefited middle- and upper-class consumers but were beyond the reach of the masses.[24] Indeed, instead of reducing poverty, dependent development had allegedly contributed to a growing income gap between the poor and the more affluent classes. At the same time, an alliance of many Third World economic, political, and military elites with multinational corporations helped keep unrepresentative regimes in power.

Modernization Theory and Dependency Theory Compared

Dependency theory offered a useful correction to modernization theory in a number of ways. It highlighted an important influence on Third World societies that previously had been largely neglected—the role of international trade, finance, and investment. Eventually, modernization theorists came to recognize that development required more than adopting new values or changing domestic political structures. Thus, dependency theory shifted the focus of research on the Third World from overwhelmingly internal factors to greater recognition of international influences.

Dependency theorists also helped redefine the concept of economic development. Whereas earlier research had stressed the importance of economic growth, *dependencistas* emphasized the significance of economic distribution. When rapid economic growth produces increased concentration of wealth and income, as frequently has happened, the poor may even end up worse off. Influenced by dependency theory and similar critiques, even establishment groups such as the World Bank reoriented their goals toward "redistribution with growth."[25]

But just as modernization theorists tended to overemphasize the internal causes of underdevelopment, early *dependencistas* erroneously attributed virtually all Third World problems to external economic forces. LDCs were often portrayed as virtually helpless pawns with little hope for development. Cardoso refined the theory by insisting that developing nations had options within the broad limits of dependency. With the proper government policies and the appropriate relationships between social classes, Third World nations could achieve associated-dependent development.

But even Cardoso's refinement fails to explain East Asia's spectacular development record since the 1960s. Those economies have been tremendously dependent—that is, very closely tied to the developed world (the core) through trade, credits, investment, and technology transfer. Indeed, they are far more globalized (integrated into the world economy) than any other part of the developing world. But contrary to what Cardoso and other dependency theorists had predicted, countries such as South Korea and Taiwan have been the economic stars of the Third World, coupling astonishing economic growth with comparatively equitable economic distribution. Although the East Asian experience does not prove that greater economic interdependence can bring similar accomplishments in Africa, Latin America, or the Middle East, it does indicate that one must look for factors beyond economic dependency to explain underdevelopment.

At the same time, however, more recent economic events in East Asia demonstrate that extensive economic linkages to the world economy and to the core also carry certain risks. To attract foreign investment, Thailand and other countries in the region kept the value of their national currencies stable and artificially linked to the dollar. In 1997, when the Thai government was no longer able to maintain the exchange rate for its overvalued currency, the baht, its worth plunged. The value of Malaysia's, Indonesia's, and South Korea's currencies soon fell sharply as well. Foreign investors, seeing the dollar values of their holdings plummet, withdrew their investments whenever possible. At the same time, local firms that had borrowed dollars from U.S. banks saw the cost of those debts in their local currencies skyrocket, forcing many companies to shut down. As many of those borrowers defaulted on their loans, international banks cut off new credit to the region, further depressing their economies. As one

---

Box 15-1

ARGENTINA: THE VOYAGE FROM DEVELOPMENT TO UNDERDEVELOPMENT

Whereas the concerns of political analysts studying the Third World have largely focused on the question of how an underdeveloped nation can become developed, Argentina poses a disturbingly contrasting question: How did it change from having been one of the world's wealthiest nations to being underdeveloped? Indeed, Argentina may be the only country in the world that changed from being economically developed to underdevelopment.

Blessed with abundant and rich agricultural and ranching lands and low population density, the country attracted huge numbers of Italian, Spanish, and other European immigrants during the late nineteenth and early twentieth centuries. Possessing a level of human capital (education, skills) rarely found in the Third World, those immigrants joined other relatively educated and skilled Argentineans in creating an industrial base that supplemented Argentina's dynamic grain and meat exports. As of the early 1930s, the country had the fifth highest per capita income in the world. Ranking behind only the United States, Canada, Australia, and Switzerland, it was far wealthier than Italy or Japan.

Today, Argentina still has one of the highest educational levels and standards of living in Latin America. But its per capita income currently ranks only 66th in the world, with per capita income roughly half that of Hong Kong, Singapore, or South Korea.[26] Beginning in the 1930s, Argentina's economic stagnation contributed to political stalemate. Bitter labor-management conflicts produced frequent unrest, the military often intervened in politics, and in the 1960s and 1970s revolutionary guerrilla groups helped provoke a brutal military dictatorship. Since the early 1980s, the military has exited from politics. But the financial crisis of January 2002 gave the country five civilian presidents in a period of just two weeks.

How did Argentina decline so precipitously? Supporters of dependency theory argue that, over time, Argentina had to pay developed nations increasingly higher prices for imported manufactured goods while the value of its agricultural exports did not rise correspondingly.

But believers in modernization theory point out that other countries that depend heavily on the same exports, including Australia and New Zealand, have fared very well economically and politically. They note that ever since Argentina's charismatic strongman, Juan Péron, rose to power in the 1940s, successive governments have spent beyond their means to win popular support. Meanwhile rich agricultural exporters failed to modernize their production techniques to stay internationally competitive. No matter which side is correct, Argentina serves as a somber reminder that achieving economic development does not guarantee keeping it.

---

observer noted, "Along the way, billions of dollars in production and hundreds of millions of jobs [were] lost."[27] Recovery took years.

Thus, the evidence regarding foreign economic penetration is decidedly mixed. Today, many political scientists agree that a full understanding of development must draw on the strengths of both modernization and dependency theories while recognizing the limits of each. In the sections that follow, we turn from general development theories to an examination of specific challenges and obstacles to development facing Third World nations today. (See Box 15-1.)

SOURCES OF POLITICAL CONFLICT

Viewers of the evening news might understandably believe that the Third World is in a constant state of upheaval. News stories stress revolutions, civil wars, riots, and **military coups** in such countries as Afghanistan, Colombia, Indonesia, Iraq, and Sierra

Leone. While, in fact, large portions of the developing world are peaceful, sharp internal divisions do plague many nations. Two particularly vexing sources of tension have been class conflict and ethnic conflict.

Class Conflict

In all nations, modern and developing alike, some people are much wealthier than others. Invariably, that inequality causes some degree of political division. In more harmonious societies, class differences merely influence the voters' electoral preferences. For example, blue-collar workers tend to vote for the Labour Party in Great Britain and the Democratic Party in the United States, whereas well-to-do businesspeople tend to support, respectively, Conservative and Republican Party candidates. Because wealth and income in the developing world are often more unequally distributed, and because the political battle for scarce economic resources is frequently more heated, class conflict in the LDCs frequently is more intense or even violent.

Unfortunately, the initial stages of economic modernization often heighten class tensions as income gaps between the poor and the social classes above them tend to widen (the Kuznets effect). In the cities, industrialization frequently expands the size of the middle class and creates a "labor elite" of skilled, unionized factory workers while many unskilled, underemployed workers are left behind in the urban slums. In the countryside, as large commercial farms expand their operations to take advantage of new export opportunities, they often evict neighboring peasant cultivators from their small, family plots.

Early economic modernization not only tends to sharpen class tensions but also increases the political capacity of previously powerless groups. For example, as the gap between rural and urban living standards widens, increased rural migration to the cities raises the literacy rate of these former peasants and exposes them to more political information from the mass media. Consequently, the newly arrived, urban poor tend to be better informed and more politically active. In time, some of these urban migrants may return to the countryside and mobilize their fellow villagers. Peasants being forced off their land by the expansion of large, commercial farms also may be radicalized. Industrialization also generates labor unions, giving workers an important vehicle for political mobilization. The growing middle class—particularly university students, professionals, and intellectuals—provides leadership for anti-establishment political parties, labor unions, or even revolutionary groups in some nations.[28]

For all those reasons, the transitional period of economic development—when a country moves out of socioeconomic backwardness toward greater modernity—often witnesses heightened class tensions. That conflict may express itself peacefully at the ballot box and through union activity. In Chile, for example, organized labor formed the backbone of Popular Unity (the UP), a Marxist coalition that elected Salvador Allende to the presidency in 1970. Eventually, however, political tensions pitting the UP government and its labor and peasant supporters against opposition parties, business groups, and parts of the middle class precipitated a brutal military coup against Allende in 1973.

The most intense class conflict in the developing world has often pitted the rural poor against local landlords and the national government. At the bottom of the political and economic hierarchy and often unable to assert their demands within the political system, peasants may turn to violence. Vietnam and China, for example, had peasant-based, communist revolutions. Peasants also played important roles in the Mexican, Cuban, and Nicaraguan revolutions. Currently, they form the backbone of guerrilla insurrections in Colombia and Nepal, and not long ago were the core of revolutionary movements in El Salvador and Vietnam.[29] Thus, although Karl Marx, the father of modern revolutionary theory, had expected class conflict to manifest itself in the tensions between urban capitalists and blue-collar workers, twentieth- and twenty-first-century revolutionary struggles in the LDCs have far more frequently been waged in the countryside. No matter how appalling living conditions for many Third World industrial workers may be, those workers are generally better off economically and politically than peasants and, hence, are less prone to join armed insurrections. Although urban labor unions may be quite militant and often support radical political parties, most still work within the framework of legal and peaceful political action.

With the fall of the communist bloc and China's current lack of interest in class struggle, however, class conflict seems to be declining as a source of political polarization in the developing world, only to be replaced by increased ethnic conflict.

Ethnic Conflict

No type of political division has brought developing nations more protracted and bitter conflict than has **ethnicity**. Throughout the Third World, people have been drawn into opposing camps on the basis of language, culture, religion, and race with an intensity that usually exceeds the influence of socioeconomic class.[30]

Of course, ethnic conflict is not limited to the Third World. It has flared up fairly recently in such disparate places as Serbia, Northern Ireland, the former Soviet Union, and Canada. But it is frequently particularly bitter in the LDCs because of the intense competition for scarce economic resources. So, although American urban politics has sometimes featured competition between Anglo-Saxons, Irish, Italians, Jews, Hispanics, and African Americans, the stakes of ethnic competition have never been as high as in Indonesia, Lebanon, and India. In those countries, contending ethnic groups frequently feel that their very survival depends on how the state distributes public-sector jobs, schools, and development projects.

Ethnic tensions have been most intense in Africa and parts of Asia, where colonial powers frequently drew national boundaries that threw conflicting ethnic groups into a single country. In India, the struggle for independence highlighted deep divisions between Muslims and the Hindu majority. Ultimately, it resulted in the establishment of Pakistan, a separate Muslim state carved out of India. In the months leading up to and following independence, communal violence between Hindus and Muslims led to some two million deaths and uprooted twelve million refugees.[31] Today, religiously based strife continues in the Indian state of Kashmir, where Islamic rebels seek independence or unification with Pakistan, and in Punjab, where the Indian military and Sikh separatists also have waged a bloody conflict.

In Africa, tribal-based civil wars have plagued the continent for decades, producing widespread destruction and vast numbers of fatalities in countries such as Nigeria, Sudan, Ethiopia, Congo, Mozambique, and Angola. Interethnic violence has also torn apart Sri Lanka, Indonesia, Lebanon, India, and other Asian and Middle Eastern nations. Ethnicity and race relations are not as volatile in Latin America, but in the recent past rural guerrilla movements in Guatemala and Peru drew support based on indigenous (native Indian) resentments against white domination.

Not all ethnic divisions have led to violent conflict, however. Although nearly all African nations have multi tribal populations, many have reached accommodations between ethnic groups. Elsewhere, in countries such as Malaysia and Lebanon past interethnic violence seems to have been brought under control. Worldwide, after 50 years of steadily rising conflict, the level of ethnic protests and rebellion within nations began falling somewhat in the early 1990s.[32] Still, ethnic conflict is likely to remain among the Third World's greatest challenges for years to come. Experience from the First World and the Second World has demonstrated that such tensions not only endure for generations but also may resurface after a long period of apparent calm. One need only look to the enduring strains between blacks and whites in the United States, between Catholics and Protestants in Northern Ireland, and between Christians (especially Serbs) and Muslims in Yugoslavia.

PROBLEMS OF POLITICAL PARTICIPATION

The intense political and economic tensions that divide many LDCs present them with a difficult dilemma. In many ethnically divided nations, large portions of the population are denied full political participation. In Iraq, for example, Saddam Hussein and his ruling elite were drawn primarily from the country's Sunni Muslim minority, and both the Shiite majority and the Kurds were denied representation. Today, following the toppling of Saddam's regime, it is the Sunnis who fear being excluded from political power. Similarly, Guatemala's large Indian population has often been denied political rights.

© AP/Wide World Photos

ESCALATING CYCLE OF ETHNIC VIOLENCE   Growing sectarian violence between Shiite and Sunni Muslims has torn Iraq apart. Militia of Shi'a radical cleric, Muqtada al Sadr, secure a road near a market east of Baghdad after the Sunni al-Qaida in Iraq had declared all-out war on the Shi'a majority.

In other LDCs, some divided by class tensions, military or single-party governments deny the entire population participation in meaningful elections. Even in the growing number of nations with contested elections, the peasantry and the urban poor often lack the resources, political skills, or connections to receive a fair hearing from government policy makers. The denial of political representation to so many citizens means that governments are not held accountable for their actions, corruption flourishes, and inadequately represented groups, such as the poor, do not get their fair share of government resources. For all those reasons, political development must create additional channels for mass political participation.

On the other hand, there is also a danger that political participation may expand faster than the nation's political institutions can accommodate. Years ago, Samuel Huntington warned that developing countries may experience an explosion of demands on the political system as formerly non-politicized people move to urban areas, attain higher educational levels, and otherwise increase their political awareness.[33] Unless more sophisticated political institutions can be created to channel their rising demands, he argued, political disorder and decay lie in waiting.

Huntington's thesis was controversial because it suggested to many readers that LDCs frequently are not ready for democracy and that some degree of authoritarianism may be necessary during the early stages of economic and political modernization to maintain stability. But he also looked to longer-term solutions through the creation of political institutions that could channel citizens' demands in an effective and orderly manner. Developing strong and effective political parties, he argued, is the key to orderly political participation, bringing together diverse groups in society and translating a wide array of conflicting demands into workable political alternatives. Other institutions also need improvement in the process of political development. Government bureaucracies, for example, must become more competent and honest so that they can better implement state policies and satisfy popular needs.

Ultimately, then, there is a delicate balance between the need for increased political participation and the dangers of an excessively rapid escalation in participation. It is probably unreasonable to expect all developing nations—many of them torn by class or ethnic divisions—to conform fully to Western standards of democracy. However, since the 1970s there has been an explosion of democratic government throughout the world, including the former communist world and the LDCs. The change has been most dramatic in Latin America, a region governed almost exclusively by authoritarian regimes at the start of that period and now composed almost entirely of democracies.

Mexico completed that transformation in 2000 when the PRI was ousted from office after 71 years as the ruling party (see Chapter 17). Although democracy has advanced far more haltingly in Africa, the number of electoral democracies on that continent has grown impressively. And in Asia, authoritarian governments have given way to democratic ones in Thailand, South Korea, Taiwan, Indonesia, the Philippines, and elsewhere. Only in the Middle East has democracy made little headway.

Although the developing world's new democratic governments have not always performed well (many are corrupt, incompetent, and even occasionally repressive), on the whole they have opened up new avenues of participation to their citizens without the resulting unrest that Huntington feared. What has caused this flurry of democratic transitions in what has been the most extensive democratic revolution in world history?

There are many reasons, but we will highlight two. The first factor involves contagion—the tendency of certain political trends or forces to spread from one country to another. From the late 1940s to the 1960s, as the former European colonies in Africa, Asia, and the Middle East gained independence, many new national leaders were attracted to Marxism because it seemed to offer them a path to rapid economic development and reduced dependency on their former colonial rulers. In countries such as Ghana, Egypt, and Indonesia, authoritarian governments (usually left-wing) offered a host of arguments (many of them self-serving) that claimed to demonstrate that meaningful electoral competition would be too divisive in ethnically and economically divided countries such as theirs. In Latin America, on the other hand, right-wing military dictatorships seized power in countries such as Argentina, Brazil, and Chile, allegedly to avert a communist threat. By the 1970s, however, as the weaknesses of military and single-party rule became increasingly apparent, democracy began to acquire new legitimacy. By the start of the 1990s, as communism collapsed in the Soviet Union and Eastern Europe, authoritarian government of any sort fell "out of style" and democracy became more fashionable. Democracy also became contagious. For example, when South Korean students—watching the local news or CNN—witnessed their counterparts in the Philippines overthrow the Ferdinand Marcos dictatorship, they began to think more seriously of toppling their own authoritarian government (and, subsequently, they succeeded).

The second important factor is that, in time, socioeconomic modernization in many developing nations has produced a more hospitable environment for democratic government. Despite serious setbacks in certain cases, LDCs as a whole have significantly raised their educational levels in the past three or four decades and often have improved their per capita incomes. Those two developments have important political implications, since there is substantial evidence that nations enjoying higher income and literacy levels are more likely to sustain democracy. For example, few countries with literacy rates of less than 50 percent have been able to sustain democracy (though there are notable exceptions, such as India), whereas countries above that point are likely to be democracies.[34] At the same time, countries that are more well off economically are much more capable of sustaining democratic government. In a study of how well democracy endured in 135 countries over a 40-year period (1950–1990), the authors found that it is most fragile in poor countries (with per capita incomes of less than $1,000) and becomes more sustainable as national income rises. "Above $6,000 [per-capita income]," they note, "democracies are impregnable and can be expected to live forever; no democratic system has ever fallen in a country where per capita income exceeds $6,055 [Argentina's level in 1976]."[35]

WOMEN IN THIRD WORLD SOCIETY AND POLITICS

In most of the developing world, full political and economic participation has been particularly difficult for women to attain. More fundamentally, women may be subjected to severe social and economic deprivation and exploitation. For example, in parts of Asia and Africa, millions of young girls—often as young as nine or ten—have been sold by their impoverished parents into arranged marriages, while thousands of women live in virtual slavery. In **fundamentalist** Islamic states such as Iran and Saudi Arabia, laws restrict the types of jobs that women can hold and the kinds of apparel they can wear.

TABLE 15.3   GENDER INEQUALITY IN THE DEVELOPING WORLD

Country	Female Literacy as Percent of Male Literacy	Gender-Related Development Index (GDI)	Gender Empowerment Measure (GEM)
Norway	a	1	1
United States	a	8	12
South Korea	a	27	59
Chile	100	38	61
China	91	64	nd
Iran	84	78	75
Guatemala	84	94	nd
India	65	98	nd
Sudan	72	110	nd
Nigeria	80	123	nd
Ethiopia	69	134	nd

[a] These data are not calculated for developed countries, but the ratio for all three countries is assumed to be around 100.

Women's Economic and Social Status

Today, in much of the developing world women continue to have fewer educational opportunities than males, shorter life expectancy, and fewer occupational opportunities in government and the private sector (see Table 15.3). To be sure, there has been progress in most of the LDCs in narrowing the educational gender gap. In 1995, for every 100 boys enrolled in secondary school in the developing world, there were only 84 girls (with obvious variations between individual countries). By the early years of the twenty-first century, there were 91 girls for every 100 boys.[36] Yet, as Table 15.3 makes clear, there is still much progress to be made.

The first column in the table indicates how the female adult literacy rate in a given country compares to the male rate. Thus, the literacy rate of women in India is less than two-thirds that of men (65 percent as high) while in Chile women and men have the same literacy rate. This offers us an indication of the educational opportunity gap (if any) between women and men. There are a small number of countries, not shown in the table, such as Jamaica, where women have a higher rate of literacy than do men (Jamaica's score is 109). At the same time, there are countries, such as Yemen (41), where women's literacy rate is less than half men's, and others, such as Chad (31), where the female literacy rate is less than a third that of men. Note that column 1 doesn't tell us anything about the national literacy rate. It only compares the two sexes. If, for example, only 30 percent of males and 30 percent of females were literate in a particular country, the score for column 1 would be 100, as the women's rate would be equal to the men's. There is no data on such gender differences available for Norway, the United States, or other developed countries, but these countries have higher than 95 percent literacy for both sexes and, a female rate that would be about 100 percent of men's. Overall, two tendencies stand out: first, very poor countries (such as India, Sudan, and Ethiopia) tend to have a greater gender gap than more affluent countries (such as Chile or Mexico); second, cultural factors are also significant—South Asia (including India) and Arab states have greater gender gaps than Latin America or East Asia.

Column 2 presents each country's ranking on the **Gender-Related Development Index (GDI)**. Basically, this begins by comparing the Human Development Index (HDI), discussed earlier in this chapter, for males and females in a given country. Thus, for each country an index is constructed for both genders that combines measurements of life expectancy, literacy, educational attainment, and income. The GDI compares the HDIs for women with those of men. The better women do relative to men, the higher the country's GDI. Finally, the countries are ranked according to their GDIs. So, Norway has the highest GDI score in the world (just as it also has the world's highest overall HDI), meaning that it has the smallest gender gap on HDI measures. GDI scores (and rankings) are available for only 177 countries. Three impoverished African nations—Sudan (110th in the world), Nigeria (123rd), and Ethiopia (134th)—have the lowest GDI rankings in Table 15.3. More generally, when we consider all the countries not on the list as well, we find that GDI scores generally correlate with income. That is, among the poorest nations, not only is the HDI score comparatively low overall, but the gap between men and women tends to be wider. Thus, most of the countries with the lowest GDI scores are poor African nations.

Finally, the last column compares each country's GEM and ranks them from first to last on this dimension. The **Gender Empowerment Measure (GEM)** is an index of three combined measures: the level of women's participation and decision-making in the economy, the level of female participation and decision-making in the political system, and the degree of women's power over economic resources. Thus, the GEM score (and ranking) is an indication of women's power in the economic and political system. It should be noted that GEM indexes are available only for 80 countries (of about 200) in the world and are generally unavailable for the poorest countries. Consequently GEM rankings are available for only five countries in Table 15.3. However, if we examine those five countries *and consider countries not included in the table*, the general pattern that we have seen for female literacy and for GDI ranking continues. The wealthiest countries in the world tend to have the highest GEM rankings (Japan, which ranks only 43rd out of 80 countries, is a notable exception), while the relatively poorer countries for which we have data had greater gender gaps. But, once again, culture also makes a difference. Norway and the other four Nordic nations had the five highest GEM rankings. Latin American nations, particularly those in the Caribbean, outperformed Asian countries. As with GDI and female literacy, Muslim nations generally performed poorly. Indeed, of the 80 countries with GEM rankings, the seven nations with the lowest scores were all Muslim. The other three Muslim countries on the list were ranked between 51st (Malaysia) and 71st (Pakistan). Even comparatively more affluent Muslim countries, such as Bahrain and Saudi Arabia, have relatively low GEM rankings.

Women as Political Leaders

If we turn our focus from the socioeconomic status of Third World women generally to the opportunities for political leadership available to women, we find a mixed picture. A surprising number of women have risen to the pinnacle of their political system, serving as prime ministers or presidents. Thus, for example, while the United States has never had a woman president, the Muslim countries of Turkey, Bangladesh, and Pakistan have all been governed by women prime ministers. So too have India and

Sri Lanka, while the Philippines have had two women presidents. On the other hand, as we will see, those women have almost all made it to those positions as heirs to a political dynasty begun by a male relative. Looking at political leadership positions below the very top, we find that the percentage of women in parliament (or congress) has risen in recent years, but still trails well behind men as it does in most advanced industrial democracies.

The list of current and past women government leaders includes Indian Prime Minister Indira Gandhi, Argentine President Isabel Perón, Nicaraguan President Violeta Chamorro, Filipino Presidents Corazon Aquino and Gloria Macapagal Arroyo, Pakistani Prime Minister Benazir Bhutto, Bangladeshi Prime Ministers Begum Khaleda Zia and Sheik Hasina Wazed, Sri Lankan Prime Minister Sirimavo Bandaranaike and President Chandrika Kumaratunga, Panamanian President Mireya Elisa Moscoso Rodríguez, and Indonesian President Megawati Sukurnoputri. Two important break-throughs took place in 2005–2006. Ellen Johnson-Sirleaf—a Harvard-trained banker—was elected president of Liberia and became Africa's first elected female head of state. At about the same time, Michelle Bachelet—a doctor, former defense minister, former political prisoner under the rule of General Augusto Pinochet, and daughter of a general who died in Pinochet's prison—was elected as Chile's first woman president. Elsewhere in the developing world, about a dozen lesser-known women also served (some briefly) as prime minister or president.

While this list is impressive, it may give an exaggerated picture of the opportunities open to women. All of the women just named assumed the leadership of their country as the widow or daughter of a former prime minister, president, or opposition leader, many of them national heroes. For example, Indira Gandhi was the daughter of India's revered first prime minister, Jawaharlal Nehru. Bangladesh's two most recent prime ministers have been, respectively, the widow and daughter of assassinated presidents. The Philippines' Corazon Aquino and Nicaragua's Violeta Chamorro were elected president following the assassination of their husbands, who had been opposition leaders against

A BREAKTHROUGH FOR WOMEN
Chilean President Michelle Bachelet addresses the Congress and the nation. She had won a decisive electoral victory, the first for a woman in a country known for its conservative social values.

their country's dictator. Argentina's Isabel Perón was the widow of legendary President Juan Perón, and Indonesia's former President Megawati is the daughter of Sukarno, the first president of the country. Some of these women proved to be very qualified. Others were not. But what brought them to the top of the political ladder was primarily their lineage.

Furthermore, all of them have had family ties and elite social status that make them very unrepresentative of other women in their country. Former Prime Minister Bhutto, for example—the daughter of a slain prime minister—was born to a wealthy land-owning family and was educated at Harvard and Oxford.[37] Similarly, Burmese opposition leader Aung San Suu Kyi, the winner of the 1991 Nobel Peace Prize, is the daughter of the country's most revered founding father and received her university degree from Oxford. For women who are not born to the nation's elite and, more significantly, are not the daughters or widows of prominent national leaders, opportunities for political leadership remain very limited (see Box 15-2). Nor does the election of a woman president or prime minister necessarily lead to improvements in the lives of the average woman in their country. Nations such as Bangladesh, India, Indonesia, Sri Lanka, and Turkey have relatively low GEMs and GDIs. For example, while Bangladesh has been led since 1991 by two women prime ministers, it currently ranks 79th among the 80 countries that report GEM scores.

THIRD WORLD POLITICAL INSTITUTIONS

Problems of inadequate political participation and ineffective government representation in the developing world are compounded by the weaknesses of political institutions, especially political parties. Parties are most effective when they can reach out to a large segment of the population, incorporate supporters into the political system, socialize them into the prevailing political culture, and build coalitions and forge compromises among contending groups in society.

In the LDCs, however, political parties often fail to provide badly needed political representation to newly politicized urban migrants, peasants, oppressed minorities, and women. All too often, they represent the narrow interests of elites or those of a single ethnic group or region. Other parties are built around a single charismatic leader without a well-defined political program. Once in power, such parties often cannot govern effectively. The **wave of democracy** since the 1970s has restored or given birth to more effective political parties in a number of countries. But, for the most part, parties—as well as other key political institutions—remain relatively weak.

Although civilian governments in the Third World generally have government structures that resemble our own, those institutions tend to operate quite differently. Congresses and parliaments are frequently subservient to the executive branch. Their legal powers are often limited, and they often rubber-stamp the chief executive's policies. The judicial branch is usually weaker still, rarely challenging the executive's authority.

Political power, then, tends to be concentrated in the hands of the executive branch and its large government bureaucracy. Even when civilian governments are overthrown by the armed forces, change is largely confined to the top, with the civilian president being replaced by a single military officer or military council and the bureaucracy headed by other military officers or by civilians loyal to the military regime.

Box 15-2

WOMEN'S REPRESENTATION
IN PARLIAMENT OR CONGRESS

Since women make up slightly over half the adult population of most countries, full gender equality in political representation would produce parliaments (a term used broadly here to include congresses) that were roughly half women. In fact, only a few countries in the world come close to that mark (women constitute 40 percent of the members of parliament in the five Nordic nations—Denmark, Finland, Iceland, Norway, and Sweden). In many developing nations, female representation is lower than in the West due partly to reduced educational and occupational opportunities for women in many countries, and cultural prejudices against women political leaders in others. As of 2006, Latin America and the Caribbean had the highest female legislative representation in the Third World (about 18 percent). Asia and sub-Saharan Africa were a bit behind with 16 to 17 percent female representation, and Arab states were well behind with only 8 percent.[38] While women in the developing world are clearly underrepresented, outside of the Arab nations their average parliamentary representation is comparable or superior to such advanced Western nations as Britain (20 percent), the United States (15 percent), France (12 percent), and Italy (11 percent).[39] Indeed, if we remove the Nordic countries from the European bloc of nations, female representatives in their parliaments

average 17.6 percent, little more than Latin America, Asia, and sub-Saharan Africa.

From 1996 to 2006, the number of women members of parliament worldwide rose from 10.1 percent to 16.7 percent. Gains in the LDCs during that period were sharpest in the Arab states (even so, they still had the world's lowest rate of female representation) and slowest in Asia (up only slightly from 13.1 to 16.4 percent, allowing Latin America to pass it as the Third World's leader). While part of this increase was related to greater educational and occupational opportunities for women or changing social values, much of the change was related to government actions expressly designed to increase female representation in the political system. These efforts have taken two forms: reserved seats for women and gender quotas for parliamentary candidates (which, in turn, can be produced in two different ways).

Under the first approach, a certain percentage of the seats in the parliament are reserved for women. Those quotas range from token representation in Jordan (with only 6 out of 110 parliamentary seats reserved for women) to quotas of near or above 30 percent in such nations as Rwanda and Iraq. Afghanistan, which recently was governed by the Taliban, undoubtedly the most repressive regime toward women in the world, has a new constitution, written under U.S. guidance, that

TABLE 15.4　THE PROPORTION OF WOMEN IN NATIONAL PARLIAMENTS
(REGIONAL AVERAGES AS OF MAY, 2006)

Region	Single House or Lower House	Upper House or Senate	Both Houses Combined
Nordic countries	40.0%	—	40.0%
Americas	20.6%	21.2%	20.7%
Europe—OSCE, including Nordic countries	19.9%	17.4%	19.4%
Europe—OSCE, excluding Nordic countries	17.7%	17.4%	17.6%
Sub-Saharan Africa	16.5%	17.6%	16.6%
Asia	16.3%	14.7%	16.1%
Pacific	11.8%	26.5%	13.8%
Arab States	8.2%	5.9%	7.7%

SOURCE: Inter-Parliamentary Union, *Women in National Parliaments* (May 31, 2006), http://www.ipu.org/wmn-e/world.htm.

(*Continued*)

Box 15-2

WOMEN'S REPRESENTATION
IN PARLIAMENT OR CONGRESS (*Continued*)

guarantees women 27 percent of all parliamentary seats. Some critics of reserved seat argue that it can result in the election of less qualified parliamentary representatives because women are guaranteed a number of seats and that it is sexist. Others feel that reserve quotas stigmatize the women who are elected. Supporters of reserved seats counter that they are necessary to overcome deep-seated prejudices against women in many societies.

A second method of raising women's representation in parliament is to establish a quota for female candidates. This, in turn, can be done in two ways: the government may mandate that women represent a certain percentage of each political party's parliamentary candidates, or the parties may institute voluntary quotas. Frequently the quota for the percentage of women candidates in each party is 30 percent, the threshold that scholars have found for "woman friendly" legislation (such as health care for women or laws protecting women against domestic violence) to be passed. Thus, for example, all Argentine parties are required to nominate women as at least 30 percent of their congressional candidates. In Costa Rica the law requires that each gender fill at least 40 percent of each party's congressional candidate list. In a number of developing nations, absent constitutional or legislative requirements, various political parties have voluntarily committed themselves to candidate quotas. Thus, for example, South Africa's African National Congress (ANC) has committed to select women for at least 30 percent of their parliamentary elections. Furthermore, they are committed to nominate women for half the posts in local government. Because the ANC dominates South African politics, its unilateral actions have raised female representation in that nation's parliament from 3 percent in the early 1990s to 33 percent in 2005. Major parties in Mexico and Mozambique have also voluntarily established quotas of 30 percent or higher.

Partly as a result of these electoral methods, a number of developing countries now have parliaments with at least 30 percent women members, at least twice the percentage in the U.S. Congress or the French and Italian parliaments. Rwanda now has the world's highest percentage of women in parliament, 49 percent. Cuba, Costa Rica, Mozambique, Argentina, South Africa, Iraq, Guyana, and Burundi all have between 30 and 36 percent. Sixteen other developing nations have parliaments or congresses with 20 to 29 percent female representation.

A caution should be kept in mind. Establishing gender quotas for candidates will likely not increase female representation in parliament unless there is also regulation of how women should be placed on the ballot. The law may require each party to field a list of candidates that is 30 percent female, but party leaders (overwhelmingly male) may nominate women primarily in districts that the party has little hope of winning (in a single-member-district system) or at the bottom of party lists (in a proportional representation system—PR). Therefore, the only highly effective quota systems are "**zipper-style quotas**" (or something similar) such as Argentina's and Costa Rica's. For example, Argentina uses PR in which voters choose from competing party lists. Congressional seats are awarded to each party in proportion to the percentage of votes their list received. If a party gains 33 percent of the national vote and wins, say, 60 of 180 seats in parliament, it sends to congress the 60 highest ranked candidates on its electoral list. The zipper-style quota requires that party lists place women in every third position starting with the top of the list. Thus, in this case, 20 of the 60 representatives that this party sends to congress would be women.

MILITARY INTERVENTION

One of the most persistent and most troublesome characteristics of Third World politics, at least until recently, has been the frequent intervention of the military in national politics. Before the 1970s and the recent worldwide wave of democracy, 59 LDCs had experienced at least one military coup attempt during the previous 40 years; 26 of those countries had witnessed four or more attempted coups. Bolivia and Venezuela topped the list with 18.[40] During the 1970s, Latin America and other Third World regions experienced continued takeovers by the armed forces— including coups in Argentina, Brazil, Chile, and Nigeria—but gradually the tide began to turn. Since the late 1970s, the number of new coups has been far more limited, and a growing number of military regimes have returned power to elected civilian governments.

Of course, coups are but the most extreme form of military intervention. El Salvador's armed forces controlled the political system for decades under the cover of carefully controlled elections. At least until recently, even elected civilian governments in nations such as Brazil, Guatemala, Nigeria, and Thailand have been subject to the military's veto power in certain policy areas. For example, the armed forces are often able to veto civilian government policies affecting national security and foreign affairs.

What accounts for the frequency of armed intervention? The answer lies less in the nature of Third World militaries than in the weakness of civilian governments and their political institutions. The military is more likely to seize power when civilian governments are inept and corrupt, when elected officials have little legitimacy or popular support, when there is internal disorder or economic chaos, or when there is a real or perceived likelihood of revolution. That does not mean that military coups under those circumstances are justified or that they are likely to improve internal conditions. And many coups are motivated solely by self-interest. For the most part, however, the more legitimate a civilian government is, the more it is backed by a strong political party, and the more effectively it governs, the lower the likelihood of a coup.

The goals of military governments are as varied as the circumstances that produce them. In the most underdeveloped political systems, military officers tend to have little professional training. In those circumstances, the armed forces may take power simply to further their own financial interests. Such coups often revolve around the personal ambitions of a single leader seeking power, wealth or, most likely, both. So-called **personal coups** (led by a dominant, charismatic figure) were once common in Central America and other parts of Latin America but have largely passed from that political scene. In recent decades, Africa has experienced a number of coups by ambitious officers, including Uganda's Idi Amin, Liberia's Sergeant Samuel Doe, and the Congo's General Mobutu Sese Seko. Most of those regimes governed disastrously. The Central African Republic's General Jean Bokassa, for example, killed and tortured thousands of his people (including schoolchildren). Declaring himself emperor, Bokassa spent millions of dollars on his coronation as emperor while his subjects suffered some of the world's worst poverty. Idi Amin's government in Uganda killed up to half a million people, particularly members of the oppressed Langi and Acholi tribes.

In the more developed Third World nations, where the officers' corps normally has greater professional training, coups are usually carried out by the military as an institution, rather than by a single officer, and they tend to have broader objectives. For example, in 1973 the armed forces of Latin America's two most long-standing democracies, Chile and Uruguay, seized power for the purpose of reordering their nations' political and economic systems. Each coup sought to crush strong leftist movements or topple a leftist government, destroy the labor movement, and create a healthy environment for business investment.

Institutional coups elsewhere also have frequently been designed to destroy radical mass movements; however, their strategies have varied. Whereas military regimes in Indonesia and Brazil had a distinctly conservative cast, the Peruvian military government tried to outflank revolutionary movements by implementing its own radical reforms—instituting one of Latin America's most sweeping land reforms, organizing the poor into government-directed unions, and introducing limited worker ownership of urban businesses.[41] But military dictatorships in Latin America and East Asia have generally been conservative, whereas in Africa and the Middle East (Ethiopia, Libya, Iraq) they have often been leftist.

Whether left-wing or right-wing, whether seeking selfish goals or perceived national objectives, most military regimes have had poor human rights records. In the most appalling cases, they have killed many thousands (Argentina, Uganda). Elsewhere (Panama, Ecuador) they have been more benign but still have harassed political opponents and the press. Ultimately, all of them, no matter how well intentioned, inhibit the spread of political participation and the development of badly needed political institutions. Although some military regimes have succeeded in specific areas—agrarian reform in Peru and Ecuador, industrialization in Brazil, rapid economic growth in Indonesia and South Korea—military rule elsewhere has generally been marked by incompetence, corruption, and repression. In Nigeria, for example, one of the world's lower-income nations, its former military ruler, General Sani Abacha, stole over $3 billion while in power (1993–1998) and previously as a power behind the throne.

As democracy has spread across Latin America and parts of Africa and Asia, the number of military governments has fallen substantially and the likelihood of future military takeovers is now much reduced. In countries such as Argentina, Brazil, Chile, Indonesia, Nigeria, and South Korea, where the military was once politically dominant, the armed forces seem committed to removing themselves from the front lines of politics. But General Pervez Musharraf's 1999 takeover in Pakistan indicates that coups will continue in the LDCs, even if at a reduced rate. And even in countries where the military does not hold power, it often continues to exercise considerable political influence from behind the scenes.

STRONG STATES, WEAK STATES

Because the private sector has often appeared incapable of dealing with many of their problems, Third World nations frequently have turned to the state (governmental authority) for solutions. For example, because it isn't sufficiently profitable for developers to build housing for the urban poor, many LDCs have created public housing agencies to address shortages in that area.

In the past, a number of Latin American governments, backed by middle-class and working-class electoral coalitions, used government institutions to promote industrial growth and expand education. Following World War II, the governments of newly independent countries in Africa and Asia were particularly inclined to intervene in the economy. Some of their founding fathers shared a socialist vision acquired during their studies in Europe. They believed that a powerful state could promote economic development in countries with inadequate private capital. Government, they argued, could also achieve greater economic and social equality and could provide better education and health care for their impoverished populations.

But leftists were not the only ones who favored a powerful state. During the 1960s and 1970s, several right-wing military regimes in South America increased state power in order to control radical labor unions and to stimulate industrialization.[42] Even in the Far East, where conservative political leaders revere the free-enterprise system, the governments of Taiwan, South Korea, and Singapore helped plan and direct industrial growth.[43]

Thus, throughout much of the Third World, the size and the formal power of the state expanded substantially during the postwar era. Large government bureaucracies were devoted to education, health care, and economic development. State enterprises often dominated banking, transportation, communications, electrical power, mining, and the marketing of agricultural products. On both the left and the right, proponents of broad government intervention felt that a powerful state was the solution to a range of socioeconomic and political problems. More recently, however, critics have blamed state intervention for many of the developing world's political and economic ills.

At the same time, however, despite the great expansion of state activities and the proliferation of government agencies, most Third World governments are actually weaker than they seem.[44] As Lynne Hammergren has noted, "constitutions and legislation often accord enormous powers of control to central governments, but . . . the limited success of . . . governments in enforcing their own legislation suggests that the extent of this control is not great."[45] Extensive governmental programs that look impressive on paper often are far more limited in their application.

The reasons for that gap vary. In some countries, powerful, vested interest groups such as agribusiness or bankers are able to block governmental initiatives that threaten their interests. Elsewhere, governments lack the financial or technical resources to satisfactorily implement proposed programs in areas such as public health, education, and transportation. And, in other instances, government agencies simply lack the trained personnel needed to implement approved legislation.

In general, governments seem to be least successful when they manage large firms such as railroads, telephone companies, and steel mills. Frequently, such enterprises face no competition, leaving them little incentive to be efficient. All too often, the size of their payroll spirals out of control as they hire loyal supporters of the government or the ruling party for patronage jobs. Finally, many of these companies lose money by design because their products are sold at a subsidized price determined by political pressures rather than by the market. Not surprisingly, consumers soon view benefits such as cheap utility and transportation prices as their right. Consequently, few governments were prepared to alienate voters by ending those subsidies.

As government spending for subsidies and other programs spiraled without commensurate tax revenues, many central governments covered their deficits by borrowing abroad. By the 1980s, many LDCs found themselves deeply in debt to foreign banks, with alarming government budget deficits and high rates of inflation. As a consequence, there has been a strong trend in recent decades toward reducing state economic involvement. Many governments—from India and Pakistan to Argentina and Mexico (see Chapter 16)—have reduced state economic regulation and embarked on **privatization** programs (the sale of state enterprises to the private sector). Although some state enterprises had been successful, others had clearly been inefficient. As large government deficits and spiraling foreign debt forced many developing nations to reduce state economic intervention, conservative economic models (labeled in the literature as "neoliberal reforms") were borrowed from the West. The aggressively conservative economic policies of Great Britain's Prime Minister Thatcher (Chapter 12) and American President Reagan influenced a number of Third World governments. Finally, the collapse of the communist Soviet bloc further discredited state-centered economies.

It is probably too early to evaluate fully the effects of privatization and government downsizing. Plagued by budgetary deficits and rampant inflation, many governments had no choice but to reduce state subsidies for basic consumer items. Undoubtedly, many privatized enterprises are being run more efficiently and are making healthier profits. Yet, there are also social costs to these changes. Since government subsidies were removed, already-malnourished urban families have been forced to pay higher (sometimes far higher) prices for bread, milk, and rice. Newly privatized companies have laid off thousands of workers in nations burdened with high unemployment.

And highly placed government officials in nations such as Mexico and Pakistan have used their inside information and influence to make fortunes in the sale of state firms. Thus, policy makers must balance the uncertain promise of longer-term economic gains with the more immediate economic and political costs of transforming their economies.

Although most analysts agree that the size of Third World governments had gotten out of hand, some worry that the pendulum has swung too far in the other direction. They argue that the state can have a positive economic influence if it channels its activities prudently. For example, working closely with the private sector, East Asian state planners have played an important role in promoting the area's economic boom.[46] Similarly, the relatively low degree of income inequality in Taiwan and South Korea was achieved, in part, through government intervention in the form of agrarian reform and education policy. Conversely, unfettered private enterprise may intensify the existing sharp economic inequalities in many LDCs. It remains to be seen how well governments will be able to balance the need for economic efficiency with demands for social justice and economic equality.

RECENT DEVELOPMENTS AND FUTURE TRENDS

The road to development has been more difficult to travel than many Third World leaders or outside analysts had originally imagined. Africa remains the most impoverished region of the developing world—devastated by civil war, dictatorship, and corruption. Famine, the result of war as well as of natural disasters, continues to plague Somalia, Niger, and Sudan. The 1990s have witnessed some signs of hope, mostly in the political realm. South Africa has created a vibrant multiracial democracy, which, whatever its limitations, has impressively reduced racial antagonisms. Between 1988 and 1994 alone, the number of electoral democracies on the African continent rose from 5 to 21.[47] In July 2002, the continent's regional organization changed its name from the Organization of African Unity (OAU) to the African Union (AU) and pledged a new commitment to promoting democratic values, defending human rights, and providing a forum for resolving internal and regional conflict. Although that constituted an important symbolic commitment to democracy, the fact that some of the continent's most repressive dictators still play important roles in the AU raised doubts about the seriousness of its intent. Today, most of the region's population still lack adequate living standards or fundamental political rights, even in countries with competitive elections. In its most recent rankings, Freedom House rated 11 sub-Saharan African nations as "Free," 16 as "Partly Free," and 12 as "Not Free." Sixteen of those nations were rated as electoral democracies.[48]

The 1980s debt crisis brought Latin America the most intense economic decline since the world depression of the 1930s. Per capita GNP diminished, unemployment rose sharply, and high rates of inflation badly eroded consumers' purchasing power.[49] Since that time, the severe inflation that had afflicted countries such as Argentina, Brazil, Mexico, Peru, and Nicaragua has been brought under control and much of the region has experienced economic growth. But that growth has been rather erratic, and some countries have suffered sharp reverses. Thus, although Argentina was growing at a very rapid clip in the early 1990s, it experienced a severe economic crisis at the start of the new century that sent living standards plunging. Since 2002 the economy has resumed growth but the rate of poverty has only fallen slowly from its record highs. And even in countries that have enjoyed more sustained economic growth, that growth often has not translated into greater employment or improved living standards for the poor.

Ironically, at the very time Latin America's economy was at its worst, the region was making impressive progress toward more democratic and responsible government. In the mid-1970s, most of Latin America had been ruled by military dictatorships, some benign and others quite ruthless. By the start of the 1990s, however, democratically or semi-democratically elected governments had been installed in nearly every country in the region. Human rights and personal liberties have improved considerably in such countries as Argentina, Brazil, Chile, El Salvador, and Uruguay, though other governments such as Colombia's and Haiti's still frequently violate their citizens' fundamental rights.

The Far East and parts of Southeast Asia have enjoyed the Third World's greatest economic success in recent decades. The economies of South Korea, Taiwan, Singapore, Hong Kong, China, Thailand, Malaysia, and Indonesia all grew at annual rates of 7 percent or more from the 1980s into the late 1990s. Using the PPP measure of GDP (see footnote 1), China now has the world's second-largest economy and is expected to pass the U.S. by 2050.* Moreover, East Asia's extraordinary growth rates have often been achieved while maintaining relatively equitable distributions of income (most notably in South Korea, Taiwan, Singapore, and Indonesia). The impressive success of the Far Eastern economic model suggests the importance of industrial exports, balanced development strategies, and a cooperative relationship between government planners and private enterprise. Still, the severe financial crisis of 1997 to 1999 threw millions of people out of work in Thailand, Malaysia, Indonesia, South Korea, and Singapore, indicating that the region's heavy dependence on the international economy has some risks.

Since 1999, Asia's economy has rebounded. Politically, however, the region has made far less progress toward democracy and the protection of human rights than has Latin America. Until relatively recently, NICs such as Taiwan and South Korea retained nondemocratic governments long past the thresholds of economic growth and literacy that allowed other countries to turn to democracy, though they have now made that democratic transition. Singapore and Malaysia, two of the most economically developed LDCs, have yet to achieve even electoral democracy. Indonesia now has enjoyed one fair and honest national election but still suffers from extensive human rights abuses, especially in its treatment of rebellious ethnic minorities. And nations such as Myanmar, Pakistan, and Vietnam have made little progress toward any kind of democracy.

* Of course, with its much larger population, China will still lag far behind the U.S. in terms of per capita income.

All of that suggests the enormous difficulty of trying to achieve economic growth, equitable income distribution, political stability, democratic government, and national autonomy simultaneously. Although many of the world's LDCs hope to become "another Hong Kong" or "another Taiwan," it is unclear how many will have the internal capabilities or external possibilities that will permit them to do so. Prospects for democracy are also clouded. Since the nineteenth century, there have been three important worldwide waves of democratization (1828–1926, 1943–1962, and 1974–present). The first two advances were followed by more limited reverse waves back to authoritarianism. So, although worldwide pressure is growing for Third World governments to democratize and honor human rights (that is, to join the "Third Wave" of democratization that has changed so many Eastern European and developing nations), it remains uncertain how effective or how permanent those pressures will be.[50] In regions such as sub-Saharan Africa, the movement toward democracy has already weakened.[51] The paths of political and economic development are challenging, complex, and sometimes difficult to predict. So far, there has been no reverse wave in the developing world. But the prospects for further democratization are low.

 WHERE ON THE WEB?

http://astro.temple.edu/~bstavis/courses/nature-of-underdevelopment.htm

Common Characteristics of Underdevelopment: Includes links to subjects such as corruption and armed conflict.

http://www.globalissues.org

Information on a number of major issues, many related to LDCs, including international trade, Third World debt, and the war on terror.

http://www.freedomhouse.org

Home page for Freedom House, a widely used and respected rating of democracy and civil liberties throughout the world.

http://www.worldbank.org/poverty/wdrpoverty/report/

World Bank report on attacking poverty.

http://www.ipu.org/english/home.htm

Inter-Parliamentary Union: Up-to-date data on the percentage of women in parliament throughout the world.

http://web.worldbank.org/data/

World Bank data on economic and social statistics.

http://womensissues.about.com/cs/thirdworld/

A guide to women's issues in the developing world.

http://web.sipri.org/contents/webmaster/databases

A reliable source of data on military spending, arms transfers, etc., for developing (and developed) countries.

◆ ◆ ◆

Key Terms and Concepts_____

(the) core
dependency theory
electoral democracy
ethnicity
fundamentalism/fundamentalist
Gender Empowerment
   Measure (GEM)
Gender-Related Development
   Index (GDI)
Human Development Index
   (HDI)
institutional coups
Kuznets effect
legitimacy

less developed countries
   (LDCs)
liberal democracy
military coup
modernization theory
newly industrialized country
   (NIC)
personal coups
political underdevelopment
privatization
Third World
traditional society
wave of democracy
zipper-style quota

Discussion Questions_____

1. Discuss the main characteristics of economic and political underdevelopment. Be sure to include as many features of each as you can. What is the relationship between political and economic underdevelopment?
2. Compare the explanations for underdevelopment offered by modernization theory with those offered by dependency theory. What are the strengths and the weaknesses of each theory?
3. What are the major economic and political problems that particularly confront women in the developing world? How well represented are women in important political offices? How have some women managed to make it to the top of the political system in a number of Asian countries?
4. What factors account for the wave of democratic change that has swept over much of the developing world since the mid-1970s?
5. What accounts for the high number of military takeovers in the politics of Third World nations? Why has military intervention been declining recently?
6. What electoral mechanisms have been used in the Third World to increase women's representation in parliament?

Notes_____

1. For an explanation of the PPP method of calculating GNP. See endnote 3 of Chapter 14. PPP offers a more accurate image of a county's standard of living and is used throughout this chapter.
2. The argument was first presented in Simon Kuznets, "Economic Growth and Income Inequality," *American Economic Review* 45, no. 1 (1955): 1–28. For a more recent discussion, see Gary Fields, *Poverty and Inequality in Development* (New York: Cambridge University Press, 1980).
3. Samuel P. Huntington, *Political Order in Changing Societies* (New Haven: Yale University Press, 1968). Huntington focuses on other causes of unrest in this book, but elsewhere he has noted the close linkage between rural inequality and peasant unrest.
4. *Nigeria: A Country Study* (Washington, DC: Area Handbook Series of the Library of Congress, 1992), pp. 133–134.
5. John Fei, Gustav Ranis, and Shirley Kuo, *Growth with Equity: The Taiwan Case* (New York: Oxford University Press, 1979); and Irma Adelman and Cynthia Taft Morris, *Economic Growth and Social Equity in Developing Countries* (Stanford, CA: Stanford University Press, 1973).

6. United Nations Development Programme (UNDP), *Human Development Report, 1997* (New York: Oxford University Press, 1997), pp. 24–26; *Human Development Report, 2004.*

7. United Nations Development Programme (UNDP), *Summary: Human Development Report 2005*, http://hdr.undp.org/presskit/hdr2005/pdf/HDR05_summary.pdf.

8. Samuel P. Huntington, "The Goals of Development," in *Understanding Political Development*, ed. Myron Weiner and Samuel Huntington (Boston: Little, Brown, 1986), p. 3.

9. Howard Handelman, *The Challenge of Third World Development*, 3rd ed. (Upper Saddle River, NJ: Prentice Hall, 2003), pp. 146–173.

10. Huntington, *Political Order in Changing Societies.*

11. Guillermo O'Donnell and Philippe Schmitter, *Transitions from Authoritarian Rule: Tentative Conclusions about Uncertain Democracies* (Baltimore: Johns Hopkins University Press, 1986); and Abraham Lowenthal, ed., *Exporting Democracy* (Baltimore: Johns Hopkins University Press, 1991).

12. See data by Freedom House published each year in the January issue of the *Journal of Democracy.*

13. *The New York Times*, "Where a Cuddle With Your Baby Requires a Bribe," August 30, 2005.

14. For a useful summary of major theories of development, see Alvin Y. So, *Social Change and Development* (Newbury Park, CA: Sage, 1990). For more challenging discussions, see Weiner and Huntington, *Understanding Political Development;* and Vicky Randall and Robin Theobald, *Political Change and Underdevelopment* (London: Macmillan, 1985).

15. The body of modernization literature is enormous. The most important works include Huntington, *Political Order in Changing Societies* (widely considered the best work in this area); Gabriel Almond and James Coleman, eds., *The Politics of Developing Areas* (Princeton, NJ: Princeton University Press, 1960); Lucian Pye and Sidney Verba, eds., *Political Culture and Political Development* (Princeton, NJ: Princeton University Press, 1965); and Cyril E. Black, ed., *Comparative Modernization: A Reader* (New York: Free Press, 1976). These works, as well as those in subsequent notes regarding dependency theory, are recommended for more advanced undergraduates.

16. Max Weber, *The Protestant Ethic and the Spirit of Capitalism* (New York: Scribner's, 1958); and Talcott Parsons, *The Social System* (Glencoe, IL: Free Press, 1951).

17. For examples of such arguments, see Parsons, *Social System;* Gabriel Almond and Sidney Verba, *The Civic Culture* (Princeton, NJ: Princeton University Press, 1963); Pye and Verba, *Political Culture;* Alex Inkeles and David Horton Smith, *Becoming Modern: Individual Change in Six Developing Countries* (Cambridge: Harvard University Press, 1974); Daniel Lerner, *The Passing of Traditional Society* (Glencoe, IL: Free Press, 1958); and David McClelland, *The Achieving Society* (Princeton, NJ: Van Nostrand, 1961).

18. Marion Levy, Jr., "Social Patterns (Structures) and Problems of Modernization," in *Readings on Social Change*, ed. Wilbert Moore and Robert Cooke (Englewood Cliffs, NJ: Prentice Hall, 1967), p. 207.

19. Huntington, "The Goals of Development."

20. Huntington, *Political Order in Changing Societies.*

21. David Collier, ed., *The New Authoritarianism in Latin America* (Princeton, NJ: Princeton University Press, 1978); and Guillermo O'Donnell, *Modernization and Bureaucratic-Authoritarianism Studies in South American Politics* (Berkeley: Institute of International Studies, University of California, 1973).

22. Theotonio Dos Santos, "The Structure of Dependence," *American Economic Review* (May 1970).

23. Werner Baer, "The Economics of Prebisch and ECLA," in *Latin America: Problems in Economic Development*, ed. C. T. Nisbet (New York: Free Press, 1969). Major early dependency studies include Andre Gunder Frank, *Capitalism and Underdevelopment in Latin America* (New York: Monthly Review Press, 1967); see also Paul Baran, *The Political Economy of Growth* (New York: Monthly Review Press, 1957).

24. The most influential work in this more sophisticated version of dependency theory is Fernando Henrique Cardoso and Enzo Faletto, *Dependency and Development in Latin America* (Berkeley and Los Angeles: University of California Press, 1979). A far more readable work with that perspective is Peter Evans, *Dependent Development: The Alliance of Multinational, State and Local Capital* (Princeton, NJ: Princeton University Press, 1979).

25. Hollis Chenery et al., *Redistribution with Growth* (London: Oxford University Press with the World Bank and the University of Sussex, 1974).

26. World Bank, *World Development Indicators Database*, 15 July 2005, GNI Per Capita (PPP) 2004, http://www.worldbank.org/data/databytopic/GNIPC.pdf.

27. Jeffrey A. Winters, "Asia and the 'Magic' of the Marketplace," *Current History* 97 (December 1998): 419. This is one of the clearest analyses of the 1997–1998 financial crisis. See also Joseph Stiglitz, "Bad Private-Sector Decisions," *Wall Street Journal* (February 4, 1998).

28. The many works on revolution include Jeffrey Page, *Agrarian Revolution* (New York: Free Press, 1975); Theda Skocpol, *States and Revolutions: A Comparative Analysis of France, Russia and China* (Cambridge, UK: Cambridge University Press, 1979); John Walton, *Reluctant Rebels: Comparative Studies in Revolution and Underdevelopment* (New York: Columbia University Press, 1984); John Booth and Thomas Walker, *Understanding Central America* (Boulder, CO: Westview, 1989), chap. 5; and Barry Schutz and Robert Slater, eds., *Revolution and Political Change in the Third World* (Boulder, CO: Lynne Rienner Publishers, 1990), chaps. 1–3.

29. Eric Wolf, *Peasant Wars in the Twentieth Century* (New York: Harper and Row, 1969); John Booth, *The End and the Beginning: The Nicaraguan Revolution* (Boulder, CO: Westview, 1985); Scott Palmer, *Peru's Shining Path* (New York: St. Martin's, 1992); and Booth and Walker, *Understanding Central America.*

30. Crawford Young, *The Politics of Cultural Pluralism* (Madison: University of Wisconsin Press, 1976); and Cynthia Enloe, *Ethnic Conflict and Political Development* (Boston: Little, Brown, 1973).

31. Young, *Politics of Cultural Pluralism*, p. 301.

32. Ted Robert Gurr, preface and "Long War, Short Peace: The Rise and Decline of Ethnopolitical Conflict at the End of the Cold War," in *Peoples Versus States: Minorities at Risk in the New Century*, ed. T. Gurr (Washington, DC: United States Institute of Peace Press, 2000), pp. xiii, 27–56; and David Carment and Frank Harvey, *Using Force to Prevent Ethnic Violence* (Westport, CT: Praeger, 2001), p. 5.

33. Huntington, *Political Order*; and Samuel P. Huntington and Joan Nelson, *No Easy Choices* (Cambridge: Harvard University Press, 1976).

34. Mitchell A. Seligson, "Democratization in Latin America: The Current Cycle," in *Authoritarians and Democrats: Regime Transition in Latin America*, ed. James M. Malloy and Mitchell A. Seligson (Pittsburgh: University of Pittsburgh Press, 1987), pp. 7–9.

35. Adam Przeworski et al., "What Makes Democracies Endure," in *Consolidating Third Wave Democracies*, ed. Larry Diamond et al. (Baltimore: Johns Hopkins University Press, 1997), p. 297. The dollar amounts quoted here are in constant dollars—that is, the effect of inflation over the years is statistically factored out—so that a per capita national income of $6,000 in 1996 would be the same as that dollar income for 1962.

36. Population Reference Bureau, "Taking Stock of Women's Progress," www.prb.org.

37. Nancy Fix Anderson, "Benazir Bhutto and Dynastic Politics," in *Women as National Leaders*, ed. Michael Genovese (Newbury Park, CA: Sage, 1993), pp. 44–47. The book contains biographies of other female heads of government.

38. Inter-Parliamentary Union, *Women in National Parliaments* http://www.ipu.org/wmn-e/world.htm. The IPU's data lumps the U.S. and Canada with Latin America and the Caribbean ("The Americas") but removing those two North American countries does not change the average.

39. Inter-Parliamentary Union, *Women in National Parliaments*, http://www.ipu.org/wmn-e/classif.htm. These figures refer only to the larger, lower house of parliament, often the most powerful house.

40. William Thompson, "Explanations of the Military Coup" (Ph.D. diss., University of Washington, 1972), *Dilemmas of Political Development*, cited by Monte Palmer (Itasca, IL: Peacock, 1989), p. 234.

41. Abraham Lowenthal, ed., The *Peruvian Experiment* (Princeton, NJ: Princeton University Press, 1975); and Cynthia McClintock and Abraham Lowenthal, eds., *The Peruvian Experiment Reconsidered* (Princeton, NJ: Princeton University Press, 1983).

42. Collier, *The New Authoritarianism in Latin America.*

43. Alice Amsden, "The State and Taiwan's Economic Development," in *Bringing the State Back In*, ed. Peter Evans et al. (New York: Cambridge University Press, 1985); Stephan Haggard, *Pathways from the Periphery* (Ithaca: Cornell University Press, 1990); and Gereffi and Wyman, *Manufacturing Miracles.*

44. Joel Migdal, *Strong Societies and Weak States* (Princeton, NJ: Princeton University Press, 1988); and Joel Migdal, "Strong States, Weak States: Power and Accommodation," in Weiner and Huntington, *Understanding Political Development.*

45. Linn A. Hammergren, "Corporatism in Latin American Politics: A Reexamination of the 'Unique' Tradition," *Comparative Politics* (July 1977): 449.

46. Haggard, *Pathways from the Periphery;* and Gereffi and Wyman, *Manufacturing Miracles.*

47. Michael Bratton and Nicolas van de Walle, *Democratic Experiments in Africa: Regime Transitions in Comparative Perspective* (New York: Cambridge University Press, 1997), p. 120. Using slightly different definitions, another expert claimed the number of democracies had jumped from 3 to 18. See Larry Diamond, *Prospects for Democratic Development in Africa* (Stanford, CA: Hoover Institute Press, 1997), appendix. See also Adrian Karatnycky, "The 1999 Freedom House Survey: A Century of Progress," *Journal of Democracy* 11 (January 2000), 187–200.

48. Arch Puddington and Aili Piano, "Worrisome Signs, Modest Shifts" *Journal of Democracy* 16 (January 2005), 103–108.

49. Howard Handelman and Werner Baer, eds., *Paying the Costs of Austerity in Latin America* (Boulder, CO: Westview, 1989), p. 2.

50. Samuel Huntington, *The Third Wave* (Norman: University of Oklahoma Press, 1991).

51. Julius Ihonvbere, "Where Is the Third Wave? A Critical Evaluation of Africa's Non-Transition to Democracy," *Africa Today* 43, no. 4 (October–December 1996): 343–368.

For Further Reading _____

Datta, Rekha, and Judith F. Kornberg. *Women in Developing Countries: Assessing Strategies for Empowerment.* Boulder, CO: Lynne Rienner Publishers, 2002.

Diamond, Larry, ed. *The Global Divergence of Democracy.* Baltimore: Johns Hopkins University Press, 2001.

_____. *Assessing the Quality of Democracy.* Baltimore: Johns Hopkins University Press, 2005.

Handelman, Howard. *The Challenge of Third World Development.* 4th ed. Upper Saddle River, NJ: Prentice Hall, 2006.

Haynes, Jeff. *Politics in the Developing World: A Concise Introduction.* Malden, MA: Blackwell Publishers, 2002.

Huntington, Samuel. *The Third Wave.* Norman: University of Oklahoma Press, 1991.

Miller, Berna, and James D. Torr. *Developing Nations.* San Diego, CA: Greenhaven Press, 2003.

Sachs, Jeffrey. *The End of Poverty.* New York: Viking Penguin, 2005.

Sklar, Richard L. *African Politics in Postimperial Times: The Essays of Richard L. Sklar,* ed. Toyin Falola. Trenton, NJ: Africa World Press, 2002.

Smith, Peter H. *Democracy in Latin America.* New York: Oxford University Press, 2005.

© Agence France-Presse (AFP)

16

MEXICO: THE BIRTH OF DEMOCRACY

◆ The Triumph of Mexican Electoral Democracy
◆ The Relevance of Mexican Politics ◆ The Origins
of Modern Mexico ◆ The Legacy of the Mexican
Revolution (1910–1920) ◆ The Postrevolutionary Order
◆ The Making of a Modern Economy ◆ The Structure
of Government ◆ Political Parties ◆ A Changing Political
Culture ◆ Voting and the Changing Electoral System
◆ Interest Groups ◆ The Fox Presidency
and the Future of Mexico

THE TRIUMPH OF MEXICAN ELECTORAL DEMOCRACY

The 1991 collapse of Communist Party rule in Russia briefly left Mexico's **Institutional Revolutionary Party (PRI)*** as the world's longest continuously ruling political party. But less than a decade later, the wave of democratic change that had transformed the Soviet Union, Eastern Europe, Latin America, and parts of Africa and Asia finally swept the PRI from power after 71 years of continuous rule. On July 2, 2000, Vicente Fox—candidate of the **National Action Party (PAN)**—was elected as Mexico's first president of the twenty-first century and the first democratically elected president in the nation's history. It was an outcome that few Mexicans would have predicted and that many, including the winners, initially found hard to believe.

For most of the twentieth century, Mexican political and economic development was structured by the country's 1910 revolution and by the "official party" that emerged from that struggle. The revolution unleashed a period of chaos and devastation, but ultimately it also laid the foundation for the nation's political and economic modernization. It spawned a ruling party that governed Mexico from 1929 to 2000, establishing political stability, improved political representation and 50 years of rapid economic growth. At the same time, however, the revolution and the PRI also introduced authoritarian rule, rampant corruption, and severe economic inequality. Because of its accomplishments and its willingness to win at any cost, the PRI won all elections of any importance until the 1980s and continued to hold the nation's all-powerful presidency until 2000.[†]

The nation continues to face serious political, social and economic problems. But since 2000 it has taken the first giant steps toward creating a more democratic and responsive political system.[1]

THE RELEVANCE OF MEXICAN POLITICS

As America's neighbor, one of its largest trading partners, a leading source of imported petroleum, and the point of origin for substantial legal and illegal immigration, Mexico's importance to the U.S. is profound. Its impressive record of growth and industrialization until the early 1980s seemed to offer valuable lessons for other developing nations. During the late 1980s and the 1990s, the country reversed its long-standing, state-centered, protectionist economic model and became a leader in "neoliberal" reform (the process of opening up the country to greater foreign trade and investment, while reducing government's role in the economy). And before the recent worldwide wave of democratization, some observers cited Mexico's modified one-party political system—featuring both political stability and regular transitions from one civilian president to another—as a political model for other Latin America nations.

More recently, however, the flaws in Mexico's economic and political development models have become more apparent. The economic crises of 1982 and 1995

---

* Mexico's three leading political parties are known by their Spanish acronyms (PRI, PAN, PRD).

[†] The ruling party had two other names before being called the PRI. Whatever the time period, however, we will always refer to the party as the PRI so as to avoid confusion.

Mexico

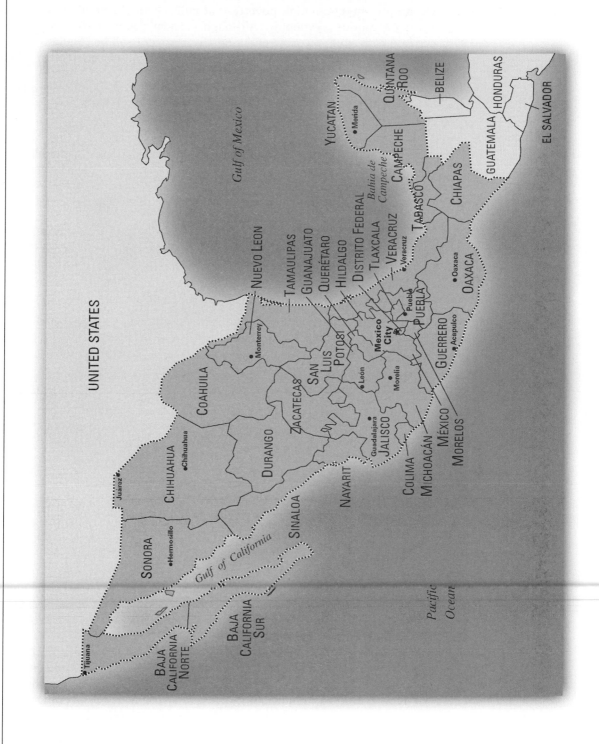

highlighted both the continuing poverty that afflicts most Mexicans and the inefficiencies of the country's economy. Although economic growth has resumed since 1996, it is too early to know how enduring that recovery will be. And although the neoliberal reforms of the 1990s were surely necessary, they also caused great suffering among the nation's poor.

At the same time, the combination of extensive political corruption, periodic government repression, and growing political opposition revealed that Mexico was not "a peculiar democracy" (as it had once been labeled) but, rather, an authoritarian system in need of reform. The slow but steady erosion of PRI dominance since the 1980s and the emergence of two major opposition parties reflected mounting discontent with the old political order. That progress culminated with Vicente Fox's 2000 presidential victory and PRI's third-place finish in 2006. But although Mexico has achieved the primary prerequisite of democratic government—fair and truly competitive elections—it still retains some of its old authoritarian characteristics.

Before looking at Mexico's current political system, however, we must first examine Mexico's past. Its colonial heritage of sharp class divisions (reinforcing racial distinctions), its weak political system in the nineteenth century, and its twentieth-century efforts—starting with its 1910 revolution—to create a strong nation-state and a more equitable society have all left indelible marks on the contemporary political scene.

The Origins of Modern Mexico

Like many developing nations, Mexico achieved independence (in 1821) with few of the prerequisites for a successful nation-state. During much of the nineteenth century, the central government was unable to control the country's regional military-political bosses. Thus, during its first 40 years of independence, Mexico was governed by some 50 presidents (including some repeats). Internal strife and government instability left the country vulnerable to foreign intervention. Consequently, Texas's secession and the subsequent war with the United States (1848) stripped the nation of nearly half its territory.[2]

In addition, Mexican society was sharply divided along ethnic and class lines. The Spanish colonial conquest had imposed European culture and religion on a large Native American population, with power concentrated in the hands of the Spanish authorities and a small upper class of whites born in the New World (*criollos*). At the same time, the largest segment of the population consisted of poor Indian or mestizo[*] peasants, who were often forced into virtual serfdom on white-owned agricultural and ranching estates. Independence failed to temper those racial and class cleavages. And even when subsequent modernization reduced racial divisions, class barriers to social mobility remained strong.

In 1876, General Porfirio Díaz established himself as the country's supreme military strongman. He was the first Mexican national leader to exercise firm control over the regional *caciques* (political bosses), and ruled with an iron fist until 1911. Attracted by Mexico's newfound stability, its favorable climate for investment, and its restrictive labor laws, foreign investors built Mexico's railroad, electrical power, and

* The term *mestizo* refers to Indians who have been integrated either forcefully or voluntarily into the dominant European culture.

telephone networks, while further developing manufacturing, mining, agriculture, and ranching. Although those investments contributed to economic growth, they also provoked a nationalist backlash. Díaz himself allegedly said, "Poor Mexico! So far from God and so close to the United States!"

THE LEGACY OF THE MEXICAN REVOLUTION (1910–1920)

The economic modernization that Díaz fostered carried within it the seeds of his regime's destruction. The expansion of plantation agriculture in the south and ranching in the north further encroached on the small farms of the beleaguered peasantry. The development of mining, petroleum, railroads, and limited manufacturing created an incipient working class that lacked the fundamental right to unionize or strike. In the cities, economic growth produced a small but influential middle class. With political and economic power in the hands of a tiny elite, this emerging group of professionals and small businesspeople had few opportunities for upward mobility and, consequently, had their own grievances.

In 1910, Francisco Madero, a wealthy political reformer who had just lost to Díaz in a fraudulent presidential election, appealed to the Mexican population, particularly the middle class, to overthrow the government. Although Madero's goals were largely modest political reforms, his call for revolt provoked the twentieth century's first mass-based revolution. In the cities, workers mobilized to fight for trade-union rights. In various parts of

© Bettmann Archive/CORBIS

ZAPATA AND HIS MEN   Despite his limited education and political experience, Emiliano Zapata was one of the most important regional military leaders of the Mexican Revolution. He is shown here seated in the center of the photo, flanked by his officers and men. A man of great personal integrity, he remains today perhaps the most revered revolutionary hero. The Zapatista rebel movement that shook Mexico in the 1990s was, of course, named after him.

the countryside, peasants and cowboys organized to regain their lands under the leadership of men such as Emiliano Zapata and Pancho Villa. For the next decade, the revolutionary struggle convulsed the nation. Before the fighting ended, it killed more than one million people (out of a total population of 14.5 million) and wiped some eight thousand villages off the map.[3] Unlike many other twentieth-century revolutions, however, the Mexican insurrection lacked a unifying political party, ideology, or charismatic leader. Peasants, workers, land owners, the middle class, and military leaders all fought for different political and socioeconomic goals. Madero himself was soon assassinated by counterrevolutionary forces. Eventually, many other revolutionary leaders—Zapata, Villa, Carranza—lost their lives in the struggle.

Although numerically superior, the peasants and workers lacked both the leadership and the organization to carry the revolution's radical wing to victory. It was the centrist forces, led by middle-class (or upper-class) military men, that emerged triumphant. Although the constitution of 1917 called for limits on foreign investment, pledged land to the peasants, and offered union rights to the workers, it would be almost two decades before Mexico's government seriously addressed most of those more radical promises.

THE POSTREVOLUTIONARY ORDER

Political Consolidation (1920–1946)

Political turmoil and bloodshed carried into the next decade. In 1929, seeking to end the perpetual conflict between regional strongmen and to stabilize the political system, Mexico's political leaders created the National Revolutionary Party (PNR), a coalition of the winning factions in the revolutionary upheaval. The party brought together various regional parties, military and civilian strongmen, and organized sectors of the civilian population. "From the beginning the PNR was envisioned as a dominant, governing party."[4] Its function was to represent and control critical sectors of the population: the peasantry, labor, the middle class, and the military. Other parties were permitted to run candidates, but for more than half a century they virtually never won at any level. In the late 1930s, the party strengthened its labor and peasant wings, and soon afterward ended party representation of the military. In 1946, its name was changed (for the second time) to the Institutional Revolutionary Party, or PRI. From its inception until the 1988 national elections, the party never lost a race for governor, lost only one election for senator, and never received less than 68 percent of the presidential vote.

The Cárdenas Era of Social and Economic Reform (1934–1940)

With the establishment of political stability, Mexico's leaders turned their attention to the revolution's still unfulfilled social and economic promises. President **Lázaro Cárdenas**'s election in 1934 was a victory for the more radical wing of the ruling (official) party. Cárdenas initiated Latin America's most far-reaching land reform, distributing some 29 million acres to the nation's peasantry.* He also expanded the country's labor movement substantially and incorporated previously excluded radical unions

---

* He distributed more land to the peasants than the combined total of all of previous presidents since the revolution. Agrarian reform reduced rural poverty and peasant unrest somewhat.

into the PRI. Finally, Cárdenas implemented many of the revolution's nationalist objectives. The revolutionary struggle, it must be remembered, was inspired partly by resentment over foreign economic involvement in critical sectors of the economy. Little was done to address that issue until Cárdenas's administration nationalized Mexico's petroleum industry and railroads. In the following decades, the government also took control of the electrical power, telephone-telegraph, and banking sectors, and established substantial footholds in steel and agricultural marketing. Although most of the economy remained in private hands, the state became the country's largest economic player by controlling most of the country's infrastructure (transportation, telecommunications, energy—most notably petroleum) and many of its largest corporations in a mixture of state-controlled and market economies known as **state capitalism**.

Government economic activity expanded further in the 1970s and early 1980s. But by the late 1980s and 1990s, a large portion of the once-substantial public sector was **privatized** (sold to the private sector) as part of a package of neoliberal reforms.

THE MAKING OF A MODERN ECONOMY

The Mexican "Economic Miracle"

Cárdenas's radical reforms (particularly those designed to redistribute resources to the poor) proved to be a short-lived deviation from the otherwise centrist path of the revolution. From the 1940s onward, state economic policy was designed to stimulate growth, with little concern for how that affected the distribution of income and resources. Agricultural credits and state irrigation projects that had formerly been directed by Cárdenas toward the peasant communities were increasingly channeled toward agribusiness. From the 1940s until the 1980s, Mexico's government, like its counterparts in most of Latin America, supported private-sector industrialization through government subsidies, tax credits, and restrictions on competing imports. At the same time, government control over the nation's labor unions restricted labor unrest and kept wages down to attract greater business investment.

Those policies led to what has been called the **Mexican economic miracle**. The country's gross domestic product (GDP) grew at an average annual rate of more than 6 percent (Table 16.1) from the 1940s to the 1980s, a more prolonged period of high growth than either the United States or Japan had enjoyed during their primary

TABLE 16.1   MEXICO'S AVERAGE ANNUAL GROWTH, 1940–1980
(AVERAGE PERCENTAGE GROWTH PER YEAR)

	1940–1950	1950–1960	1960–1970	1970–1980
Population	2.8	3.1	3.8	3.6
GDP	6.9	5.6	7.0	5.5
Agriculture	5.1	4.6	3.7	2.4
Industry	8.1	6.5	8.8	6.7
Service	7.0	5.6	6.8	5.2

SOURCE: Robert Looney, *Economic Policymaking in Mexico* (Durham, NC: Duke University Press, 1985), p. 7 (tab. 1.2).

TABLE 16.2 INCOME DISTRIBUTION IN MEXICO, 1950–2000

| | Percentage of National Income | | |
Year	Poorest 50 Percent	Middle 30 Percent	Richest 20 Percent
1950	17.4	23.7	58.9
1969	15.0	21.0	64.0
1992	18.4	27.4	54.1
2000	15.6*	26.2*	58.2*

* The 2000 data are extrapolated from the World Bank, *World Development Report, 2000/2001*, which breaks down the population slightly differently for the 40th to 50th percentiles of the population.

SOURCE: Daniel Levy and Gabriel Székely, *Mexico: Paradoxes of Stability and Change* (Boulder, CO: Westview, 1983), p. 144; Daniel C. Levy and Kathleen Bruhn, "Mexico: Sustained Civilian Rule without Democracy," in *Politics in Developing Countries: Comparing Experiences with Democracy*, ed. Larry Diamond, Juan J. Linz, and Seymour Martin Lipset (Boulder, CO: Lynne Rienner Publishers, 1995), p. 195; and World Bank, *World Development Report, 2000/2001: Attacking Poverty* (New York: Oxford University Press, 2001), pp. 282–283.

economic expansions.[5] As a consequence, within several decades Mexico changed from a predominantly rural, agricultural country to a largely urban nation with a workforce primarily employed in the service and manufacturing sectors.* Education expanded apace. Whereas only 10 percent of the population had been literate at the time of the revolution, nearly 90 percent of all Mexicans were literate by 1990.

The Other Side of the Miracle

Despite the country's dramatic record of modernization and growth, critics have insisted that the economic miracle had left too many people behind. Peasants and workers had fought and died in the revolution hoping to improve their living conditions. Champions of economic redistribution, such as Emiliano Zapata, became national folk heroes. Yet, it has clearly been the poor, especially the peasantry, who have gained least from the revolution and its aftermath.

The economic boom that began during World War II expanded the size of the urban middle class and created a significant number of better-paid industrial jobs for skilled workers. But government policies placed a higher priority on economic growth than on equitable income distribution. Table 16.2 indicates that during Mexico's extended economic expansion (1940 to 1982), the richest 20 percent of the population earned between 55 and 64 percent of the nation's income, an extremely high concentration of wealth in the hands of a few.[6] Although income concentration diminished somewhat in the 1970s, the gaps have widened again since the 1980s, enabling the country to regain its dubious distinction of being one of the Latin America's more unequal nations (Table 16.2).[7] In 2001, *Forbes* magazine's annual listing of the world's richest people indicated that Mexico, with a per capita income about one-fourth that of the United States and less than half its population, had 24 billionaires, the fourth

* In 1940, some 65 percent of Mexico's economically active population worked in agriculture. By 2000, however, only about 5 percent of the country's GDP (though perhaps two to three times that proportion of the workforce) came from agriculture, 69 percent came from the service sector, and 27 percent came from industry (see the *Economist Intelligence Unit*, April 19, 2001).

highest number in the world (behind the United States, Japan, and Germany) and more than Great Britain and France combined (the number and rank of Mexico's super-rich has since declined).

In the decades following World War II, the government's preferential treatment of large-scale, mechanized farming undermined peasant producers and contributed to rural poverty. Many peasants who could not compete with larger farms were forced to work as poorly paid agricultural laborers or migrate to the cities. Today, Mexico's rural poor are still more likely to be malnourished than their urban counterparts, less well-paid, less educated, and less likely to enjoy amenities such as electricity or clean drinking water.[8]

As a consequence of that gap, Mexico, like many developing nations, has experienced substantial rural-to-urban migration. Between 1940 and 1981, despite higher birth rates in the countryside, urban centers grew from 22 percent of the nation's population to 55 percent.[9] But because industrial development has been capital-intensive rather than labor-intensive, the cities have failed to produce sufficient employment to meet the needs of their burgeoning workforce. Consequently, even at the height of Mexico's economic boom, some 35 percent of the economically active population lacked full-time employment.[10] Since the economic crises of the 1980s and 1990s, that figure has increased sharply.

Excessive migration to cities has produced other problems as well. Mexico City's metropolitan area currently houses some 20 million people, making it one of the world's largest urban centers. Moreover, each year an additional 500,000 people migrate to the capital. Because resources have not matched that enormous growth, it has become one of the world's most polluted and most traffic-congested cities.* Millions of inhabitants live in shantytowns and slums, where they suffer from unsanitary conditions, crime, and inadequate social services. For many others who feel that neither the countryside nor the cities offer sufficient opportunities, the United States has always beckoned. Although illegal immigration obviously creates problems for U.S. policy makers, it does provide Mexico with an important pressure valve for its social and political tensions.

A number of government programs since the 1970s have sought to improve living conditions and incomes for the poor. At various times, these have included irrigation projects for poor farmers, potable water and sewage services for low-income urban neighborhoods, construction of schools and medical clinics, employment programs, and, most recently, a program granting subsidies to poor families whose children stay in school. But the benefits from these programs have failed to compensate for declining living standards caused by the country's economic crises since 1982. Nor, as we have seen, have they reduced Mexico's great income inequality.

Since the 1980s: From Boom to Bust to Recovery

During the 1970s, Mexican economic growth, as in most of Latin America, was fueled by a large infusion of loans from international banks. When President Luis Echeverría took office in 1970, support for the regime was at a low point in the wake of a government massacre of more than two hundred student protestors shortly before Mexico City hosted the 1968 Summer Olympics. Echeverría tried to rebuild the government's support by introducing a number of welfare programs and business subsidies. As spending

---

* In recent decades the government has reduced air pollution in the capital by restricting auto traffic, introducing taxis and buses with lower emissions, and moving industry out of the city. Still, pollution remains a problem, as do poor sewage and other environmental health hazards.

increased and revenues failed to rise correspondingly, the government turned to external borrowing.

Under Echeverría's successor, José López Portillo (1975–1982), fiscal deficits and external borrowing escalated further. Unfortunately, the state petroleum corporation's discovery of vast new oilfields in the mid-1970s gave the government an exaggerated sense of Mexico's projected oil-export revenues in the coming years. As a consequence, it accelerated its spending far faster than its short-term revenues grew in order to satisfy the population's increasing demands for services and benefits. Mexico's private sector shared the government's optimism about future economic growth as corporations also accelerated their borrowing from abroad. Both the Mexican government and foreign lenders (U.S., Japanese, and European banks) believed that the sharp growth of petroleum prices in the early 1970s would continue into the foreseeable future, guaranteeing Mexico sufficient funds to repay its debt. From 1970 to 1981, the government's foreign debt grew from $4.3 billion to $53 billion and private-sector external debt jumped from $1.8 billion to $20.3 billion. Other Latin American countries, including those without oil, became similarly indebted, but Mexico and Brazil led the way. When the price of oil dropped sharply in 1981, Mexico's economic boom unraveled.

President José López Portillo's August 1982 announcement that Mexico was no longer able to make payments on its debt put a brake on further loans to all of Latin America and precipitated the region's **debt crisis,** which lasted throughout the decade. For one thing, it became more difficult to receive international loans. To deal with the crisis, the Mexican government was forced to introduce **economic austerity**—belt-tightening measures including cutbacks on government spending, ongoing devaluation of the nation's currency, and policies that prevented wages from keeping pace with inflation.

From 1982 to 1988, the country experienced almost no economic growth (the GNP actually declined in three of those years), whereas the population increased by approximately 15 percent. Inflation rose sharply, peaking at an annual rate of 160 percent in 1987, but wages failed to keep pace. As a consequence, the average worker's real income (actual purchasing power) declined by 40 to 50 percent in the 1980s, wiping out many of the gains achieved during the oil boom. A United Nations study in the late 1980s revealed that over half the population was at least somewhat malnourished.

By the end of the decade, inflation had been brought under control, but living standards had not recovered.[11] Not surprisingly, support for the PRI and the government—which had been bolstered by the earlier economic boom—eroded. Finally, soon after the country resumed modest economic growth in the early 1990s, a renewed fiscal crisis in 1995 sent it into another severe depression. GDP fell by 6.9 percent that year, the worst decline since the Mexican Revolution, and unemployment increased by two million as many companies became bankrupt.[12] Although economic growth has resumed since 1996 and per capita income has returned to 1994 levels, many of the nation's poor have yet to benefit from the recent recovery.

The Structure of Government

Creating a Powerful State

As we have seen, the years from the Mexican Revolution until the early 1980s witnessed the substantial growth of state power over the economy and society. By the 1970s, as the task of managing the economy became more complex, a growing number of key government decisions were made by a new elite of highly trained government bureaucrats—often with graduate degrees in economics, public administration, or planning—rather than by elected politicians.[13] Since Mexican political institutions are often less than they seem—the Congress, for example, exercised very little independent power until recently—the discussion of Mexican politics that follows focuses less on political institutions and more on the role of the state in mediating conflicts in society over income distribution, economic growth, political rights and freedoms, and other issues fundamental to developing nations. We will also be examining the proper role and size of the state itself. And finally, we will look at Mexico's recent transition to democratic government and will discuss future prospects for Mexican democracy.

Nominally, Mexico is a federal republic modeled after the United States. Like the U.S., it features a division of federal powers between the president, Congress, and the courts. In practice, however, Mexican politics has been characterized by a tremendous concentration of power. State governments depend on the federal government for revenues, and until recently presidents could remove state governors from office when dissatisfied with their performance (although formally it was Congress that declared the post vacant). Within the national government itself, the president exercised extraordinary power, though that has begun to change after 1997 when Ernesto Zedillo (1994–2000) and then Vicente Fox (2000–2006) became the first Mexican presidents in some 70 years to lack a majority in Congress. Both men voluntarily restricted their presidential powers, some of which were transferred from the central government to state and local authorities.

The Executive Branch and the Bureaucracy

Before the revolution, Mexico alternated between rule by *caudillos* (military strongmen) such as Porfirio Díaz and periods of great instability. The chaos of the revolution and the spate of political assassinations that continued through the 1920s convinced the revolutionary elite that the country had to invest great power into the presidency. The president, no matter who held the office, dominated the political system until quite recently. Until the 1980s, even opposition newspapers and political parties hesitated to criticize the chief executive directly, focusing instead on his advisers or his policies. But, at the same time, to prevent the return of an extended dictatorship like Díaz's, the 1917 Constitution limited the president (as well as other elected officials) to a single term in office. Subsequently, the length of that term was fixed at six years.

Until 1997, "congress . . . [was] a rubber stamp, passing nearly all laws proposed by the president without effecting major modifications; the judicial branch of government . . . exhibited only a slightly greater degree of autonomy."[14] But even before the recent transition to democracy, a nation as large and complex as Mexico could not be ruled by one person. Hence, a vast bureaucratic network developed within the executive branch whose members constituted a new ruling class of administrators. At the pinnacle of that administrative elite has been the cabinet. The president has given cabinet ministers—particularly those holding such posts as finance minister and interior minister—extensive powers (subject, of course, to his approval). Under PRI governments, the cabinet also served as a stepping-stone to the presidency.

Until the election of Vicente Fox (a former governor with extensive prior experience as a business executive), presidents in recent decades had emerged from that bureaucratic elite. Typically, modern PRI presidents started their careers by attaching themselves to a patron in a powerful ministry, following him up the rungs of the administrative ladder. When their patron achieved the presidency, they were named to the cabinet and subsequently were picked by the outgoing president as the PRI candidate.

For most presidents from the 1970s through the 1990s, their presidential campaign was their first race for elected office. That pattern of political advancement through a bureaucratic, patron-client network (called a *camarilla*) has now seemingly come to an end. In the 2000 presidential election, the PRI presidential candidate was selected in a party primary. Vicente Fox, the candidate of a party (PAN) that had previously been permanently in opposition, also made his way to the presidency through a different route. He first established himself as a rancher and a Coca-Cola executive (in Mexico) and was then elected governor of his home state of Guanajuato. Indeed , in a reversal of recent patterns, all three major presidential candidates in both the 2000 and 2006 elections had previously served as state governors (or as "governor" of Mexico City).

Presidentialism (presidential political supremacy), although undemocratic, fulfilled several important functions. Symbolically, the head of state was the bearer of the revolutionary tradition and a source of unity for a geographically and socioeconomically diverse nation.[15] Ironically, when President Zedillo tried to promote greater democracy by limiting the "imperial presidency"—including renouncing his own right to handpick the next PRI presidential candidate—much of the Mexican public dismissed him as weak, so widely accepted had the idea of an all-powerful presidency become. Vicente Fox faced some of the same criticisms.

Congress

Mexico's Congress is composed of two branches, the Senate and the Chamber of Deputies, with the former holding more power over foreign policy and the latter in charge of fiscal appropriations and the budget. Between 1929 and the late 1980s, only one senator was ever elected who did not belong to the PRI. In response to public pressure for greater representation of other parties, the size of the Senate has been enlarged and the method for electing Senators has been changed several times since 1993. Currently, 128 senators are elected from the 31 states and the Federal District (Mexico City) through a complicated mix of single-member districts, proportional representation, and allocation of a seat to each second-place finisher.

Election to the Chamber of Deputies has also become more complex. Historically, deputies were elected from single-member districts. Beginning in the 1960s, however, a small number of seats in the chamber were allocated to the opposition through proportional representation (PR). The number of PR seats has been raised several times over the years in response to demands for greater democratization. Currently, 300 deputies are elected from single-member districts. Until 1988, opposition parties had never won more than a handful of those races. Consequently, to give added representation to the opposition, 200 additional deputies are now elected on the basis of proportional representation.

Given the PRI's dominance of Congress until the late 1990s and the president's domination of the PRI, it is not surprising that the national legislature rather routinely passed the president's proposed legislation. Thus, for example, between 1934 and the mid-1990s, the Chamber of Deputies approved at least 95 percent of executive-sponsored bills and in some years that figure reached 100 percent. Almost all of those bills passed the Congress without amendment.[16] In 1997, in what was proved to be a precursor of Fox's electoral upset three years later, the PRI lost its absolute majority in the Chamber of Deputies for the first time since its founding, though it remained the largest party in the chamber. As a consequence, during the second half of his presidency, Ernesto Zedillo (PRI) could no longer demand the congressional subservience to presidential desires that all his predecessors had enjoyed nor did he use the president's historical powers as party leader to pressure PRI deputies to the extent that his predecessors had. Consequently, the success rate of executive-sponsored bills dropped from 97 percent to *only* 90 percent.

Congress has become even more independent of presidential control since 2000. During the 2000–2003 congressional session, President Vicente Fox's party, the PAN, held only 41 percent of the seats in the Chamber of Deputies and was unable to form a majority coalition with other parties on many key votes. Consequently in that period Congress passed 86 percent of his proposed legislation, significantly lower than his predecessors' success rate. While 86 percent may still seem like a high success rate, "nearly every single bill [proposed by the executive branch] that could [legally] be amended was modified."[17] In the 2003 congressional elections PAN's representation in the Chamber of Deputies declined further and while it reemerged as the largest Congressional bloc in the 2006 elections, it still will be short of a majority.

Another way of measuring the extent to which presidential control over the Congress has declined during the past decade is to look at the origin of bills that *are* passed. During the 56th congressional session (1994–1997) three-fourths (74 percent) of all bills passed by Congress were originally introduced by the executive. But in the first two years of the 59th Congress (2003–2005), under Fox, only one-eighth (12 percent) of the legislation passed had been introduced by the executive branch, while 62 percent originated from the deputies themselves.[18] At the same time, most of the executive-sponsored bills that were passed were routine and uncontroversial, while most of the president's key reform proposals were rejected or substantially modified, sometimes to the point of gutting them. For example, when President Fox took office, one of his key priorities was settling the Zapatista (EZLN) rebels' seven-year-old stand-off with the government in the state of Chiapas (see Box 16-2). Toward that end, he proposed a number of constitutional amendments to improve indigenous (Indian) human rights. But when the Congress stripped key provisions, the package was rejected as inadequate by the Zapatista leadership. Here, as with some of the president's other reform legislation, he was not able to count on many of his own party's congressmen. Unlike previous presidents who hardly ever found the need to veto congressional bills, Fox used the veto five times during his first three years of office.

Some analysts initially argued that, given the president's lack of a congressional majority, he had done fairly well. Among the important presidential initiatives passed by the Congress have been a Federal Law for Transparency and Access to Public Government Information (in line with Fox's commitment to expose more government policy making to public scrutiny); a Science and Technology law (partly designed to increase the transparency of government decisions to award grants in scientific research); a federal law prohibiting discrimination based on factors such as race, ethnicity, sex, age, sexual preference, or marital status; reforms of the Federal Tax Code; and amendments to the Federal Criminal Code designed to protect child victims of sexual exploitation.[19] Various other reforms have made government more accountable to its citizens. However, by the middle of his own term, following serious PAN losses in the 2003 congressional elections, Fox had clearly become an ineffective lame duck (Table 16.3).

Table 16.3   Results of Chamber of Deputies Elections (Percentage of Seats Won)

Year	PRI	PAN	PRD
1976	80.1	8.5	—
1988	50.4	18.0	10.5[a]
1997	39.1	26.6	25.7
2000	42.0	41.4	10.4
2003	44.8	30.6	17.6
2006	24.2	41.2	32.0

[a]These votes were won by the Democratic National Front (FDN), an electoral coalition of small parties most of whom later merged into the PRD.

Source: Mexican Federal Electoral Institute (IFE); Howard Handelman, *Mexican Politics* (New York: St. Martin's, 1997), p. 75; David Shirk, *Mexico's New Politics* (Boulder, CO: Lynne Rienner Publishers, 2005), p. 217.

Unfortunately, although Congress's newfound ability to say no to the president and to reject his legislative proposals promotes greater democracy and the separation of powers (since Congress is no longer the president's lapdog), many opposition congressmen now use their votes to stymie presidential initiatives for purely partisan motives and thereby block many badly needed reforms. At the same time, a broad base of PRI and PRD congressmen opposed Fox's conservative economic policies (as opposed to his progressive political and social policies), including his desire to further privatize the economy. Critics faulted Fox with having put too much energy into passing legislation that Congress is unlikely to pass and not introducing more reforms through executive-branch actions where they are possible.[20] At the same time, the president initially made important concessions to the PRI in the mistaken belief that he could get its support for some of his major legislation. Since future presidents will often lack a congressional majority (as will Fox's successor), similar stalemates between Congress and the president may become an ongoing problem.

The Judiciary

As in the United States, the Mexican judiciary has local, state, and federal components. The degree of professionalism, however, is frequently low in local and state courts, many of which are riddled with corruption. Unfortunately, the problem has worsened in the past decade or more with the growing influence of narcotics dealers over the courts. Until recently, the Mexican judiciary has exercised limited political influence and generally has been fairly subservient to the executive branch. Judges who showed independence might face severe retribution. In 1995, for example, the government wished to prosecute several union leaders but was stymied when Superior Court Judge Abraham Polo ruled that there was insufficient evidence to issue an arrest warrant against the men. Subsequently, the judge publicly charged that he had been pressured to change his decision by the chief justice of his own court. Polo, a longtime PRI activist, refused to back down. Several months later he was gunned down by an unknown assailant.[21]

The courts sometimes do exercise a limited amount of independence and occasionally hand down decisions against the executive branch.[22] Thus, they may issue writs of *amparo*—legal documents issued to individuals who claim that their rights have been violated by a government action. Such writs can command the government to cease a particular act or to undertake a remedy. Nevertheless, the courts have used writs of *amparo* exclusively for nonpolitical cases and have refrained from challenging the political power of the presidency as the U.S. Supreme Court has done on occasion.[23]

Presidents Zedillo and Fox committed themselves to judicial reform and democratization. Zedillo introduced constitutional initiatives designed to increase the independence and the integrity of the judicial system. Perhaps the most important of Zedillo's reforms empowered the Supreme Court to declare laws unconstitutional under specially stipulated circumstances. The Court may now invalidate a law or a regulation in cases of conflict between different levels of government (a state challenge to a federal law, for example). It may also rule on any challenge to the constitutionality of a federal law if that challenge is supported by at least one-third of the members of either congressional chamber. Similarly, it can rule on state laws that are challenged by at least one-third of that state's legislature. The Fox administration attacked corruption in law enforcement and seemed to establish, for the first time ever, an honest, elite anti-narcotics unit. But it failed to pass significant court reforms. While the media has exposed political corruption more diligently in the past few years, the judicial system has often failed to convict wrongdoers.

Thus, although some progress has been made toward establishing an independent and trustworthy judiciary, there is considerable distance to go. As in most of Latin America, judicial reform has progressed quite slowly, and establishing the rule of law has been one of the greatest challenges of the transition to democracy. Still, since the end of PRI domination, higher-level courts have been somewhat more assertive and independent. Thus, for example, the Supreme Court, which had never previously ruled against a President, has done so several times since 2000.[24]

POLITICAL PARTIES

Until the late 1980s, most political scientists described Mexico as a "modified one-party authoritarian state."[25] To be sure, other parties beyond the PRI existed, but they served a purely symbolic role. As a leading observer of Mexican politics during that period noted, "Without formal opposition, elections would be meaningless. And without elections the system would lose its mask of democratic legitimacy."[26] But PRI electoral dominance began to diminish in the late 1970s and especially during the economic depression of the 1980s. Once able to attract more than 80 percent of the seats in the Chamber of Deputies, PRI dropped below 50 percent for the first time in 1997, and in 2000 they were surpassed by the PAN-led Alliance for Change (Table 16.3). In the 2006 congressional elections, the PRI finished last among the three leading parties (with less than one-fourth of the seats), an unimaginable outcome just 10 years earlier. And, most significant, Vicente Fox's presidential victory ended the PRI's 71-year choke hold on political power. Thus, Mexico has become a truly competitive multiparty system, currently dominated by three major political parties.

The Institutional Revolutionary Party (PRI)

Mexico's ruling party (later to be called the PRI) was created in 1929 and was designed to give official representation to the groups that had been part of the victorious revolutionary coalition. Although no longer in power, it remains the nation's largest party.

Beginning in the 1940s, the core of the party organization was its three occupation-ally based sectors: a labor sector to which most of the nation's blue-collar unions belonged (the Mexican Labor Confederation, or CTM); a peasant sector called the National Peasant Confederation (CNC) representing villages throughout the country; and a catchall, largely middle-class sector, including professional associations (repre-senting such groups as lawyers, doctors, and accountants), small-business associations (taxi owners and street vendors, for example), and most important, powerful white-collar unions of public employees, including teachers and many government bureaucrats.

Drawing heavily on peasant, blue-collar and white-collar votes, the PRI and its predecessors were able to win every presidential election, every gubernatorial and all but one Senate race until the late 1980s. PRI candidates were able to illegally draw on government funding and government policies to outflank the opposition. The party could also count on the television networks to bias their news coverage in favor of PRI candidates. Meanwhile, poor peasants and slum dwellers understood that gov-ernment help to their village or neighborhood (irrigation project, potable water, elec-tricity, or the like) was linked to its getting out a strong PRI vote. In the few cases when PRI candidates, despite all their advantages, were not certain of a victory, the party resorted to vote fraud. Compliant unions endorsed government economic policies, even when they damaged workers (see the description of interest groups, pp. 481–484). Mexican peasants gained the least from PRI policies and were the most disadvantaged group in Mexican society in terms of income, education, housing, nutrition, and health care. Yet, because they are so weak and marginal, they were especially depend-ent on government assistance and, hence, were more likely than any other group to vote for the PRI.

By the 1980s, however, as the government reduced its role in the economy, it became less able to channel economic rewards to its constituents. Consequently, the party shifted its emphasis from the corporatist representation just described (repre-sentation of occupational groups through their unions and associations) and instead focused on individual party membership.

Unlike other ruling parties, such as the Chinese or Cuban communists, the PRI never had a clearly articulated ideology, nor did it formulate policy as, for example, the Chinese Communist Party does. Instead, the official party was the instrument of the president and its primary purpose was to mobilize popular support for the gov-ernment and co-opt important interest groups. While President Zedillo's efforts to democratize the party in the late 1990s were often blocked by party bosses, he did end the long-standing practice of having the president pick the next PRI presidential can-didate (who, for some 70 years, was sure to win the national election).

The party's historic defeat in the 2000 presidential election has forced it to com-pete for the first time in a democratic setting without the benefit of government finan-cial support. While many political analysts predicted that, without the help of government patronage and illegal government campaign contributions, the PRI would wither away, it has, in fact, proven more resilient than expected. In 2000 it edged out the PAN as the leading party in the Chamber of Deputies and enlarged its plurality in 2003. But, as noted previously, it fell to third place in the 2006 elections. As of 2005 it held 17 of Mexico's 32 governorships. Unfortunately, convinced that President Zedillo's democratic reforms had led to Fox's presidential victory, the PRI's corrupt political bosses have reasserted their control of the party, retaking power from the economists and other **technocrats** (highly trained bureaucrats with graduate degrees in the social sciences, mostly from elite U.S. universities) who dominated the party during the last three decades of the twentieth century.

The National Action Party (PAN)

The National Action Party (PAN) was founded in 1939 as the voice of conservative Catholics who opposed the government's growing intervention in the economy and its anti-clerical position (opposition to the Church hierarchy) at that time. For nearly four decades, the party constituted the only notable opposition to the PRI. It still receives strong support from observant Catholics, but as relations between church and state have improved over the years, the party has ceased emphasizing religious issues. The PAN has considerable backing within the business community (particularly among smaller businesses that do not have direct links to the government) and among middle-class conservatives in general.

Though committed to principles of free enterprise and reduced government intervention in the economy, in recent times the party has also received support outside the ranks of conservatives by becoming the party of "good (honest) government," opposing one-party dominance and official corruption. That reformist image was enhanced by the comparative efficiency and honesty of PAN mayors and governors elected in the 1980s and 1990s when the political system began to open up. PAN strength is greatest in urban areas and in the northern section of the country, where there is considerable identification with U.S. values and regional resentment against the dominance of the central government. Ironically, the PAN mounted its successful challenge to PRI dominance in the 1990s just as the national government was adopting neoliberal economic reforms that made the PRI's economic program relatively indistinguishable from the PAN's.

Today, the PAN's electoral image is based less on conservative economics (though it still favors those policies) than on its commitment to honest government and protection of human rights. Indeed, as we will see, President Fox's cabinet included a surprising mix of PAN conservatives and nonparty, liberal, or leftist politicians and intellectuals. The Fox administration's commitment to honest government, protecting civil liberties, and exposing past government repression (most notably repression of left-wing activists in the 1960s to 1980s) initially won it at least as much praise from Mexican liberals and leftists as from the conservatives. At the same time, however, Fox's eclectic ideology and independence have alienated many leaders of his own party. After the 2000 elections, the PAN controlled the presidency, 41 percent of the Chamber of Deputies, and 36 percent of the Senate. In the 2003 elections for the more powerful congressional house, the Chamber of Deputies, the PAN suffered a significant loss of seats, making it even more difficult for President Fox to get his legislative initiatives passed. But PAN rebounded strongly in the 2006 election, taking the largest number of seats in both houses of Congress and apparently winning the presidency (although the results were still being contested at the time this book was written). And, as of 2005 it held 10 of the country's 32 governorships.

The Party of the Democratic Revolution (PRD)

For years an array of small parties, each with its own ideological slant, stood on the PRI's left. Whereas the PAN had once attacked PRI governments for excessive state intervention in the economy, the independent Marxist parties have criticized it for failing to fulfill its revolutionary promises of reduced poverty and greater economic independence from the United States. In other words, whereas the PAN has disagreed with the PRI's revolutionary ideology, the independent left has chided the official party for failing to live up to its revolutionary rhetoric.

Although many of the country's intellectuals and student activists were attracted to Marxism, leftist candidates never mounted a serious electoral challenge. The combined strength of some half-dozen leftist parties never exceeded 10 percent.

In the late 1980s, however, the major left-of-center parties finally overcame their internal conflicts and united behind the candidacy of Cuauhtémoc Cárdenas, the son of modern Mexico's most revered president, Lázaro Cárdenas. The younger Cárdenas had been elected governor of Michoacán on the PRI ticket. In 1987, however, he and several other leaders of the PRI's progressive wing were expelled from the party in the wake of their unsuccessful campaign for internal democratic reforms. Cárdenas's 1988 presidential candidacy was backed by several Marxist parties that had joined with the dissidents who had left the PRI, to form a coalition known as the National Democratic Front (FDN).

The unification of the left behind the son of the PRI's most legendary figure could not have come at a worse time for the ruling party. The economic crisis of the 1980s—bringing higher unemployment and declining living standards—had weakened PRI control over the peasantry and the urban working class. Cárdenas's campaign called for greater democratization and a rollback of President de la Madrid's harsh economic austerity policies, which had lowered Mexican living standards. Whereas the PAN's demand for less government appealed to many middle-class voters and the more prosperous regions of the north, Cárdenas's call for public works programs and a suspension of international debt payments won him considerable support among the nation's poor. The official 1988 presidential vote count showed Cárdenas surging past the PAN to take 32 percent of the vote, while the PAN received 17 percent. Carlos Salinas, the PRI candidate, barely achieved 50 percent in the official tally and reached that level only through substantial vote fraud.

Not long after the 1988 elections, the FDN dissolved and portions of that coalition formed the **Party of the Democratic Revolution (PRD)**. In the 1994 and 2000 presidential races, the party faded somewhat and Cárdenas finished a weak third both times (Table 16.4). Although the disgrace of outgoing president Salinas in 1994 (he and his brother were exposed for engaging in massive corruption) and the 1994–1996 economic crisis opened new opportunities for opposition parties, the PRD was weakened by internal squabbles and political ineptitude. Instead, the PAN reemerged as the primary challenger to PRI dominance in the 1994 presidential election. It won the presidency in 2000 and appeared to have won again in 2006.

The PRD's most important center of strength is in Mexico City, the country's vast capital. Since the capital was allowed to elect its own mayor in 1997 (before that, the mayor was appointed by the president), the PRD has held that post, considered the second-most-powerful in the political system. While generally stronger in the cities, it has also won governorships in impoverished rural states such as Chiapas and Guerrero. In the 2000 national election, the PRD lost over half of its seats in the Chamber of Deputies, but it bounced back in 2003 and especially 2006, when it gained more seats than the PRI (see Table 16.3). As of early 2005, it held the governorship of five states.

When the PRI was still in power, the PRD generally sided with the PAN on issues of political reform and human rights, while siding more often with the PRI on economic policies. President Fox's 2000 victory put the PRD in the position of having to decide whether to support Fox, a fiscal conservative with close ties to business, or join forces

TABLE 16.4   RESULTS OF RECENT PRESIDENTIAL ELECTIONS

Party	1976	1988	1994	2000	2006
PRI	92.3	50.7	53.4	36.1	22.3
PAN[*]	—	16.8	28.6	42.5	35.9
PRD[†]	—	32.5	18.0	18.9	35.3
Other	7.6	15.8	—	3.7	6.53

* The PAN boycotted the 1976 presidential election. In 2000, the PAN was the major component of the Alliance for Change coalition, which backed Vicente Fox's presidential candidacy.

† In 1988 Cuauhtémoc Cárdenas was the candidate of the Democratic National Front (FDN) coalition, some of whose members later formed the PRD. By 1994, the Party of the Democratic Revolution (PRD) had replaced the FDN. In 2000, the PRD was the primary member of the Alliance for Mexico coalition, which backed Cárdenas's presidential candidacy.

SOURCE: CFE and IFE; Pablo González Casanova, *El estado y los partidos políticos en México*, 3rd ed. (México, D.F.: Ediciones Era, 1986), pp. 132—134; and María Amparo Casar, *The 1994 Mexican Presidential Elections* (London: Institute of Latin American Studies, 1995), pp. 14.

in the Congress with its longtime enemy, the PRI, to defeat Fox's legislation. After having suffered a sharp cut in its congressional representation in the 2000 election—primarily losing seats to the PAN—in 2003, it increased the size of its share of seats in the Chamber of Deputies by 70 percent, taking seats back from the PAN (see Table 16.3). After having lost ground in the previous two presidential elections (1994 and 2000), the

STILL IN DISPUTE   PRD candidate Andres Manuel Lopez Obrador addresses a rally during the 2006 presidential race. Lopez Obrador has challenged the official vote count giving his PAN opponent a razor thin victory.

party's candidate in 2006, Andrés Manuel López Obrador, appeared to have a large lead (according to public opinion polls) for much of the election campaign. In the last two months of the race, however, PAN candidate Felipe Calderón erased that lead and apparently won the July 2 election by a hair-thin margin, although López Obrador and his supporters are still challenging the results. Until now the PRD has been dominant in Mexico City (the Federal District) and has performed well in several other states.

A CHANGING POLITICAL CULTURE

Although Mexico's political system has been characterized, until recently, as authoritarian, opportunities for political participation expanded greatly in the twentieth century, long before the 2000 election.[27] Throughout the world, the extent of political participation by individuals or groups is usually closely related to their educational levels. Since the Mexican population at the time of the revolution was overwhelmingly illiterate—and since alternative sources of political information, such as radio, had yet to be developed—levels of political involvement were predictably low.

Through the first decades of the twentieth century, many Mexicans belonged to what political scientists call a "parochial political culture."[28] That is, they lacked sufficient political knowledge to appreciate fully the impact of government policies on their lives and, consequently, tended to abstain from active political participation. But, as the country's literacy climbed over the course of the twentieth century to 92 percent, political involvement has grown. The spread of radio and television along with rapid urbanization has also added to political awareness.

At the same time, however, most Mexicans still have received fewer than six years of formal education and until recently many knew little about political parties other than the PRI. Consequently, until the last decades of the twentieth century, many did not actively follow politics. Even now, when compared to the United States, Mexicans still remain skeptical of their political institutions—political parties, Congress, the police, and the judiciary.[29] But, with the expansion of the urban middle class and increased numbers of high school and university graduates in recent decades, a growing percentage of the population actively follows politics and seeks to influence the political system. The spread of education has affected other aspects of society, including the role of women. But traditional "macho" attitudes remain a problem (Box 16-1).

VOTING AND THE CHANGING ELECTORAL SYSTEM

Although but a few generations ago voting was extremely restricted, Mexican citizens have come to view it as an important right, which they have exercised in substantial numbers even when the PRI candidates faced no serious opposition. In the presidential election of 1917, only 5 percent of the *total* national population (including minors) voted, but by the 1970s that figure approached 30 percent.[30] The PRI's total electoral dominance until recently meant that presidential elections in Mexico served a purpose different from their role in more democratic nations. They were vehicles for introducing the PRI presidential candidate (who may never have run for public office previously) to the population and a means of legitimizing his authority. In the 1982 race,

Box 16-1

THE PLACE OF WOMEN
IN A MACHO CULTURE

As elsewhere in the developing world, socioeconomic modernization in Mexico (growing literacy and educational levels, as well as urbanization), has advanced the status of women. But the country's strong *machista* (male-dominant) culture has limited progress. Many Mexicans continue to believe in male dominance. Signs of progress include a rising proportion of women in the workforce (now about 35 percent of the total) and decisions by the PRI and PRD parties (both of which had female presidents recently) to set a 30 percent quota for women on their list of candidates for the Chamber of Deputies. Still, most of the female candidates have been designated as alternates who only serve as replacements if the regular deputies are unable to serve.

One of the areas where women have faced the greatest challenge is in the behavior of the police and justice systems. For example, Claudia Rodríguez was arrested after she fought off and injured a rapist who subsequently died when medical help failed to arrive for several hours. She served a year in jail for manslaughter before protests by women activists forced her release.[31] Since 1993 more than 400 women have been murdered in the border city of Ciudad Juárez, up to half of them after having been tortured and/or sexually violated. Virtually none of the murders have been solved, and human rights groups such as Amnesty International and WOLA charge that the police and local PAN officials "have done little to investigate or prosecute those responsible" and "women can be killed with complete impunity."[32] At the same time, the police have tortured several innocent men into coerced confessions. It is widely understood that policemen are involved in at least some of the killings.[33]

for example, the PRI's Miguel de la Madrid made more than 1,800 campaign speeches, although he faced little serious opposition. The new, competitive electoral scene adds far greater urgency to the major parties' campaigns.

Clearly, the lack of a viable electoral opposition to the PRI for most of the last half of the twentieth century limited both the psychological incentive to vote and the elections' impact on government policy. Increased voter apathy and cynicism caused abstention rates (registered voters who do not actually vote) to rise from about 30 or 35 percent in the 1960s to nearly 50 percent in the 1985 congressional election.

Since the 1970s, responding to growing pressures from a more politically aware population, the national government has introduced electoral reforms that have made it easier for small parties to run candidates. It also has periodically increased the number of seats allocated to opposition parties in the Chamber of Deputies. As a consequence, the PRI's share of seats in the Chamber declined from more than 80 percent in 1972 to 39 percent in 1987 and 24 percent in 2006. The once-dominant party has lost the presidency, its majority in the Chamber of Deputies, and a significant number of state and local governments.

INTEREST GROUPS

Recognized Interest Groups

Between elections, Mexican citizens engage in a range of interest group activities. Indeed, for a less developed country, Mexico is a rather highly organized society. At the same time, until recently, most interest group activity has been controlled by the government and the PRI. As the ruling party developed, it was organized on corporatist principles. **Corporatism** involves the organization of the population into officially sanctioned interest groups based on occupational or other socioeconomic characteristics. These organizations have a direct channel of communication with the government and in some countries may be the only legally sanctioned representatives of that sector of society.[34] Thus, as we have seen, almost all Mexican labor unions, the giant peasant confederation (CNC), and a vast array of professional and small-business associations have been represented in the three sectors of the ruling PRI.

Most of Mexico's blue-collar labor unions are affiliated with the Congress of Labor (CT). Within the CT, the most powerful force is the Mexican Confederation of Labor (CTM), representing approximately six million workers. Because of its links to the PRI, the CTM used to exercise considerable influence on government policy, but that influence began to decline in the 1980s with the advent of neoliberal economic policies. But even when they had exerted the most political influence, the CTM and its member unions had not served the interests of their members very well. Most of them have been led by corrupt labor bosses who use strong-arm tactics to stay in power and are more interested in amassing wealth and power than in effectively representing their rank and file. Moreover, Mexican unions tend to organize only the more skilled and more highly paid workers, employed in modern industries such as petroleum, steel, automobiles, and electric power. Thus, as in the U.S., most of Mexico's urban workforce is not organized into unions.

During the 71 years of PRI political dominance, most labor unions were closely tied to the government, offering unwavering support in return for government favors. However, the 1980s economic crisis and the sale of most state enterprises to the private sector after 1988 reduced the state's (hence the PRI's) ability to reward unions and led to growing union independence. As the PRI's strength declined in the 1990s, the party's corporatist links with labor unions and peasant organizations began to wither, and the number of independent (non-CTM) unions has risen. The independent National Workers Union (UNT) was formed in 1997 and by 2002 included more than 100 unions and some two million workers outside the CTM and the PRI. The consequences for organized workers are likely to be both positive and negative. On the one hand, independent unions are generally more democratic and more responsive to their members' desires. On the other hand, those unions will have less influence on government policy.[35] Even with the PRI out of power, the CTM often works with the government. While the PAN has generally backed company unions rather than the CTM unions, President Fox's election did not bring the open break with organized labor that many expected. Opportunistic as always, CTM leaders tried to work with the Fox administration (2000–2006) and accepted many of his proposals, including some that are perceived as anti-labor.

Most businesses are organized into government-sanctioned chambers of industry or commerce *outside* the party structure. Mexican law "grants semiofficial status to the chambers, imposes obligatory membership, and allows the state to intervene in various facets of the chambers' operation," although state interference in business groups has usually been low.[36] Rather than serve as a hindrance, the exclusion of business organizations from the PRI allowed them a greater degree of independence than peasant and labor groups enjoyed. Some private-sector interest groups have traditionally maintained close ties to the government, particularly those representing economic activities that were established with government support. Others had more conflictual relationships with the government under the PRI but now have close ties to the PAN administration.

Mexico's huge state economic sector—growing out of the nationalization of petroleum, railroads, electricity, telephone, and telegraph—led some observers erroneously to characterize the economy as socialist. In fact, most of the nation's productive resources remain in private hands. Moreover, during the period of government nationalization (particularly in the late 1930s), the only companies taken over by the state were foreign corporations. For many years, state-owned firms provided the private sector with subsidized power, transport, and communications. Through much of Mexico's "economic miracle," powerful business interest groups (represented informally by major conglomerates known as *grupos*) maintained close links to the government and the PRI.

During the early 1970s, however, President Luis Echeverría antagonized business groups through his radical rhetoric, his introduction of price controls and agrarian reform, and his expansion of the state sector. For the first time, some powerful *grupos*, particularly those located in the industrial capital of Monterrey, allied themselves with the PAN. Businesses also showed their displeasure with government policies by transferring capital abroad. President López Portillo (1976–1982) initially improved relations with the business community but eventually infuriated it by devaluing the nation's currency and nationalizing the private banking system. President Salinas's neoliberal reforms won back the support of much of the business community for his PRI administration. But never have the bonds between big business and the government been so strong as they were under President Fox, who, after all, was a wealthy former businessman whose party (PAN) has long been linked to business.

"Outsider" Interest Groups: The Politics of Protest

For those representing the nation's poor, nonunionized, and unskilled workers, students, and other "outsiders" who lack the political clout or resources to participate in the normal interplay of Mexican interest-group politics, the political system sometimes permits an alternative form of pressure-group activity—political protest. Like the U.S. civil rights movement in the 1960s, Mexican students, peasants, and urban poor organize sit-ins, protest marches, and the like. To succeed, protests by political outsiders must attract media attention and some level of sympathy or support from within the middle class.

Protesters must walk a fine line, however. To be effective, they need to demonstrate their capacity to disrupt daily life or to arouse popular support. Yet, they must be wary not to threaten the stability of the political system or to question its fundamental legitimacy. In 1968, when huge student protests threatened to disrupt the Summer Olympics (hosted by Mexico) and embarrass the government, the students were brutally suppressed. By contrast, Mexico's most noted recent rebel group—the Zapatista guerrillas in the state of Chiapas (officially known as the EZLN or Zapatista Army of National Liberation)—while initially appearing as a threatening, armed, revolutionary group, has, in fact, evolved into a political group working peacefully within the system. (See Box 16-2.)

After the EZLN's initial, violent uprising in January 1994, the group cultivated considerable public support, halted their armed struggle, committed themselves to democratic change, and entered into negotiations with the authorities. The government, in turn, ceased its military activities against the EZLN and negotiated with them for years (without resolution).[37] The Fox administration, perhaps setting a trend, was more receptive to protest demonstrations. For example, when thousands of peasants protested

---

Box 16-2

THE ZAPATISTA REBELLION: MEXICO'S STRUGGLE FOR EQUITY AND DEMOCRACY

Much of the Mexican public looked forward to New Year's Day of 1994 with positive anticipation. On that date, the long-debated and long-anticipated North American Free Trade Agreement (NAFTA) would take effect, joining the economies of Mexico, the United States, and Canada into the world's largest free trade zone. Although NAFTA had many critics and doubters on both sides of the Mexican-U.S. border, President Carlos Salinas and his economic team saw the treaty as the symbol of Mexican economic modernization and the capstone of Salinas's neoliberal reforms, opening up the formerly insulated economy to free trade with the world's largest economy to its north.

But NAFTA's spotlight was soon stolen when—on January 1, 1994—some 600 to 1,000 peasant "soldiers" of the Zapatista Army of National Liberation (EZLN) occupied four towns in the impoverished southern state of Chiapas and held them for several days. Representatives of the media flooded Chiapas and soon enthralled Mexicans and much of the world with news of the Zapatista rebels and their ski-masked, eminently quotable, and charismatic spokesperson, the self-styled "Subcomandante [Subcommander] Marcos."[38] Although surveys showed that most Mexicans disapproved of the Zapatistas' early use of violence (a tactic soon abandoned), Subcomandante Marcos (subsequently revealed to be a former university instructor)

and the EZLN still captured the nation's imagination with their bold statements against economic inequality and injustice as well as their demands for democracy.

The government and the **Zapatistas** have sporadically pursued negotiations aimed at a peace treaty ever since, though direct negotiations have been stalled since 1996. Soon after taking office, Vicente Fox agreed to terms of a settlement that had eluded his predecessors. He permitted a "march" (actually a bus caravan) of hundreds of EZLN supporters to cities along the route to Mexico City. Upon arriving in the capital, Subcomandante Marcos and other Zapatista leaders addressed supportive crowds, as they had done along their route, and one of them ("Commander Esther") addressed the Senate. But the entire PAN Senate delegation (Fox's own party) boycotted the address and the agreement unraveled when the Congress refused to pass some of the constitutional amendments promoting the rights of indigenous peoples (Native Americans) and self-rule that Fox had promised the EZLN. In early 2006, Marcos and his supporters began a tour of the entire nation designed to convince voters that all candidates in that year's presidential campaign offered no hope for Mexico's poor and were, hence, unacceptable. Interestingly, President Fox guaranteed Marcos's safe passage on the tour (i.e., that he would not be arrested by the authorities).

(sometimes violently) against construction of a new international airport on their farmland, Fox, despite the objections of law-and-order advocates, announced that the airport would be built at a different location.

THE FOX PRESIDENCY AND THE FUTURE OF MEXICO

It is probably safe to say that after Vicente Fox's electoral victory, Mexican politics will never be the same. Now that the Mexican people have seen that they can vote out the ruling party, without negative consequences, single-party domination is unlikely to return. Not only the 2000 and 2006 presidential races but also elections for Congress, state governors, and mayors have become competitive in most parts of the country. A system of citizen electoral monitoring instituted in the 1990s and other reforms now promise an honest vote count, though the PRD's 2006 presidential candidate, Andrés

Manuel López Obrador, and his supporters have claimed that fraud contributed to the narrow victory of his PAN opponent, Felipe Calderón. Elections in Mexico's more economically developed north now frequently feature competition between the PAN and the PRI, and elections in Mexico City and in the less developed southern states generally feature races between the PRI and the PRD. In some areas, competition is intense among the three major parties. Only in a few states does one party dominate. In short, the phenomenon of competitive elections, which began slowly in the 1980s, is now firmly established. To succeed politically, candidates and elected officials from all three parties will increasingly have to be responsive to the needs of individual voters and organized interest groups.

Unlike many government leaders in other parts of the world who have run for president on the promise of democratic change but, upon taking office have been as authoritarian as their predecessors, President Fox was true to his word. For example, his government exposed past cases of political corruption (with the possibility of future prosecutions), made modest progress in reducing police corruption and brutality, and ended the previous (PRI) governments' policy of bribing journalists to receive favorable media coverage.

At the same time, Fox generally was been more responsive to grassroots demands and protests than his predecessors were. For example, he softened the government's negotiating stand with the Zapatista rebels in Chiapas and offered a peace settlement that the EZLN accepted (although it was subsequently shot down by Congress). And, as we have noted, he rejected the use of force to crush peasant demonstrators protesting the construction of Mexico City's new international airport. Thus, in a variety of ways—from the ballot box to protest demonstrations—the appeals and demands of a growing number of Mexican citizens are being heard.

But the struggle for full democracy is far from over. The judicial system, despite operating more honestly and fairly than before, is still plagued by considerable corruption and inequity. Police corruption and brutality continue, especially at the local level. And despite some impressive arrests of drug lords and their government collaborators, Mexico's drug mafia remains a dangerously corrupting force in government. Many government bureaucrats continue to demand bribes for their services. According to one authoritative estimate, in the years leading up to Fox's election, Mexicans paid $2.5 billion annually in bribes to government functionaries, averaging $100 per family.[39]

Although Congress's new independence from presidential dominance is an important step forward, all too frequently the legislature has replaced blind obedience (before 1997) with indiscriminate opposition (since 2000). Because the PAN lacks a congressional majority, President Fox has had great difficulty getting reform legislation or even many of his budget proposals passed. Of Fox's major economic initiatives, only his financial reforms (involving regulation of institutions such as the stock market, banks, insurance companies, and mortgage societies) have been passed.[40] Too often, the PRI and PRD delegations oppose his proposals merely for the sake of stymying the president. And since those two parties generally cannot reach agreement with each other, Congress often finds itself deadlocked.

Mexico's other major challenge, achieving greater economic justice and equity, remains even more elusive. President Fox has proposed a number of targeted programs designed to help Mexico's poor, but the basic structural obstacles to greater equality remain in place and in some respects have grown stronger. Fox and the PAN have been even more committed to neoliberal reforms than the previous PRI governments. Those policies, which focus on increased competition between firms, reduced government subsidies for producers, lower government regulation of business, and the consolidation of farmland into larger commercial units, are all designed to make the Mexican economy more efficient and competitive. When applied in Mexico and other developing nations, these reforms have frequently stimulated economic growth, lowered inflation rates, and reduced government budget deficits. But typically, such reforms have also widened economic inequalities, at least initially, and removed government safety nets for the poor.

Many of Fox's initiatives in the realm of social justice were widely applauded. He appointed a respected independent human rights advocate to head national security; his government revealed long-suppressed documents about the 1968 government massacre of political protestors; it allowed charges to be brought against former-president Luis Echeverría for his role (as a cabinet minister) in that massacre (ending a tradition of full immunity for all ex-presidents); opened long-secret documents on the disappearance of some 500 people killed by government security forces in the 1970s; passed laws prohibiting the use of torture against criminal suspects (a widespread practice); and introduced various measures designed to reduce police corruption, especially among units involved in the war on drugs.

While the president's efforts on behalf of clean government and human rights had some success, political corruption is still pervasive. Misconduct has crossed party lines. In Tijuana, the PRI used intimidation, vote-buying, and patronage to secure victory for its mayoral candidate, Jorge Hank Rhon. Hank, the son of a notorious party boss, had previously been convicted of smuggling. He is believed to have links to Tijuana's drug cartel, and two of his bodyguards were jailed on charges of assassinating an investigative journalist. At the same time, a senator from the Green (ecology) Party, formerly allied with Fox, was videotaped taking a bribe from a businessman who wanted to build a hotel in an ecological preserve. Within the PRD, several high-ranking Mexico City officials have been taped taking bribes and the city's director of public finance was caught gambling in Las Vegas with public funds.[41]

Lacking both a congressional majority and the political skills or desire to take on the PRI, President Fox was far less effective as president than he had been as a presidential candidate. At the same time, his control over his own party, the PAN, was limited. While Fox shared the party's neoliberal, pro-business economic priorities, his progressive social agenda was unacceptable to most of his party colleagues. For example, they saw him as too quick to give in to the demands of peasant or worker protests. They also resented the fact that Fox created his own electoral machine for the 2000 presidential election and distanced himself from the PAN. Upon taking office he appointed surprisingly few PAN members to his cabinet or as presidential advisors, and gave a number of key posts to left-of-center PRD activists who had supported his candidacy. Finally, Fox lacked political experience and a knowledge of backroom politics. He often naively assumed that if he saw a problem, he could quickly fix it. Thus, upon taking office he promised he would settle the difficult six-year-old conflict with the Zapatistas "within 15 minutes." Really believing that he could reach an accord in a matter of days or weeks, he failed to grasp the political difficulties involved. Critics accused him of being stronger on style than on substance. His tendency to make unrealistic promises contributed to voter disillusionment and falling poll ratings. Finally, despite his charismatic style and commanding presence, his flamboyant behavior and off-the-cuff comments sometimes weakened his support. Seeming strangely unaware that as president he couldn't maintain the same life style that he had enjoyed as a millionaire business executive, he created a scandal when news leaked out of his extravagant refurnishing of the president's residence, including bed linens that cost 3,800 U.S. dollars and towels that cost $400 each.

Some political analysts have voiced concerns that the more equal distribution of congressional seats among three parties, while clearly more democratic than earlier PRI domination, may doom future administrations to the same congressional-executive gridlock that plagued Fox.[42]

Despite Mexico's modest economic growth in recent years (giving it the highest per capita income in Latin America), some 50 percent of the population remains below the poverty line (making less than $2 per day).[43] Most poor Mexicans, particularly those from rural areas, still lack an adequate diet, satisfactory health care, and an education for their children that will enable them to compete in the twenty-first century. Income inequality remains among the highest in Latin America. These are great challenges that the nation will continue to face for decades.

And despite substantial democratic gains in recent years, many Mexicans remain suspicious of government institutions. Thus, when the Federal Electoral Institute declared that PAN 2006 presidential candidate, Felipe Calderón, was the victor over the PRD's Andrés Manuel López Obrador (by only 0.6 percent), the PRD challenged the tally and demanded a full recount. Hundreds of thousands of Mexico City residents joined massive protest marches, while others blocked major boulevards.

 ## WHERE ON THE WEB?

http://lanic.utexas.edu/la/mexico/

The Mexico page at the University of Texas's most extensive Web site on all of Latin America; the best source of information and links related to Mexico (including politics). Many of these links are in Spanish.

http://dir.yahoo.com/Regional/Countries/Mexico/Government/Politics/

Yahoo links to Mexican government and politics.

http://directory.google.com/Top/Regional/North_America/Mexico/

Google links to resources on Mexican society, culture, and politics.

http://www.sonoma.edu/users/w/warmotha/awmexico.html

An extended essay on Mexican politics, culture, and economics by a Mexican scholar.

◆ ◆ ◆

Key Terms and Concepts_____

caciques	National Action Party (PAN)
corporatism	Party of the Democratic
debt crisis	Revolution (PRD)
economic austerity	presidentialism
Institutional Revolutionary	privatization
Party (PRI)	state capitalism
Lázaro cárdenas	technocrats
macho (*machista*) culture	Zapatista
Mexican economic miracle	

Discussion Questions_____

1. The Mexican Revolution of 1910 dramatically changed that country's political and socioeconomic systems for the remainder of the twentieth century. Discuss the major positive and negative political and socioeconomic effects of that revolution.
2. After decades of rapid economic growth, Mexico has suffered several severe economic setbacks since the early 1980s. What caused that economic decline, and to what extent did government policy errors contribute to the economic crises of the 1980s and 1990s?
3. Discuss the relationship between Congress and the president under the PRI presidencies. Who had the upper hand and why? How has that relationship changed since the late 1990s, particularly since the election of Vicente Fox?
4. Why has Mexico's balance of strength among the major political parties created obstacles for effective government, and why is it likely to do so in the near future?
5. What factors led to the gradual decline of PRI political dominance since the late 1970s, and what factors accelerated that decline since 1988, leading, ultimately, to the 2000 presidential victory of PAN candidate Vicente Fox?
6. What have been the major successes and failures of the Fox administration?

Notes_____

1. See Vikram K. Chand, *Mexico's Political Awakening* (Notre Dame, IN: University of Notre Dame Press, 2001).
2. See Michael C. Meyer and William L. Sherman, *The Course of Mexican History*, 5th ed. (New York: Oxford University Press, 1995).
3. See Anita Brenner, *The Wind That Swept Mexico* (New York: Harper and Bros., 1947); and Judith Adler Hellman, *Mexico in Crisis* (New York: Holmes and Meier, 1979).
4. Dale Story, *The Mexican Ruling Party* (New York: Praeger, 1986), p. 21.
5. Martin Needler, *Mexican Politics: The Containment of Conflict* (New York: Praeger, 1982), p. 108; see also Miguel Ramírez, "The Social and Economic Consequences of the National Austerity Program in Mexico," in *Paying the Costs of Austerity in Latin America*, ed. Howard Handelman and Werner Baer (Boulder, CO: Westview, 1989).
6. R. M. Sundrum, *Income Distribution in Less Developed Countries* (New York: Routledge, 1990), p. 77; René Villarreal, "Import-Substituting Industrialization," in *Authoritarianism in Mexico*, ed. José Luis Reyna and Richard Weinert (Philadelphia: ISHI, 1977), p. 80; and United Nations Development Program, *Human Development Report 2000* (New York and Oxford: Oxford University Press, 2002), p. 195.
7. Manuel Pastor and Carol Wise, "The Fox Administration and the Politics of Economic Transition," in *Mexico's Democracy at Work*, ed. Russell Crandall, Guadalupe Paz, and Riordan Roett (Boulder, CO: Lynne Rienner Publishers, 2005), pp. 98–99.
8. Hellman, *Mexico in Crisis*, pp. 82–89; and Rosa Elena Montes de Oca, "The State and the Peasants," in Reyna and Weinert, *Authoritarianism in Mexico*.
9. Peter Ward, *Welfare Politics in Mexico* (Boston: Allen and Unwin, 1986) p. 17.
10. Daniel Levy and Gabriel Székely, *Mexico: Paradoxes of Stability and Change* (Boulder, CO: Westview, 1987), p. 147.
11. Nora Lustig, *Mexico: The Remaking of an Economy* (Washington, DC: Brookings, 1992).
12. Sidney Weintraub, "Detour on the Way to the Promised Land," *Hemisfile* 7, no. 3 (May–June 1996): 6–7.
13. Miguel Angel Centeno, *Democracy Within Reason: The Technocratic Revolution in Mexico*, 2nd ed. (University Park: Pennsylvania State University Press, 1997).
14. Centeno, *Democracy Within Reason*, p. 49.
15. See Carlos Monsiváis, "'En virtud de las facultades que me han sido otorgadas, . . .' Notas sobre el presidencialismo a partir de 1968," in *La transición interrumpida: México 1968–1988* (México: Nueva Imagen, 1993), pp. 113–125.

16. Jeffrey A. Weldon, "Changing Patterns of Executive-Legislative Relations in Mexico," p. 137, and Kevin J. Middlebrook, "Mexico's Democratic Transitions," in *Dilemmas of Political Change in Mexico*, ed. Kevin J. Middlebrook (London, England: Institute of Latin American Studies of the University of London, 2004), p. 24.

17. Weldon, ibid., p. 165.

18. Wayne Cornelius and Jeffrey Weldon, "Politics in Mexico," in *Comparative Politics Today* (New York: Pearson Longman, 2006), ed. Gabriel Almond et al., p. 486.

19. David A. Shirk, *Mexico's New Politics: The PAN and Democratic Change* (Boulder, CO: Lynne Rienner Publishers, 2005), p. 198.

20. Middlebrook, "Democratic Transitions" in *Dilemmas of Political Change*, p. 25; Edna Jaime, "Fox's Economic Agenda." in *Mexico Under Fox*, ed. Luis Rubio and Susan Kaufman Purcell (Boulder, CO: Lynne Rienner Publishers, 2004), p. 58.

21. *The New York Times*, June 7, 1995.

22. Needler, *Mexican Politics*, p. 90.

23. Ibid.

24. Julia Preston and Samuel Dillon, *Opening Mexico: The Making of a Democracy* (New York: Farrar, Straus and Giroux, 2004), p. 514.

25. Samuel P. Huntington, "Social and Institutional Dynamics of One-Party Systems," in *Authoritarian Politics in Modern Society: The Dynamics of One-Party Systems*, ed. S. Huntington and C. Moore (New York: Basic Books, 1970), p. 5.

26. Alan Riding, *Distant Neighbors* (New York: Vintage, 1986), p. 135.

27. See Roderic Ai Camp, *Politics in Mexico: The Decline of Authoritarianism*, 3rd ed. (New York: Oxford University Press, 1999). Excellent contemporary survey data can be found in Jorge Domínguez and Alejandro Poiré, eds., *Toward Mexico's Democratization: Parties, Campaigns, Elections and Public Opinion* (New York and London: Routledge, 1999).

28. For a discussion of political culture and types of subcultures, see G. Almond and G. B. Powell, *Comparative Politics: A Developmental Approach* (Boston: Little, Brown, 1966), pp. 27–30; and Gabriel Almond, "The Intellectual History of the Civic Culture Concept," in *The Civic Culture Revisited*, ed. G. Almond and S. Verba (Boston: Little, Brown, 1980).

29. Roderic Ai Camp, *Politics in Mexico* (New York: Oxford University Press, 2003), pp. 54–74.

30. Needler, *Mexican Politics*, p. 5. Increased voting over time resulted from higher educational levels, extending the vote to women and lowered the voting age from 21 to 18.

31. Marta Lamas, "The Role of Women in the New Mexico," in *Mexico's Politics and Society in Transition*, ed. Joseph Tulchin and Andrew Selee (Boulder, CO: Lynne Rienner Publishers, 2003), p. 136.

32. Washington Office on Latin America (WOLA), "Violence Against Women in Ciudad Juárez" (November 2, 2004), http://www.wola.org/Mexico/hr/ciudad_juarez/juarez.htm.

33. *The New York Times*, "In Mexico's Murders, Fury Is Aimed at the Police," September 26, 2005.

34. Corporatism is often associated with European fascism, and yet corporatist aspects are found not only in all of Latin America but also in many Western democracies. See Howard Wiarda, *Corporatism and National Development in Latin America* (Boulder, CO: Westview, 1981).

35. Katrina Burgess, "Mexican Labor at the Crossroads," in *Mexican Politics and Society*, ed. Tulchin and Selee, p. 100.

36. Dale Story, *Industry, the State and Public Policy* (Austin: University of Texas Press, 1986), p. 82.

37. Howard Handelman, *Mexican Politics: The Dynamics of Change* (New York: St. Martin's, 1997), pp. 82–90.

38. The Mexican journal *Proceso* is the best Spanish-language source on the Zapatista movement. Among the many books on the Zapatistas are Philip L. Russell, *The Chiapas Rebellion* (Austin, TX: Mexico Resource Center, 1995); and Neil Harvey, *The Chiapas Rebellion: The Struggle for Land and Democracy.* (Durham, NC: Duke University Press, 1998).

39. Martin Needler, "The Government of Mexico," in *Introduction to Comparative Government* (New York: Pearson Longman, 2006), p. 617.

40. Jonathan Heath, "Mexico's Economy: Are Further Reforms Necessary?" in *Mexican Governance: From Single-Party Rule to Divided Government* (Washington, DC: The CSIS Press, 2005), pp. 161–164.

41. Denise Dresser, "Fox's Mexico: Democracy Paralyzed," *Current History* 104, no. 679 (February 2005): 64–68.

42. Chappell Lawson, "Fox's Mexico at Midterm," *Journal of Democracy*, 15.1 (2004), 139–153.

43. World Bank, "Mexico Country Brief," (August 2004), http://web.worldbank.org/WBSITE/.

For Further Reading _____

Camp, Roderic Ai. *Politics in Mexico: The Decline of Authoritarianism.* 4th ed. New York: Oxford University Press, 2003.

Chand, Vikram K. *Mexico's Political Awakening.* Notre Dame, IN: University of Notre Dame Press, the Helen Kellogg Institute, 2001.

Domínguez, Jorge, and Alejandro Poiré, eds. *Toward Mexico's Democratization: Parties, Campaigns, Elections, and Public Opinion.* New York: Routledge, 1999.

Levy, Daniel C., and Kathleen Bruhn. *Mexico: The Struggle for Democratic Development.* Berkeley and Los Angeles: University of California Press, 2001.

Middlebrook, Kevin J., ed. *Dilemmas of Political Change in Mexico.* London, England: Institute of Latin American Studies of the University of London, 2004.

Preston, Julia, and Samuel Dillon. *Opening Mexico: The Making of a Democracy.* New York: Farrar, Straus and Giroux, 2004.

Shirk, David A. *Mexico's New Politics: The PAN and Democratic Change.* Boulder, CO: Lynne Rienner Publishers, 2005.

Tulchin, Joseph, and Andrew Selee, ed. *Mexico's Politics and Society in Transition.* Boulder, CO: Lynne Rienner Publishers, 2003.

PART V

INTERNATIONAL RELATIONS

U p to this point, this text has focused primarily on the domestic aspects of politics—how political behavior, institutions, and ideologies function within the boundaries of the nation-state. In Part V, we turn our attention to another important field within political science, the international relations between nation-states. In truth, domestic politics and international relations are frequently intertwined. A country's decision to go to war may be motivated by domestic politics. A nation's environmental policy may affect the purity of the air or water in neighboring states. But, in the absence of some form of regional or world government, the rules and norms of political and economic relations between sovereign states are distinct from those of domestic politics.

Chapter 17 deals with scholarly debates and approaches to the study of such issues as nuclear weapons or international law. Chapter 18 examines important contemporary issues in international relations such as world trade, human rights, and international terrorism.

READY FOR WAR   On August 30, 2006, Turkish troops parade during ceremonies marking the 84th anniversary of Mustafa Kemal Ataturk troops' victory against the Greek army.

© AFP/Getty Images

$$\boxed{17}$$

APPROACHES TO INTERNATIONAL RELATIONS

◆ International Relations versus Domestic Politics
◆ Idealists and Realists ◆ War and International Relations
◆ The Politics of Nuclear Weapons ◆ Foreign Policy
Decision Making ◆ International Political Economy
◆ International Law and Organization ◆ Ethics and
International Relations ◆ Conclusion: War, Trade, Foreign
Policy, and the Stakes of Politics

Despite the transforming effect of the terrorist attacks on September 11, 2001, and the 2003 invasion of Iraq and its troubling aftermath, domestic affairs continue to dominate the political concerns of most U.S. citizens, as they do for citizens of the United Kingdom, Japan, France, and other modern democracies. Because their access to international news is so limited, citizens in most developing countries discuss international affairs only rarely. Nevertheless, and especially in recent years, it is clear that international relations affect people everywhere in profound ways.

Many citizens immediately think of the possibility of armed conflict when they consider international relations, and indeed, wars are among the most important events in human history. Even the preparation for war transforms the allocation of economic resources and influences how nations treat their citizens. But international relations are also important when wars are not raging. Economic relations among countries dramatically change domestic conditions everywhere. Modern advances in transportation, communications, and weapons systems have created a world of complex interdependence among nations in which economic progress and national security increasingly require attention to conditions and policies in other countries.

Although international relations is basic to the study of politics and government, approaches to this field are fundamentally different from those encountered in the study of domestic politics. For example, we cannot apply the concepts of political participation through voting or interest group and party organization that we employ in analyzing domestic politics. In this chapter, we discuss the most important approaches to studying international relations, and we devote Chapter 18 to a discussion of contemporary issues.

INTERNATIONAL RELATIONS VERSUS DOMESTIC POLITICS

When we think of international politics, the first topic that occurs to many of us is the war or the threat of war in the international political scene. We study not only how wars are fought but also their causes, the complex issue of deterrence, the effects of shifts in the balance of power, strategy and tactics, the political impact of nuclear weapons, and even the ethical questions suggested by the idea of a "just war." We are sometimes tempted to assume that international relations is distinguished from domestic politics purely by its emphasis on violence.

Yet, the problem of conflict, even violent conflict, is a part of both domestic and international politics. The difference is not in the existence of conflict but in how conflict is managed. Kenneth Waltz, a leading theorist, explains the point in this way:

> The threat of violence and the recurrent use of force are said to distinguish international from national affairs. But in the history of the world surely most rulers have had to bear in mind that their subjects might use force to resist or overthrow them. If the absence of government is associated with the threat of violence, so also is its presence. . . . To discover . . . differences between internal and external affairs one must look for a criterion other than the occurrence of violence. . . . *The difference between national and international politics lies not in the use of force but in the different modes of organization for doing something about it.*[1]

Domestic politics usually takes place within a context of a generally settled order, whereas international politics takes place in a state of relative anarchy. In domestic affairs, the state assumes a "monopoly on the *legitimate* use of force, [meaning] that public agents are organized to prevent and to counter the private use of force."[2] Because such a monopoly on the use of legitimate force does not exist in international relations, Waltz describes the international arena as one in which nations engage in **self-help**; each nation must look to its own security because there is no higher authority that can consistently and effectively perform that function. Of course, forces of stability and order do exist in the international system, such as shared cultures and ideologies, and international law and organization—and they prevent some violent conflict. The difference between domestic and international politics lies in the extent to which a given actor is on its own with respect to protecting its security. Although both citizens and individual nations can be threatened with adversaries, and although both may work to defend themselves, the *primary* approach to security in domestic politics is reliance on a higher authority (for example, the police), whereas the *primary* approach to security in international politics is self-help. That idea is at the heart of contending approaches to the field.

IDEALISTS AND REALISTS

Historians and philosophers have been analyzing international relations since the time of ancient Greece. Among the earliest works in the field was *The Peloponnesian War*, written in the fifth century BCE by Greek historian Thucydides.[3] Other ancient studies include Sun Tzu's *The Art of War* and Kautilya's *Anthasastra*.[4] Those works continue to suggest insights to modern scholars. The unprecedented destruction and complex origins of World War I, however, led to rapid growth in academic study of the field, producing two sharply opposing perspectives: idealism and realism.

Idealism*

Idealists assume that war and international tensions can be prevented by establishing international law, by creating effective international organizations, by asserting rights and obligations in international affairs, and by educating citizens and leaders regarding the wastefulness of war. **Idealism** thus advocates a set of normative principles—it tells us what we *should* do. Yet, idealism also contains implicit explanations of national behavior, thus approaching the status of an empirical theory. Idealists suggest that the causes of war can be found in ill-conceived ideologies, in excesses of nationalism, and in the underdevelopment of law. If we want to know why a given war was started, we should look to those factors. On a positive note, idealism reflects the belief that effective political management can help prevent wars that otherwise

---

* Some analysts prefer the term "liberalism" or "liberal idealism" in this context. For example, a text by Charles W. Kegley, Jr., and Eugene R. Wittkopf, *World Politics, Trend and Transformation* (New York: St. Martin's, 1997), uses "liberal idealism," which they define as the assumption that "people are not by nature sinful or wicked but that harmful behavior was the result of structural arrangements motivating individuals to act in their own self-interest" (p. 19). Joseph S. Nye, Jr., in *Understanding International Conflicts: An Introduction to Theory and History*, 3rd ed. (New York: Longman, 2000), pp. 39–45, discusses "liberalism" in a broad sense, including several different meanings. We prefer to use the term *idealism* here to avoid confusion with the rather separate set of ideas associated with the term *liberalism* in social policy (as discussed in Chapter 2), and because "liberalism" is synonymous with advocacy of free trade in international political economy, as we discuss later in this chapter.

appear unavoidable: People can be brought to understand the wrongfulness of belligerent ideologies or aggressive forms of national pride, and they can be persuaded to accept a workable code of international law. Wars need not be fought.

U.S. President Woodrow Wilson (1913–1921) was a key proponent of idealism. Following World War I, his support for the creation of the ill-fated League of Nations (an international organization intended to maintain international security) was a moral mission, one that reflected a sincere belief that war could become obsolete if nations had a forum in which they could solve their differences without recourse to armed conflict. Wilson believed that war is something that humankind can "grow out of," much as adults can emerge from a rocky adolescence to become cooperative, productive citizens.

Realism

Although many people share the goals of idealism, few analysts of international relations fully accept its assumptions about the underlying forces governing international affairs. **Realism** holds that the actual motivations for national behavior are often quite different from what is implied in the public rhetoric of leaders: A nation may *claim* to act in accordance with moral, religious, or even legal principles, but its real purpose is almost always the pursuit of security and power. Because idealism is flawed as a way to explain the origins of war, charge its realist critics, it cannot serve as a blueprint for preventing war. It is necessary to identify the forces that lead to war, and then leaders can make policies that make war less likely.

Hans J. Morgenthau, an important twentieth-century realist, described the approach as the assumption that "politics . . . is governed by objective laws" and that "the main signpost that helps political realism to find its way through the landscape of international politics is the concept of interest defined in terms of power."[5] If we want to understand the behavior of nations in international affairs, according to the realist, we must begin with the assumption that everything of importance that nations do is driven by their interests in maximizing their power and security.

By emphasizing *power* and *security*, realists minimize the place of ideals as a motivating force in international relations. Proponents of realist theory have probably produced the most influential research in the field of international relations. Beginning with the assumption that "states, . . . at a minimum, seek their own preservation and, at a maximum, drive for universal domination," realism is the foundation for a wide range of useful predictions about international behavior.[6] (see Box 17-1).

For example, whereas idealists would see the outbreak of World War II as caused by the fanatical ideology of fascism, realists feel that Hitler's or Mussolini's totalitarian ideologies were less instrumental in producing the war than was the imbalance of power that developed between the two world wars. Since nations will *always* seek power and domination (regardless of the ideologies that may be in fashion at a given moment as expressed in stump speeches), realists contend that the more basic "cause" of the war was the military weakness of Great Britain, France, and the United States, which presented Germany (and perhaps Japan) with the opportunity to pursue expansionist plans.

According to this way of thinking, realists often criticize British Prime Minister Neville Chamberlain (the chief executive who preceded Winston Churchill) for his

Box 17-1

IDEALISM, REALISM, AND THE INVASION OF IRAQ

In September 2004, more than a year after the invasion of Iraq, President George W. Bush spoke to the United Nations General Assembly. He referred to terrorist attacks that had taken place after the invasion and overthrow of Saddam Hussein, including an attack on September 1, 2004 in the Russian town of Beslan that killed nearly 200 children and adults. Bush's speech is a perfect illustration of the idealist perspective, using rhetoric that echoed that of Woodrow Wilson nearly a century earlier:

In this young century, our world needs a new definition of security. Our security is not merely found in spheres of influence, or some balance of power. The security of our world is found in the advancing rights of mankind.

These rights are advancing across the world— and across the world, the enemies of human rights are responding with violence. Terrorists and their allies believe the Universal Declaration of Human Rights and the American Bill of Rights, and every charter of liberty ever written, are lies, to be burned . . . and forgotten. They believe that dictators should control every mind and tongue in the Middle East and beyond. They believe that suicide and torture and murder are fully justified to serve any goal they declare.

And they act on their beliefs.

In the last year alone, terrorists have attacked police stations, and banks, and commuter trains, and synagogues—and a school filled with children. This month in Beslan we saw, once again, how the terrorists measure their success—in the death of the innocent, and in the pain of grieving families. Svetlana Dzebisov was held hostage, along with her son and her nephew—her nephew did not survive. She recently visited the cemetery, and saw what she called the "little graves." She said, "I understand that there is evil in the world. But what have these little creatures done?"

The Russian children did nothing to deserve such awful suffering, and fright, and death. The people of Madrid and Jerusalem and Istanbul and Baghdad have done nothing to deserve sudden and random murder. These acts violate the standards of justice in all cultures, and the principles of all religions. All civilized nations are in this struggle together, and all must fight the murderers.

We're determined to destroy terror networks wherever they operate, and the United States is grateful to every nation that is helping to seize terrorist assets, track down their operatives, and disrupt their plans. . . . [M]y nation is grateful to the soldiers of many nations who have helped to deliver the Iraqi people from an outlaw dictator.*

President George W. Bush and many of his supporters have been labeled "neo-conservatives" by many commentators. Although the term has not yet acquired a widely accepted meaning, it commonly is applied to those who believe in activist government and foreign policy to achieve conservative goals. Traditional conservatives tend to be more skeptical about governmental efforts to improve societies or to spread democracy throughout the world. Thus, conservatives like columnist George Will criticized the Bush Administration's attempt to create democracy in Iraq, arguing that the effort was driven by the "Jeffersonian poetry of democratic universalism." Brent Scowcroft, a key adviser to President George H.W. Bush and a key advocate of the 1991 war to remove Iraq's forces from Kuwait, similarly criticized the 2003 invasion. His remarks were rooted in the realist school of thought, contrasting starkly with Bush's idealism.

Scowcroft, in a *New Yorker* interview, discussed an argument over Iraq he had had two years earlier with Condoleezza Rice, who was then national security adviser. "She says we're going to democratize Iraq, and I said, 'Condi, you're not going to democratize Iraq,' and she said, 'You know, you're just stuck in the old days,' and she comes back to this thing that we've tolerated an autocratic Middle East for fifty years and so on and so forth," he said. The interviewer noted that Scowcroft, with a "barely perceptible note of satisfaction" in his voice, then added: *"But we've had fifty years of peace."*** Scowcroft's conclusion embodies the realist idea that peace is more secure when nations pursue realist principles than when they act to achieve idealist goals.

*The full text of the president's speech may be found at http://www.whitehouse.gov/news/releases/2004/09/20040921-3.html.

**The *New Yorker* story, written by Jeffrey Goldberg in October 2005, is available at http://www.newyorker.com/fact/content/articles/051031fa_fact2.

(Continued)

Box 17-1

IDEALISM, REALISM, AND THE INVASION OF IRAQ
(*Continued*)

It is certainly possible to construct a realist argument to support the invasion of Iraq and the extended U.S. presence there. Despite the public speeches that embody idealism, the real reason for the invasion, according to realists who supported it, was to remove a threat to stability in the region and to assert U.S. power in order to inhibit aggression by other regimes. Those taking this view point to the fact that Libya publicly announced its decision to abandon a nuclear weapons program shortly after the invasion, and that the reason for its decision was that Libya's leaders did not want to suffer the same fate as Saddam Hussein.

It is also arguable that realist thinking led to the Bush administration's different policies toward Iraq and North Korea in late 2002. The president had argued along idealist lines in stating that no part of the "axis of evil" (which he claimed included both of those countries, along with Iran) should be allowed to have nuclear weapons, and he emphasized the dangers created by the existence of such weapons in Iraq as a justification for military action there. When North Korea admitted that it too had violated the Non-Proliferation Treaty and was working to obtain nuclear weapons, some citizens and observers felt that the United States should be equally ready to attack North Korea. After

all, both countries had violated treaties, both had nuclear bombs, and both were aggressive.

However, the difference in U.S. policy toward Iraq and North Korea indicates that the idealism of the Bush Administration was tempered by a strong element of realism. Some have argued that despite its possession of nuclear weapons, North Korea is surrounded by much stronger neighbors and that it is economically weak. Thus, economic and diplomatic pressure can be brought to bear on North Korea, possibly resulting in progress toward disarmament without war. Iraq, in contrast, is surrounded by vulnerable neighbors and has shown itself to be essentially immune to economic pressures. Moreover, North Korea does not control any strategically important resources.

Realism and idealism in U.S. foreign policy will both figure in the nation's response to problems in Iran, as discussed in the next chapter. It is often difficult to separate considerations of morality and international law from concerns for stability and power, and whatever U.S. policy turns out to be, statements and speeches justifying it will certainly contain realist and idealist notions. Which of these approaches generates the best foreign policy decisions remains the subject of a never-ending debate.

DELICATE DIPLOMACY   U.S. Secretary of State Condoleezza Rice, left, gestures while speaking with EU foreign policy chief Javier Solana during a round table meeting at an Iraqi International conference in Brussels, Wednesday June 22, 2005.

actions during the months preceding World War II. Chamberlain sought to appease Hitler as Germany moved its armies into Austria and Czechoslovakia. He refused to accelerate British defense spending in the face of the rising German military threat because he thought that doing so would be seen by Hitler as threatening. Hitler exploited the opening created, in part, by British weakness, and World War II began. Realists employ this example to support their contention that preventing wars requires a consistent recognition that all nations seek power and security, and that military weakness in critical areas will present opportunities that aggressors will exploit. The positive element in this approach is the idea that the behavior of most states is therefore predictable.

Criticisms of Both Approaches

Critics of idealism argue that an approach based on national interest and the assumption that nations will always pursue security and power provides a better foundation for explaining conflict and war. Skillful politicians may engage in florid rhetoric to persuade their citizens to sacrifice for a "moral" cause, but the objectives they most often pursue are their more concrete concerns for power, security, and self-interest.

On the other hand, critics of realism contend that realists narrowly read history as being determined exclusively by a small set of influences. Edward Hallett Carr, whose analysis of idealism and realism remains an influential statement, pointed out that realist thinking is excessively cynical. Although overt moral positions do sometimes serve simply as a cover for the pursuit of self-interest, he argues, it does not follow that the behavior of nations is as simple or predictable as realists claim.[7] Moreover, the concept of a nation's having "a" national interest is more applicable to nations that are governed by a single monarch or ruling elite (whose precise and explicit interests can be identified and acted on) than to democratic nations, whose citizens and groups have multiple and usually conflicting interests.

The U.S. and European intervention in Bosnia, the U.S. military action in Somalia in 1992–1993, and U.S. aid to central African refugees constitute significant challenges to the realist assumption that foreign policy is driven exclusively by national interest. The United States has no strategic interests in those areas. The relief efforts placed some U.S. military personnel in real danger and cost billions of dollars. Although it is fair to say that the United States did not jeopardize its security by taking those actions, it is difficult to say that U.S. interest in security and power interests lay behind them.

Similarly, some claim that British Prime Minister Tony Blair has adopted positions supporting the U.S.-led invasions of Afghanistan and Iraq that cannot be explained through realism. It is arguable that British security from terrorist attacks would be enhanced by taking a more neutral position, but he has, so far, advocated policies best explained as consistent with idealist principles.

In fact, the idea that nations pursue foreign policies *entirely* on the basis of a simple concern for self-interest is becoming increasingly difficult to defend. A recent study by a leading analyst, Robert Jervis, concludes that a "security community," defined as "a group of countries among which war is unthinkable," can influence policy. He claims that, in the contemporary world, a security community has developed among the United States, Western Europe, and Japan. The shared conviction among these countries—that war would be absurdly costly, whereas peace produces real gains—exerts real force over their policy choices.[8] Although realists would claim that the idea of a "security community" is consistent with their view (because Jervis's concept does not imply that nations disregard or act against their national interests), it certainly suggests that foreign policy choices are not a simple matter of nations acting exclusively on the basis of their independent concerns. Something larger than a nation's individual interests may shape foreign policy, and idealists would point to that observation as support for the idea that peace may be maintained or strengthened by building on these larger, collective influences.

Debates over the usefulness of realism and idealism and their many variants will not be resolved easily or quickly. Realists have always noted that the political rhetoric used to justify states' foreign policy choices usually makes it *appear* that idealistic motivations are involved; the *actual* motivations are power and security even when domestic politics requires speeches implying a higher purpose. Empirical research is unlikely to yield definitive answers to this debate partly because of the difficulty of ascertaining the motives of national leaders.

War and International Relations

The possibility of armed conflict often influences behavior even when other issues dominate relations among nations. A country's ability to attack its enemies or to defend itself in war represents a critical factor in its interactions with other nations. Thus, a great deal of scholarly attention is rightly devoted to the study of war. In this section, we consider the most widely known approaches to understanding war, and then we focus on two special issues: the balance-of-power concept and the problem of nuclear weapons.

The Causes of War: Waltz's "Images"

The fact that war is both horribly wasteful and a seemingly inescapable part of life has led philosophers and politicians to devote a great deal of attention to discovering its ultimate causes. Kenneth Waltz's classic book, *Man, the State, and War,* synthesized much of the prevailing scholarly thinking about the subject into a three-way classification of "images."[9] (In terms of the discussion in the previous section, Waltz would say that the third image is most closely associated with realism and that the first image is most closely tied to idealism.)

The First Image: Human Nature and the Causes of War The most common approach to understanding the causes of war is to look to human nature. Waltz described this "first image" of international relations as follows: "The locus of the important causes of war is found in the nature and behavior of man. Wars result from selfishness, from misdirected aggressive impulses, from stupidity."[10] To find out why World War II occurred, for example, we study Adolf Hitler's personality, his foolish ideology, and his tragic power to inspire millions of followers. Quoting Confucius, Waltz summed up the first image: "There is deceit and cunning and from these wars arise."

There are both optimistic and pessimistic versions of this first image. If the cause of war is found in human nature, then war can be ended if education and experience can correct human failings. Perhaps people can be brought to see war as wrong and avoidable. Others, who believe that war is an inherent part of human nature, imply that wars can never be fully prevented. The "laws" of human nature, they argue, are no more malleable than are the laws of physics.

Although the importance of human nature cannot be easily dismissed, it becomes quickly limited as a basis for generally understanding international conflict. Other factors must be involved. If human nature were all that mattered in the origin of wars, *then we have no way of understanding why there are periods of peace.* Since nations are not always at war (or peace), human nature cannot be the exclusive source of war. "The causes that in fact explain differences in behavior must be sought somewhere other than in human nature itself."[11]

The Second Image: The Nature of States and the Causes of War   An alternative explanation of the cause of war focuses on the nature of states. Even if people could control their aggressive impulses, the nature of the states that govern them may create conditions leading to war. The second image implies that we can explain war by looking at the ways in which different *kinds* of states increase or diminish the likelihood of war.

For example, a proponent of the second image may argue that non-democratic governments are prone to war (see Box 17-2). Such states need to repress dissent, and it is easier to do so if the citizens of such a state are unified and loyal. The leader of such a state may start a war in order to make citizens focus on a common external threat. By some interpretations, there has never been a major war between two genuinely democratic nations—an idea that seems to confirm this connection between the nature of a state's political system and its tendencies toward war. A second example of the second image idea is the conventional Marxist-Leninist interpretation of international affairs. As discussed in Chapter 2, one of Lenin's contributions to Marxist thinking was the idea that capitalist states engage in aggression because the nature of their economic systems forces them to do so.

The limitation of the second image is its assumption that the warlike (or peaceful) nature of states is entirely determined by domestic factors. Waltz points out that just as individual behavior cannot be understood apart from the societies in which individuals live, the behavior of individual *states* cannot be understood apart from the world in which they operate. Many actions taken by states reflect the nature of the international system as much as they reflect their own internal structure and domestic political needs.

The Third Image: The International System   Waltz's third image emphasizes that understanding international relations requires an appreciation of the nature of the system in which states operate. The key feature of that system is *anarchy*, as noted earlier. For Waltz, the fact that the system is anarchical creates a situation in which each state is potentially threatened, and much of international relations derives from the pervasiveness of those threats. As Waltz points out, the third image has been around a long time: "Thucydides implied an appreciation of this idea when he wrote that it was 'the growth of the Athenian power which terrified the Lacedaemonians and forced them into war.'"[15] Wars are not the consequence of human nature, or even of the nature of political systems, but of the way in which the anarchy of international relations creates insecurity.

Box 17-2

The "Democratic Peace"?

The **democratic peace** concept has gathered momentum among specialists in international relations during the last few decades. In simple terms, the more democratic a nation is, the less likely it is to be involved in a war with another democracy. There is considerable empirical support for this proposition, although it is less well established that democracies are *generally* less involved in wars—the key finding is that they rarely fight other democracies.[12]

Why should this be so? Although the matter is far from settled among political scientists and diplomats, a few themes consistently appear in discussions of the "democratic peace" phenomenon. Perhaps the root of the idea can be traced to a 1795 essay by philosopher Immanuel Kant, entitled "Perpetual Peace: A Philosophical Sketch," in which he concluded that governments that act in "responsible" ways would be reluctant to go to war. The most obvious explanation is that, in democratic systems, the people will force their leaders to avoid war because they will bear its terrible costs. Dictators, not being similarly constrained by public opinion, will initiate wars much more often.

While this makes intuitive sense, it only tells part of the story. One recent study found that, when faced with war, leaders in democratic systems are more likely to allocate a greater share of national resources to military efforts than leaders in authoritarian regimes. Voters in democratic systems dislike military defeats even more than they dislike war. Consequently, nations of all kinds are less likely to attack democratic systems, thus bringing them into war less often. Moreover, democratic leaders try to avoid defeat by being very selective about the countries they would make war upon. Because they are less reckless about engaging in war, and because would-be aggressors fear the all-out effort that democracies would make in response, the historical record indicates that democracies are less likely than non-democracies to be involved in war.[13]

A newer refinement to the "democratic peace" theory is a distinction between established democracies and newer democracies. In a 2005 book by Edward D. Mansfield and Jack Snyder, entitled *Electing to Fight: Why Emerging Democracies Go to War*, the authors found that only *mature* democracies are less likely to be involved in war.

Why would the maturity of a democracy matter? A country that has taken the first steps toward democracy, holding free elections, probably has not yet established institutions that create real accountability (such as a civilian-controlled military, a genuinely free press, and a strongly independent judiciary). In such countries, political leaders may actually be particularly motivated to take their countries to war. They realize that engaging in aggression can generate domestic support, because they can "sell" the resulting war to their citizens as a response to a past injustice at the hands of the invaded country, for example. Not being restrained by well-institutionalized legislative or judicial bodies, or by a competitive party system, leaders in emerging democracies may actually be more belligerent than dictatorships.[14]

One of the most troubling questions raised by Mansfield and Snyder's research has to do with the future of Iraq. Will Iraq be torn by an intractable civil war? Will it return to a dictatorship just as horrific as Saddam Hussein's? Mansfield and Snyder suggest that, even if Iraq continues on its path toward democracy, it will be no less likely to go to war against its neighbors than it was when it had a fascist dictatorship. The Iraqi case raises important questions about the "democratic peace" idea, even if the historical record generally supports it.

As alternative approaches to understanding the causes of war, all three images can be coherent and persuasive. Biologists and psychologists may convince us that human nature is innately aggressive, but we see that some states prevent such alleged tendencies from leading to war. Switzerland has managed to avoid direct involvement in armed conflicts for centuries. And although the anarchical nature of the international system may create widespread insecurity, nations are sometimes able to conduct themselves in ways that avoid turning insecurity into armed conflict. Along with most mainstream experts in the field, Waltz places the greatest importance on the third image, but the complexity of the origins of war makes it likely that all three approaches will continue to find able advocates.

The Balance of Power

At its core, the concept of the **balance of power** says that the *relative* power levels among competing states is the main determinant of stability in international relations and that "the behavior of individual states is explained in terms of the state of the whole system."[16] Where power is balanced, some wars will be prevented; imbalanced power invites aggression by the superior power or prompts the formation of alliances among weaker states to restore balance.

Most analysts agree that the balance-of-power concept applied most convincingly to the European "multipolar system" as it existed between 1648 and 1945. One of the clearest statements about the balance-of-power idea was made by Winston Churchill, who stated that "for four hundred years the foreign policy of England has been to oppose the strongest, most aggressive, most dominating power on the Continent." At least until World War II, the shifting balance of power in Europe prevented any one nation from dominating the world.[17]

As Waltz explains, since nations that do not preserve their own security "will fail to prosper [and] will lay themselves open to danger, . . . fear of such unwanted consequences stimulates states to behave in ways that tend toward the creation of balances of power."[18] If one state begins to threaten another state (as Germany threatened the Soviet Union and Great Britain in the 1930s), the threatened state will normally attempt to augment its power, perhaps by forming alliances (as did those two nations during that period). The aggressor's threatening posture will prompt others to make similar alliances.

The balance-of-power concept is a third-image approach because it focuses on what states do in response to the immediate character of the international system. It can also be taken as a special application of realist principles because it explains war and the avoidance of war without reference to the idealist notions that wars occur because of misguided ideologies and that they can be prevented by nurturing the love of peace. Nevertheless, a major source of confusion regarding the balance of power is that the idea is sometimes presented as an *empirical* statement (states *do* act in ways that preserve or restore a balance of power) and sometimes as a *normative* statement (states *should* act in such ways). In any event, in one form or another, the idea is one of the oldest concepts in political science. Writing in 1742, David Hume argued that "the maxim of preserving the balance of power is founded so much on common sense and obvious reasoning, that it is impossible it could altogether have escaped antiquity. . . ."[19]

A fundamental but common misunderstanding of the balance-of-power concept is the idea that balanced power and efforts to maintain balanced power always *prevent war*. As stated by Edward Vose Gulick in 1955, "The basic aim of the balance of power was to insure the survival of independent states. This . . . should be distinguished from those goals, such as 'peace' and (to a lesser degree) the 'status quo,' which were incidental to it."[20] To maintain their security, states will seek to keep power between states balanced. Sometimes power can be brought back into balance by engaging in war (perhaps to weaken an enemy); on other occasions, balancing power may require that established alliances be dismantled. The ultimate effect of the balance of power is to preserve state survival, not to secure peace.

While still useful, the balance of power is less useful in the modern world than it was a few centuries ago. The concept assumes that leaders are free to respond, quickly and with subtle precision, to a continuously changing power calculus. If an alliance with an evil tyrant or with a former enemy would improve the balance of power, such an alliance will and should be made. But modern states often find that their policy choices are constrained by economic forces, by culture, or by domestic politics. Whereas Germany's Bismarck or France's Napoleon could craft foreign policy decisions with considerable secrecy and latitude, their modern descendants are forced to carry out diplomacy in a more constrained, more public, and more complex environment. The balance-of-power idea cannot produce useful predictions of state behavior when that behavior is subject to the political demands inherent in today's democracies.

THE POLITICS OF NUCLEAR WEAPONS

Many analysts believe that the development of nuclear weapons has fundamentally changed the nature of international relations. Before the nuclear age, the military force available to major nations was a small fraction of what it is now. The largest bombs dropped in World War II before the atomic bombs that leveled Hiroshima and Nagasaki were capable of destroying no more than a city block. By contrast, a 10-megaton nuclear device, yielding the destructive power of 10 million tons of TNT, is incredibly more devastating. Such a bomb would collapse all but the strongest buildings within a radius of more than 12 miles; it would inflict immediate second-degree burns on anyone within 24 miles of the blast; it would engulf a whole city in a raging firestorm; and, under "ideal" conditions, it would produce severely destructive radioactive fallout over an area of some 100,000 square miles (roughly the size of New York, New Jersey, and Pennsylvania combined).

The availability of this kind of power not only has made war more appalling but it has changed the way nations conduct their foreign policies. In earlier eras, war was an instrument of policy through which one nation dissuaded another from doing something it opposed. Nuclear weapons have reduced the extent to which the threat of war can serve as a policy tool. A state holds nuclear missiles and bombs so that a potential aggressor will be convinced that aggression will be unacceptably costly. For that reason, it is often pointed out that—in a statement attributed to former U.S. Defense Secretary Robert McNamara—nuclear weapons are not weapons at all; they are only deterrents. The certainty of large-scale retaliation undercuts the credibility of most threats to start a nuclear war. Moreover, since the possibility exists that a nuclear power will use its nuclear weapons to retaliate for even a conventional (non-nuclear) attack, these weapons may serve as a deterrent to *any* direct aggression.

The idea of *mutual assured destruction* (MAD) thus suggests that the overwhelming destructiveness of nuclear war prevents armed conflict among nuclear powers, as long as a balance of *nuclear* power is maintained. The logic is simple, as described here in a hypothetical statement from the leader of one nuclear power to another:

We both know that the outcome of a nuclear exchange is incalculable in advance, because if such an exchange occurs, we shall probably prove incapable of limiting the damage, whether we consider ourselves under those circumstances to be rational or irrational. For on one side or the other or both there will be "rationalists" who will say that to stop now is to accept defeat. They will be joined by the irrationalists who are primarily driven by the desire for excitement, revenge, or suicide, or something else. Thus we both face the danger of escalation to mutual extinction, simply because we shall exercise all the advantages of war once we are in it.[21]

Both sides thus choose alternatives to war. In Winston Churchill's memorable words, "Peace is the sturdy child of **nuclear terror**."[22] That logic, according to many analysts, accounts for the fact that the major powers of the world have not fought each other in more than half a century. There has never been a longer period of peace among the most powerful nations on earth in all of recorded history. In fact, it may be argued not only that wars have been avoided but also that "reckless" behavior among the superpowers has been reduced. If we count the 1962 Cuban missile crisis as the last time there was a superpower conflict that brought the world to the brink of nuclear war (see Box 17-3), it has been more than 40 years since anyone came close to pushing the "button."[23]

The idea that nuclear weapons reduce the usefulness of war and the threat of war as tools of foreign policy rests on basic calculations of costs and benefits. According to Robert Jervis, fighting is rational if a country expects to be better off after the fighting than before *or* if it would be better off by fighting than by granting the concessions needed to avoid war.[24] He notes that engaging in war was rational in that sense for some countries in World War II: "Although Britain and France did not improve their positions by fighting, they were better off than they would have been had the Nazis succeeded. Thus it made sense for them to fight even though, as they feared at the outset, they would not profit from the conflict."[25] No country would improve its position by fighting in a nuclear war, however.

However, the assumption that nuclear weapons will continue to make war less likely has at least two major problems. First, it assumes that the nuclear weapons of the world are controlled by a small number of major powers, each having a sufficiently developed society so that large-scale retaliation would be costly. Although 180 countries have signed the Non-Proliferation Treaty (discussed in Chapter 18), which is a commitment to refrain from producing or transferring nuclear weapons, most observers now know or suspect that several unstable or potentially aggressive nations possess nuclear weapons. North Korea announced in October 2002 that it had a weapons program, and it withdrew from the Non-Proliferation Treaty in 2003. Iraq had a substantial program in the past, and Iran is almost certainly working on one now. Threats from those nations to use nuclear weapons may have greater credibility. Some other states, including Israel, India, and Pakistan, never signed the treaty and have recently demonstrated tests of nuclear weapons. Moreover, the possibility that a "stray" nuclear device could come into the hands of a fanatic sect or group essentially outside the control of any responsible leader is obviously destabilizing. In those kinds of situations, a nuclear war could break out, despite the influence of mutual assured destruction on the behavior of the major powers.

In addition, some analysts fully reject the idea that nuclear weapons have ever been an influence for peace. John Mueller argues that the absence of a major war since 1945 is the result of several factors that have nothing to do with nuclear weapons. The **superpowers** that emerged from World War II—the United States and

---

Box 17-3

The Cuban Missile Crisis

In October 1962, the United States and the Soviet Union had a dangerous confrontation over the existence of offensive nuclear weapons in Cuba. When U.S. intelligence discovered the missile-launching facilities under construction, President Kennedy was deeply concerned. If he did nothing, he would leave the country vulnerable, but he did not want to provoke the Soviets into a military response.

After negotiations proved fruitless, Kennedy considered several options. One was an immediate military strike to destroy the weapons. Some advisers were concerned that delay would allow the Soviets to make the weapons operational, at which point no military response would be possible without the risk that they would be launched. A second option was to set up a naval blockade to prevent any additional Soviet ships from reaching Cuba.

Kennedy chose the second option while continuing to pursue negotiations. It was an extremely tense moment, because a naval blockade is an act of war and neither Cuba nor the Soviet Union had attacked the United States. To make the blockade less provocative, Kennedy called it a "quarantine," and he instructed the navy not to try to board any Soviet ship approaching the blockade (as is normal procedure in a blockade).

The Soviets backed down, promised to remove the missiles, and the crisis passed. Some believe that they withdrew the missiles because the U.S. nuclear arsenal was so much larger than theirs at that time, making the Soviets unwilling to risk a nuclear exchange. Another possibility is that the proximity of Cuba to the United States made it possible for the United States to assemble a much stronger conventional armed force than the Soviets could assemble in a short period of time, making it likely that they would lose a conventional battle in Cuba.

We now know that the United States and the Soviet Union were far closer to nuclear war in 1962 than had previously been realized. In 1992, a conference was held in Cuba regarding the missile crisis. Top Soviet, U.S., and Cuban officials involved in that historic event spoke with amazing frankness about their thinking and strategies at the time. The most dramatic revelation was that, unknown to President Kennedy and U.S. defense and foreign policy officials, not only did Soviet troops in Cuba have tactical nuclear weapons at that time, *but also the military commander in the field had authorization to use them without having to obtain approval from Moscow!* Moreover, Castro had urged the local Soviet military commander to use his nuclear weapons if the United States launched an attack on Cuba (a definite possibility). When Robert McNamara—secretary of defense at the time of the missile crisis and a participant in the 1992 conference—learned all this, he was visibly shaken, noting that the world had come far closer to nuclear war than he had realized.

---

the Soviet Union—were relatively content with their clear dominance in world affairs, in great contrast to the unsettled situation persisting after World War I. The Soviet Union's ideology, moreover, stressed revolution rather than armed conquest. Finally, World War II demonstrated that armed conflict can escalate far beyond initial expectations, making leaders arguably more cautious about starting wars. In short, the major players in international relations may have simply become either satisfied with their situations or ideologically driven to alternatives to war, while sharing a realization that war is too costly. Mueller argues that those factors, *not the distinctiveness of nuclear weapons*, prevented war.[26]

Waltz also contends that the effect of nuclear weapons on international politics is often overstated. For example, some analysts expected that nuclear weapons would essentially equalize state power (since any one of many nations could conceivably start a war that would bring doomsday). According to Waltz, nuclear weapons did not accomplish that:

> Gunpowder did not blur the distinction between the great powers and the others, however, nor have nuclear weapons done so. Nuclear weapons are not the great equalizers they were

sometimes thought to be. The world was bipolar in the late 1940s, when the United States had few atomic bombs and the Soviet Union had none. Nuclear weapons did not cause the condition of bipolarity; other states by acquiring them cannot change the condition.[27]

Contemporary international relations seem to confirm Waltz's idea regarding the primacy of economic power. Although many factors are certainly important, the far superior economic base of the United States relative to that of the former Soviet Union was one reason for the latter state's inability to "keep up" in the arms race. The demise of the Soviet Union adds support for the view that the economic bases of a nation's power, if fundamentally weak, cannot be offset by the possession of nuclear weapons. Conversely, even without nuclear weapons, Japan and Germany have emerged as two of the most powerful players in the post-cold-war era.

FOREIGN POLICY DECISION MAKING

In recent decades, the *process* of making foreign policy has become an increasingly important area of inquiry. Politics and government in the modern era make the decision-making process itself more complex and less predictable than in earlier times. Analysts once spoke of "France" taking some step or of "Washington" or "Tokyo" preferring some alternative. Such statements implied that a single actor decided foreign policy or, at least, that a highly unified governing elite framed and implemented policies to further a single vision of the national interest. Drawing on insights derived from studies of organizations, psychology, and even economics, contemporary international relations analysts now stress that foreign policy decision making involves a wide range of often conflicting interests and actors, making it more difficult to predict and more important to understand.

Rationality and Foreign Policy Making

When we want to understand why someone made a particular choice, we generally begin by assuming that the decision maker was *rational*. We assume his or her actions were driven by an effort to achieve the objective furthered by those actions. In foreign policy, the rationality assumption means that, for example, when a nation increases or decreases defense spending, abrogates a treaty, or invades a neighbor, we consider what purpose may have been behind the actions taken. We then infer what the nation was trying to accomplish.

This assumption of rationality is often valid and useful. Many foreign policy actions do reflect a clear policy goal. But much of the work on foreign policy decision making has been devoted to discovering the ways in which foreign policy decisions are *not* "rational." For several reasons, actual foreign policy decisions may be shaped by something other than a straightforward effort to attain a clearly defined goal.

First, foreign policy decisions may be constrained or influenced by the force of *organizational routines* in the institutions involved in a nation's foreign policy system. Whereas rationality assumes that a single decision maker is free to shape his or her choices purely on the basis of a clear policy objective, the actual decision-making process requires the cooperation of an array of institutions (for example, the Ministry of Defense, the State Department, congressional committees). Even when those institutions share the same overall goals, their established routines or traditional ways of operating may affect their contributions to the decision-making process, leading to a result that deviates from the ultimate objective.

Graham Allison's study of the 1962 Cuban missile crisis demonstrated how a decision regarding the positioning of U.S. naval forces in a blockade of Cuba reflected, in part, the organizational routines (standard operating procedures, or SOPs) of the navy (see Box 17-3). The force of those routines was a factor that could have influenced policy actions, because, when the Navy was instructed to carry out President Kennedy's decision, high naval officials were drawn to the idea of implementing the president's plan by using the Navy's "standard operating procedures." Because the president had asked the Navy to arrange its ships so as to prevent Soviet ships from reaching Cuba, the Navy's first impulse was to apply its standard procedures with respect to blockade operations. According to the navy's standard procedures, the U.S. ships were supposed to be many miles from Cuba (which would have reduced the amount of time that would elapse before the arriving Soviet ships encountered them), and the U.S. forces would insist on boarding any ships approaching the blockade. If the navy's insistence on its routines had not been overcome, the *apparent* policy of the United States—as it would have appeared to the Soviets, who assumed that the U.S. actions embodied a purely rational choice—would have been much more threatening than the policy *intended* by President Kennedy. Employing the assumption of rationality, a Soviet analysis would have concluded that *Kennedy wanted to provoke war.* Although the Navy was forced to depart from its standard procedures in that case, the influence of those procedures was a real factor that had to be overcome.

The point is that in some situations, such SOPs could actually affect the content of foreign policy as it is interpreted by foreign powers, altering it from what was intended. In practice, then, foreign policy may not always be a matter of rational choices made in pursuit of a clear objective. The SOPs of the bureaucracies involved in implementing foreign policy can alter it, and policies as implemented are not always a matter of the rational choices of leaders.[28]

Second, foreign policy decisions may not amount to a rational plan to achieve a leader's clear objectives because of conflicting political influences that affect those policies. Especially in modern democracies, the actual foreign policies of nations often deviate from the policies that pure rationality would predict, because the process involves interest groups and other participants with conflicting goals. The ideal condition for rational decision making is a single leader acting in isolation, free from demands by interest groups, parties, and campaign contributors. Yet, such influences exert significant power over foreign policy choices, particularly in democratic systems.

For example, some argue that the United States sends more military aid to Israel than is demanded by the rational pursuit of the U.S. national interests; the amount of the aid is influenced, in part, by a significant lobbying effort supporting increases in such aid. To the extent that foreign policy decisions reflect an effort to accommodate diverse political demands, the decision will not be a straightforward application of "rationality."

Finally, limits on information and on time for careful deliberation can produce "irrational" decisions. A leader may fail to choose the best option because he or she did not know about it or because there was not time to consider all options. Intelligence failures have influenced policy choices in many cases, including the U.S. failure to take action to prevent the Pearl Harbor attack in 1941. In such instances, it would be inaccurate to assume that policy actions were fully informed, coherent choices in pursuit of clear objectives.

Public Opinion, Mass Media, and the Foreign Policy Process

Chief executives generally have a much freer hand in making foreign policy than in making domestic policy, in part because the public is less informed about foreign policy than about domestic affairs. Popular influences on foreign policy can be significant, however, particularly in democracies.

The idea that the public's "mood" affects decisions is a well-known axiom in the study of foreign policy.[29] The public's "mood" is a rather general matter, taking the form of, for example, greater or lesser support for "an active role" in world affairs. In the U.S., the public mood has changed significantly, strongly supporting an activist foreign policy during the years following World War II and then becoming more isolationist in the 1990s. After the attacks of September 11, 2001, many U.S. citizens became increasingly aggressive in their support of military activities. And, after years of daily reports of U.S. military deaths in sectarian violence in Iraq, the public's "mood" began to turn against the idea of an indefinite presence for U.S. troops there. The prevailing mood affects the range of choices that a leader can consider.

Of course, typical citizens in most countries have little information regarding foreign affairs. A 1994 survey reported in *Time* magazine asked citizens in Germany, Italy, France, Great Britain, Canada, Spain, the United States, and Mexico a series of four questions (what group Israel was trying to achieve peace with, the name of the president of Russia, the name of the Secretary General of the United Nations, and who was fighting at that time in Bosnia). The average U.S. citizen got a score of 38 percent, the average German was right 68 percent of the time, Mexican citizens averaged a score of less than 20 percent, and the average across all the nations was less than 45 percent.[30]

It is thus not surprising that leaders and the general public differ with respect to their opinions on several important foreign policy objectives. Figure 17.1 shows the contrasting levels of public and leadership support for a variety of foreign aid issues, based on a 2002 study by the Chicago Council on Foreign Relations.* Many of the differences are substantial, with the leaders being much more favorable to the use of foreign aid as a tool of U.S. policy in Afghanistan, Pakistan, and Russia.

Clearly, foreign policy leaders in the United States do not follow the public's opinions very closely on many matters. However, at least in modern democracies, leaders cannot ignore public sentiments, and with the influence of the contemporary mass media, public attitudes are becoming increasingly important. Before the 1950s, newspapers and radio had minimal impact, since they primarily reported information received from official military sources. Today, modern technology has enabled journalists to get information quickly and independently and to communicate with citizens almost instantly. (Camera crews were actually on the beaches in Somalia *before* the marines landed in the U.S. relief action in late 1992!) Television coverage of civilian casualties is a powerful force, and some leaders actually choose tactics that will lead to particularly disturbing pictures to influence public opinion. Iraq's Saddam Hussein was quite effective in using this technique during the 1991 Gulf War, even going so far as to have signs painted—in English—showing that certain bombed-out buildings were allegedly orphanages or baby-food processing plants.

---

* See "Worldviews 2002: American Public Opinion and Foreign Policy," at http://www.worldviews.org/detailreports/usreport.pdf.

FIGURE 17.1   OPINIONS OF LEADERS VS. U.S. PUBLIC ON FOREIGN AID ISSUES

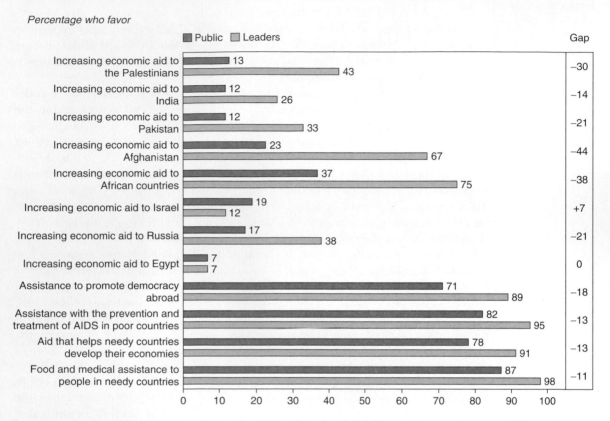

Percentage who favor

■ Public ☐ Leaders   Gap

Category	Public	Leaders	Gap
Increasing economic aid to the Palestinians	13	43	−30
Increasing economic aid to India	12	26	−14
Increasing economic aid to Pakistan	12	33	−21
Increasing economic aid to Afghanistan	23	67	−44
Increasing economic aid to African countries	37	75	−38
Increasing economic aid to Israel	19	12	+7
Increasing economic aid to Russia	17	38	−21
Increasing economic aid to Egypt	7	7	0
Assistance to promote democracy abroad	71	89	−18
Assistance with the prevention and treatment of AIDS in poor countries	82	95	−13
Aid that helps needy countries develop their economies	78	91	−13
Food and medical assistance to people in needy countries	87	98	−11

Percentages for the public and leaders calculated with "don't know" excluded. Gap equals percentage point difference between public and leader percentages. Positive sign (+) indicates a higher public percentage. Negative sign (–) indicates a higher leader percentage.

SOURCE: Chicago Council on Foreign Relations, www.cfr.org.

Some critics contend that, beyond the impact of violent images, the U.S. press was actively biased in its coverage of the Vietnam War, undermining public support for U.S. military involvement. In a famous broadcast in early 1968, Walter Cronkite (then the CBS News television anchor) indicated that, despite heavy losses, no real progress was being made in the war effort. His announcement reportedly had a great impact on President Lyndon Johnson, who halted some bombing operations shortly thereafter.[31] Cronkite made his pessimistic statement during the Tet Offensive, a large-scale Viet Cong military effort in January 1968 (named after the Vietnamese lunar New Year). According to most historians, the Tet Offensive was a significant military setback for the Viet Cong and North Vietnamese; they suffered heavy casualties and took no new territory. Nevertheless, U.S. media coverage created the widespread perception that the enemy was about to overrun U.S. and South Vietnamese forces.[32] Although historians disagree about the ultimate significance of media coverage in influencing policy choices, the influence of newspaper and television on U.S. public opinion during the Vietnam War was certainly a factor considered in the decision-making process.

The media can also be a useful *tool* of foreign policy, in addition to being an influence on it. According to K. J. Holsti, most Poles learned about the Solidarity Movement in the 1980s from British radio broadcasts and from broadcasts on Radio Free Europe and the Voice of America, two pro-U.S. radio networks. North Korea broadcasts "commentaries" intended for an audience in South Korea; the content of those broadcasts depicts South Korea as a fascist state propped up by U.S. imperialists.[33] Radio is a cheap and generally effective way of reaching a target domestic population, even in areas where illiteracy limits the effectiveness of print media.

In short, leaders usually are forced to take public views into account as they make foreign policy decisions, and the mass media are playing an increasingly important role in developing a supportive or an opposing public. Whether that is a positive development remains an open question. On the one hand, an independent, inquisitive press and an informed public may act as a restraining force, preventing leaders from taking their countries into disastrous military involvements. Perhaps the greatest impact of the heightened importance of the media and public opinion in foreign policy (especially in democracies) is that it makes leaders emphasize quick, low-casualty military options when military responses are necessary. If costly military steps are necessary to maintain national security, and if the pressure of the media and public opinion inhibits appropriate action, the country may suffer. On the other hand, political leaders may be actually tempted to take certain military steps in order to produce the "rally 'round the flag" support that the inevitable media coverage often generates.

If the foreign policy decision-making process could be more insulated from the influences of organizational routines, interest groups, and public opinion, leaders would be free to act "rationally" to achieve their goals. But if the policy in question is particularly important to a specific, organized interest, national leaders will be especially likely to respond to the pressure. The issue of time is also critical. When a policy problem can be handled quickly, public opinion will be less important because there will not be time for it to take form. Foreign policy issues that remain in the public's attention for a long period are more likely to be subject to public influence.[34]

Foreign policy decision making is not a simple process of a unified, well-informed leadership choosing the optimum alternatives to achieve a definite objective. If the process was ever that simple, it is certainly more complex now. In the modern world, the foreign policy process involves a wide range of organizational and political influences and requires access to accurate information about a staggering array of factors. Understanding the influences affecting that process, and how the process can be improved or degraded, is thus a central problem in the study of foreign policy.

INTERNATIONAL POLITICAL ECONOMY

The nature of economic relations among states has been an important subject of study for hundreds of years. In fact, until the terrorist attacks of September 11, 2001, economics had begun to surpass security concerns in foreign policy debates. Modern advances in communications and transportation make multinational corporations a common form of business organization, and their activities significantly affect prices, wages, and even economic security in many nations. The strategic value of petroleum, coupled with the geographic concentration of oil fields in a few areas, creates a volatile situation. The persistent economic underdevelopment of much of the world challenges the industrialized states that rely on them for labor and raw materials. Growing interdependence makes international political economy an increasingly important issue.

As with military affairs, in economic matters states can relate to one another in antagonistic or cooperative ways. The character of those relations depends on many things, including the nature of each country's domestic economy, its ideology and culture, and its other (noneconomic) foreign policy objectives. Although a great range of factors affects international economic relations, specialists have outlined three general approaches designed to explain them.[35]

Liberalism (or Economic Internationalism)

Employing the term *liberal* differently from its usage in common parlance, Robert Gilpin identified **liberalism** in this context as the international counterpart to free-market economics. Derived from the ideas of Adam Smith (1723–1790), the architect of classical economics, "liberal" political economy suggests that states should naturally become cooperative in economic affairs. The concept of *comparative advantage* is basic to the approach. If one state is able to produce a particular good or service cheaply and efficiently, it is said to have a comparative advantage in that area. The principles of liberal political economy imply that as long as governments do not interfere with economic affairs, nations will ultimately produce goods or services for which they have (for whatever reason) a comparative advantage.

Liberal political economy assumes that most, if not all, states enjoy a comparative advantage with respect to *some* goods or services. If governments do not get in the way, the production of all goods and services worldwide will naturally gravitate to the state or states that can produce them with the highest quality and the lowest costs. States who try to produce something for which they have no comparative advantage will quickly find that they cannot produce it at competitive prices, so goods and services will end up being produced where they can be made most efficiently. On the other hand, if a government restricts imports into its country so that a comparatively *inefficient* domestic industry is protected from competition, the good or service will be produced domestically, consuming more of the world's resources to produce them than would be consumed by the country with a comparative advantage.

Liberal political economy thus implies that the *total productivity of the world economy* will increase as goods and services are produced where comparative advantages exist. The world would suffer a net loss in output if, for example, a country that was unable to produce steel very efficiently still allocated significant resources to steel production (motivated perhaps by the prestige of producing steel). The resources of such a country could produce a more valuable output in a different usage.

Since the world economy grows indefinitely as goods and services are produced in accordance with comparative advantage, liberal political economy assumes that economic relations will normally be cooperative. Every state will be better off if all act in accordance with the principle of comparative advantage.

In regard to policy, liberal political economy advocates free trade (eliminating import restrictions and tariffs). Of course, governments are often under severe domestic pressure to restrict imports. For example, in recent decades, textile and clothing manufacturers in Thailand, Korea, Taiwan, Sri Lanka, and Malaysia have developed a comparative advantage over U.S. producers. Although U.S. consumers benefit from the importation of cheaper clothing, U.S. textile workers and many U.S. companies have demanded protective tariffs to restrict Asian imports. As you will recall from our discussion of interest groups in Chapter 6, it is likely that the domestic producers will be more influential politically than domestic consumers, and thus governments often enact import restrictions. In the light of those political realities, liberal political economy remains more a *prescription* for good policy than a *description* of how nations actually behave in economic terms.

Still, as we will see in Chapter 19, the ratification by the U.S. Congress of the North American Free Trade Agreement (NAFTA), and the Central American Free Trade Agreement (CAFTA), in 1993 and 2004, respectively, were major steps toward free trade in the Western Hemisphere. Such treaties are controversial because, in the short run at least, they may jeopardize some jobs and lead to the production of goods and services in areas with the lowest costs, which may be a result of lax environmental or safety standards.

Economic Structuralism

Unlike those who advocate the "liberal" approach, some analysts and many Third World leaders embrace a perspective that emphasizes that international political competition does not take place on a level playing field. Generally speaking, this perspective focuses on the fact that Japan, North America, and Europe have advanced industrial states, whereas most of Africa and Latin America are, on average, less advanced, and that this difference in development makes free trade unavoidably unfair.

In regard to international political economy, **economic structuralism** (closely identified with Marxist-Leninist thinking) sees states' economic relations as simply one component of the capitalist oppression that dominates all political life. Whereas liberalism claims that advancing productivity and cooperation are at least possible, economic structuralism implies that increasing conflict and exploitation will characterize international relations.*

The North–South conflict in international political economy is often interpreted from this perspective. (The term comes from the observation that, generally, the Northern Hemisphere contains countries that are wealthier than those in the Southern Hemisphere.) Those who reject liberalism because of the persistent disparities in North–South development generally oppose free-trade agreements. According to their basic argument, such agreements make it impossible for the poorer countries to gain a foothold in the international economy, since they will always be undersold by the more advanced nations in anything they produce.

Economic structuralists thus argue for strict state controls on commerce, or state ownership of all industry. In accordance with Marxist principles, they contend that public control of commerce will end exploitation of the poor, both at home and abroad, creating a system of fair compensation for workers, environmental protection, and general world prosperity.

Economic Nationalism (Mercantilism)

Ironically, both liberal (free-market) and Marxist-Leninist ideas about international political economy assume that economic relations are the primary force behind politics. For liberals, economics determines where comparative advantage exists, and economic structuralists claim that economics explains the inevitability of capitalist exploitation.

* See the discussion of *dependency theory* in Chapter 15.

A DIFFICULT BALANCING ACT   President Bush's decision to impose (and then later rescind) a tariff on steel imports reflected the difficulties that leaders face in managing domestic and international influences in trade policy.

In contrast, **economic nationalism**, sometimes termed **mercantilism**, sees *politics* as the primary force in international economic relations. It emphasizes the importance of state interests in national security, power, and industrial development, and it claims that states naturally pursue economic policies that promote those foreign policy goals.

For example, mercantilists argue that governments have a clear national interest in protecting their domestic industries from foreign competition. That national interest may outweigh the purely economic advantages associated with free trade. Even if such restrictions mean that consumers have to pay higher prices for less efficiently produced local goods and services, the state may have a legitimate interest in acting contrary to the principles of liberal political economy.

If the United States followed a policy of free trade for its steel industry, many analysts argue that domestic steel production would be severely diminished. Because Brazil or Korea can make steel more cheaply, U.S. plants would eventually shut down as buyers of steel obtained their steel from suppliers in those other countries. That was one of the arguments used to justify President Bush's decision to sign a bill establishing tariffs of up to 30 percent for imported steel in 2002. If the United States allows its steel industry to disappear, U.S. security could be threatened. In time of war, imported steel could be unavailable, and it would be impossible to produce military hardware quickly if domestic steel plants had all vanished.

However, there is a price to be paid for the tariffs, and that price is paid by consumers. It was estimated that, for example, automobiles sold in the United States cost between $100 and $300 more as a result of the new steel import policy than they would have cost without it. Perhaps as a result of these costs, President Bush ended the tariffs in December 2003.

As we discuss in Chapter 19, the growth of international trade during the second half of the last century has had many important consequences. Those favoring economic nationalism argue that one of those consequences is a reduction in the autonomy and power of nation-states. Whether for good or for ill, many analysts agree that the globalization of finance has "undermined the capacity of states to determine their own future."[36] The advancing global economy thus brings political and economic concerns into conflict in several ways, ensuring that this will be a challenge for governments for decades to come.

Each of the three main approaches to international political economy provides persuasive explanations for certain patterns or events in international affairs. The concept of comparative advantage describes an arrangement that produces an efficient allocation of productive resources, but sometimes other objectives naturally dominate a nation's foreign policy. Some analysts find Marxist-Leninist ideas helpful in explaining the economic underdevelopment of much of the Third World. Economic nationalism helps explain the motivation for seemingly inefficient economic policies based on national security needs. As economic relations become increasingly critical in international relations, the connections among domestic politics, foreign policy, and economic productivity will command increasing attention from analysts and policy makers.

INTERNATIONAL LAW AND ORGANIZATION

Although anarchy is the essential characteristic of the international system, the presence of international law and international organization suggests that the anarchy of the international system is not absolute. International law and organization can be seen as attempts to create order and stability in international relations.

International Law

International law consists primarily of traditionally recognized treaties and rights and duties. Treaties can be *bilateral* (between two countries) or *general* (ratified by a large number of countries). Some treaties are highly specific, such as a treaty in which the United States and Canada cooperate with respect to usage of the Great Lakes; some treaties apply to a broad range of related matters, such as the General Agreement on Tariffs and Trade (GATT). Other "laws" are simply traditions, such as long-accepted ideas regarding self-defense and the size of the area that each country claims as national waters.

Law is an attempt to constrain behavior. For law to be effective, there must be some way to interpret when a given action runs afoul of the law and to enforce the requirements of the law. In those respects, international law is much weaker than domestic law (in well-established political systems). The International Court of Justice (ICJ, or World Court), established as part of the United Nations, has broad jurisdiction to hear disputes about international law, but it has been ignored in many cases, thus reducing its status and influence. In some cases, the courts of individual nations apply and interpret international law (see Box 17-4).

The difficulty of enforcing international law is often severe. In 1979, Iranian students took over the U.S. embassy in Tehran, holding more than a hundred U.S. citizens hostage. The Iranian government essentially supported the students' effort and refused to recognize the jurisdiction of the ICJ to adjudicate the dispute leading to the hostage-taking. In the 1980s, the United States engaged in military activities against Nicaragua (mining harbors and funding an insurgent movement) when the country was governed by the Sandinistas, a Marxist party. When the ICJ concluded that it had

---

Box 17-4

THE WORLD COURT AND THE TRIAL OF SLOBODAN MILOSEVIC

Beginning in February 2002, the World Court (International Court of Justice) in The Hague presided over a trial of former Yugoslav dictator Slobodan Milosevic. He was charged with ordering the deaths of nearly 900 ethnic Albanians, 32 counts of war crimes, and a policy of genocide. He was also charged with 66 counts of crimes against humanity. Often called the "butcher of the Balkans," Milosevic died on March 12, 2006. If he had lived, and if the court had found him guilty, it would have been the first time that an international court ever convicted a head of state for such crimes. His death came only a few months before the four-year-old trial was expected to come to an end.

Reflecting the often problematic status of international law as a context for prosecuting criminal conduct, Milosevic's primary response to the charges was to argue that the court had no legitimate jurisdiction and that the whole trial was simply designed to concoct a rationale for NATO's bombing of Serbia in 1999. The World Court wants to try at least six other persons widely believed to be guilty of the same crimes for which Milosevic was prosecuted.

© AP/Wide World Photos

Former Yugoslav President Slobodan Milosevic at the Yugoslav war crimes U.N. tribunal in The Hague, the Netherlands, Monday July 5, 2004. He died in March 2006, before the trial was completed.

---

jurisdiction to hear a Nicaraguan complaint that the United States had violated international law with those actions, the United States refused to participate in the judicial process. When the court eventually found that the United States was in violation, its influence was severely weakened by U.S. disregard for it in this matter.

Given the weakness of international law, some analysts understandably dismiss it as empty and trivial. Even if international law is often unenforceable, however, it may still be an important factor in international relations. Law can serve as a basis for *communication*. "To present one's claims in legal terms means to signal to one's partner or opponent which [norms] one considers relevant or essential, and to indicate which procedures one intends to follow and would like the other side to follow."[37] Law can also be a source of *prestige*, since nations that can claim to abide by legal requirements enjoy greater legitimacy both in domestic politics and in foreign capitals.[38] In some circumstances, international law can be used as a *tool of policy*, strengthening a position and mobilizing domestic and allied support.

Still, international law has its liabilities. Once a state uses a provision of international law to legitimize an action, it may experience a loss of flexibility in future policy choices.

Although leaders are often "selective" in observing international law, repeatedly using it as a legitimizing tool may make it difficult or costly to disregard international law when the national interest requires it.[39]

If democracy becomes more widespread, international law may become increasingly influential. With the end of the cold war and the growing international dominance of the United States, Western Europe, and Japan, such "outlaw" states as North Korea and Iran may find it increasingly difficult to violate international law. Since superpower conflict is no longer the dominant fact in international affairs, a state that openly violates international law cannot depend on prestigious support from a superpower sponsor, who previously would have advocated the position of its client state and protected it from sanctions. The fact that the most powerful states are less divided by profound ideological conflicts increases the potential that international law will be a significant force.

International Organization

Although the individual nation-state remains the most important kind of actor in international relations, the fastest-growing force in international affairs is the **international organization** (often termed an *intergovernmental organization*, or IGO). These bodies include general-purpose organizations such as the United Nations and, with narrower memberships, the Organization of American States or the Organization of African Unity. Other IGOs are "functional" units with a more specific purpose, such as the Central American Common Market or the Association of South East Asian Nations. Whereas the number of states has more than doubled since 1950 (primarily as a result of colonies gaining independence), the number of IGOs has nearly quadrupled.

As a force in world affairs, international organization is often discussed in regard to its limitations. Many analysts felt that the failure of the League of Nations to prevent World War II demonstrated that nations will not sacrifice much of their sovereignty to an international organization. Similarly, critics note that the United Nations has been allowed to survive only because five major powers have been able to veto any significant proposed action. In other words, the UN's existence has depended on the fact that those nations did not have to sacrifice any real sovereignty in order to join it. Moreover, the United Nations has not prevented numerous "small" wars (in Vietnam and in the Persian Gulf region).

Nevertheless, the United Nations remains an important feature of the international system, and its prominence is likely to increase. Since 1945, nearly one-fourth of the international and civil conflicts that have erupted have been submitted either to the UN or to regional organizations. According to Holsti, those organizations have handled 291 cases during that time, many of which were "high-intensity" conflicts. Until 1985, only one-fourth of the submitted cases were handled successfully, but between 1985 and 1990 the success rate increased to more than one in three.[40]

As with international law, the United Nations provides a context for communication, and its approval and disapproval can provide nonviolent support for foreign policy choices. Moreover, there are signs that in the 1990s the United Nations may approach the ability to "maintain or restore international peace and security," as called for in its charter. Bruce Russett and James Sutterlin point out that the United Nations has traditionally used force often for "peacekeeping": standing between hostile forces, maintaining stability in an unsettled region, and even monitoring elections.[41]

Although it did not prevent the war, the United Nations arguably functioned to enforce "the will of the council on a state that has broken the peace" in the 1991 Gulf War. Russett and Sutterlin point out that "the Gulf action became possible because the permanent members of the Security Council cooperated on a matter of peace and security in the way originally foreseen when the UN was founded."[42] The UN has handled scores of smaller conflicts, and the demise of East–West conflict as the centerpiece of international affairs will probably make the organization even more important in the future.[43] Recently, with varying degrees of success, the United Nations has involved itself in peacekeeping operations in El Salvador, Cambodia, the states of the former Yugoslavia, Somalia, and Afghanistan (see Figure 17.2).

The growth in number and significance of other IGOs similarly reflects the more complex interdependence of the modern world. Environmental and economic issues increasingly transcend national borders, making international cooperation essential to the policy process. The heightened impact of domestic politics in democratic and newly democratic systems makes it politically useful for leaders to gain legitimacy for

---

FIGURE 17.2   UNITED NATIONS PEACEKEEPING OPERATIONS SINCE 1948

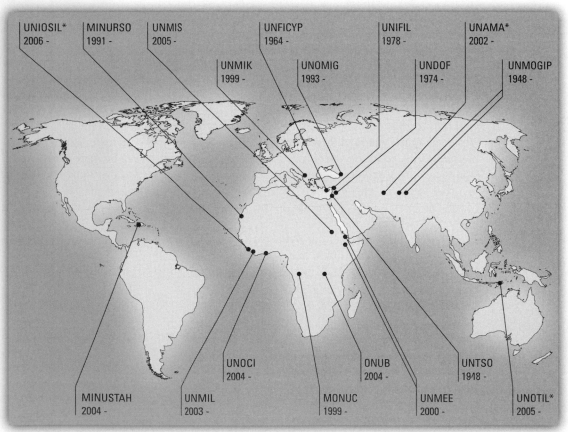

Map No. 4259 (E) R01   UNITED NATIONS
March 2006

FIGURE 17.2   (CONTINUED)

PERSONNEL

Uniformed personnel serving in peacekeeping operations	72,778
Countries contributing military and police personnel	107
International Civilian personnel	10,010
UN Volunteers	1,607
Total number of personnel serving in peacekeeping operations	89,682
Total number of fatalities in peace operations since 1948	2,242

KEY TO ABBREVIATIONS AND PERSONNEL COMMITMENTS:

UNTSO: United Nations Truce Supervision Organization
Military observers 153; international civilians 164; local civilians 139
Fatalities: 44

UNMOGIP: United Nations Military Observer Group in India and Pakistan
Military observers 43; international civilians 38; local civilians 56
Fatalities: 11

UNFICYP: United Nations Peacekeeping Force in Cyprus
Troops 859; police 67; international civilians 60; local civilians 117
Fatalities: 176

UNDOF: United Nations Disengagement Observer Force
Trrops 1,152; international civilians 48; local civilians 111
Fatalities: 42

UNIFIL: United Nations Interim Force in Lebanon
Troops 1,985; international civilians 190; local civilians 319
Fatalities: 257

MINURSO: United Nations Mission for the Referendum in Western Sahara
Troops 28; military observers 190; police 8; international civilians 121; local civilians 113
Fatalities: 14

UNOMIG: United Nations Observer Mission in Georgia
Military observers 121; police 12, international civilians 107; local civilians 186
Fatalities: 10

UNMIK: United Nations Interim Administration Mission in Kosovo
Military observers 38; Police 2,221; international civilians 797; local civilians 2,277
Fatalities: 43

MONUC: United Nations Organization Mission in the Democratic Republic of the Congo
Troops 15,044; military observers 712; police 1,087, international civilians 861; local civilians 1,656
Fatalities: 85

UNMEE: United Nations Mission in Ethiopia and Eritrea
Troops 3,149; military observers 208; international civilians 179; local civilians 217
Fatalities: 13

UNMIL: United Nations Mission in Liberia
Troops 14,867; military observers 203; police 1,028, international civilians 788; local civilians 1,363
Fatalities: 70

UNOCI: United Nations Operation in Cote d I'voire (Ivory Coast)
Troops 6,704; military observers 191; police 698; international civilians 362; local civilians 431
Fatalities: 16

MINUSTAH: United Nations Military Stabilization Mission in Haiti
Toops 7,472; police 1,761; international civilians 632; local civilians 1,329
Fatalities: 17

ONUB: United Nations Operation in Burundi
Troops 4,396; military observers 173; police 87; international civilians 318; local civilians 467
Fatalities: 21

UNMIS: United Nations Mission in the Sudan
Troops 10,000; police 715; international civilians (proposed) 1,053; local civilians 1,229
Fatalities: 2

SOURCE: United Nations Peacekeeping Operations, Background Note, February 28, 2006, http://www.un.org/Depts/dpko/dpko/bnote.htm.

their actions by appealing to international organizations for approval. Even if the "national interest" is still the driving force behind most foreign policy decisions, IGOs will undoubtedly play an ever more significant role in international affairs in the future.

ETHICS AND INTERNATIONAL RELATIONS

Most discussions of international affairs deal with explanations of state *behavior,* just as the study of domestic politics normally focuses on explaining the observable behavior of citizens, parties, and institutions. Nevertheless, the ethical dimensions of international relations have long been a subject of inquiry by politicians, philosophers, and others.

The oldest ethical perspective relevant to international affairs is pacifism. Pacifists contend that war is simply and inherently *wrong* and that any alternative (including submitting to domination by a foreign power) is morally superior to fighting. Although there have always been many individuals and religious movements that support pacifist principles, most leaders and citizens reject pacifism as an absolute guide for policy.

A much more widely accepted ethical concept is the idea of the **just war**. Richard Miller explains that the just war tradition shares with the pacifist tradition a conclusion that war is evil and should be avoided; but whereas pacifists claim that war should *always* be avoided, advocates of the just war concept feel that war can be justified under certain special circumstances.[44]

Just war theory has two components, the first pertaining to *when war is justified* and the second addressing *how wars are conducted.* War is justified when necessary to defend against outside threats, when innocent lives would otherwise be lost, when basic human rights are severely deprived, or when the future of the world community is at stake. The idea of the just war requires that war be a last resort, that only competent authorities make war (no "private" wars are just), that no "futile" fighting in defense of a cause be undertaken, and that there be no intentional attacks on civilians.[45]

The ethical issues related to war offer moral philosophers fertile ground for discussion. If the basic concepts of the just war become widely accepted, those ideas may assume some moral force, thus limiting the incidence of war. Just-war principles are obviously subject to varying interpretations, however: What appears to be a just war to one side is naked aggression to the other. However, ethical concerns have widespread impact in other foreign policy issues, notably in matters involving human rights and humanitarian assistance.

CONCLUSION: WAR, TRADE, FOREIGN POLICY, AND THE STAKES OF POLITICS

The same interests and motivations that characterize domestic politics—economics, moral disputes, ethnic and racial divisions, and political power—are also basic to the relations among states. Nevertheless, the virtual absence of central authority in international relations creates a different kind of political system from that which prevails in domestic affairs. The approaches discussed in this chapter represent different and useful ways of interpreting and predicting the behavior of states.

As we noted with respect to domestic politics, international relations is currently undergoing fundamental change. The demise of communism in most of the world, increasing economic interdependence, and contemporary concerns about nuclear proliferation and the global environment are but a few of the issues that will make international relations more complex and more critical. International organizations and law exert more force now than in previous eras in which national sovereignty was unchallenged. Chapter 19 addresses the most important of these issues in an effort to identify and evaluate the central problems in modern international relations.

 # WHERE ON THE WEB?

http://www.ceip.org

The home page of the Carnegie Endowment for International Peace. Established in 1910, the endowment conducts research and publishes the journal *Foreign Policy*.

http://www.iiss.org/

The home page of the International Institute for Strategic Studies. "The IISS is the primary source of accurate, objective information on international strategic issues for politicians and diplomats, foreign affairs analysts, international business, economists, the military, defense commentators, journalists, academics and the informed public." Members of the institute are drawn from 13 countries in Europe, North America, and Asia.

http://www.justwartheory.com/

A Web site created and maintained by Mark Rigstad, an Assistant Professor of Philosophy at Oakland University. It contains a great deal of information about just war theory, including classic texts.

http://www.wws.princeton.edu/~cis/

The home page for Princeton University's Center of International Studies, a major research arm of the Woodrow Wilson School of Public and International Affairs at Princeton University. It "seeks to promote world peace and mutual understanding among nations by supporting scholarship in international relations and national development."

http://www.csis.org/

The Center for Strategic and International Studies, a U.S. think tank with over 190 researchers focusing on national and international security, specific problems in particular geographic regions, and "new methods of governance for the global age." Many recent studies are available at no charge at the Web site.

http://www.isanet.org

The home page for the International Studies Association, the leading professional association of researchers specializing in international relations.

◆ ◆ ◆

Key Terms and Concepts_____

balance of power	just war
democratic peace	liberalism
economic internationalism	mercantilism
economic nationalism	nuclear terror
economic structuralism	realism
idealism	self-help
international law	superpowers
international organization	

Discussion Questions_____

1. How is the existence of violence different in domestic and international relations?
2. Compare the three "images" regarding the causes of war. Which do you find most persuasive in explaining the cause of the War on Terrorism?
3. What factors can lead a nation to adopt foreign policies that do not amount to a rational effort to pursue a clear objective?
4. What is a "just war"?
5. Explain how wars can be prevented by international law and international organization.

Notes_____

1. Kenneth Waltz, *Theory of International Politics* (New York: McGraw-Hill, 1979), pp. 102–103; italics added.
2. Ibid., p. 104.
3. Thucydides, *The Peloponnesian War,* trans. Crawley (New York: Modern Library, 1951).
4. Sun Tzu (sixth century BCE), *The Art of War,* trans. Samuel B. Griffith (Oxford: Clarendon Press, 1963); and Kautilya, *Anthasastra,* trans. R. Shamasastry (Mysore, India: Mysore Printing and Publishing, 1967).
5. Hans J. Morganthau, *Politics among Nations,* 5th ed. (New York: Knopf, 1973), pp. 4–5.
6. Waltz, *Theory of International Politics,* p. 118.
7. Edward Hallett Carr, *The Twenty Years' Crisis, 1919–1939: An Introduction to the Study of International Relations* (London: Macmillan, 1939).
8. Robert Jervis, "Theories of War in an Era of Leading-Power Peace," *American Political Science Review* 96 (March 2002): 1–14.
9. Kenneth Waltz, *Man, the State, and War* (New York: Columbia University Press, 1959).
10. Ibid., p. 16.
11. Ibid., p. 33.
12. Some of the most important writings on the "democratic peace" are Erich Weede, "Democracy and War Involvement," *Journal of Conflict Resolution* 28 (December 1984): 649–664; T. Clifton Morgan and Sally Howard Campbell, "Domestic Structure, Decisional Constraints, and War," *Journal of Conflict Resolution* 35 (June 1991): 187–211; Alex Mintz and Nehemia Geva, "Why Don't Democracies Fight Each Other?, *Journal of Conflict Resolution* 37 (September 1993): 484–503, Michael E. Brown, Sean E. Lynn-Jones, and Steven E. Miller, *Debating the Democratic Peace* (Cambridge, MA: MIT University Press, 1996), and David Leblang and Steve Chan, "Explaining Wars Fought by Established Democracies: Do Institutional Constraints Matter?" *Political Research Quarterly* 56 (December 2003): 385–400.
13. See Bruce Bueno De Mesquita, James D. Morrow, Randolf M. Siverson, and Alastair Smith, "An Institutional Explanation of the Democratic Peace," *American Political Science Review* 93 (December 1999): 791–807.
14. See Edward D. Mansfield and Jack Snyder, *Electing to Fight: Why Emerging Democracies Go to War*. Cambridge, MA: MIT Press, 2005.
15. Ibid., p. 159.
16. Holsti, K.J., *International Politics,* 7th ed. Englewood Cliffs, NJ: Prentice Hall, 1995, p. 17.
17. John T. Rourke, *International Politics on the World Stage,* 9th ed. (Guilford, CT: Dushkin, 2002), p. 34.
18 Waltz, *Theory of International Politics,* p. 118.
19. David Hume, *Essays and Treatises on Several Subjects,* vol. 1 (Edinburgh, Scotland: Bell and Bradfute, and W. Blackwood, 1825), pp. 331–339, quoted in *Contending Theories of International Relations* by James E. Dougherty and Robert L. Pfaltzgraff Jr. (Philadelphia: Lippincott, 1971), p. 30; Edward D. Mansfield and Jack Snyder, *Electing to Fight: Why Emerging Democracies Go to War* (Cambridge, MA: MIT Press, 2005).

20. Edward Vose Gulick, *Europe's Classical Balance of Power,* (New York: Norton, 1955), p. 30.

21. Dougherty and Pfaltzgraff, *Contending Theories,* p. 265.

22. Quoted in John Mueller, "The Obsolescence of War in the Modern Industrialized World," in *International Politics,* 3rd ed., ed. Robert J. Art and Robert Jervis (New York: HarperCollins, 1992), p. 188.

23. Robert Jervis, "The Utility of Nuclear Deterrence," in Art and Jervis, *International Politics,* p. 202.

24. Ibid., p. 204.

25. Ibid.

26. Mueller, "Obsolescence of War," pp. 188–189.

27. Waltz, *Man, the State, and War,* pp. 180–181.

28. Graham Allison, "Conceptual Models and the Cuban Missile Crisis," *American Political Science Review* 63 (1969): 689–718.

29. See Jack E. Holmes, *The Mood/Interest Theory of American Foreign Policy* (Lexington: University Press of Kentucky, 1985).

30. *Time,* March 28, 1994, p. 22.

31. As a *New York Times* reporter noted, "It was the first time in history that a war had been declared over by an anchorman." See David Halberstam, *The Powers That Be* (New York: Knopf, 1979), p. 514; See also Austin Ranney, *Channels of Power: The Impact of Television on American Politics* (New York: Basic Books, 1983).

32. See Peter Braestrup, *Big Story* (New York: Anchor Books, 1978). For a different view, see Daniel Hallin, *The "Uncensored War": The Media and Vietnam* (New York: Oxford University Press, 1986).

33. Holsti, *International Politics* p. 160.

34. Bruce Russett and Harvey Starr, *World Politics: The Menu for Choice,* 3rd ed. (New York: Freeman, 1989), p. 241.

35. Much of the text discussion is drawn from Robert Gilpin, "The Nature of Political Economy," in Art and Jervis, *International Politics,* pp. 237–253.

36. Charles W. Kegley, Jr., and Eugene R. Wittkopf, *World Politics: Trend and Transformation,* (New York: St. Martin's, 1997), p. 257.

37. Stanley Hoffmann, "The Uses and Limits of International Law," in Art and Jervis, *International Politics,* pp. 90–91.

38. Holsti, *International Politics,* p. 301.

39. Ibid., p. 92.

40. Ibid., p. 354.

41. Bruce Russett and James Sutterlin, "The U.N. in a New World Order," in Art and Jervis, *International Politics,* pp. 102–103.

42. Ibid., p. 106.

43. Ernst B. Haas, "Collective Conflict Management: Evidence for a New World Order?" in *Collective Security in a Changing World,* ed. Thomas G. Weiss (Boulder, CO: Lynne Rienner Publishers, 1993), pp. 63–120.

44. Richard B. Miller, *Interpretations of Conflict: Ethics, Pacifism, and the Just-War Tradition* (Chicago: University of Chicago Press, 1991), p. 106.

45. Ibid., pp. 13–14.

For Further Reading _____

Art, Robert J., and Robert Jervis, eds. *International Politics: Enduring Concepts and Contemporary Issues.* 8th ed. New York: Longman, 2007.

Axelrod, Alan. *American Treaties and Alliances.* Washington, DC: CQ Press, 2000.

Bardhan, Pranab, Samuel Bowles, and Michael Wallerstein, eds. *Globalization and Egalitarian Redistribution.* Princeton, NJ: Princeton University Press, 2006.

Baylis, John, James Wirtz, Eliot Cohen, and Colin Gray, eds. *Strategy in the Contemporary World.* New York: Oxford University Press, 2002.

Clark, Ian. *The Post-Cold-War Order.* New York: Oxford University Press, 2001.

Christopher, Paul. *The Ethics of War and Peace: An Introduction to Legal and Moral Issues.* 3rd ed. Upper Saddle River, NJ: Prentice Hall, 2004.

D'Amato, Anthony A. *International Law and Political Reality.* Boston: Kluwer Academic Publishers, 1995.

Dolan, Chris J. *In War We Trust: The Bush Doctrine and the Pursuit of Just War.* Burlington, VT: Ashgate, 2005.

Elshtain, Jean Bethke. *Just War Against Terror: The Burden of American Power in a Violent World.* New York, Basic Books, 2003.

Fordham, Benjamin O., and Timothy J. McKeown, "Selection and Influence: Interest Groups and Congressional Voting on Trade Policy." *International Organization* 57 (2003): 519–549.

Friedman, Thomas L. *The World Is Flat: A Brief History of the 21st Century.* New York: Farrar, Straus, and Giroux, 2002.

Goldstein, Lyle J. *Preventive Attack and Weapons of Mass Destruction: A Comparative Historical Analysis.* Palo Alto, CA: Stanford University Press, 2006.

Gibson, Martha L. *Conflict and Consensus in American Trade Policy.* Washington, DC: Georgetown University Press, 2000.

Hess, Gary R. *Presidential Decisions for War: Korea, Vietnam, and the Persian Gulf.* Baltimore: Johns Hopkins University Press, 2001.

Holsti, K. J. *Taming the Sovereigns: Institutional Change in International Politics.* Cambridge, UK: Cambridge University Press, 2004.

_____ *The State, War, and the State of War.* Cambridge, UK: Cambridge University Press, 1996.

Hoogvelt, Ankie. *Globalization and the Post-Colonial World: The New Political Economy of Development,* Baltimore: Johns Hopkins University Press, 2001.

Keohane, Robert O. *International Institutions and State Power.* Boulder, CO: Westview, 1989.

Miller, Richard B. *Interpretations of Conflict: Ethics, Pacifism, and the Just-War Tradition.* Chicago: University of Chicago Press, 1991.

Morgenthau, Hans J. *Politics among Nations.* 5th ed. New York: Knopf, 1973.

Paul, T.V., James J. Wirtz, and Michael Fortman. *Balance of Power: Theory and Practice in the 21st Century.* Palo Alto, CA: Stanford University Press, 2004.

Rousseau, David L. *Democracy and War: Institutions, Norms, and the Evolution of International Conflict.* Palo Alto, CA.: Stanford University Press, 2005.

Runciman, David. *The Politics of Good Intentions: History, Fear, and Hypocrisy in the New World Order.* Princeton, NJ: Princeton University Press, 2005.

Stern, Sheldon M. *The Week the World Stood Still: Inside the Secret Cuban Missile Crisis.* Palo Alto, CA: Stanford University Press, 2005.

Thomas, Kenneth P. *Competing for Capital: Europe and North America in a Global Era.* Washington, DC: Georgetown University Press, 2000.

Thucydides. *The Peloponnesian War,* translated by Crawley. New York: Modern Library, 1951.

Viotti, Paul R., and Mark V. Kauppi. *International Relations Theory: Realism, Pluralism, Globalism.* 3rd ed. Upper Saddle River, NJ: Prentice Hall, 1999.

Waltz, Kenneth N. *Man, the State, and War.* New York: Columbia University Press, 1959.

Walzer, Michael. *Arguing about War.* New Haven, CT: Yale University Press, 2004.

TRYING TO KEEP THE PEACE   Africa's many civil wars have tested United Nations and other peacekeeping missions. UN troops have performed with varying degrees of effectiveness, sometime participating themselves in human rights abuses. Here a crowd gathers as peacekeepers attend to the scene of a shoot-out between government and rebel forces in the Liberian capital Monrovia, as the body of a victim lies amidst the debris.

18

A CHANGING WORLD ORDER

◆ From the End of the Cold War to the Beginnings of an Uncertain Future ◆ Policing Trouble Spots: A New World Order or a World without Order? ◆ The Changing Nature of the International Arms Race ◆ Current Trends in World Trade: Economic Unification and Beyond ◆ North–South Relations ◆ Protecting the Environment ◆ Human Rights ◆ Women's Rights: A Pressing Human Rights Issue ◆ International Terrorism ◆ The Changing Face of International Relations

The title of this text, *Politics in a Changing World*, reflects the authors' keen awareness that in an era of rapid technological breakthroughs, growing political participation in much of the world, and constantly redefined ideologies, political activities and values in the twenty-first century are played out against a background of constant change. Nowhere has that been more apparent than in the realm of international relations, the interaction between nation-states, multinational alliances (economic, military, and political), **nongovernmental organizations (NGOs)**, multinational corporations, and armed nongovernmental groups (including terrorists and cross-national rebels). In all sorts of ways, economic development, technological innovation, and changing lifestyles have increased international interdependence. Problems such as illegal immigration, Third World debt, unemployment-linked trade competition, environmental decay, and drug trafficking cannot be resolved at the national level.

FROM THE END OF THE COLD WAR
TO THE BEGINNINGS OF AN UNCERTAIN FUTURE

From the close of World War II to the late 1980s, the cold war was the defining feature of the international system: a protracted confrontation pitting the United States and its allies in the **North Atlantic Treaty Organization (NATO)** against the Soviet Union and other nations of the Warsaw Pact (the Eastern European military alliance). Tensions between the two superpowers rose and fell periodically, but for each, the underlying factor shaping foreign policy was fear of the other.[1] Throughout the cold war, each side maintained a negative "mirror image" of the other.[2] Even as President Mikhail Gorbachev was about to reform the USSR, a 1985 article in the Soviet journal *International Affairs* insisted that "many facts show that modern militarism and . . . the arms race [are] the product of the . . . system of imperialism, primarily its most developed and most reactionary component—American imperialism."[3]

The United States and the USSR had been allies in World War II. But their relationship became antagonistic in the war's aftermath as the Soviet army overran Eastern Europe. The Truman Doctrine (1947) established the U.S. policy of "containment": The United States, President Harry Truman declared, would resist Soviet armed aggression and its support for communist insurgencies.[4] At the same time, the Russians felt threatened by Western "capitalist imperialism." As large numbers of former European colonies in Africa, Asia, and the Middle East gained independence in the decades after World War II, both superpowers perceived the problems of the developing world through the lens of East–West conflict. Each side extended foreign aid to developing nations primarily to counter the influence of its rival, rather than to serve the recipients' needs. For example, U.S. aid to Pakistan rose sharply when the United States wished to funnel arms to anti-Soviet guerrillas in neighboring Afghanistan, but it fell off rapidly after Russian troops withdrew. Ironically, America's desire to see the Soviet Union driven from Afghanistan led the U.S. to funnel millions of dollars to Islamic fundamentalist guerrilla groups that would later hold central roles in the Taliban government and Osama bin Laden's al-Qaeda terrorist network.

As recently as 1988, Europe was divided between Western democracies—most of them closely allied with the United States—and Central and Eastern Europe, the bloc of communist countries linked politically, militarily, and economically with the

Soviet Union. And only in the 1980s did the so-called balance of terror—the "mutually assured destruction" awaiting both sides if they went to war that had kept Europe and North America free of war for decades—begin to recede through greater mutual understanding and arms-reduction negotiations.

By 2002, so much had changed. The crumbling of communism in Eastern Europe—as symbolized so dramatically by the fall of the Berlin Wall—the subsequent collapse of Soviet communism, the reduction of the USSR from a military superpower to a secondary player, the emergence of the European Union as a major economic and political actor, and the continued spread of democracy into new parts of the Third World all seemed to promise a more tranquil and peaceful world. The United States was now the world's dominant economic, military, and diplomatic force, with no other superpower able to challenge it. To be sure, Russia retains a formidable arsenal of nuclear weapons, and its president, Vladimir Putin, sometimes expresses anti-Western sentiments. But with an enormously reduced economy and a greatly weakened military, Russia is no longer in a position to challenge the West.[5]

That doesn't mean the world felt trouble-free as we entered the twenty-first century. Far from it! The problems of world poverty, financial crises, overpopulation, environmental degradation, ethnic warfare, and political repression, just to name a few, remained enormous concerns. As the rapidly growing economic reach of vast **transnational corporations** (TNCs) controls far-flung industrial and financial empires that have little concern for national boundaries and a globalized economy threatens (or promises) to diminish the importance of the nation-state, many observers worry about such concentration of economic power and see it as a challenge to national sovereignty. Debt and other monetary crises not only have threatened the economies of nations such as Russia, Indonesia, Brazil, Thailand, and Mexico in recent years, but also periodically endanger the entire world economy. Still, as the new millennium began, the average American, and much of the world, felt safer than at any point since the start of the nuclear arms race.

All of that changed, of course, with the terrorist attacks of September 11, 2001. Suddenly, the War on Terrorism became the centerpiece of American foreign policy and a central concern of governments from Europe to Indonesia and the Philippines. The fear that worse assaults could be on the horizon heightened public anxieties—visions of nerve-gas attacks, biological terrorism, or a nuclear attack delivered not by missiles but in a backpack. At the same time, the War on Terrorism has had implications for domestic policy. In the United States and elsewhere, protections of civil liberties have been pared back, and people of Middle Eastern or other Third World origin have often found themselves under suspicion.

The end of the cold war has intensified other important security concerns—the proliferation of nuclear weapons to nations such as Israel, India, and Pakistan, and the danger of their development by so-called "rogue states" (regimes that violate their citizens' human rights, breach international law, and may support terrorism or seek weapons of mass destruction),* particularly North Korea and Iran. Some of those countries had depended on Russian military aid when that country was still a major world power, and they had been restrained from developing nuclear weapons by the USSR. Now, not only is that constraint removed, but also Russia itself is awash with

---

* The term *rogue state* is used primarily in the U.S. and is not widely accepted elsewhere. President Bush has also used the term "axis of evil."

nuclear weapons that lack adequate security protection and are overseen by underpaid military and civilian personnel who could be tempted to sell them to rogue states or terrorist organizations. To be sure, the danger of a full-scale nuclear war—an event that would dwarf the worst terrorist attack—has been removed, at least for now. And, as we will indicate, progress is being made toward dealing with many other international problems. Still, great challenges remain, with terrorism being the most terrifying and newsworthy but not the most important in our everyday lives. If they are to be successfully resolved, a greater degree of international cooperation and purpose than we have seen to date will be required. This chapter examines several critical issues that will occupy the world stage in the twenty-first century. The topics discussed are obviously not exhaustive, but they do illustrate the opportunities and the problems facing our ever-shrinking world.

Policing Trouble Spots: A New World Order or a World without Order?

In the aftermath of the 1991 Gulf War, President George H. W. Bush envisioned a **new world order** (**NWO**). The NWO would entail close cooperation among all the world's major powers to deter future aggression and maintain international stability. It "would be founded on the rule of law and on the principle of collective security."[6] In addition to stability, the NWO included a commitment to defending and spreading democracy and free-market economies throughout the world.

Clearly, international politics has not proceeded as smoothly as the elder Bush had envisioned. Subsequent wars in Yugoslavia, Afghanistan, and Iraq demonstrate how elusive world peace still is. Indeed, in some respects we may be facing a more unstable world today, since the old East–West "balance of terror" no longer inhibits regional conflicts. For example, analyst John Gaddis argued that had the cold war still been raging, the USSR would have prevented its Iraqi ally from invading Kuwait, lest it draw the Soviet Union into a war with the United States.[7]

The collapse of the Soviet bloc unleashed old ethnic hostilities in Bosnia, Macedonia, Armenia, Tajikistan, and elsewhere. Observing those events in the early 1990s, former Secretary of Defense and CIA chief James Schlesinger warned, quite prophetically, that "although the world after the Cold War is likely to be a far less dangerous place because of reduced risks of a cataclysmic clash, it is likely to be more unstable rather than less."[8] Indeed, some observers point to events since the end of the cold war—including the many internal wars in Yugoslavia, Russia, Africa, and Asia, the breakdown of the Arab-Israeli peace process, the September 11 tragedy, and the rising menace of international terrorism—as evidence of a "new world disorder." But, whether one is sanguine or pessimistic about the future of international relations, a question remains: How can the United States and its allies best police the world's most dangerous internal conflicts today (most of them in Africa, Asia, Eastern Europe, and the Middle East)?

During the 1990s, some policy planners within the Bush and Clinton administrations favored working with United Nations peacekeeping operations in selected world trouble spots. That was the framework for the Gulf War intervention that freed Kuwait from an Iraqi invasion.[9] But poorly conceived U.N. interventions in Somalia and Bosnia raised doubts about how well that body functions as a peacekeeper in difficult situations. Repeated U.N. condemnations of the massacre of tribesmen in the Sudanese region of Darfur have lacked teeth, as member states are not willing to commit substantial military forces to that region. At the same time, many in the U.S. Congress, particularly conservatives, feel that the United States should stay clear of UN-sponsored peacekeeping missions because the United Nations should never be in a position to dictate or even influence U.S. foreign policy. And foreign policy planners in the current Bush administration were divided between those (mostly in the State Department) who wanted the war against Iraq to be part of a broader United Nations operation and those (mostly in the Defense Department) who were more willing to go it alone.

In the coming years, ethnic hostilities will almost undoubtedly continue to precipitate civil or international wars in Africa, Asia, or Eastern Europe. In Bosnia, ethnic conflict among Croatians, Muslims, and Serbs caused the first war in Europe since World War II and brought unspeakable devastation and large-scale human rights violations.

In fact, most of the world's trouble spots since the end of the cold war have involved ethnic hostilities within national borders; Somalia, Liberia, Sudan, India (Kashmir), Afghanistan, and Yugoslavia come to mind. In addition, a further resurgence of Islamic Fundamentalism could provoke civil conflict in the Middle East and North Africa. These conflicts raise difficult new challenges for the international community and its most powerful member, the United States. Should the United Nations, the European community, or the United States send peacekeeping forces to contain civil wars such as Bosnia's or Liberia's? Usually, Western policy makers feel that there is insufficient reason for outside actors to intervene. When conflicts play out within a single country's borders, the international community arguably should not violate that nation's sovereignty by interceding militarily. In Washington, critics of intervention insist that such conflicts normally pose no threat to U.S. national security. Absent that threat, the United States was reluctant to put American troops in harm's way in Bosnia and limited its defense of the Kosovo Albanian population (against persecution by the Serbian government) to the use of air power. European nations have been equally reluctant to send their troops into potentially dangerous trouble spots, particularly if the United States does not take the lead.

To be sure, the United States *has* been willing to involve itself militarily when its own national interests are at stake—as in Afghanistan and Iraq. But many of the internal wars and ethnic conflicts in the Third World and Eastern Europe do not particularly affect the national interests of the United States or other major powers. Consequently, neither the U.S. nor NATO nor other powerful actors have been willing to send peacekeeping forces to end horrendous civil wars or other forms of brutality in Rwanda, Mozambique, Congo, and the Sudan even though those conflicts have collectively killed millions of people.

Supporters of United Nations and U.S. peacekeeping missions argue that many internal ethnic quarrels spill across national borders and they may create international conflicts that could threaten U.S. national interests or even world peace. They point out, for example, that had the war in Kosovo (a province of Serbia) continued unchecked, it could have spilled over into Albania, Macedonia, and Greece. A second argument for peacekeeping interventions is that if the United States is to maintain its status as a world leader, it cannot succumb to isolationism and must assume some responsibility as the "world's policeman." Proponents of that position note that the United States lost status in Western Europe when it initially failed to assume leadership during the Bosnian crisis. Finally, some who favor international intervention into internal ethnic conflicts and massacres raise a moral challenge. For the international community to sit back and allow mass starvation in Somalia, tribal genocide in Rwanda and Burundi, or death camps in Bosnia, they argue, makes it as morally bankrupt as those who did nothing to help the Jews escape Hitler's genocide.

Despite such moral arguments, however, outside governments are understandably reluctant to risk the lives of their nations' soldiers to save the lives of civilians in far-off nations. Nor is it realistic to expect external intervention every time there is a human rights crisis. Therefore, the question of where and when to intervene will continue to be a major issue facing the United Nations, NATO, and the United States, among others.

THE CHANGING NATURE
OF THE INTERNATIONAL ARMS RACE

East–West Disarmament

The reform and subsequent collapse of the Soviet Union were closely associated with a series of agreements between the world's two greatest nuclear powers reducing their nuclear capabilities and with it the possibility of nuclear war. Since the late 1980s, first the USSR and then its major successor state, Russia, have reached a series of agreements with the United States significantly reducing their nuclear arsenals. In 1988, they signed the Intermediate-Range Nuclear Force (INF) Treaty calling for the destruction of more than 2,500 missiles between them. That treaty constituted "the first formal agreement that actually reduced the number of nuclear weapons in existence rather than just slowing down the rate of increase. . . ."[10]

Three years later, START I (the Strategic Arms Reduction Treaty) was signed, requiring both the U.S. and the Soviets to reduce the number of deployed strategic nuclear warheads to 6,000. On December 1, 2001, both Russia and the United States announced that they were in compliance with those terms. Following the collapse of the Soviet Union, President George Bush and Russian President Boris Yeltsin had announced yet further nuclear weapons reductions. Yeltsin also declared that Russian missiles would no longer be targeted at U.S. cities. START II, signed in 1993, mandated further cutbacks of strategic nuclear weapons to 3,000–3,500 for each country.

Because Russia's parliament failed to ratify that treaty until April 14, 2000, the deadline for compliance has been extended until the end of 2007. Finally, in a rather unexpected move, Presidents George W. Bush and Vladimir Putin announced in May 2002 that their countries would reduce the number of their strategic nuclear warheads to 1,700–2,200 by the close of 2002 (the Strategic Offensive Reductions Treaty, SORT). Critics of that agreement note that the warheads are to be placed in storage and not destroyed and, furthermore, that there are no provisions for verifying compliance.

Although many analysts see these as serious flaws and although the treaty has yet to be ratified by either country, the SORT accord still is likely to contribute to the ongoing process of substantially reducing nuclear arsenals. On the other hand, in June 2002 the United States withdrew from the 1967 Anti-Ballistic Missile Treaty, a treaty that had limited its signatories' ability to build antimissile defense systems, which would have made it less likely that either side would launch an offensive attack.

The Dangers of Nuclear Proliferation

Ironically, at the very time that the prospects for global nuclear war are receding, there has been an increase in actual and potential **nuclear proliferation** to the Third World, increasing the possibility of regional nuclear conflicts. In fact, the very collapse of the Soviet Union created another possible source of proliferation. Because Russian professionals, including nuclear scientists and technicians, now draw very low salaries, some may have been hired by Third World nations seeking to develop their own weapons programs. There has also been concern that nuclear weapons or components will be sold abroad by Russian military officers wishing to enrich themselves. While those fears now have receded, other developments have been troublesome. Currently, India and Pakistan have tested nuclear weapons. Israel almost certainly has them. North Korea recently has claimed to have nuclear weapons and, while its claim cannot be verified, it definitely has a program capable of eventually producing them.

Several factors make Third World proliferation particularly worrisome. First, two potential nuclear powers—Iran and North Korea (Libya, formerly in that category, has terminated its nuclear program)—are considered rogue states with records of belligerence that do not inspire confidence. Others—India, Pakistan, and Israel—with nuclear capabilities are embroiled in bitter regional conflicts with each other or with non-nuclear nations. Finally, even if all new nuclear powers were to try to act responsibly, the chances of war by miscalculation increase greatly as the world's nuclear club grows.

The Nuclear Non-Proliferation Treaty (NPT) came into effect in 1970 and currently has 189 national signatories. Its purpose was to prevent the spread of nuclear

© AP/Wide World Photos

IRAN: A NUCLEAR THREAT?   An Iranian security official, dressed in protective clothing, walks inside that country's Uranium Conversion Facility. Iran's 2005 decision to restart uranium conversion and exclude international inspectors raised Western fears that the country was planning to build nuclear weapons.

weapons beyond the hands of the five countries (the U.S., the Soviet Union, Britain, France, and China) that possessed them at that time. The treaty prohibited countries with nuclear weapons from giving or selling them to non-nuclear countries and from sharing with them weapons technology (though China and France did not become signatories until 1992). One difficulty with the treaty is that it allows countries without nuclear weapons to develop nuclear energy for peaceful purposes even though such uranium enrichment programs can fairly easily be converted to weapons production. Enforcement depends on inspections by the International Atomic Energy Agency (IAEA), an arm of the United Nations.

So far, the NPT has been fairly effective but not totally so. For one thing, some countries—including India, Israel, and Pakistan—never signed the treaty. India and Pakistan have announced that they have nuclear weapons, and while Israel has refused to confirm that it has them, it is widely believed that it has 100 to 300 warheads. Others (such as North Korea) have withdrawn from the NPT, while still others have evaded inspection. South Africa secretly developed some nuclear weapon in the 1980s but dismantled its program and its weapons in 1990 and signed the NPT the following year.[11] Iraq apparently had a nuclear weapons program for a number of years, but seems to have abandoned it in the early 1990s, years in advance of the U.S. invasion. As new countries have developed nuclear weapons, the risk increases of further proliferation. Israel is believed to have assisted the South African program. Pakistan has now admitted that the father of its nuclear weapons program, Abdul Qadeer Khan, had sold Libya and North Korea technology and equipment for building nuclear weapons (Libya has since abandoned its program and agreed to IAEA inspection).

Clearly, the two most worrisome cases at the present time are North Korea and Iran, the former because of its unpredictable and belligerent behavior, the latter because of its association with Islamic extremism and terrorism. The North Korean weapons program dates back to the 1960s or 1970s. From that regime's perspective, it was threatened by the deployment of U.S. nuclear weapons to South Korea as early as 1958 (all such U.S. weapons were, however, removed by 1991). Despite later signing the Nuclear Non-Proliferation Treaty and an additional pact with the United States promising to dismantle its plutonium program, North Korea continued its clandestine weapons program. In early 2003 it became the first nation ever to withdraw from the NPT. Later that year it reactivated a reactor at its main nuclear complex and announced a joint program with Iran to develop long-range ballistic missiles with nuclear warheads. The North Koreans now claim to have nuclear weapons, though they have yet to test them. Equally ominously, they have been testing missiles capable of delivering such weapons. Six-Party Talks (involving both Koreas, the U.S., China, and Japan) designed to dismantle North Korea's program have accomplished nothing, and the prospects for progress seem very dim.[12]

Iran's nuclear energy program dates to the late 1960s and received assistance during the 1970s from the United States and West Germany. Its purpose was to produce energy for internal consumption so that Iran could export petroleum being used for that purpose. As a signatory to the Nuclear Non-Proliferation Treaty, Iran allowed inspection by the IAEA. Following the Islamic Revolution of 1979, which overthrew the Shah (emperor), a U.S. ally, the program was frozen and during the Iran-Iraq War of 1980–1988 the entire nuclear program was suspended. Nuclear energy development was resumed in the 1990s, and in 2002 the United States accused Iran of seeking to develop nuclear weapons at secret plants, a claim rejected a few months later by the IAEA, which said its international inspectors had found no evidence to support the American charge. By 2004, however, the Director General of the IAEA, Mohamed ElBaradei, had accused Iran of not fully cooperating with inspectors. As with the North Korean case, the U.S. has taken a harder line on this issue than its allies. For example, a leaked, confidential IAEA report in 2004 again asserted that, contrary to U.S. claims, there was no evidence of an Iranian nuclear weapons program. Britain, France, and Germany have held periodic talks with Iran in which the European nations have offered to give Iran assistance for its nuclear energy program if it would agree to stop uranium enrichment. In response, Iran did voluntarily suspend uranium enrichment in 2004, but resumed activity in late 2005. While there is debate as to what Iran's plans are and when, if at all, it might develop nuclear warheads, the prospects are worrisome. Not only does that nation have links with Middle Eastern terrorist groups, but it has very hostile relations with Israel. In fact, Israel has hinted that if it becomes convinced that Iran is close to developing a nuclear weapon, it could launch a preemptive conventional air attack on Iranian nuclear facilities just as it had done to Iraq in 1981.

The post-cold-war world will be hard-pressed to contain the Third World nuclear arms race and possible regional nuclear wars. As nuclear know-how spreads and as it becomes easier to deliver nuclear weapons in small packages, the possibility that a group such as al Qaeda may acquire nuclear capability, though currently unlikely, remains ominous.

CURRENT TRENDS IN WORLD TRADE: ECONOMIC UNIFICATION AND BEYOND

A very different contemporary international concern is economic, cultural, and political globalization. Unlike other issues discussed in this chapter, it presents both potential opportunities and possible dangers. As a trip to any nearby shopping mall quickly reveals, the world is becoming more interconnected. Labels on garments indicate that they were made in an array of developing countries such as Honduras, Guatemala, Turkey, Sri Lanka, and Indonesia. Simple electronic goods such as clock-radios come from Malaysia and Thailand, and computer keyboards and computers come from Mexico, Brazil, South Korea, and Taiwan. Even the customers and the sales staffs in malls located in major cities such as Los Angeles, Chicago, Boston, and Miami include people born in dozens of other nations.

The most talked-about economic and political phenomenon of the early twenty-first century is **globalization**—the enormous spread of economic activity, political interactions, mass culture, and ideas across national borders, often in de facto defiance of national sovereignty. Through the World Wide Web, e-mail, and the mass media, the quantities of international communications and cross-cultural contacts are growing enormously. "Hollywood" movies are now among the primary exports of the United States. And an estimated one billion people worldwide have access to CNN news broadcasts.[13] For some, globalization is a positive development, promising economic growth, greater cross-cultural understanding and cooperation, and even the spread of democracy. For others, it threatens to spread American imperial dominance and destroy cultural diversity. Thus, Benjamin Barber warns of globalization that would force "nations into one homogeneous global theme park, one McWorld, tied together by communications, information, entertainment, and commerce."[14]

FIGURE 18.1   GROWTH IN THE WORLD TRADE, 1913–2001

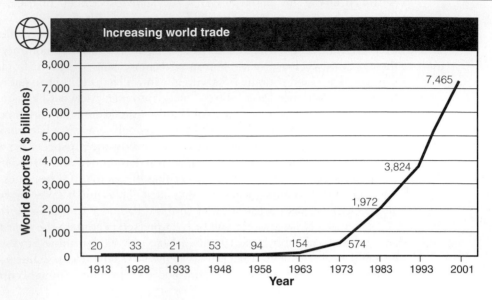

SOURCE: IMF, *World Economic Outlook*, May 2002, on the Web at http://www.imf.org/. As presented in John T. Rourke, *International Politics on the World Stage*, 9th ed. (Guilford, CT: McGraw-Hill—Dushkin, 2003), p. 410.

Perhaps nowhere has the growth of international economic links been more impressive and important than in the realm of world trade. As Figure 18.1 indicates, on the eve of World War I (1913) the total value of world trade was a mere $20 billion annually. During the next 50 years, it grew gradually to an annual rate of $154 billion in 1963. At that point, international trade began to spiral rapidly upward, increasing by 700 percent from 1973 to 1993, and then nearly doubling in the following eight years (1993–2001). That unprecedented growth was stimulated by a number of factors, including improved transportation technology; the rapid growth of the world economy from the late 1940s to the 1990s, particularly in the United States, Western Europe, Japan, China, and East Asia; and the creation of multinational economic unions and free-trade agreements such as the North American Free Trade Agreement (NAFTA), the **European Union (EU)**, APEX (Asian-Pacific Economic Cooperation), and MERCOSUR (an agreement of four South American nations); worldwide free-trade agreements and enforcement mechanisms through the General Agreement on Tariffs and Trade (GATT) and its successor, the World Trade Organization (WTO); and the explosion of exports by **newly industrialized countries (NICs)**, particularly in East Asia.* For example, today more than 40 percent of Taiwan's, South Korea's, Singapore's, and Hong Kong's respective GNPs are devoted to exports. The volume of trade varies according to the rate of global economic

* The term NICs refers to countries (and the city of Hong Kong) in East Asia (especially South Korea, Taiwan, Singapore, and Hong Kong) and in Latin America (especially Argentina, Brazil, and Mexico) that have recently developed substantial industrial manufacturing and export capacities. More recently, countries such as Thailand and Malaysia have joined that club.

growth, and the 2001–2002 recession in the United States and other industrialized nations resulted in stagnant trade growth. But the volume of trade picked up in 2003 and grew rapidly in 2004.[15]

The beginnings of today's globalized economy can be traced to the early years after World War II. In 1947, seeking to rebuild the world economy, the United States and 22 other nations signed the General Agreement on Tariffs and Trade (GATT), designed to remove barriers to international trade.[16] By 2006, the World Trade Organization (WTO), the successor to the GATT, had 149 member nations (with some 30 others negotiating for admission). Between them, they conduct more than 97 percent of world trade.[17] With the recent addition of China to its membership rolls, the WTO is continuing the process of opening up most of the world's markets to **free trade** (international trade that is relatively unrestricted by quotas, tariffs, or other barriers).

The newly emerging economic order has several important features that will influence interstate relations and economic conditions worldwide in the coming century. First, the international division of industrial production has shifted. During the 1960s and 1970s, the first East Asian NICs—South Korea, Taiwan, Hong Kong, and Singapore—enormously expanded their exports of low-cost, labor-intensive consumer goods, such as garments, footwear, textiles, and inexpensive consumer electronics.

Taking advantage of their low wage scales at the time, they were able to undersell Western producers of those items. In the 1980s and 1990s, these "East Asian tigers" emerged from underdevelopment and, as their wage scales rose substantially, they shifted to production of more expensive, technology-intensive products, such as computers, computer software, automobiles, and steel.[18] In Latin America, more industrially developed countries such as Brazil, Mexico, and, to a lesser extent, Argentina have also increased exports of sophisticated industrial products. At the same time, production of components, lower-end industrial exports, and apparel has been transferred to less-advanced, cheaper-labor countries in East Asia (including China, Malaysia, and Thailand) and to Latin America's more recent export manufacturers, such as Honduras and Costa Rica.

Overall, a significant share of the world's industrial production and exports (especially labor-intensive manufacturing) has shifted from the developed to the developing world. The NICs can no longer be ignored as trade competitors. Not only have many former textile- and shoe-manufacturing towns in the American South and New England seen their production shift to East Asia and Latin America, but also modern Brazilian, Mexican, and South Korean steel mills can compete successfully with producers in Germany, France, and the United States.

The developing nations are now both major suppliers to U.S. firms and consumers and major consumers of American products—trading partners and competitors. In 2000, China replaced Japan as the nation with whom the United States has the largest trade deficit. Table 18.1 indicates how critical the U.S. market is to Third World exporters. At the same time, however, Third World NICs and other developing economies are also major importers of U.S. products. Currently, some 40 percent of U.S. exports are destined for the Third World.

Another important trend in world trade is the growing importance of services as an exportable commodity, particularly from the United States. As a portion of the world's industrial production has moved to Asia and Latin America in recent years, the service sector (banking, insurance, computer services, social services, education, health care, and the like) has represented a growing portion of the American GNP and exports.

TABLE 18.1 TOTAL EXPORTS (MANUFACTURED AND NONMANUFACTURED) OF SELECTED DEVELOPING NATIONS (FIRST HALF OF 2001)

	Total Exports (billions)	Exports to U.S. (billions)	Percentage to U.S.
Mexico	$68.89	58.05	84.3
Brazil	26.31	5.59	21.2
Chile	9.14	1.57	17.2
China	144.63	41.20	28.5
South Korea	75.52	16.68	22.1
Hong Kong	80.87	14.91	18.4
Thailand	33.29	6.86	20.6
Indonesia	30.85	4.64	15.0

SOURCE: *The New York Times*, July 1, 2001.

Currently, over one-third of the value of world trade is in services, with the United States playing a major role.

Finally, a third major development has been the emergence of regional trading blocs and investment zones. We have already referred to the most important of those, the European Union and NAFTA. Starting with the European Coal and Steel Community (1952) and the creation of the European Economic Community (1958), Western Europe has moved steadily toward a fully integrated economy. Today, a tourist or a businesswoman traveling to any significant Western European nation except Switzerland, Norway, and Great Britain—or a U.S. firm investing in the region—must work with only a single currency, the Euro, which has replaced the French franc, the German deutschmark, and other national currencies. The single currency caps a half-century of steadily growing economic integration resulting in virtually a single economy for most of Western and Southern Europe. The combined Gross National Product of all EU members exceeds that of the United States and recently grew further as it expanded its borders, though expansion has had its problems (see Box 18-1).

Unlike other regional trading blocs, the EU has gone beyond trade and fiscal unification, moving toward growing political unity as well. For example, the European Court of Justice has the authority to overturn decisions made by courts in EU member states, thereby overriding national sovereignty to some degree.[19] The popularly elected European Parliament passes legislation in a number of policy areas that is binding on all members. Significantly, parliamentary members have not organized themselves into voting blocs by country but, rather, have organized by political orientation, with most representatives aligned with either the conservative or the socialist blocs. Very slowly and carefully, the EU had been moving toward the creation of a loose political union, a process recently slowed by a popular backlash (Box 18-1).

In East Asia, less-formal economic zones have developed based on trade and investment. As China has opened its doors to foreign investment, Hong Kong and Taiwanese businessmen have moved in to forge strong economic ties. Since June 1997, Hong Kong (a former British colony) has been administered by China, producing even closer economic bonds between the two. At the same time, Japan has established

Box 18-1

A VOTER BACKLASH AGAINST FURTHER EUROPEAN INTEGRATION

In 2004, the European Union undertook its biggest expansion ever (in terms of the number of member states) by admitting eight Eastern European and two Southern European countries, thereby increasing the Union's membership from 15 (Austria, Britain, Belgium, Denmark, Finland, France, Germany, Greece, Ireland, Italy, Luxemburg, the Netherlands, Portugal, Spain, Sweden) to 25 with a combined population of more than 450 million. In addition to the tiny island-nations of Cyprus and Malta, the expansion brought in eight former members of the Soviet-led Warsaw Pact—the Czech Republic, Slovakia, Estonia, Latvia, Lithuania, Hungary, Poland, and Slovenia—thereby creating a united Europe stretching from Ireland to the Russian border. If they are able to meet EU economic and human rights standards, Bulgaria, Romania, Croatia, and Turkey may also join in the coming years.

Subsequent events, however, suggested that Europe's political and diplomatic elite were too far ahead of some of their national populations in their desire for a more-integrated Europe. A proposed new European Constitution would have created a single EU foreign minister (with a coordinated European foreign policy), streamlined EU administration, given the European parliament broader jurisdiction, and otherwise advanced integration. Ratification required approval by all 25 member nations. Since the constitution was supported by most of the region's major political parties and leaders (including all of the national governments), most analysts anticipated the document would pass the parliaments of all the member states.

But as unanticipated voter resistance surfaced in a number of countries, 10 members decided to make their countries' ratification of the constitution contingent upon the voters' approval in a national referendum. Early public opinion polls suggested that, while British voters might vote no, the constitution had majority support in the rest of the countries with referenda. As voting approached, however, the tide began to turn against the constitution. After nine countries had approved the document (two of them through referenda), voters in France and the Netherlands soundly rejected it within days of each other in 2005. Since the leaders of the two dominant political parties in France supported the constitution, as did 90 percent of the Dutch parliament, the referendas' results were a stunning rejection of those nations' political elites.

The reasons for the rejections were varied and not always directly related to the constitution itself. Some feared that companies would move jobs from the richer nations (the 15 previous members of the EU) to the 10 new members, which have substantially lower wage levels. Others feared a flood of immigrants from the new members and, more so, from Turkey's large Muslim population should that country be admitted in the future. Traditionally liberal Dutch voters had been shocked by an Islamic extremist's assassination of filmmaker Theo Van Gogh. Others were expressing their unhappiness over the adoption several years earlier of a common currency, the Euro, which was widely seen as inflationary.[20] In any event, with the constitution defeated, the EU must figure out what to do next. Most Europeans still favor the union, but many fear it is changing too quickly. Thus, the EU will survive but it is less clear what direction it will take.

---

important trade and investment links with Thailand, Malaysia, and Indonesia. Those ties, however, are bilateral (between two countries), rather than the multinational arrangements found within the EU.

In North America, the United States, Mexico, and Canada have created NAFTA, which, at the time it took effect (1994), became the world's largest free-trade zone. Initially subject to bitter opposition in the United States from many labor unions and from independent presidential candidates Ross Perot and Ralph Nader, NAFTA for the most part merely cemented the already growing economic ties among the three nations.[21] Today, the United States is Mexico's largest trading partner, while Canada and Mexico are currently the first and third largest trading partners of the United States.

Subsequently, the Clinton and Bush administrations have called for the eventual incorporation of much of Latin America into a hemispheric American free-trading zone (AFTA). There is little immediate prospect of that happening, but meanwhile Latin American countries have been expanding existing free-trade agreements with each other, forging new ones, and opening their doors to investment and trade from both within and outside the region.

These changes mark a dramatic shift away from the economic nationalism that had previously characterized Latin American trade policy. Supporters of free trade argue that it will force the region's formerly protected companies to become more competitive and will allow Latin America to emulate East Asia's rapid, export-based, economic growth. But critics of the new, "outward looking" development model worry that, at least in the short run, the relatively unrestricted entry of American, East Asian, and European goods will drive less competitive local firms and farmers out of business and create substantial unemployment. Both sides of the debate, however, recognize that, one way or another, Latin America must inevitably join North America, Europe, and Asia in an increasingly interdependent world economy.

North–South Relations

One type of international economic and political relation that has often been particularly sensitive over the years is the relationship between the world's advanced, industrialized nations (referred to as "the North") and the less developed, Third World countries ("the South"). The demise of Western colonialism—from Indian and Pakistani independence in 1947 through the independence of almost all of Africa's last remaining colonies in the 1980s and 1990s—produced a steadily growing number of sovereign Third World nations. The United Nations General Assembly became a forum in which developing nations expressed their views and aired their grievances. Many of them, subscribing to theories of dependency and Western imperialism (see Chapter 15), blamed the capitalist nations of North America and Europe for their own economic difficulties. Others held the United States and the Soviet Union equally culpable for spending billions on the arms race while ignoring the needs of the world's poor.

Unhappy with international trade patterns and desiring more foreign assistance, they demanded that more attention be paid to **North–South relations** (particularly to issues pitting developed nations against underdeveloped countries) and less to the East–West conflict (between the West and the Soviet bloc).

Yet, ironically, the end of the cold war has, for the most part, had a negative impact on the developing world. Whereas the Soviet Union once provided significant economic and military aid to countries such as Cuba, India, Syria, and Iraq, contemporary Russia, having suffered an economic meltdown (Chapter 13), is no longer a donor of Third World development aid. At the same time, developing nations have less leverage over the United States, which, during the cold war, often gave foreign aid to keep Third World countries from falling into the Soviet sphere of influence or succumbing to communist insurgencies. As a consequence, since the early 1990s, foreign aid has constituted a dwindling percentage of the U.S. federal budget. During that time, Japan replaced the United States as the world's largest foreign aid donor.

Still, as a consequence of economic interdependence, increased trade, and the emergence of the United States as the world's diplomatic and military superpower, developing nations are, if anything, more deeply in the American sphere of economic and political influence. In the past, many Third World leaders maintained that the Western industrial powers had victimized Africa, Asia, Latin America, and the Middle East, first through colonialism, and then through unjust postcolonial economic and political ties known as neocolonial relations. Consequently, they argued, the developed capitalist nations have a moral obligation to aid Third World development. Today, lacking alternative backing from the Soviet bloc, Third World leaders have generally abandoned their anti-Western rhetoric. Instead, they look to foreign aid and, increasingly, improved trade relations with the North to help them escape poverty.

Trade and Investment

Although increased North–South trade seems inevitable and is increasingly seen as desirable, the *terms* of that trade remain a source of controversy. As we saw in Chapter 15, Third World analysts have maintained that, over time, international "terms of trade" have deteriorated for developing countries that depended on the export of commodities. In other words, they argued that, over time, the prices of commodities such as copper, cotton, coffee, or sugar (the less developed countries' major export) have increased at a slower rate than have the prices of manufactured imports such as tractors or television sets. Consequently, over the years, they contended, a country such as Costa Rica has had to export more and more bananas to pay for the same number of imported automobiles. Years ago, economists at the United Nations Economic Commission for Latin America (ECLA) produced extensive statistics on Latin American trade that supported that position. More recent economic data, however, show no consistent pattern in the comparative prices of Third World commodity exports and their manufactured imports. Commodity prices, it seems, can rise or fall sharply in a rather short period of time. Therefore, Third World exporters are at a disadvantage in some years and benefit in others.

That point, however, suggests a different kind of obstacle to economic growth in the LDCs. Commodity prices often fluctuate wildly over time, making it difficult for developing nations to anticipate their future export revenues. How, then, can countries such as Chile make long-term development investments without some idea of their anticipated income from copper exports? In an attempt to remedy that problem, from the 1960s into the 1990s many commodity exporters tried to create international cartels of sugar-, coffee-, or cocoa-growing nations, which, when the price of a crop or mineral export dropped too low, could limit the supply and thereby restore prices to an acceptable level.

Industrialized nations reject the notion that international trading arrangements are unfair and view commodity cartels as an unreasonable restraint on international trade. Ultimately, with only the exception of OPEC (the Organization of Petroleum Exporting Countries), efforts to create these cartels were short-lived and failed to control world prices. Such arrangements depend on the willingness of all, at least most, cartel members to limit their exports of, say, sugar, when the price drops too low. But that is precisely the time when sugar-exporting nations are most desperate for export revenues and, therefore, the temptation to export more is irresistible.

For the last two decades or so, principles of free trade have gained wide international acceptance. Even were Third World countries to try artificially controlling the volume and price of their exports or limiting their imports, pressures from the IMF, the World Bank, and the world's richest nations would force them to stop. Moreover, as increasing numbers of Asian and Latin American countries have diversified their exports, adding manufactured goods to their traditional exports of crops and minerals, they too have benefited from free trade. Whereas Brazil may have once favored a coffee cartel to control that crop's volatile price, today it is more concerned with reducing trade barriers to its export of airplanes, weapons, and shoes. Indeed, aircraft have recently replaced coffee as Brazil's leading export.

But, while the world's industrialized nations have pressed developing nations to accept free trade, they have violated its principles by offering their own agricultural producers some $300 billion annually in subsidies, putting Third World farmers at a considerable disadvantage. In 2003, the G20 alliance of "Southern" nations (later expanded to 22), led by Brazil, China, and India, challenged the industrialized nations in WTO negotiations over a new treaty, demanding that the North end its agricultural subsidies. The following year, in the so-called Doha (Qatar) round of negotiations (named after the city where the talks started), a general agreement was reached calling for the North to lower its agricultural subsidies and the South to lower tariff barriers to manufactured goods. But final agreement on a new WTO treaty has so far been stymied by disagreements over technical issues and Doha negotiations were suspended in 2006.

In the past, foreign investment was also a frequent source of North–South friction. Lacking capital and technological expertise, most developing nations have long solicited some foreign investment. But often they have done so warily. For one thing, some transnational corporations (TNCs) have meddled in the domestic politics of their host countries, bribing local officials or even trying to topple unfriendly governments. For example, International Telephone and Telegraph encouraged the CIA to destabilize Salvador Allende's democratically elected socialist government in Chile. Even when TNCs do not act irresponsibly, host countries are frequently uncomfortable having their most important natural resource (and primary export) controlled by foreigners, as the United Fruit Company did in many banana-exporting countries. More recently, however, as free-market ideals have triumphed in the international community, attitudes toward foreign investment have changed. Countries that were once wary now yearn for more investment. For example, China, once the most forceful voice against "capitalist imperialism," is now the Third World's largest recipient of foreign direct investment. Brazil's recently departed president, Fernando Henrique Cardoso, once the most articulate spokesman for dependency theory (and its associated suspicion of foreign investment), vigorously courted investments by transnational corporations during his two terms in office.

The Debt Crisis

A final issue in North–South division concerns the Third World's foreign debt. Starting in the 1970s, many developing nations, particularly in Latin America, incurred substantial external debts in order to invest in economic development projects, compensate for international trade deficits, and cover budget deficits. Initially, those loans were secured primarily from Western and Japanese commercial banks that saw LDCs as profitable clients. When OPEC raised petroleum prices sharply in the 1970s, United States, Japanese, and European banks accumulated billions of "petrodollars" (money generated by oil-exporting nations), which they were happy to lend to such nations as Argentina, Brazil, Mexico, South Korea, Indonesia, and Nigeria.

By the early 1980s, the developing world (excluding the Middle East's petroleum-exporting nations) had accumulated a total foreign debt exceeding $700 billion.[22]

By the end of the twentieth century, Third World debt had climbed to $2,060 billion.[23] Some of those loans were invested wisely in roads, schools, or factories, helping to stimulate economic growth. But some went to less productive uses: covering short-term budget deficits, making payments for imported consumer goods, or purchasing armaments. Too often, a substantial amount of money was wasted because of corruption and poorly designed economic policies. Latin American nations, by far the largest Third World debtors, borrowed most of their money at variable interest rates, as did countries in Africa (Asian debtors generally locked into fixed rates). As interest rates shot up at the end of the 1970s, those countries were often unable to keep up with their payments. Thus, by the end of the decade many LDCs were burdened with debts that were taking up large, and growing, portions of their export earnings, their national budgets, and their gross national products.

In 1982, when Mexico—the developing world's second-largest debtor—announced that it was unable to pay the interest on its foreign debt, the international banking system faced a serious crisis. Loans to Latin America equaled up to two-thirds of the net corporate assets of some international banks. Unwilling to expose themselves any further in the wake of Mexico's partial default, they curtailed additional loans to the developing world. The consequences for Latin American and African economies were disastrous, since those countries had depended on a steady inflow of new credit to maintain their economic growth. So they went into a steep economic decline that lasted until the early 1990s and from which some have yet to recover fully.

Ultimately, new funds were provided to most debtors, often for the purpose of allowing them to roll over their old debts. To secure that additional credit, however, countries such as Argentina, Brazil, Mexico, and Nigeria had to agree to stringent economic austerity programs, often designed by the International Monetary Fund (IMF). These programs required debtor nations to slash government spending, devalue their currencies, and privatize state-owned enterprises in order to reduce sharply their budgetary and trade deficits. The immediate effects were devastating. Governments were forced to cut social services such as health care and education, to reduce subsidies for food and other basic necessities, and to lay off government employees. Throughout Africa and Latin America, economies plummeted and living standards dropped as much as 40 percent.

As their economies staggered under the weight of measures needed to correct budgetary imbalances, many LDCs complained that they would never recover unless they were granted some form of debt relief. Although initially unsympathetic to such requests, the U.S. government ultimately responded modestly. In 1989, Treasury Secretary Nicholas Brady introduced a plan allowing debtors to reduce their obligations to private banks if they met stringent IMF or World Bank criteria for economic reform. By the 1990s, the worst of the **debt crisis** seemed to have passed, at least in Latin America. After a decade of stagnation, a number of countries have resumed economic growth. Still, major debt crises in Russia, East Asia, Mexico, and, most recently, Argentina since the mid-1990s suggest that many countries are not out of the woods yet. In Africa, already the most impoverished region of the developing world, debt payments often soak up funds badly needed to improve the economy and to fight malnutrition and diseases such as AIDS. These problems have led to a worldwide movement of concerned citizens seeking to persuade their governments to forgive the debts of the most poverty-stricken nations (see Box 18-2).

Responding to calls for debt relief, in 1996 the World Bank initiated a program, called the Heavily Indebted Poor Countries initiative (HIPC), which enabled a number of very

---

Box 18-2

ROCKING THE DEBT: BONO MAKES AFRICA'S
EXTERNAL DEBT A HOT ISSUE

At first glance, few topics seem more dry and less hip than Third World debt. Not surprisingly, the issues of foreign exchange rates, balance of trade, commodity prices, and variable interest rates do not normally attract the interest of rock stars. But the huge external debt that so many Third World nations accrued during the 1960s and 1970s took a terrible toll, the effects of which are still being felt, especially in sub-Saharan Africa.

Africa is home to 16 of the 17 poorest nations in the world (as measured by per capita income).[24] Although the total size of that continent's debt is actually much smaller than Latin America's, it constitutes a much higher percentage of its foreign export revenues and GDP. Currently, in some African nations, annual debt repayments account for as much as 60 percent of the country's export earnings.[25] That means that most of the income received for coffee or copper exports must be spent on interest payments rather than on roads, factories, or electric power plants. And because most of the debt is owed by the region's governments (rather than the private sector), debt payments consume a major portion of the national budget, taking away funds that would otherwise be used to fulfill critical needs in education and health care. To take one extreme example, between 1972 and 1986 allocations for education in Zaire, one of Africa's largest countries, fell from 15.2 percent of the national budget to 0.8 percent.[26] And for most of Africa, the debt burden continues to take its toll. In some countries, including those ravaged by AIDS,

the cost of debt payments dwarfs government expenditures on health care.

In the past decade, a number of grassroots NGOs have tried to put a human face on the suffering that lies beneath the dry statistics on the foreign debt. One such group, Jubilee 2000, has pressured the world's wealthiest nations to forgive the debts of Africa's poorest nations. Although nobody doubts that corrupt and ineffective African governments bear much of the responsibility for their own countries' debt crises, various NGOs argue that it is unfair to make starving villagers and AIDS victims pay the cost.

Africa's debt has become a more trendy topic in recent years since the rock star Bono, of the famed Irish group U2, became Jubilee's most prominent spokesman. Like other famous music and film stars who have campaigned for political or social causes (such as Sting, who has been a highly visible advocate for human rights and the environment), he has given much wider visibility to what might otherwise have been an obscure issue. But unlike most celebrity advocates, Bono is also extremely knowledgeable about the nuances of the African debt issues and has been quite persuasive in his conversations with powerful political leaders who formulate Western debt policy toward the LDCs. Columbia University's Jeffrey Sacks, perhaps the most influential American economist analyzing debt issues, has joined with Bono in a series of visits to the finance ministers of the world's eight largest economic

---

poor nations to reduce their loan payments to the Bank if they agreed to channel those savings into education, health care, and other vital social services. As of 2004 the program had produced more than $31 billion in debt forgiveness. More recently, British Prime Minister Tony Blair championed debt relief, and in 2004 his government committed itself to cancelling $180 million annually in poor-country debt. And, changing its prior objections to debt cancellation, the Bush administration has come to support the idea of some relief. Interestingly, the United States' overthrow of the Saddam Hussein regime in Iraq had some effect here. Following the U.S. occupation, it cancelled its share of Iraqi debt and pressured other nations to do the same, arguing, in part, that the Iraqi people should not have to pay the debt of a corrupt dictator. Debt relief advocates argued that countries such as Congo (formerly Zaire) and Nigeria should get the same consideration.

Of course, some critics argue that a policy of debt cancellation could induce poor governments to take further loans with the expectation that they will not have to pay

powers, arguing for debt relief. And, indeed, at their 1999 summit in Cologne, Germany, the Group of Seven (G7)—the group of leaders from the world's major economies—promised to cancel up to $100 billion of Africa's $300 billion debt. Although the amount of subsequent relief fell well short of that total, Cologne still provided helpful debt relief. It is true that many other actors and factors beyond Bono and Jubilee 2000 influenced that decision, but the importance of star power should not be discounted.

© AP/Wide World Photos

ROCKING THE DEBT Irish Rock Star Bono has become perhaps the leading spokesperson for a campaign to convince Western governments to cancel the foreign debt of Africa's most impoverished nations. Here he is joined by Irish singer Bob Geldof and Italian singer Jovanotti at a news conference in Italy.

them back. At the same time, many supporters of debt relief argue that it is not enough. They note that developed nations give their own farmers $300 billion yearly in subsidies. As a consequence, they have a tremendous advantage when competing with Third World farmers in the international market.[27]

PROTECTING THE ENVIRONMENT

Worldwide concern for the environment has grown steadily since the birth of the ecology movement in the 1960s. In the United States, it has expressed itself through celebrations of Earth Day; the growth of Greenpeace, the Sierra Club, and other environmental groups; and a spate of congressional legislation designed to clean our air, water, and soil. In many Western European nations, environmentalists have become an

© AP/Wide World Photos

BURNING THE ENVIRONMENT   Each year, Indonesian farmers and plantation owners (like their counterparts in Brazil and elsewhere) burn vast areas of jungle or forest to clear land for farming. In the short run, this creates an unhealthy haze over part of Indonesia and neighboring Malaysia. In the long run, it contributes to global warming. Here Indonesian soldiers try to contain the fire.

electoral force. **Green Party** candidates, for example, have won seats in the European (EU) Parliament and in the national parliaments of several EU states.

Indeed, the German Green Party recently held the balance of power in the German parliament and had several cabinet posts as a junior partner in the Social Democratic–Green Party governing coalition. The ecology movement originally focused on domestic remedies such as the U.S. Clean Air Act, but environmentalists soon realized that many important ecological problems cross national borders and are amenable only to international solutions. For example, acid rain from the United States destroys Canadian forests. Industrial pollution on the Rhine River flows through Switzerland, France, Germany, and the Netherlands. The smoke and ash from fires intentionally set to clear jungle in Indonesia brings health problems to neighboring Malaysia and Singapore. Preserving the ozone layer, slowing global warming, and protecting endangered sea life are but a few of the environmental concerns that can be addressed only through international agreements.

Frequently, however, ecological concerns pit global needs against national sovereignty. For example, European and North American environmentalists are extremely concerned about the rapid decimation of the Third World's tropical rain forests. Possible consequences include depletion of the world's oxygen supply, intensification of global warming, destruction of endangered species, and loss of potential medical cures from jungle plants. But nations such as Brazil, Indonesia, and Malaysia view their forests as valuable sources of exportable hardwood timber,

ECONOMIC DEVELOPMENT AND ECOLOGICAL
CONCERNS

Like the United States and other industrialized nations, Third World countries face difficult trade-offs between economic needs and ecological considerations. Often, the poor recognize the dangers of industrial waste and other environmental hazards but must accept them to survive. In an impoverished village outside Bahia de Salvador, Brazil, villagers catch and eat fish containing dangerously high levels of mercury emitted from nearby industrial plants. Well aware that the mercury will eventually kill or paralyze many of them, they continue to fish. "What is better," asked one poor villager, "to die of starvation now or to die from the mercury later?" Like many U.S. politicians, Third World political leaders and bureaucrats often give the immediate needs of economic development precedence over long-term ecological concerns. When one of this text's authors questioned the environmental consequences of a Jamaican development project he was visiting, he received a frosty reply from a government economist: "You Americans raped your environment in order to become a wealthy industrialized nation," he said. "We Jamaicans insist on the right to do the same." Still, environmental movements have begun expanding in many Third World nations.

suitable locations for plantations and cattle ranches, and potential areas for resettlement of landless farmers.

Because they are desperate for foreign exchange—particularly when faced with huge external debts—these countries are usually reluctant to accept environmental regulations that would reduce their export capacity. With some justification, they complain that the industrialized nations now pointing an accusatory finger at the Third World have already depleted their own forests at an earlier stage of development and continue to be the major sources of air and water pollution (see Box 18-3). That argument highlights the fact that developing nations are not the only perpetrators of environmental destruction. By 1990, industrialized countries—with only 25 percent of the world's population—consumed 75 percent of its energy and 85 percent of its forest products. Industrialized nations also were responsible for 75 percent of global warming.[28] Since that time, the developed world's contribution to global warming has fallen to about 57 percent of the world's total, largely because China's emissions along with the rest of Asia's have grown dramatically.[29] So, even today, industrialized nations contribute far more to many types of ecological damage than do developing countries. Furthermore, the United States uses far more fossil fuel (primarily petroleum and coal) per capita and per dollar of GNP than do Western European nations and Japan.

Only in the last 30 to 35 years, as the magnitude of worldwide ecological damage has been recognized, have there been a growing number of international treaties aimed at preserving the environment. In 1997, during negotiation of the Kyoto Climate Change Protocol (an international agreement aimed at reducing global warming), the United States resisted European pressures for stronger emission restrictions. Eventually, a treaty emerged requiring signatories by 2010 to reduce to their 1990 levels emission of carbon dioxide and other greenhouse gases believed to contribute to global warming. But in 2001, shortly after enough nations had satisfied the Kyoto agreement to put it into effect, the Bush administration surprised and angered much of the international community by announcing that the United States would not abide by the treaty because it would limit American economic growth and because some scientists rejected a number of the treaty's assumptions. Some observers argue that had President Clinton received Senate approval for the treaty in 1997 (not a certainty), it might have been possible to meet the U.S. commitments by 2010. But, some argue, by not presenting the treaty to the Senate for three years and letting greenhouse emissions continue to climb, the Clinton administration had left office with the U.S. no longer able to meet the treaty's demands.[30] The United States also has long resisted clean-air regulations designed to reduce acid rain, despite strong pressure from Canada. In all of those cases, the United States has placed economic growth ahead of environmental safeguards, even when that decision has antagonized many of our allies. Similarly, Norway and Japan, nations with important fishing industries, have resisted international treaties designed to protect whales.

Throughout the world, environmental issues apply to what social scientists call "collective goods" and "the tragedy of the commons." A collective good is a good or service to which a community (including a community of nations) has free access, such as ocean fishing waters beyond national boundaries. The tragedy of the commons describes a "situation in which [actors] have an incentive to increase their consumption of a collective good even though their consumption will [eventually] significantly reduce either the quality or the supply of that good."[31] Thus, every country with an ocean coast has access to international fishing waters. For each vessel and each nation's fleet, their near-term interest lies in catching as much as they can (particularly poor fishermen who need the catch to provide for their families). In the long term, if everybody maximizes their catch, supplies of salmon, cod, and the like will be depleted. But, absent some enforceable international agreement, no boat or country will reduce its catch while its competitors do not. Similarly, although it is obviously in the collective interest of all nations to protect the world's ozone layer, its air, and its water, each nation seeks to maximize its own economic output (even at the expense of the collective good) while hoping that other nations make the necessary sacrifices.

There are some cases where a country's economic interests and environmental concerns can be reconciled. For example, environmental NGOs such as the World Wildlife Federation have arranged a number of "debt for nature swaps" in which they have purchased external debt notes of countries such as Ecuador and Bolivia at highly discounted prices.* Then they have canceled those debts in return for a commitment from the debtor government to protect an agreed-upon area of forest from exploitation. In countries such as Costa Rica, the rain forest and other environmentally threatened resources have been developed into an economic resource through "ecotourism." In most cases, however, international environmental efforts will have to reconcile trade-offs in two difficult areas. First, as we have seen, environmental protection will have to be weighed against pressures for economic growth; second, the sovereignty of independent nations will have to be balanced against the need for international cooperation.

---

* Since banks did not expect to recoup their loans, many sold debt notes (for as little as 10 percent of their face value) to purchasers who were willing to assume the risk. Thus, the World Wildlife Fund could have bought (and retired) $100 million of the Bolivian debt notes for as little as $10 million.

HUMAN RIGHTS

Even more than environmental issues, human rights concerns can raise fundamental conflicts between the emerging values of the global community and the sovereignty of individual states. Recent history has been replete with violations of human rights. Not long ago, the world recoiled in horror when the Khmer Rouge government murdered a million Cambodians and when Hutus massacred 500,000 Tutsi in Rwanda. Governments in Myanmar, Syria, Iran, China, Sudan, and Colombia, among others, at times imprison, torture, or kill members of the political opposition.

International NGOs monitoring human rights, such as Amnesty International and Human Rights Watch, have raised public consciousness of political repression. The media have brought some of these horrors into our living rooms, and celebrities such as Sting have popularized the global campaign for human rights. Although various governments, international agencies, and NGOs have different definitions of human rights and apply different standards, there is a growing consensus over the unacceptability of two fundamental types of violations: the execution, imprisonment, or torture of individuals because of their political beliefs, and repression based on race, religion, or ethnicity.

In formulating their foreign policies, some governments clearly are more strongly guided by human rights concerns than are others. Nations such as Sweden, Canada, and the Netherlands have been particularly outspoken. President Jimmy Carter first raised human rights to the forefront of U.S. foreign policy. Since the end of the cold war, the United States had been freed of its earlier dilemma—namely, what its policy should be toward countries such as South Korea, pre-revolutionary Iran, and El Salvador, which were important allies in the cold war but serious violators of human rights. In the past, U.S. foreign policy makers frequently turned a blind eye toward human rights abuses by our allies. Since the early 1990s, however, as the threat of communism has ended and democratic freedoms have advanced in much of the world, the U.S. commitment to defending human rights has strengthened. At the same time, however, many independent human rights groups have accused the United States of violating the rights of prisoners from the Afghan conflict being held at the U.S. base in Guantanamo Bay, Cuba.

Whatever their moral concerns, however, rarely have countries intervened individually or collectively in the internal affairs of even the worst human rights violators. There are several reasons for that reluctance. Sometimes, governments feel that intervention would have little effect. For example, many analysts felt that Western democracies could do little in the short run to reduce Chinese political repression in the wake of the 1989 Tiananmen Square massacre and argued that foreign pressure would actually be counterproductive. Leading human rights groups disagreed. In other instances, as we have noted, geopolitical considerations have led world powers to overlook human rights violations by their own allies.

Ultimately, however, a fundamental reason that foreign intervention on behalf of repressed victims is so rare is that it breaches a basic tenet of international law. The principle of nonintervention is "the most important embodiment of the modern idea that states should be treated as autonomous entities."[32] International organizations such as the United Nations or the Organization of American States (OAS) were created to deter international aggression, not domestic repression. Even when the United Nations determined that human rights violators in Bosnia should be brought to trial before the International Court of Justice in the Hague (the Netherlands), American and European peacekeeping troops were reluctant to arrest well-known Serbian war criminals for fear of upsetting Bosnia's fragile peace.

There have been recent indications of changing Western attitudes toward the balance between human rights concerns and respect for national sovereignty. These slowly shifting views may ultimately change international law. In 1998, when former Chilean dictator General Augusto Pinochet was in London for medical treatment, the Spanish government asked Britain to extradite him to Spain so that he could be put on trial for the murder of several Spanish citizens who were killed in Chile by Pinochet's security forces. Even though that request violated existing legal practices that protected a former government leader from prosecution by a foreign nation and even though the abuses had not taken place on Spanish or British soil, the British courts ultimately decided that Pinochet could have been turned over to the Spanish courts except that he was too old and allegedly no longer mentally competent to stand trial.

In a more far-reaching departure from the principle of sovereignty, a recent Belgian law allows that country to try accused human rights violators who enter Belgium even if neither they nor their victims are Belgian and the abuse did not take place on Belgian soil. Reacting to passage of that law, Israeli Prime Minister Ariel Sharon canceled a planned visit to Belgium lest he be arrested and charged with human rights crimes involving the massacre of Palestinian refugees in Lebanon.

Occasionally, individual nations and international organizations have also censured human rights violators by means short of direct intervention. For example, the United States, the British Commonwealth, the European Union, and much of the Third World invoked trade and cultural-exchange sanctions against South Africa in response to that nation's apartheid policies of racial segregation and repression. Some governments have curtailed foreign aid to pressure human rights violators. In the recent past, the United States has suspended military assistance to Uruguay, Chile, and Guatemala for that purpose. Currently, most Western countries have suspended aid to Myanmar for the same reason.

The end of the cold war seems to have elevated the importance of human rights concerns in international relations. Not only has democracy developed greater worldwide stature, but also Western powers have felt somewhat less compelled to placate Third World allies that violate human rights standards. With the spread of world terrorism, however, there has been some backsliding. Just as the U.S. often had been hesitant to criticize human rights violations in countries that were cold-war allies, so too the United States now seems prepared to overlook these violations in countries that are allies in the war against terror. Hence, countries such as Russia (whose war in Chechnya involves substantial rights violations), China, Pakistan, and Tajikistan have escaped censure.

Although many scholars and diplomats laud the growing world concern for human rights, the question of international enforcement remains controversial. Third World nations tend to fear that human rights issues could be used as a wedge for Western (or UN) intervention in their internal affairs. There is also the question of consistency. If international sanctions can legitimately be invoked to protect democratic rights in Myanmar or Kenya, should they not be used to protect Catholics in Northern Ireland or Native Americans in South Dakota? The international system has yet to settle on universal standards for answering such questions. What we can say, however, is that, in the post–cold-war world, Western nations and key international organizations seem more inclined to incorporate human rights criteria in formulating their foreign policies.

WOMEN'S RIGHTS: A PRESSING HUMAN RIGHTS ISSUE

Statistics and case studies make it clear that in many nations, particularly in the developing world, women have fewer career opportunities, suffer a disproportionate share of the poverty, enjoy fewer political rights or political power, and are more often the victims of exploitation than are men. As with many of the issues discussed in the chapter, there is controversy as to which of these problems are the proper subject of international action. For example, religious custom may mandate the veiling of women or, in some countries, deny them certain opportunities such as the right to drive a car. Elsewhere, local custom may permit or encourage practices such as arranged marriages, child brides, or educational limitations for girls and women. Unfair as such practices may seem, they are generally protected by national sovereignty. There is no international compact, for example, that would force Saudi Arabia to let women vote or drive or that would end bridal dowries in India. But, international concern has grown in recent decades over acts of violence and brutality routinely inflicted on women in various nations.

For many years human rights groups primarily focused on assisting "prisoners of conscience," people who had been imprisoned and often tortured or executed on the basis of their political or religious beliefs. In time, rights activists increasingly examined genocide and other massive abuses perpetrated by governments against particular ethnic groups or religions. With the rise of the women's rights movement, greater attention has been paid to systematic violations of women's rights such as their exclusion from the political system, forced marriages, systematic brutality by husbands against their wives, forced prostitution and the international sex trade, and forced female circumcision. Added together, these violations surely make women the largest group of victims of rights abuses.

Women's rights issues began to get serious international attention in the 1970s, prompted primarily by the growth of the feminist or women's rights groups in the western industrialized nations. Declaring 1975 to be International Women's Year, the United Nations staged the first UN conference on the status of women in Mexico City, with 133 member states attending. After that, three more UN-sponsored World Conferences on Women were held at five-year intervals, each of them designed to develop strategies and approaches to improve the status of women worldwide. At the same time, the UN has worked closely with NGOs engaged in such activities as combating violence against women and reducing female poverty.

Worldwide, forced labor generates about $31 billion annually, half of that earned in the United States and Europe. Much of that total (especially money generated in the West) comes from the involuntary sexual exploitation of women (forced prostitution). A substantial portion of the women involved are drawn from Eastern Europe and the developing world. By one recent estimate, more than 700,000 women and children are trafficked *out of* those regions (with far more forced into prostitution or other forms of forced labor *within* those areas). By another estimate, two million women and children are sold into the sex trade annually (the total within and across national borders). In India alone, an estimated total of 200,000 girls from Nepal, many under the age of 14, work as sex slaves.[33] In 2000 the U.S. Congress passed the Victims of Trafficking and Violence Protection Act, which enhanced the capacity of women victims to bring suit or testify against international traffickers by allowing them to stay in the U.S. temporarily or longer and offering them legal assistance. Since 1996, the European Union has also taken measures, involving its members and cooperating with the U.S. and other nations, to combat human trafficking. But, such efforts have failed to make a serious dent in this trade, as many Third World governments have not been responsive to the problem and developed nations have not given the issue the priority it deserves.

Other instances of widespread violations of women's human rights are equally disturbing. In some countries, most notably Pakistan, many women become the victims of "crimes of honor." Women who are accused of having either premarital or extramarital sex are considered to have brought dishonor on their family. At the very least, they may be banished. In many cases they are executed, often by their father or brother. Pakistani civil and religious courts treat these crimes very differently from other homicides. Perpetrators are given a much lighter sentence or, in most cases, go unpunished. Of the several thousand "honor" murders committed in Pakistan each year, only about 10 percent are even brought to trial. In hundreds, if not thousands, of cases each year, **honor killings** are covered up as "kitchen accidents" after the woman has been set on fire.

Many women are also killed by their families for rejecting an arranged marriage or seeking a divorce. Even more shockingly, husbands, fathers, or brothers often execute women who have been raped with the justification that the victim has brought dishonor on her family. In other cases, women have been killed merely because their relative suspected them of having an unacceptable relationship with a man. In one Pakistani village two brothers killed a man whom they had forbidden to walk past their house and talk with their sister. Then they killed the sister. As one human rights worker told Amnesty International, "the distinction between a woman being guilty and a woman being alleged to be guilty of illicit sex is irrelevant. What impacts on the man's honor is the public perception, the belief in her infidelity. It is this which blackens honor and for which she is killed . . . It is not the truth that honor is what it's about, but public perception of honor."[34]

INTERNATIONAL TERRORISM

The use of terrorism as a political tactic is not new. During the nineteenth century, for example, anarchist revolutionaries in Russia, Italy, Spain, and other parts of Europe and Latin America carried out assassinations and bombings for the purpose of destroying organized government and capitalism in order to create a new political and economic order. But the September 11 attacks on the World Trade Center and the Pentagon created death and destruction in the heart of American society on a scale never previously seen. Suddenly, the United States seemed vulnerable despite its vast military and economic power.

Although 9/11 was the most dramatic and horrendous attack of its kind, it was not the first terrorist action against the United States undertaken by an Islamic fundamentalist group. Al-Qaeda terrorists had previously bombed U.S. military housing in Saudi Arabia in 1996, American embassies in East Africa in 1998, and the navy ship *USS Cole* off the coast of Aden in 2000. Since September 11, terrorist bombings apparently linked to al-Qaeda killed almost 200 tourists in a Bali (Indonesia) night club, killed a similar number and wounded more than 1,000 people in bombings of several Madrid commuter trains in 2004, and killed 56 while wounding some 700 passengers on London subway trains and a bus in 2005. In Iraq, thousands of people have died since the fall of the Saddam Hussein regime as a result of terrorist activity.[35] At the same time, it is important to realize that terrorist activity long predates today's radical Islamist groups and that in recent times there have been many non-Islamic terrorist groups ranging from the Irish Republican Army to paramilitary organizations in Colombia.

Despite its growing frequency, however, there is still not total agreement as to what constitutes terrorist activity. Some analysts have questioned why only violence perpetrated by nongovernmental actors is considered terrorism. Why, they ask, are Palestinian suicide bombings and the Bali assault called terrorist acts whereas Russia's intentional bombing of Chechen civilians, Israel's retaliations against Palestinian civilians, and the Guatemalan army's massacre of more than 100,000 Indian villagers are not similarly labeled? Another debate pits those who support the causes of alleged terrorists against those who oppose them. As more than one observer has noted, "Your terrorist is my freedom fighter." Many Catholic Irish Americans took that position when they contributed substantial funds to the Irish Republican Army (the IRA), who were seen as heroes by some and terrorists by others.

The U.S. Department of Defense defines terrorism as follows: "The calculated use of violence or the threat of violence to inculcate fear; intended to coerce or to intimidate governments or societies in the pursuit of goals that are generally political, religious, or ideological."[36] For our purposes, we will further define a terrorist act as an act of violence carried out by nongovernmental actors against civilians or against soldiers who are not engaged in acts of war. This doesn't suggest that the intentional killing of civilians by the military (as in Chechnya, Guatemala, or Sudan) is any less immoral or reprehensible than bombings by terrorists. It simply indicates that the latter atrocities need another name such as the term "state terrorism." Ironically, the great expansion toward globalization in recent decades has unwittingly contributed to the surge in international terrorism. The spread of capitalism, Western values, and Western culture—encompassing democracy, McDonald's, and R-rated Hollywood movies, among many other things— have led many in the Third World, most notably Islamic fundamentalists, to feel that they are being engulfed, enslaved, and spiritually polluted by westernization. Living in societies that have little military power and limited international influence, some of these people see terrorism as their only means of defending themselves and preserving their religious and ideological values.

So, precisely at a time when wars between nations are becoming less common, and war between major military powers is almost unimaginable, terror has become perhaps the leading cause of uncertainty in international relations. Precisely because terrorist groups such as al-Qaeda live in the shadows and cannot be targeted the way Iraq, Afghanistan, or other nations could be, and because one never knows where, when, or in what form the next attack will take place, terrorists arouse particularly acute fears. In 2006, for example, Britain unearthed plans by Islamic terrorists to blow up as many as ten transatlantic passenger planes using liquid explosives.

They are also dangerous because of their capacity to create havoc with very limited resources. The only weapons held by the men who killed more than three thousand people on September 11 were box cutters. And although the Bush administration has revived plans for building a "star wars" missile defense system, many experts believe that the greatest threat of nuclear attack comes not from missiles but from a terrorist's backpack (see Box 18-4). It is a threat that is not likely to go away for many years to come.

Box 18-4

WAR IN IRAQ AND THE WAR ON TERRORISM

Both President Bush and leading administration figures such as Secretary of Defense Donald Rumsfeld have frequently depicted the war in Iraq (begun March 29, 2003) as part of the international war on terrorism. The strongest and most controversial claim of a link between Iraq's Saddam Hussein and international terrorism was Vice President Richard Cheney's assertion that the leader of the September 11 attack on the United States had met five months earlier in Prague (Czech Republic) with senior Iraqi intelligence officials and that there might be a link between Saddam and the 9/11 attack.[37] While President Bush distanced himself from that claim, he and other administration officials insisted that there was "a relationship" between Saddam's government and al-Qaeda, links that helped justify military action against Iraq. Administration supporters drew on CIA and other intelligence to insist that there was clear evidence of Iraqi logistic, financial, and intelligence support for al-Qaeda.[38]

Critics of that assertion argue that, while there may have been some contacts between al-Qaeda and the Iraqi regime, any "relationship" was minor and inconsequential. For one thing, they said that it was unlikely that a secular ruler, Saddam, and a fundamentalist leader, Osama bin Laden, would form an alliance, especially

since al-Qaeda had backed a fundamentalist revolt against Saddam several years previously. In mid-2004, well after the U.S. invaded Iraq, the bipartisan "September 11 commission" (officially the National Commission on Terrorist Attacks Upon the United States), which had been appointed by President Bush to investigate the 9/11 attacks, stated that its review of relevant intelligence data had disclosed limited communications between the Iraqi government and al-Qaeda, but no evidence of a "collaborative relationship." When questioned by a *Washington Post* reporter, a "senior FBI official and a senior CIA analyst concurred with the [commission's] finding." One year earlier, an official British Intelligence report, which had been leaked to BBC news, had reached the same conclusions.[39]

Both the U.S. and British governments continue to stand by their earlier assertions of such collaboration. Since there undoubtedly was some evidence of contacts between Saddam Hussein's government and international terrorist groups such as al-Qaeda, the debate revolves around two issues: first, the accuracy of relevant intelligence data (for example, the September 11 Commission staff concluded that the alleged meeting in Prague between Iraqi intelligence officers and a future 9/11 terrorist never happened); second, whether any

---

THE CHANGING FACE OF INTERNATIONAL RELATIONS

Important new political phenomena are often difficult to predict. Nowhere is it more difficult than in the area of international relations, where so many unaccountable actors and factors are at play. The end of the cold war was scarcely anticipated five years before it happened. Few could have predicted how the events of September 11, 2001, would change the nature of world politics and even international finance. Today, as U.S. and allied forces face an uncertain future in Iraq, as scientists warn of a possible worldwide pandemic from Asia-born avian flu killing millions of people, we don't know what other major developments may take place in the next five to ten years. Similarly, settlements of struggles such as the Arab-Israeli conflict, which seemed within reach not long ago, now seems increasingly remote in the wake of the Israeli invasion of Lebanon.

Some trends seem likely, however. While there seems almost no likelihood of a new arms race between world powers, nuclear proliferation will remain an ongoing danger. Should democracy take root in Russia, Eastern Europe, and such nations as South Korea and Taiwan, it would bode well for the prospects for world peace. Until

contacts that might have been made led to any meaningful cooperation (i.e., is there any evidence of cooperation beyond the fact that an al-Qaeda official and an Iraqi official had coffee together at a restaurant?).[40]

Of course, following the overthrow of Saddam Hussein's regime, even if Iraq's government ever did aid terrorist organizations, it obviously no longer does. Yet, in a June 28, 2005, address to the nation, President Bush insisted "Our mission in Iraq is clear. We're hunting down the terrorists. We're helping Iraqis build a free nation that is an ally in the war on terror."[41] This argument has three components: first, that the enormous number of suicide bombings in Iraq coming from al-Qaeda and other terrorist groups means that Iraq has become a magnet for terrorists from other nations, who can then be attacked by the U.S. and Iraqi armies (like drawing moths to a flame); second, that both the U.S. and al-Qaeda (from whose ranks many, though not all, of the terrorists emerge) have placed their prestige on the line in Iraq and if we defeat terrorism there it will be a major blow to international terrorism, just as failure to establish a stable, democratic Iraq would be a blow to the United States; finally, that if a stable, democratic government is established in Iraq, not only will terrorism decline there, but the democratic example would spread to other Middle Eastern nations, with a corresponding drop in terrorism.

Critics of those arguments counter with the following assertions. First, while the war has drawn many terrorists to Iraq, there is no evidence that the supply of suicide bombers is dwindling (to the contrary, attacks have increased). More important, they argue that the war has also mobilized many new converts to Islamic fundamentalism and terrorist movements throughout the Muslim world. They note, for example, that support for terrorism has apparently been growing among young Muslims living in Europe (and perhaps elsewhere) and that since the start of the war, such militants have committed major terrorist attacks on Madrid and London. Second, they contend that, even if terrorism were defeated in Iraq, there is little reason to believe that this would diminish terrorism elsewhere. Martyrdom, of course, is a major aspect of militant Islamic fundamentalist movements (witness the heroic status granted suicide bombers in Israel) and some contend that when Muslim fundamentalist movements have been beaten back militarily (as in Israel and the Russian war in Chechnya) it has only led to an increase in terrorism. Finally, while most opponents of the Iraq war share the Bush administration's desire for a stable democracy in Iraq, they point to the ongoing ethnic conflict there and the high level of Sunni opposition to the new constitution as evidence that this is unlikely to happen in the foreseeable future.

now, at least, democratic nations have never waged war against one another (or virtually never, depending on how one defines democracies).[42]

Small wars will continue to rage in the Third World. Some conflicts—such as Middle East hostilities or ethnic violence in Africa—seem more intractable than even pessimists had imagined. Future competition among the world's major powers, however, seems likely to be primarily economic, rather than military or ideological. That conflict will pit the United States against Japan and the European Union, with newly industrialized countries such as South Korea, Taiwan, Mexico, and Brazil likely to play important secondary roles. Third World poverty, protection of the environment, ethnic conflict, and human rights are likely to demand increasing attention. Solutions to those problems will be extremely difficult to achieve and may require new levels of international cooperation.

 WHERE ON THE WEB?

http://www.terrorismanswers.com/havens/afghanistan.html
Council on Foreign Relations: information on terrorist history in Afghanistan.

http://www.academicinfo.net/terrorism.html
Links to a wide variety of scholarly articles, papers, and other online resources on terrorism.

http://www1.worldbank.org/economicpolicy/globalization/

The World Bank presents an optimistic picture of the benefits of globalization.

http://www.ifg.org/

Web site for the International Forum on Globalization, a research institute critical of the negative effects of globalization.

http://www.hri.ca/

Human Rights Internet—A human rights gateway.

http://www.hrweb.org/

History of the human rights movement and links to leading human rights groups.

http://europa.eu.int/

The European Union (EU) online.

◆ ◆ ◆

Key Terms and Concepts_____

debt crisis
European Union (EU)
free trade
globalization
Green Party
honor killings
newly industrialized countries
  (NICs)
new world order (NWO)

nongovernmental organizations
  (NGOs)
North Atlantic Treaty
  Organization (NATO)
North–South relations
nuclear proliferation
transnational corporations
  (TNCs)

Discussion Questions_____

1. How has the prospect of nuclear war decreased in some respects since the end of the cold war, and how in other respects has the prospect of nuclear conflict increased?
2. In what ways has protection of the environment become an international issue? Why must solutions to some environmental problems transcend national boundaries?
3. What are the principal arguments in favor of substantial external debt cancellations for the poorest developing nations? What are some arguments against cancellation?
4. Discuss how international efforts to protect human rights (including the prosecution of leaders who violate those rights) may come into conflict with the doctrine of national sovereignty. In what ways has the international community begun to change the balance between human rights principles and principles of national sovereignty?
5. Discuss some of the difficulties and complications of defining what constitutes an act of terrorism.
6. In what ways are Third World women particularly victimized by human rights abuses and, therefore, in need of special protection?
7. Why did French and Dutch voters recently reject a proposed new EU constitution? What did those votes suggest about the future of economic and political unions between allied states?

Notes_____

1. For a picture of how each nation saw the world during the cold war, see Walter S. Jones, *The Logic of International Relations* (New York: Harper Collins, 1991).

2. Urie Bronfenbrenner, "The Mirror Image in Soviet-American Relations," in *Analyzing International Relations*, ed. William Coplin and Charles Kegley, Jr. (New York: Praeger, 1975), pp. 161–166.

3. Y. Katasonov, "Socio-Economic Factors of the Arms Race," *International Affairs* (January 1985): 47.

4. The concept of containment was first developed by diplomat George Kennan writing under a pseudonym. See "X," "The Sources of Soviet Conduct," *Foreign Affairs* (July 1947): 566–582. Later, Kennan charged that foreign policy makers had misinterpreted his arguments.

5. See *Transition to Democracy in Eastern Europe and Russia: The Impact on Politics, the Economy and Culture*, ed. Barbara Wejnert (Westport, CT: Praeger, 2002).

6. Bruce Russett and James Sutterlin, "The U.N. in a New World Order," *Foreign Affairs* (Spring 1991): 69.

7. John Lewis Gaddis, "Toward the Post–Cold War World," *Foreign Affairs* (Spring 1991): 111.

8. James Schlesinger, "New Instabilities, New Priorities," *Foreign Policy* (Winter 1991–1992): 4.

9. Gaddis, "Toward the Post–Cold War World."

10. James Lee Ray, *Global Politics* (Boston: Houghton Mifflin, 1990), p. 375; see also Marshall Shulman, "The Superpowers: Dance of the Dinosaurs," *Foreign Affairs* (Winter 1987–1988).

11. Wikipedia, "Nuclear Non-Proliferation Treaty," Web site visited August 39, 2005, http://en.wikipedia.org/wiki/Nuclear_Non-Proliferation_Treaty.

12. Robert Norris and Hans Kristensen, "North Korea's Nuclear Program, 2005," *Bulletin of the Atomic Scientists* (May/June 2005): 64–67.

13. John T. Rourke, *International Politics on the World Stage* (New York: McGraw-Hill—Dushkin, 2002), p. 42.

14. James Barber, *Jihad vs. McWorld: How Globalism and Tribalism are Reshaping the World* (New York: Ballantine, 1996), p. 4.

15. Summary of United Nations, *World Economic Situation and Prospects 2004*, http://www.un.org/esa/policy/wess/wespp2004pressrelease.pdf.

16. Jack Finlayson and Mark Zacher, "The GATT and the Regulation of Trade Barriers: Regime Dynamics and Functions," *International Organization* (Autumn 1981): 561–602.

17. World Trade Organization Web page; available at http://www.wto.org.

18. Gary Gereffi, "Rethinking Development Theory: Insights from East Asia and Latin America," *Sociological Forum* (Fall 1989).

19. Geoffrey Garrett, R. Daniel Kelemen, and Heiner Schultz, "The European Court of Justice, National Governments, and Legal Integration in the European Union," *International Organization* 52 (1998): 149–176.

20. "French Referendum on the European Constitution," Wikipedia, en.wikipedia.org, visited August 28, 2005; "Dutch Reject EU Constitution," CNN Web site, June 1, 2005, www.cnn.com/2005/WORLD/europe/06/01/dutch.poll/.

21. Robert Pastor, *Integration with Mexico* (New York: Twentieth Century Fund Press, 1993), pp. 14–15, 42–50.

22. For an early summary of the debt crisis and its consequences, see Howard Handelman, "Consequences of Economic Austerity: Latin America and the Less Developed World," *Britannica Book of the Year: 1990* (Chicago: Encyclopaedia Britannica, 1990), pp. 192–193.

23. World Bank data quoted in http://www.globalissues.org/Trade Related/Debt/Scale.asp.

24. United Nations Development Program, *Human Development Report 1999* (New York: UNDP and Oxford University Press, 1999), pp. 136–137.

25. Nikoi Kote-Nikoi, *Beyond the New Orthodoxy* (Brookfield, VT: Avebury, 1996), p. 15.

26. Bill Turnbull, *The African Debt Situation*; available at http://www.thewhitefathers.org.uk/302dt.html.

27. "Can Africa Get Out of Debt," *Time Europe* Web site (October 3, 2004), www.time.com/time/europe/magazine/; "Debt Forgiveness Gathers Steam," *Christian Science Monitor* (September 30, 2004).

28. "Women, Population and the Environment," in *Great Decisions: 1991* (New York: Foreign Policy Association, 1991), p. 65.

29. International Energy Agency, *World Energy Outlook 2002.*

30. Thomas C. Schelling, "What Makes Greenhouse Sense," in *International Politics*, ed. Robert J. Art and Robert Jervis (New York: Pearson Longman, 2005), p. 542.

31. Alan Lamborn and Joseph Lepgold, *World Politics in the Twentieth Century* (Upper Saddle River, NJ: Prentice Hall, 2003), p. 418.

32. Charles Beitz, *Political Theory and International Relations* (Princeton, NJ: Princeton University Press, 1979), p. 71; quoted in Ray, *Global Politics*, p. 497.

33. "Sex trade's reliance on forced labour," BBC News (May 12, 2005), http://news.bbc.co.uk/2/hi/business/4532617.stm: Jan Jindy Pettman, "Gender Issues," in *The Globalization of World Politics*, 3rd ed., ed. Jon Baylis and Steve Smith (New York: Oxford University Press, 2005), p. 678; "Sex Slavery: The Growing Trade," CNN archive Web site (March 8, 2001).

34. "Pakistan: Cost of a Lie," in *Le Monde Diplomatique*, English version, May 2001, http://mondediplo.com/2001/05/13pakistan.

35. However, more Iraqis corrently die from sectarian violence (Shi'ia versus Sunni) than from terrorist bombings.

36. Available at http://www.terrorism.com/terrorism/bpart1.html.

37. Vice President Cheney on "Meet the Press" (September 14, 2003); "Iraq, 9/11 Still Linked by Cheney," *Washington Post* (September 29, 2003).

38. Stephen Hayes, "Case Closed," *The Weekly Standard* (November 24, 2003).

39. "Al Qaeda-Hussein Link Is Dismissed," *Washington Post* (June 17, 2004); "Leaked Report Rejects Iraqi al-Qaeda Link," BBC News (February 5, 2003), news.bbc.co.uk.

40. "Iraq, Al Qaeda, and What Constitutes a Relationship, *Christian Science Monitor* (June 22, 2004).

41. Presidential Address (June 28, 2005), "Iraq, War on Terror." The White House Web site.

42. Jack S. Levy, "Domestic Politics and War," *Journal of Interdisciplinary History* 18, no. 4 (Spring 1988): 653–673. Some scholars challenge these findings.

For Further Reading _____

Art, Robert J., and Robert Jervis, eds. *International Politics: Enduring Concepts and Contemporary Issues.* 7th ed. New York: Longman Pearson, 2005.

Baylis, John, and Steve Smith, eds. *The Globalization of World Politics: An Introduction to International Relations*, 3rd ed. New York: Oxford University Press, 2005.

Enloe, Cynthia. *Bananas, Bases and Beaches: Making Feminist Sense of International Politics.* Berkeley: University of California Press, 2000.

Ignatief, Michael. *Human Rights as Politics and Idolatry* . Princeton, NJ: Princeton University Press, 2003.

Kunibert, Raffer, and H. W. Singer, eds. *The Economic North–South Divide: Six Decades of Unequal Development.* Cheltenham, UK, and Northampton, MA: Edward Elgar, 2001.

Nacos, Brigitte L. *Terrorism and Counterterrorism: Understanding Threats and Responses in the Post-9/11 World.* New York: Penguin Academics, 2006.

Neack, Laura. *The New Foreign Policy: U.S. and Comparative Foreign Policy in the 21st Century.* Lanham, MD: Rowman & Littlefield, 2003.

Nye, Joseph S. *The Paradox of American Power: Why the World's Only Superpower Can't Go It Alone.* New York: Oxford University Press, 2002.

Rifkin, Jeremy. *Biosphere Politics.* New York: HarperCollins, 1992.

Welch, Claude E., Jr., ed. *NGOs and Human Rights: Promise and Performance.* Philadelphia: University of Pennsylvania Press, 2001.

World Bank. *Globalization, Growth, and Poverty: Building an Inclusive World Economy.* New York: Oxford University Press, 2002.

PART VI

EPILOGUE

Politics is inherently difficult to predict and impossible to predict completely. Chapter 19 analyzes a number of issues, discussed earlier in the text, that are likely to be of ongoing importance in the coming decades. These include international terrorism, the worldwide spread of democracy, women's growing role in politics, and ethnic conflict. Many of these issues—be they the trade-off between civil liberties and the war on terrorism or the proper balance between economic growth (so badly needed in the developing world) and environmental protection—raise fundamental questions first discussed in the preceding chapters of the text.

This final chapter also reiterates the text's insistence that so many of the vital decisions and issues affecting all of our lives are either political in nature or are, at least, influenced by political factors.

© EMPICS /Landov

19

POLITICAL PROSPECTS AND CHALLENGES AT THE BEGINNING OF THE TWENTY-FIRST CENTURY

◆ International Terrorism ◆ Economic Globalization
◆ The Spread of Democracy ◆ The Global Environment
◆ Women and Politics ◆ Nationalism and Ethnic Conflict
◆ Information Technology and the Mass Media

Our review of political science and political events in this text suggests that some political issues are ongoing, sometimes dating back to the time of ancient Athens, while specific political events are ever-changing and often difficult to anticipate. As the twenty-first century began, some eternal debates and questions continued: What is the proper role of government? What role, if any, should government play in stimulating economic growth or reducing societal inequalities? What should be the relationship between religion and government? These are but a few of the questions that generate political debate and conflict across national boundaries and across time.

At the same time, however, specific political developments or trends, even those of monumental proportions, continually surprise us. Changes in the political world continue to challenge both the skills of politicians and the analytical abilities of political scientists. Major world events—such as the collapse of Soviet-bloc communism, the astonishing growth of the Chinese economy (unexpectedly based primarily in capitalism), the rise of global terrorism, and the extensive spread of democratic government worldwide—are all paradigm-changing developments that were not anticipated by most political scientists, journalists, or government analysts a decade earlier or even less.

In other parts of the world, hopeful signs of peaceful progress are mixed with daunting roadblocks. The conflict in the Middle East took a dramatic and deadly turn after the Israeli and Palestinian negotiators failed to reach a peaceful settlement in the summer of 2000. The emergence of more moderate Palestinian leadership—following the 2004 death of Yasser Arafat—and Israel's 2005 unilateral withdrawal from Gaza improved the prospect for peace, but it is still unclear what will be the long-term effects of the victory by the hard-line party, Hamas, in the recent Palestinian elections, or whether Israel is willing to give an incipient Palestinian state a sufficient portion of the West Bank to make that state viable. After a period of greatly heightened tensions between India and Pakistan (over the disputed region of Kashmir), those countries have begun a cautious detente, but a solution of the Kashmir problem remains elusive and extremists from either country certainly could derail the process. North Korea's October 2002 announcement that it had nuclear weapons, and was pursuing a program to construct more of them, substantially raised the stakes for diplomacy in that part of the world. Iran's recent decision to resume nuclear power development without international monitors raises some dangerous prospects in that region.

In the United States, the 9/11 tragedy and President Bush's resolute response helped heighten his popularity and propelled him to reelection in 2004. Since that time, however, public concern and dissatisfaction over the war in Iraq (and, to a lesser extent, over the federal government's response to hurricane Katrina's devastation) caused the president's approval ratings to decline in late 2005 and fueled a growing sense of malaise among many Americans. Those and many other incidents and events provide ample evidence that we are in a period of fundamental political change. And as we move further into the new century, we find that many of the problems that people face not only have become more serious but also have become more directly perceived as *political* problems.

It is thus increasingly important to understand politics and government. At the same time, current events call into question some of the accumulated knowledge of political science. In this concluding chapter, we briefly examine a number of the critical political transformations that are now unfolding in the world and that will have significant consequences as we move further into the twenty-first century. Many of these developments raise fundamental political debates over long-standing issues previously discussed in this book.

INTERNATIONAL TERRORISM

The terrorist attacks of September 11, 2001, produced a substantial restructuring of international affairs. The subsequent War on Terrorism brought the United States into a more prominent role in international affairs as it extended or strengthened its military presence in new areas, most prominently in its invasions of Afghanistan and Iraq. To be sure, there have been no terrorist attacks on the U.S. since 2001 (at least up to the time this chapter was written). But the wave of suicide bombings in Iraq, periodic suicide bombings in Israel and, especially, the bloody bombings on several Madrid commuter trains (2004) and on London subway trains and a London city bus (2005) have kept the threat of terrorism very much on the front burner (see Box 19-1).

Much as U.S. foreign policy from the late 1940s through the late 1980s was directed through the prism of the cold war with Soviet communism, so too has U.S. foreign policy since 9/11 been built substantially around the war on terrorism. Just as Third World nations were judged during the cold war by how susceptible they were to communist insurgency (Vietnam) or, conversely by how much they supported America's cold war efforts (South Korea), today countries are judged by how vulnerable they are to terrorist attacks (Saudi Arabia, Indonesia) or by how much they support Washington's war on terrorism (Pakistan, Kazakhstan, Romania).

While most sovereign states subscribe, in one form or another, to the U.S. goal of fighting international terrorism, particular aspects of that policy have sometimes not been well received, including by our European allies. Thus, for example, European public opinion, even in Britain, the United States' staunchest ally, is overwhelmingly opposed to the U.S. military efforts in Iraq. At the start of that war, Germany's and, especially, France's refusal to join the military alliance that invaded Iraq caused considerable tensions with the United States. More recently, the influential human rights monitor, Human Rights Watch, has alleged that CIA aircraft made stops in European airports (in locations including Britain, Sweden, Spain, and Ireland) on their way to deliver terrorism suspects to secret overseas jails (in Afghanistan, Thailand, and several Eastern European countries) where they could be tortured. While such charges have not been proven to date (the U.S. government has refused to confirm or deny them), they have eroded relations with Western Europe and provoked numerous condemnations from that region's political leaders and mass media. The European Council (of the EU) has launched an investigation and warned that if it can be determined that Romania has housed such prisons, as alleged, its application for European Union membership will be denied.[1] Britain and Australia have complained to the United States about a number of their citizens who have been held without charges in the U.S. military base in Guantanamo Bay (Cuba). At the same time, in a break with tradition, a high-ranking International Red Cross official condemned conditions for prisoners (terrorism suspects) at that base.[2]

The war on terrorism has also raised concerns in the U.S. Members of civil liberties groups and many citizens are disturbed by alleged violations of due process in the handling of suspected terrorists or supporters at Guantanamo and elsewhere. Critics warn

Box 19-1

Terror Escalates in Western Europe: Madrid and London

Terrorism has been no stranger to Western Europe, as a wide variety of radical groups have emerged since the 1970s. Spain's ETA, Italy's Red Brigade, Germany's Red Army Faction (Baader Meinhoff Gang), and a number of small, right-wing hate groups, to name but a few, engaged in kidnappings, murders, assassinations, and bombings, particularly during the 1970s and 1980s. The Irish Republican Army (IRA) used terrorist violence in Northern Ireland and England as part of their efforts to reunify the north with the Republic of Ireland. And militants of the PKK (the leading Kurdish separatist party and military group) periodically assassinated Turkish diplomats in Europe and kidnapped European tourists in Turkey. Some of these groups were moved by visions of a Marxist revolution. Others acted in the name of ethnic separatism. Occasionally there also were instances of state-sponsored terrorism, as in 1988, when agents of the Libyan government blew up Pan Am Flight 103 over Lockerbie, Scotland, killing 270 people.

During the 1990s, there were hopeful signs that terrorism in the region might decline. With the collapse of Soviet communism and the capture of key European terrorist leaders, Marxist revolutionary groups such as the Red Brigade, Baader Meinhoff, and Greece's November 17 were decimated. A 1998 cease-fire called by the Basque separatist group, ETA, though short-lived, reduced the subsequent level of terrorist activity in Spain. But the rise of al-Qaeda and other Islamic extremist groups in the 1990s brought a new terrorist threat, one magnified by the region's large Muslim population. Today, the 15–20 million native-born and immigrant Muslims residing in Western Europe constitute more than 5 percent of its total population, rising to 10 percent in France and 7 percent in Holland.

On March 11, 2004, Islamic extremists (apparently linked to al-Qaeda) detonated 10 coordinated bombs on four crowded commuter trains in Madrid, Spain, killing 192 people and wounding about 2,000 others. The attack traumatized Spaniards, and two days later more than 10 million people (about one-fourth of the nation's population) demonstrated against terrorism in cities throughout the country. In Madrid itself, some two million people, marching in the rain, expressed their grief with chants such as "It's not raining, Madrid is crying."

Sixteen months later, on July 7, 2005, radical, Islamic suicide bombers simultaneously set off bombs in three trains in the London underground (subway). An hour later, a fourth bomber detonated a bomb on a double-decker bus. In all, 52 people were killed beyond the bombers themselves, and another 700 or so were wounded. Like the Madrid bombings, these attacks took place during the morning rush hour, a time designed to maximize fatalities and injuries. Two weeks later, four would-be suicide bombers again attempted

---

that actions taken in this emergency setting may set precedents that will undermine basic rights and freedoms in more "normal" times. For example, a report by the Reporters' Committee for Freedom of the Press claimed that more than one thousand non–U.S. citizens had been secretly imprisoned on immigration charges, that the Pentagon had disregarded a 1992 agreement that had allowed open press coverage of combat situations, and that there was a danger that military tribunals could replace more open trials of people accused of terrorism.[3] And, at the close of 2005, a leaked government document revealed that President Bush, in the war on terrorism, had authorized hundreds or perhaps even thousands of wiretaps on phones and e-mail communications in the U.S. without court authorization. Although some of these allegations are unproven and controversial, they suggest that the U.S. government response to international terrorism is increasingly becoming an issue in both international and domestic politics as they provoke a serious debate over the correct balance between national security and civil liberties. For example, President Bush claimed that Congress's authorization of the war on terror had given him legal authority to conduct the wiretaps. Many senators, including some Republicans, disagreed.

to set off bombs in London underground trains and a public bus. This time, miraculously, in all four cases only the bomb detonators exploded (causing no damage), not the bombs themselves. While nobody was hurt in the second round of attacks (the would-be bombers fled, but were later apprehended), they put Londoners further on edge and increased anxieties throughout Western Europe.

Although similar in many respects, the Madrid and London terrorist assaults had different political impacts. The bombings in Madrid came but three days before national parliamentary elections. Initially, the Spanish government of conservative Prime Minister José María Aznar blamed the attacks on ETA, the Basque separatist group, despite evidence to the contrary. It is widely believed that his government did not admit that the likely perpetrators were Islamic terrorists because that would confirm the fears of many Spanish voters that the country had exposed itself to the threat of terrorism when it sent troops to join the U.S.-led coalition in Iraq. Very shortly, however, the government had to admit that it was an Islamic, not an ETA, attack. Voter reaction to the government's apparent deception and the electorate's overwhelming desire to pull Spanish troops out of Iraq enabled the Spanish Socialist Workers' Party—which had trailed in opinion polls prior to the train bombing—to win the national elections. Soon afterwards, the new socialist prime minister, José Luis Rodríguez Zapatero, ordered the withdrawal of Spanish troops from Iraq.

In Britain, the political effects of the London bombings were quite different. Although there had been growing public opposition to the Iraq war, especially within Prime Minister Tony Blair's own political party, antiwar sentiment was not as intense as in Spain. More significantly, the London attacks took place only months after Blair had led his Labour party to a historic third consecutive victory and were unlikely to impact the electorate until the 2009 or 2010 parliamentary elections. Thus, in the wake of the terrorist attack, Blair remained committed to Britain's role as the United States's primary ally in that war.

The combined effect of the two transport attacks on the rest of Western Europe, however, was to increase anxieties and intensify security procedures. In 2006, these concerns were further intensified when British intelligence agencies averted a plot by several dozen British-born Muslims (of Pakistani extraction) to blow up some ten passenger planes. Another effect, unfortunately, was to raise a veil of suspicion around the region's entire Muslim population. Most research indicates that fewer than 10 percent of European Muslims support radical Islam and the vast majority opposes the use of violence. Since almost all of the Madrid and London bombers were residents of Spain or Britain and many were second-generation citizens who spoke their nation's language fluently, not surprisingly there has been a backlash—sometimes descending into racism—against the region's Muslim population.

Few, if any, serious critics question airport screenings of passengers and their baggage, even if such measures do constitute some invasion of privacy. At the other end of the spectrum, most Americans and their political leaders would oppose unrestricted wire tapping of all phone conversations involving Muslim-American citizens and residents even if it might strengthen national security. In between those two polar extremes, however, lies a wide area of debate in which a society must determine whether some potential security measures in the battle against terrorism (such as denying the right of *habeas corpus* to U.S. citizens suspected of links to terrorist groups) are currently necessary infringements on civil liberties or are not worth their cost in personal freedom.

In 2001–2002, only two to three months after the 9/11 attacks, Darren Davis and Brian Silver conducted a representative survey of almost 1,500 Americans to assess popular attitudes regarding the proper balance between civil liberties and security. They found that, in the abstract, a majority of respondents (55 percent) agreed with the statement that "we should preserve our freedoms above all, even if there remains some risk of terrorism," while only 45 percent felt that "in order to curb terrorism in this country, it will be necessary to give up some civil liberties." That is to say, even on the heels of 9/11, most Americans believed that anti-terrorist measures should not infringe significantly on this country's civil liberties.

When asked to evaluate specific trade-offs between civil liberties and security, however, commitment to individual rights was sometimes weaker. To be sure, 92 percent of Americans opposed **racial profiling** (such as carrying out additional airport security checks on dark-skinned or "Arab-looking" passengers) and 77 percent opposed giving government authorities "the right to search a property *without a warrant* "solely on the suspicion that a terrorist act or other crime is being planned there. At the same time, however, 60 percent felt that high school teachers should not criticize America's antiterrorist policies, but instead, "should defend America's policies in order to promote loyalty to our country." And, while a slight majority opposed allowing the U.S. government to indefinitely detain non-citizens who are suspected of belonging to a terrorist organization (without bringing charges), almost half (47 percent) supported it.[4]

Since the threat of international terrorism will likely persist for a long time, this debate will be with us for many years. Public opinion and government policy regarding any trade-off between security and civil liberties will probably change in either direction, depending on how great the threat of terrorism on American soil is perceived to be.

Economic Globalization

International trade, communications, and investment expanded tremendously during the last decades of the twentieth century and will surely continue to grow in coming decades. Economic globalization is characterized by increased world trade, the freer international flow of finances (banking, stock market transactions), growing international migration of labor, increased transfer of technologies across borders, the growth of more powerful multinational corporations (MNCs), greater influence for world institutions such as the World Bank, the International Monetary Fund (IMF), and the World Trade Organization (WTO), and, consequently, greater dependence of almost all national economies on the world economy. Citizens and political leaders now realize that jobs, wealth, and economic security increasingly depend on forces beyond their immediate borders. The debate about the global economy has led to energetic and occasionally violent demonstrations in the United States, Europe, and Latin America as opponents of free trade and other manifestations of globalization contend that these trends harm the interests of workers, lead to environmental damage, and create additional problems around the world. Often these critics charge that globalization has widened the gap between rich and poor nations, increased income disparities within developing nations, and on balance, increased Third World poverty.

Undoubtedly, as we have seen (Chapter 15), the spread of multinational corporations in the Third World has sometimes had disastrous effects as, for example, the mercury and arsenic pollution of Indonesian waterways by the world's largest gold mining company—the U.S.-based Newton Mining Corporation—and the destruction of Indonesia jungles by Japanese logging companies. But, it is not always clear how many of these problems can be charged to globalization. For one thing, in most cases economic development—long before globalization—has had significant environmental costs (smokestack emissions, auto emissions, runoff from chemicals used in farming). With proper environmental controls, such damage can be limited to some extent, but can't be eliminated. While some multinationals have been guilty of serious environmental destruction, many Third World corporations have a comparable record. Sometimes it is politically more expedient for developing nations to enforce environmental standards on foreign corporations than on national firms (though it is also true that some MNCs have greater financial resources to bribe their way around government regulations). The key issue in this policy area, then, may not be globalization but, rather, the willingness and capacity of Third World governments to pass and actually enforce appropriate environmental regulations that apply to both international and national corporations.

Let us turn to a second area of dispute regarding globalization, namely that it has increased poverty, especially in less-developed countries. In fact, data from sources such as the World Bank and the United Nations Development Program indicate that during the past two to three decades (encompassing the greatest increases in globalization), world rates of extreme poverty, rather than rising, have fallen significantly. Thus, according to World Bank data, the percentage of the developing world's population living in "extreme poverty" (defined as living on less than $1 per day, adjusted for inflation) declined from 40 percent in 1980 to 21 percent in 2001. Between 1980 and 2002, life expectancy in developing countries rose from 60 years to 65. Changes in income distribution have been limited, both between the world's richer and poorer nations and among the populations of individual developing nations.[5]

While the decline in poverty, along with improved life expectancy and literacy, cannot be linked definitively to economic globalization, it must be noted that these improvements did take place during the period of most rapid globalization. Moreover, the most dramatic reductions in poverty—in China and East Asia and perhaps more recently in India—took place in the very countries that had linked themselves most closely to the world economy.[6] Still, considerable debate persists among respected economists over the magnitude of reductions in Third World poverty. Thus, for example, Shaohua Chen and Martin Ravallion, economists at the World Bank, analyzed 454 household surveys of poverty in 97 developing countries, dating from 1981 to 2000. They estimated that the absolute number of people living in extreme poverty had declined by 390 million during that two-decade period, about twice as many as had been reported in previously published World Bank statistics. At the same time, however, they insisted that all of this improvement had basically taken place in China (where extreme poverty fell by an astonishing 400 million people during those two decades) and, to a far lesser extent, in the rest of East Asia (with a more modest regional decline of 45 million). Elsewhere in the developing world, their data indicated, the absolute number of people living in extreme poverty had actually *increased* (by 55 million), although the *percentage* of the population mired in extreme poverty (given population growth during those two decades) had not changed substantially. Poverty had remained relatively constant in Latin America and had risen sharply in Africa.

More significantly, the experience of the many people living on per capita incomes between $1 and $2 per day (a measure of "poverty" less severe than the "extreme poverty" of those living on $1 or less per day) had been relatively static. Thus, although the percentage of Third World people living either in poverty or extreme poverty (everyone living on $2 per day or less) fell between 1981 and 2000, it only fell from 67 percent of the Third World's population to 53 percent.[7] Many of the people who had escaped from "extreme poverty" had only made it into "poverty."

All of these data suggest that there is some disagreement over the extent to which Third World poverty has diminished in percentage terms, but there is widespread agreement that it *has* fallen. While economic globalization has not benefited *all* parts of the Third World, and while, at least in the short run, some countries and some groups (including displaced workers in the U.S.) may have been harmed by it, most economists believe that, on balance, globalization has generally benefited the developing world and its poorer citizens.

As we have noted, economic gains for the poor (and the population generally) in recent decades have been most dramatic in Asia, with results less clear in Latin America and deteriorating conditions in Africa. The problems of trade deficits and international debt have made Argentina's economy seriously unstable, and economic problems continue in Brazil and Venezuela. But, again, it is the region that has been most integrated into the global economy (Asia) whose living standards have grown fastest and the region least integrated (Africa) whose economy has performed most poorly.

Still, the globalization of commerce brings a number of important forces and values into conflict. Although experts disagree about the magnitude of the gains from free trade and growing cross-national flows of finance, labor, and technology, most observers find globalization has had significant wealth-enhancing effects. On the other hand, it has not produced increased wealth evenly, and it has led to economic disruptions and increased restraints on many governments. Integrating national power into the new realities of the global economy will be a major challenge for political leaders in the coming decades. We are likely to see deepened tensions among business interests, environmental activists, consumer interests, agricultural groups, labor unions, and human rights organizations. The globalization debate also raises long-standing differences between those who believe society's interests are best served by free trade and a minimum of government economic intervention and those who feel that international trade and investment as well as other aspects of a market society must be regulated and sometimes restricted in order to save much of the population (not just the poor) from the ravages of what critics call "savage capitalism" (i.e., unrestrained capitalism). Those tensions will be a significant force in both international and domestic politics for the foreseeable future.

THE SPREAD OF DEMOCRACY

The decline of communism during the 1980s and 1990s in Europe was paralleled by an equally dramatic spread of democracy, not only in the former Soviet bloc but in Latin America and parts of Africa and Asia as well. During that period, dictatorships gave way to popular, competitive elections and majority rule in such diverse places as Chile, Russia, the Philippines, South Africa, South Korea, Taiwan, and Central/Eastern Europe.

For more than 30 years, Freedom House, a respected human rights institute, has asked a large panel of experts to evaluate the countries of the world on two dimensions: first, *political rights*, a measure of the extent to which a nation's elections are free and fair; second, *civil rights*, a measure of a how well a country protects its citizens' freedom of association, belief, and press, as well as their religious, economic, ethnic, and other rights. Each country is awarded a score of 1–7 (1 being the highest score and 7 the worst) for each of these two dimensions, and the average combined score is used to rank the country as either "free," "partly free," or "not free."[8] During the past three decades, the total number of countries categorized as free or partly free has risen dramatically, while the number that are not free has fallen correspondingly. Between 1972 and 2005, the number of countries classified as "free" more than doubled from 42 to 89. The total of "partly free" nations rose from 36 to 58, while the number of countries that are "not free" declined from 67 to 45 in 23 years.[9] Of course, the scores for particular countries may change each year in either direction as some become more free and others, such as Russia (which slipped from "partly free" in 2003 to "not free" in 2004), become less free.

As we noted in Chapter 15 when most of the countries of Africa, Asia, and the Middle East achieved independence in the years after World War II (from the late 1940s to the early 1960s), many analysts felt that these countries were not ready for democracy and first needed to achieve stability under some form of benevolent, authoritarian rule. They also pointed to the economic and/or social advances made under **mobilization regimes** in China, Cuba, and South Korea under military rule.

Events over the past few decades, however, have made political scientists and other analysts doubtful about the alleged advantages of nondemocratic regimes. The absence of effective political competition tends to makes one-party or no-party systems less responsive to their citizens than competitive systems are. Even nondemocratic governments that seemingly seek to improve living standards for most of their citizens often make major mistakes that remain uncorrected because competing policies and independent criticisms are not considered.

For example, Mao Zedong's plan to increase food and industrial production through the Great Leap Forward (see Chapter 14) led to colossal mismanagement and unintended mass starvation. No alternative party platform or scholarly criticism existed to suggest a better solution to China's problems. Finally, revelations about recently deposed dictatorships in nations as diverse as Chile and Romania have revealed a significant degree of corruption and nepotism. Even regimes that started off with good intentions seem to confirm the observation of British statesman Lord Acton that "power tends to corrupt, and absolute power tends to corrupt absolutely." Industrialization and the accompanying growth of mass literacy and a professionally trained middle class generally encourage wider political participation and ultimately intensify pressures for democracy. Almost all analysts agree that countries with higher GNPs and higher literacy rates are more likely to be democratic, although the relationship is by no means direct or automatic. Events in Eastern Europe, Latin America, and, more recently, Africa have also shown that pressures for democracy can be contagious—the transition to democracy in a few countries tends to spread to their neighbors through a "demonstration effect" or what Samuel Huntington called "snowballing."

None of this suggests that democracy will become universal in the foreseeable future or even that the process of democratization in a particular country is irreversible. For the most desperately poor nations of the world—predominantly in Africa and parts of Asia—the socioeconomic foundations for democracy do not yet seem to be in place. Moreover, as our case studies of the United States, Great Britain, Russia, China, and Mexico have indicated, some political cultures seem more supportive of democratic government than others are. It is certainly overly optimistic to predict that virtually all nations will become democratic, even in the long run. Currently, countries that have not even made the transition to semi-democracy (i.e., those that remain "not free") are heavily concentrated in Sub-Saharan Africa (where per capita income and literacy generally remain extremely low) and the Arab world (where democracy may be inhibited by cultural factors, by the ongoing conflict with Israel—which militarizes politics—and, in some countries, by the state's domination of the major source of income, the petroleum industry, which provides added power to authoritarian regimes).

In fact, the spread of democracy, so vigorous from the early 1970s to the early 1990s, has slowed appreciably since that time. Thus, for example, of late the number of "free" countries has remained static, only growing from 88 in 1997 to 89 in 2005, while the number of "partly free" nations increased modestly from 53 in 1999 to 58 six years later.[10] While some additional countries are likely to embrace democracy in the coming years—much as Ukraine and Georgia recently have done—leading analysts generally believe that for now the "wave" of multiple transitions has likely come to an end. Fortunately, unlike the world's two previous waves of democratization (1828–1926 and 1943–1962), the most recent wave (which began in 1974 in Portugal and essentially ended about 25 years later) has yet to be followed by a "reverse wave" of collapsed democracies (although that has happened in a few cases such as Pakistan and Russia).[11]

The main reason that the pace of democratization has slowed down and is likely to continue to advance slowly, at best, is simply that most of the countries with the social and economic preconditions for maintaining democracy (at least moderate income and literacy levels) already have become at least partially free. Stated slightly differently, those countries that remain "not free" as of 2005 were frequently very low-income and/or low-literacy nations such as Afghanistan, Cambodia, Chad, Eritrea, Haiti, Laos, Myanmar, Pakistan, and Zimbabwe. To be sure, there is not a *perfect* correlation between democracy and per capita income or literacy. Countries such as Cuba and Singapore have relatively high Human Development Indices or HDI (a composite statistic measuring life expectancy, education, and literacy), but rank much lower in the Freedom House democracy scores. Conversely, such nations as Mali and Mongolia had low HDI scores, yet were rated as "free" by Freedom House. On the whole, however, the correlation between socioeconomic development and democracy is a strong one. Of the 25 nations with the world's highest HDI scores, 24 were rated "free," one country (Singapore) was "partly free," and none were evaluated as "not free." At the other end of the scale, among the 25 countries with the lowest HDI scores, only two were "free," 12 were "partly free," and 11 were "not free."

At the same time, however, the 49 countries currently rated as "not free" by Freedom House include a number of nations that have higher HDI scores than one might have expected. That is, they have HDI scores which are usually associated with "free" or "partly free" political systems. Two groups stand out. The first consists of former republics of the Soviet Union (including Russia, Belarus, Azerbaijan, and Tajikistan). While their previous, communist government gave these Soviet Republics comparatively high literacy rates and moderate HDIs, it also created an entrenched power elite whose leaders often were able to control the new government after the collapse of the USSR. Even in Russia, which had made important strides toward democracy under Presidents Mikhail Gorbachev and Boris Yeltsin (1985–1999), current President Vladimir Putin, a former KGB (Soviet secret police) agent, has installed a government (with a number of his former KGB comrades appointed to key posts) that has rolled back much of his predecessors' progress toward democracy. Of the 15 former republics of the Soviet Union, only three (Estonia, Latvia, and Lithuania) moved to full democracy immediately after the collapse of the USSR. More recently Ukraine has joined that group, while Russia—by far the largest and most powerful former republic—has regressed from a ranking of "partly free" to one of "not free."

The second group of countries that stand out within the "not free" category is the Arab nations, especially petroleum-exporting countries. For example, Libya, Saudi Arabia, Qatar, the United Arab Emirates, and Oman, all have middle- or upper-level HDI scores but low Freedom House ratings. As noted earlier, many analysts have attributed this discrepancy to Islamic aspects of their political cultures. Specifically, they argue that the Muslim religion's rejection of a separation between Church and State and the inferior status it assigns to women present serious obstacles to democratic government.

More recently, however, Alfred Stepan and Graeme Robertson have demonstrated that, while Muslim nations as a group tend to less democratic, if one separates the world's 47 predominantly Muslim nations into two groups—the 16 Arab-majority countries (in North Africa and the Middle East) and the 31 Muslim countries that are predominantly non-Arab (such as Malaysia, Turkey, Bangladesh, Mali and Pakistan)—and if we also control for economic development (i.e., compare poor Muslim countries to poor non-Muslim nations, more economically developed Muslim nations with more economically developed non-Muslim countries), we observe a very different pattern. It turns out, say the authors, that, while Arab countries are far less likely to be democratic than are non-Muslim countries at the same level of economic development (indeed, Lebanon is the only Arab country to have achieved democracy), *non-Arab* Muslim countries are actually just as likely to be democratic as are non-Muslim countries at similar economic levels. Indeed, Muslim, non-Arab countries such as Bangladesh, Gambia, Mali, Niger, and Nigeria are democratic "overachievers" in that they have been more democratic than we might have expected based on their low economic development. Thus, conclude Stepan and Robertson, something about Arab society has limited democratic development, because it is not a problem for Muslim nations outside the Arab world.[12]

Once again, these issues are part of a more fundamental debate. Some scholars, for example, have posited a fundamental "clash of civilizations" between Western societies, which gave birth to and embraced democracy, and the Islamic world, which allegedly holds values that are fundamentally antithetical to democracy.[13] As we have just observed, others argue that it is mistaken and counterproductive to view Islam as inherently undemocratic. Experts also disagree as to how many of the recently democratized nations will revert to authoritarianism ("a reverse wave") and how many new nations will join the democratic community in the foreseeable future (a possible "fourth wave"). Like the controversy over Islam, this debate has clear policy implications. For example, are American pressures likely to cause additional transitions to democracy or will such pressures be futile in countries that are not "ready for democracy"?

THE GLOBAL ENVIRONMENT

During the past half-century, humankind has greatly expanded its ability to alter the environment for better or worse. Until the age of rapid industrialization and nuclear energy, the behavior of nations primarily affected only the land, water, and air within their borders. In recent years, however, we have come to recognize that government decisions regarding industrial production and the use of natural resources may influence the global environment as well.

For example, many scientists feel that global warming will eventually imperil the world's food supply and threaten the earth's coastal regions with flooding. Physicians prepare for a rapid rise in skin cancer as the fragile ozone layer is depleted. International traffic in petroleum increasingly threatens large bodies of water with oil spills. And a nuclear power accident, such as the one that occurred at the Soviet-era nuclear plant in Chernobyl, can spread radioactive fallout through much of northern Europe. There are many unsafe reactors still functioning in the former Soviet Union and elsewhere.

Increasingly, political leaders are beginning to recognize that solutions to problems like these will require some government regulation and a high level of international cooperation. Change may be slow, but progress in such matters as the control of global warming, preservation of endangered species, and protection of rain forests challenges existing concepts of political power and, as we noted in Chapter 18, raises issues of national sovereignty. Much of our understanding of politics until recently assumed that states and their citizens act in their own interests. Environmental issues create a unique political context because effects of decisions made in any single nation frequently transcend its borders. Perhaps more than in any other policy area, environmental policy suggests that a new kind of politics is gathering momentum.

Much of the debate over environmental issues will center around three basic issues: First, what is the proper trade-off between environmental protection and economic growth? Second, what are the best mechanisms for protecting the environment? Finally, to what extent does this require state intervention and to what extent is the market better equipped to handle it?

The answer to the first question is linked, in part, to an individual's or group's beliefs about the degree of danger posed by current or anticipated environmental degradation. Take, for example, the issue of global warning. As we have seen, environmentalists and their scientific backers argue that the emission of greenhouse gasses from industry and automobiles is already warming the atmosphere and has begun to have such negative effects as the melting of the polar icecap, with dire consequences for the future unless industrial and vehicular emissions are controlled (as called for in the Kyoto Treaty). Many industry spokespersons and their scientific backers insist either that the threat of global warming has yet to be demonstrated (President Bush's position) or that this threat has been exaggerated and can be dealt with by coming technological changes. In refusing to sign the Kyoto Treaty, the Bush administration argued that the treaty's limits on greenhouse emissions would curtail U.S. economic growth in return for unproven benefits. Although environmentalists argue that it is possible to protect the environment without significantly limiting economic growth or constraining certain lifestyles, there are certainly cases where governments and citizens must choose. Should the government impose higher taxes on SUV's and other gas guzzlers? Is Brazil's or Indonesia's income from lumber exports and cattle ranching (on cleared jungle) worth the destruction of large tracts of jungle? Should a dam be built in the state of Washington that would produce electricity but would damage the spawning of salmon?

Even when there is a consensus on protecting the environment, there is often disagreement over the best way to accomplish that goal. While virtually everyone believes that *some* environmental controls are needed (for example, prohibitions on dumping toxic chemicals such as mercury into the water system), analysts often disagree over whether environmental protection is better achieved through government controls or through free-market mechanisms. One example of antipollution market incentives was created by the 1990 Clean Air Act Amendments, which gives each electric power company a quota for allowable sulfur-dioxide and nitrogen oxides emissions, major contributors to environmentally destructive acid rain. Utilities whose emissions fall below their allowable quota may then sell "licenses to pollute" to other companies that have exceeded their quotas (and are thereby effectively fined by having to buy such licenses). Polluting thus becomes an added business expense to those companies that fail to meet their target, while other firms profit by reducing pollutants below the target levels. While such market approaches frequently have been effective, many environmental analysts feel that they are too often inadequate, making government regulation necessary.

WOMEN AND POLITICS

In most of the world, the status and the role of women today are very different from what they were at the beginning of the last century. As previously noted, in recent decades, women have served as the elected leaders (presidents or prime ministers) of Great Britain, France, Iceland, Ireland, Israel, Norway, Argentina, Panama, Bangladesh, India, Pakistan, the Philippines, and Sri Lanka. In 2005 Germany elected its first female prime minister and Liberia elected Africa's first woman president. Women are currently represented on the U.S. Supreme Court, in the U.S. cabinet, in numerous governors' mansions, and in virtually all major legislative assemblies around the world. They have even explored outer space. In less high-profile professions women have also assumed leadership positions in law, medicine, the sciences, and education. Particularly in developed nations, women commonly work now in occupations that were largely closed to them only a few decades ago: architecture, public safety, and front-line service in the armed forces.

For thousands of years of human civilization, women played subordinate and limited roles in all major cultures. A great many of those restrictions have been substantially eroded in the past 90 years. That does not mean that progress has been universal or unidirectional. We noted (in Chapter 15) that in much of the Third World, modernization has often initially brought a deterioration in the condition of the female poor. In nations such as Iran and India, and even in highly modernized societies such as Japan, women are far from equal. The global trend, however, seems to be in the direction of greater equality.

The ongoing liberation of women has many causes. Important leaders and grassroots movements induced nations to change their policies in many instances. In the United States, for example, early in the twentieth century Susan B. Anthony and the suffragettes helped advance the case for extending voting rights to women, and in recent years Betty Friedan, Gloria Steinem, Eleanor Smeal, and contemporary feminist organizations such as the National Organization for Women (NOW) continue to place gender issues on the national agenda. Feminism as a political movement is more advanced in northern Europe than in the United States, while far more modest movements seek equality for women in many parts of the developing world.

Modern technology has also been critical. The development of safe and effective birth control has enabled women to pursue educational and career plans without interruption for childbirth, and modern technology has made the long-exaggerated physical differences between the sexes far less relevant. Those advances have been of greater consequence to women living in the more affluent nations of the world or coming from the middle and upper classes of the Third World. Yet, women continue to encounter barriers that do not affect men, even in the most "advanced" nations. In other nations, women remain subject to religious and governmental laws that limit their freedom in profound ways. Despite impressive advances, many battles are yet to be won in the fight for equality between the sexes.

Nevertheless, the growing equality of women has changed the politics of much of the world, and it will continue to do so in the future. As women achieve leadership positions in government and business, societies will need to adapt in important ways. Changes in public policy will be demanded increasingly as family responsibilities are no longer assumed to be women's primary domain. Laws governing sexual harassment and discrimination will be strengthened as the workplace mixes men and women more equitably. A stronger female presence in political institutions will often also bring greater diversity to political discourse. In 1996, for the first time, a majority of women voted for a different presidential candidate (Clinton) than did a plurality of men (Dole), a pattern repeated in 2000 and 2004, although the gender gap in voting narrowed in the most recent election. Had John Kerry attained the same percentage of the female vote in 2004 as Al Gore did in 2000, he would have defeated George Bush. In short, the political agenda, and the people who control it, will be fundamentally changed as women assume new roles in government.

As we have seen, recent gains in the proportion of women elected to parliamentary or congressional seats, especially in Latin America, have often been related to the establishment of gender quotas or reserved seats for women (Chapter 15). Quotas in candidate selection may be established voluntarily by individual political parties (including Britain's Labour Party, South Africa's ANC, and all significant parties in Denmark, Norway and Sweden) or by legally imposed candidate quotas—often 30 percent—in some 41 countries worldwide, including Belgium, France, Argentina, Costa Rica, Rwanda, Tanzania, and Uganda. India mandates that 30 percent of the seats in each of the thousands of village councils nationwide be held by women.

Quotas such as these, like quotas in other occupations such as civil service or police work, raise important questions about public policy and equality: Are guaranteed quotas for women discriminatory toward men, or do they simply correct past discrimination against women? Does requiring that 10 or 30 percent of each party's parliamentary candidates be women ultimately have the effect of creating a virtual "ceiling" beyond which it becomes difficult for women to climb (a criticism voiced by some feminists)? Similar arguments can be made regarding affirmative action for underrepresented racial, religious, or ethnic groups. For example, to address the economic superiority of Malaysia's Chinese minority, the government has established quotas guaranteeing Malays (the ethnic majority) a percentage of university admissions, homes in new housing developments, the civil service, government contracts, and the like. As with gender quotas, supporters of such policies defend them as a necessary correction of discrimination and prejudice, while opponents criticize them for interfering with equal opportunity and a purely merit-based allocation of government leadership positions, employment, or other public resources.

WOMEN'S RIGHTS IN THE MUSLIM WORLD   In some Muslim nations women have begun to organize to defend their rights. Here, in the Indonesian capital of Jakarta, women protest domestic violence, pornography, female trafficking, and prostitution.

NATIONALISM AND ETHNIC CONFLICT

The power of ethnic loyalties has long shaped domestic and international politics. Like many contemporary ideologies, nationalist beliefs became most clearly articulated in nineteenth-century Europe, when cultural traditions were strongly linked to national heritage and pride. "The doctrine [nationalism] holds that humanity is naturally divided into nations, that nations are known by certain characteristics which can be ascertained, and that the only legitimate type of government is national self-government."[14]

Nationalism became a force for democratic government and artistic achievement, on the one hand, and for brutality and aggression on the other. It was a primary factor contributing to numerous wars in the nineteenth and twentieth centuries as citizens were motivated to expand their territories in accordance with extreme visions of nationhood.

World War II, the last and most devastating of the international wars attributable to European nationalism, had a rather contradictory effect. It contributed to the demise of the British, French, and other European empires in Africa and Asia, setting off a chain of nationalist and interethnic struggles on those two continents. In Western Europe itself, however, the horrors of World War II inspired the major powers (most notably the historic rivals Germany and France) to set aside their nationalist competition and move toward economic, political, and military cooperation. The cold war (1947–1989) and the Soviet threat also fostered Western European cooperation.

In Eastern Europe, communism kept nationalist tendencies in check at two levels. Internationally, the Soviet Union required these countries to join together in military and economic pacts (the Warsaw Pact and Comecon), regardless of their feelings about one another or the USSR. Equally important, communist rule placed a firm lid on subnational interethnic hostilities.

The end of the cold war and the erosion of Marxist ideology have occasionally unleashed ethnic conflict and nationalism as a significant force in parts of Russia and East/Central Europe, most notably the bloody disintegration of Yugoslavia. No longer muted by Marxist-Leninist ideology or single-party discipline, long-standing hostilities among Croatians, Serbs, and Bosnians erupted into war. The war in Bosnia was soon followed by Serbian government repression against a rebellion by the country's ethnic-Albanian minority in the province of Kosovo. Previously, a similar breakdown of centralized communist control led to the collapse of the Soviet Union into 15 different nations. In several of these former Soviet republics, interethnic conflicts continue to rage and threaten stability.

The conflict in Chechnya illustrates this trend. The more than one million Chechens are an indigenous group of mountain herdsmen and farmers who have lived in the North Caucasus region for millennia. They speak their own language, are mostly Sufi Muslims, and have a strong ethnic identity. They have resented and defied control by Russia or the Soviet Union for centuries—dating back to their successful resistance to Peter the Great's invasion in 1722—and have suffered greatly for that, particularly under Stalin (who deported most of the Chechens to Siberia and Soviet Central Asia in 1944, where they remained until 1957). The Chechens declared their independence from Russia in 1991, but Moscow did not recognize the declaration and sent troops in 1994 to quell the rebellion. After three years of savage fighting and many thousands of deaths (mostly Chechen civilians), the Russians negotiated a cease-fire and troop withdrawal in 1996–1997. However, when subsequent negotiations broke down and violence resumed, the Russian military returned to Chechnya in force in 1999 and claimed to have ended the rebellion by 2001. However, reports indicate that Russian soldiers are killed almost daily as the rebels continue small-scale attacks. At the same time, more than one thousand Russian civilians have been killed by Chechen terrorists operating outside Chechnya in various parts of Russia. Thus, that ethnic conflict continues, and genuine peace is not yet in sight.

As noted in Chapter 15, in much of Africa and Asia, nationalism and ethnic conflict have been major sources of instability since independence. Particularly in Africa, arbitrarily drawn colonial boundaries often divided ethnic groups (tribes) into different colonies or threw antagonistic groups together in the same colony. In Asia and the Middle East, religious tensions have been equally disruptive in such countries as India, Indonesia, and Iraq. In recent decades millions have died as a result of tribal, religious, or other ethnic conflicts (or ethnically related conflicts) in Angola, Congo, India, Nigeria, and elsewhere.

Contrary to common perceptions, after rising steadily for the previous 50 years, the level of ethnic protests and rebellions within states has actually *diminished* somewhat since the start of the 1990s and the end of the cold war (though that level is still higher than it was prior to 1980).[15] Still, if we look back at the 60 years since the end of World War II, the most frequent arenas for violent conflict have not been wars between sovereign states, but rather internal strife tied to cultural, tribal, religious, or other ethnic animosities. According to one recent estimate, "nearly two-thirds of all [the world's] armed conflicts [at that time] included an ethnic component. [Indeed], ethnic conflicts are four times more likely than interstate wars."[16] Estimates of the number who have died are difficult to reach and often disagree. But, according to a respected study by political scientists David Laitin and James Fearon, "Since the end of World War II, 16.5 million people have died in internal conflicts [mostly ethnically based], compared with 3.3 million in interstate wars."[17] Other estimates of ethnic conflict place the death toll at 20 million or more. Today, ethnic hostilities threaten to break up countries such as Afghanistan, Iraq, Liberia, and Uganda. In such countries as India, Iraq, the Philippines, and Kenya, tensions among groups with different religions, languages, and tribal membership sometimes dominate domestic politics. Moreover, ethnic divisions may be harmful even when they do not lead to violence. Research by a number of economists and political scientists has indicated that in Africa and elsewhere, the more ethnically diverse a country is, the more poorly it tends to perform economically.[18]

The current resurgence of nationalism and ethnic conflict in parts of Europe and its continued role in the Third World may contribute to violence and instability in the coming years. Although not always features of nationalism, racism and other kinds of hatred of people of different backgrounds are often present when nationalist feelings are strong. Perhaps no other force more directly threatens many newly developing democracies in the Third World, Eastern Europe, and the former Soviet Union. According to Zbigniew Brzezinski, ethnic and religious beliefs are more "tightly binding" than abstract principles such as democracy and capitalism.[19] Even in Western European nations such as France, Austria, and Germany, ethnic unrest by Third World immigrants and white racist opposition to immigration pose a challenge to democratic institutions.

International affairs will become increasingly complex as the bipolar world of the cold war is replaced by a less ordered array of tensions among diverse nations. One of the greatest challenges of this new century will be to extract from nationalism its most positive aspects and to tame its destructive forces. If recent trends continue, the majority of wars and war deaths in the coming decades are very likely to come from civil wars within nations rather than between nations. As we have observed, in all, civil conflicts at the close of the twentieth century and the start of the twenty-first have resulted in the deaths of millions of people (through war or starvation) in the former Yugoslavia, Angola, Congo, Rwanda, Sudan, Afghanistan, Indonesia, Sri Lanka, and elsewhere. More than 3.3 million have died in the Democratic Republic of the Congo alone in ethnic conflict that is still ongoing.

INFORMATION TECHNOLOGY AND THE MASS MEDIA

The impact of the changes in contemporary political life will be amplified as a result of the development of new and emerging information technologies and their use by mass media throughout the world. In previous eras, only a few people were immediately informed about even major events and wars. (The United States and Great Britain actually fought a major battle in the War of 1812 several days after a treaty was signed ending the conflict.) Large parts of the world remained ignorant of many significant incidents and conditions. People therefore focused their attention more closely on local concerns. In a very real sense, the demand for *change* itself is a response to knowledge about conditions in other places; one cause of the movement toward modernization in developing nations is the information brought by foreigners about life in more advanced countries. Without such information, people are less driven to demand improvements in their lives.

We are now in the midst of a revolution in communications technology that will doubtless accelerate the forces of political change throughout the world. The power of instant media images of such events as the war in Iraq, the fall of the Berlin Wall, ethnic massacres in Bosnia, Rwanda, and Darfur (Sudan), the plight of tsunami victims in Southeast Asia and hurricane victims in New Orleans, and countless other happenings affects political choices. Without modern mass media, perhaps the fall of communism in Poland in 1989 would have remained an isolated event instead of serving as the trigger of a much larger movement.

When we acknowledge that the mass media can transform our awareness of world events, we immediately encounter the problem of *control*. A free press is essential to the open debate and criticism that are basic to democracy, but the press is not free in most countries. Despite recent progress, Freedom House's 2006 report on press freedom reported that only 73 of the 186 nations analyzed had a relatively free press. Of the remaining nations, 54 were ranked as "partly free" and 67 were classified as "not free."[20] Today many governments still require the dissemination of some stories and statements

© AP/Wide World Photos

JANJAWEED HELL   Sudanese Arab armed militias, called Janjaweed, with unofficial government support, have killed or driven to starvation some 200,000 black tribesmen and forced a million more to flee into refugee camps as part of a program of "ethnic cleansing" in that country's Darfur region.

and prohibit coverage of others. In still others, journalists are sometimes harassed, imprisoned, or even assassinated.

Mass media are also potentially subject to control by the dominant interests outside government. Those who pay the bills are often able to exert control. A newspaper in a small town that is dominated by a single manufacturing facility (which also buys much of the paper's advertising space) will be unlikely to publish news stories critical of that facility. On a broader level, some critics have noted that in industrial democracies, major corporations are the primary source of funds for both news and entertainment programming, and so corporate interests are taken into account by media leaders.

However, there are hopeful signs that the press has become freer in most parts of the world. According to data provided by the United Nations, there was a significant improvement in "press freedom" between 1980 and 2000, an improvement that was noticeable in both rich and poor countries.[21] Despite that progress, serious restrictions remain. Freedom House's surveys suggest that almost all of the gains in press freedom, just noted, since 1980 came in the 1980s and very early 1990s and that improvements for the rest of the 1990s were far more limited. And according to the Committee to Protect Journalists, some 36 journalists were assassinated worldwide in 2005, often to silence critical investigations of the government.[22]

The problem of media control will become an increasingly important political issue. Government control appeals to many who are disturbed by the influence of dominant business interests, but the record of government-controlled media is dismal (in cases where state-owned news outlets have editorial independence—as with the British and the Canadian Broadcasting Company—they face competition from privately owned outlets). Nevertheless, a free and open information network is a vital component of modern democracy. The Internet is perhaps the most "open" communications medium ever constructed, and governments are currently grappling with the problems and opportunities it creates. Managing the freedom *and* the diversity of the media will be increasingly difficult and critical to effective government in the years to come.

The contemporary world is changing in many other ways, of course. Relations among different races, religions, and linguistic groups are becoming better in some areas and worse in others; technology will present new questions for public policy in numerous contexts; advances in transportation and communication will alter international economic and military relationships; the eventual demise of petroleum as the dominant source of energy will change both our everyday lives and the allocation of wealth between producing and consuming nations.

What is common to the elements of change in the modern world is that they all affect *political* life, and the choices they present will be made largely by political systems. Existing political institutions may not always be satisfactory, as illustrated by the current widespread disillusionment with U.S. and European political parties. New political forms may be developed, such as the neighborhood associations often used by the poor in both developing and industrialized nations. Regardless of the kinds of governments and institutions that people create in the years ahead, however, the solutions to people's problems will inevitably involve politics. The words of Nobel laureate Thomas Mann, written a century ago, continue to ring true today: "In our time, the destiny of man [humankind] presents itself in political terms."[23]

Key Terms and Concepts_____

mobilization regimes   racial profiling

Notes_____

1. *BBC News* (November 30, 2005), http://news.bbc.co.uk/1/hi/uk/4482640.stm, "Europe in Uproar Over CIA Operations," *Los Angeles Times* (November 26, 2005), www.LATimes.com: World News; *BBC News* (November 28, 2005), "EU warned on 'secret' CIA jails, " http://news.bbc.co.uk/2/hi/europe/4478766.stm.

2. *BBC News* (October 10, 2003)."Red Cross Blasts Guantanamo," http://news.bbc.co.uk/2/hi/americas/3179858.stm.

3. See the report titled "Homefront Confidential: How the War on Terrorism Affects Access to Information and the Public's Right to Know," available at http://www.rcfp.org/news/2002/0314report.html.

4. Darren W. Davis and Brian D. Silver, "Civil Liberties vs. Security: Public Opinion in the Context of the Terrorist Attacks on America," *American Journal of Political Science* 48, no. 1 (January 2004): 28–46.

5. Data comes from the World Bank PovertyNet, "Overview," http://web.worldbank.org/.

6. For a study that links reductions in Third World poverty to globalization, see Surjit Bhalla, *Imagine There's No Country* (Washington, DC: International Institute for Economics, 2002).

7. Shaohua Chen and Martin Ravallion, "How Have the World's Poorest Fared since the Early 1980s?" (Washington, DC: Policy Research working paper, No. WPS 3341, 2004).

8. Arch Puddington and Aili Piano, "The 2004 Freedom House Survey: Worrisome Signs, Modest Shifts." *Journal of Democracy* 16, no.1 (January 2005): 103–108; see also www.freedomhouse.org.

9. Freedom House, "Freedom in the World," http://www.freedomhouse.org/template.cfm?page=15&year=2005 and Larry Diamond, *Developing Democracy* (Baltimore: The Johns Hopkins University Press, 1999), p. 26.

10. Puddington and Piano, "The 2004 Freedom House Survey," and Adrian Karatnycky, "The 1998 Freedom House Surveys: The Decline of Illiberal Democracy," *Journal of Democracy* 10, no.1 (January 1999): 112–125.

11. Larry Diamond, "Is Pakistan the (Reverse) Wave of the Future," in Larry Diamond and Marc F. Plattner (ed.), *The Global Divergence of Democracy* (Baltimore: Johns Hopkins University Press, 2001), pp. 355–370.

12. Alfred Stepan and Graeme B. Robertson, "An 'Arab' More Than 'Muslim' Electoral Gap," *Journal of Democracy* 14, no.3 (July 2003).

13. Samuel P. Huntington, *The Clash of Civilizations and the Remaking of World Order* (New York: Simon & Schuster, 1996).

14. Elie Kedourie, *Nationalism* (London: Hutchinson University Library, 1961), p. 9; quoted in *In Defense of Politics*, 2nd ed., by Bernard Crick (Chicago: University of Chicago Press, 1972), p. 78.

15. Ted Robert Gurr, "Preface" and "Long War, Short Peace: The Rise and Decline of Ethnopolitical Conflict at the End of the Cold War," in *Peoples versus States: Minorities at Risk in the New Century*, ed. T. Gurr (Washington, DC: United States Institute of Peace Press, 2000), pp. xiii and 27–56; David Carment and Frank Harvey, *Using Force to Prevent Ethnic Violence* (Westport, CT: Praeger, 2001), p. 5.

16. Monica Duffy Toft, *The Geography of Ethnic Violence: Identity, Interests, and the Indivisibility of Territory* (Princeton, NJ: Princeton University Press, 2003), p. 3; see also Peter Wallensteen and Margareta Sollenberg, "Armed Conflicts, Conflict Termination, and Peace Agreements, 1989–1996," *Journal of Peace Research* 34, no. 3 (1997): 339–358.

17. "Causes of World's Civil Wars Misunderstood, Researchers Say" *Stanford University News Service* (9/24/02), http://www.stanford.edu/dept/news/pr/02/civilwar925.html. Since that research was conducted, many thousands of additional lives have been lost due to ethnic conflict in Darfur (Sudan), Liberia, the Ivory Coast, and elsewhere.

18. For analysis of ethnic division and economic growth in Africa, see William Easterly and Ross Levine, "Africa's Growth Tragedy: Policies and Ethnic Divisions," *Quarterly Journal of Economics* 112 (November 1997): 1203–1250; Daniel N. Posner, "Measuring Ethnic Fractionalization in Africa," *American Journal of Political Science* 48 (October 2004): 849–863.

19. See Zbigniew Brzezinski, *Global Turmoil on the Eve of the Twenty-First Century* (New York: Scribner's, 1993).

20. Freedom House, "Freedom of the Press 2006" http://www.freedomhouse.org/template.cfm?page=70&release=356.

21. The report is available at http://www.undp.org/hdr2002/facts.html.

22. Committee to Protect Journalists, "From Iraq to Philippines, murder is top cause of journalists' death in '05." http://www.cpj.org/Briefings/2006/killed_05/killed_release_03jan05.html.

23. Quoted in Crick, *In Defense of Politics*, p. 157.

For Further Reading _____

Anderson, Charles W. *A Deeper Freedom: Liberal Democracy as an Everyday Morality*. Madison: University of Wisconsin Press, 2002.

Barney, Darin. *Prometheus Wired: The Hope for Democracy in the Age of Network Technology*. Chicago: University of Chicago Press, 2000.

Bartoli, Henri. *Rethinking Development: Putting an End to Poverty*. Washington, DC: Brookings, 2001.

Boxill, Bernard, ed. *Race and Racism*. New York: Oxford University Press, 2001.

Carment, David, and Patrick James, eds. *Wars in the Midst of Peace: The International Politics of Ethnic Conflict*. Pittsburgh: University of Pittsburgh Press, 2001.

Eisenstadt, Shmuel N. *Paradoxes of Democracy: Fragility, Continuity, and Change*. Baltimore: Johns Hopkins University Press, 1999.

Graham, Mary. *Democracy by Disclosure: The Rise of Technopopulism*. Washington, DC: Brookings, 2002.

Hardin, Russell. *Liberalism, Constitutionalism, and Democracy*. New York: Oxford University Press, 2000.

Norton, David L. *Democracy and Moral Development*. Berkeley and Los Angeles: University of California Press, 1991.

Olson, Mancur, Jr. *The Rise and Decline of Nations*. New Haven, CT: Yale University Press, 1982.

Spragens, Thomas A., Jr. *Reason and Democracy*. Durham, NC: Duke University Press, 1990.

GLOSSARY

Absolutism The concentration of tremendous political power in a single source, such as an absolute monarch. (**Ch. 13**)

Adversarial Democracy The kind of democratic politics created by the use of a single-member-district electoral system. Since the winning party receives all of the representation from each district, there is usually no need to form a coalition with minority parties. *See also* Consensual Democracy. (**Ch. 4**)

Adversarial System A legal system in which an independent judge (sometimes with a jury) hears arguments presented by two opposing sides before rendering a decision. (**Ch. 9**)

Agents of Political Socialization Individuals, groups, and institutions—such as the family, schools, churches, or labor unions—that transmit political values to each generation. (**Ch. 3**)

Allocation of Resources The distribution of a society's wealth among its members. Resources may be allocated authoritatively, by government action, or by the workings of a market system. (**Ch. 1**)

Anarchism The opposition to government in all forms. The advocates of this ideology believe that government is unnecessary and inevitably harmful and divisive, and that people would coexist peacefully without it. (**Ch. 2**)

Appellate Courts Courts that hear appeals from decisions made by trial courts. Normally, appelate courts do not hear new evidence, but instead respond to claims that a trial court misinterpreted the law or made a procedural error.

Aristocracy The most prestigious echelon of a stratified society. In Great Britain aristocratic families have a royal title, often dating back centuries. (**Ch. 12**)

Articles of Confederation The basic agreement among the former British colonies in America ("states") that governed the relations among them and the powers of the national congress until the Constitution was ratified in 1789. (**Ch. 11**)

Authoritarian Systems Non-democratic (dictatorial) government that exercises extensive control or authority over society. (**Chs. 1, 5, 13, 14, 15, 16**)

Balance of Power The relative levels of military strength among potential adversaries. Many "realist" theorists of international relations feel that the balance of power is the most important factor in explaining the outbreak of war. (**Ch. 17**)

Basic Law A body of law that supersedes other laws; for example, the U.S. Constitution is basic law in that statutes that contradict it are invalid. (**Ch. 9**)

Behavioralism An approach to political research that emphasizes observation of individual political behavior, as contrasted with approaches that focus on political documents and laws. (**Ch. 1**)

Belief System An ordering of opinions and attitudes held together by some broader ideological theme or pattern; not a random assortment of beliefs. (**Ch. 4**)

Bicameralism The division of the legislature into two chambers, or "houses." (**Chs. 7, 11**)

Bolsheviks The Marxist faction in the Russian Revolution headed by Vladimir Lenin. The Bolsheviks evolved into the Soviet Communist Party, and the term is sometimes used more broadly to describe Marxist-Leninists. (**Ch. 13**)

Budget Formulation The process of forming a proposal for a government's budget, including plans for both revenues and expenditures. (**Ch. 8**)

Bureaucracy The government organizations, usually staffed with officials selected on the basis of expertise and experience, that implement (and sometimes make) public policy. (**Ch. 10**)

Bureaucrat A person working for the public sector who is appointed on the basis of training and experience; usually applied to an official with a specified realm of authority. (**Ch. 10**)

Caciques Mexico's regional political bosses or strongmen. (**Ch. 16**)

Candidate Evaluation The personal appeal of an electoral candidate. Candidate evaluation may be positive or negative, and where it is a strong factor, it may exert greater influence on vote choices than party identification or voters' opinions about issues. (**Ch. 4**)

Capitalism An ideology advocating private property and minimal government. Also, the third stage of "prehistory" in Marxist ideology; in this stage, ownership of capital becomes the basis for political power and industrial workers are exploited by those who own factories. (**Ch. 2**)

Cárdenas, Lázaro Mexico's most revered recent leader, President Cárdenas introduced a series of economic and political reforms in the 1930s that benefited the nation's poor and strengthened the role of the state in the economy. (**Ch. 16**)

Catchall Parties Parties that try to appeal to a wide range of social classes and groups and, hence, have a relatively poorly defined policy program or ideology. The Democratic and Republican parties in the United States have fit in this category in the past, but are becoming more well defined. (**Ch. 5**)

Central Committee Consisting until 1990 of 400 to 500 members, the Soviet Central Committee included leading members of the Communist Party who nominally approved key policy decisions and elected the Politburo. With rare exception its votes were dictated from above, although there was far more debate and open discussion as Gorbachev's reforms advanced. Ruling communist parties in nations such as China and Vietnam also have central committees. (**Ch. 13**)

Charismatic Authority The ability to evoke allegiance and loyalty from citizens or subordinates by virtue of image, speaking skills, and the generation of emotional responses. (**Ch. 8**)

Checks and Balances The principle, associated most prominently with U.S. government, holding that arbitrary, irresponsible government power is best prevented by establishing a system in which each part of the government can check the actions of the others. (**Ch. 11**)

Chief Administrator An individual who manages and coordinates the implementation of programs through administrative agencies; one of the primary roles of modern chief executives. (**Ch. 8**)

Christian Democrats Political parties and their supporters who profess a political doctrine usually linked to the Catholic Church. Important in Latin America and Europe, these parties range from right of center to left of center ideologically. (**Ch. 5**)

Citizen Participation The practice of involving citizens in the bureaucratic decision-making process. (**Ch. 10**)

Civil Law The body of law pertaining to efforts by private parties to gain compensation for injuries inflicted by other private parties; for example, one person suing another for damages arising from libelous statements is a civil law matter. (**Ch. 9**)

Civil Society The network of groups such as labor unions, business associations, church groups and the like that can influence the political system but are independent of government control. (**Ch. 13**)

Classical Political Philosophy A body of political philosophy, based on the ideas of Plato (427–347 BCE) and his student Aristotle (384–322 BCE); associated

with a distrust of democracy and efforts to envision the just state. (**Ch. 1**)

Coalition Government A government formed, usually when no single party has a majority in Parliament, from a coalition of parties. In countries such as India and Israel, where frequently no single party wins a majority in Parliament, national elections are followed by negotiations between possible coalition partners since the prime minister must have the backing of a parliamentary majority. (**Ch. 12**)

Coercive Authority The authority that a leader enjoys by virtue of possessing the power to force compliance with his or her demands. (**Ch. 8**)

Collectives A term used to describe cooperatively owned factories and other enterprises. These are neither state-owned nor private enterprises. (**Ch. 14**)

Collectivization The process, common to many leftist revolutionary societies, of bringing private farm plots under the control of large collectively administered units. Although collective farms are technically run by the farmers who belong to the unit, they are generally under some degree of state control. Often collectivization involves considerable repression of peasants and landowners. This was especially true in the Soviet Union under Stalin, where millions died. (**Ch. 13**)

Command Economy A highly centralized, communist economy in which key decisions on production, employment, and the like are made by a powerful state and party bureaucracy. (**Ch. 13**)

Committee System The way in which committees are empowered in a legislature. Committees in some systems are quite powerful, independently determining which bills become law, whereas in other systems committees normally have little influence. (**Ch. 7**)

Common Law A set of principles first developed centuries ago by British courts in efforts to establish a basic code of fairness for situations in which no statutory law applied. (**Ch. 9**)

Communalism The first stage of "prehistory" in Marxist ideology; in this stage, society's productive capacity is so undeveloped that each person must consume everything he or she produces to survive, making slavery or other forms of exploitation economically impractical; sometimes termed "primitive communism" (**Ch. 2**)

Communes Highly collectivized agricultural units that were introduced to China in the late 1950s and subsequent decades. Because the commune system involved enormous state intrusion in their lives, the peasantry generally resented them. (**Ch. 14**)

Communism The stage in Marxist ideology in which "true" human history begins; in this stage, technological development has advanced to the point at which scarcity of resources no longer exists, and there is no class conflict or exploitation. (**Ch. 2**)

Conflictual and Consensual Political Cultures In consensual political cultures, citizens tend to agree on basic political procedures as well as the values and general goals of the political system. Conversely, conflictual political cultures are highly polarized by fundamental differences over those issues. (**Ch. 3**)

Connecticut Compromise The decision made, in drafting the U.S. Constitution, to divide the legislative power into two chambers, with the upper chamber designed so that each state would have two members in it regardless of population. Smaller states had been reluctant to support the Constitution if all legislative power were to be placed in a single chamber with districts allotted to states on the basis of population. (**Ch. 11**)

Consensual Democracy The kind of democratic politics created by the use of proportional representation electoral systems. Since a party does not have to win a majority of the votes in any state or district to gain parliamentary representation, this arrangement is said to force several parties to form an inclusive coalition and to govern in a more consensual manner. *See also* Adversarial Democracy. (**Ch. 4**)

Conservatism An approach to political life that sees traditional values as important in solving social problems. Edmund Burke (1729–1797) produced a landmark statement of conservatism in his criticism of the French Revolution, arguing that it destroyed aristocratic and religious traditions and would destabilize and coarsen French society. (**Ch. 2**)

Constituent Services Activities by legislators to obtain information, favors, and exceptions to regulations for their constituents, normally by making requests of administrative officials. (**Ch. 7**)

(The) Core A term used by dependency theorists to refer to the highly developed, capitalist nations that dominate the world economy. (**Ch. 15**)

Corporatism A political system in which citizens are represented in government by major interest groups. In its most advanced form, it involves the organization of the population into officially sanctioned interest groups based on occupational or other socioeconomic lines. (**Ch. 16**)

Council Housing Public housing built for the poor by the local government council. (**Ch. 12**)

Coup d'État An irregular, nonconstitutional removal of a head of state. (**Ch. 8**)

Criminal Law The body of law pertaining to the prosecution and punishment of those accused of crimes. (**Ch. 9**)

Cult of Personality An effort, commonly encountered in totalitarian political systems such as Soviet Russia or Nazi Germany, to glorify a political leader and develop a cult following behind him. Cults of personality developed around Joseph Stalin and Mao Zedong, for example. (**Ch. 13**)

Cultural Revolution Mao Zedong's effort (1966–1976) to revitalize China's revolutionary spirit and to cleanse the nation of real or alleged antirevolutionary cultural aspects. It involved a reign of terror in which hundreds of thousands, perhaps millions, were killed. (**Ch. 14**)

Debt Crisis The severe economic downturn suffered in the 1980s by nations in Latin America and Africa, arising from their inability to repay outstanding international debts. (**Chs. 16, 18**)

Declaration of Independence The formal statement, written primarily by Thomas Jefferson and adopted by the Second Continental Congress on July 4, 1776, that the 13 American colonies were independent of British control. (**Ch. 11**)

Defendant The person accused of a crime or sued by a plaintiff in a civil action. (**Ch. 9**)

Delegate Model An approach to representation in which the representative acts in accordance with the expressed preferences of the constituency that elected him or her. (**Ch. 7**)

Democracy A system of government in which government is ultimately accountable to the citizens. Although democracy literally means "government by the people," in practice it normally means that the people can select and remove those that govern them. (**Ch. 1**)

Democratic Peace The idea that something about the nature of democratic government makes it very unlikely that democratic states will go to war with other democracies. (**Ch. 17**)

Democratic Revolutionary Party. *See* Party of the Democratic Revolution (PRD).

Deng Xiaoping Leader of the Chinese political system from the 1970s to 1997 and architect of the nation's transformation to a more market-based economy. (**Ch. 14**)

Dependency Theory A theory once supported by many scholars that suggested that the Third World's underprivileged position was attributable to the control that powerful capitalist nations held over them.

Dependency involves a measure of economic and political control by developed nations (the core) over less developed ones (the periphery). (**Ch. 15**)

Deregulation A movement in public policy, most widespread in the United States and Great Britain in the 1980s, that involved removing or reducing regulations on private-sector activity, generally on the assumption that much government regulation is wasteful, counterproductive, and unnecessary. (**Ch. 2**)

Devolution The transfer of political power from a central government to regional or local government. (**Ch. 12**)

Diplomacy The communications and negotiations among national leaders regarding matters of foreign policy. (**Ch. 8**)

Dual Democratic Legitimacy A characteristic of presidential systems; the fact that the chief executive and the legislature are separately elected means that both institutions can claim to represent the people, and when these institutions disagree over policy, gridlock can ensue. In parliamentary systems, only the Parliament can claim democratic legitimacy, and the chief executive (prime minister) is elected from that body. (**Ch. 7**)

Dual Transition A simultaneous transition from a command economy to a free market and from communist rule to democracy. (**Ch. 13**)

Duma The lower house of the current Russian parliament. (**Ch. 13**)

Economic Austerity A set of government economic policies, often imposed as the result of pressure from the international financial community, designed to reduce inflation, trade deficits, and budget deficits, and to facilitate repayment of the country's external debt. Such policies, at least in the short run, generally lead to reduced living standards, especially for the poor. At the same time, they may be necessary to restore a nation's economic health. Hence, the precise form that they take is subject to heated debate. (**Ch. 16**)

Economic Determinism The idea that economic forces govern changes in the nature of societies; largely, but not exclusively, associated with Marxism. (**Ch. 2**)

Economic Internationalism (Liberalism) An approach to international political economy that emphasizes the benefits of free trade among nations. It is associated with classical liberal economics; often termed "liberalism" in this context. (**Ch. 17**)

Economic Nationalism An approach to international political economy that focuses on the importance of national interest and national power, holding

these to be more important than the economic efficiency gains that may be obtained through free trade; also termed "mercantilism." (**Ch. 17**)

Economic Structuralism An approach to international political economy associated with Marxist-Leninist thinking; it emphasizes the persistent economic inequalities separating poor and rich countries, and focuses on how state economic systems produce a structure of dependency and inequality. (**Ch. 17**)

Electoral Democracy A political system that features competitive (free and fair) government elections but may not respect fundamental civil liberties. *See* Liberal Democracy. (**Ch. 15**)

Elite Theory The idea that a single, generally unified elite dominates society; typically contrasted with pluralism. (**Ch. 6**)

Emergency Leadership The effort by a chief executive to initiate, coordinate, and energize governmental activities in time of crisis. (**Ch. 8**)

Environmentalism An ideology holding that the issues pertaining to the state of the physical environment, and policies directed toward it, are of primary importance. The most intense advocates of this ideology argue that environmental problems supersede other issues, such as economic development, poverty, and international relations. (**Ch. 2**)

Ethnicity A type of group identification in which individuals identify with people like themselves (and set themselves apart from other people) on the basis of race, religion, culture, language, nationality, and the like. Examples of ethnicities in the United States include Irish-Americans, Afro-Americans, Catholics, Italian-Americans, Jews, and Gypsies. (**Ch. 15**)

European Union (EU) The Western European trade and economic organization that binds together 25 of the region's nations. It is the successor to the European Community (EC) but involves a more intensive and geographically extensive union. (**Chs. 12, 18**)

Evolutionary Change A process of gradual, interrelated change, as distinguished from more rapid, and often disruptive, revolutionary change. (**Ch. 12**)

Expert Faction That faction of Chinese Communist Party leadership in the 1960s and 1970s that favored assigning management positions to trained experts even when they were not the most ideologically "correct" citizens. (**Ch. 14**)

Extended Republic The idea, associated with James Madison, that political disputes would be less violent and destabilizing if the political system were extended to comprise all the states (rather than continuing to resolve most political disputes independently in each of the states). (**Ch. 11**)

Falun Gong A Chinese spiritual sect stressing meditation and exercises. The government has repressed the movement, with hundreds allegedly dying while in police custody. (Ch. 14)

Fascism An ideology that emphasizes extreme appeals to national unity, hatred of foreigners and ethnic minorities, and complete obedience to the state. (Ch. 2)

Feminism An ideology that advocates equal rights for females. Some versions of feminism also identify specific feminine traits, such as compassion and sharing, that proponents claim will improve society as women achieve more leadership positions. (Ch. 2)

Feudalism The second stage of "prehistory" in Marxist ideology; in this stage, land ownership becomes the basis for political power and farm workers are exploited by those who own the land. (Ch. 2)

Fixed Jurisdictions The bureaucratic principle holding that agency officials should have clearly established areas of activity or specialization, making it possible to determine who is responsible for any given decision or program. (Ch. 10)

Folkways The norms and traditions observed in a legislature pertaining to the way members treat one another and expect to be treated. (Ch. 7)

Formal-Legal Analysis An approach to political science that emphasizes the study of laws, constitutions, and official institutions. (Ch. 1)

Free-Rider An individual who enjoys the benefits of a collective effort without contributing to it. (Ch. 6)

Free Trade Export and import commerce between nations that is relatively unimpeded by tariffs, quotas, or other government-created barriers to trade. (Ch. 18)

Fundamentalism A belief among some Christians, Hindus, and Muslims that the holy book must be accepted literally and that traditional religious values must be protected against the intrusions of the modern world. *See* Islamic Fundamentalists. (Ch. 15)

Fundamentalist Somebody who believes in religious fundamentalism. *See* Fundamentalism *and* Islamic Fundamentalists. (Ch. 15)

Gender Empowerment Measure (GEM) A statistical measure of how much gender equality or inequality exists in a given country or set of countries regarding economic and political power. (Ch. 15)

Gender Gap A difference between men as a group and women as a group with respect to some specific criterion, such as support for a given political party. (Ch. 4)

Gender-Related Development Index (GDI) A composite index that compares women's life expectancy, educational level, and income to that of men in the same society. It compares the Human Development Index (HDI) of women to that of men. *See also* Human Development Index. (Ch. 15)

Glasnost The opening up of Soviet politics under Mikhail Gorbachev's government. *Glasnost* allowed greater media freedom and freedom of speech in an attempt to remedy the faults of Soviet communism through more honest discussion. (Ch. 13)

Globalization The spread of economic activity, political interactions, mass culture, and ideas across national borders, often in de facto defiance of national sovereignty (Ch.18)

Glorious Revolution The removal of King James II by the British Parliament in 1688, firmly establishing parliamentary dominance over the monarch at a time when royalty elsewhere in Europe still based their authority on divine right. (Ch. 12)

Government The people or organizations that make, enforce, and implement political decisions for a society. (Ch. 1)

Government Functions The basic tasks that governments perform in healthy, developed political systems. (Ch. 1)

Grand Jury A group of citizens who determine whether there is sufficient evidence to charge (or indict) a person or persons with a crime. (Ch. 9)

Great Leap Forward China's ultimately disastrous effort (1958–1961) to rapidly accelerate industrial and agricultural production through the use of mass mobilization and other radical techniques. (Ch. 14)

Green Parties Political parties with a platform primarily devoted to protecting the environment. Taking a strong stand on ecological issues such as global warming and pollution, these parties have been most successful in Western Europe but exist in other regions as well. (Ch. 18)

Gulag The extensive network of prison camps to which millions of Soviet citizens were sent under Stalin. (Ch. 13)

Hierarchical (System) Political or social system in which people have clearly understood ranks, from a governing elite down to the lowest ranks of society. (Ch. 5)

Hierarchy The bureaucratic principle holding that clear lines of super- and subordinate status should exist in organizations. (Ch. 10)

Homogeneous Societies Societies that lack sharp class, racial, regional, or ethnic divisions. (Ch. 12)

Honor Killings Murders committed by male family members against female relatives who have allegedly dishonored the family. The women may have committed adultery or engaged in extra-marital sex, married someone who is unacceptable to the family, rejected an arranged marriage, or even been the victim of rape. Some 5,000 women are murdered annually in honor killings, mostly in the developing world. Many of them had not even committed the "sins" of which they are accused. (Ch. 18)

Human Development Index (HDI) A composite measure of life expectancy, school enrollment, literacy rate, and per capita income used to evaluate living standards. (Ch. 15)

Human Rights The principle that all people, regardless of their culture, their level of economic development, or the type of political system in which they live, are entitled to certain freedoms and privileges. (Ch. 1)

Human Rights Act Legislation passed by Parliament in 1998 that gave Britain its first written Bill of Rights drawn from the European Union's Convention on Human Rights. (Ch. 12)

Idealism An approach to international relations holding that wars are caused by evil and ignorance and that they can be avoided by nurturing a spirit of international community and justice. (Ch. 17)

Ideology A more or less coherent system of political thinking. (Ch. 2)

Income Distribution A measure of how the wealth of a society is shared among its members. Usually we speak of the *equality* of income distribution. (A highly equal income distribution is one in which the difference in income between the poorest and the richest segments of the population is not great.) (Ch. 1)

Incumbency Advantage The political advantages enjoyed by those in office over challengers. These advantages include the ability to manipulate news coverage, free mail privileges, and the power to grant favors to constituents. (Ch. 11)

Individualism A way of thinking that emphasizes individual interests, needs, and rights in contrast to social or communal interests, needs, and rights. (Ch. 2)

Industrial Democracy A highly industrialized nation or society with a democratic political system. (Ch. 12)

Inquisitorial System A system of criminal law in which the judge acts as a representative of the state, seeking information from the person or persons accused of a crime in an effort to determine guilt or innocence. (Ch. 9)

Institutional Coups Military takeovers carried out by the armed forces as a unified institution rather than a coup led by a single military strongman. Such coups tend to have some motivating ideology or plan of action. (Ch. 15)

Institutional Revolutionary Party (PRI) The party that ruled Mexico continuously from its formation in 1929 until 2000. (Ch. 16)

Interest Articulation The process of expressing concerns and problems as demands for governmental action. (Ch. 1)

Interest Group An organization that attempts to influence public policy in a specific area of importance to its members. (Ch. 6)

International Law The body of law consisting of treaties (both bilateral and general) and traditionally recognized rights and duties pertaining to the relations among states. (Ch. 17)

International Organizations Organizations whose members are individual nation-states. Such organizations may be general, dealing with a wide range of issues, or they may be designed to address only a single set of problems. (Ch. 17)

Iron Triangles The idea that interest groups, legislative committees, and bureaucratic agencies in a given policy area engage in continuing interaction, and that they act together to perpetuate policies and programs, resisting change and control. (Ch. 10)

Islamic Fundamentalists An extremely devout minority within the Islamic religion whose members believe in a traditional and literal interpretation of the Quran, the Muslim holy book. They reject many aspects of modern life and reject such Western cultural influences as Hollywood movies, rock music, and "immodest dress" as corrupt threats to traditional, conservative Islamic values. Some fundamentalist Muslims support the use of violence to advance their cause; others do not. (Chs. 2, 3)

Judicial Activism The principle holding that judges should follow their own values in deciding how to interpret statutes and provisions of basic law. (Ch. 9)

Judicial Restraint The principle holding that judges should be reluctant to overturn legislative or executive laws and decisions, doing so only when absolutely necessary. (Ch. 9)

Judicial Review The power of courts to overturn or void actions or laws that they feel are unlawful or inconsistent with basic law. (Ch. 9)

Justice The quality of being righteous, fair, and deserved. (Ch. 9)

Just War The philosophical tradition that attempts to define the conditions under which war is just and those under which it is not. (Ch. 17)

Kuomintang (KMT) The Chinese nationalist party that toppled the imperial government but, following a prolonged civil war, was overthrown nearly forty years later by the Chinese Communists.

Kuznets Effect The observed tendency of income distribution to become more concentrated in the earlier stages of economic development, before becoming more egalitarian in later stages. (Ch. 15)

Leadership Recruitment The process through which a political system attracts its leadership. In most countries, political parties play a critical role in this process. (Ch. 5)

Legitimacy A government's or a state's basis for claiming authenticity, the right to rule. (Ch. 15)

Leninist (Parties or Principles) V. I. Lenin, the leader of the 1917 communist revolution in Russia, argued that in a revolutionary society, the communist party must have absolute power and strict party discipline within the party must commit its members to support all the leadership's decisions. At least until 1989, all ruling communist parties adhered to these principles, and even most communist parties that were not in power enforced Leninist unity within the party itself. (Ch. 5)

Less Developed Countries (LDCs) Countries in Africa, Asia, Latin America, and the Middle East that have less developed economic and political systems including greater poverty and more conflictual politics. (Ch. 15)

Liberal Democracy A political system characterized by both free and fair elections (electoral democracy) *and* respect for civil liberties, including a free press (media), free speech, and freedom of religion. (Ch. 15)

Liberalism (1) A political ideology stressing tolerance for diverse lifestyles and opinions and demanding public assistance for those in need. (2) An approach to international political economy holding that trade barriers are counterproductive and wasteful. (Chs. 2, 17)

Libertarianism An ideology advocating minimum government and maximum individual liberty. (Ch. 2)

Lobbying Efforts by groups or individuals to influence public officials through formal and informal contacts with them. (Ch. 6)

Long March The PLA's difficult 6,000-mile trek fleeing the KMT in 1934–1935. Though they suffered enormous losses in the march, the Chinese Communists planted the seeds of their eventual victory. (Ch. 14)

Macho (*Machista*) Culture A culture, common in many parts of Latin America, in which men display and are expected to display an assertive, sexist attitude and accompanying behavior. Men dominate personal relationships and public life. (Ch. 16)

Majority Rule A decision-making principle that holds that when individuals disagree about which alternative is best, the choice taken will be that which the larger number of individuals prefer. (Ch. 1)

Malapportionment A condition in which legislative districts are of very different sizes, making the vote of a citizen in a district with a large population effectively less influential than the vote of a citizen in a district with a small population. (In the United States, the Supreme Court required states to correct malapportionment in the 1962 *Baker v. Carr* decision.) (Ch. 4)

Mao Zedong The leader and theoretician of the communist revolution in China. Mao's stress on the role of the peasantry in Third World revolutions and his belief that underdeveloped nations could experience communist revolutions had a profound impact on Marxist thinking and on revolutionary movements in Africa, Asia, and Latin America. (Ch. 14)

Marbury v. Madison The U.S. Supreme Court case from 1803 which, for the first time, held an act of Congress unconstitutional. Most historians believe that the opinion in this case established much of the power of the Supreme Court. (Ch. 11)

Marginal Seats Legislative seats won by a small electoral margin; incumbents in these seats cannot be confident that they will be reelected. (Ch. 11)

Marxism A comprehensive political and economic ideology based heavily on the writings of Karl Marx (1818–1883). It offers an explanatory theory of historical development and calls for class struggle (political struggle, either peaceful or violent) between the working class and the capitalists. Marxist thought is the basis of communist and radical socialist ideology. (Ch. 2)

Mass Parties Parties growing out of the working class movement, usually with a socialist orientation. (Ch. 5)

Member of Parliament (MP) A Member of the British Parliament (House of Commons). (Ch. 12)

Mercantilism An approach to international political economy holding that states pursue their national interests in making international economic policies, especially those pertaining to trade. (Ch. 17)

Mexican Economic Miracle The period of dramatic economic growth and industrialization from the 1940s until the 1982 debt crisis and the country's subsequent deep recession. (Ch. 16)

Military Coup A sudden seizure of full government power by the armed forces. The word *coup* is a shortened version of "coup d'état," which means "a blow at the state." (Ch. 15)

Missouri Plan An approach for selecting judges. Adopted by Missouri in 1940, the plan allows the governor to select judges from a list of candidates compiled by a nominating commission made up of legal experts and citizens. (Ch. 9)

Mobilization Regime An authoritarian regime that tries to mobilize (energize) its population behind government goals through the use of political institutions (most often, political parties) and ideology. (Ch. 19)

Modernization Theory A popular academic theory that attributes underdevelopment to the Third World's traditional cultural values and weak political and economic institutions. To modernize, the theory suggests, Third World nations must borrow (and possibly adapt) Western values and institutions. Modern values are transmitted through urbanization, increased education and literacy, as well as through greater exposure to the mass media. (Ch. 15)

Modern Political Philosophy A body of political philosophy associated with Machiavelli (1469–1527), Hobbes (1588–1679), Locke (1632–1704), and others. In contrast to "classical" political philosophy, modern political philosophy places greater emphasis on individualism and on pragmatic concerns about how government works. (Ch. 1)

Multiculturalism The idea that cultural diversity is valuable and that measures should be taken to ensure that cultural traditions other than the dominant one are preserved and respected. (Ch. 2)

National Action Party (PAN) One of Mexico's major parties (along with the PRI and PRD), it now holds the presidency. It is a conservative, pro-Catholic party with close links to the business community. Its strong stance against government corruption and in favor of democratic reform has helped it gain power. (Ch. 16)

Nationalist Party (KMT, Guomindang) China's first important, modern political party. Led by reformist elements and traditional warlords, it rose to power with the overthrow of the old imperial dynasty. (Ch. 14)

Nationalization The process whereby the government takes control of an economic enterprise, as when Great Britain nationalized the railroads and steel mills after World War II. (Ch. 12)

Natural Law A moral or ethical standard grounded in some concept of nature or divinity. (Ch. 9)

Neofascist Parties Political parties that support a modified, and usually toned down, form of fascism with an emphasis on supernationalism, ethnic prejudice, and, in Europe, a commitment to limiting or ending further immigration. (Ch. 5)

New Labour The title that Prime Minister Tony Blair and his supporters gave the Labour Party after it largely abandoned socialism and converted to a more centrist political ideology. (Ch. 12)

Newly Industrialized Countries (NICs) Countries in East Asia and Latin America—including Taiwan, South Korea, Hong Kong, Mexico, and Brazil—that have expanded their industrial capacities dramatically in recent decades and have become important international economic actors. (Chs. 15, 18)

New World Order (NWO) A concept proposed by President George Bush following the end of the cold war and the Allied victory over Iraq in the 1991 Gulf War. As envisioned by its proponents, it would entail close cooperation among the world's major powers to deter future aggression and would maintain international stability based on the rule of law and collective security. The vision has largely faded and proved to be of little utility during the conflicts in Bosnia and Iraq. (Ch. 18)

Nomenklatura The list of positions (some one million) within the Soviet Communist Party, the government bureaucracy, the military, state-owned business enterprises, labor unions, the media, cultural organizations, and professional groups for which appointment required party approval. The term more commonly referred to the hundreds of thousands who held important posts, constituting a tremendously powerful and privileged elite. (Ch. 13)

Nondecisions Problems and issues not addressed by a political system. Elite theorists often point to nondecisions as evidence that elite forces successfully steer government away from actions that would threaten elite interests. (Ch. 6)

Nongovernmental Organizations (NGOs) Organizations that are active and often influential in areas such as education, health care, the environment, and promoting the needs of the poor, but have no formal links to government. They can be very influential in developing nations. (Ch. 18)

No-Party Regimes A political system in which there are no organized political parties, often because the government has banned them. (Ch. 5)

North Atlantic Treaty Organization (NATO) A defense community established by the United States and many of its Western European allies during the cold war. Its purpose was to defend Europe against a possible attack by the Soviet Union and its Eastern European allies in the Warsaw Pact. It has survived the end of the Cold War. (Ch. 18)

North–South Relations Economic and political relations between the more economically developed nations of the world (the North) and the developing nations of the South. (Ch. 18)

Nuclear Proliferation The spread of nuclear weapons or of the capacity to produce nuclear weapons to additional countries, most notably in the developing world. (Ch. 18)

Nuclear Terror The idea that the prospects of nuclear war are so horrible that nations avoid it, even when their national interests would have led to war in the absence of nuclear weapons. (**Ch. 17**)

Oligarchy The relatively small group of multi-millionaire or billionaire businessmen in Russia who often gained their wealth illicitly after the fall of communism and who now control most of the economy. Individually they are known as oligarchs, and collectively they are called the oligarchy. (**Ch. 13**)

Ombudsman A person who attempts (or an office that attempts) to resolve the problems that individual citizens have with administrative agencies and programs. (**Ch. 7**)

One-Child Policy A Chinese government population-control policy that penalizes urban families that have more than one child and most rural families having more than two children. (**Ch. 14**)

Open Door Policy Deng Xiaoping's policy of opening up China to economic, trade, and cultural exchange with the West and then with Japan, Hong Kong, and Taiwan. (**Ch. 14**)

PAN. *See* National Action Party.

Parliament The entire British national legislature consisting of the elected House of Commons and the House of Lords (with inherited or appointed seats). In common usage, however, *Parliament* refers only to the far more influential House of Commons. (**Ch. 12**)

Parliamentary Supremacy The idea that the Parliament enjoys sovereign power, and that no court or executive can abrogate its decisions. (**Ch. 9**)

Parliamentary System A system of executive–legislative relations in which the legislature elects the chief executive. (**Ch. 7**)

Party Discipline The capacity of a party to have its legislative representatives vote as a unified bloc. (**Ch. 12**)

Party Identification A citizen's sense of attachment to a political party. (**Ch. 4**)

Party of the Democratic Revolution (PRD) A coalition of Mexico's leftist, nationalist parties originally headed by Cuauhtémoc Cárdenas, the son of the legendary former president, Lázaro Cárdenas. In 1988, heading a predecessor coalition to the PRD, Cárdenas mounted a formidable challenge to the ruling PRI. In a symbolically important election, the PRD gained control of Mexico City in 1997, led by Cuauhtémoc Cárdenas, who became the first popularly elected mayor of the giant metropolis in more than 70 years. The PRD is one of Mexico's two major opposition parties (along with the PRI) that now control the Chamber of Deputies. It expresses the unhappiness felt by many of Mexico's poor over their country's severe economic setbacks in recent years. (**Ch. 16**)

Party Platform The set of policy orientations officially held by a political party. (**Ch. 5**)

Patronage The practice of selecting bureaucratic officials on the basis of their political support for the elected official with the power to appoint them; contrasted with appointment on the basis of neutral competence or expertise. (**Ch. 10**)

Patron-Client Relations Relations between a politically or economically powerful figure (the patron) and a less powerful individual, often a fairly dependent person such as a Third World peasant (the client). The patron (for example, a local political party boss) gives the client services or goods that he or she needs (a job in the civil service, financial credit, or a welfare payment, for example) and, in return, the client agrees to vote for or even campaign for the patron's political party. (**Ch. 5**)

People's Liberation Army (PLA) China's Red army, which, under Mao Zedong's leadership, carried out the communist revolution. (**Ch. 14**)

Perestroika The restructuring of Soviet political and, especially, economic institutions introduced by Communist Party Secretary Mikhail Gorbachev. The goal was to make communism more humane and more efficient. (**Ch. 13**)

Personal Coups Coups led by a single military strongman, such as Somoza in Nicaragua, with little in the way of long-term goals other than increasing the power and wealth of the leader. (**Ch. 15**)

Personalistic Party A political party whose primary purpose is to further the political career of one person, the party leader. Sometimes the party is actually named or nicknamed after that leader, as, for example, the Peronist party in Argentina (nicknamed after its founding leader, Juan Perón). (**Ch. 5**)

PLA. *See* People's Liberation Army.

Plaid Cymru A Welsh nationalist political party. (**Ch. 12**)

Plaintiff The person who brings a legal action against another person for damages in a civil suit; the "complaining party." (**Ch. 9**)

Pluralism The idea that there are many centers of political power in society (typically contrasted with elite theory or other views holding that a single class or group dominates society). Also, the condition of having many centers of power in a society. (**Ch. 6**)

Policy Initiation The first steps taken to make or change policy. Executives and administrators have increasingly taken over this function in industrial democracies. (**Ch. 7**)

Politburo The highest-ranking decision-making body of the now-defunct Soviet Communist Party. Its roughly 12 to 16 members represented the power elite of the party and made most key political and economic decisions until it was stripped of much of its power shortly before the fall of the Soviet Union. Other ruling communist parties (such as China, Vietnam, and Cuba) also had politburos at their helms. (**Ch. 13**)

Political Action Committee (PAC) Organization established to gather and disburse campaign contributions to candidates in the United States. (**Ch. 11**)

Political Aggregation The process through which a political system reduces the multitude of conflicting societal demands to a manageable number of alternatives. Frequently this is done through programmatically oriented political parties. (**Ch. 5**)

Political Culture The pattern of individual attitudes and orientations toward politics among the members of a political system. (**Ch. 3**)

Political Development The idea that nations become modern by acquiring certain capacities and capabilities. The term is sometimes considered controversial because it implies that traditional (or "underdeveloped") nations will change along a known path to become similar to the Western industrial democracies. (**Chs. 1, 15**)

Political Economy The study of the impact of government on economic conditions, including analysis of alternative public policies and different systems of government. (**Ch. 1**)

Political Liberalization The process of loosening authoritarian controls over society and allowing a higher degree of political freedom. (**Ch. 14**)

Political Party An organization that unites people in an effort to win government office and thereby influence or control government policies. (**Ch. 5**)

Political Resocialization The active effort by government to transform society's political culture. Political resocialization is common during radical revolutions (such as Maoist China's) or after a mobilized country has suffered a defeat in war (as in the postwar de-Nazification efforts in Germany). (**Ch. 3**)

Political Socialization The process of creating a shared political culture among the members of a political system, typically from one generation to another. It may also entail changes over time that lead to a gradual transformation of the culture. (**Chs. 1, 3**)

Political Subculture The distinct political orientations of a region, a class, an ethnicity, or a race found within a larger political culture. (**Ch. 3**)

Political Underdevelopment A condition marked by lack of state and national autonomy, weak government institutions, weak political parties, limited opportunities for popular political participation and articulation, and instability. (**Ch. 15**)

Politico Model An approach to representation in which the legislator alternately represents constituents in accordance with the delegate model and the trustee model (see definitions), depending on the nature of the issue and the degree of public concern about it. (**Ch. 7**)

Politics The process of making collective decisions in a community, society, or group through the application of influence and power. (**Ch. 1**)

Popular Consultation A regularized process through which citizens can make known their preferences regarding governmental policies and decisions; a key component of democracy. (**Ch. 1**)

Populist (Parties) Political parties that try to build a broad electoral coalition of working-class, middle-class, and, sometimes, business-community voters, often by promising a wide range of government programs that would benefit each sector of the coalition. (**Ch. 5**)

Positive Law Laws made by governments; normally contrasted with "natural" law. (**Ch. 9**)

Postmaterialism A somewhat distinctive set of political orientations common to many individuals in industrial democracies who were politically socialized during the era of postwar affluence. Postmaterialists tend to be somewhat less concerned with ideology or with economic issues and more concerned with issues such as grassroots political participation, the environment, and civil liberties. (**Ch. 3**)

Postwar Settlement An unspoken agreement between Europe's labor or socialist parties and allied labor unions, on the one hand, and conservative parties and the business community, on the other. The right agreed to accept a welfare state in return for the left's agreement to abide by the ground rules of the free-market system. (**Ch. 12**)

Power Elite The name given to the set of forces that, in C. Wright Mills's interpretation, dominates American society; it consists of the leaders of the military, corporate, and political establishments. (**Ch. 6**)

PRD. *See* Party of the Democratic Revolution.

Presidential "Character" Developed in the study of the U.S. presidency, the idea that the behavior of individual presidents is largely determined by basic elements of their personalities and character. (**Ch. 11**)

Presidentialism Concentration of political power in the hands of the national president (**Ch. 16**)

Presidential System A system of executive–legislative relations in which the chief executive is elected independently of the members of the legislature. (**Ch. 7**)

President's Cabinet The secretaries of the cabinet-level departments in the executive branch of the U.S. government. (**Ch. 11**)

PRI. *See* Institutional Revolutionary Party.

Primaries Elections held to select candidates for a general election. (**Ch. 11**)

Princelings Children of high-ranking Chinese government and Communist Party officials who use their connections and privileged position to enrich themselves and gain power in the growing private sector. (**Ch. 14**)

Privatization The process whereby the government transfers state-owned enterprises (such as petroleum companies or electric power) to the private sector through the sale of stock. (**Chs. 12, 13, 15, 16**)

Proletariat The Marxist word used to describe the working class. The proletariat were viewed by Karl Marx as the greatest victims of capitalist exploitation and, hence, the ones who would bring the communist revolution to fruition. (**Ch. 13**)

Proportional Representation An electoral system in which parties receive seats in the legislature in proportion to the share of the popular vote they receive. Voters choose between party lists in larger, multi-member districts, rather than choosing a particular candidate. (**Ch. 4**)

Public Opinion Polls Data on the opinions, demographic characteristics, and vote choices of citizens; nearly always estimated by gathering information about a sample of the larger population of citizens. (**Ch. 4**)

Public Schools The term used to describe Great Britain's most elite private schools (pre-university). The meaning of term *public* here is totally different from its meaning in reference to U.S. schools. (**Ch. 12**)

Racial Profiling The practice of associating certain illegal or potentially dangerous behavior (such as drug dealing or terrorism) predominantly with particular races or ethnic groups (normally minority groups) and the use of that "profile" by government authorities to target those groups more heavily for investigation (such as special airport searches or auto searches on the highway) or even arrest. (**Ch. 19**)

Rational Choice An approach to political theory distinguished by its application of economic principles, particularly the assumption that individuals seek their own interests in making political decisions. (**Ch. 6**)

Rational-Legal Authority The authority that a leader enjoys when his or her actions are consistent with established legal principles. (**Ch. 8**)

Realism An approach to international relations that emphasizes the role of national interest in explaining the causes of war and conflict. (**Ch. 17**)

Red Faction That faction of Chinese Communist Party leadership in the 1960s and 1970s that favored assigning all leadership and management positions in society to those individuals who proved themselves most committed to Maoist, communist ideology. (**Ch. 14**)

Red Guards Young people who became the shock troops of China's Cultural Revolution and helped enforce its terror. (**Ch. 14**)

Redistricting The process of redrawing the boundaries of legislative districts; necessary to avoid malapportionment as populations grow at different rates in different areas. (**Ch. 4**)

Reds versus Experts The name given to a debate in the 1960s between those Chinese leaders who favored maximizing the use of Maoist ideology as a driving force in society (the Reds) and those who felt that concessions needed to be made to technical expertise (the Experts). (**Ch. 14**)

Representative Authority The authority that a leader enjoys when it is perceived that he or she is representative of the "people" or the "majority." (**Ch. 8**)

Representative Bureaucracy The idea that non-elected bureaucrats may be, in practice, more closely representative of the citizens than elected legislators or executives. (**Ch. 10**)

Responsibility System The program giving China's peasantry control over their own family plots. It was the opening step in the conversion of the nation's collective farms to private holdings. (**Ch. 14**)

Responsible Parties Parties that can demand discipline from members elected to a legislature, who almost always vote in accordance with the party platform. (**Ch. 7**)

Routines Patterns of bureaucratic activity that become established. (**Ch. 10**)

Rule Adjudication The process of applying governmental rules to individual cases. (**Ch. 1**)

Rule Execution The process of implementing or carrying out policy decisions. (**Ch. 1**)

Rule Making The process of establishing laws, orders, edicts, regulations, and other authoritative acts by government. (**Ch. 1**)

Self-Help The idea that in the international system, states cannot rely on protection provided by a higher power (as citizens can rely on government to protect them from criminals). (**Ch. 17**)

Shays's Rebellion An uprising in Massachusetts in 1786–1787 challenging the foreclosures of farm mortgages and demanding government action to improve the position of debtors. (**Ch. 11**)

Shock Therapy Drastic government measures designed to reduce rampant inflation, large budget deficits, and troublesome trade deficits. Typically, shock treatment involves currency devaluation, slashes in public spending, layoffs of public employees, restraints on wages, and other painful measures that, at least in the short run, reduce popular living standards. (**Ch. 13**)

Single-Member Districts An electoral system in which each electoral district has one representative in the legislature; sometimes called "winner-take-all" because, in contrast to proportional representation systems, parties receiving fewer votes than the winner get no representation from that district. (**Ch. 4**)

Social Capital The density of associational involvement (belonging to groups ranging from church choirs to the League of Women Voters) in a town, region, or country and the norms and social trust that these group activities produce. (**Ch. 3**)

Social Class. *See* Socioeconomic Status.

Social Democrats Political parties and their supporters who adhere to a non-Marxist, moderate form of socialism. (**Ch. 5**)

Social Movement Broad mobilization of ordinary people [seeking] a particular goal or goals. (**Ch. 5**)

Socialism The fourth and final stage of "prehistory" in Marxist ideology; in this stage, following a revolution by the workers exploited under capitalism, the state is governed in the interests of the workers; also an ideology advocating social equality, public ownership of industry, and a lesser role for private property. (**Ch. 2**)

Socialist (Party) In Western Europe where socialist parties are most influential and often govern, the terms *socialist* and *socialism* have shed the Marxist meaning found in the previous definition of socialism. Instead, they have become left-of-center, democratic parties that favor working class and middle-class economic interests and a somewhat more active state. Often used interchangeably with the label *social democratic*. (**Ch. 5**)

Socioeconomic Status (SES) A person's position in society, with regard to income, educational attainment, and occupational status. (**Ch. 4**)

SOEs (State-Owned Enterprises) Firms, primarily in industrial manufacturing, still owned by the communist government. (**Ch. 14**)

State Capitalism An economic system in which most of the economy is owned and managed by private enterprise but the state controls important segments (such as Mexico's giant petroleum industry) and uses its economic wealth and political power to help direct the economy. (**Ch. 16**)

State Duma. *See* Duma.

Statist Favoring a large role for the government (the state) in national life, especially the economy. Statist parties generally favor extensive government programs for welfare, economic development, and the like, whereas antistatists prefer a more limited government role. (**Ch. 5**)

Statute A law passed by a legislature. (**Ch. 7**)

Statutory Interpretation The process of deciding how statutes apply to particular contexts; normally a task of courts. (**Ch. 9**)

Statutory Law The body of law created by acts of the legislature; distinct from provisions in constitutional law, law made by judges, and administrative regulations. (**Ch. 9**)

Suffrage The right to vote or the exercise of that right. (**Ch. 12**)

Superpower A state whose military strength is of a higher order than that of all but the other superpowers. (**Ch. 17**)

Superpresidentialism Extreme concentration of political power in the hands of the president. (**Ch. 13**)

Supreme Soviet The Soviet Parliament, which, until Gorbachev's reforms, functioned as a rubber stamp for decisions made by the Communist Party leadership. The post-Soviet, 1993 constitution replaced it with a new, democratically elected parliamentary structure. (**Ch. 13**)

Symbolic Leader Serving as the unifying symbol of the nation; a key function of modern chief executives. (**Ch. 8**)

Technical Responsibility The idea that bureaucrats may be controlled by their own sense of professional standards, even when public control is weak or absent. (**Ch. 10**)

Technocrat A highly trained bureaucrat, often with a graduate degree in the social sciences (frequently from a developed country). In recent years many modernizing societies, such as Mexico, have increased the technocrats' power at the expense of that of elected politicians in the belief that technocrats can render more impartial, scientifically guided administrative decisions. (**Ch. 16**)

Term Limits The idea that legislators should be allowed to serve only a limited number of terms. A movement to enact term limits gained momentum in the United States during 1992. (**Ch. 11**)

Thatcherism The philosophy of the British Conservative Party's right wing as espoused by former Prime

Minister Margaret Thatcher. Thatcherites rejected much of the welfare state and sought substantial reductions of state intervention in the free market. (Ch. 12)

Third Generation The new generation of leadership, led by President Jiang Zemin, that took over after Deng Xiaoping's death. This generation began to turn power over to a fourth generation of leaders at the 2002 party congress. (Ch. 14)

Third World A category of nations in Africa, Asia, Latin America, and the Middle East that share two primary characteristics: they are politically and/or economically less developed; and they are neither industrialized democracies (the First World) nor former members of the Soviet–Eastern European bloc of communist nations (the Second World). The term "Third World" is used interchangeably with "developing nations" and "less developed countries" (LDCs). (Ch. 15)

Tiananmen Square Located near Beijing's imperial Heavenly City, it has been the locale of major political gatherings in communist China. In 1989 it was the center of student pro-democracy demonstrations, and the June 4 massacre there made it a symbol of China's ongoing political repression. (Ch. 14)

Tories Members or supporters of the British Conservative Party. (Ch. 12)

Totalitarian Government A form of authoritarian (non-democractic) government in which the government exercises near-total control over all forms of political activity and organized societal activity. Such extreme control is very rare and perhaps only Nazi Germany, the USSR under Stalin, and China under Mao exercised it. (Chs. 1, 5, 15)

Traditional Authority The authority that derives from a leader's embodiment of long-standing, widely accepted social and political traditions. (Ch. 8)

Traditional Societies Societies that tend to stress long-standing beliefs; evaluations of individuals based on their ethnicity, class, or other innate qualities rather than on their abilities; and other pre-modern social values. (Ch. 15)

Transnational Corporations (TNCs) Large corporations with holdings in many nations and in some cases corporate ownership in more than one country. Also referred to as multinational corporations. (Ch. 18)

Trial and Appellate Courts The two basic levels of courts in most judicial systems. The evidence pertaining to a case is presented in trial courts, whereas appellate courts normally rule on claims that trial courts made errors of law or procedure. (Ch. 9)

Trustee Model An approach to representation in which the representative acts in accordance with his or her independent judgment, regardless of the wishes of the constituency that elected him or her. (Ch. 7)

Two-and-One-Half-Party System A national party system in which two parties are predominant but a third party presents a significant challenge, as in Great Britain. (Ch. 5)

Vanguard Party A term used by Vladimir Lenin to describe the Communist Party as an enlightened elite acting in the best interests of the working class. (Ch. 13)

Vertical Power Russian President Vladimir Putin's efforts to concentrate political power in the hands of the federal government and, in turn, in his own hands. (Ch. 13)

Vote of No Confidence A vote by the Parliament expressing its unwillingness to support the prime minister and his or her cabinet. (Ch. 12)

Voter Turnout A measure of how many voters actually vote in a given election. (Ch. 4)

Warlords Regional military leaders who exercised much of the local power in the Chinese imperial order. (Ch. 14)

Watergate Refers to the wide-ranging patterns of illegal and abusive activities of the Nixon administration during 1972–1974. The Watergate is the name of an office and apartment building in Washington, DC, in which a burglary associated with the Nixon reelection effort took place. (Ch. 11)

Wave of Democracy One of three periods in world history since 1828 when a substantial number of countries were making a transition to democracy. (Ch. 15 and 19)

Welfare State The arrangement of public services, regulations, and programs of income redistribution that are established to provide a basic standard of living to all members of society. (Chs. 2, 12)

Zapatista A member of the Chiapas revolutionary group known as the EZLN (Zapatista Army of National Liberation). (Ch. 16)

Zhou Enlai Mao's longtime associate who served many years as China's premier. He was the most cosmopolitan of China's early communist leaders and helped shape its foreign policy in the Maoist era. (Ch. 14)

Zipper-Style Quota An electoral system for a legislature or parliament that is based on proportional representation and the introduction of quotas for women or other underrepresented groups. Women candidates are given a guaranteed share (often 30 percent) of candidates on the party list and are alternated from the top of the list (those who are most likely to win seats) to the bottom in accordance with that quota. See also Proportional Representation. (Ch. 15)

PHOTO CREDITS

INDEX